Anthony Eden, Anglo-American Relations and the 1954 Indochina Crisis

Anthony Eden, Anglo-American Relations and the 1954 Indochina Crisis

Kevin Ruane and Matthew Jones

BLOOMSBURY ACADEMIC
LONDON • NEW YORK • OXFORD • NEW DELHI • SYDNEY

BLOOMSBURY ACADEMIC
Bloomsbury Publishing Plc
50 Bedford Square, London, WC1B 3DP, UK
1385 Broadway, New York, NY 10018, USA
29 Earlsfort Terrace, Dublin 2, Ireland

BLOOMSBURY, BLOOMSBURY ACADEMIC and the Diana logo
are trademarks of Bloomsbury Publishing Plc

First published in Great Britain 2019
Paperback edition published 2021

A catalogue record for this book is available from the British Library.

A catalog record for this book is available from the Library of Congress.

ISBN: HB: 978-1-3500-2117-4
         PB: 978-1-3500-2119-8
         ePDF: 978-1-3500-2116-7
         eBook: 978-1-3500-2118-1

Typeset by Integra Software Services Pvt. Ltd.

To find out more about our authors and books visit www.bloomsbury.com
and sign up for our newsletters.

For Amir
(MCJ)

For Mark O'Donnell and Richard Smyth
(KJR)

Contents

Acknowledgements   viii

List of Abbreviations   x

Map   xii

1   Introduction: Anthony Eden, Anglo-American Relations and the 1954 Indochina Crisis   1

2   Indochina, 1951–1952: The Chinese Dimension   19

3   Indochina, 1952–1953: The Vietminh Dimension   33

4   Indochina, 1953: Dimensions Converge   49

5   Vietnam in the Shadow of the Bomb, 1953   63

6   From Bermuda to Dien Bien Phu, 1953–1954   77

7   Uniting for Action, March–April 1954   89

8   Disunited Inaction, April 1954   105

9   'He Lied to Me', April 1954   119

10   25 April 1954: 'The Day We Didn't Go to War'   133

11   The Geneva Conference: Opening Skirmishes   147

12   The Fall of Dien Bien Phu, May 1954   163

13   'The Most Troubled International Scene I Can Ever Recall'   179

14   Geneva: Phoenix Rising, June 1954   193

15   The Geneva Settlement, July 1954   207

16   SEATO, 1954–1955   223

17   Geneva Suborned   237

18   Conclusion: Eden, Indochina and Suez   255

Notes   263

Bibliography   312

Index   325

Acknowledgements

The old cliché that it takes longer to write history than to make it contains (like all clichés) more than a grain of truth. This book, with its focus on a single year of the Indochina War, has been three decades in the making. Off and on for much of that period, Matthew Jones and I talked about 'doing something' on Indochina, but despite the prompting of friends and historians – most persistently Geoffrey Warner and most recently Fred Logevall – we never quite got round to it. In early 2016, however, having both just completed major projects and with a decent stretch of unallocated research time before us, we stopped prevaricating and settled to our task. We hope the result is worth the wait.

Over the years, more Indochinese-related encouragement, wisdom and advice have come my way than I can possibly salute in a short acknowledgement. However, in addition to Geoffrey and Fred, I would like to single out the following for especial thanks: James Ellison, always my go-to sounding board; Sean Greenwood, who first set me on the road to Indochina (albeit via the EDC); John Young, that willing reader and sage critic; Jim Latham, for RDM; and my family – Vanessa, Niamh, Fiontan, Eimear and Sam – for their love and support during the often trying creative process. And I can hardly forget Matthew Jones! Aves vehement to that fine historian and good friend.

Lastly, as this study has two authors, we each have a dedicatee – or in my case, dedicatees: Mark O'Donnell, my alternative FDR, and Richard Smyth, my alternative Churchill.

KEVIN RUANE, Canterbury, November 2018

I have incurred many debts in researching the material for this book and during the final stages of writing up. The first and most obvious is to my co-author, who has been a close travelling companion on our Indochina journey over many years, and whose initial suggestion it was to collaborate on this common project, where ideas, resources and countless words have been pooled and exchanged. Beyond anything else it has been great and rewarding fun to work with someone of such generosity of spirit and abiding good sense.

Several friends have offered encouragement and support over the years, and I want to thank Bob Brigham, Alec Hoffmann, Richard Immerman, Fred Logevall, David Milne, Rudolf Muhs, Andrew Preston, Andy Rotter, David Ryan, Bevan Sewell, Brad Simpson, Sarah Snyder, Arne Westad and John Young. My colleagues at the Department of International History at the LSE help to make it a wonderful place to be based as an academic. However, my greatest debt, as always, is to my family, who make it all possible: Amir, Anya, Alec and Sofia.

MATTHEW JONES, London, November 2018

In addition, we would both like to thank our publisher, Bloomsbury Academic. In particular, Emily Drewe, for taking on our double act in the first place, and Beatriz Lopez (early on) and Dan Hutchins (latterly) for their patience, support and high professionalism.

KJR and MCJ

List of Abbreviations

AEC – Atomic Energy Commission, USA

ANZUS – Australia, New Zealand, United States Pact, 1951

CIA – Central Intelligence Agency

COS – Chiefs of Staff, UK

CPG – Central People's Government, PRC

CR – Centre of Resistance, Dien Bien Phu

DPC – Defence Policy Committee, Cabinet, UK

DRV – Democratic Republic of Vietnam

EDC – European Defence Community

FEC – French Expeditionary Corps

FPSA – Five-Power Staff Agency

FO – Foreign Office, UK

FORD – Foreign Office Research Department

HMG – His/Her Majesty's Government

JCS – Joint Chiefs of Staff, USA

JPS – Joint Planning Staff

MAAG – Military Assistance Advisory Group, USA

MOD – Ministry of Defence, UK

NATO – North Atlantic Treaty Organisation

NKVD – People's Commissariat for Internal Affairs, USSR

NSC – National Security Council, USA

PAVN – People's Army of Vietnam

PRC – People's Republic of China

RVN – Republic of Vietnam

SEATO – Southeast Asia Treaty Organisation

USSR – Union of Soviet Socialist Republics

VNA – Vietnamese National Army

WEU – Western European Union

Map French Indochina

1

Introduction: Anthony Eden, Anglo-American Relations and the 1954 Indochina Crisis

Tuesday, 20 July 1954, was possibly the longest day in history. In Geneva, a city renowned for the production of highly accurate timepieces, the participants in an international conference tasked with ending the Indochina War – the bitter eight-year conflict between France and the communist-led nationalists of the Vietminh – found their day extended by several hours. The conference had ground on for three months, but now, thanks to French Premier Pierre Mendès-France, its climacteric drew near. On being appointed in June, Mendès-France vowed to secure peace with honour for France within a month. If he failed, he would resign, and the war, which had already cost so much French blood and treasure, would go on. In calendar terms, the Mendès-France deadline translated to midnight, 20 July.

For Anthony Eden, the British Foreign Secretary, the prospect of ongoing war in Indochina was the stuff of nightmares. Co-chair of the Geneva conference (alongside his Soviet counterpart, Vyacheslav Molotov), Eden regarded this Cold War hot war as 'the most dangerous and acute of the problems' confronting him during his post-war (1951–1955) Foreign Secretaryship.[1] Should the peace process fail to deliver a settlement, the United States – the Republican administration of Dwight D. Eisenhower – appeared ready to intervene militarily in Vietnam, the crucible of the war, at the head of an international coalition in support of France. If that happened, Eden was convinced that the People's Republic of China (PRC) would enter the war on the side of the Vietminh, a move that could trigger American military retaliation (conventional and nuclear) against the PRC itself. If the Soviet Union, allied to China since 1950, then became embroiled, the conditions for a possible third world war would be in place.

The Indochina War had begun in 1946 as a colonial conflict with the French seeking to retain their imperial primacy in Vietnam, Laos and Cambodia in the face of the challenge posed by the Vietminh under veteran communist revolutionary Ho Chi Minh.[2] In 1950, Indochina entered the arena of the Cold War when the Chinese communists, fresh from their triumph in the Chinese Civil War, began supplying the Vietminh with arms and advice, and the United States commenced a military assistance programme to help France, its partner in the North Atlantic Treaty Organisation (NATO). Thereafter, while the French and Vietminh confronted one another as of old, the war was also a Sino-American war-by-proxy which, if it ever developed into a direct

US-PRC clash, could draw in Britain, America's closest ally, and the Soviet Union, the PRC's powerful patron. In the event, the outbreak of the Korean War in June 1950 distracted international attention, but with the signing of a Korean armistice in July 1953, Indochina came into its own as the Asian Cold War's most incendiary problem.

By the start of 1954, US aid to France was covering nearly 80 per cent of the cost of the French war effort, but it was the Vietminh, a formidable military force with strong "rice roots" political support, who were in the ascendant. In February 1954, the United States, the UK, France and the Union of Soviet Socialist Republics (USSR) summoned the Geneva conference with the object of converting the Korean armistice into a peace treaty. The French government, under pressure from a disillusioned public and parliament, succeeded in adding Indochina to the Geneva agenda to assess first-hand the communist world's attitude towards a possible negotiated solution. The conference was scheduled to open on 26 April, but its purpose, from an Indochinese standpoint, was transformed in mid-March by the onset of the decisive battle of the war at Dien Bien Phu, a remote corner of north-west Vietnam where a 12,000-strong French garrison found itself surrounded by 40,000 Vietminh troops. The US government, for whom a non-communist Indochina was a national security priority, suddenly faced the possibility not just of a French defeat in the battle but a collapse of French morale and endurance elsewhere in Vietnam. Even if the line was held militarily, US policymakers worried that a disaster at Dien Bien Phu would lead to a crumbling of support for the war in metropolitan France and change Geneva from a diplomatic reconnaissance mission into a new "Munich", the scene of a French sell-out to the Vietminh.[3]

Wedded to a geostrategic outlook which posited Vietnam as the starter-domino in what Eisenhower dubbed 'the "falling domino" principle', the US administration engaged in a frantic inter-agency investigation of options.[4] On 29 March, the US Secretary of State, John Foster Dulles, announced his government's response: 'united action', an American-led coalition comprising, inter alia, the UK, Australia and New Zealand, to intervene in Vietnam to shore up the French position.[5] In London, this prospect set alarm bells ringing. The Conservative government of Winston Churchill was fearful lest US-orchestrated intervention prompt PRC counter-intervention, a full-scale war between the United States and the China, and even general war with the Soviet Union. British concerns were heightened by the knowledge that North America lay beyond the range of the present generation of Soviet bombers, a fact which meant that the UK and the other European NATO countries, not the United States, could pay a terrible price if American policy in choices in Asia led to global war. 'All we hold dear', Churchill predicted, 'ourselves, our families and our treasures', would be at risk of immolation if the Soviet Union ever launched an airborne nuclear assault on the British Isles.[6]

United action was born of the trauma of the Korean War in which US forces did the bulk of the fighting and the dying – some 34,000 killed – in a supposedly collective UN campaign.[7] In March 1954, just eight months on from the Korean armistice, the Eisenhower administration and the US Congress determined that salvaging the French position in Indochina should be a genuinely shared international undertaking. With no possibility of UN 'police' action on the Korean model due to the nature of the struggle (part colonial, part civil, with no clear-cut external aggression present), coalition-building devolved to America and a small number of allies with an interest in Indochina and Southeast Asia. An important consequence of this decision to proceed only on a multilateral basis was the gifting of a power of veto over US policy to any ally failing to see the problem and the solution in like-minded terms.

Britain was one such ally. With the backing of Churchill, the Cabinet and the Chiefs of Staff (COS), Eden proceeded to play that veto for all it was worth. The imminent Geneva conference had to be given a chance to effect a peaceful solution, he insisted, and that meant there could be no question of UK support for diplomacy-wrecking military action. With Australia and New Zealand reluctant to enter a coalition without Britain for reasons of Commonwealth solidarity, US hopes for united action collapsed into disunited inaction and Anglo-American relations became strained almost to breaking point.[8] Thereafter, in contemplating the negotiating prospects, Eden knew that a failure to end the war through diplomacy would free the United States to return to the charge in promoting a military solution with all its escalatory dangers. Against this, a successful outcome at Geneva would contain America.[9]

Peace, however, would not come from British desiring but from French and Vietminh readiness to compromise. For two months, from April to June, Eden despaired as the French negotiating team at Geneva proved incapable of setting never mind following a clear diplomatic course. At a harshly realistic level, the French knew that the loss of the Dien Bien Phu garrison – news of which reached Geneva on 7 May – marked the end of their imperial mission and that they should look to exit Indochina on the best terms they could get; but at an emotional, patriotic level, they blanched at the thought of so great a national humiliation and considered fighting on, albeit with the United States as a co-belligerent. French vacillation at Geneva hobbled the peace process until June when the National Assembly in Paris, reflecting the restiveness of France at large, propelled Mendès-France, a long-standing critic of the war, into the premiership. Eden was delighted by the new French leader's tunnel-visioned approach to peace, while the Soviets and the Chinese, who had become nervous themselves about US escalation, began to lean on the Vietminh to offer concessions to France. Even so, the chances of securing a settlement within Mendès-France's stringent deadline remained 'on a knife-edge', Eden recalled; on one side lay peace; on the other lay what he had feared from early on, 'the beginning of the third world war'.[10]

As Mendès-France's month played out, Eden was relieved to discover that a majority of the delegations at Geneva shared his assessment of the consequences of failure. By the time that decision day (20 July) dawned, an outline agreement, including the partitioning of Vietnam into a Vietminh north and non-communist south, had crystallized. The principal dissenters were the Americans who refused to endorse any settlement predicated (as partition was) on the surrender of people and territory to communism. However, as Geneva entered its final lap, the Americans found themselves outnumbered by the proponents of compromise. Not just Britain, but France, China, the Soviet Union and the Democratic Republic of Vietnam (DRV, the Vietminh as a state entity) agreed that peace was preferable to allowing the fighting to continue as a potential catalyst for global war. Of the Indochinese states, the quasi-independent governments of Laos and Cambodia embraced the peace agenda, but the anti-communist Vietnamese, deploring partition, sided with the United States.

As the final day of the conference wore on, a comprehensive settlement was tantalizingly close to realization, but by dusk it was clear that the finer details of the accords would not be worked out before the expiration of the Mendès-France deadline. It was an anxious moment. Was the conference – and with it the chance of peace – about to collapse? At this point, the story goes, a decision was made to stop the clocks at the Palais des Nations, the former home of the League of Nations and the venue of the conference. In effect, time stood still until the agreements were definitively concluded in the early hours of the following day, after which the clocks were reset and restarted.[11] Even if the story is apocryphal, the Geneva accords ending the Indochina War were formally recorded as being reached at midnight on 20 July, a concession to Mendès-France who was able to continue in office. Closing the conference on the afternoon of 21 July, a weary but relieved Eden congratulated the assembled delegates, including some grim-faced Americans and Vietnamese, on a job well done. 'We had stopped an eight-year war and reduced international tension at a point of instant danger to world peace,' he told them. That 'achievement' was 'well worth while'.[12]

As the title indicates, *Anthony Eden, Anglo-American Relations and the 1954 Indochina Crisis* examines the events of 1954 from the particular perspective of Eden, widely acknowledged at the time as the principal facilitator, if not architect, of the Geneva settlement. A second, complementary perspective is Anglo-American relations in that Eden's Indochinese diplomacy pitched the so-called special relationship into a serious crisis of its own. The historical literature on 1954 is extensive, but there is little sustained attention devoted to the interaction of these two issues.[13] There are, however, good reasons for taking an Eden-centric approach. History is lived forwards, not backwards, but in Eden's case, the 1956 Suez crisis, which brought about his ignominious resignation as Prime Minister in January 1957, has cast what Anthony Adamthwaite calls 'a retrospective blight' over much of his earlier career.[14] In modern British political word-association, 'Eden' invariably begets 'Suez' as a first response, certainly when the game is played at the level of public-historical memory – witness, in this connection, how Eden always comes bottom of media-generated league tables of Britain's best or greatest prime minister or else tops those polls seeking to establish the UK's worst leaders.[15] This book offers a corrective to this perception by freeing Eden from the shadow of Suez. The debate about his Middle East policy after he became Prime Minister in 1955 and the dissection of his misjudgements, misapprehensions and mistakes about Egypt will go on.[16] But it is important to recall another Eden – one of the dominating figures in British foreign policy from the mid-1930s to the mid-1950s, an adroit and oft-times successful Foreign Secretary in the Second World War and the early Cold War, and a statesman of international repute and respect. In terms of his skill in the cut-and-thrust of high-level and high-stakes international negotiations, Eden deserves to stand alongside the finest diplomatists to have represented the UK on the world stage.

Other than the Liberal Sir Edward Grey, Eden was the longest-serving Foreign Secretary of the twentieth century.[17] Born in June 1897 to landed gentry in County Durham, Eden was educated locally before going to Eton, but what might have been a seamless transition from school to university was interrupted by the Great War. In September 1915, aged eighteen, Eden joined the British Army; serving with the 21st

(Yeoman Rifles) Battalion of the King's Royal Rifle Corps, he saw action on the Western Front, won the Military Cross for bravery and became (in 1918) the youngest Brigade Major in the Army. Eden's Great War experience was searing for him personally (two brothers were amongst the war-dead) and critical in shaping his later foreign policy outlook, especially his commitment to peace and collective security and his faith in the war-avoiding properties of international diplomacy.[18]

Demobilized in 1919, Eden studied Oriental languages (specializing in Persian and Arabic) at Christ Church, Oxford, and after graduating (with a Double First) in 1922, he toyed with becoming a barrister before deciding on a career in politics. In December 1923, he entered parliament as a Conservative MP. Within three years, he was appointed Parliamentary Private Secretary to the Foreign Secretary, Sir Austen Chamberlain. In 1931, when a National coalition government was formed, he was made Under-Secretary of State at the Foreign Office, and in 1935, he entered the Cabinet for the first time as Minister for League of Nations affairs. Blessed with matinée idol good looks, easy charm, exquisite manners and impeccable dress sense, and now the highly visible embodiment of an organization on which so many people's hopes for lasting peace rested, Eden was amongst the best known and most popular politicians in the country. However, his decorous public image hid from view some less-attractive character traits; vain, petulant, impatient and quick to anger, he was capable of spectacular histrionics. Although these private eruptions tended to subside as quickly as they arose, some who witnessed them wondered whether so thin-skinned and volatile an individual was cut out for a long-term career in the Westminster-Whitehall pressure cooker.

In December 1935, aged thirty-eight, Eden was made Foreign Secretary, the youngest holder of the office since Lord Granville in 1851. His international inheritance, though, was troubled: Nazi Germany, Fascist Italy and Imperial Japan were a growing menace in Europe and Asia, while a chain of crises (German reoccupation of the Rhineland, the Spanish civil war and escalating Japanese aggression in China amongst them) made for a testing tenure. There were also difficulties closer to home. By the start of 1938, appeasement had emerged as Prime Minister Neville Chamberlain's preferred response to the Fascist challenge in Europe, and as Number 10 arrogated to itself important aspects of diplomacy vis-à-vis Germany and Italy, Eden grew restive. In February 1938, nine months into Chamberlain's premiership, he resigned. Later, in his history of the Second World War, Churchill portrayed Eden as a noble-minded anti-appeaser.[19] In truth, his decision to leave the government was prompted as much by pique at Chamberlain's intrusion into his ministerial territory as by objections to appeasement per se. Either way, he was not out of office for long. On the outbreak of war in September 1939, Eden was made Dominions Secretary; in May 1940, when Churchill succeeded Chamberlain, he became Secretary of State for War; and at the end of 1940, he was appointed Foreign Secretary for the second time.

For the remainder of the war, Eden could be counted amongst Churchill's closest advisors and confidants. Both men were later extravagant in their praise of one another and the effectiveness of their partnership. Even if locked in separate rooms, 'put any questions on foreign policy to us and nine times out of ten we would give the same answer', Churchill maintained. Eden, too, remarked on their almost telepathic congruity of outlook.[20] The closeness is further attested by Churchill's anointing of Eden as his political successor.[21] However, this flawless version of the Churchill-Eden relationship has long since been debunked by historians; that there was genuine compatibility, personal and political, is not in doubt, but they also disagreed more regularly than either publicly admitted.[22]

One of the most persistent points of friction concerned the United States. For many people, Churchill has come to personify the 'special relationship', a construct he virtually willed into existence during the war before declaring it 'special' in his Fulton (Iron Curtain) speech in 1946.[23] Churchill was persuaded that Britain's wartime prospects and post-war security depended on maintaining the closest and most harmonious working relationship with the United States. He was not so foolish as to suppose that this combination could ever be one of equals or that it would be devoid of rivalry, and he experienced plenty of frustrations in dealing with America's wartime President Franklin D. Roosevelt. But for all that, he brought a romanticism to UK-US relations – envisioning at one time an amalgamated Anglo-American super-state – to which Eden was entirely immune.[24] If anything, Eden saw too close an association with the United States as a threat to UK autonomy and a check on its freedom to advance its national interests.[25]

In 1943, troubled by what he regarded as Churchill's overly trusting relationship with Roosevelt, Eden confided to his diary that 'I am most anxious for good relations with the U.S. but I don't like subservience to them and I am sure this only lays up trouble for us in the future.'[26] Two years later, as the war drew to a close, he insisted with regard to the Americans that 'we couldn't allow them to dictate our foreign policy and if they were wrong we would have to show independence'.[27] This perception of the United States as a rival as much as an ally constituted the 'most important single element in his diplomatic outlook', Eden biographer David Dutton has shown. Intellectually, he understood the importance of good Anglo-American relations but the 'practical experience of working with the United States … left him deeply troubled'.[28]

Labour's landslide victory in the July 1945 General Election sentenced Eden to more than six years in opposition. As Churchill busied himself delivering acclaimed set-piece orations at international venues (Fulton, Zurich, Strasbourg) or else writing his mammoth history-cum-memoir of the Second World War, the task of rebuilding the shattered Tory party fell heavily on Eden. As the great man's acknowledged heir, he soon grew resentful at Churchill's intermittent leadership and impatient for the succession. The Conservative defeat in the February 1950 General Election might have brought about a change at the top but the Labour victory was so wafer-thin that Churchill, with another election beckoning, stayed in harness. The election duly came in October 1951. For Churchill, the Conservative triumph, albeit with a modest overall majority, was a moment of sweet if delayed revenge for the mauling of 1945.

When Churchill got down to constructing his peacetime administration, his first decision was to send Eden back to the Foreign Office. For his part, Eden was happy to return to King Charles Street, but he did not expect to be there for long; like most politically sentient observers, he assumed that Churchill, his ambition to return to power now sated, would soon step down in his favour. But everyone, Eden included, assumed wrongly, and it would be three-and-a-half years before Churchill finally retired. For now,

Eden got on with running British foreign policy amidst increasing Cold War tensions; US-Soviet nuclear rivalry; multiple threats to UK interests in Asia, the Middle East and the Mediterranean; the ongoing transformation of Empire into Commonwealth; and bleak economic prospects. In dealing with these and other challenges, Eden set as his lodestar the avoidance of war and, by extension, the preservation of peace.

'My world began in war,' Eden wrote of his Great War experience. 'It has been spent in war, its preparation and its aftermath,' he added in reference to the Second World War in which, on a personal level, he lost a son to add to the brothers who perished in the First World War.[29] Now, as Foreign Secretary for the third time, his overriding aim was to ensure that the Cold War remained just that, a *cold* war. 'Hatred of war is good,' he had told the House of Commons back in 1938 as Europe edged closer to cataclysm. 'It is sane and it is healthy. But fear of war is not so good, for fear of war paralyses the will.'[30] By the early 1950s, Eden's outlook had changed because the nature of war had changed. In the nuclear era, with the United States and the Soviet Union developing ever more powerful weapons of mass destruction – Britain itself would join the nuclear club in 1952 – he still hated war, but he had come to fear it, too. In the interwar period, international statesmanship had failed and global tragedy ensued. In a nuclear-armed world, a similar failure, brought on by a paralysis of international diplomacy, could not be permitted.

From this standpoint, none of Eden's post-war achievements are more deserving of study than his role in preventing the 1954 Indochina crisis from escalating into a showdown between the rival Cold War blocs. For those historians who have looked closely at Eden's crisis management, his successful opposition to US-led military action in Vietnam in advance of the Geneva conference, and his equally successful efforts thereafter in holding the negotiations together until the French and Vietminh were ready to conclude an agreement, has been deemed worthy of high praise.[31] Many of Eden's biographers echo this judgement. According to Robert Rhodes James, he not only 'prevented the eruption of a super-Power conflict in Southeast Asia', but his 'strategy and tactics' provided 'models to be followed by anyone with serious interest in the diplomatic arts'.[32] Even Randolph Churchill, a jealous contemporary and a mostly spiteful biographer, acknowledged that Eden's 'talent for negotiation was never seen to better advantage' than in his Geneva 'triumph'.[33]

Historians have also singled out 1954 as Eden's 'annus mirabilis'. Aside from Indochina and Geneva, he is lauded for his vital contribution to preserving NATO in the destabilizing aftermath of the crash of the European Defence Community, the scheme by which West Germany was to provide forces to augment Western security; to resolving the question of the status of Trieste; to brokering the agreement ending a complex international dispute over Iranian oil; and to the understanding with the Egyptian government which paved the way for UK military disengagement from the Suez Canal zone. In aggregate, these accomplishments make 1954 Eden's 'most successful year as a diplomatist', his 'amazing series of diplomatic achievements' marking the 'high point' of his career.[34] By its close, he had been awarded the Wateler Peace Prize by the Carnegie Foundation, was named 'Politician of the Year' by the traditionally anti-Conservative *Daily Mirror* newspaper, and had been inducted by the Queen into the Most Noble Order of the Garter. 'Seldom in history has Britain and a

British Foreign Secretary been so highly revered in the councils of the world,' recalled Anthony Nutting, one of Eden's close associates at the Foreign Office.[35]

'Let the end try the man,' remarks Prince Hal in *Henry IV* (Part 2), a favourite play of the Shakespeare-loving Eden.[36] In this book, Hal's premise is reversed insofar as Eden and Indochina, the jewel in the crown of his annus mirabilis, are tried in their own right and not in the light of Eden's end, his 'Suezide', as David Reynolds has put it.[37] A major Cold War crisis containing serious Hot War perils and a British statesman, derided or dismissed today but at the top of his diplomatic game in 1954 in working to preserve world peace, hardly require justification as subjects for historical scrutiny. But the present study is also in part a response to an earlier treatment, James Cable's *The Geneva Conference of 1954 on Indochina*. Cable occupies a unique position in the story of 1954 as a participant-scholar; a junior member of the UK delegation at Geneva, he became, in retirement, a distinguished historian, his account of the Indochina crisis being a short but sparkling example of his scholarly brilliance. Cable endorsed the historiographical consensus regarding Eden and his diplomacy, but in doing so he offered two observations which have served as additional spurs to write this book. First, 'The Geneva Conference is one of those events which require periodical reassessment if their lasting significance is to be appreciated.' Second, 'Only literature lasts: history requires constant revision.'[38]

From the thrust of this introduction, it might be inferred that the Cable-inspired reassessment and revision that follow will be consensus-reinforcing. At one level, that inference would be correct: Eden's handling of the crisis does deserve credit. However, this book goes beyond previous studies in identifying the wellspring of his diplomacy, the source of his readiness not just to disassociate the UK from US policy but to seek to thwart the United States over Indochina at the risk of damage to the "special relationship", What, then, brought Eden to adopt such a provocative posture? In a word: fear. More particularly, the fear, already alluded to, of nuclear war. And a fear intensified, ironically, not by the actions of the USSR but by the US government's insistence in 1953–1954 that nuclear weapons had acquired 'conventional status' in America's military arsenal and were a legitimate recourse in a range of circumstances below the global war threshold.[39]

One of those circumstances was war with China. According to the Eisenhower administration, Korea had been (in Dulles's words) 'a strategic mistake', an American blood sacrifice incurred in combatting a symptom, not the cause, of communist aggression.[40] Should a new communist-inspired crisis break out on mainland Asia, the Eisenhower administration told the British in late 1953, it intended to deal with the matter at root by targeting the PRC.[41] In 1954, when Indochina became that crisis, Eden, the Cabinet and the COS all feared that US intervention under the banner of united action could provoke – and was perhaps intended to provoke – a level of direct PRC counter-intervention sufficient to justify American retaliation against China. More worryingly still, the most bellicose American happened to be the top military man in the United States: Admiral Arthur W. Radford, Chairman of the Joint Chiefs of Staff (JCS), whom the British were convinced was 'spoiling for a fight' and 'raring for a scrap'.[42] If or when it happened, 'Radford's war with China', as Eden called it, would almost certainly involve the unleashing of US nuclear arms in keeping with the tenets of the Eisenhower administration's national security strategy, the much-vaunted New Look.[43]

Unveiled at the start of 1954, the New Look emphasized massive nuclear retaliation as a deterrent to Sino-Soviet aggression and relied on asymmetrical strategic response should deterrence fail.[44] To the British, it was immediately apparent that if China went beyond indirect support for the Vietminh and sent its armies into Vietnam, the Americans would not allow themselves to become entrapped in another Korean-type "meat-grinder" war but would launch a bombing offensive against military targets in China and institute a naval blockade of PRC ports. Adding to the asymmetry of response – and to what the Foreign Office saw as the 'cataclysmic potentialities' of the New Look – China's use of conventional force in Indochina would be countered by US unconventional (nuclear) means in hitting back at the PRC.[45]

With the Vietminh doing so well on their own without direct Chinese support, there was no pressing reason for the Central People's Government (CPG) to deepen its involvement. However, from his dealings with top military and political figures in the US government, not just the gung-ho Radford, Eden doubted that Washington decision-makers would draw any distinction between unprovoked Chinese aggression (unlikely going into 1954) and Chinese intervention prompted by prior American-led action. In the latter scenario, too, the response would be to bomb and blockade the PRC. The Eisenhower administration sometimes tried to assuage British concerns by pointing out that a Kremlin guided by self-interest would never act to save China if, by so doing, it risked a direct confrontation with a much more powerful US. But American readiness to gamble with British national security impressed no one in London. If the US analysis was wrong, it would be the UK, home since 1948 to American atomic bomber bases, not the United States, which would be sitting in the 'bull's-eye' of a Soviet nuclear riposte.[46]

In the historiography of the Indochina crisis, the nuclear issue is either skirted or ignored altogether (one distinguished scholar has even asserted that 'the atomic bomb did not play any role in the ending of the Indochina conflict').[47] In contrast, this book argues that Indochina was not just a nuclear-infused crisis, it was the first international crisis of the *thermo*nuclear era. By a coincidence of timing seldom appreciated in the literature, the war reached its climax in 1954 just as the UK government, parliament and public were trying (like world opinion generally) to come to terms with the emergence of a new and terrifying engine of destruction, the hydrogen bomb. The USSR claimed to have tested its first thermonuclear weapon in August 1953. In February 1954, on the eve of Indochina crisis, the United States confirmed publicly that it had itself been a thermonuclear power since late 1952 and was in possession of a stockpile of deliverable H-bombs. Hundreds of times more powerful than the atomic bombs used against Japan in 1945, and capable of generating radioactive "fall-out" on a scale which extended the geographical killing zone far beyond detonation point, the H-bomb provided the Churchill government with a chilling reminder of the consequences for the UK if the situation in Indochina spiralled out of control and a general war ensued. With his mind wracked by visions of 'a frightful war which will be the end of everything', Churchill confessed that '[m]y thoughts are almost entirely thermo-nuclear'.[48] So were Eden's. But while the Prime Minister fretted, his Foreign Secretary acted to remove at least some of the catalytic conditions tending towards another world conflict.

Although *Anthony Eden, Anglo-American Relations and the 1954 Indochina Crisis* accepts the "Eden triumphant" consensus amongst British scholars, it is far from uncritical in its treatment of 'the man of Geneva', as Eden was popularly acclaimed in the wake of the conference.[49] In a departure from works which focus primarily on 1954, this book charts the development of the UK approach to Indochina from October 1951, when Eden resumed charge of British foreign policy, through to and then beyond the Geneva conference. In adopting this longer-term perspective, and in accepting that the true art of crisis management is to avoid a crisis in the first place, Eden's handling of Indochina down to 1954 emerges as erratic and inattentive. Several opportunities to help the French get to grips with the Vietminh threat were squandered during this time, a negligence explicable in part by the constraints imposed on creative policymaking by Treasury instructions to limit UK overseas commitments at a time of economic difficulty. Still, the fact remains that prior to 1954, Eden possessed no Indochina policy worth its name.[50] That he rose to the occasion and managed the crisis itself with great skill is not in question. The point, rather, is that the crisis might have been averted, or more realistically attenuated, if Eden and the Foreign Office's Asia experts had been able to convert their instincts about what was required in Indochina into a policy for persuading the French to take early and requisite military and political action.

Eden was neither the first nor the last Foreign Secretary to fail to respond to a deteriorating international situation until the warning signs flashed red. As he advised readers of *Full Circle*, the first of his three volumes of memoirs published in 1960, it should be 'remembered that the events which I now describe were never seen in isolation at the time, but were constantly entangled with a dozen other problems which were vexing us simultaneously'.[51] This was true. At the same time, *Full Circle*, though sound on the crisis, is not an entirely accurate guide to Eden's approach before 1954. Take his claim that he had concluded as early as 1952 that the French could not win the war and that some kind of negotiated settlement was 'the outcome to work for'.[52] In reality, Eden and the Foreign Office held on to a vision of French military success until at least the spring of 1953. Even when Eden agreed at the start of 1954 to examine the pros and cons of a negotiated settlement, he did so not because he believed the war was ripe for diplomatic resolution but because the French government, under domestic pressure, felt obliged to explore all exit options. Given French military and political weakness in Indochina, Eden and his advisors struggled to see how direct negotiations between France and the Vietminh, China, or the USSR could produce an acceptable settlement – meaning one that did not risk the communization of all of Indochina.

British gloom extended to the partitioning of Vietnam, the division of the country into a communist north and a non-communist south along a line reflecting the Franco-Vietminh balance of power. Here, again, *Full Circle* is an unreliable guide. According to Eden, at the start of 1954 he alighted on the idea of 'some form of partition as a solution which might … effect a settlement that would hold'.[53] In actual fact, Eden suspected that partition would lead in quick time to Vietminh absorption of southern Vietnam and possibly Laos and Cambodia. All of which presents us with an irony. Eden's reputation as peacemaker in 1954 is founded on Geneva and partition – on a conference he did not really want, at least in its Indochinese form, and on a solution about which he harboured grave reservations. And yet, perversely, that reputation is merited. The pivot point for Eden was the start of the battle of Dien Bien Phu on 13 March 1954. When the Eisenhower administration reacted to early French reverses by proposing united action, Eden's nervousness about a wider war interacted with more recent thermonuclear fears to effect a fundamental alteration in his attitude. Geneva, the unwanted conference, suddenly became central to British efforts to negate US-led intervention. By the same token, partition, the unwanted solution, acquired new utility as the key to a successful diplomatic outcome. A settlement, Eden averred, even a flawed partition arrangement in Vietnam, would do a service to peace by drawing the sting of the immediate crisis even if it could not save Indochina in the long run. To put it bluntly, but not inaccurately, Eden was ready to entertain the eventual loss of Vietnam rather than accept the risks attaching to a continuation of the war.

To appreciate both the magnitude of Eden's decision and the depth of the fear of US policy which inspired it, we need to recall the importance of Indochina from a British standpoint in the early 1950s. According to the COS, a non-communist Tonkin (the northern third of Vietnam and the cockpit of the war) was as essential to the defence of Indochina as a non-communist Indochina, 'the front-line of the Cold War in Asia', was to the defence of Southeast Asia.[54] The Foreign Office shared this outlook. In a paper prepared for Eden following his return as Foreign Secretary in 1951, officials described Tonkin as 'the bottle-neck through which the forces of Chinese or Chinese-sponsored Communism would swamp the whole of South-East Asia'. They continued:

Once [Tonkin] is lost, the next position where effective military defence would be possible is the Isthmus of Kra [in Thailand]. A withdrawal to that position would mean the almost certain loss of the rice-producing areas of Indo-China, Siam [Thailand] and Burma, on which much of South-East and South Asia at present depends for food. Malaya and Singapore might be untenable. Communism would have reached the frontiers of Burma and East Pakistan. Another important stage would have been reached in the itinerary of world Communism which, according to Lenin, leads from Moscow, through Peking and Calcutta to Paris. It is therefore of the greatest importance that the French should continue to hold the line in Tongking.[55]

As the second most important member of the Western Alliance behind the United States, the UK was contributing more than its fair share to the containment of communism in Western Europe and the Middle East. As to Southeast Asia, there, as elsewhere, international obligations and national interests were interconnected. Before 1954, whenever Eden contemplated Indochina, his 'chief concern' was for Malaya where the UK was fighting to quell a communist insurgency, smaller in scale than the Vietminh challenge to the French in Indochina but still a danger demanding effort and sacrifice to combat.[56] Like planners in the Ministry of Defence, Eden saw Indochina as a geostrategic bulwark against the spread of Chinese or Chinese-backed communism southwards, a development which, if came to pass, would add greatly to UK difficulties in dealing with the Malayan Emergency.[57]

Should it come to general war, British policymakers accepted that Southeast Asia would not be a defence priority (Western Europe, the Middle East and the Mediterranean were more immediately critical to national security). But in the Cold War, the containing of communism in the region was imperative.[58] Moreover, Malaya's rubber and tin resources were a tremendously valuable export asset to an ailing UK economy, a fact which, on its own, merited investment in the security of the colony and the region in which it was cocooned.[59] In sum, Churchill's Conservative government was as cognizant as its Labour predecessor of Indochina's importance at the heart of Southeast Asia's Cold War defence and as a security-screen shielding resource-rich Malaya and other UK regional interests.[60] Reflective of this assessment, Eden told the House of Commons in February 1953 that Indochina was the 'strategic key to South-East Asia' and avowed that its non-communist future 'must be a matter of vital concern to the whole free world'.[61]

Yet, just over a year later, that same Eden was preparing to surrender Tonkin under a partition arrangement worked out with the Soviets, Chinese and Vietminh at the Geneva conference. What had happened? Although Eden still worried that partition would only delay rather than prevent the communization of Indochina, this concern had been trumped by a greater fear: a third and nuclear world war brought on by US intervention in Vietnam. Eden appreciated that the security of Malaya, like the rest of non-communist Southeast Asia, would be harder to assure with Ho Chi Minh triumphant in Indochina, but on the balance, 'that in itself is not a reason for intervening', he maintained. 'We do not want to bring a greater disaster upon our heads by trying to avert the immediate one.'[62]

Frightened of what he saw as 'the dangers of the alternative courses of action which the US government were likely to favour if a settlement were not … secured by negotiation', Eden devoted himself to making Geneva work.[63] Flexible, pragmatic and non-ideological where peace was concerned (his relations with the Soviets were much closer at Geneva than with the Americans), Eden preferred to redraw the containment line in Southeast Asia to exclude some if not all of Vietnam rather than fight to hold that line at the risk of war with China and the USSR.[64]

Historians have sometimes remarked on Eden's aversion to planning in foreign policy and suggested that his default preference was for intuitive or spontaneous diplomacy.[65] In this book, a case is made in support of a somewhat more strategic Eden.[66] Indochina, in and of itself, is not a good example; as previously noted, Eden was devoid of a settled policy until the crisis erupted. However, his Indochinese diplomacy in 1954 was informed by a number of guiding principles which could be classified as strategies.

In June 1952, Eden presented a paper – 'British Overseas Obligations' – to the Cabinet which sought to determine which of the country's many and costly international responsibilities could be shed in order to make its foreign policy more affordable.[67] Following the outbreak of the Korean War and the accompanying general war scare in 1950, the Labour government launched a rearmament programme of such urgent ambition that defence spending rocketed in the space of a year from 8 per cent to more than 14 per cent of gross national product. The connected diversion of resources from the productive economy saw a balance of payments surplus of £300 million become a deficit of £370 million by the time the Conservatives returned to power.[68] Dealing with the parlous state of the economy was amongst the new government's most pressing concerns, but despite strenuous efforts to right the deficit, the economic indicators remained forbidding going into 1952. 'Never in my life have I faced an ordeal of this kind,' reflected Churchill. 'It was worse than 1940.'[69] 'British Overseas Obligations', produced mid-year, was Eden and the Foreign Office's response to the crisis.

'The essence of a sound foreign policy is to ensure that a country's strength is equal to its obligations,' Eden's paper argued. But it was now 'clear that rigorous maintenance of the presently-accepted policies of Her Majesty's Government at home and abroad is placing a burden on the country's economy which it is beyond the resources of the country to meet'. His paper went on to scrutinize the UK's global commitments one by one before concluding that there were in fact no major obligations (NATO or UN membership, for example) which could be safely jettisoned. Some minor adjustments might be possible – relinquishing responsibility for the security of the Falkland Islands was one – but any financial savings would be far outweighed by the damage done to Britain's standing in the world. Even a modest retreat would be interpreted as a 'failure of will and relaxation of grip', Eden stated. And 'once the prestige of a country has started to slide there is no knowing where it will stop'. How, then, could economies be made? The solution – the strategy – the Foreign Office came up with was to take two areas of the world, the Middle East and Southeast Asia, in which the UK presently bore a disproportionate share of the financial, material and military cost of security, and relocate them within the framework of new NATO-type security organizations. 'Our aim should be to persuade the United States to assume the real burdens in such organisations, while retaining for ourselves as much political control – and hence prestige and world influence – as we can,' Eden advised an approving Cabinet.[70]

This method of managing Britain's economic decline while maintaining its international status has been termed 'power-by-proxy'.[71] In regard to Southeast Asia, prior to the return of Eden and the Conservatives, a regional defence organization had been a Foreign Office aspiration. Now, in June 1952, with no sign that the UK was likely to be admitted to ANZUS in the near future – its exclusion from the September 1951 Australia/New Zealand/US Pacific Pact had been a stinging humiliation – it became an objective.[72] However, for the next two years the British tried in vain to engage the interest of the Americans. Playing its own version of power-by-proxy, the US government, with myriad drains on its resources elsewhere in the world, was content for the UK to retain primary responsibility for area defence.[73] But then, in March 1954, with Dulles's call for united action, the United States seemed at last to have accepted the collective ideal. The British, though, were suspicious; on closer inspection, London policymakers concluded that united action was a sleight of hand, a cynical attempt by the Eisenhower administration to win Congressional approval for US intervention in Vietnam by establishing a veneer of international cover. In rejecting the plan as it applied to Vietnam, the Foreign Office, at the behest of the Cabinet, pressed the Eisenhower administration to reconfigure its ideas to make them the foundation stone of a Southeast Asia Treaty Organisation (SEATO). In addition to helping realize power-by-proxy, Eden saw SEATO as a means of protecting Southeast

Asia if Indochina was lost to communism. Equally, if Geneva ended in a settlement, SEATO might stand as a guarantor of the peace.

Power-by-proxy was Eden's conception. And though it failed to achieve its aim in Southeast Asia (SEATO, when eventually formed, was a hollow version of what was envisaged in 'British Overseas Obligations'), it did influence his 1954 crisis management. Furthermore, by its very existence, power-by-proxy gainsays the argument that Eden had no interest in planning. This defence can even be extended. Eden was an advocate of two other concepts, or strategies, inherited from Labour and destined, like power-by-proxy, to impact on his approach to Indochina. The common denominator is China, specifically the competing and conflicting Anglo-American approaches to dealing with the PRC's emergence as the dominant power in Asia. These concepts (containment-and-compromise and dual containment) will be addressed fully in later chapters, but it is useful, from a contextual standpoint, to consider briefly how it was that China was such a 'black spot' and 'major irritant' in UK-US relations.[74]

In truth, British and American policies on China were moving in opposite directions from the very start. In January 1950, three months after the birth of the People's Republic, Attlee's Labour government accorded de jure recognition to the CPG. The Democratic administration of Harry S. Truman not only refused to follow the British lead but continued to recognize Chiang Kai-shek and the anti-communist Chinese nationalists – losers in the civil war and now largely confined to Taiwan – as the legitimate rulers of the immense Chinese land mass. In London, policymakers struggled to understand the US position; Washington enjoyed diplomatic relations with Moscow, hence ostracism of Beijing was inconsistent and potentially counterproductive. According to Foreign Office China experts, the PRC and USSR might share a common ideology (their union solemnized in the February 1950 Sino-Soviet treaty), but the ultra-nationalism of the Chinese Communist Party, when melded with China's traditional xenophobia, suggested that Sino-Soviet relations would be anything but smooth. This being so, diplomatic contacts might offer openings to the West to drive a wedge between China and the USSR. Beyond this, the Labour government's desire to protect long-standing UK business and commercial interests in China spoke in favour of a modus vivendi with the PRC, as did concern for the security of the Crown Colony of Hong Kong.[75]

Viewing diplomatic recognition as an act of moral approval, the US government was unmoved by British arguments. Even if it had been minded to ape UK pragmatism, the rise of McCarthyite anti-communist fundamentalism in the United States in early 1950 reduced the Truman administration's room for manoeuvre on China before the outbreak of the Korean War eliminated it altogether.[76] By then, Anglo-American differences had spilled over to the United Nations where the United States insisted that Chiang's regime remain the sole representative of China in all UN organs, including the Security Council, and the British favoured the transfer to the communists of all Chinese prerogatives. To avoid a damaging split, the Labour and later the Conservative government publicly deferred to American preferences while working privately to change US thinking.[77]

This, though, did not prevent UK China policy generating misunderstanding and bitterness in the United States, with the China lobby, McCarthyites and others traducing the British as 'Communist sympathizers' or 'greedy materialists' and likening

London's approach to 'appeasement of bandits, robbers and murderers'.[78] The Truman administration, too, grew frustrated with the placatory thrust of UK policy, especially following PRC entry into the Korean War. With Chinese troops killing US soldiers from late 1950 onwards, the Attlee government's insistence – born of a fear of a wider war involving the USSR – that the conflict be confined to the Korean peninsula rather than extended to China was not always appreciated in Washington. Anticipating Admiral Radford on Indochina in 1954, US strategists countered that there might be no end to wars like Korea unless or until communist aggression in Asia was dealt with at source, and that meant targeting the PRC.[79] In the event, the United Nations sided with the UK in the strategic debate, much to the frustration of those in the US government in favour of a bold approach.[80] 'United Kingdom policy was broadly speaking to use the carrot and the stick' in dealing with the PRC, a senior Foreign Office official summed up in late 1951, 'whereas United States policy involved the use of the stick alone'.[81]

Responding to these developments, the British Foreign Office evolved two methods of handling the PRC – and of handling US policy towards the PRC – which would hopefully reduce the chances 'of the Americans taking the bit between their teeth and going ahead, without consulting any of their allies, on steps which may have consequences affecting us all'.[82] The first was 'containment-and-compromise'.[83] Given that the PRC could not be wished out of existence, the British believed that lasting peace in Asia hinged on a general settlement with China. This was the compromise side of the strategy. For the three years of the Korean War, Labour and Conservative governments alike were forced to emphasize containment, but the ultimate object, a modus vivendi with China, was never abandoned. To the contrary, as Labour Foreign Secretary Ernest Bevin put it in February 1951, if the Chinese communists were handled prudently, 'a settlement of the East can keep peace for a hundred years'.[84]

In public, too, Labour and Conservative leaders stressed their enduring commitment to an Asia-wide settlement negotiated with the PRC once the fighting in Korea was ended.[85] With the signing of the July 1953 Korean armistice, the strategic recalibration began. As the later chapters of this study will demonstrate, Eden's readiness to engage directly and constructively with PRC Premier and Foreign Minister Zhou Enlai on Indochina at Geneva in 1954 confirmed the post-Korea restoration of compromise to a position of precedence over containment. In contrast, American policy seemed to Eden to still be fuelled by a vengeful desire to punish the PRC, to reverse the communist revolution or at the least to destroy China's future war-making potential.

This brings us back to British nervousness over united action in 1954. Based on recent experience, the Churchill government feared that the United States would manipulate the Indochina crisis to provide the opening to target China which had been denied to it during the Korean War. In reaction to this possibility, Eden brought into play the second inherited concept, dual containment. Existing in sketchy form under Labour, dual containment filled out after 1951 as the British repeatedly, if unsuccessfully, pressed the Americans to join in a collective defence of Southeast Asia. Historians Geir Lundestad and Michael Lind have shown how the United States pursued its own form of dual containment in Europe and East Asia after 1945, its policies predicated on keeping out new enemies (the Soviet Union and China) and keeping down old ones (Germany and Japan).[86] By the early 1950s, the UK also perceived twin dangers in need of containing, the one posed by Chinese communism, the other posed by the United States and its minatory approach to the PRC. Leaving aside other considerations, including power-by-proxy, in 1954 a Southeast Asian defence organization became for Eden an instrument of dual containment – a construct which, if it could be realized, would not only deter Chinese aggression but would curb US adventurism by making Washington answerable to allies, not just to itself, for its policy choices.

The irony, as will be seen, is that by the end of the Indochina crisis, Eden had begun to wonder whether the UK's ability to hobble US unilateralism might actually be greater outside than inside SEATO.

*

Although Eden is the main focus of this book, the Indochina stage was graced by a rich and varied cast of actors, some of whom, it could be argued, are equally deserving of the accolade 'Man of Geneva'. Eden himself recognized a plurality of effort at Geneva. In June 1954, with the conference recessed for a short time, he paid tribute in the House of Commons to Molotov, Zhou Enlai and Mendès-France whose shared commitment to the peace process gave him hope that a settlement might yet be reached. Of the American Secretary of State, he made no mention.[87] That is hardly surprising. As Eden told Dulles to his face the previous month, 'the trouble with you, Foster, is that you want World War Three'.[88]

As has been established, the Indochina crisis spawned an acute secondary crisis in Anglo-American relations. And here, it is fair to say, basic UK-US policy differences were greatly exacerbated by the personal animosity that Eden and Dulles felt towards one another. They had never really got on, their mutual mistrust predating 1954, but Eden's refusal to back united action so outraged Dulles that their relationship became increasingly acrimonious.[89] As Dulles's associates testified, the US Secretary never really got over Eden's 'breaking of faith'.[90] Moving forward two years to 1956, when the Egyptian government's nationalization of the Suez Canal Company precipitated another international crisis, the Anglo-American dramatis personae was almost identical to the Indochina cast-list: Eisenhower was still US President and Dulles still headed the State Department, and though there was no Churchill on the UK side, Eden was present in his elevated position as Prime Minister. Intriguingly, though, the roles they played in 1956 were a reversal of those they inhabited in 1954. Now it was Eden's turn to press for military action (in this case to recover the canal and, if possible, topple Nasser and his government), while Eisenhower and Dulles publicly promoted international mediation and a peaceful solution.

Noting this 1954–1956 co-relation, a number of historians have argued that Eden may have derived an exaggerated sense of Britain's independence in the international arena as a result of his triumphs in 1954, especially his success on Indochina. More particularly, he developed a recklessly inflated notion of how far the UK could operate independently of the United States. Geneva, lest it be forgotten, was not just a victory for peace; it was in many ways a victory for Britain over America, and for Eden over Dulles. According to this line of argument, Eden's Indochina-inspired overconfidence led him to downplay the likely American reaction to his scheme for resolving the Suez crisis. In approving military action to recover the canal, Eden was content to work in cahoots with France and Israel but opted to leave the United States in the dark until the very last moment. This proved to be a colossal misjudgement, and the scale of US hostility, once fully revealed, left him stunned.[91]

Is it taking things too far to suggest that Dulles 'stored up his resentments' from 1954 until a chance presented itself in 1956 to get his own back on Eden? Was Dulles really driven by a thirst for revenge – a thirst slaked by the draconian US economic sanctions imposed on the UK in November 1956 which triggered a run on the pound, compelled the government to halt military action in Egypt and launched Eden into political oblivion? Is this taking human agency too far?[92] To reiterate, the aim of this book is to take Eden and Indochina out of the shadow of Suez. In so doing, however, the part – if any – that Indochina played in Eden's 'Suezide' must also be interrogated.

2

Indochina, 1951–1952: The Chinese Dimension

Anthony Eden began 1951 in opposition and in predictive mode. There was, he suspected, 'a very dangerous year' ahead for Asia, where the 'threat to peace' was 'urgent'. The Korean War was the main worry – a big Chinese offensive had just begun – but Indochina, where the Franco-Vietminh war was now in its fifth year, was a growing concern.[1] In the final months of 1950, the French Expeditionary Corps (FEC), which had largely contained the Vietminh since 1946, suffered a series of major reverses – cumulatively, 'the greatest colonial defeat since Montcalm died at Quebec' – in the mountainous north of Tonkin which left the People's Army of Vietnam (PAVN) in control of the supply lines from the People's Republic of China, its increasingly generous benefactor. Over the course of 1951, however, the French slowly recovered their morale, if not the lost territory, so that by the time that Eden took over at the Foreign Office in the autumn the situation in Tonkin had begun to stabilize.[2] Like many war-watchers, Eden attributed the improvement in the French position to the 'brilliant' leadership of General Jean de Lattre de Tassigny.[3]

The 61-year-old de Lattre arrived in Indochina in December 1950 to take on the dual responsibility of High Commissioner and Commander-in-Chief and soon acquired the moniker *Roi Jean*, a testament both to his leadership skills and an imperious personality. De Lattre's first priority was to thwart a powerful PAVN thrust towards Hanoi in the Red River delta, the hub of the French position in Tonkin. This he accomplished between January and March 1951 with victories at the battles of Vinh Yen, Mao Khe and Dong Trieu, a sequence of success which left thousands of Vietminh troops killed or wounded. The flow to Indochina of increasing quantities of US military supplies, including aircraft to deliver napalm bombs, gave the French a decisive advantage in these battles, with one PAVN survivor remembering Vinh Yen as 'a burning tomb'.[4]

To further secure Hanoi, as well as Haiphong, Tonkin's main port, de Lattre ordered the construction of hundreds of concrete blockhouses-cum-forts along the delta's extensive landward perimeter. The so-called de Lattre line eventually fanned out in a rough semicircle from the coast at Baie d'Along inland as far as Vinh Yen and Viet Tri before looping southwards to the sea again near Phat Diem. This defensive chain was intended to protect the delta and its 10 million inhabitants from Vietminh main-force assaults, but the PAVN commander, General Vo Nguyen Giap, scarred by recent defeats, opted to avoid set-piece engagements and prioritized lower-level mobile (or guerrilla) warfare. In dealing with this particular challenge, the de Lattre line would prove to be a porous barrier. Nevertheless, as French reporter Lucien Bodard noted, de Lattre had 'blazed like a splendid comet' in the Indochinese firmament in 1950–1951. Thanks to his inspired and inspiring leadership, some in Paris, Hanoi and Saigon dared to think not just of recovery but of victory.[5]

Significantly, de Lattre was not one of the optimists. Conscious of the limited manpower and resources likely to be made available to him by his government, he accepted that there was 'little chance of a miracle'.[6] On a visit to London in October 1951, he told the British Chiefs of Staff of his 'nightmare': direct Chinese intervention to prevent a Vietminh defeat. French intelligence assessed that the PRC could muster 150,000 troops for action in Vietnam in an emergency. De Lattre could 'deal with Ho Chi Minh', he maintained, 'but not with Ho Chi Minh reinforced in this way'. If China entered the war, France would require allied assistance. In any event, Indochina was no longer a purely French concern. Tonkin was 'the keystone to the defence of South East Asia', an area which, if lost, would leave 'no possible line of resistance to Communism short of the Suez Canal ... [and] once Communism had penetrated as far as Suez, then it would not be long before it infiltrated into North Africa [and] Europe might well find herself out-flanked to the South by Communist infiltration'. In making his case, de Lattre was preaching to the converted with both the Chiefs of Staff and the Labour Foreign Secretary, Herbert Morrison, already persuaded of the need for a coordinated Western policy for deterring – or meeting – Chinese aggression in Southeast Asia.[7]

On 25 October 1951, election day in Britain, Morrison proposed to the US and French governments that they join with the UK in top-level military discussions on Southeast Asian security.[8] Twenty-four hours later, the Conservatives having been returned to power, the Morrison initiative became the Eden initiative. 'Tongking is vital in the defence of South-East Asia', a Foreign Office brief for the new Foreign Secretary pointed out. However, because of the UK's limited and already overstretched military resources, not to mention an economy in crisis, any help for the French could only be offered within the framework of an agreed Anglo-American-French policy for sharing the burden for the defence of Southeast Asia generally. Predicting 'British Overseas Obligations' and power-by-proxy, the Foreign Office hope was that if the United States could be persuaded to shoulder responsibility for dealing with Chinese aggression against Indochina, Britain's contribution to regional security could be limited to its ongoing anti-communist effort in Malaya. Still, the first step was agreement on military objectives 'at Chiefs of Staff level', hence the Morrison/Eden initiative.[9]

The French responded quickly and enthusiastically to the British proposal, but the US government, or at any rate the Pentagon and Joint Chiefs of Staff, evinced little interest in defence coordination. In November, when the French sought a pledge of US air support if China attacked Tonkin, General Omar Bradley, Chairman of the Joint Chiefs of Staff, rebuffed them on the ground that the United States could not take on additional commitments while the Korean War remained such a drain on its resources.[10] Adding urgency to French entreaties was intelligence pointing to a significant build-up of Chinese forces along the Sino-Tonkin border.[11] PRC invasion rumours were a staple of the war but up to now none had proven true. From the standpoint of international communist strategy, the Vietminh were doing a good job on their own account in diverting French strength (and American money and military hardware) away from Western Europe, and it was hard to see what Beijing – or Moscow – would gain from a shift to active belligerency. That said, by December British intelligence suspected that there might be some substance to the latest French claims. At the least, the reports provided an excuse to relaunch the Morrison/Eden proposal. On Christmas Eve, the Foreign Office instructed the British Ambassador in Washington, Sir Oliver Franks, to convey to the Truman administration 'our view that tripartite military talks should take place without delay'.[12]

Three days later – a full two months on from the launch of the Morrison/Eden initiative – the US Joint Chiefs relented and agreed to participate in staff talks.[13] Continued rumours of Chinese action 'on a large-scale' strengthened the Anglo-French case for tripartite planning.[14] In time, these reports would turn out to be as vacuous as their predecessors, but even if the Chinese were not poised to make an immediate move on Tonkin, there was no guarantee they would not seek to open a second front in connection with Korea at some point in the future. And a threat that could not be dismissed, US planners belatedly accepted, was a threat that must be catered for.[15]

On New Year's Eve 1951, Churchill, Eden and a large retinue of advisors headed to the United States for talks with the Truman administration. For Eden and the Chiefs of Staff, the visit provided an opportunity to raise the issue of Southeast Asian security ahead of the tripartite staff talks which were now scheduled to take place at the Pentagon in mid-January. More generally, the visit would take the temperature of the Anglo-American partnership which had lately 'become very difficult to manage', the Foreign Office briefed Eden, 'owing to the increasing disparity of power within it'.[16] The Prime Minister was keen to make the UK-US relationship "special" again after what he held to be six years of neglect under Labour – too keen, in the view of some in the British party who worried that he might concede US primacy in Asia, a part of the world which rated low in his estimate of UK global interests, if this helped secure American support for the British position in the Middle East, especially Egypt, a Churchillian priority.[17]

Amongst this troubled contingent was the Foreign Secretary. In Rome a few weeks earlier, Dean Acheson, the US Secretary of State, conferred with Eden about the Korean armistice negotiations which had begun the previous July and were now centred on the north-south border town of Panmunjom. If an armistice was signed only to be broken by the Chinese, that would be 'the trigger', Acheson said. 'We should have to go after them ... if they jump on us, they will be for it ... no holds will be barred.' Eden emerged from this encounter convinced that the United States would 'rise in its wrath' if provoked by the Chinese, and by the time he arrived in Washington he was anxious to establish the UK's right to judge an Asian crisis on its merits. After all, what the Americans considered a casus belli might be viewed by the British as lower-level skirmishing meriting a proportionate not a disproportionate response. Eden was also mindful of the fact that the present generation of Soviet bombers lacked the range to reach North America but could easily get to East Anglia where the previous Labour government had granted the US Air Force bases for its atomic-capable B-29 super-fortresses. If the United States acted unilaterally and provocatively in an Asian crisis, whether in Korea or over Indochina, Britain would bear the brunt of Soviet atomic retaliation if general war ensued.[18]

Churchill was not particularly sympathetic to Eden's Asian concerns. 'I do hope that Anthony will meet the Americans over China, which really does not matter to us,' he confided to Lord Moran, his personal physician, soon after arriving in Washington. 'Then they in turn might meet us about Egypt or Persia, which matter a lot. After all, what Conservative in England is in favour of Chinese Communists?'[19] Churchill's interest in Asian affairs had waned since Indian independence, and he was invariably unhappy when tensions with Washington over communist China threatened to impact negatively on Anglo-American relations in other areas.[20] 'The ferment in the Far East hardly seemed to interest him,' Moran observed; 'when China was the subject of discussion you could see that he had not got the facts in his head.'[21]

The Asian Cold War came up in informal Anglo-American discussions aboard the presidential yacht, the *Williamsburg*, on the evening of Churchill and Eden's arrival (5 January). The Prime Minister commended the Americans for their commitment in Korea and sympathized with US losses. The value of this sacrifice, however, could be seen in Europe as much as in Asia in the NATO defence build-up prompted by North Korea's aggression. On Southeast Asia, Acheson suggested that the time had come for the United States and its allies to decide whether the region 'was worth fighting for' if the Chinese engaged in main-force aggression. 'If it was', then 'how could effective resistance be offered[?]'. Eden personally had no doubts on that score: Southeast Asia *must* be defended. But that required allied planning. The French 'could handle Indo-China if it did not become a second Korea with major Chinese intervention', he remarked in an echo of de Lattre. 'If this happened, there would have to be major decisions.'[22] This was the closest that Anglo-American leaders came to discussing Southeast Asian security. Instead, there was tacit acceptance that the issue could be left to the tripartite Chiefs of Staff when they met the following week.

The Asian Cold War was the topic of a more formal discussion on 6 January when Churchill and Eden met with Acheson, Bradley and the US Secretary of Defense, Robert Lovett. Korea again dominated with the Americans making clear their determination to bomb and blockade China if the communists wrecked the armistice negotiations or undermined an emergent settlement (though Bradley insisted that population centres would not be bombed and that, in the first instance at least, atomic weapons would not be used). On the British side, Eden refused to be bounced into giving advance approval to any dangerously escalatory action.[23] At a further meeting the next day, this time with Truman present, Acheson provided an Asian tour d'horizon. In Korea, 'the Chinese had ceased to take the armistice talks seriously'. If the PRC attitude portended a resumption of the heavy fighting of 1950–1951, UN forces could cope as long as American air power was deployed 'not only on the other side of the Yalu River, but also against air-fields in other parts of China', and as long as the US Navy was free to operate against Chinese ports. Moving on to Taiwan, Acheson reaffirmed American support for Chiang Kai-shek, 'in spite of the weakness and corruption of his regime'. In the Pacific, the 'key to the position' was Japan and it was 'essential to save Japan from Communism'. On Indochina, the administration's hope was that the staff talks would produce 'an agreed course of action' for dealing with the Chinese threat. Meanwhile, US military aid, already considerable, would continue to be given to France to combat the Vietminh.[24]

No sooner had Acheson finished than Churchill expressed his wish to 'help the United States in every way possible'. In Asia, 'there could be no UK priority or equality of leadership'. To the contrary, the 'role of leader squarely belonged to the United States and the UK will do its utmost to meet US views and requests'. This doubtless pleased the President who, in anticipation of the British visit, had expressed 'a strong desire to obtain agreement from Mr Churchill … that he and the UK would go all out for us in Asia'.[25] When Eden spoke, he tried to claw back a little of what the Prime Minister had conceded. Asia must be viewed as a strategic whole, he argued, with the Americans committed in Korea and the British and French committed in Malaya and Indochina, respectively. Allied unity in containing communism across this huge area was a pressing matter.[26] This appeal was greeted coolly by a US administration pursuing its own line on power-by-proxy. A State-Defense brief on Southeast Asia, prepared for Truman in advance of the British visit, recommended that if Churchill and Eden demanded a greater level of US involvement in Southeast Asia, the President should give 'as responsive a reply as possible without at the same time taking the heart out of British and French determination to defend the area by their own means'. It had been 'apparent for several years that the UK wishes to maximise American commitments in Southeast Asia', but any proposal for a 'command set-up' should be resisted.[27]

For Churchill, the climax of the visit was an address to a joint session of Congress, the third time he had been accorded the honour. Aside from his standard refrain about Anglo-American comity, the speech, delivered on 17 January 1952, was notable for a loaded reference to Korea. 'We welcome your patience in the armistice negotiations,' he told his audience, 'and our two countries are agreed that, if the truce we seek is reached only to be broken, our response will be prompt, resolute and effective'.[28] Warmly received on Capitol Hill, the Korean section of his address generated criticism at home where the *Manchester Guardian* accused the Prime Minister of giving way to American preferences for 'carrying the war to China', and the *Daily Herald* condemned his approval of an American attack on China, presumed to be nuclear in nature, which could spark a world war and bring 'ruin for us all'.[29]

Churchill had done no more than articulate publicly a decision taken privately by his Labour predecessor Clement Attlee, a point he was quick to make in parliament on his return from America when the opposition moved to censure him for warmongering. It was the old Labour government, he revealed, not the present Conservative one that had departed from the principle of limiting the war to Korea. In May 1951, the Cabinet, with Attlee in the chair, secretly approved the bombing of targets in China, albeit in heavily prescribed circumstances (if, for instance, UN forces came under attack from aircraft launched from bases inside the PRC). Churchill supported this undertaking and urged all parties to show trust in the judgement of the Americans. Labour was undone and the government survived the censure vote.[30]

In public, Eden backed Churchill's 'trust America' position, but in private he had been 'horrified' by the way the British had been treated in Washington. The Americans were 'polite [and] listen to what we have to say', he told the Cabinet on his return, 'but make (on most issues) their own decisions'. This was regrettable but tolerable as long as those decisions were measured.[31] But what, one wonders, would Eden have made of Truman's diary entry for 27 January, just over a week after he and Churchill had left for home. The President often used his diary as a pressure release, but this particular entry, occasioned by indications that the Chinese were secretly planning an offensive in Korea while talking peace at Panmunjom, is unusually angry. The time had come, Truman felt, to hit China and hit it hard.

> It seems to me that the proper approach now would be an ultimatum with a ten day expiration limit, informing Moscow that we intend to blockade the China coast from the Korean border to Indo-China, and that we intend to destroy every military base in Manchuria, including submarine bases, by means now in our control and if there is further interference we shall eliminate any ports or cities necessary to accomplish our peaceful purposes ... We did not start this Korean affair but we intend to end it for the benefit of the Korean people, the authority of the United Nations and the peace of the world ... This means all out war. It means that Moscow, St. Petersburg, Mukden, Vladivostok, Pekin[g], Shanghai, Port Arthur, Dairen, Odessa, Stalingrad and every manufacturing plant in China and the Soviet Union will be eliminated. This is the final chance for the Soviet Government to decide whether it wants to survive or not.[32]

As 1952 wore on, the British – both political and military leaders – reluctantly concluded that American thinking about China was a dangerous admixture of emotion and vengefulness. Truman's diary entry is an extreme expression of this attitude, and to be sure, the President never spoke publicly in such terms. Even so, when Eden encountered similar attitudes in his dealings with US officials, even in moderated form compared with Truman's dyspeptic outburst, they troubled him greatly.

The three-power staff talks on Southeast Asia took place at the Pentagon on 11 January 1952, a dark day for France. Two months earlier, de Lattre had been diagnosed with cancer. He returned to France for medical treatment but by the end of the year it was being whispered in Paris that de Lattre's comet was fading fast. He died on the day the staff talks began. After the largest funeral seen in Paris since that of Marshal Foch in 1929, de Lattre, posthumously promoted to the rank of Marshal of France, was laid to rest at his home village of Mouilleron-en-Parads alongside his son, Bernard, killed on duty in Vietnam the previous year.[33]

Notwithstanding the masses who turned out to pay their respects to de Lattre, the fact was that after more than five years of fighting, public opinion in France was wearying of the war.[34] It remained to be seen what impact the disappearance of so formidable a champion of the cause would have on the staying power of the French government, parliament and people. For now, the FEC fought on against the Vietminh. As for China, the Vietminh's ally, the task before the US, UK and French military leaders when they assembled at the Pentagon was to decide on a common position on PRC aggression. The importance of the Chinese dimension of the Indochina problem at this time is reflected in the high level of representation: General Bradley, the JCS chief, led for the Americans; Field Marshal Sir William Slim, the Chief of the Imperial General Staff, for the UK; and General Alphonse-Pierre Juin, head of the French General Staff, for France.

De Lattre was no more, but the fear that had haunted him in the final phase of his life lingered. According to Juin, 350,000 Chinese troops were believed to be massing on the Chinese side of the Sino-Tonkin frontier. If the PRC invaded, France would stage a fighting withdrawal in the north. As long as Anglo-American air and naval support was speedily forthcoming, he was confident that Hanoi and the Red River delta, as well as Annam (the centre) and Cochinchina (the south), could be held. In response, neither Bradley nor Slim was prepared to commit to local defence in Tonkin, both claiming that their respective military resources were already overstretched. The Americans felt that the issuance of a warning to China that 'further active aggression' beyond Korea 'would result in retaliation not necessarily confined to the area of aggression' might have deterrent value. But what if the warning was ignored? To Bradley, the answer was to bomb and blockade China. The Western Alliance risked military exhaustion if it kept battling communism in 'fringe areas' like Korea and Vietnam. Aggression must be dealt with at source, and in Asia that meant China. But what kind of bombing? Conventional or unconventional? This, Bradley admitted, was a poser. 'If you have a limited number of atomic bombs, do you use them on China or should you save them for someone else?' Slim, for his part, was non-committal on bombing but agreed that a warning might sow 'some doubt in the Chinaman's mind'.[35]

This focus on China rather than Indochina, and the working assumption on the US side that Tonkin (and perhaps all of Indochina) could not be saved in the event of PRC aggression, disheartened Juin. Recognizing the implications for French morale, Bradley and Slim agreed to the setting up of an 'Ad Hoc Committee' to consider in more detail not just the kind of action to be taken against China but measures to defend Vietnam *in* Vietnam, the 'fire-brigade' option. Australia and New Zealand would also be invited to participate.[36] The staff talks therefore closed on a note of harmony, but afterwards Juin could barely hide his disappointment at the lack of any reassurance for Indochina from the Americans who steadfastly refused to commit 'a man, a ship, or an aeroplane' if China attacked Tonkin.[37]

The Ad Hoc Committee – composed of US Vice Admiral Arthur C. Davis, French General Paul Ely and British Air Chief Marshal Sir William Elliot – convened at the Pentagon on 25 January 1952. On the question of countering a PRC invasion, the committee could only replicate the disagreements of the staff conference. The Americans parried French pressure to commit to local defence in Tonkin and adhered to their preference for action against China itself. The British, too, saw little hope of successful local defence, but this did not produce automatic backing for the American approach. Neither bombing nor blockade would compel the PRC to withdraw from Tonkin, Elliot felt, while 'the danger of this action resulting in general war' involving the USSR 'was unacceptably serious'. Davis agreed: bombing and blockade would not save Vietnam, but that was not the object. US thinking was predicated on reducing China's 'capacity for further aggression' beyond Vietnam. If it served as the catalyst for direct action against China, Vietnam's sacrifice could lead to the salvation of the rest of Asia. Besides, Davis pointed out, 'All retaliatory action carried an equal risk of extending the conflict.' In the end, this fundamental Anglo-American (and Franco-American) disagreement prevented the Ad Hoc Committee reaching unanimous recommendations.[38]

In London, the Foreign Office and the Ministry of Defence drew the same conclusion, namely that the US Joint Chiefs, if not the Truman administration generally, were looking for an excuse or justification to destroy the Central People's Government. Shackled by the UN in Korea, the US military evidently regarded Vietnam as a more promising springboard from which to attack China. 'I have the impression that as usual the Americans are trying to entangle us,' Sir William Strang, Permanent Under-Secretary in the Foreign Office, concluded. 'In fact, it looks as though the tripartite talks as a whole have proved to be an entangling operation: objective: war with China.'[39] Air Chief Marshal Sir John Slessor, Chief of Air Staff, despaired of a US policy driven by 'blind petulance'. His fellow service chiefs concurred. 'We must face the fact that naval blockade and widespread bombing of China means general war with China, which we have no certainty would not lead to Global war by the invocation of the Sino-Russian treaty.' The Americans needed to be reminded that the 'object of any action against China is not revenge for her evil doing'.[40]

Anglo-American differences were sufficiently worrisome for Elliot to take time out from a visit to London in February to drive to Chartwell, Churchill's family home in Kent, to give the Prime Minister a first-hand briefing. If China invaded Indochina, the British Chiefs of Staff were not opposed to retaliation per se, Elliot explained, but they did want it confined to rail communications and airfields leading to the area of aggression – in this case Tonkin – 'not therefore widespread bombing all over China'. Blockade, he added, would only be effective if action was taken against Soviet ports in East Asia, a move rejected in the Korean context as recklessly escalatory. Elliot's overall conclusion – 'We are opposed to general war with China or to action which we feel might (almost involuntarily) involve Soviet Russia and lead to global war' – was seconded by Churchill.[41]

Inconclusive as they were, these two rounds of military discussions confirmed for the British that the Americans were far from complacent about containing communism in Southeast Asia. Yet the satisfaction London policymakers ought to have derived from this revelation was offset by anxiety about the draconian retaliatory measures favoured by the US Joint Chiefs if China attacked Vietnam. 'The Americans considered that the Russians would start a global war when they wished to do so and not before, regardless of what might happen in the Far East,' the Chiefs of Staff reflected, whereas in the British view, 'global war might start, not particularly because either side wished it, but because an extension of war in the Far East – which was admittedly likely to follow retaliatory action against China – could gradually lead to a situation where global war became unavoidable'.[42]

Even if war with China remained confined to Asia, the Foreign Office worried that there would still need to be a substantial redeployment of troops and military resources from Europe and the Middle East. But was this sensible in terms of the West's global priorities? In a war with the Soviet Union ('enemy number one' and the only power 'that can threaten our very existence') the defence priorities were the UK and the North Atlantic area followed by the Middle East and Southeast Asia. Now, however, in a time of Cold War, these priorities were in danger of being turned 'upside down'. The UK's strategic reserve was committed in the Middle East, notably Egypt, dealing with 'enemy number three', nationalism, while the demands of coping with 'enemy number two', China, were creating a haemorrhage of resources from Europe to Asia. The Korean War, along with the campaigns in Indochina and Malaya, 'constituted a serious enough strain in all conscience', Eden's advisors counselled. Could the West afford another large-scale war in Asia that denuded the defence of Western Europe and the Middle East and left these 'hot war strategic priorities' vulnerable to attack from 'enemy No. 1', the USSR? In sum, if the Chinese made an aggressive move on Vietnam, the Western response had to be 'limited to the theatre of attack'.[43]

Historian Anthony Short has found it 'hard to avoid the impression that, if only hypothetically, the US was preparing for war' with China.[44] This may have been true of the American military, but the political authorities in Washington seem to have been more conflicted. In public, Acheson played the anti-Chinese hard man (in testimony before the Senate Foreign Relations Committee he pronounced himself in favour of warning the PRC, vis-à-vis Indochina, that 'if you fellows come in ... you will be pasted').[45] Contrary to this and the menacing tone he adopted when he met Eden in Rome in late 1951, Acheson sometimes succumbed to private doubts about the wisdom of the JCS position. It was too much to expect America's allies to 'agree to give us complete support, furnish all the ground troops and leave us complete freedom for any action we wished to take and not involve us in any united command', and even more so 'in view of the fact that ... the action contemplated would not achieve the desired result of protecting Southeast Asia unless it accomplished it by a defeat of China which would undo what looked like an early conquest'. In an effort to harmonize its political and military outlook, the US government, at Acheson's prompting, embarked on a wholesale review of its Southeast Asian policy, a process which dragged on into mid-1952. As a result, further tripartite discussions were put on hold.[46]

While they waited on the Americans, the British honed their own thinking. The effectiveness of any action against China should not be judged in terms of how far it contributed to 'undermining or destroying the Central People's Government', a Foreign Office study reiterated in March.[47] In a paper for the Defence Committee that same month, the Chiefs of Staff cautioned that American plans could not save Indochina but would run the risk of 'total war'. Even if the USSR behaved with restraint, US actions might still 'make things much worse' in Korea, invite a PRC attack on Hong Kong and 'go a long way to do what [we] have always agreed we should not do, i.e. throw China more and more, and perhaps irretrievably, into the Russian camp'. The American military outlook 'is inspired not by cool strategic reasoning but by vengeful petulance – backed by political pressure to do *something* – without thinking out where it is going to lead'.[48]

The Prime Minister agreed. A blockade would be 'futile' if it excluded Soviet ports, he observed. Yet to include them would be 'a direct challenge to the Soviet Government, with consequences which no one could foretell'. As to bombing, Churchill thought that air action against Chinese lines of communication inside PRC territory and adjacent to the front would not 'raise the decisive issues'. In general, though, he considered it 'silly to waste bombs in the vague inchoate mass of China, and wrong to kill thousands of people for no purpose'.[49] Another COS submission to the Defence Committee in April commented that while 'we are supporting American policy in both Korea and Japan, the part of Asia of greatest interest to the Americans, they are not committed to any measures to the containment of China in South-East Asia, where the main British interests lie'. What was needed was a coordinated Anglo-Franco-American policy for deterring or repulsing Chinese aggression in a proportionate manner. Foreshadowing the dual containment thinking which would influence Eden in 1954, the Chiefs of Staff noted that the United States was at present answerable only to itself for its actions, but if some kind of tripartite planning machinery was put in place, the British and French might be able to exercise some restraining influence over US policy. Such machinery – and in due course perhaps a NATO-esque structure – would straddle the extremes of doing too much to punish China (the US approach) and doing nothing (which the British agreed was unthinkable). By its very existence, a Southeast Asian defence organization would provide 'tangible evidence' that the Western powers possessed 'a co-ordinated policy' and would serve as a less provocative deterrent to Beijing than a warning about the dire consequences of wrongdoing.[50]

In May 1952, Eden and Acheson met in Paris. The US administration's policy review was now complete and awaiting the President's approval, Acheson revealed. Its core conclusion was that it would be nothing less than 'disastrous for the position of the Western Powers if South-East Asia were lost without a struggle'. The US military still favoured 'vigorous counter-action', including bombing and blockade, if the PRC committed a new aggression. Knowing that this news would be 'distasteful' to Eden, the US Secretary assured him that the administration had no plans for 'an all-out attack on China' and that the United States would 'do nothing in that area which would provoke a third world war'. The likelihood was that the PRC would continue its indirect support for the Vietminh, but as insurance against 'a general war by accident', Acheson proposed a deterrent warning to China.[51]

Eden was indeed dismayed. By reaffirming the rectitude of existing policy, the three-month US policy review had terminated at its point of departure. All he could do was restate how 'strongly opposed' the British government still was 'to any course of action in S. E. Asia which would be likely to result in a war with China' and alert Acheson to the dangers of issuing any warning while Anglo-American thinking was so far apart on the purpose and the risks of action against the PRC.[52] What Acheson did not vouchsafe was that the review – NSC 124/2, finally signed off by Truman in June – maintained that if British or French 'concurrence' was unobtainable with regard to China, 'the United States should consider taking unilateral action'.[53]

It was not just Eden but British policymakers generally who were downcast. For some time, the Churchill government had regarded a coordinated defence plan for Southeast Asia as a much needed end in itself as well as a first move in the direction of a fully fledged regional defence organization. In both cases the aim was to deter Chinese aggression by demonstrating allied cohesion – initially, UK, US and French unity, and then more widely. From a national interest standpoint, and again anticipating the arguments Eden would advance in 'British Overseas Obligations' in June, the Foreign Office and Ministry of Defence also saw a Southeast Asian NATO as a way to transfer some of the present burden of regional defence to the United States.[54] Now, policymakers were obliged to invest a defence organization with an additional utility: the shackling of American power. In Southeast Asia, the UK recognized twin threats, one posed by Chinese communism, the other by American unilateralism. In pushing for allied defence coordination, the Foreign Office sought to give effect to dual containment. The objective was to 'stem the torrent of American Sinophobia' with a view to 'harnessing it to constructive purposes ... diverting it from the fruitless swamp of Korea, and the dangerous rapids of Formosa [Taiwan], into the dynamos of South East Asian defence'. The ideal, a security arrangement encompassing the Far East as a whole, 'might also (by including provision for Allied consultation) operate as a check on precipitate unilateral action by the Americans'.[55]

Events in Korea underscored the need for such a check. On 23 June, in one of the largest operations of the war, five hundred US aircraft bombed Chinese power plants on the Yalu river, making 'a pretty good mess'.[56] The plants were not on PRC territory but they did supply airfields in Manchuria and came perilously close, in the view of the Foreign Office, to an unprovoked extension of the war, a point the British would have made to the Americans had they been consulted.[57] Eden was angry and upset, but Churchill, having all but conceded leadership in Asia to the United States at the start of the year, was inclined to view the decision to mount the attack as 'within the competence of the United Nations Commander', General Matthew Ridgway.[58] To the Prime Minister, China was a localized problem ('you can take it that for the next four or five years 400 million Chinese will be living where they are now ... They cannot swim, they are not much good at flying and the Trans-Siberian railway is already overloaded').[59] Eden, in contrast, regarded the PRC, or more specifically a Sino-American showdown, as a potential catalyst for general war with the USSR. Accordingly, while agreeing to hold his tongue in public on the bombing, the Foreign Secretary intended to make 'clear in private conversation' with the Americans that the UK 'ought to have been consulted in advance and would expect to be so consulted on any future similar occasion'.[60]

Eden got his chance at the end of June when Acheson arrived in London for scheduled talks. The US Secretary was contrite, up to a point. When Eden demanded 'no more surprises', Acheson conceded that the British should have been apprised in advance – and would have been but for a bureaucratic 'snafu' – but refused to accept that the UK had 'an absolute right' to be consulted even on issues of shared concern like Korea.[61] The following week, Churchill told the House of Commons that full-scale war with China would be a 'great mistake'. At the same time, he reminded MPs of the 'terrible cost' the Americans were bearing in Korea and suggested that they deserved admiration for their restraint not criticism (such as the Labour opposition had ventilated) for alleged minatory proclivities. On the question of consultation on the Yalu bombing, the Prime Minister was frank. 'As we were not informed, we could not know,' an admission which provoked noisy protests and not just from the Labour benches. Still, Churchill refused to deviate from his "trust America" position, and in the end the government survived an opposition vote of censure by a comfortable margin.[62]

US intelligence subsequently estimated that the amount of electric power available in North Korea had been reduced by 90 per cent as a result of the bombing, but to Eden the success of the operation was not the issue. The problem was American unilateralism. As such, the episode reinforced the conviction of the Foreign Office, as well as the Chiefs of Staff, that a security system in Asia, including the still unprotected Southeast Asian front, was urgently needed.[63] Nor were the British the only ones thinking along these lines. For Robert Schuman, the French Foreign Minister, the Yalu bombing likewise 'proved the need for some kind of permanent tripartite body for consultation'.[64] However, nothing could be done to realize this objective until Anglo-American differences on retaliatory action against China were reconciled.

The Truman administration, wary about entanglement in Southeast Asia but cognizant of the dangers of ongoing disunity, proposed a new round of defence talks in the summer of 1952. This time, the military men were to be given 'political guidance', Acheson suggested. In other words, those forms of action which were militarily viable but politically objectionable were to be ruled out in advance in an effort to improve the chances of consensus.[65] This proposal went nowhere for one simple reason: both the State Department and the Foreign Office largely shared the viewpoint of their respective military experts and therefore fashioned political terms of reference reflective of their national military perspective. Echoing the US Joint Chiefs of Staff, Acheson felt that limiting the response to a PRC invasion of Tonkin to the area of the aggression 'would not hurt the Chinese very much' when the object ought to be to 'hurt' the PRC 'as much as we could'. It was 'futile and a mistake to defend Indochina in Indochina … we could not have another Korea'.[66] The Foreign Office, in line with the COS position, advocated the creation of 'allied machinery' through which Southeast Asian security could be organized. Action in this regard would provide 'tangible evidence' of Western determination to resist aggression and, in so doing, contain China.[67]

Any lingering chance of Anglo-American agreement on political guidance was extinguished when Eden insisted that the words 'if possible' be excised from the following caveat in the UK working draft: 'action, at any rate to begin with, should if possible be confined to the area of aggression'. When his advisors objected that the Truman administration would regard the new phraseology as excessively constraining, Eden bridled: 'No. This gives the Americans a freer hand than I am prepared to endure'.[68] When it came to winning the Prime Minister's backing for his outlook, Eden took advantage of Churchill's publicly expressed worry about the Western powers being 'sprawled about in China' at the cost of the NATO effort in Europe. The Foreign Office's version of political guidance minimized that danger, Eden told him. At the same time, 'we must play our part in collective resistance if China erupts again'. This could be done most effectively 'if there is advance consideration' within the framework of a coordinated allied defence system.[69] Here once more the outline of dual containment is discernible. It was present again in August when Franks wrote to Eden to stress that the creation of a defence organization had become urgent, 'not only because we want to do all we can to ensure the defence of South East Asia but because it is most desirable to influence American thinking and planning before an emergency happens'. As things stood, 'if Chinese aggression occurred the Americans would very likely rush into action which we would feel ill-advised'.[70]

By the end of the summer all sides had accepted that political guidance was a dead letter and the US government duly proposed – and the British and French agreed – that the next round of talks should revert to a solely military basis.[71] In October, US, British, French, Australian and New Zealand staff representatives gathered at the Pentagon. From a military viewpoint, the conference report noted, the five delegations accepted that 'a combination of all coercive measures' (local defence of Vietnam, interdiction of Chinese lines of communication, a blockade of PRC ports and the bombing of all targets of military significance in China) 'offers the best prospect of causing Communist China to cease an aggression'. However, this agreed conclusion obscured as much as it revealed, not least UK misgivings about those measures favoured by the Americans which risked war with China and general war with the USSR. The outcome of the talks also confirmed the failure of Air Chief Marshal Elliot and his team to persuade their US counterparts of the value of deterrence via demonstrable unity within a coordinated defence. The problem, Elliot told the Chiefs of Staff, was that the Americans were determined to 'be left free to pursue their own military policies … without any international intervention'.[72] The Pentagon conference thus capped a year of 'disappointingly few results', the Ministry of Defence reflected. The reason was the 'unwillingness' of the US Joint Chiefs 'to be tied to any specific commitments in South-East Asia or to discuss in detail measures to deter the Chinese from aggression'. British negotiators had also to deal with the Truman administration's avidity for 'widespread retaliatory action' if China made a move on Vietnam – action, UK military experts judged, which would be 'both ineffective and provocative of global war'.[73]

The Foreign Office was equally dismayed by the failure to dent 'the American determination to retain freedom of military action', and officials consequently approached 1953 seeking to involve the United States in collective defence for the same reasons that had sustained them during 1952.[74] One was the need to enhance regional security by making the deterrent to China more potent. Another derived from anxiety about US unilateralism. As the Head of the Southeast Asia Department, John Tahourdin, pointed out, the absence of any allied defence coordination left 'hanging over all our heads the danger that the Americans may, by unilateral action, drag the western world into a full-scale war with China – or worse'.[75] Finally, from the standpoint of power-by-proxy, the longer a coordinated defence for Southeast Asia remained an ideal rather than a reality, the longer the UK would have to go on shouldering a disproportionate share of the burden of area security.

Having said all this, there was an unexpected and constructive development towards the back end of 1952. At a meeting of the North Atlantic Council in Paris in December, the French, taking advantage of the presence of UK and US foreign and defence ministers, proposed the establishment of a Five-Power Staff Agency (FPSA) for Southeast Asia (with Australia and New Zealand invited to complete the quintet).[76] It was a limited concept confined to intelligence interchange with some planning functions, all without commitment to governments. In fact, it was so modest that even the Americans could find no grounds for objection. Eden, however, was dubious about British involvement despite his advisors pointing out that the agency might form the nucleus of the security grouping that was the UK's regional priority.[77]

Eden eventually relented, but his initial hesitancy is instructive. By the end of 1952, the Foreign Secretary's approach to Indochina had altered in important ways. The change-process dated from the previous August when Rob Scott, supervising Under-Secretary for Asian affairs in the Foreign Office, produced a much-discussed position paper. Remembered by Eden as 'one of the ablest members of our Foreign Service', Scott offered a stocktake on the Chinese dimension of the Indochina problem and adumbrated the dangers should the United States opt for a forestalling war. 'We are not considering a campaign in which we fire the first shot,' Scott reminded his colleagues; hence it was imperative that the ongoing five-power military consultations 'should not be allowed to develop into an examination of action to be taken against China for the sake of giving an outlet to pent-up American emotions'. From there, Scott's paper pivoted to the Vietminh dimension. For more than a year, the overwhelming focus on a hypothetical Chinese menace had blinded UK (and US) policymakers to two real, present and connected dangers: Vietminh success in the field and, in France, war-weariness bordering on defeatism. Chinese aggression could never be ruled out and the Western powers needed to plan appropriately. Nonetheless, Scott called for urgent consideration of measures 'to stiffen and invigorate the French to deal with the *present* situation in Indo-China' which could well become critical when serious fighting resumed in the autumn.[78]

By December, when the French began lobbying for the FPSA, Eden had not only embraced the Scott thesis but suspected a Gallic plot whereby under cover of organizing to defend Indochina against the external Chinese threat, the French were really seeking a greater commitment from their allies to deal with the internal Vietminh threat. For Eden, planning to counter PRC aggression was one thing, British boots on the ground in the Red River delta quite another. The Chiefs of Staff acknowledged Eden's concern about back-door internationalization of the war; Air Chief Marshal Sir William Dickson, Slessor's successor as Chief of Air Staff, thought that the French saw the Staff Agency, in part at least, as a means to 'resolve their current difficulties in Indo-China'. On balance, however, the service chiefs, along with the Foreign Office's Asian experts, argued that the risk that the Agency might 'to some extent [be] used for current operations in the theatre' was worth taking if it helped accustom the Americans to working with allies in Southeast Asia.[79] 'I suppose that the planning is without commitment,' Eden commented in giving his belated approval.[80]

✶

The FPSA would prove to be of limited worth over the next two years. In any event, even as the Agency came into being, the Vietminh dimension was beginning to supersede the Chinese dimension as the British government's most pressing Indochinese concern.[81] The time had come to stop 'pursuing this will-o'-the-wisp' – a coordinated allied policy for dealing with Chinese aggression – 'while shutting our eyes to the present reality of the mounting danger of the war against the Viet Minh', warned the Head of the Foreign Office's Southeast Asia Department.[82] The FPSA was all well and good. But it offered a solution, or the makings of a solution, to the Indochina problem as it stood at the start of 1952, not as it stood going into 1953.

Indochina, 1952–1953: The Vietminh Dimension

Back at the start of 1952, British Indochina-watchers were as one in seeing the passing of General de Lattre as the gravest of blows to French prospects. On 2 January, as news of the de Lattre's illness spread, the UK Ambassador in Paris, Sir Oliver Harvey, wrote to Eden warning that the French public were 'heartily sick' of a war which no longer seemed to be *their* war. On one level, it was being fought for Vietnamese, Cambodians and Laotians whose independence could hardly be denied come the end of the conflict; on another level, the French were manning the battlements of freedom in Southeast Asia, a Cold War responsibility which, if relinquished, the Americans would probably take up. It followed, the Ambassador averred, that unless the United States increased its financial and military assistance for the war effort, and unless the concurrent Korean armistice talks could be extended to prospect a general settlement of all Asian Cold War problems, including Indochina, 'France may well feel that she has done her duty' and look to 'extricate herself as well as she can'.[1]

Nine days later, de Lattre was dead. With the 'disappearance of the Frenchman who almost succeeded in raising the *sale guerre indo-chinoise* into the *guerre glorieuse pour la civilisation*', Harvey wrote again to Eden, despondency threatened to infect the French body-politic.[2] This view was echoed by the British Minister in Saigon, Hubert Graves, who thought it had taken 'a personality as strong as de Lattre's' to ensure that wavering politicians in Paris continued to invest in the war effort.[3] Even as the General lay dying, no less a figure than Robert Schuman, the French Foreign Minister, went public with the view that 'if an armistice can be concluded … on honourable terms, France would not hesitate to make peace'.[4] This was not defeatism. It was political pragmatism, a minimum gesture to placate a disillusioned domestic constituency. Soon, though, more than the minimum would be needed.

In February came news of the French withdrawal from the garrison town of Hoa Binh, located beyond the Red River delta defence perimeter and astride the main Vietminh north-south line of communication. The order to evacuate had been issued by General Raoul Salan, the new Commander-in-Chief in Indochina, on the ground that locking up eighteen battalions in static defence made no strategic sense. It is likely that the order would have been given even if de Lattre had lived. But coming when it did, the retreat was taken by the French press and public opinion as a setback not unconnected with the demise of *le Roi Jean* and consequently pressure mounted on the (consecutive) administrations of Edgar Faure and Antoine Pinay to explore the potential for an early end to French involvement in the war. The obvious exit options were the transfer of full sovereignty to the Associated States (as Vietnam, Laos and Cambodia were formally designated following the grant of semi-independence in 1949–1950) followed by FEC disengagement and the probing of the communist side as to its attitude towards a negotiated settlement.[5]

The pressure on the French government was all the greater as NATO plans to rearm the Federal Republic of Germany within a European Defence Community (EDC) neared completion. Responding to US pressure in 1950 for a West German contribution to European security, France had proposed the creation of a multi-nation European Army as a vehicle for raising German divisions without recreating a national German Army. By 1952, this scheme had been transformed into a six-member (France, West Germany, Italy, Netherlands, Belgium, Luxembourg) supranational EDC to sit within NATO. But regardless of form and nomenclature, the prospect of German rearmament was distressing to a great many people in Western Europe whose memories of German militarism were both recent and painful. France was an exemplar. Critics of the Indochina War and critics of the EDC, as well as those with dual animus, were wont to argue that the early return of French troops from Southeast Asia to Europe would not only strengthen national security but so boost the NATO manpower pool that there might be a need to rearm Germans after all. Even if the EDC remained a going concern, the repatriation of French forces would ensure that the French numerical contribution to the community would exceed that of West Germany, a psychologically comforting superiority which even the EDC's supporters craved.[6]

In public, the French government's regular expressions of determination to stay the course in Indochina were increasingly accompanied by signals of willingness to consider communist peace proposals if they respected French interests and assured the freedom of the Associated States. Reacting to intelligence 'from too many different sources to be ignored', officials in the British Foreign Office wondered if the French might already be secretly trysting with the Chinese or the Vietminh.[7] The Chiefs of Staff, in a paper for the Cabinet's Defence Committee in mid-March, suggested that if back-channel peace negotiations were already in train, the French, given the weakness of their bargaining position, could only be looking for a cloak to disguise the nakedness of a decision to cut and run. And once the French were gone, there was 'little doubt' that 'power would be seized, in a short space of time by the Communist-dominated forces'. Regardless of how it occurred – Chinese invasion, Vietminh military victory, French political collapse, negotiated retreat – the service chiefs were adamant that the loss of Vietnam would be calamitous:

> The impact … upon the neighbouring countries, Burma and Siam [Thailand], would be to raise the morale of the existing Communist element at the expense of the present Government, whose position would rapidly become precarious. Should they be unable to withstand the pressure of Communist influence, and become pro-Communist, or be replaced by pro-Communist Governments, this would bring Communism to the threshold of Malaya … If the present Siamese Government fell and were replaced by a Communist-controlled government, a great deal more could and would be done from Siamese territory to assist the

rebels [in Malaya]. Moreover, the fall of Indo-China, Burma and Siam to the Communists would convince every Chinese in Malaya that the Communists would sooner or later triumph there also and might make even the Malays more disposed to compromise with the Communists and to withdraw their support from the Government. The internal situation would, even if reinforcements were sent, seriously deteriorate and might get out of control in a comparatively short time. The cutting off of rice supplies from Burma and Siam would also lead to a catastrophic deterioration in the internal situation in Malaya.

Inspired by the possibility of a Chinese invasion of Tonkin, since 1951 the Ministry of Defence had been working on a contingency plan (code-named *Irony*) for British forces to occupy the Songkhla position in southern Thailand on the narrow Kra isthmus to create a military barrier to protect Malaya. Now the Chiefs of Staff extended their purview to include occupation of Songkhla 'as soon as it became clear that the French position in Indo-China was collapsing'.[8] The Defence Committee, with Churchill chairing, approved the new concept (codenamed *Ringlet*), but its members were unanimous in seeing French victory – or failing that, French readiness to continue the fight until the Associated States were capable of maintaining their own security – as the only really acceptable outcome from a British and free world standpoint. In advancing these scenarios, Churchill and his colleagues were equally unanimous that the UK, with an over-heating economy and over-stretched military resources, could provide no practical support to France.[9]

At first sight, the policy sanctioned by the Defence Committee was contradictory and self-defeating. The government was convinced that 'the key to the defence of Malaya lies in Indo-China' and deemed it 'a British interest that the French should stay'.[10] To that end, however, the French were to be offered no material assistance, only words of encouragement, even though it was agreed that if Indochina was lost, the UK would have to reinforce Malaya at considerable cost and at some risk to European security as a result of transferring British forces from West Germany, the obvious reinforcement source. Viewed in these terms, was there not a case for short-term sacrifices on behalf of France to negate the need for greater sacrifices in the future?[11]

As it happens, the Defence Committee *did* recognize the value of speculating to accumulate but concluded that it should be the United States that did the speculating. An increase in American aid, policymakers agreed, would be 'one of the most effective means of buttressing the French will to continue the struggle'. Yet even here, the deleterious impact of a dire economic situation on imaginative diplomacy is discernible in the Defence Committee's hesitancy about approaching the Truman administration to do more for Indochina in case a hike in aid to France would produce a concomitant reduction in the amount of US mutual security assistance to the UK.[12]

The 'tragic ... spectacle of the might, majesty, dominion and power of the once magnificent and still considerable British Empire having to worry ... how we can pay our monthly bills', as Churchill put it, left the Conservative government's Indochina policy rooted in hope: that China would not invade Vietnam, that the French would not quit and that the Americans, of their own volition, would increase military assistance to France while maintaining current aid levels to Britain.[13]

In the spring of 1952, the Pinay administration adopted what, to the Foreign Office, was a reassuringly robust public position on the war. For France to abandon the Associated States, declared Jean Letourneau, the new High Commissioner in Indochina, would not only represent a dereliction of national duty but would undermine the foundations of the French Union and call into question France's status as a front-rank power.[14] The Americans, too, were pleased. A negotiated settlement of the war was anathema to a Truman administration anxious to get the French to think victoriously.[15] Against this, as Ambassador Harvey reminded the Foreign Office, the 'desire' for an end of the war was 'almost universal' inside and outside the French parliament.[16]

In Indochina, meanwhile, the French authorities claimed that the Vietnamese National Army (VNA) was fast approaching the size and competence that would allow France to begin a safe phased withdrawal of its Expeditionary Corps. The object was to complete a full transfer of defence responsibility to the Vietnamese by 1955. After several false starts, a VNA had come into being in July 1951, largely at de Lattre's urging. Compulsory military training and conscription followed.[17] By March 1952, the authorities in Paris, Hanoi and Saigon were investing increasing faith in what they called (tastelessly) *jaunissement*, literally the 'yellowing' of the war, as an exit strategy. To Graves and the British Legation in Saigon, however, the French were living in a fantasy world. The chances of the VNA, an overwhelmingly conscript army of unproven mettle and morale, ever becoming a match for Giap's highly motivated, battle-hardened forces were remote.[18]

A perceptive editorial in the *Times* in April 1952, circulated in the Foreign Office, drew attention to a conceptual and structural problem inherent in the VNA, namely the difficulty of attracting the best and the brightest of the Vietnamese to fight when the French were adamant that future independence for Vietnam would be contained and constrained within the framework of the French Union. Although the VNA was 120,000-strong, only about one-third of its troops were in regular regiments. The balance was made up of a motley array of manpower from anti-communist religious sects, militant Catholics organizations and other sectional groups. The editorial went on:

The French are doing all they can to expand the regular regiments but two serious handicaps have to be overcome. In the first place the shortage of Vietnamese officers means that senior regimental posts are held by Frenchmen; in the second, some of the most promising recruits for commissioned rank hesitate to come forward because they are dissatisfied with the present political arrangements in Indo-China. The Vietnamese army is making good technical progress, but it has not yet become the kind of focal point of Vietnamese patriotic fervour that General de Lattre … hoped and expected. As more Vietnamese cadets emerge from the excellent new officers' training schools, the commissioned ranks of the army will contain fewer Frenchmen. The process would be greatly speeded up if the youth of the country could be persuaded that victory over the Viet-Minh forces would bring them the political independence which they want. Only the French, with their long experience of the shortcomings as well as the strength of Vietnamese nationalism, can find the answer to this problem of reconciling its aspirations to the obvious limitations inherent in 'independence within the French Union'.[19]

Despite these difficulties, the French government was determinedly optimistic in public. In June 1952, Paris announced that six VNA divisions would be combat-ready by the end of the year, news greeted with scepticism in London. Already unsettled by Graves's pessimistic reporting, the Foreign Office's Southeast Asia Department now worried that the French, in their desperation to be free of the war, were preparing to hand-over 'willynilly' to a Vietnamese army incapable of maintaining security unaided.[20] Eden shared this concern; French government ministers, in oft-remarking that outright victory in the war was impossible because the Chinese would never allow the Vietminh to lose, displayed a 'thoroughly defeatist attitude'.[21]

The Americans were also sold on the VNA. The US military assistance programme, begun in 1950, went beyond the provision of arms and equipment to include advising the French on how to get the best out of Vietnamese recruits based on the American experience in training South Korean armed forces. An early French withdrawal from Vietnam would be a 'disaster', Acheson told Eden in May 1952, but with committed US support there was a 'fair prospect' they would 'hold on' until the Vietnamese could cope on their own.[22] The following month, the Truman administration announced an increase in aid 'especially devoted to assisting the French in the building of the National Armies of the Associate States'.[23] Eden thought the appropriation, worth $150 million, 'generous by any standards'. All told, the US taxpayer was picking up more than 40 per cent of the cost of the French war effort (a percentage which would nearly double over the next two years).[24]

In Saigon, the UK Jeremiah-in-chief Hubert Graves found it impossible to share American confidence in the French, let alone the Vietnamese. With US dollars banked, what was to stop the French playing out time until the expanded Vietnamese army took over in 1955? If this was the French intention, the High Command in Indochina would probably prioritize defensive operations to minimize FEC casualties in the transition phase. To Graves, this was the opposite of what was required. The Vietnamese should be bequeathed a security problem of manageable proportions and that required the French to break the back of Giap's forces by adopting a forward strategy based on short-term but large-scale reinforcement of the FEC from the professional French army in Europe.[25] In London, the Foreign Office concluded that the Graves solution was fine in theory but impossible to bring about in practice given the febrile state of French politics and popular dislike of the war.[26] Its prospects receded further in July when military authorities in Paris announced that FEC units would henceforward be withdrawn pari passu with the combat-readiness of Vietnamese units. There was still time for the French to embrace the 'psychology of victory' and 'smash the Vietminh', Graves told the Foreign Office. But not much.[27]

Despite Foreign Office coolness, by the autumn Graves's remedy had managed to acquire a number of powerful adherents. With heavy fighting about to resume in Indochina following the rains, both the Chiefs of Staff and the Minister of Defence, Lord Alexander, stressed the urgent necessity of an 'all-out effort by the French' serviced through early redeployment of up to four divisions of French troops from

Europe.[28] 'Surely not', an incredulous Eden minuted when he first learned of this recommendation. 'I cannot conceive that the transfer of four French divisions to Indo-China under present circumstances is discussable.'[29] The Chiefs of Staff begged to differ. 'What we wished to see achieved', the new Chief of the Imperial General Staff, General Sir John Harding, pointed out, 'was that, as a result of a major military operation by the French and Vietnamese forces, a sound military position would be established ... thus allowing the French to withdraw the bulk of their forces without the Communists being in a position to take over control again.'[30]

As the year wore on, the reinforcement lobby swelled to include the Office of the Commissioner-General for the UK in Southeast Asia, British governors, ambassadors, heads of missions and colonial administrators in the region, the UK Commanders-in-Chief in the Far East, the British Embassy in Paris and the War Office in London.[31] Meanwhile, events in Vietnam, and their impact in France, continued to disturb British observers of all stripes, pro- or anti-reinforcement. Shortly after the start of the fighting season in October, the PAVN overran several French posts in the Thai country in north-west Tonkin. The Pinay administration did its best to minimize the significance of the losses, while in Vietnam, Salan mounted a counteroffensive, operation Lorraine. Even so, the reverses still dismayed French opinion and generated renewed pressure on the government to explore the potentialities of a negotiated settlement. This, in turn, troubled the British. In view of the unfavourable politico-military balance in Indochina, the Foreign Office's Southeast Asian experts contended, any diplomatic arrangement worked out between the French and the Chinese or Vietminh would expose all of Vietnam, Laos and Cambodia to the threat of early communization.[32] It was becoming clear to Eden and the Foreign Office – as it had been to Harvey for some time – that a 'respectable departure' from Indochina would be 'welcomed by every shade of opinion'.[33]

In November 1952, the Chiefs of Staff again ventilated their view – this time 'most strongly' – that reinforcement of the FEC from Europe and the adoption of an aggressive strategy in Vietnam were imperative. The task of persuading the French government to take the necessary action was the job of diplomats, not military men. The issue 'must not be shirked', Eden was told. It was 'a political matter with which you in the Foreign Office must deal'.[34] The Foreign Secretary was taken aback. The Chiefs of Staff 'firmly "pass the buck" to us', he told his advisors at the start of December. 'What do we do?'[35]

No one in the Foreign Office denied the benefits that would accrue from a forward French military policy, and not just in Vietnam. As Deputy Under-Secretary Pierson Dixon observed, Indochina was becoming 'a running sore that is spreading over to Europe'. In May, an EDC treaty had been signed in Paris, but the scheme, which was central to NATO defence plans for the future, would not become operative until the treaty was ratified in the legislatures of all six member states. By the autumn, Indochina was impeding French approval. As Dixon noted, the authorities in Paris, faced with the prospect of rearmed Germans in the EDC, 'which, because of the Indo-China drain, may well outnumber the French', were disinclined to put the EDC treaty to the vote.[36] In the end, however, after giving the matter a good deal of consideration, Eden and his senior advisors decided against broaching reinforcement with the French on the grounds that the obstacles were simply too daunting.

The most obvious hurdle was the widespread French desire to reduce not add to the human and financial cost of the war. In total, and leaving aside US financial offset, the defence of Indochina since 1946 had cost France more than twice the amount of money it had received under the Marshall Plan. As for the toll in blood, before the onset of the new fighting season, over 30,000 French or French Union soldiers, along with 1,500 French officers, including many of the best graduates of St. Cyr, had been killed.[37] Even if French leaders were prepared to accept the logic of reinforcement, the Foreign Office struggled to see where the troops would come from. Alert to the danger of inviting Chinese intervention, the Chiefs of Staff maintained that additional troops must be French. But France – like the UK – was overstretched in terms of its military commitments. The French Union offered no solution; the FEC was already swollen with troops from Morocco, Senegal and other colonial territories, but their fighting quality was adjudged to be greatly inferior to that of reinforcements drawn from the optimum source, the regular French army.[38] Yet with only five full-strength French divisions currently in Europe, any suggestion that up to four of them be sent to Indochina was certain to go down badly with the French government, parliament and public. Nor did conscription provide the answer. While British national servicemen were deployed in Malaya, their French counterparts were barred by law from operating in theatres of active military operations.[39] Then there was the EDC. No French government would take the 'risk' of reinforcing Vietnam, Harvey reminded the Foreign Office, 'not only because of the resulting weakening of the defences of Western Europe but because of the increased disequilibrium between France and Germany that would result'.[40]

Impressive in themselves, these difficulties comprised only part of the reason the Foreign Office objected to reinforcement. The other was the likely price the French would insist on if they were to consider complying with British recommendations. To even suggest reinforcement, officials agreed, would expose the UK to demands for a quid pro quo. The Pinay administration was unlikely to ask for British troops to be sent to Vietnam, but money or military supplies might well be requested. Alternatively, or additionally, the French might set a European price in the form of a British undertaking to station extra troops on the continent to maintain NATO's overall strength during the time it took redeployed French forces to clear up Vietnam. Even the Chiefs of Staff conceded that an approach to Paris on reinforcement might be used as 'a lever to force the UK to commit forces to the European Defence Community' and so ease French fears of being swamped by Germans.[41]

Despite the advantages of a forward strategy in Indochina, the Foreign Office ruled out paying any of the projected costs to facilitate French reinforcement. UK economic and military resources were already at breaking point while politico-military compensation for France in Europe was rejected for reasons connected with the sanctity of sovereignty over British armed forces. What would happen, Eden wondered, if the war dragged on despite an influx of French reinforcements? Was there not a danger of the Americans pressurizing the British to convert a temporary troop commitment to the supranational EDC into a permanent undertaking? Eden did not want to take that chance. As he told a concurring Cabinet in December 1952, Britain 'cannot join the Community nor merge any part of its forces in the Community'.[42]

British troops making good the deficit in Western Europe's defence caused by French reinforcement appeared to be a more viable proposition because the UK commitment would be to NATO and not to the EDC. Even here, however, Eden harboured strong objections. The problem was partly a question of manpower: no regular forces could be spared, while the strategic reserve was already committed, mostly in policing the Suez Canal zone. But even if the troops were available, Eden had already rejected precisely this undertaking in the context of the EDC. For over a year, the French had been seeking a pledge from the Churchill government to maintain UK forces in Europe at existing strength for the foreseeable future. Such a pledge, they argued, would provide a safeguard against a revival of German militarism and therefore improve the EDC's ratification prospects in the National Assembly. Eden, though, was unyielding. In Cabinet in early December, he insisted that 'we had already gone as far as we could'. Besides, a troop pledge would circumscribe Britain's freedom to dispose of its armed forces as it saw fit and might even represent 'the first step on a slippery slope to which there might be no end' short of UK membership of a federal United States of Europe. Eden, in sum, was unwilling to do more for France in Southeast Asia than he was ready to do for France in Europe over the EDC.[43]

As 1952 drew to a close, it was 'generally agreed' in the Foreign Office that 'something drastic must be done to save Indo-China'. The issue devolved to finding a way to persuade the French to reinforce without laying the UK open to unwelcome or unfulfillable demands for compensation. The answer, the Foreign Office finally concluded, was for the Americans to do the persuading – if they could be brought to share the British view of the urgency of the situation. When it came to dishing out unpalatable advice, the United States was in a much stronger position both to influence French policy and absorb any demands for recompense.[44]

The climax of the reinforcement debate in Whitehall coincided with the conclusion of the 1952 US Presidential election which saw Republican Dwight D. Eisenhower win the White House and the Republican Party gain control of the Senate and House of Representatives for the first time since the Great Depression. In London, the Foreign Office's Asia specialists looked forward putting UK views on Indochina to the new administration at the earliest possible moment in order to influence the shape of Republican policy at its formative stage of development.[45] Indeed, British policymakers saw the changing of the guard in Washington as an opportunity to recalibrate Anglo-American relations right across the board. Over the preceding eighteen months, Truman and the Democrats had developed what, to British minds, was a disturbing penchant for unilateral decision-making on matters of mutual UK-US concern. Now, with Eisenhower in the White House, there was a chance to start afresh.[46]

However, this opportunity did not come without problems and even risks. Out of office since 1933, the advent of the Republicans was greeted with some unease and foreboding in London. When Churchill learned of Eisenhower's victory, he sent him a message of 'sincere and heartfelt congratulations', but in private he confessed to being 'greatly disturbed' and worried that 'this makes war much more probable'.[47] The Republicans not only lacked recent experience of government, Churchill reflected, but Eisenhower, fine soldier that he was, could well find himself out of his depth politically and the plaything of the viscerally anti-communist Republican Old Guard not to mention the McCarthyites.[48] As Martin Gilbert has shown, Churchill's unease about the shape of US foreign policy under the Republicans interacted with his growing fear of nuclear war and his awareness of Britain's vulnerability to nuclear assault to give him 'a new sense of mission' to be a Cold War peacemaker. This aim, 'more than any other consideration, was the underlying motive of his remaining years of power'.[49]

Because of Eisenhower's political inexperience, UK policymakers anticipated that his Secretary of State would exercise a more than usually determining influence over US foreign policy. It was with dismay, then, that Churchill, Eden and many others in London learned of Eisenhower's choice: John Foster Dulles. In terms of background and experience, the 64-year-old was the obvious man for the job having 'trained for diplomacy ... as Nijinsky was trained for the ballet'.[50] Based on his recent record as the Republican Party's foreign policy frontman, however, some in the Foreign Office considered Dulles anti-British while others feared that he would adopt a diplomatic modus operandi predicated on securing American objectives regardless of the sensibilities of US allies, the UK included. Today, historians tend to view Eisenhower as a clued-up and proactive foreign policy president, albeit one who was content at the time to let Dulles occupy the spotlight and appear as though he was running the show. The British certainly fell for the trick. Convinced of the US Secretary's near-omnipotence as the shaper and mover of foreign policy, they came to look on Eisenhower as little more than (in Churchill' words) 'a ventriloquist's doll'.[51]

Dulles had acquired notoriety in Britain during the US election campaign by promising that a Republican administration would roll back communism and liberate Eastern Europe from Soviet domination. Was Hot War being written into the new administration's Cold War script? There had also been menacing talk of relying much more heavily on nuclear weapons as instruments of US national security. Intended to distance the Republicans from the Democrats, whose containment policy was derided by Dulles for perpetuating rather than seeking to win the Cold War, this assertive rhetoric added to the sense of unease felt by Churchill and others in the UK government.[52] As to the Asian Cold War, it was evident from the moment in the election campaign that Eisenhower pledged to 'go to Korea' to assess the situation for himself that a Republican administration would not permit the war, and American losses, to continue indefinitely.[53]

A week after the US election result was declared, Eden met Dulles in New York. 'It was now generally admitted that ... the war in Korea was a strategic mistake which would have to be corrected,' Dulles observed. There was 'no point in our first eleven being held down on a barren peninsula by the enemy's second eleven'.[54] Dulles did not go into details but the British concluded that the new administration would seek to accelerate the development of the South Korean armed forces to relieve the United States of the primary defence burden; as Eisenhower avowed during the campaign, if Asia continued to be the locus of Cold War hot wars, 'then let it be Asians against Asians, with our support on the side of freedom'.[55]

In London, the Foreign Office further speculated on the possibility of a new US-led offensive in Korea in order to persuade the Chinese of the wisdom of an early armistice or else weaken the communist side prior to the start of any staged transfer of defence responsibility to South Korea. Unlike the French in Vietnam, the United

States already had the firepower in-theatre to launch such an assault. But would the Republican administration also seek to target China directly? During the election, Eisenhower avoided any discussion of extending the fighting beyond Korea. Although the China lobby was keen to confront the PRC directly, the Foreign Office expected the President – who claimed never to have seen a 'feasible plan for attacking China' – to be cautious.[56] This was reassuring. As Churchill reminded the Cabinet in the wake of the US election, to widen the Korean conflict into war with China would be 'a grave mistake'.[57]

The British obtained further pointers to the shape of Republican policy when Selwyn Lloyd, Eden's Minister of State, met Dulles in New York in December. Korea 'should be seen in its true perspective which was the right wing of a general Far Eastern front of which the centre was Formosa [Taiwan] and the left wing Indochina', Dulles argued. He was also 'more worried' about Indochina than Korea due to Vietnam's critical geostrategic position in Southeast Asia and its potential to wreck the EDC in Europe. That said, 'if the French could be induced to leave their ground troops there and even reinforce them' it might be possible to conduct 'a major cleaning up operation with the object of leaving a situation in which hostilities would be limited to small guerrilla activities'. This kind of operation 'would have to be accompanied by a deterrent to the Chinese to stop them intervening'.[58] Eden found Lloyd's report encouraging. In particular, Dulles's readiness to view the Asian Cold War as a single front 'represents the conversion of America to a view which we have long held and have put to the Truman administration without effect'.[59]

On the wider Anglo-American front, Churchill visited the United States in January 1953 in the hope of extracting from the President-elect a public affirmation of the centrality of the "special relationship" to the new administration's foreign policy. As Eisenhower's diary confirms, he returned home disappointed:

> Mr. Churchill … has fixed in his mind a certain international relationship he is trying to establish – possibly it would be better to say an atmosphere he is trying to create. This is that Britain and the British Commonwealth are not to be treated just as other nations would be treated by the United States in our complicated foreign problems. On the contrary, he most earnestly hopes and intends that those countries shall enjoy a relationship which he thinks will recognize the special place of partnership they occupied with us during World War II. In certain cases he would like to make the connection a matter of public knowledge … Winston is trying to relive the days of World War II [when] he had the enjoyable feeling that he and our president [Roosevelt] were sitting on some rather Olympian platform with respect to the rest of the world and directing world affairs from that point of vantage. Even if this picture were an accurate one of those days … in the present international complexities, any hope of establishing such a relationship is completely fatuous.[60]

Alongside his failure to wring a public declaration of US-UK specialness out of Eisenhower, Churchill's concerns about Republican Cold War extremism were mostly confirmed and he headed back across the Atlantic in expectation of 'rough weather …

ahead in dealing with the Republican party' and disappointed in Eisenhower who did not seem to have 'much political maturity'.[61]

The first storm cloud arose in East Asia. Following the outbreak of the Korean War in June 1950, President Truman ordered the US 7th Fleet to the Taiwan straits where it had been on patrol ever since. Officially, the Fleet's mission was to neutralize the straits, preventing a nationalist attack on the mainland as much as a PRC assault on Taiwan. Unofficially, as Truman privately admitted, the Fleet was dispatched to 'stop crooked old Chiang Kai-shek being mopped up by the communists'.[62] Neutralization was maintained until the 1952 election when the Republicans began pressing for the Fleet's withdrawal in order to free Chiang to attack the mainland. The idea of a nationalist re-conquest of China was an absurdity but the threat of some form of US-backed military action, if it forced Beijing to divert troops from Korea to bolster coastal defences, might ease the pressure on the UN Command. Accordingly, in his first State of the Union address on 2 February 1953, Eisenhower announced the termination of the 7th Fleet's mission.[63]

The Churchill government was disconcerted. When it first learned of what impended, the Foreign Office warned the State Department that de-neutralization could provoke a hostile Chinese reaction elsewhere, even an attack on Hong Kong, and was likely to have negative repercussions on the Korean armistice negotiations.[64] UK policymakers understood the domestic political context in which Eisenhower was forced to operate; having promised decisive action on China during the election, and with the China lobby ready to hold him to account, the removal of the Fleet was an early earnest of the administration's commitment to follow through on campaign pledges. Nevertheless, Eden was still disappointed to discover that British cautionary advice counted for so little in Republican Washington.[65] So was Churchill. 'What I do hope', he wrote to Eisenhower, 'is that where joint action or action affecting our common destiny is desired, you will let us know beforehand so that we can give our opinion and advice in time to have them considered'.[66]

Despite his private unhappiness, Eden held back from open criticism of the Eisenhower administration. The de-neutralization decision should be viewed in its 'correct perspective', he advised the House of Commons on 3 February. The original deployment had been a US decision, hence the UK had little locus standi to counsel against annulment, a comment which failed to placate an opposition keen to charge the government with supine support for aggressive US policies in Asia.[67] When Dulles arrived in London the following day for scheduled talks, Eden seized the chance to insist on 'good arrangements' to ensure timely consultation in the future. Keen to put the matter to rest, the US Secretary did not demur.[68] Back in the Commons on 5 February, Eden told MPs that he was 'quite confident that we shall develop with the new Administration the type of collaboration which will make it impossible for any step which could have far reaching international reactions to be taken without our having an opportunity to express our views beforehand'.[69]

In America, Eden's certitude embarrassed Dulles who was accused by sections of Congress and the press of handing the UK a right of veto over US foreign policy. A close examination of the British record of the London talks does suggest that Eden – possibly deliberately – employed a more committal form of language in parliament than had been agreed with Dulles. However, when the media storm broke in America, Eden was unapologetic. Any repetition of unilateral decision-making on matters of shared UK-US concern would be 'disastrous', he cabled the new British Ambassador in Washington, Roger Makins. One of the ambassador's first jobs was to 'ensure that the new Administration understands that the future of Anglo-American relations depends on their readiness to treat us reasonably as a partner'.[70]

Makins had his work cut out. In an effort to limit the damage to his reputation, Dulles told newsmen in Washington that America's international partners, even supposedly special ones, had no given right to consultation. 'In dealing with our allies', he said, 'the United States Government must strike a balance between allied unity and American freedom of action ... To be committed to "consultation" on every step is to be exposed to veto by those consulted, with consequent handicaps on freedom of action'. Excessive consultation reduced action 'to the lowest common denomination of boldness and capacity among the consulting nations'. All would be well, Dulles felt, if America's partners just had 'faith in the United States and show[ed] trust in the fundamental decency and moderation of American objectives'.[71]

The 'unleashing of Chiang' (as it was dubbed in the US press) overshadowed the Dulles visit to London but the two foreign ministers still managed to cover other ground, including Indochina. The war was 'top of the National Security Council's agenda', Dulles confirmed, and the administration was seeking 'ways and means' to provide extra help to France so that the 'problem could be resolved or at least reduced to manageable proportions within eighteen months'. However, it was apparent from other comments made by Dulles that the US administration was more concerned to assist France with the development of the Vietnamese armed forces than to press the French government to reinforce or adopt a forward strategy.[72]

Officials in the Foreign Office greeted this disclosure with rather more equanimity than would have been the case a few months earlier. The reason was an important shift in the French approach to Indochina. At the end of January, Harvey spoke with Letourneau in Paris. The 'only possible policy was to build up the Vietnam Army so that the French could withdraw their forces', Letourneau contended. In saying this, he carefully avoided committing himself 'about how long it would take to get the Vietnamese ... to the point of being able to take over the burden'. Letourneau 'implied' that it was 'improbable that the French would be able to pull out entirely in the foreseeable future'. The Vietnamese 'would in a year or two become strong enough' to take over internal security duties and this would permit French forces to be 'very much reduced ... in three or four years' time'. On reinforcing the FEC preparatory to the handover, Letourneau revealed that the French General Staff had debated this possibility only to conclude that the difficulties were 'too great'.[73] Reading Harvey's dispatch, the Foreign Office's Southeast Asia Department instantly seized on a 'most important' development. Hitherto, the French had planned to start the rundown of the FEC in 1953 and complete the process in the winter of 1954–1955. Now Letourneau was peddling vagueness ('foreseeable future', 'a year or two', 'three or four years').[74]

From Saigon, Graves concluded that there had been 'a change of policy'. In consequence, French prospects were 'decidedly better than they appeared three months ago and we may get through the critical period 1954–5 without the collapse which, on the earlier reckoning, seemed so likely'. The Foreign Office shared this sense of deliverance or temporary deliverance; it was 'increasingly clear' to officials 'that the French now have no intention of pulling out before the Vietnamese forces are ready' and that the 'urgency' of reinforcement had consequently 'receded'.[75] Equally, it was more than ever apparent to British observers that victory was not the French objective. As Letourneau observed, the French 'could no more solve the problem in Indo-China than the British could solve it in Malaya or the UN in Korea'. The solution had to be found 'by political means – and not by military means'.[76] With this, the reinforcement debate, first set in train by Graves nine months before, seemed to have run its course.[77]

On 5 March 1953, Eden arrived in Washington for scheduled talks with Dulles to be greeted by the news that Joseph Stalin was dead. As a result, he spent more time than planned with the President mapping out an Anglo-American response to the passing of the Soviet dictator. Caution prevailed. Both Eisenhower and Eden felt that time was needed to evaluate fully the implications of this momentous event. In the nuclear age, there was a danger that public opinion in NATO countries could become excited at the prospect of a thaw in East-West relations, hence a reduction in the risk of nuclear war, simply because of a change at the top in Moscow. The Western powers needed to base their policy less on wishful thinking and more on hard-nosed realities. The deeds of the post-Stalin Kremlin leadership had to be the gauge against which the prospects for détente were measured.[78]

The news from Moscow reduced the time available to Eden for discussion of other issues, but he still managed to pursue one of his top agenda items, namely 'to extract indications of authoritative American thinking in regard to Korea and Indo-China' and to impress upon the administration 'the importance of proper consultation before final decisions are taken' in both areas.[79] In talks at the State Department, Dulles restated his belief in the 'unity of the whole front' in Asia and in the connected importance of 'creating a threat of pressures in the center (mainland China)' so as to make it 'less likely that the Chinese Communists would send increased forces to help the Communist rebels in Indo-China or to send additional forces into Korea'. The main advantage Moscow gained from the Korean War, Dulles felt, was the tying down of large numbers of American troops which might otherwise be deployed to strengthen security in Western Europe. Indochina likewise generated European consequences by freezing progress on the EDC. It was as much for Eurocentric as any other reasons that the US administration favoured a 'policy of disengagement', the substitution of local forces in Korea and Vietnam for US and French forces respectively. There was no question of relying 'exclusively' on local troops. To the contrary, there would need to be 'stiffening from the outside'. Nevertheless, the object must be to make the USSR 'tire of supplying equipment for [wars] in Asia which instead of engaging United States and French troops [were] being mainly waged against locally raised forces'.[80]

In Indochina, Dulles wanted the French to incentivize the Vietnamese to fight hard by making a public promise of full independence. As for Korea, he revealed that US military planners were considering new offensive operations, possibly an advance to the Korean 'waist' to shorten UN lines. This could bring 85 per cent of Korean territory under UN jurisdiction and create the conditions for an economically self-sustaining and defensible free Korean state.[81] Eden made little recorded response to Dulles's adumbration of disengagement and concentrated instead on extracting an assurance of consultation if the United States planned to intensify operations in Korea. And by consultation, he meant the soliciting of British views *before* the event. He was not looking to 'impose a veto on any action', only to ensure that his government would 'not be taken by surprise'. Dulles, though, was tepid. When asked directly by Eden if he would commit to the principle of consultation, he said he 'would assume so'.[82] Eisenhower, in contrast, was much more forthcoming in telling Eden that there would 'of course be consultation before any major step was taken', an assurance which, to Eden, invalidated Dulles's circumspection.[83]

At the end of March, a delegation of French ministers, led by Pinay's successor René Mayer, visited Washington. After three days of talks, Mayer committed his government to prosecute the war with vigour and to further develop the Vietnamese armed forces 'with a view to destroying the organized Communist forces' within two years. Eisenhower, in return, agreed to treat sympathetically any French requests for extra military assistance.[84] Significantly, the Americans were not prepared to pledge more money and arms there and then. Instead, they asked the French to come up with a plan for Indochina which offered a 'reasonable prospect of a successful end to the war within a fairly short time'.[85]

Mayer was disappointed not to have secured a no-strings American commitment to increased military assistance, but the US administration had been adamant. Eisenhower was extremely sensitive to the mood on Capitol Hill where the Republican Party leadership was pressing for value for money in mutual security investment and where there was talk of linking further backing for the war to French guarantees on performance. A recent *Life* magazine editorial, redolent of Congressional attitudes, likened the French Chamber of Deputies to a 'bedroom farce' in which 'Marianne expects her American sugar daddy to slip another billion-dollar note down her stocking'.[86] From the President's perspective, a more proactive French military strategy, forward strides in expanding and training the Vietnamese army, and an enlightened approach to political side of the war – the matter of *real* independence for the Associated States – were not only necessary in and of themselves but essential in terms of maintaining Congressional support.[87]

In the Foreign Office, officials were dismayed by the US administration's seeming acceptance of optimistic French assessments about the capabilities of the Vietnamese armed forces. To other observers beyond King Charles Street, not least the erstwhile members of the reinforcement lobby, it was hard to imagine how the Vietnamese could cope on their own even after another two years of training – unless, that was, the FEC, strengthened by an injection of French troops from Europe, moved to the offensive and destroyed Vietminh's main-force formations. But this kind of bold solution did not feature on the American agenda. Nor was it going to materialize of its own accord. The Chiefs of Staff, always mindful that the security of Malaya depended on a non-communist Vietnam, were particularly troubled on this count. The 'policy of expanding the Vietnamese army is not a satisfactory substitute to providing more French troops from elsewhere', they insisted.[88]

Since February, when the French extended the timetable for the handover to the Vietnamese, the pressure on the Foreign Office from the Ministry of Defence and other agencies to raise reinforcement with the French had tailed off. But it was always liable to increase again when the illusion upon which Franco-American thinking rested – that Vietnamization would be enough on its own to contain the Vietminh – was exposed. That moment was about to arrive.

4

Indochina, 1953: Dimensions Converge

In the month following Stalin's death, a new collective leadership emerged in Moscow with Georgi Malenkov (Chairman of the Council of Ministers) primus inter pares alongside Lavrenti Beria (NKVD chief) and Vyacheslav Molotov (Foreign Minister). The new men in the Kremlin, particularly Malenkov, were soon talking publicly of the need for improved East-West relations, a shift in the Soviet government's outlook which the press in Britain and elsewhere hailed as the onset of a communist peace offensive predicated on détente.[1] In Washington, the US government remained cautious. The Kremlin needed to act, Eisenhower decided, not just talk.[2] But the British Prime Minister felt that words were sufficient, for now at least. Driven by instinct not analysis, Churchill declared that 'we must not cast away a single hope, however slender', of reducing international tension. His goal was an early summit meeting with Malenkov, an objective which set him at odds not only with the wary Americans but with many in his own government, including the Foreign Secretary. Against this, Churchill's summitry chimed with wider British and West European opinion; in an age of rising nuclear anxiety, the public at home and abroad were more than willing to give peace a chance.[3]

While the post-Stalin leadership in Moscow was experimenting with the language of détente, in Indochina the Franco-Vietminh struggle remained a model of localized Cold War violence. On 14 April, the PAVN invaded northern Laos, committing an estimated 30,000 troops to the operation. Taken unawares, the French High Command was forced to airlift substantial reinforcements and supplies from Vietnam.[4] The PAVN continued its advance in the days that followed and got to within twelve miles of the royal capital, Luang Prabang, before the onset of the monsoon in early May combined with supply problems to cause Giap to withdraw his forces back to Vietnam.[5]

The crisis gave US policymakers a jolt. In the National Security Council (NSC) at the end of April, Eisenhower 'expressed great disappointment over the developments in Laos'. Until the Vietminh attack, 'he and most other people had imagined that in due course, however slowly, the French would succeed in overcoming their enemies. This confidence had now been shattered'.[6] In London, as we have seen, confidence had been in short supply for some time. For the Churchill government, the invasion underscored the speciousness of French claims that the war would be so reduced in scope within two years that the Associated States would be able to cope on their own. Beyond this, it bred fears of a Vietminh annexation of northern Laos and a concomitant communist threat to Thailand. In British geostrategic assessments, Thailand occupied a vital buffer position between Malaya and a potentially communist Indochina. Recalling Thailand's accommodation with Japan in 1941–1942, UK strategists suspected that 'expediency rather than principle' would determine the Bangkok government's response to a Vietminh success in Indochina, with anti-communism likely to be rejected in favour of a pro-communist quasi-neutrality.[7]

By the spring of 1953, the Malayan Emergency was 'well in hand', according to General Sir Gerald Templer, the High Commissioner in Malaya.[8] Lord Salisbury, chair of the Cabinet's Malaya Committee, went even further; excited by statistics suggesting that the number of people killed by communist insurgents over the previous year was around one-quarter of those who perished in road traffic accidents in the colony, he pronounced Malaya to be 'at peace'.[9] However, this good progress could easily be arrested if the Vietminh gained control of upper Laos, for the danger to Malaya would then be 'sharp'.[10] According to the Colonial Office, the Malayan Communist Party would be 'encouraged not only to renew with fresh vigour their campaign of violence but also to intensify their efforts to subvert the mass of the people'. Moreover, with Malaya dependent on Thailand for 40 per cent of its rice, any cut in the importation of that staple – a likely consequence if Bangkok adopted a pro-Vietminh outlook – 'would have a disastrous effect'.[11]

Malaya's external security was just as worrying. Following the Vietminh invasion of Laos, the Malaya Committee and the Chiefs of Staff reviewed plans for occupying Songkhla. It would 'only be a matter of time – perhaps a very short time – before the Siamese [Thai] Government succumbed to Communism in the event of a French collapse', the COS contended. If that happened, Malaya's land frontier would become vulnerable to infiltration by Chinese or Chinese-backed guerrillas. Advance units of the Chinese People's Liberation Army could reach the northern border of Malaya within four months of a Vietminh takeover of Indochina. For this reason, the Chief of the Imperial General Staff, Field Marshal Sir John Harding, insisted that plans for occupying Songkhla be brought to an advanced state of readiness.[12] In the Foreign Office, long-standing political reservations about the Songkhla strategy now resurfaced. For one thing, the Bangkok government was unlikely to look sympathetically on measures designed to serve British rather than Thai interests.[13] For another, what would happen if the Thai authorities denied entry to British forces? The UK would then have to invade Thailand, an aggressive move likely to provoke outrage in the United Nations and elsewhere, including America. The predominant foreign influence in Thailand was the United States, which maintained a Military Assistance Advisory group and a Special Technical Aid Mission in the country, and the Eisenhower administration might well take a very dim view of British actions.[14]

It fell to Churchill to oversee the UK response to the crisis. In early April, Eden went on sick leave – in all, he would be away for six months with intestinal problems requiring two complex and dangerous operations – and Churchill took over the Foreign Office. In this dual Prime Minister/Foreign Secretary capacity, he chaired a meeting of the Cabinet's Defence Committee on 29 April. Acknowledging but rejecting Foreign Office concerns, the committee recommended that Songkhla be occupied 'immediately if the security of Malaya on the landward side was in danger as a result of events in Indo-China or Siam.[15] As to informing the Americans, the Chiefs of Staff were torn between giving advance warning (thus inviting a possible veto) and presenting the United States with a fait accompli at the risk of damaging relations. Churchill's instinct was to bring Eisenhower fully into the picture, but as PAVN pressure on Laos eased in the days following the committee's discussion he had second thoughts. 'Plans are being prepared, but it may well be two, three or four months, or *never* before they will become urgent,' he wrote to Salisbury on 2 May.[16] No approach was made to Washington. Instead, the Chiefs of Staff were left to perfect their plans 'to occupy the Songkhla position, preferably with but if necessary without the approval of the Siamese [Thai] Government'.[17]

The ease with which PAVN forces by-passed French fortifications en route into Laos confirmed for British observers the failings of static defence. However, the French High Command, far from accepting that locking up large numbers of troops in strategic "hedgehogs" was surrendering the initiative to the enemy, began preparing for a renewed threat to Laos in the autumn by bolstering existing redoubts on the *Plaine des Jarres* at cost to the security of the Red River delta. The 'evil genii of the French Army were indeed Vauban, Maginot and Beau Geste,' UK officials in Vietnam lamented. In France, too, there was dismay at the negativity of military leadership. Sensitive to public opinion, but also nervous about the overall strategic picture, the Mayer government announced at the start of May that General Salan was to be replaced as Commander-in-Chief. The British approved. As the UK mission in Saigon put it, Salan had determined 'never to stay and fight (or better still go and fight) the Vietminh'.[18]

Foreign Office officials flagged a further danger thrown up by the Laotian crisis, namely the 'possibility that France, faced with military reverses may once again turn to the idea of compromising with the Vietminh'. With its watching brief on the French political scene, the Western Department assessed that just over half of the Chamber of Deputies opposed the war. This did not necessarily equate to a majority in favour of negotiations but it did reflect deep unhappiness at the way the war was being prosecuted. That said, further military setbacks could well lead to serious pressure on Mayer to seek a diplomatic solution. For the time being, the Foreign Office expected the FEC 'to muddle along'. But looking ahead, officials feared that the French were embarked on a course that would end in 'material and moral defeat, not only for themselves but for the Western world'.[19] The UK Legation in Saigon concurred. Only a few months before, the talk had been of 'winning the war' – such was de Lattre's legacy – but now 'the climate of opinion is so altered that the problem ... is whether the Red River Delta can be held at the opening of the next campaigning season'.[20]

US policymakers were also disillusioned with Salan and the High Command ('a poor lot', Eisenhower complained). In addition to an injection of 'forceful and inspirational' military leadership, the US administration wanted the French government to make a 'clear and unequivocal public announcement ... that [it] seeks self-rule for Indochina and that practical political freedom will be an accomplished fact as soon as victory against the communists is won'. To the President and his top advisors, this political aspect – finding ways to encourage the non-communists to fight hard – was a vital complement to the military prosecution of the war.[21] On 8 May, the French government announced that General Henri Navarre, Chief of Staff of French NATO forces in Europe, would succeed Salan. Eisenhower had hoped for a dynamic leader but Navarre had a rather different reputation: brave but remote, confident with a keenly analytical mind, a desk officer more than a man of action.[22] The UK Commissioner-General for Southeast Asia, Malcolm MacDonald, met Navarre shortly after his appointment. 'Small unimpressive man – pigmy', he wrote, slightingly. 'First impression not a De Lattre'.[23]

To Navarre's credit, he threw himself into his task with seriousness and commitment. But what exactly was that task? In his memoirs, Navarre recalled the instructions given to him by Mayer: go to Indochina, study the situation, report back, but 'don't ask for too many reinforcements'. It was a telling caveat. From the outset, Navarre's mission was not to destroy the Vietminh but to create military conditions sufficiently favourable to negotiate 'an honourable way out'.[24] Six years into the war, French and French Union sacrifices were enormous. The metropolitan French death toll included 3 generals, 8 colonels, 18 lieutenant colonels, 69 majors, 341 captains, 1,140 lieutenants, 3,683 NCOs and 6,008 soldiers. To this could be added 12,019 French legionnaires and African troops and 14,903 Indochinese troops killed, 20,000 missing in action and 100,000 wounded. The stomach for even greater sacrifices was simply not there, Mayer and his colleagues concluded.[25]

As previously noted, the Eisenhower administration had been looking to link its military assistance programme to a French plan for victory. It remained to be seen how the Mayer government's more limited objective of negotiations from strength would go down in Washington – if, that is, the French came clean to the Americans. But at least the US policy of help for self-help was constructive. In comparison, UK policy was a study in passivity with the Defence Committee's conclusion on 29 April that little could be done to assist the French in Laos epitomizing the Churchill government's approach.[26] The goal of French victory (or at least French maintenance of the status quo) without significant British investment was by no means new. Now, though, in the spring of 1953, a number of government figures, conscious of the importance to the UK of a non-communist Indochina, began to lobby for a greater level of commitment. The insider rebellion was prompted by Churchill's decision, endorsed by the Defence Committee, to reject a French request for the loan of forty mothballed York transport aircraft to help with operations in Laos. 'We seem to give a flat rejection to everything the French ask', the Minister of State at the Foreign Office, Selwyn Lloyd, complained; 'cannot we be more positive?'[27]

The Secretary of State for War, Antony Head, not only shared Lloyd's perplexity but decided to raise the matter at the very highest level. In a letter to the Prime Minister on 30 April, Head confessed his 'very grave concern' at 'our decision that nothing whatsoever can be done to help'. Aware of how thinly Britain's military resources were spread, Head nonetheless argued that the 'consequences of French defeat ... are so far reaching that I do not feel that even a remote chance of avoiding it should be neglected'. The loss of all of Southeast Asia, which could well flow from a Vietminh triumph, would have profound economic as well as political and geostrategic consequences for Britain, to say nothing of its damaging impact on the Cold War balance of power. 'Is it certain beyond doubt that the military situation in Indo-China is beyond salvation? Is it absolutely certain that a high level approach by yourself to the President followed by a joint offer of maximum help within our capacity in exchange for some guidance and say in the conduct of the war would be abortive?'[28] Head perfectly clarified the issue which the government had so far ducked. If saving Indochina from communism was essential, the UK had to do more to aid the French in their struggle. A new approach was needed, one which overrode the Treasury-imposed imperative of avoiding additional defence commitments, for 'in supporting the French effort as presently conceived', Michael Joy of the British Legation in Saigon warned, 'We are ... backing an almost certain loser.'[29]

Astonishingly, within six weeks of Head's letter to Churchill, the UK would possess a new and assertive Indochina policy. This development is remarkable not just in light of the hesitancy which had marked the Conservative government's approach over the previous twenty months but because it occurred while Churchill was in charge of British foreign policy. The Prime Minister, as we know, regarded the Asian Cold War as a sideshow compared with the situation in Western Europe and the Middle East. As for Laos, following the Vietminh attack he remarked that he had managed to 'remain ignorant about these outlandish areas all his life' and it was 'hard' on him that they should 'come to tease him in his old age'.[30] And yet, for all this, Churchill turned out to be the catalytic agent behind a major shift in UK policy.

Initially, the Prime Minister gave Head and those who thought like him little encouragement. There were 'a lot of things happening which we rightly view with anxiety', he wrote on 2 May, and it was doubtful whether 'these anxieties would be diminished by our becoming involved in the immense regions concerned'. The Americans had responded to the Laotian situation with an offer of transport aircraft to the French, hence 'we were quite right not to dissipate further our own limited and over-strained resources'.[31] From this, the prospects for any new approach to Indochina appeared unpromising. Yet, far from hampering progress in this direction, the Prime Minister was soon leading a public assault on French foreign policy in general and Indochina policy in particular.

Blinkered as Churchill was on Asia, he still invested the war in Indochina with importance for European reasons. In 1950, the outbreak of one Asian war, in Korea, had initiated Western rearmament and helped convert the North Atlantic Treaty into a fully fledged defence organization, NATO. Three years on, to Churchill's dismay, another Asian war, in Indochina, was preventing the completion of the West's defence buildup in Europe. Buckling under the strain of six years of costly struggle, the French could hardly meet their financial and manpower contributions to NATO. At the same time, French law prevented national servicemen from serving in active war zones, and this limited the manpower available for Indochina. Additionally, in the year since the EDC treaty was signed, successive governments, concerned that the drain of Indochina would see French troops outnumbered by German troops in the EDC, had refused to seek the treaty's ratification by the National Assembly. 'The root of all evil in Europe and in Indochina', Churchill told Head, 'is the French refusal to adopt two years' national service and send conscripts abroad as we do. Their political infirmities have prevented them from doing this and they have so weak an army that they can neither defend their own country nor their Empire overseas. They have however been successful in ... weakening NATO and all that it stands for'.[32]

Although the Foreign Office suspected that any French government seeking to change the law on conscription would be committing 'political suicide', Churchill still brought a refreshing urgency to the Indochina problem, not to mention a readiness to deliver home truths to the French. On 11 May, in a speech in parliament best remembered for his call for a post-Stalin East-West summit, he declared that if France 'wishes to preserve the authority and life of the French Union, she should take more effective steps herself'. He recommended the adoption of the British national service model and the deployment of conscripts to combat zones. If the French had done this earlier, 'they would ... have had much less difficulty in maintaining their positions in Indo-China and could also have developed a far stronger army in defence of their own soil in line with their allies'.[33]

Those Foreign Office officials looking for a ministerial lead in holding the French to account for their failings in Indochina were delighted. True, conscription was not the answer, but in Eden's time in charge of foreign policy since 1951, nothing remotely as frank had been said to the French, even in private. 'Churchill only did it because of Europe', recalled one member of the Southeast Asia Department. 'But that didn't matter. The French had been sleep-walking and he woke them up.'[34] The Mayer government was understandably upset by this public dressing-down, but when the French Embassy sought an assurance from the Foreign Office that Churchill had not deliberately set out 'to hurt French feelings', it drew a blank.[35]

Even before Churchill's speech, some in the Foreign Office had attempted to fashion a new approach on Indochina. On 7 May, the Under-Secretary responsible for Southeast Asia, Rob Scott, responding to the stimulus of Lloyd and Head, produced a memorandum recommending a more dynamic policy. Thanks to Churchill's readiness to challenge the French – his speech in parliament came just four days later – what might have been just another paper exercise was taken seriously by the Foreign Office hierarchy. Scott maintained that the Indochina War could still be won if four conditions were met: inspiring military leadership allied to an offensive strategy; unstinting support for the war effort from the government in Paris; an enlightened approach to the political aspect of the problem; and – controversially – reinforcement from Europe. Scott was aware that pressing the French would generate 'certain additional commitments for this country', but in view of the high value attaching to a non-communist Indochina, the government, he recommended, should now 'accept the consequences for ourselves of this advice'.[36]

Praising Scott's 'excellent analysis', Sir William Strang, the Foreign Office's Permanent Under-Secretary, summoned senior officials to a meeting on 21 May.[37] By then, Navarre's appointment had been announced, Churchill had delivered his public broadside to the French and (ironically) the facilitatory Scott had departed for Washington to take up a new position as Makins's deputy. All those present – including Europeanists hitherto averse to the reinforcement thesis or to any weakening of NATO in favour of Southeast Asia – not only agreed with Scott's four points but felt that the situation in Indochina had become so critical following events in Laos that there needed to be an early showdown with the French. Officials made one significant modification to Scott's thesis, however; instead of the UK paying whatever price the French demanded to bring about reinforcement, Strang and his colleagues preferred to make 'a supreme effort to rally the French to their responsibilities as a Great Power'. To this end, the government needed to come up with incontestable arguments in support of Scott's four points and then put them directly to the Mayer government. The only unresolved issue was the method of 'presentation of the problem as we see it to the French'.[38]

Unwittingly, the French provided the answer to this question. On 20 May, Mayer proposed a meeting of French, British and American leaders to discuss the international situation. Eisenhower responded positively, as did Churchill, and a date, mid-June, and a venue, Bermuda, were quickly settled. Here was the opening the Foreign Office sought. At Bermuda, the Prime Minister could take up where he had left off on 11 May and tackle French leaders face-to-face on Indochina. But no sooner had Bermuda planning begun than the Mayer government collapsed and France was plunged into a month-long political crisis. Eventually, towards the end of June, Joseph Laniel, a centre-right deputy from Normandy, succeeded in forming a government. In securing his majority in the National Assembly, Laniel pledged to 'put all his energy into ending this bloody war' through negotiations. In the interim, Vietnamization would be intensified in order to turn 'a French war supported by Vietnam' into 'a Vietnamese war supported by France'.[39]

Due to the political turmoil in Paris, the Bermuda conference had been put back to early July. In London, the Foreign Office, working closely with the Chiefs of Staff and other concerned Whitehall agencies, used the delay to perfect the brief on Indochina that Churchill would use at the conference. Completed on 24 June, the brief stands as the most comprehensive statement of British policy on Indochina since the Conservatives returned to power. Strategically, the paper noted, Indochina was 'the key to the defence of South-East Asia and hence of the Indian Ocean'. Economically, 'a threat to South-East Asia is a threat to Malaya, the most important single source of surplus dollars in the sterling area'. And geostrategically, the loss of Indochina would not only be a victory for world communism but 'a catastrophe which would gravely affect France's world position'. The threat to UK and other Commonwealth interests in Southeast Asia was growing in direct proportion to the deterioration in the French position. With their current politico-military approach, the French were 'drifting towards an eventual defeat'. To avert disaster, a resolute lead from Paris was 'indispensable'. The French had failed to grant 'real independence' to the Indochinese and this left Bao Dai, ex-emperor of Annam and Vietnamese Head of State, struggling to shed the colonial puppet label. Militarily, the negativity of French strategy meant that the initiative 'rests squarely with the Vietminh', while French claims that the Vietnamese armed forces would soon be able to cope unaided were 'entirely fallacious'.[40]

Since the problem was politico-military, the solution needed to be similarly dual in nature. In the first place, France should bestow upon Vietnam a level of independence comparable to that enjoyed by members of the British Commonwealth, including the right of secession from the French Union. Militarily, an offensive strategy, predicated on French reinforcement from Europe, was necessary to destroy or at least weaken Vietminh forces prior to any handover to the Vietnamese. The French would doubtless raise objections to these recommendations, but so great were the stakes, and so dire was the French predicament, that the time had come for UK diplomacy to confront the authorities in Paris with a stark choice: either live up to the responsibilities which went with front-rank power status or else accept that France could no longer be regarded as a serious player in international affairs.[41]

To the disappointment of all concerned in the Foreign Office, Churchill failed to confront the French because he never actually made it to Bermuda. On 23 June, the Prime Minister hosted a dinner at Number 10 Downing Street in honour of his Italian counterpart. Towards the end of the evening, Churchill became unwell and by the following morning it was clear to his doctor and close advisors that he had suffered a stroke. Had Eden been fit, this would have been the end of Churchill's premiership. In the Foreign Secretary's absence, however, a small group of politico-medical crisis managers – amongst them Salisbury and Rab Butler, the Chancellor of the Exchequer – deferred any constitutional decision until Churchill's condition became clearer. An obfuscatory medical bulletin was issued explaining that the Prime Minister was in need of 'a complete rest'. The reality of his condition was further concealed when the Fleet Street press barons, secretly apprised of the situation, agreed to avoid comment or speculation in their newspapers.[42] In the end, only Churchill's family and closest colleagues knew the truth – and for that same reason they were the only witnesses to his astonishing recovery. By 1 July, he was cabling Eisenhower to say that he was 'not without hope' of carrying on.[43]

Bermuda, though, was off. Even if Churchill made the speediest of recoveries, the autumn (by which time heavy fighting would have resumed in Vietnam) was the earliest point at which a rescheduled conference could happen. Churchill's misfortune thus robbed the Foreign Office and the Chiefs of Staff of the chance to challenge the French in advance of the new campaigning season. A substitute conference of US, French and British Foreign Ministers was arranged for Washington (10–14 July) and some in the Foreign Office wanted to use this Little Bermuda, as it became known, to 'push the French' on Indochina 'to the very limit of good manners and even beyond'.[44] But Lord Salisbury, who took over from Churchill as acting Foreign Secretary, chose Korea – where, after two years of negotiation, an armistice was close to completion – as his primary Asian focus. Although he had kept 'generally in touch' with international affairs over the last few years, Salisbury found it a tall order 'to go and negotiate at Washington over a number of horribly complicated problems only after a week in the Office'. Through no fault of his own, he was not the man to confront the French on Indochina.[45]

Then again, would a fit Churchill have been? In retrospect, it is hard to imagine the Prime Minister, at seventy-eight, mastering so detailed a brief on a subject of oscillating interest to him. And even if he had collared French leaders, Harvey, for one, did not think it would have made a difference. The French were 'more interested in discussing the possibilities of reaching a peaceful conclusion of the conflict than of considering whether fresh resources might be assembled in order to win a military victory', he pointed out. The challenge facing Churchill and British diplomacy generally would have been 'much more that of keeping the French up to their present mark than of persuading them to go beyond it'.[46]

Looking back, Harvey was right. Supported by a burgeoning cross-section of war-weary political and public opinion, the Laniel government was looking to negotiate. The nascent Korean armistice and the spectacle of the United States (albeit under the

UN flag) preparing to come to terms with the Chinese communists was an additional spur: if the Americans could settle for a result short of victory in Korea, why should the French not do the same in Indochina where they had been fighting twice as long?[47] De Lattre always believed that 'the Korean and Indochina wars were "one war" and that ... there must be "one peace"', but now, in the summer of 1953, the Americans rejected this correlation.[48] If anything, the Eisenhower administration's willingness to compromise in Korea hardened its opposition to similar negotiations on Indochina.[49] Privately, Dulles still viewed Korea as a 'strategic mistake'; surrounded on three sides by sea, and bordered to the north by China and the USSR, the geostrategic impact of Korea's loss to communism was absorbable, 'but if Indochina goes, and South Asia goes, it is extremely hard to insulate ourselves against the consequences'.[50]

If the French were no longer committed to obtaining an outright military solution – and that was the import of Laniel's successful prime-ministerial pitch to the French National Assembly – was there any point in the British exhorting them to greater efforts and sacrifices? The policy contained in Churchill's Bermuda brief was a policy for war at a time when the French were starting to think of peace. The one solace from a British standpoint was that Laniel seemed to be a negotiator-from-strength. The same could not be said about any future French premier. Just a few days before Laniel secured his constitutional majority, the Radical deputy Pierre Mendès-France fell a mere thirteen votes short of forming a government. Mendès-France, the Foreign Office noted, had campaigned on a platform which not only opposed the Indochina War (and the EDC) but called for early negotiations with the Vietminh.[51]

For a time in the summer of 1953, the seriousness of the Laniel government's commitment to a negotiated settlement and, by extension, the degree to which it no longer sought victory, was obscured by the announcement of two initiatives which, prima facie, went some way towards fulfilling the recommendations in Churchill's Bermuda brief.

On 3 July, Laniel issued a 'solemn declaration' in which he pledged to 'perfect' the independence of Vietnam, Laos and Cambodia. The Associated States were invited to send representatives to France to begin negotiations as soon as possible. Two days earlier, a debate in the US Senate revealed considerable support for linking further increases in American assistance for the war effort to serious French efforts to make Indochinese independence a reality. Whether cause and effect – disgruntlement on Capitol Hill followed by Laniel's declaration – was at work, the fact remained that the French government had committed itself publicly to the kind of political advance which UK policymakers had long regarded as necessary to detach non-communist nationalists from the communist-controlled Vietminh.[52]

Hard on the heels of Laniel's declaration came the second initiative. Following a fact-finding tour of Indochina, General Navarre had drawn up a new plan of campaign. During the forthcoming fighting season, French forces would start to transition from defence to offence. Initially the emphasis would be on pacification in Cochinchina and Annam and on stabilizing Tonkin and the Red River delta. Large-scale engagements with the PAVN were to be avoided in 1953–1954 prior to the launch of offensive operations in 1954–1955. Essential to the success of the Navarre Plan, as it soon became known, was the further expansion of the Vietnamese armed forces with a view to taking over from the FEC in the future. 'Vietnamisation' was 'the very foundation of my plan', Navarre recalled, for 'without it, there was no way out'.[53]

On 17 July, Navarre presented his plan to the French Chiefs of Staff, who approved it in principle, and then made a similar presentation to the Committee of National Defence the following week. One of his objects, he explained, was to create a mobile reserve complete with air support to undertake offensive operations in 1954–1955. To give effect to his vision while the VNA was developing, Navarre requested immediate reinforcements to the tune of twelve infantry battalions, drawn if possible from Europe. Backing the plan, the committee promised eight additional infantry battalions, one engineer battalion and an increase in transport aircraft, artillery and naval support, less than Navarre asked for but more than he feared he might get.[54] On 30 July, the Quai d'Orsay informed the British Embassy in confidence of what had been agreed. Public disclosure would come in due course. For the moment, the French government needed time to consider how best to handle the popular-political reaction to the news that the military commitment was to be increased. In London, the Foreign Office was staggered. 'The moral of all this is never say die!', an incredulous Head of the Southeast Asia Department remarked of the decision on reinforcement, while the Paris Embassy applauded a 'courageous' decision that would cause 'uproar when the news comes out'.[55]

The Laniel government had a further reason for keeping the decision under wraps: uncertainty about American financial backing. Implementation of the Navarre Plan, including the recruitment, training and arming of a further 135,000 Vietnamese troops, required a substantial cash injection from the United States. Back in March, the Eisenhower administration had insisted that the French produce a politico-military plan for victory as a sine qua non of continued military aid. Judging from the US NSC's agreement to allocate a further $385 million to France on top of the extensive funds already pledged for 1953–1954, Laniel's declaration and the Navarre Plan met this requirement.[56] News of the US aid package was made public in a Franco-American communiqué on 30 September. The French undertook to make 'every effort to break up and destroy the regular enemy forces in Indochina', to 'carry through … plans for increasing the Associated States forces' and to commit their own troops to 'assure the success of existing military plans'. For their part, the Americans confirmed that the extra money was intended to 'make it possible to achieve these objectives with maximum speed and effectiveness'.[57] On the eve of the new campaigning season, the French seemed to have come up with a blueprint which promised if not victory then at least a reversal of the losing trend. The Americans, in underwriting that blueprint, evidently thought likewise.

In the British Foreign Office, however, officials had already concluded that there was less to the French grand design than met the eye. With regard to Laniel's solemn declaration, it emerged that Indochinese independence was to be perfected within the framework of the French Union which meant that France would retain considerable control over foreign, defence and financial-commercial policy. As defined by the Constitution of the Fourth Republic, the French Union was not a grouping of equals but a combination of states under and answerable to the Presidency of the Republic. Comparisons with the British Commonwealth, although often made, were inappropriate. The assimilationist philosophy underpinning the French imperial mission was reflected in the French Union's plethora of centralized institutions, a bureaucratic nexus with no parallel in the Commonwealth. Moreover, France's position in the French Union was explicitly predominant and not, as in the case of Britain in the Commonwealth, first amongst equals.[58] In practice, the Associated States could never truly be free *and* members of the French Union. Yet, as Churchill's Bermuda brief pointed out, the right of secession from the Union was the minimum demand even of moderate nationalists.[59]

By September, the British Mission in Saigon was reporting local responses to Laniel's initiative that were 'apathetic or fatalist where not critical'. Bao Dai was particularly bitter. 'What do they mean "perfect"?', he snapped. 'What's the matter with the French – they're always giving us our independence. Can't they give it to us once and for all?'[60] Preliminary discussions between France and the Associated States got under way later in the year, but while Laos soon accepted (and was granted) independence within the French Union, a similar arrangement for Cambodia and Vietnam proved elusive and negotiations in both cases dragged on into 1954.[61]

As British faith in the Laniel declaration waned, so British scepticism about the Navarre Plan waxed. In public Navarre employed the rhetoric of victory, but London policymakers doubted that this was really the objective.[62] These suspicions were warranted. Privately, the Committee of National Defence, whose decisions were binding on the French Cabinet, was no longer committed to military victory. The orders issued to Navarre reflected this. As General Paul Ely, the Army Chief of Staff, recalled, the aim was to 'create military conditions that would allow the government to negotiate a satisfactory, honourable solution to the Indochinese affair'. Navarre's task was 'to prove that the Vietminh had no chance of winning by force of arms' so that Ho Chi Minh would be compelled 'to negotiate'.[63]

From the UK Foreign Office's standpoint, even if the Navarre Plan proved to be less ambitious than its packaging suggested, it was reassuring that Navarre himself was more cognizant than his predecessor of the need to inflict serious damage on the Vietminh in advance of negotiations or a FEC rundown. However, much hinged on the arrival of the reinforcements Navarre had been promised, and seasoned Indochina-watchers in Whitehall preferred to wait until 'the troops are on Indo-Chinese soil' before getting too carried away.[64] This proved to be wise self-counsel. Navarre had asked for twelve battalions, had been promised nine, but in the end would receive only seven, the majority hailing from North Africa and judged by UK military experts to be much inferior in quality compared with troops from the professional French army in Europe. Political expediency eroded the Laniel government's good intentions insofar as domestic criticism of reinforcement was always going to be less vociferous if the manpower came from the French Union rather than France.[65]

By early September, the Foreign Office and UK posts in Southeast Asia had concluded that the Navarre Plan was probably a reworking of the old policy of minimizing French casualties and playing out time before handing the war over to the Vietnamese. As the Foreign Office's Southeast Asia Department reflected, the depressing likelihood was that the 'well-organised, trained and equipped modern force' that was the PAVN would overwhelm the Vietnamese National Army and propel Ho Chi Minh to power within a short space of time following FEC evacuation. The most to be expected from the Navarre Plan was 'the avoidance of what previously looked like almost certain military disaster' when serious fighting recommenced.[66] Later, in his memoirs, Navarre confirmed the accuracy of these British reservations. Soon after taking over from Salan, Navarre realized that there was no possibility of winning the war. Even if he had concluded otherwise, his political masters in Paris were only interested in creating military conditions that would permit France an 'honourable way out'. To that end, Navarre was told to keep casualties low. As for the extra troops granted to him, these were not reinforcements at all but merely advance replacements for his projected 1953 losses.[67]

French interest in a negotiated Indochina settlement deepened as peace in Korea drew nearer. At Little Bermuda in mid-July, Georges Bidault, the French Foreign Minister, told Dulles and Salisbury that 'French public opinion would not tolerate a situation in which an armistice in Korea was not matched by similar progress towards a peaceful solution in Indo-China'. Bidault proposed that the Korean Political Conference, which was to convene pursuant to the armistice to map out the country's post-war future, be extended to take in Indochina. Dulles and Salisbury demurred on the ground that this would complicate the search for a Korean settlement, but Bidault persisted. French soldiers were dying every day, he reminded them, and it was 'important to avoid the impression that Indo-China was kept as an ... open wound while things were being patched up in Korea'.[68]

This juxtaposition eventually made some impression on Salisbury. The UK government was on record as favouring a modus vivendi with China encompassing the whole Asian Cold War front once peace was restored in Korea, and on reflection, Salisbury felt that if the Korean conference made good progress, and if the Chinese raised the question of Indochina of their own accord, 'we should keep an open mind and be prepared to seize such opportunities as might offer'. Dulles, in contrast, declared himself 'greatly surprised and disturbed' that the French should prefer talking to rather than fighting communists. In London, the Foreign Office saw no cause for such wonderment; to the contrary, it was obvious to Asian specialists that the French planned to 'muddle along' in Vietnam 'until an armistice in Korea creates a new situation in the light of which they will seek a settlement by negotiation'.[69]

The Korean armistice was finally signed on 27 July 1953. Back in 1949–1950, following the birth of the PRC, Britain's China policy proceeded along two lines, 'containment and compromise'.[70] While the Korean War was ongoing, containment took precedence. But the UK government's hopes for a broad Asian settlement were never abandoned. 'The fighting [in Korea], while it continued, was an absolute bar to any improvement in the general situation in the Far East,' Selwyn Lloyd told the House of Commons on the day of the armistice, 'but now that the fighting has ceased we can once more look forward with hope'.[71] In Washington, the US administration sounded a more negative note. The United States, Dulles announced, had no intention of buying a satisfactory outcome in the Korean Political Conference – a unified and democratic Korea, for example – at the cost of concessions to China. This meant, inter alia, that Chiang Kai-shek and the Chinese nationalists would not be unseated at the United Nations in favour of Mao Zedong and the Chinese communists.[72]

When the United States and South Korea went on to conclude a mutual defence treaty, Ambassador Makins in Washington composed a dispatch to Salisbury reflecting on the frustrations and emotions aroused in America by the recently ended conflict. Alongside US readiness to invest in South Korea's future security, there was fierce opposition to rewarding the PRC for killing 34,000 Americans by giving it satisfaction not just on UN representation but on control over Taiwan (which Beijing deemed a rebel province of China, not a separate state), or in relaxing Western trade restrictions, Makins reported. The war just ended also offered clues to how the United States might handle a new war elsewhere in Asia. In Korea, Makins wrote, there had been 'increasing impatience with allies', 'disillusionment with the United Nations' and a desire to 'go it alone'. There was particular resentment towards the UK for insisting on confining the conflict to the Korean peninsula. The 'concept of a war for limited objectives' was 'wholly alien and repugnant to American mentality', and blame for the costly stalemate 'was increasingly being laid on external factors', including the attitude of America's allies.[73]

It was inevitable that the Korean armistice would impact on French attitudes towards Indochina. In August, the French Ambassador in London, René Massigli, channelling Bidault, told Salisbury that the pressing matter was how to bring the Franco-Vietminh struggle 'within the ambit of the [Korean] Political Conference' in order to initiate Franco-Chinese dialogue. Maurice Dejean, Letourneau's successor as High Commissioner, considered it 'essential that the Chinese should be induced to disinterest themselves in Indochina'. Unless that happened, he saw 'no hope'.[74] The French displayed no comparable interest in talking to Ho Chi Minh at this point. Negotiations with China could be packaged for public consumption as international diplomacy whereas dealing with Ho would, by French lights, legitimize the DRV, dismay Bao Dai and his followers and encourage nationalists elsewhere in the French Union to pursue their political aims through force of arms.[75] Realistically, there would have to be direct Franco-Vietminh engagement at some point; it was just a question of timing. 'Nobody here seems to believe any longer in a complete defeat of the Viet Minh,' Patrick Reilly of the British Embassy in Paris reported to the Foreign Office. The 'basic aims' of the French government were to 'find some diplomatic means of persuading the Chinese Government to withdraw their support from the Viet Minh' and then 'to negotiate with the Viet Minh from strength'.[76]

The Korean armistice impinged on the Indochina problem in other ways. For the previous two years, the French had worried that peace in Korea would be followed by an increase in PRC military assistance to the Vietminh or even direct Chinese intervention. As the Panmunjom negotiations neared a climax, the French managed to persuade the British and Americans to accept an 'addition' to the Joint Policy Declaration which the UN Command was to issue in conjunction with the armistice agreement. Published on 7 August, the Declaration stated that 'if there is a renewal of the armed attack [in Korea] … we should again be united and prompt to resist'. Moreover, the 'consequences of such a breach of the armistice would be so grave that, in all probability, it would not be possible to confine hostilities within the frontiers of Korea'. Then came the French add-on: 'We are of the opinion that the armistice must not result in jeopardising the restoration or the safeguarding of peace in any other part of Asia.' This was an implicit but unmistakable warning to China that an attack on Vietnam would not just nullify the Korean armistice but risk full-blown war with the United States or US-led UN forces.[77]

French hopes that progress in the Korean Political Conference would lead to discussions with China on Indochina were eventually dashed because there was no progress. Under the terms of the armistice, the Korean conference was to convene within three months of the end of hostilities, but this timetable was soon in trouble. In August, the UN General Assembly resolved that membership of the conference should include all participants in the UN Command plus the two Koreas and China. The Soviet Union and India would also participate as interested but neutral parties. The Americans immediately objected to the USSR's designation as a neutral; the Soviets, they insisted, were de facto belligerents insofar as they supplied China and North Korea with military assistance and should participate in the conference under that heading. This was the cue for a behind-the-scenes argument between the United States and the UK, the latter backing USSR involvement on the ground that no Korean settlement was likely to be lasting without Soviet support. In the end, to American displeasure, the General Assembly again voted in favour of Soviet involvement, although the USSR's status remained unresolved.[78]

For the remainder of 1953, the future of the Korean Political Conference remained in flux. Rather than proceed with the conference proper, the UN General Assembly approved preparatory talks. These got underway at Panmunjom on 26 October with Arthur Dean representing the United States (and in absentia South Korea and the United Nations), Huang Hua the PRC and Ki Sok Pok the North Koreans. Two months of acerbic exchanges ensued with the communists insisting that the USSR attend the main conference as a neutral and the Americans equally insistent on according the Soviets belligerent status. In mid-December, the Chinese accused the Americans of conspiring with the South Koreans to subvert prisoner-of-war exchanges. That was too much for Dean. Citing 'rude, arrogant and insulting' communist diplomacy, he promptly walked out never to return.[79]

Well before then, policymakers in London and Washington had begun to worry that China might be using the armistice as a smokescreen behind which it could resupply and reinforce its armies prior to renewing hostilities. As both the UK and US governments were aware, the wording of the Joint Policy Declaration could be used to justify war with China if the armistice collapsed. For the British, this prospect rekindled apprehensions about American retaliatory preferences – bombing, blockade, even an assault on China with nuclear arms – and prompted fears that Korea, if mishandled, could be a catalyst for general (nuclear) war with the USSR. Unless, that was, Indochina got there first.[80]

Vietnam in the Shadow of the Bomb, 1953

On 2 September, in a speech in St. Louis, Missouri, the US Secretary of State drew an explicit linkage between Korea and Indochina. If China invaded Vietnam, this 'second aggression', following on from the PRC's intervention in Korea, 'could not occur without grave consequences which might not be confined to Indo-China'. Dulles took some of the edge off this warning by adding that peace could be had in Indochina 'if Red China wants it'. A successful Korean conference could lead to 'an end of aggression and restoration of peace' elsewhere.[1] In Paris, the Laniel government welcomed this statement, the first time a senior US government figure had publicly acknowledged even the possibility of a negotiated end to the war.[2]

The same day that Dulles spoke in St. Louis, *Pravda* hinted that the USSR, too, had some interest in Indochinese diplomacy. Hailing the Korean armistice as a 'victory for the forces of peace and democracy', the Soviet organ suggested that the people of Vietnam might yet see 'the settlement of French-Vietnam relations by means of direct negotiations'.[3] In Britain, the press seized on the apparent congruity of US and USSR views, the *Manchester Guardian* noting that if 'these two countries support negotiations then there seems some reason to feel that they may be attempted'.[4] On 3 September, China joined in with an editorial in the *People's Daily* which argued that by 'applying the principle of settling international disputes through negotiation', France could 'get out of its mess in the Vietnam war'.[5] The Vietminh, however, were in no hurry to talk. 'We are always for peace,' Ho Chi Minh told the *Vietnam News Agency*, 'but we know that peace can only be achieved through the victory of our long and hard resistance'.[6]

In the Foreign Office, officials agreed that the Americans, Soviets and Chinese appeared to have opened the door to negotiations. But the Southeast Asia Department found it hard to believe that any of them would cross the threshold. Despite what Dulles said in St. Louis, the United States was unlikely to approve of early negotiations in view of French military and political weakness in Vietnam, while the USSR, despite its public position, probably favoured the continuation of a war which sapped France militarily in Europe, jeopardized the EDC and destabilized NATO. As for the Chinese, they might dangle the prospect of negotiations before the French but only in the hope of winning a Western ally in their campaign for UN representation and control of Taiwan. Nor did British policymakers feel it safe to assume any basic divergence between Ho Chi Minh and his Sino-Soviet patrons despite their apparently differing perspectives. For the time being, then, the British position, and ultimately the American and French positions, remained unchanged: progress on the Korean Political Conference was the litmus test of the sincerity of the communist bloc's interest in peace in Asia.[7]

For the French, the jambing of one door to negotiations with China was offset by the possible opening of another. Building on what had been agreed at Little Bermuda, the Western powers sent an official Note to the USSR in August proposing a four-power foreign ministers meeting on Germany and Austria. The Soviet government countered with a proposal for a five-power conference, with China as the extra participant, and a brief to survey the full international scene. Publicly, the Western powers stuck to their four-power concept, but in private their unity was strained. Aside from the British, who were already predisposed to diplomatic engagement with China, the French were attracted by a five-power meeting insofar as it offered an alternative forum within which to gauge PRC attitudes to Indochina. The United States was wholly *un*attracted. For the moment, the United States, UK and France presented a solid front to the outside world, but it would not take much to expose the fragility of this unity.[8]

As 1953 drew to a close, the dilemma Indochina posed for British diplomacy had almost completed its transformation from an issue of war to an issue of peace. Back in June, at the time of the abortive Bermuda conference, the Churchill government had developed a policy predicated on encouraging the French to press if not for military victory then for military ascendency. That policy had then been reworked to take into account mounting evidence that a negotiated solution was the Laniel administration's preferred way forward. By September, the Foreign Office had become anxious that negotiations in present circumstances (without, that is, prior French military success) would be tantamount to giving Indochina away. Nor was there much confidence in the Foreign Office or Ministry of Defence that the Navarre Plan would deliver the level of battlefield primacy necessary for the French to secure a peace with honour.[9] A question must be asked at this point. If the British recognized the limitations of the Navarre Plan, why did the Americans not do so too? For an answer, we need to consider the Franco-American relationship in its Indochinese setting.

To guarantee continued, let alone increased US military assistance, the French had developed the habit of telling the Americans what they wanted to hear.[10] In Washington in March 1953, Letourneau assured the Eisenhower administration that France was determined to 'break the back' of Vietminh resistance, but a little later, talking to the Australian Foreign Minister, he confided that there was 'no possibility of France winning the war'.[11] Similarly, at the end of August, Laniel told the US Ambassador in Paris, Douglas Dillon, that the 'Viet Minh were now at the peak of their power and on the way down'. Laniel was 'confident of victory in a fairly short period of time if the funds were available'.[12] Laniel's performance – like Letourneau's – was typical of the general French approach. To ensure that its real goal, negotiations from strength, was underwritten by US dollars, the French government tended to exaggerate the scope of its ambition. Victory was a ruse, not an objective. 'Nobody believes any more that it is possible to beat the Viet Minh militarily,' former premier René Mayer admitted privately. 'Nevertheless, in order to induce Washington to grant France sizeable direct assistance, the notion has been propagated that additional efforts might yield decisive results.'[13]

The Laniel government was forced to tread a fine line as it sought to placate both the Americans and its domestic polity. The US-French communiqué of 30 September

1953, for example, emphasized French willingness to destroy the Vietminh as a regular military force in return for which the Americans agreed to bankroll the Navarre Plan. This trade-off went down poorly in France where the press not only attacked the United States for turning the French Expeditionary Corps into US mercenaries but accused Laniel of playing a double game by talking of peace to the French people while promising military victory to the Americans. A well-placed source in the Quai d'Orsay later confirmed to the British Embassy in Paris that the wording of the communiqué had been shaped to appeal to the United States rather than French opinion. The 'American public would expect the emphasis to be placed on French determination to fight hard'. But in reality the policy of the Laniel government was 'to negotiate a peace in Indochina as soon as their position is sufficiently favourable'.[14]

In a statement issued on 2 October, Laniel sought to quell the outcry over the communiqué by explaining that the new US appropriations would ease the expense of expanding the Vietnamese army. Vietnamization, Laniel felt, offered France its best exit option. As for peace negotiations, these could only be safely conducted from strength, a position France did not presently enjoy.[15] So far, it seemed, so robust. But a few days later, Maurice Schumann, Bidault's deputy at the Quai d'Orsay, told the Voice of America that if it was down to France alone, negotiations would already be in train, but Bao Dai and his government opposed any compromise with the communists. These inconsistencies did not go unnoticed in the British Foreign Office. The French premier spoke of negotiations from future strength whereas Schumann implied that immediate negotiations, ipso facto from weakness, might be contemplated in defiance of Bao Dai. Either way, British officials were left to reflect on how 'very, very thin is the present veneer of determination on the part of the French'.[16]

A further question needs to be asked. Why did a fiscally conservative US government wedded to curbing mutual security spending agree to invest an extra $385 million on top of an already huge Indochinese outlay in a French military plan which, as far as the British were concerned, was unlikely to ensure a non-communist future for Vietnam? Why, having decided that Korea was an unwinnable war, did the Americans conclude that Vietnam offered a better prospect? In actual fact, far from blindly accepting French assurances of success, the Eisenhower administration backed the Navarre Plan conscious of its shortcomings – but aware, too, that there was no practicable alternative. 'Washington leaders felt they had no choice but to go along,' historian Ronald Spector has shown. If negotiating with the communists from weakness was unacceptable, 'then the only choice was to bankroll the Navarre plan and hope for the best'.[17] Also influencing administration attitudes was a belief that Laniel's was probably the last French government that would fight the war with any degree of élan and a corresponding fear that a successor would, in the words of a State Department study, be 'committed to seek a settlement on terms dangerous to the security of the United States and the Free World'.[18]

There was also a subtle but discernible element of self-deception about the American approach to Indochina. Convinced that there was no acceptable substitute to military victory, and having made the preservation of a non-communist Vietnam one of its foremost foreign policy priorities, the Eisenhower administration could hardly have admitted publicly, or even to itself, that the Navarre Plan was badly flawed. To have done so would have meant confronting the unhappy truth that only large-scale US intervention with air, naval and probably ground forces could rescue the situation. But the Republican administration, like US opinion at large, was unwilling to entertain the thought of another costly commitment on the Asian mainland so soon after the termination of the unpopular Korean experience. US policymakers therefore sought to convince themselves that the Navarre Plan held (as the French, for their own reasons, said it did) a reasonable prospect of success. In September 1953, Charlton Ogburn of the State Department's Far Eastern Affairs bureau suggested to colleagues that US policy was based 'on an article of faith' which had so far gone unquestioned, namely that 'the French cannot and must not fail'. With mounting evidence that the French might well fail, Ogburn thought it wise to consider alternatives. His superior, Philip Bonsal, Director of the Office of Philippines and Southeast Asian Affairs, disagreed: 'We cannot *let* the Navarre Plan fail.' Within the US government, Bonsals outnumbered Ogburns.[19]

"Bonsalism" even infected the Oval Office. In Eisenhower's view, Vietnam was the key to the defence of Indochina and Indochina the key to the security of the rest of Southeast Asia. The problem lay in persuading the US public and Congress of this reality and its concomitant, the need to continue to invest in the French war effort. Leaving aside ignorance ('Many Americans', Eisenhower suspected, 'thought that Saigon was something to eat'), the prospect of victory, and publicly asserting that prospect, was necessary to win domestic support for 'an all-out effort in Indochina for a year or 18 months'. If there was no successful outcome by 1955, that 'would be the end of the Aid'.[20] The authors of the *Pentagon Papers* later remarked that the 'temptation to "go along" with the French' sprang from an '*expectation* of victory' within the Eisenhower administration which got in the way of any objective analysis of the Vietnam situation until reality finally hit home in the spring of 1954.[21] The contrast with the British is marked. 'The outlook is far from encouraging,' the Foreign Office's Southeast Asia experts concluded in September 1953, 'since either a strong Vietminh military attack or an offer by them to negotiate (both equally dangerous) might cause the final collapse of morale in France and the Associated States'.[22]

In Vietnam, the new fighting season got off to a slow start due to the Red River delta remaining flooded longer than usual. At the same time, and much as the UK Foreign Office had feared, the arrival of new French troops in-theatre proved to be reliefs, not net reinforcements as Navarre had requested. Between July 1953 and January 1954 the number of French and Foreign Legion soldiers in the FEC actually declined. Like Salan before him, Navarre was instructed by his political masters to 'adjust your aims to the means you have at your disposal'.[23]

In October, Giap ordered his armies westwards in the direction of Laos in a move which presaged a possible renewal of the PAVN invasion of the spring. The French countered with Operation Castor, launched on 20 November. Some 2,500 paratroopers and equipment were air-dropped into the Nam Yum valley in the Thai country close to the sparsely populated village of Dien Bien Phu and astride the main invasion route into Laos. If Giap did make a thrust in that direction, the French would be waiting for him. Further troops and supplies soon followed as the French set about constructing a fortified *base aero-terrestre*. Located 180 miles west of Hanoi and deep in enemy-held territory, Dien Bien Phu was entirely dependent on air supply. Encased in minefields and barbed wire, the redoubt boasted an interconnected network of nine Centres of Resistance (CRs) complete with lookout posts, communication centres and underground dugouts. The Nam Yum valley, in which the base nestled, was ten miles long, five-and-a-half miles wide and crested by wooded hills.[24]

To begin with, Navarre did not see Dien Bien Phu as the site for a climatic engagement. The base, which was operational by December, was initially intended to bolt the door into Laos. Looking ahead, Dien Bien Phu certainly had potential as a mooring point for offensive operations inside enemy territory, but the Navarre Plan was predicated on consolidation rather than offensive action in 1953–1954. Before long, though, Dien Bien Phu became an *abcès de fixation*. In some ways, this suited Navarre. If the Vietminh chose to accept the challenge of destroying the entrenched camp, Giap's forces would have to cross the open valley floor in strength and expose themselves to superior French firepower. On 3 December 1953, Navarre declared that he was ready for battle on the grand scale if that was what Giap wanted.[25]

The man Navarre chose to command the garrison was Colonel – later General – Christian Marie Ferdinand de la Croix de Castries, a 51-year-old cavalryman with a martial lineage stretching back to the Crusades and a reputation as a ladies man; all nine CRs were given female code names, allegedly named for the commander's former lovers (Anne-Marie, Beatrice, Claudine, Dominique, Eliane, Francoise, Gabrielle, Huguette and Isabelle). 'Dienbienphu must become an offensive base,' Navarre told de Castries, somewhat in defiance of the philosophy of the plan that bore his name. 'That's why I've picked you.'[26] Hubris was not confined to senior commanders. 'If they [the Vietminh] attack', Second Lieutenant Jean Fox wrote to his family, 'there'll be plenty of yellow meat in the barbed wire.'[27]

Shortly after Castor commenced, the PAVN invaded Laos via the Annamite mountains. By the end of the year, Thakhek had been captured and the country effectively cut in half. The Vietminh would maintain the military pressure during the first weeks of 1954, advancing on the royal capital, Luang Prabang. As a protective screen for Laos, Dien Bien Phu was clearly not working. As an *abcès de fixation*, it was doing better. By February 1954, Giap had thirty-three battalions within striking distance of the base, 'the biggest concentration of Viet Minh troops ever realized in the Indo China War', according to the British Joint Intelligence Committee.[28] Initially, US military experts questioned the wisdom of diverting so many French troops (12,000 rising to a peak of just over 15,000) and so much military hardware from the critical Red River delta. However, Navarre maintained that if the enemy was sucked into a large-scale frontal attack, the garrison's strength and firepower must be sufficient to ensure victory. Giap and his military advisors, recalling the horrendous mauling de Lattre meted out to the PAVN in 1950–1951, and second-guessing Navarre's approach at Dien Bien Phu, had serious misgivings about accepting battle.[29]

In October 1953, shortly before the French infested Dien Bien Phu, Anthony Eden returned to the Foreign Office after a six-month convalescence following life-saving intestinal surgery. In career ambition terms, he was impatient to take possession of Number 10 Downing Street. In Cold War diplomatic terms, he retained a strong dislike of Churchill's top-level summitry and much preferred a lower-level Foreign Ministers approach to East-West relations. To his dismay, Eden discovered that during his time away Churchill had turned his quest for a summit into an overwhelming justification, or excuse, for clinging to power despite his own serious health issues.[30]

On the wider international scene, Eden had to deal with the continuing saga of German rearmament and the EDC, as well as complex negotiations concerning Trieste, Egypt and Iran. It was Asia, though, that was the 'theatre that causes us all most immediate concern', he told the House of Commons on 5 November. Korea was an especial worry. 'We and our Allies are working very hard to bring about this conference because we know that if once we can achieve a Korean settlement then we can move on to the wider relaxation of tension in the Far East, and what a relief that would be to us all.'[31] Privately, the British government still wondered whether Chinese stalling on the conference might portend a resumption of hostilities. If the war reopened, the United States had made it abundantly clear that it would not become mired again in fighting on the ground in Korea but would target China directly and accept, in the process, the possibility of general war. At a meeting of the Defence Committee, the British Chiefs of Staff surmised that the USSR would probably seek to avoid war with the Western Alliance over the next several years and concentrate on extending its power and influence by non-military methods. There was, however, a danger that general war might arise 'unintentionally' if a localized Asian problem escalated out of control.[32]

In November, the Chief of the Imperial General Staff, Field Marshal Harding, identified Korea as an obvious catalyst in this regard. The United States 'meant to go all out' if the armistice collapsed, he reminded his fellow service chiefs, 'driving the Chinese out of Korea and ... reunifying the country by force of arms'. In pursuit of this objective, the Americans would do 'everything in their power' to hurt China. The UK had to resist such extreme measures, including the 'unrestricted use of unconventional weapons against China', on the grounds that they would 'increase world tension and heighten the risk of general war'. Retaliation should be confined to the maximum military effort *within* Korea. If direct action was to be taken against the PRC, it should be strictly limited to conventional bombing of airfields and lines of supply to the Korean front and to a naval blockade covering the Chinese coast from the Kwantung peninsula to the Yalu River (thereby excluding Soviet ports). Nuclear arms, the Chiefs of Staff agreed, were weapons of last resort to be employed only 'if defeat seemed imminent'.[33]

The perplexing communist attitude to the Korean Political Conference also served to revive British interest in dual containment and, more specifically, in a collective defence organization for Asia to deter or meet PRC aggression while simultaneously functioning as a shackle on US adventurism. Notwithstanding the creation of the Five-Power Staff Agency, the Foreign Office felt that there was still 'a long way to go before we can expect to see the United States committed to participation in any more formal piece of defence machinery' in Asia, 'with political strings attached, on the lines of NATO in Europe'. In the absence of a coordinated Allied approach, Southeast Asia remained the weakest link in the Western Alliance's containment chain.[34] In a memorandum approved by the Cabinet on 26 November, Eden rehearsed the difficulties preventing an agreed Anglo-American approach to the Asian Cold War. The principal difficulty was the 'American attitude towards China'. Many Americans, including governmental decision-makers, seemed 'disinclined to accept the fact that Communism in China has come to stay, responsive to suggestions that the Chinese people could and should be assisted to liberate themselves by intervention from outside, and suspicious of attempts to reduce China's dependence on the Russians by establishing commercial or diplomatic contacts with Peking'. Britain, he argued, should aim 'to convince the US Government, and encourage them to convince American opinion, of the rightness of our own approach'. This was 'based upon acceptance of the facts of the situation, the avoidance of provocation, gradual progress towards more normal trading and diplomatic relations, and the need to keep a toe in the door in case divergencies between China and Russia develop and can be exploited'.[35]

Even as Eden was expounding his thinking in Cabinet, an opportunity to begin the UK-US reconciliation process had arisen. At the beginning of November, the USSR rejected the latest Western offer of a four-power foreign ministers meeting on European problems and again proposed a five-power meeting on world affairs. The impasse encouraged Churchill to resurrect the idea of an East-West heads of government summit. As a first step, he suggested to Eisenhower that the Bermuda conference, in stasis since the summer, be reactivated. Eisenhower – and Laniel – proved agreeable and early December was set aside for a tripartite conclave.[36] On 26 November, the day that Eden's paper on Asia was tabled in Cabinet, the Soviet government abruptly changed tack: a four-power foreign ministers meeting on Germany and Austria was acceptable after all.[37] In addition to providing the British, French and Americans with a chance to discuss the world scene, the reconstituted Bermuda conference thus offered a timely opportunity to compose a formal tripartite invitation to the USSR to attend a foreign ministers council.

In France, Indochina continued to exercise both parliamentary and public opinion. At the end of October, the National Assembly held a full-dress debate on the war. In a strong defence of his government's policy, Laniel insisted that the launch of the Navarre Plan would prove to the Vietminh that there was 'no longer the least hope of obtaining the departure of French and French Union troops by force'. On negotiations, he said that a peaceful solution remained his goal but this could only be secured from a position of strength, such as the Navarre Plan promised to create, and in agreement with the Associated States.[38] A month later, on 29 November, Laniel's commitment to negotiation from strength was tested when the Stockholm news magazine *Expressen* published an interview with Ho Chi Minh in which the Vietminh leader revealed a readiness to discuss peace. 'If as a result of the lessons of these years of war the French Government wish ... to resolve the question of Vietnam by means of negotiations', Ho remarked, 'the people and government of the Democratic Republic of Vietnam are ready to examine the French proposals'.[39]

The Foreign Office in London and the State Department in Washington both suspected that Ho had been levered into making his offer by the USSR and China. In recent weeks, Moscow and Beijing had stated publicly that there was no international problem which could not be solved through diplomatic dialogue, and the Ho interview seemed to reflect the peace motif of post-Stalin communist propaganda.[40] Evidence emerging since the end of the Cold War supports this contemporary Anglo-American assessment but only up to a point. The Chinese were keen to win French and wider international support for their foreign policy goals (admission to the United Nations, a resolution of the Taiwan issue in their favour, increased trade with the West). To this end, the Central People's Government concluded that a moderate, constructive approach to Indochina would reap benefits by exposing the 'contradictions' between France and the United States. At the same time, PRC leaders were fearful that if the situation in Vietnam spiralled out of control, US intervention on the side of the French would drag China into another major conflict when it had hardly begun the recovery process following its costly campaign in Korea. The USSR, in its post-Stalin incarnation, also inclined to the view that the war was becoming ready for diplomatic resolution. Given this Sino-Soviet outlook, and given the Vietminh's reliance on PRC and USSR military supplies, the DRV leadership could not easily deflect pressure to consider a negotiated settlement.[41] But were the Vietminh minded to resist? Recent research on the DRV perspective shows that Ho and his comrades had their own reasons for considering a diplomatic compromise, including war-weariness amongst their followers, morale problems in the PAVN, a realistic assessment of the limits of their overall strength vis-à-vis the forces that France, the French Union and the Vietnamese could still muster, and concern about American intervention. To be sure, Sino-Soviet pressure existed. But so did Vietminh agency.[42]

The most immediate consequence of the Ho interview was the destabilization of Franco-Vietnamese relations. In October, a congress in Saigon of non-communist nationalists, convened with Bao Dai's blessing, outraged French opinion by passing a resolution demanding Vietnam's withdrawal from the French Union as part of a full independence package. In France, the resolution was taken by many people as an insult considering the great loss of blood and treasure in Vietnam since 1946. 'Let them stew in their own juice', French President Vincent Auriol fumed. 'We'll withdraw the expeditionary force.'[43] As Philippe Devilliers and Jean Lacouture later reflected, 'Everyone in France now knew what had been clear enough from the start; even if France won the war, it would have to leave Indochina.'[44] A month after the Saigon congress, at a point of tension in Franco-Vietnamese relations, along came Ho's *Expressen* interview.[45]

Publicly, the Laniel government dismissed the Ho démarche as '98 per cent propaganda'; if the DRV was serious, it needed to provide detailed proposals which the French would then scrutinize 'in consultation' with the Vietnamese.[46] This stress on a role for the State of Vietnam was a correct response from the leader of the French Union. In reality, the surge of 'contemptuous anger' in France following the Saigon congress had been so great that Vietnamese sensibilities were unlikely to prevent a diplomatic settlement of the war if DRV terms were acceptable to France.[47]

The Bermuda conference opened on 4 December 1953. At a public relations level, the meeting was intended to reaffirm UK, US and French unity in the face of the Kremlin's 'peace offensive', and judging from the communiqué issued after four days of talks, it was mission accomplished.[48] In truth, the Western allies struggled to reach unanimity on many of the issues before them at a tense and acrimonious conference. 'The inside story on Bermuda is ... not to be trusted on ordinary paper which doesn't have some fireproofing', one Foreign Office official wrote afterwards. 'The words would scorch it.'[49]

Churchill set the tone. Annoyed at the presence of the French, whom he regarded as gatecrashers at an Anglo-American party, he was rude to Laniel and Bidault and was generally irascible. Aside from the French, Churchill's bad form owed much to the absence of American support for his pet project, a summit with the Soviets. Eisenhower crudely but effectively rejected Churchill's thesis that there had been a change for the better in Soviet foreign policy since Stalin's death. 'Russia was a woman of the streets,' he declared, 'and whether her dress was new, or just the old one patched, it was certainly the same whore underneath'. The United States 'intended to drive her off her present "beat" into the backstreets'.[50] With this, Churchill's hopes for an early top-table meeting with Malenkov were sunk. Instead, the three powers dispatched an invitation to the USSR to attend a four-power foreign ministers meeting in Berlin. The offer was quickly accepted and late January 1954 set for the opening of quadripartite discussions on European questions.[51]

Indochina was the subject of a conference plenary on 7 December. Bidault struck an optimistic note in maintaining that the Vietminh had reached the 'ceiling' of their numerical strength and now faced 'military stagnation'. France had reinforced the FEC, the Vietnamese army continued to grow and overall the military picture was 'greatly improved as compared with last year'. On the political front, his government remained committed to perfecting the independence of the Associated States. As for negotiations, Bidault said that talking to Ho Chi Minh would be 'useless' but discussions in an international setting – a five-power conference, for example, possibly flowing from the forthcoming Berlin meeting – offered a more hopeful vista. France would coordinate its approach with the Associated States, but at the same time, the French people 'must not see before them an endless dreary plain on which they were expected to continue marching while elsewhere in the world hostilities ceased'.[52]

In response, Churchill heaped praise on France for its 'valiant effort'. Eisenhower, too, was generous in his appreciation and promised that the United States would continue to back the French war effort to the greatest practicable degree. The President was less enamoured of talk of negotiations with China, however. The term 'five-power meeting', he remarked, held 'unpleasant connotations' in the United States.[53] Later, in his diary, Eisenhower identified an end to military aid to the Vietminh as one of several conditions the PRC needed to fulfil before the United States would treat it as 'a respectable member of the family of nations'. On the other hand, if the French were bent on seeking Beijing's help in negotiating an end to the war, he wondered whether there was any point in continuing the US military assistance programme for Indochina.[54]

When China was discussed later that same day, Anglo-American differences were much in evidence. A month earlier, Eden told the House of Commons that the Conservative government remained committed to a general settlement in Asia and to 'peaceful relations with China'.[55] When he made the same point at Bermuda, Dulles conceded the need for a common China policy on the part of the Western powers but offered the American rather than the British approach as a model for emulation. The PRC should be exposed to 'maximum pressure', economically, politically and militarily short of war. Against this, 'friendliness', as practised by Britain, had nothing to recommend it. Eden's campaign to win the Americans over to the wisdom of UK thinking on China had a long way to go.[56]

Although China and Indochina, along with relations with the USSR and the EDC's ratification prospects, took up a good deal of time at Bermuda, none of these issues turned out to be the 'foremost matter at the conference', Jock Colville, Churchill's private secretary, noted in his diary. That prize went to Korea.[57]

On 3 December, just before he left Washington for Bermuda, Eisenhower chaired a meeting of the National Security Council to consider the kinds of military action to be taken if the communists wrecked the Korean armistice and full-scale fighting resumed. As summarized by Admiral Arthur W. Radford, Chairman of the Joint Chiefs of Staff, the US military's preferred 'concept of operations called initially for a massive atomic air strike which would defeat the Chinese Communists in Korea and make them incapable of aggression there or elsewhere in the Far East for a very considerable time'. Eisenhower approved. Expressing himself with 'great emphasis', the NSC minutes tell us, the President offered 'the opinion that if the Chinese Communists attacked us again we should certainly respond by hitting them hard and wherever it would hurt most, including Peiping [Beijing] itself', and that this 'would mean all-out war against Communist China'. With that, the President took off for Bermuda.[58]

In a one-to-one meeting with Churchill on 4 December, Eisenhower outlined his administration's proposed response to a reopening of the Korean War. The targets for nuclear punishment would be purely military, he stressed. Astonishingly, Churchill 'quite accepted' the US approach and suggested that his conversation with the President would 'put him in a position to say to Parliament that he had been consulted in advance and had agreed'.[59] When Eden learned of what the Americans were planning, he was horrified. US proposals threatened to 'unleash a third world war' with 'prospects' in the nuclear age 'too horrible for the human mind to contemplate'.[60]

Late that night, Eden wrote to Churchill to say that 'we have agreed that if there were a breach of the armistice by China our reaction would be prompt, resolute and effective', a reference to Churchill's January 1952 address to the US Congress. The Joint Policy Declaration of August 1953 further stated that 'in all probability the conflict could not be confined to Korea' if fighting resumed. The government thus 'recognised that it would probably be impossible to avoid bombing Chinese aerodromes beyond the Yalu'. At the same time, Eden went on, 'We have never given, or been asked to give, approval to widespread bombing of China proper nor, of course, to the use of atom bombs, or to a blockade.' In case Churchill somehow thought that war with China could be limited geographically, Eden reminded him that if the USSR came to the PRC's aid it would be in Europe, not Asia. And in that case, the UK would be in immediate danger.[61]

Anglo-American leaders dined together the following evening. With his mind focused by Eden's counsel, Churchill proceeded to rescind his earlier approval and now 'strongly resisted' US policy. If general war resulted from US action against China, Soviet nuclear bombardment of London and other UK cities would bring appalling levels of death and destruction. Some people might survive 'under mounds of flaming and contaminated rubble', Churchill supposed, but they would have 'nothing to do but take a pill to end it all'.[62] Eisenhower was perplexed. There was no logical reason why a USSR driven by self-interest would attack in the West just because America used nuclear weapons in the East, he contended. The targets in China would be limited to those supporting the Korean front; hence provocation of the Kremlin would be minimal. But these arguments failed to sway either Churchill or Eden.[63]

British fears of what a shift from Cold War to hot war would bring had grown year-on-year since the USSR tested its first atomic weapon in August 1949 (two further Soviet atomic tests had been reported in the West in 1951 and pointed to a nuclear arms programme of some momentum). Concentrating British minds was the fact that the present generation of Soviet bombers had the operational range to reach Western Europe but not North America. Hence, as Eden was acutely conscious during the Korean discussions at Bermuda, it would be the UK and Western Europe, not the United States, that felt the full heat of Soviet nuclear attack in time of general war.[64]

By a chronological coincidence, British nuclear anxieties would peak the following spring at precisely the moment that the Indochina crisis came to a head, but they were already running high at the time of Bermuda. Given the importance of this convergence, and its impact on UK policy on Indochina and the Asian Cold War as we approach 1954, it is appropriate to reflect a little on the roots of British nuclear thinking.

Following the UK General Election in October 1951, the new Conservative government made enhanced Anglo-American nuclear cooperation one of its key national security objectives. In particular, the Churchill administration was keen to establish the principle of full UK-US consultation before American nuclear weapons were used against the USSR. Under the previous Labour government, the US Air Force had been granted atomic bomber bases in East Anglia, a move the Conservatives supported even though it meant that the UK became (in Churchill's words) an American 'aircraft carrier' sitting at the top of the Soviet nuclear targeting list. Forward bases were essential for the United States if it was to conduct an effective air campaign against the USSR in time of war, but equally, given Britain's exposed position, the Conservative government demanded the right to be consulted if or when the United States proposed to launch a nuclear attack on the USSR.[65] In the event, the best that Churchill could wring from the Truman administration was a public undertaking in January 1952 that the launch of US atomic bombers from the UK would be a 'joint decision ... in the light of the circumstances prevailing at the time', a phrasing which gave the Americans ample scope for evasion in time of crisis.[66]

The British hoped to overturn the restrictions of the 1946 US Atomic Energy Act (which drastically limited the scope of American nuclear relations with other powers) and obtain 'full cooperation' on nuclear war planning once the UK became a nuclear power in its own right.[67] That moment arrived in October 1952 with the successful test of a plutonium device; it had taken seven years, but Britain had finally caught up with the United States and the Soviet Union, not in size of arsenal or in delivery methods, obviously, but in possession of the article. Or so it seemed. The following month, the UK was again left standing when the Americans announced the success of a test in the Pacific 'contributing to thermo-nuclear weapons research'.[68] In Britain and elsewhere, newspapers immediately concluded that the United States had the hydrogen bomb, a terrifying instrument of destruction vastly more powerful than atomic bombs, but the Truman administration, when pressed for confirmation, was coy.[69] We now know that the test of 1 November 1952, code-named Ivy-Mike, involved a thermonuclear device the size of a house and delivered a destructive yield of 10.4 megatons, around five hundred times more powerful than the bomb used against Hiroshima.[70]

Following Churchill's January 1953 visit to the United States and his first-hand experience of the extreme anti-communism of right-wing Republicans, the British government began to worry about a US-initiated nuclear showdown with the USSR.[71] In terms of the UK's safety, it made little difference whether general war was caused 'by the United States by mistake' or 'by Russia on purpose', as one Foreign Office official put it; either way, the Britain would suffer terribly.[72] Working on the assumption that 132 Soviet weapons 'of the Nagasaki type' managed to penetrate the country's air defences, the Cabinet's Home Defence Committee estimated that 1,378,000 people would die instantly, 750,000 would be left badly injured, over 2 million homes would be destroyed and a further 10 million left uninhabitable.[73] Recent research shows that the USSR in the early 1950s possessed nothing like this level of destructive capacity, but for the Churchill government at the time, perception equalled morbid reality.[74]

Since 1945, UK defence planners had become accustomed to thinking in atomic terms and to evaluating the destructiveness of new weapons according to multiples of the power of the Nagasaki or Hiroshima bombs. Thermonuclear weapons, however, with a destructive yield many hundreds and potentially a thousand and more times greater than the bombs used on Japan were almost beyond comprehension. Atomic bombardment might be survivable for a proportion of the UK population, but assault by hydrogen bombs could be the end of all things. 'It is so awful,' Churchill said of the H-bomb, 'that I have a feeling it will not happen.'[75] He was wrong. In August 1953, Moscow announced to the world that it had tested a thermonuclear weapon.[76] The Prime Minister's first reaction was that 'we were now as far from the age of the atomic bomb as the atomic bomb itself from the bow and arrow'. His second reaction was to redouble his efforts to arrange an East-West summit, the essential first step towards détente and a world made safe.[77]

Four months on from the Soviet H-bomb, Churchill was at Bermuda trying but failing to persuade Eisenhower to agree to meet Malenkov. Then again, it was also at Bermuda that Churchill, to begin with at least, leant support to a US policy for dealing with a reopening of the Korean War which risked triggering the very nuclear war he was so keen to prevent. Perhaps, Eden mused, Churchill had not fully understood what Eisenhower told him.[78] What is more certain is Eisenhower's annoyance when, at Eden's prompting, Churchill withdrew his support for US policy on Korea. 'British thinking – apparently both governmental and personal thinking – still looks upon the use of the atom bomb as the initiation of a completely new era in war,' the President wrote in his diary. 'Even more than this, it looks upon any decision of this kind as a policy question of the gravest import.' He continued:

This feeling unquestionably arises out of the fact that ... they see themselves as the initial and possibly principal, target of a Soviet bomb offensive. They apparently cling to the hope (to us fatuous) that if we avoid the first use of the atom bomb in any war, that the Soviets might likewise abstain. Our thinking, on the other hand, has come a long way past this kind of conjecture and hope. Specifically we have come to the conclusion that the atom bomb has to be treated just as another weapon in the arsenal. More important than this, we are certain in our own minds that the Soviets will do whatever they calculate their own best interests dictate. If they refrain from using the atom bomb, it will be for one reason only – because they believe that their position would be relatively worse in atom warfare than if this type of warfare were not employed.

Churchill and Eden 'stated time and again that they had no thought of recoiling from necessary decisions in this regard; their idea seems to be that there should be, probably will be, a sufficient time immediately after the outbreak of war to make necessary decisions'. For Eisenhower, however, an iron-clad commitment to consult London would not only retard instant reaction in the heat of crisis but bestow upon the British a 'veto' over measures designed to protect US national security. This, he avowed, could not happen.[79]

*

As we approach the crisis year of 1954, it is right to dwell on the nuclear discussions at Bermuda for the simple reason that they were still fresh in Churchill's and Eden's minds when they were called upon to formulate a response to the Indochinese climacteric. In the lead-up to Bermuda, the United States made plain its determination to react with firmness to open Chinese intervention in Vietnam; at the conference itself, although the Americans confined discussion of nuclear retaliation to the Korean context, the British were left in no doubt that the consequences of a PRC invasion of Tonkin would be equally devastating for China and equally likely to create conditions threatening of global war.

Reflecting on Bermuda, Churchill and Eden differed in their estimates of the impact their counsel had made on the Americans. Writing to the Queen, the Prime Minister thought that Eisenhower and Dulles had been 'impressed by the dangers' laid before them.[80] The Foreign Secretary was less sure. The Americans, he suspected, still intended to 'hit back with full power' and 'go for China with all the weapons at [their] command' should a crisis occur in – or beyond – Korea.[81] Interestingly, Eden's phraseology was similar to that employed by Eisenhower ('hit them with everything we've got') in a private briefing of Congressional leaders on Korean policy on his return to Washington.[82] The British, it seemed, had some grounds for nuclear nervousness.

6

From Bermuda to Dien Bien Phu, 1953–1954

What the British were given at Bermuda in December 1953 was a preview of the Eisenhower administration's new national security strategy, NSC 162/2, better known as the New Look. Signed off by the President in October, the New Look's aims resembled the old Democrat strategy of containing and weakening the Soviet bloc over the long term by maintaining global defensive positions of great strength. When it came to means, however, the Republican approach was quite different. To maximize American military power yet balance the defence budget, the New Look emphasized primary reliance not on expensive large-scale conventional armed forces, as had been the case under the Democrats, but on more cost-efficient nuclear arms. The deterrent power of these weapons was obvious. Should the communists nonetheless commit aggression, the Republican administration was prepared to consider massive nuclear retaliation with a seriousness which set it apart from its predecessor. Another notable feature of the New Look was asymmetrical strategic response: in a public rendering of what the British had been told privately, Dulles proclaimed in late December that if there was 'a renewal of hostilities in Korea or an invasion of Indo-China', the US 'reaction would not necessarily be confined to the particular theatre chosen by the communists for their operations'. In other words, if China hit Vietnam, America might hit China.[1]

The New Look was formally unveiled in a speech by Dulles in New York on 12 January 1954. Referring to the 'massive retaliatory power' at America's disposal, he said that the administration had taken a 'basic decision' to 'depend primarily upon a great capacity to retaliate, instantly, by means and at places of our choosing'. A direct attack by the USSR on the United States or its allies would be an obvious casus belli, but Dulles indicated that local communist aggression, as had occurred in Korea, would henceforward also merit crippling nuclear punishment both on the battlefield and against its source, be it the USSR or China. 'Local defense will always be important,' he conceded, but local defence 'must be reinforced by the further deterrent of massive retaliatory power'. The New Look also promised value for money by prioritizing nuclear weapons over conventional arms, an approach which allowed for cuts in overall defence expenditure without jeopardizing national security. In sum, America would have a 'maximum deterrent at a bearable cost', the proverbial 'bigger bang for the buck'.[2]

Intended to impress, worry and therefore contain the USSR and China, the New Look ended up frightening America's allies. The British, post-Bermuda, were edgier than most. Following Dulles's speech, Foreign Office officials feared that the 'likelihood of atomic warfare (by the USA or the Soviet Union) in the event of new armed conflict involving Communist forces is increased', while 'the very nature of the retaliatory power at the Americans' disposal is such that any decision to retaliate becomes one of cataclysmic potentialities'. Perhaps, they comforted themselves, Dulles was indulging in a 'brand of sales talk' designed to appeal to domestic opinion, particularly the Republican right, and in practice the administration would be sensible.[3] For Eden, however, rhetoric and reality were conjoined. In a memorandum prepared for the Defence Committee at the end of January 1954, he rated it a near certainty that the United States would employ the 'most effective weapons at their disposal', including nuclear weapons, if the communists broke the peace in Korea. Because of the ruinous implications of this policy for the UK should general war ensue, he proposed to make plain to Washington that 'we cannot agree to such action in advance and must insist upon being consulted at the time before it is taken'.[4]

As to Indochina, the British government entered the new year with a policy consisting of two negatives and an aspiration: no negotiations until the French achieved a position of military strength, no outlay of meaningful UK financial or military assistance to the French to help them achieve that position, and the hope that the French would continue the fight with an offensive spirit so that when the time came for the Vietnamese to assume responsibility for security, the Vietminh threat would have been reduced to manageable proportions.

This, though, is not the impression readers of Eden's memoirs, *Full Circle*, published in 1960, would gain. British success – Eden's personal success – in bringing an end to the Indochina War is presented therein as the climax of a long-term diplomatic strategy. According to Eden, the Conservative government concluded as early as 1952 that 'the chances of winning the war in Indo-China were ... slender' and that a negotiated settlement 'seemed to me to be the outcome to work for ... Two years were to pass before it could be realised'.[5] In fact, the British retained visions of a positive military outcome for at least a year beyond when Eden claimed that a negotiated solution became the centrepiece of his policy. It was only the emergence of the centre-right Laniel government in France in June 1953 and its insistence on exploring negotiation options which compelled UK policymakers to investigate the implications of a diplomatic settlement. But here, too, Eden's memoirs are misleading. As we will see, that examination, undertaken in early 1954, concluded that there was no compromise which could safeguard Indochina's non-communist future unless – or until – the French reversed the tide of war. In *Full Circle*, however, Eden tells us that 'at the beginning of 1954 my thoughts began to turn to the possibility of some form of partition as a solution which might bring hostilities to an end and effect a settlement that would hold'. The Berlin conference 'provided me with an opportunity to develop this idea'. That the Churchill government eventually embraced negotiations, and partition, is not in question. But the process leading to that point was more complex than Eden allowed.[6]

The Foreign Office devoted a good deal of time in January 1954 to preparing for Berlin. Although European issues were top of the conference agenda, policymakers fully expected the USSR to use the occasion to renew its proposal for a five-power conference. If that happened, Berlin might prove a test for Western unity. In Cabinet on 11 January, Eden explained that while Britain was open-minded about negotiations with the Central People's Government, as were the French for Indochina-related reasons, the Americans strongly opposed diplomatic dialogue with the Chinese beyond the (presently inert) Korean Political Conference. Aware of these differences, the Soviets might be tempted to use the China issue to divide the Western powers, especially if confronted by a firm tripartite front on Germany, Austria and the EDC. In this, they could not be allowed to succeed – 'Western unity must survive the Conference unimpaired,' Eden determined.[7]

Given the scale of the Eisenhower administration's negativity towards a five-power meeting, unity required the British and French to align themselves with the Americans. But what would happen if the Soviets adapted their proposal and offered a five-power conference focused not on world affairs but on Asia, with Indochina given equal top-billing alongside Korea? Would Bidault hold strong in that eventuality? The war in Indochina was 'exceedingly unpopular in France', Harvey reported in mid-January, 'and the great majority of people would certainly be in favour of ending it on any tolerable terms'.[8] If the Soviets threw Indochina into the mix at Berlin, and if the French responded positively, the British would be faced with a dilemma. Should they make common cause with the French in line with their established commitment to a general Asian settlement? Against this, the Foreign Office was convinced that negotiations on Indochina were unwise with the French position so parlous. And what of the Americans? Britain would not just be backing an ally, France, in agreeing to meet China, but supporting an enemy, the USSR. What kind of strain would that place on Anglo-American relations? In the end, policymakers decided that the "special relationship" should take precedence. If the USSR laced a five-power conference proposal with the prospect of a Indochina settlement, Western unity had to hold and that meant the British and French joining the Americans in rejecting the offer. Contrary to what Eden wrote in his memoirs, he approached Berlin intending to hinder not advance a negotiated solution for Indochina.[9]

And yet, over the course of three weeks at Berlin, something happened to alter the diplomatic dynamic. On 18 February, the closing communiqué stated that a further foreign ministers meeting would take place at Geneva, beginning on 26 April, on the Asian Cold War. The Berlin four, the People's Republic of China and 'other interested States' would attend. There were two items on the Geneva agenda: Korea and 'the problem of restoring peace in Indo-China'.[10] The 'something' that happened was that Eden reversed his thinking on a five-power meeting and on how best to maintain Western unity on the China issue.

The Berlin conference opened on 25 January 1954, its sessions alternating between cold and cheerless locations in the Western and Soviet sectors of the city. 'All the Frenchmen bite their nails; half the Americans chew gum; none of the Russians ever smile,' Evelyn Shuckburgh, Eden's Principal Private Secretary, noted in his diary.[11] At the first session, Molotov wasted no time in attempting wedge-driving by proposing a three-point agenda: Germany, Austria and – first for discussion – the convening of a five-power conference on the international situation.[12] Dulles crackled with indignation. Not content with trying to catapult China to great power status, he railed, the USSR proposed to replace the United Nations and run the world through a five-power directorate.[13]

Eden initially kept his own counsel, but that evening he cabled Churchill asking him to seek the Cabinet's agreement to a change in the UK's negotiating position. Having gone to Berlin intending to join the Americans in blocking a Soviet play for a five-power conference, he now felt that the French, with their many Indochinese preoccupations, 'would be embarrassed if their Western allies adopted a wholly unconstructive attitude.'[14] Alongside this concern, Eden was disinclined to give the Soviets an easy propaganda victory by allowing Molotov to spin opposition to five-power talks to show how the UK and France were in thrall to the US administration's aggressive approach to China. After just a day in Berlin, Eden was asking himself 'whether a Five-Power conference, definitely confined to the Far East and beginning with Korea' (in other words, not covering the global scene) 'would really be so harmful', especially in light of the failure to get the Korean Political Conference off the ground. Molotov had not proposed such a meeting, but he might.[15]

The Bermuda conference also impacted on Eden's attitude. It was just six weeks since Eisenhower and Dulles revealed to the British their nuclear plans for dealing with a collapse of the Korean armistice. To Eden, anything that concretized the peace, including talking to the Chinese, would eliminate Korea as a proving ground for the New Look. At a broader level, once in Berlin, Eden seems to have sensed an opportunity to score a rare but worthwhile victory for Britain's policy of diplomatic contact with China over the American policy of ostracism. Recognizing the same opportunity, the Cabinet backed the Foreign Secretary in his desire to reverse course. Conveying the news to Eden on 27 January, Churchill said he was 'sure it would make the world safer if the Five Power Conference including China could be brought on to the scene as soon as possible'.[16]

By then, Eden had detected a potentially exploitable chink in the armour of Dulles's resistance to communing with the PRC. At an eve-of-conference meeting of Western delegations, the US Secretary remarked that it might be worth trying to jump-start the stalled Korean Political Conference. The next day, when Molotov made his bid for a five-power conference, Eden ('a sea anemone covered with sensitive tentacles all recording currents of opinion around him') saw his opening. Noting both Dulles's Korea comment and how keen the Americans were to preserve a united Western front at the conference, he calculated that if faced with a firm Anglo-French consensus in favour of a five-power conference, the US Secretary would grumble but acquiesce, especially if the meeting was confined to Korea.[17] If Molotov persisted in pressing for a five-power meeting with a global remit, however, the British and French would stand with the Americans in opposition.[18]

Dining with Molotov on the third evening, Eden's diplomatic cunning was given free rein. It was unrealistic to expect agreement on a five-power meeting with a worldwide agenda, he observed, but a conference centred on Korea, with China participating alongside other interested parties, was a more viable proposition. In this way, Eden sowed the seed: Molotov was primed to accept a Western offer on these lines, if one were made; alternatively, if the Russian made such an offer on his own account, Dulles, as Eden knew, would probably assent, as would Bidault.[19] 'Some slight sign of Eden desire [to] play intermediary role with Molotov', a suspicious Dulles cabled Eisenhower.[20]

Then again, someone had to talk to the Soviets outside the stultifying correctness of the conference chamber. That was diplomacy. With Dulles frightened of one-to-one meetings with Molotov in case 'McCarthy … sees pictures of him being matey', it fell to the British Foreign Secretary to assume the role of East-West bridge-builder.[21] Alone later with Dulles, Eden peppered him with reasons why a five-power meeting on Korea was nothing to fear.[22] The success of his efforts was evident when Dulles told the conference on 28 January that while he would always abhor the principle of a five-power conference, a meeting with China on 'matters of practical fact where the circumstances made such meetings necessary' might be arranged. Korea was an obvious contender, but Dulles insisted that all the countries involved in the late war, not just the Berlin four and the PRC, should be involved.[23]

At the end of January, the conference shifted its formal agenda emphasis to Germany and Austria on the understanding that the five-power question would be revisited near the end of proceedings. Informally, the issue remained a live topic of debate. On 1 February, Molotov told Eden that he was prepared to drop his global agenda and support a Korean conference at Geneva in April with China and all other interested states. Eden was delighted but he still had his work cut out to secure Dulles's definitive consent. 'Molotov has just agreed to date & place of Far East Conference if we can agree to have one!', he wrote to his wife, Clarissa. 'Typical of our tortuous methods.'[24] Over the next few days, Eden and Dulles held further discussions. 'British strongly press for some "constructive" move on our part in Asian area', Dulles informed Eisenhower on 6 February.[25]

Molotov, meanwhile, continued to fight for recognition of the PRC's status as a great power. The participants in the putative Korean conference should be formally invited by the USSR, the United States, UK, France and China, he argued. As an inviter rather than invitee, the PRC would occupy a position of equality within an informal "Big Five". Dulles, needless to say, objected. Increasingly reconciled to a conference on Korea, the US Secretary still refused to be party to any move, even a procedural one, which elevated the PRC's international standing.[26] To the contrary, Dulles wanted to insert a reference to China's 'aggressive' behaviour into the section of the Berlin communiqué dealing with the Asian conference, a move Molotov denounced. So did Eden, privately; the Soviet Foreign Minister had been trying to 'negotiate helpfully' and deserved better.[27] Enlisting Bidault's aid, Eden managed to block the American caveat. Eden was 'a problem' at Berlin, Dulles said later, especially in his refusal to entertain 'any language' in the communiqué 'which appeared to impugn the good faith of the Chinese Communist Government'.[28]

Midway through the conference, the Western powers had become resigned to the fact that Soviet intractability on Germany meant that European questions would defy resolution. So great was the level of popular expectation in Western Europe that détente was in the offing – a hope that Churchill had done much to inculcate – that the British, French and Americans were keen to ensure that failure was laid at the door of the Soviets. Onus-shifting was easy on Germany as the USSR's refusal to countenance free all-German elections as a prerequisite to negotiating a German peace treaty was unacceptable to even the most détente-minded of observers. In contrast, a Western refusal to respond positively to the Soviet proposal for a conference on Asia, where the Cold War was hottest, would be less easy to justify and could produce a sharp reaction in the European NATO states.[29]

In working for an Asian conference, Eden and his advisors were aware of this propaganda aspect of the situation. Mostly, though, they were animated by the need to find 'some means to get the Americans and Chinese Communists together at the same table, since until this is done we can make no progress towards reducing tension in the Far East and thus enable the Americans and ourselves to extricate ourselves from Korea and the French from Indochina'.[30] In pursuit of this aim, Eden enjoyed the backing of the Cabinet. Even Churchill, whose natural instinct was to side with the Americans in the Asian Cold War, was 'anxious' that Berlin 'should not end as a manifest failure' but lead instead 'to other meetings, which may possibly be more fruitful'. American hypersensitivity on China was a problem, the Prime Minister admitted. But the UK was 'not bound always to speak with one voice with US'.[31]

As Berlin entered its closing stages, Eden redoubled his efforts to find a compromise that would 'meet the bear without parting us from the eagle'.[32] Molotov, however, held out for China to be recognized in the communiqué as a Geneva convenor while Dulles opposed according the PRC any such distinction. In the end, it was a Churchillian intervention that helped bridge the divide. Why not 'slur over' the difference between convening and invited states by 'lumping all the participants in one category', he suggested. This 'would not confer on China the special status desired by Molotov' but leave it 'open if obscure'. If the United States and USSR accepted this formula, then Berlin would be 'au revoir and not goodbye'.[33] Dulles and Bidault proved amenable, but Molotov stuck to his position until the very last moment before giving his consent. Eden had some sympathy for his Soviet counterpart. The USSR was probably 'nervous' of the Chinese 'now Stalin is dead' and concerned that the PRC would do 'something rash and involve R[ussia] in it', he surmised. From that standpoint, a conference which helped reduce tensions in Asia ought to recommend itself to the USSR as much as to the UK. At the same time, to prove to the Chinese that he had negotiated strongly on their behalf, Molotov had to go down to the wire before accepting the Churchill compromise.[34]

Unanimity obtained, on 18 February the Berlin communiqué stated that the representatives of the United States, France, UK, USSR, PRC, North Korea, South Korea and 'the other countries the armed forces of which participated in hostilities' would meet two months hence to consider the post-armistice future of Korea.[35]

The 1954 Geneva conference is of course best remembered for Indochina, but for much of the time at Berlin, Eden and Dulles were united in resisting Bidault's entreaties to expand the Geneva agenda. The priority for Eden was to get the Korean Political Conference going in some form. Here, the French predicament in Indochina helped insofar as it guaranteed Bidault's backing for a meeting with the PRC and left Dulles and his objections outvoted two-to-one. But Bidault was also determined to have Vietnam, Laos and Cambodia covered by the Asian conference.[36] For nearly three weeks, the British and Americans gave the Frenchman no encouragement, but as Berlin reached its climax, Eden and Dulles began to rethink their position, albeit for reasons to do with Europe more than Asia.

Throughout the negotiations on Germany, Bidault had held firm in the face of Soviet pressure to jettison the EDC. Nor did Bidault waver when Molotov 'hinted broadly' at the possibility of a 'bargain in which France would be helped to solve the Indo-China problem in return for agreement for a 5 power conference and abandonment of the EDC'. Molotov offered no specifics but the implication was that the USSR would lean on the PRC and DRV to give the French an honourable way out of Indochina if, in return, the French killed off the EDC.[37] This worried Bidault's allies. If Molotov 'can concoct a plausible Indo-China/EDC deal then we shall really be in trouble', General Alfred Gruenther, the NATO Supreme Commander, wrote to Eisenhower.[38] In the end, Bidault's stalwart defence of the EDC earned him the gratitude of Eden and Dulles. At the same time, the Anglo-Americans knew that the EDC was deeply unpopular in France, where the loss of sovereignty over the French army seemed to many people an excessively high price to pay to rearm Germans. Viewed in the context of French domestic politics, Bidault's pro-EDC stance at Berlin could yet be a pyrrhic victory for the Western Alliance if the National Assembly retaliated by voting out the Laniel government. The man thought most likely to form a successor administration was Pierre Mendès-France, 'the Cassandra of the Fourth Republic', whose hostility to the EDC was matched only by the strength of his opposition to the war in Indochina.[39]

On 10 February, the Churchill Cabinet decided that it was 'important ... to meet Bidault's point of view on Indo-China in order to strengthen his hand over EDC when the conference is finished'. At Berlin, Eden had already reached the same conclusion: Indochina should be put on the Geneva agenda, not because the war was ready for diplomatic resolution but to help prolong the life of a pro-EDC government in Paris.[40] A similar calculation informed American thinking. Dulles saw danger in Indochinese negotiations but ultimately accepted a dual Korea-Indochina conference for EDC reasons. In some accounts, it is suggested that Bidault threatened Dulles that the scheme would be scuppered unless he got his way; in others, the Frenchman reportedly promised to deliver EDC ratification if Indochina was added to the Geneva agenda.[41] Whatever the truth of the matter, Dulles was certain that unless Bidault returned to France 'with something to show on Indochina', the Laniel administration would fall and be replaced by a successor with 'a mandate to end the war ... on any terms [and] oppose French ratification of EDC'.[42]

Some Berlin reflections are called for. Firstly, the summoning of the Geneva conference was a triumph for the Churchill government's pragmatic China policy and a corresponding defeat for the Eisenhower administration's more doctrinaire approach. It was also a personal victory for Eden, who successfully outmanoeuvred Dulles. In this last regard, some in the British delegation were nervous about the potential damage to Anglo-American relations and even questioned Eden's motives. The Foreign Secretary was 'so keen to get a conference, so as to have some "success" to go home with that he seems to forget how terribly dangerous this topic is for Dulles', Shuckburgh wrote.[43] Eden wanted for neither ambition nor vanity, but on this occasion good PR was the product not the driver of his diplomacy. Moreover, he knew himself that Dulles had taken a political risk in agreeing to meet the Chinese and even praised his 'courage' in doing so when briefing the Cabinet on his return to London.[44]

What Eden underestimated was the scale of that risk. This only became clear when Dulles got back to Washington and found himself pilloried by the Republican Old Guard for agreeing to commune with the Chinese. There were snipes about Dulles's support for 'a Far Eastern Munich' and rumours that Eisenhower was looking for a new Secretary of State 'more rigid on the China issue'.[45] Dulles hit back strongly in a televised news conference on 24 February in which he asserted that the Chinese 'will not come to Geneva to be honoured by us but rather to account before the bar of world opinion'. With these words, he shored up his domestic positon but only by foreclosing on constructive US-PRC dialogue at Geneva.[46]

Reflecting further on Berlin, it is worth reiterating that while the Geneva conference is most associated with Indochina in historical memory, at its moment of conception it was regarded by the Western powers as a de facto Korean Political Conference. In the British Foreign Office, officials felt that as far as Indochina went, the West was 'not necessarily committed to working out a final settlement by negotiation but rather to discussing where and how the first steps towards a negotiated settlement might be taken'.[47] Bidault, meanwhile, thought in public relations terms. In order to placate restless French opinion, he had to appear interested in a settlement, but as an Indochina diehard he had no intention of giving much away at the negotiating table. Whether Bidault's ministerial colleagues were of the same mind remained to be seen.[48] The Americans also put the stress on Korea – the 'sole objective is to negotiate a peaceful agreement for a unified independent Korea', US Under-Secretary of State General Walter Bedell Smith argued.[49] On Indochina, Washington policymakers saw Geneva as a 'holding action' to soothe French opinion, help keep a pro-EDC French government in office and buy time for the Navarre Plan to make a difference.[50] As Dulles reflected in a cable to the State Department at the close of the Berlin negotiations, his compliance on Geneva arose primarily 'from necessity [of] avoiding break with France which would imperil both Indochina and EDC'.[51]

Whatever the British, American and French governments thought privately, the prospect of Indochina negotiations was well received in many quarters.[52] Inevitably, the potentialities of peace were most keenly debated in France. Alongside press speculation, several prominent political and military figures suggested that an end to Chinese support for Ho Chi Minh was the goal to aim for. Denied PRC backing, the Vietminh threat would wither to a level which the Vietnamese could deal with on their own. At that point, the FEC's mission could be terminated. The French press dubbed this line of thinking the Markos hypothesis, so named for the Greek communist leader Markos Vafiadis whom the USSR cast aside during the Greek Civil War. Defence Minister René Pleven, Navarre and Bidault were all reported to be thinking in these terms.[53]

The flaw in the Markos hypothesis was that the French had nothing with which to tempt the Chinese into dropping the Vietminh. The Americans, though, had a very great deal. According to Pleven, US willingness to compromise on issues of importance to the Central People's Government – American derecognition of Nationalist China and recognition of the PRC, acceptance by Washington of communist control of Taiwan, the lifting of the US veto on communist representation at the United Nations – might persuade Mao Zedong, the PRC leader, to do business on Vietnam.[54]

In London, the Foreign Office was astonished at the way the Laniel government expected the Americans to turn their China policy upside down to deliver France from its Indochinese predicament. Ivone Kirkpatrick, Strang's successor as Permanent Under-Secretary, charged Laniel and Pleven with possessing 'no principles and no idea even of where expediency lies'. Eden, a Francophile by nature, lamented that the French 'become daily more hopeless and contemptible'.[55] The Americans themselves were quick to administer what *Le Monde* called a 'cold douche to French hopes that the United States might buy off Chinese support to the Vietminh'.[56] There was 'no possibility whatsoever' of concessions to China, the US Embassy told the Foreign Office in amplification. 'Exchange of performance for Communist promises is a swindle'.[57]

With the Chinese negotiating track blocked, would the French reach out to the Vietminh? In March, the British Embassy in Paris discovered that the Quai d'Orsay was considering two possible outcomes should Laniel depart from his publicly stated positon and deal directly with Ho Chi Minh. One was Vietminh participation in a national coalition government, the prelude to French military withdrawal and Vietnamese independence. The other was the partition of Vietnam into a Ho Chi Minh north and a Bao Dai south.[58] London policymakers saw peril in both scenarios. Likening a coalition to a 'Trojan Horse', Foreign Office Asia experts predicted that the Vietminh would quickly suborn the government. In a telegram from Saigon – one of several praised by Eden for the 'impressive' quality of their analysis – Graves warned that a coalition was not 'a solution' but 'a capitulation'.[59] Officials had no more liking for partition, despite Eden's claim in *Full Circle* that he had long since made up his mind that this was the way out for France. A more accurate recollection came from the Head of the FO Southeast Asia Department, John Tahourdin, who maintained that the government 'had no Indo-China policy', on partition or anything else, 'until the crisis loomed'.[60]

The first serious British examination of negotiating options was produced by the Foreign Office's Research Department (FORD) on 26 February 1954, a week after the announcement of the Geneva conference. The study worked on the pessimistic if realistic premise that French 'military victory ... is not to be expected' and that some variety of diplomatic solution was inevitable. The 'key' in this regard was the Central People's Government for whom Vietminh control of Vietnam was an 'essential part of Chinese policy and strategy'. From a PRC perspective, the 'collapse of the Viet Minh would involve the establishment, indirectly, of American power on the very frontier of China, and they can accept such a situation no more in the case of Vietnam than they could in the case of Korea'. The study went on to consider whether there was any compromise which could satisfy Chinese security needs while saving something from what threatened to be 'the wreck of the Associate States system'. A coalition held chimerical allure; as the Sovietization of Eastern Europe had shown, once communists got into government it was only a matter of time before the whole state was subverted. Accordingly, there was really 'no recourse but a partition of Vietnam'.[61]

This, though, was a counsel of despair. At best, FORD argued, partition would postpone not prevent a communist takeover:

The urge for reunion will be strong: despite differences between North and South, there is a strong spirit of Nationalism which will conduce towards reunion; and it is to be feared that the greater dynamism of the Communist leaders in contrast to the divided counsels and lack of general effectiveness of the non-Communist leaders will in the upshot result in a reunion under Viet Minh auspices.

Uninviting as this prospect was, FORD found it difficult to perceive any alternative other than 'the complete and immediate surrender of the whole country to the Communist cause', whereas there was 'a faint hope that a partition might satisfy the Chinese for the time being' and bring about a solution 'which, even if short-lived, would at least gain time and would at least enable the French to escape, without excessive discredit, from the burden which is having such grave consequences elsewhere than in Indo-China'.[62]

This downbeat verdict set the tone for the ensuing Foreign Office discussion with all who commented agreeing that partition was a *least bad* solution. The assessment of British representatives in Southeast Asia was similarly qualified. To Graves, partition meant 'defeat by instalments', while MacDonald described the coalition-versus-partition debate as 'a choice between two evils, both so evil that I hope that neither of them will be seriously pursued'. As for the Chiefs of Staff, they did not mince words: partition would be 'a victory for Communism' and a 'serious strategic defeat' for the West.[63]

Around this time, Clarissa Eden fell ill and her husband absented himself from London to oversee her convalescence.[64] Politics was another distraction with Churchill hinting that his resignation was 'drawing near' only to reverse course and declare his determination to stay on until his summitry ambitions had been satisfied.[65] Despite these personal and political upsets, Eden still kept abreast of the Foreign Office exploration of partition. One paper prepared for his attention defined the UK goal at Geneva as 'peace in Indo-China' but only on terms that 'do not expose the whole of the country to Communist domination', something which partition could not assure.[66] When Denis Allen, Deputy Under-Secretary for Asian affairs, told a Soviet diplomat that 'any solution which left Communism in a position of influence in Indochina was unsatisfactory to us', he earned an approving 'Good' from the Foreign Secretary.[67]

Turning to the battlefield situation in Vietnam, neither Eden nor the Foreign Office's Indochina experts saw the contest brewing at Dien Bien Phu as the decisive confrontation of the war. The hope was for a French triumph, obviously, but even if the Vietminh emerged victorious, there seemed to be no objective reason why the French should not continue the fight elsewhere. Even at peak strength, the garrison numbered just over 15,000, less than 7 per cent of combined French and French Union strength. However, as Graves had been telling the Foreign Office for months, the French domestic scene was now as critical as the military front. The war could 'be lost very easily by a spate of defeatism in Paris' such as a disaster at Dien Bien Phu might spawn.[68]

A disaster, however, was not what General Navarre anticipated. Intelligence suggesting that the PAVN was in possession of Chinese-supplied artillery gave him pause for thought, to be sure, but as he told reporters at a news conference on 19 February, the likelihood was that the current campaigning season would end in a 'dead heat'.[69] Navarre was wrong, as we know. Later, he would claim that the fate of Dien Bien Phu was sealed the day before (18 February) when the Berlin communiqué summoned the Geneva conference. Without the prospect of negotiations and the linked imperative of improving their diplomatic hand through battlefield success, 'it's likely the Viets wouldn't have attacked'.[70] In actual fact, we now know that it was in early December 1953 that the DRV leadership decided to accept the challenge thrown down by the French at Dien Bien Phu. The news from Berlin did not start the countdown to the battle but it did increase the pressure on Giap to deliver a victory which the Vietminh could convert into negotiating currency.[71]

During the first weeks of 1954, a steady stream of visitors flew in to Dien Bien Phu to view the preparations – French generals, ministers and journalists, American military types and even a British novelist, Graham Greene. All were struck by the cosmopolitan composition of the soldiery. In total, the FEC numbered 52,000 Frenchmen, 30,000 North Africans, 19,000 Foreign Legion, 18,000 West Africans and 53,000 Vietnamese under French command (as opposed to serving with the VNA). The garrison, comprising seventeen different nationalities, was a microcosm of this multinational war machine. Sightseers were assured by de Castries that the base was impregnable. If dubious visitors pointed to the surrounding hills and asked about the danger of enemy shelling, they were told that any artillery the Vietminh managed to establish would be too far away to be anything more than an irritant. 'We were absolutely convinced of our superiority in defensive fortified positions,' recalled Navarre; 'we were absolutely persuaded that a fortified position could hold out easily at odds of three to four against'.[72]

Despite Giap's memory of the napalm-infernos of Vinh Yen, Mao Khe and Dong Trieu in 1951, he and the Vietminh's political leadership decided to accept those odds.[73] A huge flow of material aid from China helped instil confidence. During the first three months of 1954, the PRC funnelled 200 trucks, 10,000 barrels of oil, 100 cannons, 3,000 guns of various kinds, 2,400,000 rounds of small arms ammunition, 60,000 artillery shells and 1,700 tons of grain to the PAVN. At a psychologically sustaining level, Giap would regularly remind his troops of what was at stake: it was 'not Dien Bien Phu or Hanoi, but the whole of Vietnam that is the prize of this battle'.[74]

Overnight on 12–13 March, the Vietminh scattered leaflets around Dien Bien Phu. On one was written, in French, 'Dienbienphu will be your grave'. Another showed a crude cartoon of Navarre's hand pushing French soldiers towards a field of daggers. The leaflets were laughed off by de Castries and his men but in retrospect they were chillingly prophetic.[75] Just after 5.00 pm on 13 March 1954 the storm broke. With a threefold advantage in numbers, possessed of PRC-supplied firepower far heavier and accurate than the French anticipated, and with legions of civilian porters enlisted to transport supplies to the front, the PAVN launched a murderous artillery barrage from concealed hillside positions. This was followed by human-wave assaults – consistent with Chinese advice to 'annihilate' the French – which quickly overwhelmed three of the outlying CRs (Beatrice, Gabrielle and Anne-Marie). Worse still from a French standpoint, the airstrip, so vital to the garrison's survival, was now exposed to Vietminh artillery and anti-aircraft guns. Landing or take-off became suicidal, and before the month was out, Dien Bien Phu was reliant on risky airdrops of supplies.

For the Vietminh, however, these gains, though substantial, came at the cost of very heavy casualties, and on 18 March Giap ordered a halt to the attack to resupply and reinforce.[76]

That same day, Navarre spoke publicly of inflicting 'such heavy losses on the enemy that the latter's back will be broken'.[77] What else could he say? That Giap had Dien Bien Phu in a noose? In London, the Chiefs of Staff began to entertain the possibility, even the probability, of a French defeat which could set off a 'chain of events that would sooner or later have a serious effect on the situation in Malaya'.[78] In the Foreign Office, some officials clung to the view that Dien Bien Phu was just one battle and that the French could absorb a defeat. From Paris, Harvey put them right. 'If the fortress is carried by assault', he reported, 'the effect will not only be to weaken the French bargaining position at Geneva, but radically to change the attitude of the French Government towards the conference'. There would follow 'such an outcry in Parliament and in the country that the Government will probably be faced with the alternatives of either resigning or virtually adopting the Left-wing Opposition policy of negotiations with Ho Chi Minh at almost any price'.

The outcome of the war might well be determined by the result of a single battle after all.[79]

*

Following a twelve-day lull, Giap resumed the attack on 30 March. Dien Bien Phu had become 'a deadly trap', Bidault recalled. 'We had counted on our superior artillery and our air force; but the Viet-Minh artillery turned out to be lethal and invulnerable to our counter-attacks because it was hidden underground or sheltered by slopes'. Enemy anti-aircraft fire also posed an unexpectedly serious threat. 'We had counted on maintaining a regular supply service to Dien Bien Phu, but the air strip soon became almost unusable. The size of the fortress got smaller and smaller, as more and more outposts were captured, and we soon could do nothing to help except parachute arms, food and medical supplies'.[80]

As the Dien Bien Phu perimeter contracted, the British government began to look more positively on the Geneva conference. Diplomacy, policymakers came to see, might yet preserve some part of Vietnam which, if military events were left to run their course, could be lost in its entirety. As a corollary of this new emphasis on negotiations, the Foreign Office revisited partition. If southern Vietnam could be saved, along with Laos and Cambodia, this would provide some kind of containment barrier to the north of Malaya. Doubts persisted about the longevity of partition but these were now outweighed by another danger – the escalation of the war through American or American-led military action.[81] For the British, a successful outcome at Geneva came to be seen as the best if not the only way of avoiding a wider war, even a general war with the communist bloc, hence to containing America.

Uniting for Action, March–April 1954

On 21 January 1954, in the course of his annual budget message to Congress, President Eisenhower made a brief but pointed reference to Indochina. There, he said, French forces 'are holding back Communist efforts to expand into the free areas of Asia'. The United States was supplying substantial military assistance 'to enable these gallant forces to sustain an offensive that will provide the opportunity for victory'.[1] There was no mention of the French fighting to achieve a level of battlefield success that would permit them to negotiate peace from strength. The emphasis was on victory. Nothing that occurred at the Berlin conference when it opened four days later changed the American government's basic outlook in this regard.[2]

While supportive of the administration's indirect if costly backing for the French, the US Congress was constantly on guard lest any more direct forms of help were in the offing. Six months on from the end of the Korean War, there was deep reluctance on Capitol Hill, and in the country generally, to see the United States drawn into another land war in Asia. In that connection, the Pentagon's announcement on 7 February that two hundred US Air Force technicians would be heading to Vietnam to help maintain B-26 bombers supplied to the French was greeted with considerable concern. Was US aid to France about to take a more direct turn? And why had Congress not been consulted?[3]

Remembering President Truman's decision to commit US forces in Korea in 1950 without express Congressional authorization and the political difficulties this had caused the Democrats as the war dragged on, the Eisenhower administration was quick to offer reassurance. In testimony before the Senate Foreign Relations Committee, Under-Secretary of State and presidential confidant Walter Bedell Smith said that no similar undertakings would be made in future without due consultation.[4] On the decision to send technicians itself, however, Eisenhower was unrepentant. 'Don't think I like to send them there,' he told Congressional leaders. 'But we can't get anywhere in Asia by just sitting here in Washington doing nothing. My God, we must not lose Asia. We've got to look this thing right in the face.'[5]

Congress would bulk large in the administration's thinking on Indochina in the months ahead. Eisenhower had spent much of his first year in office resisting the Bricker Amendment, a proposed shackle on the independence of the White House in foreign policymaking. The Amendment ('a damn thorn in our side', Eisenhower called it) eventually foundered but the administration remained extremely sensitive to Congressional opinion.[6] While conceding Eisenhower's vote-winning ability in 1952, many in the conservative establishment never accepted him as a natural-born Republican. It helped that Vice-President Richard Nixon was a card-carrying member of the Old Guard, but many on the right of the party still felt that Eisenhower needed watching.[7] The President, for his part, sought to cooperate with Congress as far as practicable but his efforts to build a bipartisan consensus in foreign policy were regularly undermined by the Republican right. 'I should set quietly about the formation of a new party' based on 'the middle way', he confided to his diary.[8] He also had regular run-ins with the Republican majority leader in the Senate, William F. Knowland, a China lobby stalwart determined to hold the administration to account on Asia, while McCarthy continued to exert a corrosive influence on US politics with his 'extravagant and often baseless charges' of communist sympathies on the part of individuals and groups.[9]

Like the US Congress, the British Foreign Office had wondered whether the decision on aircraft ground crews betokened a shift towards more direct forms of US involvement, the more so in light of Eisenhower's publicly ventilated victory thesis. On 8 February, Makins met with Smith at the State Department. The French 'were not aiming so much to win a war, as to get in a position in which they could negotiate', the American complained. The administration was doing all it could to persuade the French 'that their negotiating position would be pretty hopeless unless they negotiated from strength', but there was 'no intention of sending American troops to Indo-China'.[10] Two days later, Eisenhower told reporters that 'no one could be more bitterly opposed to ever getting the United States involved in a hot war in that region than I am. I cannot conceive of a greater tragedy for America'.[11] All of which sounded unequivocal. Yet, looking back, there was a tension, a contradiction even, in the US government's approach. On the one hand, senior figures from the President down agreed that Vietnam must be saved from communism. On the other hand, those same figures abjured the thought of US involvement in another Asian land war. But what would happen if the PAVN's military momentum brought the Vietminh to the brink of victory? Or if the Laniel administration's will to continue the war collapsed? How was non-intervention to be reconciled with the imperative of keeping Vietnam, Indochina and all of Southeast Asia on the right side of the Cold War divide?

Back in 1954, British policymakers struggled to square the administration's non-intervention stance with ongoing American press comment, some of it apparently based on insider information, that military options were under active consideration.[12] On 13 February, Michael Joy of the British Embassy in Washington shared with the Foreign Office his view that 'many people in the administration were convinced that deeper involvement is coming'. There was a 'feeling' in US policymaking circles 'that China was disastrously thrown away: a stitch in time would have saved nine … The application of this (partly emotional) doctrine to Indochina is clear'.[13] Makins likewise detected a 'growing conviction' on the part of the administration 'that the United States could not stand idly by if the threat of a Communist Indo-China became acute'.[14] In short, when Eisenhower or Smith denied that military action was under consideration, the British did not believe them. And rightly so.

. The US government had begun secretly debating the merits of intervention some weeks earlier. On 8 January 1954, Indochina was the subject of extended discussion in the National Security Council. Although policymakers anticipated a French victory in the approaching battle at Dien Bien Phu it seemed prudent to weigh the options if the Vietminh prevailed. On the question of American military action, the President was forthright. He 'simply could not imagine the United States putting ground forces anywhere in Southeast Asia, except possibly in Malaya, which we would have to defend as a bulwark to our off-shore island chain'. The key to winning the war 'was to get the Vietnamese to fight' and he could see 'no sense in even talking about United States forces replacing the French' since that would cause the Vietnamese to 'transfer their hatred' to America. 'I can not tell you ... how bitterly opposed I am to such a course of action'. Vietnam 'would absorb our troops by divisions!' But then the contradiction manifested itself. 'We could nevertheless not forget our vital interests in Indochina,' Eisenhower reminded the NSC. Likening the situation in Vietnam to a 'leaky dike', he reasoned that 'it's sometimes better to put a finger in than to let the whole structure be washed away'.[15]

Where the President was conflicted about the correct course of action, others were more confident. Admiral Radford, the JCS chief, insisted that the United States should 'do everything possible to forestall a French defeat at Dien Bien Phu', although he had in mind air action not ground forces. 'Weren't the stakes worth it?,' Radford asked. 'We were already in this thing in such a big way that it seemed foolish not to make the one small extra move which might be essential to success'. By the close of the meeting Eisenhower had shifted towards the Radford position to the extent that he mused aloud on how a 'little group of fine and adventurous pilots' flying carrier-launched bombers devoid of US insignia could make a valuable contribution without America becoming directly involved in the war.[16]

The following week, the President approved NSC-5405, 'United States Objectives and Courses of Action with respect to Southeast Asia', a policy statement reaffirming the high value the administration attached to Indochina as the keystone in the arch of communist containment in the region. While direct PRC intervention could never be ruled out, NSC-5405 noted, the immediate threat to Indochina came from the military effectiveness of the Vietminh coupled with the growing fragility of metropolitan French resolve to continue the fight. For now, the Laniel government was committed to the war. But any successor would probably seek early negotiations with the communists despite the absence of 'any prospect for acceptable terms'. As to US policy, NSC-5405 recommended increased military aid to enable French and French Union forces to pursue an 'aggressive military, political and psychological program'. The Vietnam National Army should continue to be expanded and trained to take on the security burden from mid-1955. On the political plane, the French needed to hurry up and deliver the independence Laniel had promised in July 1953.[17]

In approving NSC-5405, Eisenhower ordered the setting up of a committee of senior policymakers to examine military options if – as Smith put it – 'things go bad in Indochina regardless of our assistance'.[18] Meeting for the first time on 29 January, the committee comprised Smith (in the chair), Radford, Central Intelligence Agency (CIA) chief Allen Dulles, Deputy Secretary of Defense Roger M. Kyes and Special Assistant for National Security C. D. Jackson. In marked contrast to the anti-intervention line he would adopt with Makins when he met him the following week, Smith maintained that 'the importance of winning in Indochina was so great that if worst came to the worst he personally would favor intervention with US air and naval forces – though not ground forces'. Radford agreed. The United States 'could not afford to let the Viet Minh take the Tonkin delta. If this were lost, Indochina would be lost and the rest of Southeast Asia would fall'. When Radford proposed that military plans be drawn up as an insurance policy, no one on the committee disagreed.[19]

Smith met Makins again on 19 February. During the previous few days, the US press had carried stories – apparently based on further leaks from within the administration – suggesting that bombing and blockade of China was on the NSC/JCS agenda in connection with Indochina. Referring to these reports, Makins said to Smith that if war plans were being put in place, he presumed they would only be actioned in the event of overt Chinese intervention in Vietnam, a remote contingency given how well the Vietminh were doing on their own. Smith quickly corrected him: 'in the event of such intervention or of a French collapse and withdrawal'.[20]

Based on this and other indicators of administration thinking, the Foreign Office was sure that some degree of military planning was going on in Washington. On 24 February, Allen wrote to Scott (now Makins's deputy) to say that American entry into the Indochina War 'would not necessarily help the military situation if its only result was to bring about a corresponding increase in the scale of Chinese intervention'. Geneva must be given a chance, and the risks attached to negotiations, including a settlement based on partition, 'might have to be accepted if the only alternative seemed to be the enlargement of the war through increased intervention from the outside'. Parliament and the country 'might in the last resort take some convincing that the risk was not one that we ought to accept in the interests of peace'. Remembered by Cable as enjoying 'influence over Eden', Allen had sketched out what would soon become the official British position with regard to both military intervention and the Geneva conference.[21]

On 2 March, the Smith committee produced a report for the President outlining a programme of action to bring about the 'defeat' of the Vietminh 'without resort to overt combat operations by US forces'. As such, it represented a compromise between what Radford thought essential and Eisenhower considered politic. Working on the premise that the French would survive the current campaigning season and go on to turn the tide of the war in 1954–1955 in accordance with the Navarre Plan timetable, the report recommended an expansion of the US Military Assistance Advisory Group (MAAG), first established in Vietnam in 1950, to enable it to play a greater role in operational planning and in training the Vietnamese armed forces. There should also be further augmentation of the French Air Force with US personnel to maximize effectiveness. Full independence for the Associated States remained another priority. If the French proved responsive to American advice, and if the Chinese stayed out of the war, the Smith committee concluded that there was 'promise' of 'ultimate victory'.[22]

This was not exactly a blueprint for direct US military intervention such as the British suspected the Americans to be working on. In fact, the report exhibited little anxiety over the outcome of the battle brewing at Dien Bien Phu and was in essence a plan for victory without recourse to US belligerency.[23] That being so, negotiations with the communists did not feature. As Dulles told the NSC on 26 February, the French were unlikely to push for a settlement at Geneva 'provided there was no real military disaster in Indochina prior to and during the conference', a view replicated in the Smith committee report. Few Washington policymakers thought that such a calamity impended. Geneva was to be endured not utilized. Once the conference had come and gone with nothing given away, the business of winning the war could recommence.[24]

Over the next fortnight, the British Embassy closely monitored the Eisenhower administration's growing obsession with Indochina. On 10 March, Scott wrote to Allen to say that Vietnam now had 'top priority' but American decision-makers were 'baffled and frustrated and do not know what to do'. Against this, they knew what they would *not* do: they would not accept a negotiated settlement at Geneva likely to lead to communist domination of Southeast Asia, and they would not send ground troops to fight in Indochina. 'It is very important that you in London should realise the importance attached here to Indo-China,' Scott continued:

> It is *the* issue of the moment, outranking Germany, Middle East, Korea, and all other 'sore spots'. So, when I say that Indo-China has 'top priority', I mean precisely that. Next, when I say that the Americans will not accept a settlement likely to lead to Communist domination, I mean that this will be their attitude however much the French incline to a settlement on any terms. If the French push through a settlement of which the Americans disapprove, then we shall be in for an 'agonising reappraisal' with a vengeance. The consequences could be far reaching, affecting the whole of French-American relations and reacting on the North Atlantic Treaty Organisation. Finally, when I say that the Americans will not intervene with combatant forces in Indo-China, I do not mean that come what may they never will. All I mean is that this is their present policy. The general trend is against adventures overseas. This trend will not be easily reversed.

Scott's remark about an 'agonising reappraisal' referenced a controversial speech delivered by Dulles at the NATO Council in Paris in December 1953. Frustrated by the failure of the French parliament to ratify the treaty to bring the EDC (and with it West German rearmament) into being, Dulles warned that further delay might oblige the United States to reconsider its whole relationship to European security. This was hard-nosed diplomacy – a threat, not even particularly veiled, that unless the French gave the EDC a green light, the Eisenhower administration would reconsider its relationship with NATO and possibly embrace a 'peripheral defence' of Western Europe, a move that would see US troops leave the continent.[25] By the spring of 1954, the prospect of the agonizing reappraisal not only remained in its original European form – the French having not yet ratified the EDC – but seemed poised to take in British and French non-compliance with US policy preferences in Southeast Asia. Troubled by this linkage, on 18 March Eden circulated Scott's letter to Allen to the Cabinet.[26] By then, the battle of Dien Bien Phu was into its fifth day.

Despite the early loss of Anne-Marie, Beatrice and Gabrielle, the Eisenhower administration had remained sanguine about the prospects for a victory or at least a defensive victory for the French in the Nam Yum valley. In the National Security Council on 18 March, Eisenhower commented positively on French air supremacy, the high combat value of US-supplied napalm and the impressive strength of the French fortifications. Dulles even wondered whether 'pessimistic' French reports 'might be designed as a build-up to exaggerate the extent of their final victory'.[27] Two days later, when French Army Chief of Staff General Paul Ely turned up in Washington, Americans' illusions were quickly dispelled.

Meeting with Radford, Allen Dulles and a number of other top administration figures on the evening of his arrival (20 March), Ely put the odds on the Dien Bien Phu garrison's survival as no better than '50–50'. A defeat, he opined, would have 'serious adverse effects' and not just in Vietnam. French public opinion might revolt against a continuation of the war and the Laniel government would be compelled to seek a negotiated settlement at or before Geneva on whatever terms the communists offered.[28] The main purpose of the Ely mission was to secure a guarantee of US air intervention if the PRC air force entered the war – Chinese MIG-15s had been sighted in the skies of Tonkin in early March – but the General also succeeded in puncturing the Eisenhower administration's complacency about Dien Bien Phu. 'Indochina problem getting graver', Jim Hagerty, Eisenhower's press secretary, recorded in his diary.[29]

Dawning American realism was not accompanied by consensus as to what should be done beyond ramping up military aid to France. On 22 March, Ely met the President at the White House. Radford was also present. After listening to a report on the battlefield situation, Eisenhower ordered that everything possible be done to satisfy French material needs, including the supply of additional B-26 bombers, C-47 transports and helicopters.[30] There is nothing in the documentary record to indicate that more direct forms of US assistance were discussed during the Ely mission, but in his memoirs the Frenchman recounted how, towards the end of his stay, Radford told him privately that if the Laniel government made a formal appeal for American help at Dien Bien Phu, US air strikes against Vietminh positions would soon follow. Sixty B-29 heavy bombers, operating from the Philippines, could drop an average of 450 tons of explosives per raid. The President's approval, Radford suggested, could be obtained 'without difficulty'.[31]

Later, in 'a battle of the memoirs', Radford denied encouraging Ely to press for US bombing.[32] At the time, however, the pugnacious JCS chief was without question the administration's foremost champion of military action in Indochina and, if needs be, the bombing (conventional and nuclear) of China.[33] On 24 March, Radford wrote to Eisenhower advising that preparations be put in place to act 'promptly and in force possibly to a frantic and belated request by the French for US intervention' at Dien Bien Phu, a request which, if Ely is to be believed, Radford had encouraged the French to make.[34] Whatever the truth of the matter, others in the administration, not least the President and the Secretary of State, were nervous that even limited air action could generate unstoppable momentum towards a ground commitment and a new Korea. Recalling the February furore over the dispatch of aircraft technicians, Eisenhower and Dulles knew that any far-reaching military decisions would need political underpinning. Irrespective of his rights under the Constitution as Commander-in-

Chief, the President was not about to send bombers into action at Dien Bien Phu without advance consent from Congress.[35]

In the end, it may be that something was lost in translation: Radford had little French; Ely's English was poor. Nevertheless, the Frenchman returned to Paris convinced that American air intervention at Dien Bien Phu was to be had for the asking. Nor did Ely waste any time before telling ministers and military chiefs about Radford's 'extraordinaire ouverture'. Rather than make an immediate appeal to Washington, however, the French Committee for National Defence preferred to assess the ramifications of US intervention, in particular whether air strikes (operation *Vautour* as the French now dubbed the purported Radford plan) would bring China into the war. To that end, a special envoy was dispatched to Hanoi to consult with Navarre.[36]

In public, the US administration continued to express confidence in the French. 'I do not expect there is going to be a communist victory in Indochina,' Dulles told a news conference on 23 March.[37] Asked by a reporter for a 'soldier's appreciation' of Dien Bien Phu, Eisenhower felt that the 'odds' were 'all in favour of the defender'.[38] In private, however, the administration debated with mounting seriousness the merits of military action. On 24 March, Eisenhower told Dulles that he 'agreed basically that we should not get involved in fighting in Indochina'. The 'basically' is a telling reflection of his conflicted mindset. Indeed, Eisenhower went on to suggest that if the necessary 'political pre-conditions' were in place, he would not 'wholly exclude the possibility of a single strike' against the Vietminh at Dien Bien Phu, 'if it were almost certain this would produce decisive results'.[39]

Radford, meanwhile, lobbied for a much greater level of intervention and was backed by Vice-President Nixon and Air Force Chief of Staff Nathan F. Twining, but the influential Chief of the Army, General Matthew Ridgway, was not only sceptical about the efficacy of US action at or beyond Dien Bien Phu but concerned that any such intervention 'would greatly increase the risk of general war'.[40] Without Ridgway's backing, Radford would struggle to shift his interventionist ambitions from planning to realization.[41] As for Dulles, he seems to have been as torn as Eisenhower: publicly upbeat about French prospects, in private he feared the consequences of French defeat ('We could lose Europe, Asia and Africa all at once if we don't watch out').[42] On 24 March, Dulles told Cabinet colleagues that the United States needed to help the French to 'win in Indo-China'. There would probably have to be 'fairly strong action' involving risks, but 'these risks will be less if we take them now rather than waiting for several years'.[43]

On 25 March, the President chaired another meeting of the National Security Council. According to Radford, the time had come to intervene either in concert with the French, with allies if the French withdrew, 'or, if necessary, unilaterally'. Defense Secretary Charles Wilson concurred. Eisenhower, however, was clear that 'Congress would have to be in on any move … to intervene' and that a multilateral approach was much more likely to garner support on Capitol Hill than a unilateral variant. He went on to ponder which countries might 'join us in a broadened effort to save Indochina', given that UN police action on the Korean model was ruled out by the absence of clear-cut external aggression. The 'free nations' of Southeast Asia, including the Philippines and Thailand, were obvious candidates, as were the UK, Australia, New Zealand, France and (possibly) Nationalist China. Reluctant as he was to involve the United States militarily, Eisenhower accepted that the loss of Vietnam could well bring about 'the fall of all of Southeast Asia to the Communists' and he therefore tasked the NSC Planning Board with exploring the circumstances and conditions under which the United States might yet enter the war.[44]

With military planning intensifying, the State Department, mindful of Eisenhower's insistence on a multilateral approach, worked on a political framework for intervention. By 29 March, the administration was ready to go public with its response to the crisis. That morning, Eisenhower met Republican legislative leaders to alert them to the possibility that 'within the space of forty-eight hours, it might be necessary to move into the battle of Dien Bien Phu in order to keep it from going against us'. In that case, he would be 'calling in the Democrats as well'.[45] At 9.00 pm that evening, Dulles delivered a speech to the Overseas Press Club in New York which he hoped would 'puncture the sentiment for appeasement before Geneva'.[46] Having cleared the text with the President, Dulles told his audience that 'the imposition on South-East Asia of the political system of Communist Russia and its Chinese Communist ally by whatever means would be a grave threat to the whole free community'. The United States 'feels that the possibility should not be passively accepted but should be met by united action'. Dulles's reference to the extension of communism 'by whatever means' was particularly loaded insofar as it suggested that America was preparing to respond forcefully not just in the case of a Chinese invasion of Vietnam, which was unlikely, but if the PRC maintained its present indirect backing for the Vietminh.[47]

The Secretary of State was vague on how united action would function in practice. This may have been a deliberate ploy to keep the communists guessing as to what impended, but given that it was barely four days since Eisenhower had spoken to the NSC of the need for a broadened international effort on Indochina, Dulles's speech had more than a hint of improvisation about it. With Congress certain to bridle at the prospect of unilateral US intervention, the State Department prioritized the lining up of allies ahead of any detailed consideration of how a united action coalition would work. Should it issue a warning to China to cease its support for the Vietminh on pain of punishment? Or should it muster its collective strength and enter the war on the side of the French? Should it pursue both of these aims at the same time? Dulles gave no real clues in his speech, although it is worth recalling his recent assertion in Cabinet that America's goal should be to help the French to *win* in Indochina. Was this to become the coalition's goal, too? If so, somebody needed to tell the French who (as Ely had tried to explain in Washington) were no longer fighting for victory only for a sufficiency of battlefield success so that they could then negotiate a peace with honour.[48]

Whatever the overall goal of united action, US policymakers were agreed on one thing: British support was critical. The administration had been pleased when Thailand and the Philippines responded quickly and favourably, but the UK was the big catch. If America's closest and strongest ally was on board, a powerful alliance would begin to take shape. As important as any UK military contribution was the political and moral value of its adherence. For one thing, Australia and New Zealand might be more inclined to participate in a united action coalition on grounds of Commonwealth solidarity. For another, that same Commonwealth factor might deter India from encouraging other Asian nations to denounce a coalition as a neocolonial intrusion in Asian affairs.[49] It had been with these kinds of considerations in mind that Dulles summoned Makins to the State Department on 27 March to pass on the gist of the speech he planned to deliver forty-eight hours later. He was 'anxious' to provide advance notice, Makins reported to Eden, because he was 'not sure that what he was going to say would be in complete harmony with your views'.[50] This, as we will see, was the understatement of the 1954 Indochina crisis.

At the very moment the Eisenhower administration was seeking UK backing for an approach on Indochina that risked war with the PRC and potentially global war with the USSR, the British government, parliament and public were trying – and mostly failing – to come to terms with the terrifying implications of the hydrogen bomb. This chronological convergence is rarely if ever acknowledged in the large literature devoted to the Indochina crisis.[51] Yet, in important determining ways, the British government's response to the US call for united action was shaped by a deep-seated fear of nuclear war, by recognition of the UK's vulnerability to Soviet nuclear attack, and by Eden and Churchill's memory of how Eisenhower and Dulles had spoken at Bermuda of normalizing the use of weapons of mass destruction. In short, Indochina in 1954 needs to be recognized as the first international crisis of the thermonuclear age.

Several developments ensured that the Churchill government remained in a state of heightened nuclear nervousness after Bermuda. At the start of February 1954, the Eisenhower administration confirmed that the 1952 Ivy-Mike test had been 'the first full-scale thermo-nuclear explosion in history' and that the United States possessed a growing H-bomb arsenal.[52] The President followed this with a Special Message to Congress in which he declared that the hydrogen bomb 'today dwarfs in destructive power all atomic weapons' and reaffirmed what he told the British privately at Bermuda, namely that nuclear weapons 'have today achieved conventional status in the arsenals of our armed forces'.[53] Amidst this flurry of thermonuclear news, Eisenhower wrote a long personal letter to Churchill on 9 February, the contents of which unnerved both the Prime Minister and his senior advisors. Littered with emotive phraseology about the 'stupid and savage individuals in the Kremlin' and the need to 'throw back the Russian threat and allow civilization, as we know it, to continue its progress', the letter depicted the Cold War as an epic Manichean contest. What would happen, Eisenhower wondered, if communism won that struggle?

> It is only when one allows his mind to contemplate momentarily such a disaster for the world and attempts to picture an atheistic materialism in complete domination of all human life, that he fully appreciates how necessary it is to seek renewed faith and strength from his God, and sharpen up his sword for the struggle that cannot possibly be escaped.[54]

At any other time, the President's message might have been taken by the British as a think-piece, but in the thermonuclear context of February 1954 it acquired an unsettling quality. The Prime Minister 'broods a great deal about the atomic and hydrogen bomb', Harold Macmillan, the future British premier, wrote in his diary. 'The destructive power of the [H-bomb] is frightful. All London in one night ... Will the Americans put off the "show down" again until the Russians have caught them up for a second time? Or will they go for pre-emptive war?'[55] Eisenhower's message (which Salisbury, the minister in charge of UK nuclear policy, thought 'most sinister') hinted at the latter.[56] Recalling Bermuda, Eden insisted that Churchill reply to Eisenhower thus: 'I take it that you are referring ... to the spiritual struggle. Otherwise your words might suggest that you believe war to be inevitable. I certainly do not think so and I am sure you do not either.'[57]

Any reticence Churchill felt about challenging Eisenhower evaporated when Sterling Cole, Chairman of the Joint Congressional Committee on Atomic Energy, issued a statement on 17 February providing details about Ivy-Mike. A similar weapon used against a modern city would wreak 'absolute destruction over an area extending three miles in all directions' and 'severe-to-moderate damage' for up to seven miles from ground zero.[58] Churchill was horrified. With the UK (unlike the United States) within range of Soviet bombers, he poured his fears into his reply to Eisenhower on 9 March:

> You can imagine what my thoughts are about London. I am told that several million people would certainly be obliterated by four or five of the latest H-Bombs. In a few years these could be delivered by rocket without even hazarding the life of the pilot. New York and your other great cities have immeasurable perils too, though distance is a valuable advantage at least as long as pilots are used. Another ugly idea has been put in my head, namely, the dropping of an H-Bomb in the sea to windward of the Island or any other seaborne country, in suitable weather, by rocket or airplane, or perhaps released by submarine. The explosion would generate an enormous radio-active cloud, many square miles in extent, which would drift over the land attacked and extinguish human life over very large areas. Our smallness and density of population emphasizes this danger to us.

Churchill renewed his appeal for Eisenhower's backing for a summit – which struck him as more necessary than ever – before closing in terms redolent of Eden's advice. 'I understand that in speaking of the faith that must inspire us in the struggle against atheistic materialism, you are referring to the spiritual struggle, and that like me, you still believe that War is not inevitable.'[59]

While Eisenhower's response was awaited, there was another disturbing development. At the start of March, the US Atomic Energy Commission announced that a series of tests was underway in the Pacific. No details were given but the press in America and elsewhere presumed – correctly – that thermonuclear science was involved. Unlike operation Ivy in 1952, operation Castle was intended to test weapons which could be carried by US bombers. The first blast, code-named Castle-Bravo, produced a staggering yield of 15 megatons, nearly twice as powerful as American experts had predicted. Content to make the fact of the test public, the Eisenhower administration had no plans to discuss its nature or impact. Soon, though, this policy of minimal disclosure was in tatters.

On 14 March, a Japanese trawler, the *Lucky Dragon*, reached its home port of Yaizu with its crew suffering from severe radiation sickness, victims of Castle-Bravo. The US Navy had warned vessels to avoid the area in which radioactive contamination was assessed to be a potential hazard, but the *Lucky Dragon*, operating on the edge of this exclusion zone, was showered in toxic ash. The trawler's fate and the scale of the nuclear fallout set off a wave of 'radioactivity hysteria' in Japan and caused an international outcry against the Eisenhower administration's apparently out-of-control testing regime.[60] In a concession to public alarm, the US authorities extended the Pacific exclusion zone to 450 miles out from the proving ground but otherwise refused to disrupt its programme. If mapped on to Western Europe, this new danger zone would cover the whole of the British Isles, most of France, all of Holland and Belgium, and Germany as far east as Frankfurt. The message to the people of the UK and Western Europe was terrifyingly stark. In the event of general nuclear war, if you survived the blast and the heat of the H-bomb, the death-cloud would get you anyway.[61]

Viewed against this fraught backdrop, Eisenhower's reply to Churchill, sent on 19 March, was less than reassuring. While admitting to 'grave concern at the steady increase in methods of mass destruction', the President saw no reason to rush to meet the Soviet hierarchy at a summit.[62] As well as disappointing Churchill, Eisenhower's message, coming six days into the battle of Dien Bien Phu, did little to reduce the British government's fears of a wider war with China and the USSR brought on by American intervention in Vietnam. In Cabinet on 22 March, Eden reminded his colleagues that the logic of the New Look meant that the United States 'will soon assume that *any* action by them is atomic ... They will have all their armaments attuned & fitted for atomic weapons *only*'. He was seconded by Salisbury. The US Strategic Air Command was 'turning over to H. bomb as standard weapon'. With East Anglia home to atomic-capable US B-29 bombers, this made the UK a prime target for the USSR and underlined the literally life-and-death difference between the UK and US situations: unlike Britain, the 'US can't be attacked with this by R[ussia] for 5 years or so'.[63]

Nuclear nervousness was by no means the preserve of the British Cabinet. To the contrary, just as the Indochina crisis was coming to a head, the UK at large was succumbing to a bad case of H-bomb fever. 'Very great excitement everywhere', Shuckburgh wrote in his diary, 'as if people began to see the end of the world'.[64] On 1 April, in the midst of the tumult provoked by Castle-Bravo and the *Lucky Dragon*, a *Daily Mirror* editorial questioned the ability of the government and its aging leader to handle the American 'horror-bomb problem'.[65] What the *Daily Mirror* and its four million readers did not know – what nobody outside the Whitehall policymaking elite knew – was that Eden and the Foreign Office were at that very moment mapping out a plan to prevent US intervention in Vietnam sparking a full-scale Sino-American conflict and potentially a global war with the Soviet Union.

The day the *Daily Mirror* published its critical editorial, Eden gave his approval to 'Policy towards Indo-China', a memorandum prepared by the Foreign Office in consultation with the Chiefs of Staff and the Joint Intelligence Committee. Intended as the main steering brief for the UK delegation at the Geneva conference, the paper constituted the most comprehensive statement of the British position on the war since the Conservatives returned to power. 'Policy towards Indo-China' began by rehearsing established principles – the need to support France in resisting the Vietminh and in building up the Associated States to ensure their survival when the Expeditionary Corps withdrew. However, the paper went on to warn that recent military developments, dovetailing with political upset in Paris, raised doubts as to whether the French would see the war through to a successful conclusion. Indeed, the Laniel government seemed bent on reaching a diplomatic settlement with China or the Vietminh. In either case, the French would be negotiating from weakness; hence the outcome was unlikely to assure the long-term non-communist orientation of Vietnam, Laos and Cambodia.[66]

As French resolve weakened, so the possibility of deeper American involvement increased, the paper continued. The Eisenhower administration had several options in this connection: an expansion of the existing military assistance programme; a large injection of US advisors to take over the training of local armed forces; the deployment, under US command, of Nationalist Chinese or South Korean forces to support the French; and direct American intervention with air, naval and possibly even ground troops. Of these possibilities, the latter would be the most effective if the aim was to tip the military balance back in France's favour. But it was also the most high-risk. 'Any direct intervention by the armed forces of any external nation ... would probably result in Chinese intervention, with the danger that this might ultimately lead to global war,' the paper stressed. 'Our influence should therefore be used against these more dangerous forms of deeper United States involvement.' By a process of elimination, the provision of more American military assistance coupled with a bigger US role in training the Vietnamese seemed to be the most hopeful way forward – as long as the French were willing to carry on. Here, Dien Bien Phu was crucial. A victory in the battle, and the French would probably continue. A defeat, and the pressure on the Laniel government to negotiate peace 'at almost any price' might become irresistible.[67]

'Policy towards Indo-China' argued that a successful outcome to the Geneva conference would negate US intervention. But Eden and his diplomatic team needed to apply caution. The UK was not directly involved in the war and could not dictate to the French, only support them in seeking a settlement on the best terms possible. At the same time, the Americans were certain to oppose any compromise with the communists. In conclusion, the paper acknowledged that an entirely satisfactory outcome to the war, either from a general Western or specifically British standpoint, was no longer to be expected. At Geneva, the UK delegation should thus 'strive for the adoption of the least disadvantageous course'. This meant partition which, though imperfect, 'might salvage more from the general wreck than any other'.[68]

By an irony of timing, 'Policy towards Indo-China' affirmed British opposition to US or US-led intervention just as Dulles was issuing his clarion call for united action. The American Secretary of State spoke in New York on 29 March. By then, the document was complete and awaiting approval by the Chiefs of Staff and the Foreign Secretary. In giving that sanction on 31 March and 1 April, respectively, neither saw reason to revisit the paper's conclusions in light of Dulles's statement.[69]

Moscow and Beijing reacted angrily to the prospect of US-led united action. According to *Pravda*, it was a 'transparent slanderous provocation intended exclusively to poison the atmosphere on the eve of the Geneva conference and to intensify tension in international relations', while the Chinese *People's Daily* warned that a new Korean

War was suddenly a real prospect.[70] Sino-Soviet assessments were not dissimilar to those of the French government. Unlike *Vautour*-type air strikes, united action would do nothing to help the French at Dien Bien Phu, Bidault complained, but might well 'torpedo' the Geneva conference and 'prevent France from ending the Indochina war'.[71]

On 30 March, Ambassador Makins called on Dulles at the State Department in search of enlightenment about united action. Apart from offering an assurance that the administration was not planning anything 'silly' like sending American troops to Vietnam, Dulles confined himself to generalities about the need for the United States and UK to help the French avoid a 'sell out' at the Geneva conference.[72] If Makins returned to his Embassy little wiser about US policy, the arrival on his desk two days later of 'Policy towards Indo-China' *ought* to have made his own government's position clear to him. It is right to stress the caveat, however. In a covering telegram, the Foreign Office suggested that the time had come to 'face the possibility that the conditions for a favourable solution … may no longer exist'. According to Cable, much of the confusion and rancour which would affect Anglo-American relations in the weeks ahead originated with this message. Having decided definitely that a military solution was unacceptable, the Foreign Office needed to spell this out more clearly to Makins. Instead, in observing that a satisfactory outcome *may* no longer exist, the telegram implied that it *might* still exist. That, Cable felt, 'was no way to tell an ambassador notoriously solicitous for the preservation of good Anglo-American relations' that the UK policy paper 'was to be interpreted in the manner most displeasing to Mr Dulles'. The Churchill government opposed a military solution, period. The Ambassador should have been told this. Instead, he was left to his own pro-American interpretative devices.[73]

On the afternoon of 2 April, Makins, accompanied by Scott, met again with Dulles and other State Department officials, including Smith. All but admitting that united action was an improvisation, the Americans said that they presently had no 'specific plan in mind' either to forestall a French defeat or contain the wider communist threat to Southeast Asia. As instructed by London, Makins pointed out that the situation in Vietnam was possibly beyond military salvation and that a negotiated settlement, with partition the 'least damaging' option, should be considered. Dulles objected that any diplomatic compact would delay not prevent the communization of the region. The alternative to a negotiated settlement was military action, or at least the prospect of such action, he argued. If it was 'made plain to the Chinese that continuation of aid to Viet Minh was dangerous for China, they would desist, and the Russians would use their influence in the same direction'. Warming to his theme, Dulles said that the Joint Chiefs of Staff believed that the Western powers already enjoyed such military superiority in Asia that if the Chinese continued to interfere in Vietnam, bombing and blockade of the PRC should follow. There were obvious perils in taking this course of action but those radiating from the loss of Vietnam were even greater.[74]

Here, finally, was confirmation of what the Foreign Office suspected. Military options *were* under active consideration in Washington, with an attack on China regarded as preferable to direct intervention in Vietnam. Makins was taken aback. The British government had 'not contemplated any action which would carry with it the prospect of an extension of the war', but this might be the outcome if the PRC ignored an Allied injunction to abandon the Vietminh. In response, Dulles repeated that the 'primary objective was to keep the French in the war' for which purpose a demonstration of collective Allied determination would be a morale boost. In addition to the United States and UK, he envisioned France, Australia, New Zealand, Thailand, the Philippines and the Associated States as coalition partners. If it came to war with China, this ten might be expanded to twelve by bringing in South Korea and Nationalist China.[75]

Although disturbed by US thinking, Makins advised the Foreign Office to apply caution. A 'decision to range ourselves with the fundamental American decision or dissociate ourselves from it cannot be long delayed and will have a profound effect over the whole field of Anglo-American relations'. On balance, Makins favoured going with the Americans:

> If we align ourselves with the Administration we shall be able to bring our influence continually to bear upon them. We now have an opportunity to retrieve the damage to our world position and to Commonwealth solidarity which the ANZUS Pact [formed in 1951 without the UK] has undoubtedly caused and to work for a security system in the Far East in which we shall have our rightful place. The Americans will certainly desire our cooperation and would, I believe, be ready to listen to our views as well as support us elsewhere even though our contribution in resources was small. If we decline to work with the Administration they will certainly be discouraged, but I think in the end they will do the best they can with Australia, New Zealand, Philippines, Siam [Thailand], etc., and without us will be more likely to take South Korea and Formosa [Taiwan] finally to their hearts. All this would weaken our position in the Far East and the security of our interests there. It would affect our relations with the United States everywhere.

Closing, the Ambassador observed that American opinion had developed rapidly in the five days since Dulles first flagged up united action. It was now likely, he judged, that 'public sentiment', along with 'influential groups' in Congress, would back firm action on Indochina.[76]

In speaking with Makins, Dulles had indicated that some kind of warning to China – implicit, perhaps, in the sense that the formation of a united action coalition would send a message to Beijing – was the US government's current focus. What he did not tell the Ambassador was that the administration was simultaneously giving serious consideration to armed intervention in Vietnam.

The Vietminh had returned to the charge at Dien Bien Phu on 30 March. An intense artillery bombardment was followed by a series of concentrated frontal assaults on the Eliane and Dominique CRs. Although bloodied, the French held firm but their perimeter was again reduced. Three days later, his own forces having sustained heavy losses, Giap abandoned human-wave tactics and opted for siege warfare. A network of trenches, many new, others dug in advance and now activated, soon enveloped the base. Unlike the static trenches of the Western Front in the First World War, these shifted and constricted the French fortress and enabled the Vietminh to get within assault distance of CR's in some safety. Alongside what Giap referred to as *grignotage* (nibbling) tactics, Vietminh artillery kept up a steady bombardment. 'Although I am doing all I can to avoid it', Navarre informed Laniel, 'the fall of the entrenched camp has become a possibility sooner or later'.[77]

On 1 April, Eisenhower told the National Security Council that the 'plight' of the garrison raised once more 'the question whether the United States ought not to consider any kind of intervention'. Military action carried 'very terrible risks' but the issue could not be deflected. However, rather than debate options there and then, he preferred to confer privately with 'certain of the members of the National Security Council'.[78] There is no record of what was discussed in this elite assembly but its import can be inferred from Hagerty's diary. 'Indochina situation getting really hot', he recorded. The President was of the opinion that 'US might have to make decision to send in squadrons from two aircraft carriers to bomb Reds at Dien Bien Phu'. Hagerty then quoted Eisenhower directly: 'Of course, if we did, we'd have to deny it forever'.[79] Was the President toying with the idea of unmarked US aircraft delivering a series of short, sharp air strikes? Possibly. But the record of Dulles's telephone calls that same day indicates that Congressional backing for intervention in the war was also on the agenda.[80]

By the time that Eisenhower met with Dulles, Radford and Wilson at the White House the following morning (2 April), a Congressional resolution had been drafted. Identifying 'the Chinese Communist regime and its agents in Indochina' as the enemy, the resolution authorized the President to employ naval and air power 'to assist the forces which are resisting aggression in Southeast Asia'. After perusing the text, Eisenhower said that it 'reflected what, in his opinion, was desirable'. But he also felt that the correct 'tactical procedure' was 'to develop first the thinking of congressional leaders' before sending it to the Hill.[81]

Dulles and Radford agreed with the President on this point but otherwise held differing views on the purpose of the resolution. To Dulles, it would legitimize US involvement in a united action coalition to deter further Chinese interference in Vietnam and potentially serve as the kernel of a future Southeast Asia defence organization. To Radford, the resolution was the legal basis for immediate and if necessary unilateral military action in Vietnam. For now, the JCS chief, faced with opposition from, amongst others, the President, the Secretary of State and Ridgway, had no choice but follow rather than lead. 'Hell, if we had let Raddy go, he would have been in there with a whole carrier fleet', Thruston Morton, a Dulles aide, later recalled. 'Raddy had it all figured out, how he could get carriers in the area and bomb the hell out of them.'[82]

On the morning of 3 April, Dulles and Radford met Congressional leaders, four Republicans and four Democrats, at the State Department. Radford provided a military briefing before handing over to Dulles. The President needed to know if he could rely on the support of Congress if he determined that national security necessitated the deployment of US air and naval power in Southeast Asia, he explained. Ground troops were not presently part of the plan. In the ensuing discussion, the British came in for a good deal of criticism for failing to rally immediately to the united action banner. Democratic Senator Richard Russell was not alone in suggesting that if the UK 'flinched' it would be 'necessary to reconsider our whole system of collective security from the standpoint of dependability'. By the end of the meeting it was clear that there was substantial Congressional support for such action as the administration deemed necessary. There was, though, an important caveat: there could be 'no more Koreas with the United States furnishing 90% of the manpower'. If or when it came, action must be truly united. To this end, Dulles undertook to obtain 'definite commitments from the English and other free nations'. If he secured allied backing, the 'consensus' was that a resolution 'giving the President power to commit armed forces in the area' stood a good chance of endorsement.[83]

Afterwards, Dulles rang Eisenhower at Camp David to say that the meeting 'went pretty well', although it also 'raised some serious problems'. Amongst these was the 'position of Britain'. It would be 'hard to get the American people excited' unless the UK government joined in with united action. With Eisenhower's approval, Dulles began work on a presidential message to Churchill.[84] As of 3 April, the future of united action seemed to be largely in the hands of the British. Like a diplomatic domino effect, if the Churchill government approved American plans, then other countries, including the UK's Commonwealth partners Australia and New Zealand, were likely to do so, and then Congress, the final domino, would grant the President the necessary authority to send US forces into Vietnam.[85] What the Eisenhower administration did not yet realize was that it had gifted a veto power over its plans to an ally more than ready to use it.

Disunited Inaction, April 1954

While the State Department got on with drafting a presidential message to Churchill, details of the Dulles-Radford-Congressional meeting began 'leaking in all directions'. In point of fact, it was from the US press that the British first learned of the existence of a second variation on united action. Hitherto, as far as the Foreign Office knew, the Eisenhower administration's plans were predicated on the issuance of a warning to China to cease its support for the Vietminh. Now it appeared that united action also encompassed intervention in Vietnam.[1]

The press stories were corroborated by Commonwealth sources. In Washington on 4 April, Dulles briefed his ANZUS pact colleagues Sir Percy Spender, Ambassador of Australia, and Leslie Munro, Ambassador of New Zealand, the Australian's account of the meeting finding its way to London soon after. Dulles wanted to form 'an ad hoc alliance' for the 'specific purpose of giving direct military support to French and Vietnamese in Indo-China', Spender recorded. The proposed members – the Dulles ten – would be encouraged to affirm their readiness to join a coalition 'within a short period of time'. Although armed intervention was not anticipated prior to Geneva, Dulles felt the need for 'at least some form of declaration of common concern and of common intention to give military assistance of a direct kind which could then quickly be worked out'. Radford, who was also present, observed that intervention would be 'primarily if not wholly supporting action by Naval and Air Forces'. Dulles saw 'little danger' of PRC counter-intervention. Nor was the administration thinking of using 'unconventional weapons'.[2]

Two days earlier, when Dulles met Makins, China had occupied centre stage. Now it was Indochina. The US Secretary further emphasized 'the key position of the United Kingdom', Spender noted. The administration 'could not carry Congress and American public opinion along in giving direct military assistance to Indo-China unless United Kingdom was prepared to do likewise'. There was a secondary precondition to united action, Dulles added: the French must 'give without delay complete political independence' to the Associated States.[3]

Given the focus Dulles placed on Britain – the State Department's account confirms that he 'stress[ed] at length how the attitude of the United Kingdom was the key to the problem' – it is curious that the Churchill government was left to discover the nature of US plans via a combination of American press comment and Antipodean sharing.[4] However, a cable from Dulles to Ambassador Winthrop Aldrich in London on 1

April shows that indirection was probably deliberate. Dulles had been 'disappointed at Eden's attitude' at Berlin in pressing for the Geneva conference, while the British in general still could not grasp that 'if Indochina goes' the rest of Southeast Asia 'will be directly threatened'. Dulles intended to talk 'very frankly to Australians and New Zealanders here regarding problem ... in hope they will press British to stand firmly with us'. From this, it would seem that Dulles preferred not to put united action version #2, intervention in Vietnam, to the Churchill government until he was sure that the Australians and New Zealanders were 'willing to urge the British in the right direction'.[5] In the event, both the Canberra and Auckland governments were consumed by indecision. Fearful of offending the Americans, on whom their external security rested, they were equally concerned to maintain good relations with Britain.[6] A few days later, an impatient Dulles had to 're-emphasise' to Spender and Munro 'his hope' that they would 'use their influence' with the UK 'to secure its adhesion to the coalition', but Australia and New Zealand continued to avoid committing themselves one way or the other until the UK had pronounced.[7]

Eisenhower was also calculating in his handling of the British. In instructing Dulles to prepare a letter to Churchill on united action, he insisted that it be framed 'on a personal basis to be sure he sees it' rather than on an official basis lest it be routed to Eden whose opposition to US plans, on past form, was anticipated.[8] After altering the State Department draft to reflect his own instincts and writing style, Eisenhower dispatched the message a little before midnight, Washington time, on 4 April. Earlier that evening, White House aide Sherman Adams tells us, the President confided to his inner circle his readiness 'to send American forces to Indo-China under certain strict conditions', most notably 'joint action with the British'.[9]

In his letter, Eisenhower revealed to Churchill his fear that regardless of the outcome at Dien Bien Phu, the French might not fight on for long. But no matter how Vietnam succumbed to communism – on the battlefield or at the negotiating table – 'the ultimate effect on our and your global strategic position ... would be disastrous'. Laos, Cambodia, Thailand, Burma and Indonesia would follow Vietnam into the communist fold, the danger to Malaya would be 'direct', and Australia and New Zealand would be imperilled. Robbed of essential trade outlets in Southeast Asia, Japan would look to the China market at the risk of absorption into the communist bloc via politico-economic osmosis. To insure against these calamitous consequences, Eisenhower felt that 'serious and far-reaching decisions' were needed. Since there was no conceivable negotiated solution which could guarantee Indochina's non-communist future, there was little point looking to Geneva for deliverance. He then invoked the agonizing reappraisal: if united action failed to materialize, US public and Congressional opinion might ask questions about America's involvement in the NATO 'cooperative system'.[10]

Turning to practicalities, Eisenhower argued that the objective for America and its allies must be to persuade the Chinese to end their support for the Vietminh while increasing Western support for the French. This could be done by building a 'coalition composed of nations which have a vital concern in the checking of Communist expansion'. The United States 'would expect to play its full part' in such a combination. He went on:

The important thing is that the coalition must be strong and it must be willing to join the fight if necessary. I do not envisage the need of any appreciable ground forces on your part. If the members of the alliance are sufficiently resolute it should be able to make clear to the Chinese Communists that the continuation of their material support to the Viet Minh will inevitably lead to the growing power of the forces arrayed against them … If we grasp this one together I believe that we will enormously increase our chances of bringing the Chinese to believe that their interests lie in the direction of a discreet disengagement. In such a contingency we could approach the Geneva conference with the position of the free world not only unimpaired but strengthened.[11]

Here was confirmation, albeit in a personal communication from President to Prime Minister, that the Americans contemplated united action in the form of military intervention in Vietnam. So what had happened to Dulles's China focus? Or was united action to be effectuated on two fronts, China and Vietnam, at the same time? For now, Eisenhower was less interested in details than in securing Churchill's support for the principle of taking a stand. In pursuit of this, he balanced the stick of the agonizing reappraisal with the carrot of American help to defend Hong Kong, a long-standing British objective. He also played on the Prime Minister's vanity and sense of himself as the great anti-appeaser of the 1930s. 'If I may refer again to history, we failed to halt Hirohito, Mussolini and Hitler by not acting in unity and in time. That marked the beginning of many years of stark tragedy and desperate peril. May it not be that our nations have learned something from the lesson?' Closing, the President offered to send Dulles to London to fast-track coalition-building.[12]

Even shorn of its carefully calibrated cajolery, a personal presidential appeal like this would normally have elicited what Eisenhower sought, namely Churchill's support on grounds of Anglo-American solidarity. But these were not normal circumstances, they were thermonuclear circumstances, and so Churchill – who was 'more worried by the hydrogen bomb than by all the rest of my worries put together' – held back.[13] Fear of the H-bomb in Britain and Western Europe, the Americans were coming to see, was not only widespread but an increasingly destabilizing phenomenon. 'Some feel the British Isles could be wiped out, and so they better make a deal on the best terms possible with the Russians,' Dulles told Lewis Strauss, Chairman of the Atomic Energy Commission, on the day (29 March) he delivered his united action speech. 'Something needed to be done to moderate [the] wave of hysteria' which was 'driving our Allies away from us. They think we are getting ready for a war of this kind. We could survive but some of them would be obliterated in a few minutes'.[14]

Strauss, ironically, added to the panic in the United States and abroad when he went on to tell a news conference in Washington on 31 March that a hydrogen bomb could be made 'as large as you wish, as large as the military requirement demands'. A single bomb could 'destroy a city', New York, for instance.[15] Appalled, the Eisenhower administration rushed out a clarification – only the island of Manhattan would be devastated and not, as Strauss implied, the New York metropolitan area with its 3,500 square miles – but the damage was done. 'H-BOMB CAN WIPE OUT ANY CITY' ran the banner headline in the *New York Times* the next day, the overture to similar headlines in the UK press.[16] In light of the scale of H-bomb anxiety in Britain, Eisenhower's appeal to Churchill to back united action, a scheme which risked conflict with China and a nuclearized Soviet Union, could hardly have been worse timed. By a further chronological irony, the President's letter reached Downing Street on 5 April, just as the Prime Minister was heading to the House of Commons for a full-dress debate on the H-bomb called by the opposition in response to public panic over thermonuclear developments.

Opening the debate, Labour leader Clement Attlee, sensitive to the mood of the country, adopted a non-partisan, statesman-like tone. Churchill, in contrast, replied with a highly politicized attack on the previous Labour (Attlee) government for its failure to maintain the wartime nuclear agreements he had reached with President Roosevelt. One of these, the 1943 Quebec agreement, embodied the principle of mutual US-UK consent to the use of weapons of mass destruction. Conservative MPs sat in embarrassed silence as their leader was drowned out by Labour boos and catcalls. Lord Woolton, the Conservative Party Chairman, witnessed the debate from the Peers' Gallery. Churchill, he concluded, was 'out of touch with what the country, and indeed the world, wants from him'.[17]

Also watching was the US Ambassador. It had been a painful spectacle, Aldrich cabled Dulles the next day, with implications which went far beyond the H-bomb. Editorials in that morning's *Times* and *Manchester Guardian* were representative of 'thoughtful feeling of great part of country' in expressing concern about the impact of the debate on Anglo-American relations. Divested of its Tories-versus-Labour political content, Aldrich felt that the argument came down to the degree to which the UK felt able to go along with the United States on major international issues which carried a risk of war.[18]

Indochina was a very live case in point. In view of public nervousness arising from the New Look, massive retaliation, the H-bomb, the *Lucky Dragon* and fallout, would – or could – the Churchill government endorse united action? In Washington, Dulles was 'distressed' at the 'position in which Churchill had been placed' in parliament and prey to 'apprehension that this … might make it difficult for the United Kingdom to commit itself to a firm decision in the immediate future'.[19] Churchill's perfunctory two-line reply to Eisenhower's letter, sent to the White House on the morrow of the H-bomb debate, did little to ease this concern. 'I have received your most important message … We are giving it earnest Cabinet consideration.' The Prime Minister did, however, accept the offer of a Dulles visit to London.[20]

As it prepared for the US Secretary of State – he would fly in on 11 April – the Foreign Office remained unsure as to what exactly united action entailed. To judge from Eisenhower's letter to Churchill, US thinking was either evolving rapidly (with intervention in Vietnam in process of superseding a warning to and action against China) or else it was being made on the hoof. Of the two possibilities, the latter seemed as likely as the former. A full week after Dulles announced united action, Makins was complaining that the State Department had still not given much thought to 'procedure'.[21] But just as the Foreign Office was beginning to think that China was no longer the primary focus of united action, Dulles told the House Foreign Affairs Committee on 5 April that ongoing indirect PRC assistance to the Vietminh should be considered an act of aggression. China, he indicated, was 'getting awful close' to the kind of behaviour that would justify a US-led military response.[22]

President Eisenhower, meanwhile, continued to decry the idea of unilateral US intervention, his strength of feeling inadvertently adding to the UK's importance as a maker or breaker of united action. Late on the evening of 4 April, the French government conveyed to Washington a fraught request for US air support at Dien Bien Phu. Having consulted Navarre (whose initial worries about a violent PRC reaction had been attenuated by the seriousness of the garrison's position), Laniel was anxious to move quickly.[23] Coalitions and long-range plans for Southeast Asian security were all well and good, the French pointed out, but the immediate priority was to save the garrison. The Laniel government duly proposed that US bombers should target Vietminh artillery, anti-aircraft batteries and supply lines at Dien Bien Phu. In making his appeal, Laniel did not fail to mention that Radford had encouraged Ely to believe that a presidential go-ahead was a formality.[24]

Having just written to Churchill emphasizing *united* action, Eisenhower was obliged to revisit *unilateral* intervention. Notwithstanding Radford's alleged role in events, the President told Dulles in an early morning telephone call on 5 April that he would not 'risk our prestige' in what threatened to be a 'defeat' at Dien Bien Phu. Besides, without Congressional support, intervention 'would be completely unconstitutional & indefensible'.[25] Later that day in Paris, US Ambassador Dillon informed Bidault that the French appeal – which Dulles labelled 'hysterical' – had been rejected at 'the highest level'. The Frenchman was crestfallen. The 'time for formulating coalitions has passed', he commented. France's future in Indochina depended on the outcome at Dien Bien Phu and he 'prayed God they would be successful'.[26]

The President's unilateralist animus was also on show when the National Security Council met on 6 April. Amongst the tabled papers was an eye-opening NSC Planning Board estimate of US force levels if it came to intervention – 35,000 naval and 5,600 air personnel backed by an undetermined number of ground troops. These figures were based on the assumption that tactical battlefield atomic weapons would be available for use. If this nuclear dimension was ruled out, force levels would increase substantially.[27] The Council itself began by discussing the likely Chinese reaction to any US/Allied military involvement in Indochina, with the CIA predicting 'a better than fifty percent chance' of PRC counter-intervention. Radford, however, supported by Defense Secretary Wilson, was less interested in Chinese hypotheticals than in the existing military situation. With the PAVN pressing hard at Dien Bien Phu and Vietminh infiltration of the Red River delta an ongoing problem, he said that remedial military action was urgently needed. Sensing where the Admiral was going, Eisenhower interjected to say that there was 'no possibility whatever of US unilateral intervention … and we had best face that fact'. Dulles, agreeing, reminded the meeting that it was 'hopeless' to expect Congressional support unless united action was made flesh. He then gave colleagues an update on his efforts in this regard; on the plus side, Australia and New Zealand were 'disposed to try to join with us' and he was confident that Thailand and the Philippines would also 'come along'; on the negative side, the UK was being 'most difficult'. The uproar in the UK over the H-bomb had not helped:

The British Government was at present in the doldrums. Prime Minister Churchill had almost collapsed in Parliament during the debate on the hydrogen bomb. The paralysis of the British Government was almost as serious as that of the French. Despite all these difficulties ... [he] would not exclude the possibility that the British would come along with us. For one thing, the danger to Malaya would be considerable if the British do not agree to do something to defend Indochina. For another, the British would have to anticipate heavy pressure from Australia and New Zealand, whose interests and security were heavily involved.[28]

Dulles either misjudged the British or was overly reliant on the skewed assessment of London's attitude given to him by the pro-American Makins. Leaving aside Churchill's parliamentary ordeal, the UK government possessed a clear, thought-out position on Indochina based on opposition to coalition-building and military action before Geneva and support during the conference for a settlement based on partition of Vietnam. This was not paralysis. Dulles also exaggerated the extent of Australian and New Zealand support for US policy, but being ignorant of *Ringlet* and *Irony*, his puzzlement at the Churchill government's confidence that Malaya would hold is understandable. Overall, Dulles was hopeful about the prospects for united action, but he cautioned that if the United States 'failed to get results in its efforts to build up a regional grouping, it would certainly be necessary to contemplate armed intervention', a remark which hinted that the Secretary of State, if not the President, was prepared in extremis to embrace unilateralism. For now, the priority was to organize a coalition ahead of the Geneva conference, an imperative which brought Dulles back to the 'crucial importance' of Britain:

If we can get the United Kingdom to line up with us throughout Asia in resistance to Communism, and if the United Kingdom is prepared to risk the loss of Hong Kong in order to save Malaya, all of this might prove to be the beginning of a real United States policy in Asia. We have in fact lacked such a policy largely because the United Kingdom had proved consistently unwilling to go along with us on any significant policies or objectives in Asia. The chance may now be at hand, at long last, to win the British over to our side. The peril in Southeast Asia might forge the needed unity because the British stake in Malaya is so great and because Britain's two children, Australia and New Zealand, are likewise imperilled. If the British come in now they will gain assets for their position in Australia and New Zealand. If they do not, Britain will lose its remaining influence in the ANZUS countries ... It was also a means of compelling the British and some of the others to re-examine their colonial policy, which had proved so ruinous to our objectives, not only in Asia, but in Egypt, Iran, and elsewhere. The effort to compel these changes could, of course, have the effect of tearing the free world coalition to pieces. Nevertheless, we could not go on forever avoiding these great issues. The peoples of the colonial states would never agree to fight Communism unless they were assured of their freedom.

Dulles ended with the agonizing reappraisal. If the UK and France refused to cooperate, 'we might have to recognize that [they] were solely European powers'. In that case, 'the United States would be required to make a complete reappraisal of its entire basic policy respecting the free world coalition'. According to the NSC minute-taker, at this, a 'temporary silence' descended.[29]

Again, some comment is in order from the British perspective. Firstly, in *Ringlet* and *Irony*, the Churchill government believed it had some chance of defending Malaya without risking Hong Kong. Second, policymakers would have been nonplussed by the suggestion that the UK had been 'consistently unwilling' to go along with the United States in Asia. To the contrary, since 1950 multiple British approaches to the Americans to participate in a collective defence arrangement in Southeast Asia had been rebuffed. Third, Dulles evidently resented the UK's refusal to derecognize the PRC and actively support Nationalist China to bring its China policy into line with that of the United States. He also seemed incapable of conceding that the British approach might possess certain virtues. Finally, the Churchill government would have been outraged by the implication that its colonial policy was somehow on a par with that of France, especially in regard to Malaya where, unlike the French in Indochina, the UK had pledged to bestow full independence once the communist insurgency was quelled.

As the meeting drew to its close, the President's Special Advisor, Robert Cutler, echoing Radford's earlier point, suggested that all the attention being given to coalition-building and regional security was ridiculously futuristic considering the gravity of the immediate communist threat to Vietnam. Wilson agreed. The Pentagon, he said, was 'very concerned' that the military situation was 'moving with great rapidity in the wrong direction'. Eisenhower, however, sought to end the meeting where he began it by declaring 'with great conviction' that the United States on its own 'could not intervene in Indochina and become the colonial power which succeeded France'. At the same time, he admitted that the implications of the loss of Vietnam for the rest of Southeast Asia left the United States 'directly behind the 8-ball'. There were 'certain areas' of the world where 'we cannot afford to let Moscow gain another bit of territory', and Dien Bien Phu 'may be just such a critical point'. Once again, the President had voiced the contradiction inherent in his own and wider US thinking. Alarmed by the consequences that could flow from a Vietminh-dominated Vietnam, he and others (though not Radford) feared to take the military action required to shore up the cornerstone of Southeast Asia's security unless America's allies shared the effort and the consequences. But if Vietnam was worth saving, how could the United States avoid becoming involved militarily and if necessary unilaterally?[30]

As a codicil to this important discussion we should note the absence of any NSC interest in the Geneva conference and negotiations as an alternative method of crisis management. In a report tabled at the meeting, the Smith committee recommended that the United States oppose any political settlement and continue to seek 'military victory'.[31] For his part, Dulles declared Geneva a 'phoney' and stressed that if he went to Switzerland at all, he would be 'back in a week'.[32] In London on 6 April, Aldrich called at the Foreign Office to convey directly to Eden the administration's view that 'any settlement negotiated in the immediate future could only result in ultimate complete control of all Indo-China by the Communists'. What Washington wanted was 'the strong support of the United Kingdom' for united action. Aldrich also revealed that the French had requested American air intervention at Dien Bien Phu. Perplexed, Eden thanked him for the information, but the next day, to the Foreign Secretary's relief, the French Embassy confirmed that the request had been turned down.[33] This maladroit manoeuvre by Aldrich struck Eden as 'US diplomacy at its worst' and strengthened his commitment to the Geneva process. At one level, the prospect of negotiations operated as a potential brake on American-led military action; at another level, the actuality of negotiations offered the prospect of ending the war in Indochina and preserving peace in Southeast Asia.[34]

Over the next few days, the Eisenhower administration's disdain for Geneva grew so blatant that an editorial in the *Times* admonished the Americans for their 'premature and imprudent' expectation that the conference must 'fail'.[35] Whether or not the editorial was inspired by Eden – who was close to Iverach McDonald, the paper's Foreign Editor – it certainly reflected his views. When the UK High Commission in New Delhi reported that the Indian government was 'reluctant to believe that Americans are definitely out to wreck Geneva conference', Eden underlined the words 'reluctant to believe' and added in the margin of the telegram: 'But Why[?].'[36] The Eisenhower administration's negativity even reached Dien Bien Phu. There, amidst the mud, blood and gore, one of the garrison's doctors, Lieutenant Sauveur Verdaguer, wrote to his wife that 'for all sorts of reasons, it's high time this ended'. The only problem was that 'these fucking Americans want to torpedo the Geneva Conference'.[37]

At 11.00 am on 7 April, the Churchill Cabinet met to decide a response to American proposals – or, rather, to respond to what ministers currently understood American proposals to be. Intervention in Vietnam was presently the subject of intense conjecture in the US press and on Capitol Hill, was the object of the recent (abortive) French approach to the Washington, and had featured prominently in Eisenhower's personal letter to Churchill of 5 April. Eden, however, presented the Cabinet with a memorandum focused on the only aspect of united action which the Americans had so far conveyed directly to the UK government via normal politico-diplomatic channels, the China option.

In some respects, Eden's paper noted, Dulles's New York speech was a welcome (if overdue) show of US interest in Southeast Asia's security. As such, united action might yet provide a springboard for the relaunch of British designs for an Asian NATO to 'remove the anomaly of our exclusion from ANZUS' and enhance the security of Hong Kong and Malaya. That, though, was for the future. In the present, Eden had 'grave misgivings' about building a coalition and issuing warnings ahead of Geneva insofar as Beijing was bound to interpret these moves negatively and probably boycott – and so wreck – the conference. The 'fundamental weakness' of the US plan was the 'assumption' that the PRC could be intimidated into abandoning Ho Chi Minh. 'There is a distinction between warning China that some specified further action will entail retaliation, which might be an effective deterrent, and calling upon her to desist from action in which she is already engaged.' Eden found it hard to see what threat would be sufficiently potent to make China 'swallow so humiliating a rebuff ... without any face-saving concession in return'. And what would happen if the Chinese dismissed a warning? The answer, presumably, was that the coalition would have to 'withdraw ignominiously or else embark on warlike action against China'.[38]

During the Korean War, Eden's memorandum continued, the Chiefs of Staff had concluded that bombing China would be militarily ineffective even when combined with a naval blockade of the Chinese coast. In the current Indochinese context, this action would be worse than ineffective: it would give China 'every excuse for invoking the Sino-Soviet Treaty and might thus lead to a world war'. The time for a warning was later, Eden argued. If Geneva produced a settlement based on partition of Vietnam, the Chinese might be told that any attempt to upset the peace would be met with retaliation. This would be 'far more likely both to deter China and to be acceptable to British (and French) public opinion'. The paper ended with a reiteration of united action's one redeeming attraction: for the first time, the United States seemed genuinely interested in participating in a security system in Southeast Asia. For that reason, Eden recommended making known to the Americans the UK's doubts about the wisdom of military action ahead of Geneva while simultaneously expressing interest in a defence organization as a contribution to regional stability.[39]

For many years, the only account of this meeting available to historians was the carefully moderated official minutes prepared by Cabinet Secretary Norman Brook.[40] With the release of Brook's original handwritten record, however, we can now access ministerial opinions omitted from the printed minutes. For example, the extent of Churchill's nervousness at the thought that the Americans 'might go it alone' in Vietnam 'if we don't go along with them' becomes much clearer. At a moment of acute thermonuclear unease in Britain, the Prime Minister feared that a war with China, if it led in turn to general war with the USSR, 'would expose us to awful danger'. As for Eden, he was clearly cognizant of Britain's power of veto over US plans:

> AE: Declaration won't hearten French or frighten China. And Russia might take it as excuse for not coming to Geneva. I don't want any declaration before Geneva – tho' we should make a plan. Two telegrams just received from Spender [Australian Ambassador to Washington]. He says Dulles stressed Key position of U.K. Has met Congressional leaders: satisfied Congress would support Dulles' plan but not unless U.K. would join in direct military help to Indo-China. U.S. would have to re-consider plan if U.K. wouldn't join.

With Dulles due in London in a few days' time, Eden framed the dilemma facing the government in bald terms: 'If he comes, and we can't accept his plan, US/UK cooperation will be injured. But if we accept it, it kills Geneva.'[41] After the meeting, Churchill wrote again to Eisenhower begging for more time before delivering a final verdict on united action. The issue 'raises many problems for us', he explained, 'and I am sure you will not expect us to give a hurried decision'.[42] Reading between the lines, Eisenhower concluded that 'the British had little enthusiasm for joining us in taking a firm position'.[43]

As agreed in Cabinet, the Foreign Office began preparing a modified version of US proposals to put to Dulles. Drafted by Allen, the emergent paper recommended that no warning be issued to China and no defence organization be pursued prior to Geneva. After the conference, planning for a Southeast Asian version of NATO could proceed apace. Even then, however, should the Americans continue to favour a warning to

China, it should not be generalized but focused specifically on safeguarding whatever compromise had been reached at Geneva. Allen worked on the assumption that the Indochina War would end in the partition of Vietnam and that the southern half of the country, together with Laos and Cambodia, would be candidates for membership of a defence pact. Thailand, too, should be brought in to make implementation of *Ringlet* and *Irony* easier in an emergency. As for the present situation in Vietnam, although Dien Bien Phu seemed doomed, neither the Foreign Office nor the Chiefs of Staff expected a general French collapse before the Geneva conference. Accordingly, the coalition envisaged by the Americans was not to be regarded as 'a temporary expedient to meet the present emergency in Indo-China but a lasting alliance for the defence of our common interests', and not just in Southeast Asia but across the wider Asian spectrum, including Hong Kong. Crucially, the 'terms of this alliance should not involve the commitment of United States or British ground forces to Indo-China'.[44]

On 7 April, Eden cabled Makins complaining about the 'haphazard' way the US administration was approaching the crisis and advising the Ambassador to be careful in his dealings with the State Department to avoid committing the government to anything remotely resembling 'joint action'.[45] Disturbed by this message, Makins responded with a series of telegrams in which he attempted to explain the 'cross-currents' of US thinking which had 'confused and probably irritated' the Foreign Secretary. The main problem was the extent to which improvisation was driving US crisis management, with the decision to launch united action taken 'at the top level … before the ways and means of executing this decision either on the political or on the military side had been worked out'. When America's allies raised difficulties, Dulles was forced to do 'a certain amount of rationalising' and he was now thinking less in terms of a warning to China than in building an ad hoc coalition which, by its mere existence, would demonstrate allied unity and hopefully deter the PRC from maintaining its aid to the Vietminh. Makins trusted that Eden would not allow the inconsistencies in US thinking 'to prejudice your consideration of an extremely important decision of the American Administration to extend their world responsibilities'.[46]

The Ambassador also thought that Dulles would be 'open to argument' on methods and procedure, but he would want to know – and in advance of Geneva – whether the UK would 'accept the substance' of the US plan for united action. In addition to coalition-building, Dulles sought a common negotiating position, to prevent 'Communist success at the conference table', and wanted to examine ways to retrieve the military situation in Vietnam 'by air and naval action' (though this action would probably be taken after Geneva). The US Secretary did not want to have a 'totally useless trip'. Rather, he sought advance assurance that 'you were not going to turn him down … [H]e thinks we have reached a turning point in our affairs' and from 'a psychological point of view' there was 'some risk in this visit unless you are prepared to entertain the substance of his proposals favourably'.[47]

There is no record of Eden's immediate reaction to these telegrams. However, based on what we know of his thinking, he would surely have agreed with the assessment of his Southeast Asia advisors that Dulles not only had 'a queer way of framing policy and conducting diplomacy' but that the reconfigured US plan was 'only slightly less obnoxious than before'.[48]

In the lead-up to Dulles's visit, the talk on Capitol Hill was all about Vietnam and the disappointing attitude of America's allies. Senate majority leader William Knowland was particularly outspoken. 'We cannot have an effective system of collective security if some of these nations that have received our help want to stand on the sidelines now that the chips are down and let this nation assume the burden alone.' If the British and others wished to delay taking a position on united action until the outcome of Geneva was known, Knowland suggested that Congress in turn should hold off approving appropriations for NATO. In the Foreign Office, officials had one word for this juxtaposition: 'Blackmail'.[49]

The Eisenhower administration could not ignore Congressional opinion, but it could – and did – seek to shape it to its own ends. On 10 April, Makins reported to the Foreign Office that the US government's 'campaign to create an atmosphere in which Congress and the public could be brought to accept increased American participation in the war in Indo-China … is making remarkable headway'. There had still been 'no public hint' of precise plans, but many Americans were 'convinced' that intervention was coming. James Cable in the Foreign Office's Southeast Asia Department, noting the administration's 'striking' efforts to prepare the domestic ground for military action, observed drolly that 'Mr. Dulles will no doubt tell us he is only acting under pressure from public opinion'.[50]

The best-known example of opinion-forming occurred on 7 April when Eisenhower used his weekly news conference to enunciate the 'falling domino' principle. Vietnam was posited as the trigger domino whose fall to communism would set off a chain reaction taking in the other countries of Southeast Asia, endangering America's 'island defensive chain' of Japan, Taiwan and the Philippines, and threatening Australia and New Zealand. Add to this the surrender of millions of people to communism and the accretion of economic and industrial strength to the Sino-Soviet bloc that would come from unfettered access to Southeast Asia's natural resources, and it became plain, Eisenhower said, why the 'possible consequences of the loss are just incalculable to the free world'.[51]

Within the administration, Radford did not need domino metaphors to tell him what was at stake. Remembered by Eisenhower as 'a man of tough conviction', Radford remained the most ardent proponent of US military action in Vietnam, if needs be unilaterally and if necessary with nuclear weapons.[52] The same day that the President unveiled the domino theory, Radford sent an emissary, US Navy Captain George Anderson, to talk in secrecy to the State Department's Doug MacArthur. According to military assessments, Anderson said, 'three tactical A-weapons, properly employed' would 'smash' the Vietminh at Dien Bien Phu. His chief, Radford, wanted to know whether State would agree to atomic weapons being so employed in the context of US intervention. MacArthur could not vouch for Dulles, but speaking personally, he felt that the matter 'raised … very serious questions affecting the whole position of US leadership in the world'. He also doubted that the French would agree. Even making an approach to Paris was dangerous in that it was bound to leak and cause 'a great hue and cry throughout the parliaments of the free world', especially amongst the NATO powers, 'notably the UK'. If the Chinese intervened directly, 'that would be a different matter'. Further than this MacArthur refused to go. Nor do Dulles and Radford appear to have had an opportunity to discuss the subject with one another before the Secretary of State left for London.[53]

MacArthur was right. Any suggestion that the United States was seriously considering atomic options would have shocked the British whose nuclear anxieties showed no signs of abating. At the end of March, the White House approved the public release of the US Atomic Energy Commission's (AEC) film of the 1952 Ivy-Mike test. On 8 April, a *Pathé* newsreel entitled 'H-bomb', a six-minute distillation of the longer AEC version, began showing in cinemas around the UK. Over the following three weeks – the high tide of the intervention crisis in Vietnam – moviegoers were treated to jaw-dropping footage of thermonuclear destruction. 'Mike was power, the kind of titanic energy released by stars,' the commentary boasted. At one point, in unintentional homage to Strauss, a silhouette of the Manhattan skyline was transposed over the Ivy-Mike fireball. A hydrogen bomb dropped on any other comparable-sized city – London, for instance – would achieve an identical result: 'complete, utter, absolute annihilation'. For many people in Britain, in and out of government, the AEC footage was not just an historical record of an American scientific achievement but an omen of what might be in store for them if general war broke out.

Before we turn to the Dulles visit to London, it needs to be emphasized that while the British were critical to the future of united action, the French also occupied a pivotal position. This may sound like a statement of the obvious but the literature on the war does not always acknowledge how critical it was to US plans that the French Expeditionary Corps kept on fighting, even if disaster overtook Dien Bien Phu, and that the French government resisted the siren songs of a negotiated settlement during the time it took to put together a united action coalition. The problem for the Eisenhower administration was that these essentials were by no means shared by the Laniel government. On 7 April, Bidault contacted Dulles to say that in view of the French public's emotional investment in the outcome at Dien Bien Phu, never mind the actual military investment, defeat would make it very difficult for France to continue the war 'even with full American military support'. If the battle was lost, Bidault said he would do his best to resist the clamour in France for immediate FEC evacuation, and he would 'never negotiate with Ho-Chi-Minh'. But Dulles needed to understand that his viewpoint was increasingly out of kilter with wider public and even governmental opinion.[54]

Dulles was not pleased by this news. The United States was doing all it could to meet French needs short of active belligerency, he cabled Dillon in Paris. Now, in the wake of the US rejection of the French appeal for air support, the Laniel government was trying to 'place upon us responsibility if Dien Bien Phu should fall'. Dulles hoped that Bidault's remarks were no more than the 'hasty reflex of a deeply harassed man'. If not, Dillon would have his work cut out in restoring to the French 'a sense of perspective which the times require'.[55] Dulles still believed that a French military collapse in Indochina generally was unlikely before the rains set in. Even if Dien Bien Phu succumbed, the defenders would still have done serious damage to Giap's army. The real danger 'the bad situation in Paris'.[56]

The next day (8 April) the Laniel government again pressed for US military intervention. United action was welcomed as an 'indication of increased solidarity between the United States and France', the French Ambassador in Washington, Henri Bonnet, told Dulles. But the 'immediate problem is the outcome of the battle for Dien Bien Phu'. As for negotiations, French public opinion set great store by Geneva and, in consequence, there was concern that the construction of a coalition might 'jeopardize in advance the chances of obtaining peace'. Dulles struggled to contain his annoyance. The French attitude was based on the 'fallacy' that to get something out of Geneva they must go to the conference in a weak position, he countered, whereas US policy was designed to allow France to negotiate from strength. When Bonnet repeated that precipitate moves on united action would turn Geneva into a 'farce', Dulles reached for the agonizing reappraisal. 'If it became necessary for the US to base its defenses on the shores of this country – all right,' he snapped. 'The French were apparently afraid if we all stood together. But it was crazy to think that the US would be drawn into a war … to save one outpost such as Dien Bien Phu.'[57]

On 9 April, Laniel spoke in the French National Assembly. 'Two imperatives dictate our attitude at present', he declared; 'first of all, to make every effort to hold out at Dien Bien Phu and with the aid of our allies maintain our military effort; next to undertake in complete freedom the conversations at Geneva so that they may achieve the results which we are seeking, namely a peace which will respect the interests of the peoples [concerned].'[58] Later that day in London, Massigli, acting on Bidault's instructions, handed Eden a detailed account of Bonnet's meeting with Dulles. After reading it, Eden observed that UK and French 'minds were working on parallel lines' in wanting to make a success of Geneva. The same could not be said for Anglo-American minds and lines.[59]

*

On 10 April, Dulles arrived at Washington airport for his flight to London. As he prepared to board his aircraft, he told reporters that the spread of communism in Southeast Asia could be arrested only if 'all of the free peoples who are now threatened unite against the threat'. In Vietnam, the administration's 'purpose is not to extend the fighting, but to end the fighting … [It] is not to prevent a peaceful settlement at the forthcoming Geneva Conference, but to create the unity of free wills needed to assure a peaceful settlement.' In going to Europe, he was embarking on 'a mission of peace through strength'.[60] Dulles then asked Makins, who had gone to the airport to wish him bon voyage, to cable ahead to London to tell Eden that he had 'never' had in mind a 'verbal warning to the Chinese'. Rather, he wanted to build a coalition which, by its very existence, would send a clear message to the PRC, 'just as the formation of NATO had been a warning to the Russians' in 1949. He wished to insure against 'continuing misunderstanding' on this point.[61]

So there it was. The issue which had so disturbed the British for the previous twelve days had, it seemed, been a non-issue. Then again, the UK government had not been alone in its reading (or mis-reading) of US policy. For Richard Casey, Australia's Foreign Minister, it was evident that the Americans had favoured a 'stern warning' to the PRC which, he felt, would make the Chinese 'resentful and irritable at Geneva, and might even tip them over the edge'.[62] As recently as 7 April, Eisenhower's press chief noted in his diary that 'Indo China really getting rough – Dulles been in touch with Ambassadors of UK, France, Australia, New Zealand, Philippines & Thailand to seek joint warning to Red China not to move in.'[63]

Perhaps Dulles's thinking evolved rapidly over the next three days so that by the time he spoke to Makins at the airport, a warning to China had disappeared as an option. In that case, why admit that it had ever existed in the first place? Whatever the truth of the matter, Dulles's inconsistency did nothing to eliminate the suspicion in London that with Radford on the loose, Communist China, not the Vietminh, was the real target of American plans.

9

'He Lied to Me', April 1954

Dulles arrived in London on Palm Sunday, 11 April 1954. Following dinner that evening at the American Embassy, the British and American foreign ministers had the first of what were destined to be difficult and subsequently much disputed discussions on Indochina. It was becoming clear, Dulles began, that the French 'could no longer deal with the situation' in Vietnam, 'either politically or militarily on the present basis and on their own resources'. If their position collapsed and all of Indochina was lost, the consequences for Southeast Asia would be grave. The battle at Dien Bien Phu was entering its 'crucial phase'. A French defeat could hasten FEC disengagement or bring about a dangerous politico-diplomatic compromise with the communists, perhaps both.[1]

The US Secretary went on to reveal that three weeks earlier, the Joint Chiefs of Staff had proposed intervention with naval and air forces (a falsification, both chronologically and insofar as only Radford was four-square behind military action). On reflection, the administration decided that it should not act alone, hence the call for united action. To proceed now, Dulles continued, two prerequisites must be fulfilled: first, the French needed to give the Associated States 'real independence'; second, there must be tangible proof that America's allies, 'especially the United Kingdom, Australia and New Zealand', took 'an equally grave view of the situation' and were prepared to act.[2]

Dulles then turned to what he called 'some public misconception' of his proposals. 'He had not had in mind the immediate issue of any warning statement directed specifically against China,' he explained. 'He had rather thought that the formation of an *ad hoc* coalition, which might eventually develop into a defense organization for South East Asia on the ANZUS or NATO model, would in itself constitute an effective deterrent against further Chinese intervention.' Dulles felt that

> only if some action of this kind were taken now, would it be possible to arrest the further deterioration of the situation in Indo-China and thus avoid having to deal with an even more serious situation later on. It was indispensable that the whole area should be denied to communism and, provided our united determination to achieve this was made clear at this stage, he did not think the result would be to provoke further Chinese intervention.

Such action would rather be 'a deterrent', Dulles averred. Moreover, 'the evidence of solidarity before the Geneva Conference could only have a good effect upon the negotiations there'.[3]

Responding, Eden delineated between the two aspects of the US plan. The first, which he welcomed for many reasons, including power-by-proxy, was collective security in Southeast Asia. The British government was ready to examine the practicalities of creating a defence organization, including membership; here, Eden felt it was 'particularly important' that India and the other Asian Commonwealth states, along with Burma and Indonesia, should not be 'deliberately excluded'. The second aspect of the American plan was what to do about Indochina. Because of the controversy which would flare over what had (or had not) been agreed in London, it is worth carefully noting Eden's words. 'If there were to be any question of Allied intervention, military or otherwise, or of any warning announcement before Geneva, that would require extremely careful consideration. It was doubtful whether the situation in Indo-China could be solved by purely military means and we must at least see what proposals, if any, the Communists had to make at Geneva.'[4]

In discussing the communiqué to be issued at the close of their talks, Eden suggested to Dulles that the text be limited to Indochina, in particular to what was happening at Dien Bien Phu, 'with a warning that we should not allow the prospects of the Geneva Conference to be prejudiced by military action'. He was 'doubtful about making any immediate mention of a decision to begin discussions about the possibility of concluding a South East Asia security arrangement if that were agreed upon'. These post-prandial exchanges ended in agreement that Allen and MacArthur would get together the next morning to draft the communiqué and map out a programme of action for realizing a regional defence system.[5]

To judge from the cable Dulles sent to Smith after this meeting, the UK Foreign Secretary got his viewpoint across reasonably effectively. 'Eden indicated a real willingness to consider defense arrangements in SE Asia on the basis of united action but he is obviously against implementation of any coalition prior to Geneva,' Dulles commented. 'I believe he would strongly and actively support such action if Geneva fails.' His overarching 'impression' was that the British were 'thinking not so much in terms of holding Indochina as in looking to possible arrangements for holding remainder of Southeast Asia if Vietnam goes'.[6] If the Americans had cause for disquiet, it centred on Eden's solicitousness towards Indian opinion, an adjunct of his interest in securing the widest possible Asian backing for a defence organization. Dulles had proposed the United States, UK, France, Australia, New Zealand, the Associated States, Thailand and the Philippines as founder members. In this formulation, Asian participation amounted to three French colonies and two American clients, a line-up that repelled Eden. But extending Asian involvement was itself problematic: the neocolonial nature of US relations with Thailand and the Philippines, to say nothing of French colonial primacy in Indochina, was off-putting to genuinely independent Asian nations; India, Burma, Sri Lanka and Indonesia were committed to Cold War neutrality, which ruled out involvement in any anti-Chinese construct; and Pakistan seemed more interested in joining the Middle East defence organization which the Western powers were presently developing. Nevertheless, going into the Dulles talks,

Eden's view vis-à-vis India and other Asian neutrals was that 'we ought to try to get them', if not as members then as benevolent supporters. Besides, to make any kind of success of the Indochina negotiations at Geneva, Eden knew that the good offices of India, the de facto leader of the non-aligned Asian bloc, would be critical.[7]

By contrast, the US government took a cynical view of the neutralism of 'Nehru and his tribe' – as Eisenhower referred the Indian Prime Minister Jawaharlal Nehru and his people – which to American eyes possessed a decidedly pro-Beijing bias.[8] This attitude was shared by the 'violently anti-Indian and ... anti-Nehru' Knowland and the Republican Old Guard.[9] Because US-Indian relations were 'very bad', the Commonwealth Relations Office cautioned the Foreign Office ahead of Dulles's arrival, the Americans were wont to accuse the UK of 'dragging our feet ... in South-East Asia because of far too tender a regard for Indian susceptibilities'.[10] This assessment was borne out during the Anglo-American talks at the US Embassy on 11 April. When Eden championed Indian involvement in Southeast Asian security, Dulles, whose dislike of Cold War neutralism was well known, countered by proposing pact membership for anti-communist states like Nationalist China, South Korea and even Japan. That, for the moment, shut Eden up.[11]

At the meeting of Anglo-American officials the next morning, MacArthur gave Allen a draft declaration of common purpose, limited for now to the United States and the UK but intended to have multi-nation applicability. The declaration asserted that the defence of the Associated States was vital to the security of Southeast Asia and the Western Pacific and called on the countries of the free world to 'combine their efforts' to deal with the communist danger.[12] Allen reacted negatively. The draft carried 'a commitment to clean up the Communists in Indochina' and he 'doubted that HMG could undertake such a course of action, at least until after efforts for settlement had been explored at Geneva'. In addition, the British Chiefs of Staff judged that 'such a commitment would involve sending forces, including ground troops into Indochina which, in turn, might result in an all-out war with China, possibly involving the use of atomic weapons ... In such circumstances world war might even result if the Soviets honoured their commitments under the Sino-Soviet Treaty'.[13]

When the principals met that afternoon, Dulles described the declaration as 'preliminary thoughts', but Eden still felt pressured. 'The [UK] Secretary of State', the British record notes, 'said that he could agree to no more than to engage in *preliminary* discussions on the *possibility* of forming a mutual security system [emphases added]'. Rebuffed, Dulles tried to pin Eden down on the communiqué. A first draft, prepared by Allen and the State Department's Livingston Merchant, committed the UK and the United States to examine 'the possibility of establishing a collective defence', a formula close to that which Eden had just adumbrated. However, timing was all-important. It would be 'difficult' for the UK government 'to give an undertaking in advance of the Geneva Conference regarding action to be taken subsequently', Eden explained.[14]

Changing tack again, Dulles suggested that in seeking to halt the spread of communism in Southeast Asia, surely 'Indo-China was the place for such intervention', a remark which further indicated that united action was predicated on fighting in Vietnam. According to Dulles, the deployment of air and naval forces might yet stave off a French military collapse, avoid a giveaway peace at Geneva and renew 'the possibility of victory'. The 'last thing the United States desired was involvement in Indo-China', he said, but it would be 'a greater evil not to make a stand in Indo-China now and to allow the whole area to crumble rapidly'. Dulles was 'confident' that if the necessary conditions were in place, Congress 'would authorise the President to use United States air and naval forces, and possibly even land forces'.[15]

This was clever diplomacy. Dulles played on the British desire for a regional defence organization in the post-Geneva period by setting as the price for US backing for this long-term UK goal a commitment from Eden to support military action in Vietnam in the present. No wonder the Foreign Secretary was studied in his reply. With Geneva drawing near, British public opinion 'would be firmly opposed to any present commitment to become involved in what was an unpopular war'. After Geneva, the position might be different. Still Dulles did not give up. Remarking that a widening of ANZUS had become 'desirable' and that its geographical scope might be extended to cover Malaya, in a single verbal swoop he erased three years of American opposition to two key British objectives. Eden, though, would not be shifted. In line with the advice of the Chiefs of Staff, he reiterated that military intervention in Vietnam could not be kept limited to air and naval action; hence in trying to solve the immediate problem, a larger and much more dangerous one might be created.[16]

The remainder of the meeting was given over to considering the make-up of a regional pact if or when it materialized. Eden remained keen to secure 'wider Asian membership', especially Indian adherence. Even if (as was likely) Nehru refused to participate, the invitation, in tandem with full Anglo-American disclosure of what was being planned, might deter India from denouncing the pact as a neocolonial construct. Dulles, however, preferred to launch the project with his original line-up of ten and feared that an 'open invitation' would lead to 'embarrassing requests' from Taiwan and South Korea to join the club.[17] While the British were 'obviously opposed to organizing united action prior to Geneva', the US Secretary cabled Washington afterwards, 'I think they have moved forward considerably as a result [of] our discussion', especially in terms of their willingness 'to state publicly' in the communiqué 'their readiness to examine possible collective defense measures'.[18]

Eden circulated a draft of the communiqué to a small gathering of Cabinet colleagues that evening. He had 'contrived' to insert 'an expression of hope that the Geneva conference would lead to the restoration of peace in Indo-China', he explained, and had 'excluded … any statement which might commit us to provide direct military assistance in Indo-China'. Eden further revealed that the United States was 'ready for the first time to accept a commitment to the defence of Malaya', and possibly Hong Kong, 'a notable advance'. The Americans seemed to think that Malaya could not be defended unless Vietnam held, and assumed that a promise of US help with Malaya, albeit under the aegis of ANZUS, would be matched by a UK promise to help with Vietnam. With *Ringlet* and *Irony* on the stocks, he had felt able to reject this linkage. Eden's colleagues commended his handling of the talks, but they also reminded him of the importance of maintaining UK-US 'solidarity in an area in which previously the Americans had shown some reluctance to become committed'.[19]

Eden, Dulles and their advisors met for a final time at the Foreign Office on the morning of 13 April to go over the communiqué. Britain and the United States, the final text ran, were 'ready to take part, with the other countries principally concerned, in an examination of the possibility of establishing a collective defence, within the framework of the Charter of the United Nations, to assure the peace, security and freedom of south-east Asia and the western Pacific'. This terminology represented a retreat by Dulles who had pressed for an examination of collective defence 'measures' only to be reined in by a nervous Eden who felt that such phrasing implied a commitment to action in Vietnam. The British preferred collective defence 'system' but the Americans objected to the inference that such a system should be put in place *before* united action was applied to Vietnam. In the end, the looser 'collective defence' bridged the divide. The communiqué also expressed the hope that Geneva would produce a peaceful settlement and that the 'unity of defensive purpose' of Britain, America and their partners would help ensure 'an honourable peace'.[20]

The question of which countries could be deemed 'principally concerned' with Indochina proved harder to resolve. Eden still insisted that 'every effort should be made to secure the co-operation of the Asian countries themselves'. Dulles demurred. It was his 'hope' that 'any indication that India was being invited would be avoided'. Far better to limit the plan to Southeast Asia, which meant confining consultations to Dulles's preferred ten (Australian and New Zealand involvement was justified by the communiqué's reference to the western Pacific). In the end, it was agreed that when Eden reported to parliament, he should say that membership required further consideration. As to 'next steps', the Foreign Secretary chose his words carefully: '*Possibly* it might be desirable *at some stage* to set up a working group of experts [emphases added].' Given what followed, it is right to italicize those conditionals.[21]

On more Vietnam-specific matters, Dulles, who was due to fly direct from London to Paris, proposed to make 'a great effort' to convince Laniel and Bidault of the 'capital importance' of granting full independence to the Associated States. With regard to Geneva, 'we should all show the greatest ingenuity in our search for means of enabling the Chinese to withdraw from Indo-China without serious loss of face', a remark which indicated that the Americans were still looking for a PRC climbdown. Finally, in an echo of his position at Berlin, Dulles objected to Indochina being discussed at Geneva until the four convening powers, the United States, UK, France and the USSR, had agreed amongst themselves which other countries were to be invited to take part in that phase of proceedings. Although China would attend the conference, Dulles was determined to avoid giving the impression that the negotiations in their Indochina form were a de facto five-power conference in which the PRC enjoyed a status of equality alongside the Berlin four. With this, the meeting, and Dulles's intense but seemingly productive sojourn in London, came to an end.[22]

On the afternoon of 13 April, Eden went to the House of Commons where he gave MPs an account of the discussions and read the text of the communiqué into Hansard. Attlee followed with comments broadly supportive of the government's position, but Labour left-wingers, led by Aneurin Bevan, condemned Eden's support for a regional pact as 'a surrender to American pressure' which Asian Commonwealth and Asian neutral opinion would resent as helping shore-up colonialism in Indochina. 'I do not regard my negotiations with the United States as a question of somebody always giving way to someone else', Eden retorted. The shared UK-US aim in Southeast Asia was to build 'something comparable to the NATO organisation that exists in Europe'. That said, there was no 'definite commitment' to bring a pact into being. The government had merely agreed to an examination of potentialities, an exploration which itself would be 'greatly influenced by what happens at Geneva'. Taking aim at critics who had predicted that the government would join with the US administration in 'some fulminating declaration' about China, Eden said that the merest glance at the communiqué would show 'that we are as anxious as they are – and perhaps more so – to see the Geneva Conference succeed'.[23]

Most of the British press, if not the Bevanites in parliament, thought that Eden had done a decent job of restraining the Americans. The 'urgency apparently felt by Mr. Dulles for some new gesture or statement of policy before the Geneva conference ... has not found so enthusiastic an echo in London', the *Times* commented. It was also clear that the countries of Southeast Asia 'are not to be stampeded into security before the Geneva conference has given the Chinese Communists a chance to show their intentions'.[24] This was also the view of the Foreign Office. 'The talks with Dulles went quite well', Shuckburgh recorded, 'and he settled for a much milder statement on S. E. Asia – *not* committing us to fight in Indo-China – than we had feared'.[25]

Dulles, meanwhile, flew on to Paris. At around the same time that Eden was addressing the House of Commons, the US Secretary was telling Bidault the news of the British government's readiness to enter into discussions on regional security. Without a show of allied unity, he explained, the US public and Congress might be reluctant to continue the presently high level of investment in the French war effort. United action would also prove to the Chinese that regardless of what happened in Indochina, Southeast Asia as a whole was off limits. Having said this, Dulles did not see the war as a lost cause. Nor, by extension, did he believe the French should settle at Geneva. Bidault listened carefully but was clearly distressed. Public disillusion was now so great that 'France must have an opportunity to negotiate an honourable peace', he told Dulles. The Laniel government had no intention of handing Vietnam over to the communists, but it could not survive politically if it gave the impression that it had decided in advance that negotiations would lead nowhere. It was from a desire to protect the diplomatic prospect that French ambivalence about US plans for a regional pact arose. Echoing Eden, the Frenchman argued that timing was the issue: 'We must give Geneva a chance and see what happens there.' If or when the conference failed, that would be the moment to look at area defence.[26]

Dulles met twice more with Bidault and once with Laniel during a 36-hour stay in the French capital. In these meetings he tantalized his hosts by holding out the possibility of US intervention in Vietnam as an alternative to diplomacy if the now familiar American conditions (the formation of a united action coalition and a French grant of full independence to the Indochinese) were fulfilled. Neither Laniel nor Bidault offered him satisfaction; hence the communiqué issued at the end of the talks confined itself to emphasizing how at Dien Bien Phu and elsewhere in Indochina the 'independence' of the Associated States was 'at stake'. The real meaning of the document was subtextual. There would be no united action, or at least no French support for united action, until the Geneva conference had run its course.[27]

As Dulles conferred with the French, Eden set down his thoughts in a telegram to Makins. He was keen 'to ensure that my own views are impressed on the United States Government before their own ideas harden'. Coming less than twenty-four hours after he had last spoken to his American counterpart, this was a little odd. Did Eden feel that the outcome of the London talks had somehow lacked precision? Or did he wish to ensure that an Ambassador known for his pro-American sympathies was apprised first-hand of his outlook? Either way, Eden asked Makins to stress three points in dealing with the State Department. First, that any collective defence arrangement should be a permanent structure not a contrivance to meet the present emergency; secondly, every effort should be made to bring along Asian opinion, especially the Asian Commonwealth and neutrals; and thirdly, any defence pact must be consonant with the UN Charter. With an eye to Geneva, Eden added that he was 'not convinced that no concession could be made to Communists in Indo-China without inevitably leading to Communist domination of the whole of South East Asia, particularly if we have the proposed security system'.[28]

This comment is revealing. Hitherto, British assessments of partition had been fatalistic in concluding that a communist Vietnam would be the ultimate – if temporarily delayed – outcome. For all that the Foreign Office wanted to give Geneva its head, officials had been uneasy about this "least bad" solution.[29] Now, prompted in part by Allen, the Foreign Secretary had alighted on a way to add durability to partition by making the proposed defence organization a guarantor of a settlement. Here was a pointer to the future, but the sequencing was critical; premature action in realizing regional security would not only jeopardize the chances of Geneva producing an agreement but would alienate India and wider Asian opinion.[30]

On 16 April – Good Friday – Makins, armed with Eden's instructions, met with Merchant at the State Department. Dulles had been 'generally well satisfied with his discussions in London' and wished to begin consultations on regional defence 'as soon as possible', Merchant said. To this end, the US administration planned to hold a briefing meeting on 20 April for Washington-based ambassadors from Dulles's proposed member states. 'I presume that I can agree to such a proposal', Makins cabled Eden.[31] He presumed too much. 'I feel very strongly that any such meeting … would be a grave mistake which could have very serious consequences at this time', was Eden's first reaction, penned on the copy of the Makins telegram couriered to him at his country home in Sussex where he was spending the Easter weekend. Returned to the Foreign Office for conveyance, Makins received the response the next day.[32]

Overnight, Eden's indignation swelled. On 17 April, he fired off two further telegrams to Makins. Declaring himself 'surprised' by the Dulles initiative, he insisted that 'we reached no definite agreement in London', either on the procedure for moving forward on collective defence or on membership. The summoning of an ambassadorial meeting might look innocent, 'yet the fact that this group has met so soon will inevitably attract the widest publicity, and the countries invited will be regarded as already formally constituting the organisation envisaged'. Aside from the fact that membership 'was expressly reserved in London', to call 'a mass meeting to meet Dulles before India has spoken', and before other Asian neutrals had been consulted, 'gives every pretext for criticism'. Worse still, summoning the ambassadors of Laos, Cambodia, Vietnam,

Thailand and the Philippines – colonial 'puppet' or US 'stooge' governments – while ignoring genuinely independent area states would be 'fatal to the whole plan'. In view of all this, Eden instructed Makins to have nothing to do with Dulles's meeting.[33]

After digesting the contents of these telegrams on Easter Sunday morning (18 April), Makins set off to the State Department. Meeting with Smith, he explained that he would not be attending the meeting two days hence. According to the report the Ambassador sent to Eden afterwards, Smith made no particular comment other than to undertake to put Dulles in the picture. The US record, in contrast, has Smith expressing 'amazement'.[34] Makins returned to Foggy Bottom that afternoon to see Dulles. Displaying considerable sangfroid, the US Secretary read aloud from the US record of the London discussions. This was 'unequivocal' in positing pact consultations in advance of Geneva, Makins told Eden. Dulles 'thought you were both agreed on procedure', namely to start with a small number of obvious candidate states, leaving the door open for wider accession in due course. Reluctantly, Dulles had to accept that this was not the case, but as invitations had been issued to the embassies concerned and the meeting was already generating press comment, cancellation would be embarrassing. In these circumstances, Dulles thought it best to announce a broadening of composition and turn the occasion into a general Geneva briefing. Those states making up the UN Command in Korea and not originally invited would be added to the list. The press would be informed that with time running out it made sense to discuss the Geneva conference en bloc rather than in smaller combinations. Makins 'strongly' recommended to Eden that he be permitted to take part in this reconstituted meeting.[35]

Eden dealt with the incoming cables from Washington on Easter Monday, 19 April. Both Allen and Shuckburgh, his closest advisors, had been given the Bank Holiday weekend off, while Kirkpatrick, the head of the Foreign Office, was at home recovering from flu. This left no one on duty in King Charles Street with the combination of rank, experience and audacity to restrain the Foreign Secretary from venting his spleen in a further string of telegrams to Makins. Denying that any concrete understanding had been reached with Dulles in London to proceed forthwith to construct a pact around a small nucleus of states approved by the United States, Eden said that the 'only hope' of general Asian adherence was to begin, at the appropriate time, with as many states as possible. To go ahead with the Associated States, Thailand and the Philippines would 'not only discourage subsequent adherence, but invite direct attack at [the] forthcoming Colombo meeting of Asian Prime Ministers', a reference to a scheduled gathering of the prime ministers of India, Pakistan, Burma, Indonesia and Sri Lanka on 28 April, two days into the Geneva conference.[36]

As for what should happen next, Eden felt he had no choice other than to accept the proposed adaptation of the ambassadorial meeting, and UK involvement therein, but he wanted it understood by participants and press that its primary purpose was to coordinate thinking on the Korean phase at Geneva. Any linkage to defence planning for Southeast Asia was to be avoided. If Dulles wished to make further public comment on that subject, he should stick to the wording of the London communiqué and not 'add glosses which I might be unable to accept and might feel obliged to dispute'.[37] The on-duty under-secretary at the Foreign Office over the Easter weekend was Roderick

Barclay who thought it wise to caution Makins privately that the Foreign Secretary 'is very concerned about the explosive possibilities of this matter'.[38]

Makins hardly needed the primer: the telegrams pouring into his embassy spoke for themselves. 'I am not aware that Dulles has any cause for complaint,' Eden remarked in another message. Aside from the question of competing interpretations of the London communiqué, 'I should have thought anyone could have foreseen the reactions such a meeting must have on the Colombo Conference, to which we attach importance, to say nothing of Geneva.' He went on:

> Americans may think the time past when they need consider the feelings or difficulties of their allies. It is the conviction that this tendency becomes more pronounced every week that is creating mounting difficulties for anyone in this country who wants to maintain close Anglo-American relations. We at least have constantly to bear in mind all our Commonwealth partners, even if the United States does not like some of them.

Rejecting the Philippines and Thailand as in any way representative of Asian opinion, Eden ended by warning that unless 'a real effort' was made to include genuinely independent states, 'I fear the whole of this scheme may be prejudiced, which I deplore'.[39]

When first told by Makins that Eden had blocked British participation in the ambassadorial get-together, Dulles had held his emotions in check. In private, however, he gave them full vent. 'Eden ... double-crossed me,' he raged to his sister. 'He lied to me!'[40] U. Alexis Johnson, a Dulles aide, recalled how his boss felt 'betrayed' by Eden and that the resulting 'antipathy' and 'friction' continued 'as long as both of them were in office'.[41] In a similar vein, Dillon remembered Dulles talking of 'a complete breaking of faith'.[42] Historians, too, have come to see Easter 1954 as the moment when the already fragile Eden-Dulles relationship was damaged beyond repair; henceforward, existing UK-US policy differences on Indochina would be magnified by the antipathy which the British Foreign Secretary and the American Secretary of State bore for one another.[43] Two months on, Makins reported that the issue still 'rankles with Dulles and his senior advisers' who were feeling 'sore' with the British in general and Eden in particular. A 'smouldering resentment' permeated the State Department.[44]

Because of the severity and consequences of the Eden-Dulles falling out, it behoves us to try to get to the bottom of what happened. According to Cable, the London communiqué, a 'vacuous formula' allowing both the British and Americans to interpret it according to their lights, must bear some of the blame.[45] In a telegram from London on 13 April, Dulles told Eisenhower that the communiqué 'indicates a large measure of acceptance of our view of the danger and necessity for united action'. The British, he conceded, were 'extremely fearful' of ground intervention and did not share the American view that the loss of northern Vietnam must perforce set the Southeast Asian dominos toppling. Despite such differences, Dulles was 'satisfied that a very big step forward has been taken in bringing British thinking into harmony with our own'.[46] When he got to Paris, Dulles was explicit in telling Bidault that the UK government would 'take part at once in an informal working group in Washington' on Southeast Asian defence 'in which their Ambassador would participate'.[47]

As we have seen, the British, too, felt the London talks had gone well. The communiqué and its contents 'were so favourable to us, and so far from what Dulles's speeches before he came here led everyone to suppose he would demand', Shuckburgh wrote.[48] Did the British somehow misread Dulles? Did they misconstrue his reasonableness? Was he so compliant because he felt that he had won the argument over pre-Geneva action? These questions defy definitive answers, although even Eisenhower admitted privately that his Secretary of State was 'not particularly persuasive in presentation and, at times, seems to have a curious lack of understanding as to how his words and manner may affect another personality'.[49]

Beyond this, Dulles may have felt the need to spin the communiqué in his favour for domestic political reasons. On his return to Washington, he was attacked by the Republican Old Guard for creating a 'paper' pact which 'studiously eliminated' from its ranks South Korea and Nationalist China, America's main anti-communist allies in Asia, out of undue respect for British 'prejudices' towards Chiang Kai-shek and South Korea's leader Syngman Rhee.[50] Privately, Dulles railed against Knowland and his ilk 'for failing to back up Administration on foreign policy,' and it is possible that his swift and of necessity publicized move to get Southeast defence planning started may have been an attempt to deflect further brickbats. But in spinning the communiqué, he perhaps swerved away from what the British, or Eden at any rate, believed had been agreed, especially on the timing of the next step.[51]

A post-mortem undertaken by the British Embassy in Washington provides support for the American interpretation of the outcome of the London talks. In a letter to Kirkpatrick, Makins confessed to being 'almost as taken aback' as Dulles by Eden's hostility to the meeting of ambassadors. The American record was 'unequivocal in the sense that it had been agreed that consultation should take place as soon as possible, and in any case before the Geneva Conference'. In comparison, the Foreign Office record was 'very scrappy'.[52] An entry in Shuckburgh's diary a little later adds to the case against Eden:

> According to what Denis [Allen] says, we are getting very near to having cheated the Americans on this question of starting talks on SEA [South-East Asian] security. Denis told me ... at lunch today that when Dulles was in London A.E. *did* [original emphasis] indicate that we should be willing to start such talks at once, provided we were not committed to any action in Indo-China. The American record showed that, but ours was obscure on the point and A.E. has always denied it.[53]

A decade on, Eden's alleged betrayal of Dulles was still being talked about in the Foreign Office. In November 1964, as the United States edged closer to full-scale war against North Vietnam, officials considered the likely impact on Anglo-American relations of warning Lyndon B. Johnson's Democratic administration of the dangers of military intervention. Whatever was said, Edward Peck, Assistant Under-Secretary for the Far East, cautioned his colleagues, it was essential not to 'repeat what Lord Avon [Eden] did in 1954, when he allowed Mr. Dulles to expect British support for a forward policy in Indo-China only to let him down with a public bump a couple of weeks later'. If the Johnson administration 'did decide on a really tough policy and HMG are uncertain of their ability to support this to the bitter end', the lesson of 1954 was that 'we ought to voice our doubts at the very beginning'.[54]

Apportioning blame for the Eden-Dulles misunderstanding has become a feature of the historiography of 1954. Here, Dulles has his critics. Ted Morgan likens him to 'a travelling salesman with his foot in the door'; having tried and failed in London and Paris 'to push a product' that neither the British nor French wanted to buy, he was 'not giving up' and decided, on his return to Washington, 'to force the issue'.[55] Victor Bator has similarly accused Dulles of trying to offset 'his defeat in London' by going 'ahead with his own plan, hoping that Eden would not brave open defiance of a *fait accompli*'.[56] For other scholars – the majority, it must be said – Eden is the villain of the piece.[57] From his unique vantage point as participant in and historian of the crisis, James Cable represents the many in arguing that the Foreign Secretary's Easter weekend telegrams 'were the petulant reaction of a cornered rabbit' and a 'deplorable performance' which 'lastingly impaired relations between Eden and Dulles'.[58]

There is, though, a case to be made in support of Eden, and not just retrospectively. Against the finger-pointing of Makins, Shuckburgh and Allen we can juxtapose the findings of a review of the British record of the London talks undertaken by the Foreign Office's Southeast Asia Department. The Dulles 'initiative' – the summoning of ambassadors for 20 April – 'came as a complete surprise to us since the Foreign Office interpretation of the London talks was that there would be full consultation before any definite step was taken or any proposal was made public'. The 'main trouble' was the 'almost indecent haste of Mr. Dulles in trying to rush into these preliminary consultations … without any prior agreement with ourselves'.[59] Kirkpatrick made a similar point to Makins. 'It seems clear that we and the Americans have different ideas about how matters were left at the conclusion of the talks in London,' he wrote.

> No very clear conclusions were reached … In my view, the Secretary of State was right in thinking that the Americans had not been given any sort of 'all clear' to go ahead with consulting a selection of other interested powers. On the contrary, I think the next step should have been for the State Department, in the light of Dulles' talks in Paris, to inform us of what had passed in Paris and to consult us about how and when the next step should be taken. Consequently I am not surprised that the Secretary of State objected when he learnt of the American intention to proceed forthwith to call the meeting in Washington.[60]

Like the Southeast Asia Department, Kirkpatrick had worked on a presumption of advance notice before anything further was said or done. So, it seems, did the Americans, at least to begin with. In a cable to Eisenhower in the midst of his London visit, Dulles said that he had 'told Eden after we completed this trip we would get in touch with British to see how best we might proceed in organizing united will to resist aggression in SEA. One possibility was to establish informal working group in Washington'. Dulles, however, did not get in touch. To the contrary, he went straight ahead and called the meeting of ambassadors, a de facto working group.[61] Similarly, when Smith spoke with Spender in Washington on 15 April he revealed that 'the Secretary had told Eden following his return to Washington we would contact British [to] examine how [we] might best proceed in organizing united will [to] resist aggression [in] Southeast Asia. One possibility might be [to] establish informal working group in Washington to which Eden agreed and said Makins would be available'.[62]

Arguably, the violence of Eden's outburst when Dulles summoned his 20 April meeting was not connected to any dispute over the principle of defence planning but to the lack of prior consultation. Had he been approached (as he seems to have expected he would be), Eden would have been able to restate his reservations about pre-Geneva action or else insist on secret and initially bilateral UK-US planning rather than open and multilateral discussions. The American record, which Makins and some in London valued above the British record, is in fact less than unequivocal.

In the end, the strongest argument against Eden reneging on a precise promise – and in favour of straightforward crossed wires – is that precipitate action on a defence grouping ran counter to all his hopes for Geneva. To put it another way, his determination to make a success of Geneva is difficult to reconcile with his approval of measures that could see the conference stillborn.

At Dien Bien Phu, meanwhile, the French garrison, augmented by reinforcements parachuted in between 9 and 12 April, continued to hold out bravely. 'I salute you and your men whose exploits bring glory to France and are an example which inspires us all,' Churchill wrote to de Castries.[63] On the diplomatic front, Dulles was due back in Paris on 21 April ahead of a gathering of the North Atlantic Council. Despite the false start, he remained keen to get a Southeast Asian defence working group up and running as soon as possible. It was 'wise to strike while the iron was hot', he told Makins, 'and it was hot at present'. Congress was 'ready to contemplate additional American involvement now'.[64] At the same time, the US government carried on with secret preparations for possible military action in Vietnam, Radford continually updated contingency plans and senior White House staff were placed on a one-hour muster warning in case urgent decisions were required.[65]

In London, in contrast, the Foreign Office's focus remained the diplomatic prospect. A Southeast Asia Department paper, 'Pros and Cons of Partition', completed on the eve of the NATO meeting, admitted that partition remained a far from ideal compromise. In a negative-positive sense, it was preferable to a continuation of the war and the ongoing deterioration in the French position. However, in a wholly positive sense, peace in Indochina was the best antidote to US plans for a military solution; hence partition represented 'a move away from the risk of war'. A north-south/Vietminh-French division might also find favour with the Chinese (whose security on the Sino-Vietnamese frontier would be assured), war-weary French public opinion, Asian neutrals and the United Nations. On the other hand, the Americans and the Associated State of Vietnam were sure to object to any such surrender. Finally, on a point of geostrategic detail, it was essential for Malaya's security that Laos and Cambodia ended up on the non-communist side of any division.[66]

This Foreign Office study accompanied Eden as he headed to Paris for the North Atlantic Council. Running late, he had a 'wild drive' to Heathrow in the morning on

22 April, and then, on landing at Orly, police outriders were required to ensure that his car got him into central Paris in time for a luncheon meeting with Dulles.[67] It was an uncomfortable encounter. According to the American record, Eden responded 'very frankly' to Dulles's invitation to 'clear up any misunderstanding' arising from their last meeting: 'When he had agreed in London last week to [an] informal working group' he had

> overlooked [the] Colombo conference ... He felt it would be most undesirable to give any public indication of membership in program for united action before the end of the Colombo conference. The establishment of a working group of ten countries we [the United States] envisaged would certainly be known and since it would not include three Commonwealth countries, there would probably be criticism emanating from Colombo which would be most unhelpful at Geneva.[68]

The British record of the luncheon makes no mention of a memory lapse. Instead, Eden said he had been struck (*after* Dulles left London) by the close proximity of the opening of the Geneva and Colombo conferences, and this, he felt, demanded caution. The Colombo factor was not the reason he blocked UK participation in the ambassadorial gathering; rather, it was a supplementary consideration buttressing his primary objection, namely its damaging impact on the Geneva peace process and the potential to estrange neutral Asian opinion.[69]

Quite what Dulles made of this is unclear. If Eden had forgotten about the Colombo conference, did it make that much difference if the five Asian prime ministers condemned regional defence planning individually or collectively? Another possible explanation for Eden's odd manoeuvre is that he was persuaded by his advisors that a gesture was needed to calm a fevered Dulles. As Cable reminds us, 'most of those with access to Eden and influence over him tended to favour conformity with American polices'. Both the Southeast Asia Department of the Foreign Office and Lord Reading, one of Eden's parliamentary under-secretaries, supported a more independent position 'but carried little weight'.[70] Just as Geneva could not succeed without a constructive communist contribution, Eden knew it would struggle to prosper in the teeth of American hostility. Hence the need for fence-mending. But only a little. The original reasons for his negative reaction to the US government's initiative still stood.[71]

Eden's act of contrition – staged or otherwise – seems to have gone some way towards salving Dulles's amour propre, though Smith was reported to be fuming ('you know God damned well you just don't forget about something like the Colombo Conference').[72] The US Secretary was pleased to learn that the British remained committed to the principle of regional security and had 'no objection to our discussing together very secretly the form and outline of the plan' – Eden even suggested a 'double-tier system' for a security organization of full and associate members. 'Of one thing I was sure', the Foreign Secretary said, 'we could not gain security in South-East Asia by force of arms alone. We must have Eastern opinion with us'. Dulles did not dissent, although he suggested pointedly that he would agree to Indian association if Eden agreed to South Korean and Taiwanese association. As for the immediate situation, Dulles had spoken that morning to Bidault who was so depressed by the latest news from Dien Bien Phu that 'we might be faced at Geneva with a sudden collapse of French will'.[73]

With the crisis intensifying, it is worth reflecting on whether Eden's insistence on the widest possible South and Southeast Asian support was tactical – a means, that is, of frustrating American plans for intervention in Vietnam. Winning over India and other Asian neutrals to the idea of a Western-engendered security system, let alone persuading them to become members or associates, would be a complicated and drawn-out process, as Eden assuredly realized. Moreover, some of the Foreign Secretary's privately held views on India and its Prime Minister were distinctly uncomplimentary: Nehru struck him as 'a miserable little Indian Kerensky,' and he predicted that within a decade, 'India will have either broken up into little pieces because of this man, or gone Communist while he fiddles around, complaining about the Americans'. For the most part, Eden shared the Foreign Office consensus that the Indians were 'intolerably high-minded advocates of woolly agreements that conceded everything unrelated to Indian national interests'.[74]

Despite these private eruptions, there is no reason to question Eden's basic sincerity in wanting, if not broad Asian adherence, then certainly Asian support in principle for regional defence. Top of his list were the Asian Commonwealth states of India, Pakistan and Sri Lanka and the ex-Commonwealth state of Burma. By the same token, there is little doubt that he was aware that working to bring the Colombo powers into line would operate as a check on dangerous US initiatives before Geneva. Thereafter, the Colombo powers might be persuaded to join in the guarantee that would need to be attached to an Indochina settlement.[75] The Americans themselves, however, acquired early and never shed the suspicion that Eden's Asian fixation was a pretext for obstruction. This opinion was shared by the authors of the *Pentagon Papers* who later insisted – without any evidential underpinning – that it was 'clear' that 'the British were restrained by the Indians'.[76] To Eden, though, what really mattered was restraining the Americans. And in that task, the Colombo powers, other than Pakistan perhaps, were to prove valuable allies.

25 April 1954: 'The Day We Didn't Go to War'

While the diplomats talked, soldiers continued to die at Dien Bien Phu. On 20 April, General de Castries took stock. It was a mournful tallying. Since the start of the battle, the area of the base had shrunk by almost half. With the airstrip unusable, the garrison relied on airdrops of vital supplies which sometimes fell (literally) into enemy hands. Of the 12,000 men-at-arms in position when the fighting began, only 2,300 could now be considered able-bodied. The field hospital overflowed with wounded. With no time, space or energy to bury the dead, the corpses piled higher, the sight and stench of the dead adding to the demoralization of the living. 'I didn't think we could hold out much longer,' de Castries later recalled. 'Our perimeter was shrinking, the supply problems were growing, and I was contemplating getting the garrison out.'[1]

In truth, the time for rescue missions or breakouts was fast disappearing. With the arrival of the rains, expected any day soon, relief by land would become impossible and further supply and reinforcement by air rendered even more hazardous. And then there was the next PAVN offensive to contend with following a recent lull in hostilities, an attack Navarre predicted would be 'très très dur'.[2] Privately, the French Commander-in-Chief began to entertain thoughts of a ceasefire locally at Dien Bien Phu and possibly more generally across Vietnam. To continue fighting through the rainy season while simultaneously negotiating at Geneva would surrender all the advantages to the Vietminh and leave the French and their Vietnamese allies in a hopeless position. As for US intervention, Navarre was torn. 'What is certain,' he advised the government in Paris, 'is that internationalization of the war is the end of French influence in Indochina – in one definitive stroke it draws down one hundred years of effort and eight years of sacrifice'. Even as matters stood, Navarre felt, 'it is much more for the United States that we are fighting than for ourselves.'[3]

The deteriorating military situation provided the backdrop to a difficult encounter between Bidault and Dulles on 22 April at the start of the NATO Council in Paris. Dillon and Ely were also present. Dulles had set out for the French capital in search of a 'course which will not involve us in war or cause a loss of territory'.[4] What Bidault told him dented those hopes. The position at Dien Bien Phu was 'virtually hopeless', the Frenchman admitted. All that could save the garrison was 'massive' US air intervention, in effect the implementation of *Vautour*. Bidault had previously opposed internationalization for reasons of patriotic pride (an American takeover of a French war was a bitter pill to swallow) but had changed his mind; if surrendering direction of the war was what it took to save the garrison, so be it. Knowing that united action had become a Dullesian *idée fixe*, Bidault hoped that the United States would not make intervention contingent upon British participation given Eden's negative view of military action. As to that other Dulles fixation, a regional defence organization, if Dien Bien Phu fell, French opinion was unlikely to embrace any such scheme. With people in France looking to Geneva for a way out, the US proposal for a coalition was already construed in some quarters as calculated to damage the prospects for a negotiated settlement and to keep France fighting America's war.[5]

In Washington, Eisenhower was angered by Dulles's report of this meeting and had no hesitation in rejecting Bidault's appeal for air support at Dien Bien Phu. Nor was the President's ire confined to the French. The British had signally failed 'to appreciate the seriousness of the situation at Dien Bien Phu and the probable result on the entire war of defeat at that place'. Dulles, who had Eisenhower's 'complete support', needed to have it out with Eden. 'The British must not be able merely to shut their eyes and later plead blindness as an alibi for failing to propose a positive program.' The Churchill government should get on board with united action in order to insulate the rest of Vietnam, and Southeast Asia, from the consequences of a Vietminh victory at Dien Bien Phu.[6]

With Washington six hours behind Paris, Dulles had not received this instruction by the time of his luncheon encounter with Eden on 22 April. The US Secretary was 'most gloomy' about the French position, Eden wrote afterwards, and argued that the United States, Britain and France needed to work out the 'maximum concessions which the French could offer at Geneva in order to secure a settlement with the Communists'. This was a substantial modification to Dulles's previously uncompromising attitude to the conference, but his interest in united action remained very much intact. The negotiating prospects of the Western powers would be strengthened if the communists 'knew we were working with like-minded people to unite in defense of southeast Asia'.[7] Eden was perplexed by Dulles's 'stories of complete French moral surrender'.[8] Were the Americans deliberately exaggerating the French plight in an attempt to bounce the UK into agreeing to immediate defence planning for Southeast Asia or even intervention in Vietnam? Personally, Eden found it 'hard to believe' that the position at Dien Bien Phu, though undeniably bad, was 'so immediately desperate as Mr. Dulles suggested' and he proposed to meet Bidault, 'without the Americans', to get to the truth of the matter.[9]

Eden's chance came that night at a dinner of the Brussels Pact powers. Bidault was far from his best – 'worn out, garrulous, ironical and obscure' – and decidedly 'hysterical' about Dien Bien Phu, according to Shuckburgh. Nevertheless, from what Eden divined, it was 'pretty clear' that the French that morning had rejected the American call for a regional approach and a united action coalition in favour of an exclusive focus on Dien Bien Phu. Piqued, Dulles had collapsed into 'extreme pessimism', Eden concluded. One way or another, it had been 'a confusing, difficult and depressing' first day in Paris.[10]

Officially, Friday 23 April was devoted to NATO affairs, but it was the worsening situation in Vietnam that most preoccupied the Western powers. Chairing a post-luncheon NATO plenary, Bidault struck Shuckburgh as borderline drunk. 'Frightful impression of mental collapse, coupled with a histrionic show of courage and morale' in the face of the news 'pouring in' from Dien Bien Phu, 'all bad'.[11] Laniel was less emotional but equally pessimistic when he met with the State Department's Doug MacArthur. If Dien Bien Phu fell, his government would find it impossible to avoid reaching a settlement at Geneva, 'even if unfavorable'. The prospects for EDC ratification, which were bound up with the fate of Indochina, would be reduced to negligible proportions. However, according to French military experts, US intervention at Dien Bien Phu 'with about 200 to 300 carrier aircraft' (bearing French insignia to disguise the US role) could stave off disaster both in Vietnam and Europe. But *Vautour* needed to happen very soon; otherwise the bombing would be 'meaningless'. MacArthur was flabbergasted. The picture Laniel painted 'seemed to be catastrophic'. In effect, he was saying that 'the fall of an outpost in Indochina must result in the abandonment of that area and the destruction of the [NATO] collective defense system which we had together developed for the defense of Western Europe'. Laniel agreed that it was illogical. But Dien Bien Phu had become 'a symbol in the minds of the French people and Parliament' who were 'no longer capable of reasoning about it'.[12]

Mid-way through the afternoon's NATO meeting, Bidault was handed a copy of an urgent message from Navarre, the gist of which he shared with Dulles at the close of proceedings. In Navarre's judgement, the situation at Dien Bien Phu was now so desperate that the options had dwindled to two: either a US aerial bombardment of Vietminh positions and lines of communication or an immediate ceasefire, not just in northern Vietnam but throughout Indochina. An 'exhausted', 'confused' and 'rambling' Bidault gave 'the impression of a man close to the breaking point', Dulles cabled Eisenhower. But for all Bidault's contortions, the dilemma confronting the United States was real and pressing.[13]

A few hours later, the dilemma was Britain's as well. At pre-dinner drinks at the Quai d'Orsay, Dulles drew Eden aside and told him about Navarre's appeal. Eden was aghast. Air intervention could not save the fortress but would have 'far-reaching consequences' if China was provoked into entering the war directly. And what of the Soviet reaction? Dulles agreed that bombing could not affect the outcome of the battle but he thought it might have a psychologically bolstering impact on the French who would see that they had powerful allies in the fight. There was still no objective reason why the loss of one battle should lead to a military surrender throughout Indochina. Nor could the Geneva negotiations be allowed to turn into a forum in which the French simply gave and the communists took. Accordingly, if Eden 'felt able to stand with him', Dulles was ready to recommend to Eisenhower that he seek 'war powers' from Congress 'of the widest character' to move armed forces into Vietnam. An agitated Eden begged Dulles not to take any decisions without prior UK-US consultation. To this, Dulles assented.[14]

Returning to the US Embassy after dinner, Dulles cabled Eisenhower. The 'situation here is tragic' with France 'almost visibly collapsing under our eyes'. The loss of Dien Bien Phu could see the government 'taken over by defeatists'. In Bidault's view, Dulles reported, if the United States was to help at Dien Bien Phu, the French 'would as a matter of honor go on fighting' even if US air action failed to save the fortress. But if Dien Bien Phu was lost without any American intervention, Bidault saw 'no hope of any French reaction, other than acceptance of defeat and probably left-wing government which would hold office on sufferance of Communists, although probably without open Communist participation'. Against this, Dulles closed, there was the need to balance Eden's 'fear that United States intervention might initiate World War Three'.[15]

As Dulles was composing his cable to the White House, Eden was telling Shuckburgh the 'grave news' that his American opposite number was readying himself to 'urge Eisenhower to take steps which would lead to all-out American intervention', hence to 'US war with China and incalculable consequences'. A shaken Shuckburgh advised that the priority was to stiffen the Laniel administration's resolution. With Geneva in mind, continued French resistance beyond Dien Bien Phu, especially in the Red River delta, together perhaps with American 'noises off', might prise an acceptable settlement from the Chinese and Vietminh. But the stiffening exercise would not be easy with Bidault 'on the verge of collapse' and other French politicians talking of a rerun of 1940.[16] 'I am fairly hardened to crises', Eden later wrote, 'but I went to bed that night a troubled man'.[17]

The memory of Bermuda added to Eden's upset. Earlier in the day, Dulles spoke to the NATO Council on the subject of nuclear weapons. His aim was to try to lower the temperature of the H-bomb fever infecting America's European allies. In the event, his insistence that 'it should be our agreed policy ... to use atomic weapons as conventional weapons against the military assets of the enemy whenever and wherever it would be of advantage to do so' was deeply unsettling in the context of the intensifying crisis in Indochina. Nor did Dulles give anything away on consultation. If possible, the United States would share its thinking with allies before unleashing its nuclear arsenal, but 'we must make sure that the methods of consultation ... do not themselves stand in the way of our security'. In other words, 'under certain contingencies, time would not permit consultation without itself endangering the very security we seek to protect'. Was Vietnam such a contingency? Or Dien Bien Phu?[18]

Saturday 24 April saw Paris warmed by gentle sunshine. 'Another glorious day', Shuckburgh wrote, 'but not for us'.[19] At 3.45 pm, Eden met Dulles at Dillon's residence. Radford (who had just flown in from Washington) was also present. The Americans appeared to have cooled on the idea of a symbolic air strike at Dien Bien Phu. According to Dulles, the President 'had not the power to act with such speed'. In any event, as Eden has previously pointed out, it was 'perfectly clear that no intervention could now save the fortress'. At the same time, Dulles remained convinced that there was 'no chance' of preventing a disaster throughout Vietnam when Dien Bien Phu succumbed unless the United States and the UK both showed willing to enter the war. Despite Laniel and Bidault's insistence that they wanted help at Dien Bien Phu, Dulles felt that an Anglo-American undertaking to join the fight elsewhere in Indochina would boost morale and encourage the French to carry on. According to Bao Dai, the Vietnamese, too, were ready to fight on. Therefore, 'if the British would go along with us', Eisenhower was ready to ask Congress to approve US military intervention. But 'an essential element in securing such approval would be the fact that it was firmly based on joint action'.[20]

Eden demanded to know what kind of a UK commitment the Americans had in mind. Radford suggested that a number of Royal Air Force (RAF) squadrons could be diverted from Malaya or Hong Kong and that an aircraft carrier might be sent to the Gulf of Tonkin. Eden remained sceptical – the more so because 'the French had not painted anything like so desperate a picture to us'. To the contrary, they had given the impression that they would continue the war regardless. Eden also doubted that an Anglo-American contribution confined (as Radford suggested) to air or naval power would decisively alter the tide of war but it would have a negative effect on world opinion generally and on China and the USSR in particular. Was Vietnam worth 'a world war'? Radford had little truck with such concerns. He had 'never thought the Chinese would intervene', partly through lack of resources and partly because of the vulnerability of the PRC to American retaliation. In any event, maybe the time had come to confront the Chinese head-on, to 'go after the source' of communist aggression in Asia through 'offensive action' instead of constantly dealing with its symptoms in places like Korea and Vietnam. The USSR would launch the Third World War when it wanted, Radford said. It would not be provoked into war simply to protect or preserve China. To run scared from decisive action would leave the Western powers and the non-communist states in Asia in danger of 'being nibbled to death'. If the British were not careful, he added, this would be their fate in Malaya. Passing over the chance to mention the Songkhla strategy, Eden focused instead on what he saw as the fundament of the meeting. The Americans were 'confronting British opinion with about as difficult a decision as it would be possible to find,' and he proposed to fly back to London that evening to consult the Prime Minister, the Cabinet and the Chiefs of Staff.[21]

Radford, 'whom we did not think very intelligent', was 'obviously raring for a scrap', Shuckburgh recorded. What the Americans wanted was 'for US/UK more or less to take over the conduct of the war, push the French into the background and hope that the locals will be so inspired by this spectacle that they will rally against the Communists ... We were deeply disturbed by this'.[22] Eden confided his own fears to his wife. 'The Americans want to go in but won't unless we agree,' Clarissa wrote in her diary. 'Anthony says he won't agree and if they go in it will mean fighting China & setting off a Third World War. Admiral Arthur Radford is spoiling for a fight.'[23] The Canadian Foreign Minister, Lester Pearson, who saw Eden after the meeting, described him as 'almost frightened ... to death' by Radford. [24]

There was a further tripartite meeting at the Quai d'Orsay later that afternoon limited, on American insistence, to the foreign ministers and a single advisor each. Dulles asked Bidault straight out whether France would continue the war after the fall of Dien Bien Phu. The Frenchman's response was tortuous. Defeat would yield potentially 'irreparable' consequences and would probably be followed by a Vietminh offensive against the Red River delta. In France, the government would come under great pressure to bring the war to an immediate end. Nevertheless, the Americans 'knew what his policy and that of his government was'. In actual fact, the Americans, like the British, were struggling on both counts, and so Dulles asked again 'point blank' if France would sue for a ceasefire *before* Geneva. No, Bidault said. That very day, de Castries had been ordered to fight on until all ammunition was exhausted. At this, Dulles produced a letter which he hoped Bidault would find 'helpful'. He would send it to the French Foreign Ministry via the normal channels once he had received approval from Washington. The letter expressed regret that the time had passed for air strikes at Dien Bien Phu. However, if the French so wished, the Eisenhower administration was ready to activate the legal-constitutional processes necessary to permit the President 'to move armed forces into Indo-China and thus to internationalise the struggle against Communism and protect the whole south-eastern region of Asia as a whole'. From the fleeting glimpse Eden was given of this letter, it was unclear whether British support remained a sine qua non of US action, but he nevertheless made clear to Dulles and Bidault that there was nothing in the London communiqué committing the UK to join the fight. Recalling the crossed wires of ten days earlier, Eden 'wanted no misunderstanding on this'. As the meeting closed, Bidault agreed that Dulles could send him the letter. It might 'be useful at some stage'.[25]

It is impossible to say whether – as is sometimes suggested – the curious incident of the Dulles letter in the afternoon was the product of collusion on the part of the US and French foreign ministers to 'shake Eden' and effect a change in British policy.[26] But shaken Eden was. It was 'quite clear that we shall have to take a decision of first class importance, namely whether to tell the Americans that we are prepared to go along with their plan or not', he cabled Churchill.[27] In his diary, Shuckburgh expanded on what this decision entailed:

> If we refuse to co-operate with the US plan, we strain the Alliance. If we do as Dulles asks, we certainly provoke the bitterest hostility of India and probably all other Asiatic states and destroy the Commonwealth. Also, a war for Indo-China would be about as difficult a thing to put across the British public as you could find. Nothing should be done before Geneva, then, even supposing Indochina could be saved by force of arms, which was extremely doubtful – unless, as Radford seemed to want, the 'source of the trouble', China, was attacked, and then what about the Soviet-Chinese alliance and what price the third world war?[28]

Dulles emerged from the tripartite discussion reasonably satisfied. Bidault was 'obviously tired' but still 'in full control of himself'. In his 'present mood ... he may endeavour to limit the effects of the loss of Dien Bien Phu'. If so, Dulles told Washington, 'we will at least enter the Geneva conference without the French Government definitely committed to some disastrous course of action'.[29]

Later, in his memoirs, Bidault made the remarkable claim that Dulles – possibly just after this meeting – 'ask[ed] me if we would like the US to give us two atomic bombs' for use at Dien Bien Phu, an offer he declined on the grounds that 'our side will suffer as much as the enemy' and 'we will be risking a world war'.[30] It has been suggested that neither Dulles nor any other top administration figure 'seriously advocated the use of nuclear weapons at Dienbienphu', although staff discussions and planning were in train for a nuclear response to large-scale Chinese intervention on the Korean model.[31] However, before we dismiss Bidault's recollection as the fevered imagining of a man close to a nervous breakdown, we should note that other French figures – senior diplomat Jean Chauvel, Bidault's Minister of State at the Quai d'Orsay Maurice Schumann, and General Ely amongst them – have corroborated the claim.[32] Moreover, a Pentagon study in early April proposed that up to six 31-kiloton atomic bombs delivered from US Navy carrier aircraft in daylight could be used to great profit against the Vietminh at Dien Bien Phu.[33] 'You could take all day to drop a bomb,' US Air Force Chief Nathan Twining later attested, 'make sure you put it in the right place

... and clean those Commies out of there and the band could play the *Marseillaise* and the French could come marching out ... in great shape'.[34]

When Dulles learned of the French claim he was 'totally mystified ... It is incredible that I should have made [the] offer since the law categorically forbids it'.[35] Incredible? Or plausibly deniable? As Fredrik Logevall reminds us, given the persistent nuclear buzz in US policymaking circles during the crisis, and given too Dulles's fear of the consequences of the loss of Dien Bien Phu, it is 'entirely possible Bidault heard what he claimed to have heard'.[36]

The US offer (the Dulles letter) to intervene in Vietnam was formally passed to the Quai d'Orsay at 9.00 pm, Paris time, on 24 April. In it, Dulles maintained that regardless of what happened at Dien Bien Phu, 'the position in Indo-China can be held by the collective action of the free nations having vital interests in the area'. France 'can count upon us', he ended, 'and we hope that we can count upon you'.[37] But could either count on the British?

Dulles had been 'in a fearfully excited state', Eden told Iverach McDonald, 'saying that America was ready for action ... and that all America was waiting for was agreement by Britain ... I was put on the spot'.[38] Unlike the earlier Anglo-American divergence over united action, when UK support, though critical to the Eisenhower administration's design, was still sought in conjunction with that of several other countries, the Churchill government was now the sole determinant. 'I laid before Eden essentiality of prompt combined action regarding Indochina if situation was to be saved', Dulles cabled Eisenhower late on 24 April. 'I emphasized that for us to act, British participation was necessary and I added that I hoped we could bring with us other countries.'[39] For immediate purposes, though, the UK would be enough.

As the Dulles letter was being delivered, Eden, accompanied by Shuckburgh and Allen, was flying from Orly to Heathrow. On landing, a government car drove them to Chequers. Arriving at 11.30 pm, the weary travellers found the Prime Minister waiting for them 'in a silken two-piece suit, covered by a silk dressing gown'.[40] After a stiff drink and a cold supper, Eden handed Churchill a summation of the British position which Allen had composed during the journey. The document had eight points:

1. We do not regard the London communiqué as committing us to join in immediate discussions on the possibility of Allied intervention in the Indo-China war.
2. We are not prepared to give any undertaking now, in advance of Geneva, concerning UK military action in Indo-China.
3. But we shall give all possible diplomatic support to the French Delegation at Geneva in efforts to reach an honourable settlement.
4. We can give an assurance now that if a settlement is reached at Geneva we shall join in guaranteeing that settlement and in setting up a collective defence in South East Asia, as foreshadowed in the London communiqué, to make that joint guarantee effective.
5. We hope that any Geneva settlement will make it possible for the joint guarantee to apply to at least the greater part of Indo-China.
6. If no such settlement is reached we shall be prepared at that time to consider with our Allies the action to be taken jointly in the situation then existing.

7. But we cannot give any assurance now about possible action on the part of the United Kingdom in the event of failure to reach agreement at Geneva for a cessation of hostilities in Indo-China.
8. We shall be ready to join with the United States Government now in studying measures to ensure the defence of Siam [Thailand] and the rest of South-East Asia including Malaya in the event of all or part of Indo-China being lost.[41]

Approving the document, Churchill grew nostalgic. 'We have thrown away our glorious empire, our wonderful Indian Empire, we have cast it away', words which a cynical Shuckburgh decoded as 'why should we fight for the broken-down French colonial effort after that?'[42]

Early the next morning, Bidault replied to the American offer of help *beyond* Dien Bien Phu by asking yet again for help *at* Dien Bien Phu. A 'massive intervention of American aviation' could still save the situation, he informed the US Embassy in Paris. Indeed, the unprecedented concentration of Vietminh forces and military matériel ringing the base offered an opportunity to deliver a shattering blow to the enemy's war-making capacity.[43] At around the same time, Eden and Churchill were driving from Chequers to Number 10 Downing Street. There, at 11.00 am, the Cabinet, or as many ministers as could be mustered at short notice on a Sunday, gathered in emergency session.

Eden began by outlining the background to the latest twist in the crisis before recommending that the American proposal for 'some dramatic gesture of Anglo-American intervention in Indo-China' be rejected. The US Congress was more likely to grant the administration war powers if action was a US-UK rather than a unilateral US affair. To that end, 'participation by token British forces' might be all that was required. But in line with the outlook of the Chiefs of Staff, who were also present, Eden questioned whether air action, which was what the Americans were proposing, would be effective in retrieving the position. With the recent Korean experience in mind, it was likely that 'no military aid to the French could be fully effective unless it included the provision of ground troops'.[44]

The Cabinet shared the Foreign Secretary's misgivings. Whatever the Americans might say, ministers felt that air or naval intervention was 'bound to lead to our committing ground forces', an undertaking which neither the British public nor parliament was likely to endorse. The Cabinet further suspected that the Eisenhower administration was looking to use the crisis as an excuse, or justification, for war with China. Dismissing Radford's judgement that action could be taken against the PRC 'without drawing the Soviet Union into the conflict', Eden warned that 'anything like open war with China' could escalate into 'a third world war'. The government should therefore 'decline to give any immediate undertaking to afford military assistance to the French in Indo-China'. The eight-point memorandum put to Churchill the night before – and now approved by the Cabinet – would operate as general guidance for the UK delegation at the Geneva conference. With regard to the possible structure of peace, it was 'inevitable that large parts of Indo-China should fall under Communist control', Eden observed, 'and the best hope of a lasting solution lay in some form of partition'. Hitherto seen as a temporary fix, partition might endure if a Southeast Asian defence organization, once formed, guaranteed the demarcation line. The UK aim at Geneva should be to lend the French all possible support in seeking an honourable settlement, but diplomacy would not be helped by 'premature military intervention'.[45]

In giving its unanimous backing to Eden's approach, the Cabinet agreed that the UK's 'primary role' in any collective security system, beyond supporting partition in Vietnam, should be the defence of Malaya, with the Americans assuming the burden elsewhere in Southeast Asia. In a notable departure from the secrecy of the past, ministers authorized Eden and the Chiefs of Staff to disclose to the Americans, if or when appropriate, the existence of *Ringlet* and *Irony*. Summing up, the Prime Minister said that it would 'clearly be ill-advised to encourage the Americans to take precipitate military action in Indo-China'.[46]

Churchill and Eden went straight from Number 10 to the Carlton club for Sunday lunch, after which Eden planned to return briefly to the Foreign Office before flying to Paris to update Gladwyn Jebb, Harvey's successor as Ambassador, and thence onwards to Geneva where the conference would open the next day. However, these plans were thrown into disarray when the French Ambassador turned up at the Foreign Office at 2.30 pm with a copy of Bidault's response to Dulles's offer of help. Massigli explained that his government still believed that Dien Bien Phu could be saved. The Americans, so recently opposed to action at Dien Bien Phu, had apparently undergone an eleventh-hour conversion to the French (or Radford/*Vautour*) bombing thesis. Massigli recounted how the previous evening in Washington, Under-Secretary Smith told Bonnet that while the administration still rejected unilateral American intervention, an immediate declaration by the United States, Britain, France, the Philippines and the Associated States proclaiming their determination to resist communist expansion in Southeast Asia and to use 'eventual military means' could make all the difference. The State Department urged the French to do 'everything in their power' to persuade the British to join in this declaration. According to Massigli, once assured of a minimum of British support, Eisenhower would seek Congressional approval for carrier-launched air strikes at Dien Bien Phu within the next seventy-two hours.[47]

Eden was appalled at this ratcheting up of the crisis and angered at the roundabout way the news had reached him (Massigli via Bonnet via Smith). Yet again, he told Massigli, 'we were being asked to authorise a military operation in whose efficacy none of us could have any confidence, but the political outcome of which could be of the gravest character for us all'. The Ambassador claimed to understand this, but equally, because 'the Americans have declared their willingness to act, dependent upon our [UK] attitude', Massigli 'trusted we would consider the effect on French opinion and elsewhere of our refusal'.[48] After the Frenchman left, Foreign Office officials vented their fury at the way the Americans had set them up as 'whipping-boys' for any failure to act at Dien Bien Phu.[49]

The Cabinet was obliged to reassemble at 4.00 pm to consider the French démarche. Referring to Radford's 'conviction that the time was ripe for the Western Powers to show that they were ready to take direct military action to check the ambitions of Communist China', Eden restated his belief that the People's Republic of China, not the Vietminh, was the real American target. Air action at Dien Bien Phu would not only invite counteraction by the PRC, it might well be intended by Radford to provoke a Chinese response that the United States could then use to justify hitting back at the PRC through bombing and blockade. Thereafter, Eden continued, if 'the United States began to wage open war against China, there was a grave risk that the Soviet Union would feel obliged to intervene' and this 'might therefore be the first step towards a third world war'. With the Chiefs of Staff of the same mind, the Cabinet wasted little time in reaffirming its earlier decision to refuse to support any military operation in Vietnam. Speaking for his colleagues, Churchill said that 'what we were being asked to do was in effect to aid in misleading Congress into approving a military operation which would itself be ineffective and might well bring the world to the verge of a major war'. Personally, he had 'no doubts that this request must be rejected'.[50]

The drama of the day's two meetings is evident even in the stolid official record, but for a greater sense of the tension, as well as additional insight into ministerial thinking, we need to look elsewhere. Macmillan missed the morning meeting but attended in the afternoon. If the government agreed to the proposed declaration, he wrote in his diary, Eisenhower would seek Congressional authorization to use American air power immediately. 'This will produce a "show down" – in other words, either Russia must come to the aid of China (this means World War 3) or abandon China (this means almost fatal blow to Russian prestige).' The French government, 'in desperation, clutch at this American straw to save themselves – and perhaps the 4th Republic'. Eden had 'no doubt that we ought to refuse to take part'. Nor did Eden believe that 'such a bare-faced plan' would win the support of parliament, people or Commonwealth.[51]

Another important source, Brook's notebook, has Eden telling the Cabinet that while there had been 'no talk yet of using atomic bombs', in Paris 'Dulles made it clear that US would feel free to use atomic weapons in retaliation – not necessarily in place they had been attacked'. On the Commonwealth reaction, it was already clear, said Eden, that Canada 'deprecates' military intervention and that Australia would probably 'follow our lead'. As for Churchill, Brook records his wish to 'avoid a row with U.S.' along with his reluctance to see Britain enter into an 'indefinite military commitment' in Vietnam. 'We mustn't lose our influence with U.S. But we shouldn't go into *this* [original emphasis].'[52] Given Churchill's default inclination to back the Americans in most instances in Asia, these remarks must have come as a relief to Eden who was certain that the government 'would fall if it tried to agree' with US plans.[53]

Looking back, the fate of united action was sealed in the Cabinet room of Number 10 Downing Street on the afternoon of Sunday, 25 April 1954. A few months later, the American journalist Chalmers Roberts published an article in *The Reporter* in which he reconstructed the Dulles-Radford-Congressional meeting of 3 April from an insider source (later revealed as Democrat John W. McCormack). Roberts credited legislative leaders with setting the conditions – including British support – which stymied US intervention in Vietnam. He entitled the article 'The Day We Didn't Go to War'.[54] In truth, 25 April is a more critical date insofar as a British green light, had it been forthcoming, would have opened the way for at least some level of American-led action. When Roberts interviewed Eden a little later, he asked him who he thought had spiked the US plan. Eden pondered for a moment and then replied: 'I guess I did.'[55]

To round off the events of 25 April we need to look at what happened in and between Paris and Washington over the previous twenty-four hours to bring the United States to the brink of war, Britain permitting. After Eden had left for London, Dulles, accompanied by MacArthur and Dillon, went to the Matignon to confer with Laniel. The news from Dien Bien Phu was 'very bad', the French premier disclosed. The fortress would likely be lost within a few days. When that happened, his government would fall and its successor would settle for peace at any price. Laniel then added his own plea for US air intervention to the request already lodged by Bidault. Dulles was sympathetic but non-committal about action at Dien Bien Phu but was more positive about intervention elsewhere in Vietnam. However, he reiterated his government's conditions: first, that 'the United Kingdom ... agree to join us in the military defense of Indochina'; second, that the Associated States were accorded 'real and complete independence'. On this last point, Laniel set the record straight: negotiations with the Vietnamese were close to completion, with Vietnam's relationship to the French Union the only unresolved issue. In that case, Dulles said, intervention hinged on the British and 'we were prepared to do everything in our power to make them see the seriousness of the situation'. The French, too, should plead their case directly to the Churchill government.[56]

With this, Dulles headed to Orly for his flight to Geneva. Around the same time, Dillon cabled the State Department offering some personal reflections. The Ambassador suspected that the full French Cabinet was unaware of the mounting number of requests for US help at Dien Bien Phu and that it was a quartet of Laniel, Bidault, Pleven and Schumann who were leading the charge with Ely lending military backing. Dillon himself was in favour of *Vautour* which, if launched, would strengthen the position of the fight-on group in the government vis-à-vis defeatists. Contrariwise, if the United States refused to help, the fact would soon become public knowledge and lend credence to the already widespread suspicion in France that 'US desires that French personnel should contrive to bear the full burden of the fighting against the Communists'. Given that the Laniel government would probably collapse when Dien Bien Phu perished and be replaced by a coalition tasked with negotiating a settlement under the most unfavourable of conditions, Dillon felt that *Vautour* was 'the only way to keep the French Union forces fighting ... and so to save Indochina from Communist control'.[57]

Dillon's analysis made an impression in the State Department and clearly informed Smith's handling of his meeting with Bonnet on the evening of 24 April (Washington time), the encounter which in turn prompted Massigli's call on the Foreign Office and brought about the second British Cabinet meeting on 25 April. However, there is nothing in Smith's account to suggest that he encouraged the French to believe that US intervention was to be had at Dien Bien Phu as opposed to more widely in Vietnam. In this specific respect, Smith disagreed with Dillon's prescription. He also reminded Bonnet of the 'impossibility of direct United States intervention without Congressional authority', which would only be forthcoming 'as the result of a declaration of intention by the several nations most immediately threatened in Asia, in concert with ourselves'. In view of the imperative of British adherence to any such declaration, Smith advised the French to impress upon the Churchill government 'the sense of urgency and the necessity for concerted action'.[58]

From this, the possibility emerges that the French, acting on US instructions to urge the UK to agree to intervention in Vietnam generally, deliberately conveyed the impression to the British that the Americans now wanted air intervention at Dien Bien Phu. In fact, the only action the US administration favoured was *beyond* Dien Bien Phu. A few days later, when Eisenhower learned that the French had, in effect, sought 'unilateral American intervention' in the battle, he called it an 'astonishing' interpretation of US policy.[59] As for Dulles, he disliked the idea of bombing at Dien Bien Phu solely as a fillip to French morale and insisted that a US, or better still a US-UK, or wider allied promise to help elsewhere in Vietnam offered the best chance of persuading the French to keep up their war effort when (rather than if) the fortress capitulated. Arriving in Geneva on the evening of 24 April, Dulles cabled Smith to say that for all the force of Dillon's pro-*Vautour* analysis, the 'risk' of France quitting Indochina after defeat at Dien Bien Phu should be accepted 'rather than intervene under present circumstances' in the final phase of the battle.[60] The Churchill Cabinet, it would appear, had not only said no to the Americans but to the French as well.

Following the second Cabinet meeting on 25 April, Eden and his advisors flew from London to Paris in an RAF Hastings to pick up Clarissa Eden, who would be joining her husband at Geneva, and to update Jebb, before continuing on to Switzerland. As the aircraft taxied to a halt at Orly, Shuckburgh peered out of the window 'and there was Bidault on the tarmac, waiting for our reply'. Eden had expected to meet the Frenchman at Geneva, but here he was, nervous and twitchy. And so it was that in a passenger lounge in the terminal, 'over a pot of hydrangeas', Eden delivered the Cabinet's 'negative decision'. Dejected, Bidault said that the news from Dien Bien Phu was slightly better, and there was a feeling that 'the fortress could still be held for a little while longer if help were in prospect'. He hoped that the Americans would go ahead on their own with air strikes. France was 'on the edge of the slope', militarily in Vietnam and politically in Paris.[61]

After bidding Bidault au revoir, Eden took to the air again. 'As we flew on', he later wrote,

> I thought of the many occasions when I had visited Geneva before the war, in the days of the League of Nations, and of the international conferences I had experienced in the city. I was back again after seventeen years, and I should need good fortune if we were to stop this dispute being the first in a chain of events leading to another catastrophe.[62]

The Hastings landed at Geneva's Cointrin airport at 9.00 pm, having encountered stormy weather in its descent. The UK party was then driven to the Beau Rivage, the hotel overlooking Lac Léman which Eden had often used when on League of Nations business. There, as Shuckburgh's diary recounts, turbulence of a different kind awaited them:

> Immediately Dulles came round to see us (we were not very welcoming) to hear the result of our journey to London. We [Eden, Dulles, Shuckburgh and Merchant] had a disagreeable session ... D. seemed to have no explanation for

having failed to tell us what he had told the French, but he did say (thereby in effect denying Bedell Smith) that he was against any air strike to save Dien Bien Phu. He thought it would be ineffective and that 'we do not yet have the political basis for taking military action'. So the whole Bedell Smith incident was little more than an attempt to bounce us, and to shift the blame for the fall of Dien Bien Phu on us.[63]

In his own report to London, Eden said he had taken Dulles to task for informing him 'second hand' about the apparent US volte-face on action at Dien Bien Phu. Consistent with the Cabinet's recommendations, he told the Americans that 'if an acceptable settlement could be arrived at we were ready to guarantee it'. If Geneva failed, 'we were prepared to examine that situation. But we were not prepared to intervene now'. Dulles insisted that he had never been a 'partisan of an immediate air strike' at Dien Bien Phu but did fear that the French would 'throw in the sponge' if there was not some show of Anglo-American solidarity.[64]

Later in the meeting, when the Americans expressed scepticism about the UK's ability to defend Malaya if Vietnam was lost, Eden revealed in outline form the Songkhla strategy (*Ringlet* and *Irony*). Dulles took note but preferred to think in terms of preserving Vietnam, not offsetting the consequences of its communization. The French 'ought to be made to feel that if despite the loss of the fortress, they were willing to fight on, they would get help', he said. If the British believed that the remainder of Southeast Asia could be held if all of Indochina fell to communism, that was 'a serious error'. Eden, standing his ground, said that the British Chiefs of Staff adjudged that only the deployment of ground troops in Tonkin 'on a considerable scale' could make any impact and that air strikes at Dien Bien Phu would serve no useful purpose. However, as he indicated in Paris, he saw value in a preliminary UK-US study of regional defence. This was all 'disheartening', Dulles replied, insofar as in camera discussions would do nothing for French morale. The meeting thus ended poorly. 'It seemed to me that the prospects of French capitulation were increased in the light of the British position,' Dulles told the State Department later. The UK was ushering France towards 'an unconditional surrender'.[65]

Dulles had arrived at Geneva on 24 April, a day ahead of Eden. Addressing reporters on the tarmac at Cointrin, he said he had come to Switzerland 'on a mission of peace made necessary by communist aggression in Asia', both in Korea and Indochina. 'We hope to find that the aggressors come here in a mood to purge themselves of their aggression.'[66] From the outset, it seemed, Dulles was on crusade. In a telegram to Eden two days later, Makins averred that the Eisenhower administration had been 'knocked off idea of immediate intervention' thanks to the Cabinet's veto of British involvement in united action. But things could change and the President was 'likely to have greater volume of Congressional support for action ... to stop the spread of Communism in South East Asia than for almost any other measure he could propose'.[67] Together, Dulles's purging statement and Makins's warning strengthened Eden's conviction that the only sure way to neutralize the danger of Indochina escalating into a clash between the Cold War power blocs was to make a success of Geneva. 'I am beginning to think Americans are quite ready to supplant French and see themselves in role of liberators of Viet Nam patriotism and expulsers or redeemers of Communist insurgents in Indo-China,' he told the Foreign Office. 'If so they are in for a painful awakening.'[68]

As he set about his task, Eden was aware of the diplomatic value of the various minatory statements issuing forth from American sources at this time. The 'Russians & Chinese are terrified of the Americans' bellicosity', he noted, and fear was an exploitable commodity.[69] Shuckburgh concurred. If the communists were 'scared by Dulles's "noises off", with air lifts, security pacts, threats of atomic war', they were more likely to offer the French reasonable terms.[70] However, the prospect of US military action had to remain just that, a *prospect*. Actualization could not be permitted. The diplomatic purchase, Eden maintained, lay in keeping 'the enemy … in doubt as to what action might be taken by the Free-World'.[71]

Within the Eisenhower administration, meanwhile, there was perplexity and irritation that the New Look had terrified allies as well as enemies. The 'attitude' of the Churchill government in particular 'is one of increasing weakness', Dulles complained to the President. The 'British seem to feel that we are disposed to accept present risks of a Chinese war and this, coupled also with their fear that we would start using atomic weapons, has badly frightened them'.[72] The President was also frustrated. The British were in the grip of 'a morbid obsession that any positive move on the part of the free world may bring upon us World War III'. He also thought them fearful for the security of Hong Kong if they took part in any action against China's proxies in Vietnam. But 'if the Communists would take a good smacking in Indo-China they would be more likely to leave Hong Kong severely alone for a long time'.[73]

If the British were not in a smacking mood, the Americans, ironically, had only themselves to blame. Having decided that Indochina must be saved from communism, and having articulated publicly the dire consequences for the United States and the West generally that its loss would bring, the Eisenhower administration was under severe self-imposed pressure to make united action a reality. This, in turn, explains the lack of sympathy in Washington for the UK's contrary position. Yet the fact remains that the Churchill government's worries about a wider war – and ultimately a general nuclear war – had been ignited by Eisenhower and Dulles at Bermuda and fanned by the US administration's muscular nuclear posturing in the weeks that followed. British opposition to united action was a real problem for the Americans, but it was a problem of their own making.

*

In terms of Geneva, then, the British attitude to US military action in Vietnam was more complex than it first appears. When UK policymakers contemplated the consequences likely to flow from US or US-led intervention, they were all unsettling and had, as their culmination point, the Third World War. But the *threat* of American action, or even hints of US bombing and blockade of China, could be utilized to secure concessions from the communists. The French held a similar view. 'Lightning should not strike during [the] conference', Bidault warned, 'but occasional rumbles of distant thunder were useful'.[74] The American thunderer-in-chief was Radford, but as Eden and Churchill were about to discover, he was by no means beyond hurling lightning bolts.

11

The Geneva Conference: Opening Skirmishes

On 26 April, the day the Geneva conference opened, the Chairman of the US Joint Chiefs of Staff arrived in London on a mission approved by President Eisenhower.[1] Taking advantage of Eden's absence, Radford intended to make a last-ditch attempt to sell united action to UK military and political authorities. Meeting with the Chiefs of Staff at the Ministry of Defence, he avowed that the fall of Dien Bien Phu would create 'a very grave situation', not just in Indochina and Southeast Asia but in Europe, too. Accepting that air strikes could no longer save the French garrison, he was convinced that immediate intervention elsewhere in Vietnam by a coalition of powers led by the United States and the UK 'might prevent a complete collapse and encourage [the French] to go on fighting'. Intervention would require not only air and naval forces but 'the build-up of substantial land forces'. America, though, would not be contributing ground troops since the 'Asian countries' had 'plenty of manpower'. Radford also restated his belief that PRC counter-intervention was unlikely and Soviet involvement even more so. But even if he was wrong, 'Russia and the Communist Bloc are going to get relatively stronger', especially in nuclear arms, and it was 'in our interests to take a risk now'.[2]

The British record of this meeting indicates that Radford spoke without interruption, but afterwards, the Secretary of the COS committee commented that the Admiral's exposition 'had in no way altered the views of the Chiefs'.[3] Ensconced at Geneva, Eden had been confident that General Harding and his colleagues would withstand whatever Radford threw at them. The Prime Minister was a different matter. With Radford due to dine at Chequers that same evening (26 April), the Foreign Secretary was on edge lest Churchill, in his anxiety to heal the rift in Anglo-American relations, agree to 'Radford's war against China'.[4]

The dinner was an intimate one. Apart from the two principals the only other guests were a Radford aide and Jock Colville, Churchill's private secretary, who has left us a vivid account of the evening. Radford told Churchill that 'the fall of Dien Bien Phu, and failure of the United States and Great Britain to take appropriate action would be a great victory for the Communists and a turning point in history'. To prevent this, the US Congress was ready to approve US intervention as long as 'England was willing to co-operate'. Consider the future if Vietnam was lost 'and there was Communist infiltration elsewhere in S. E. Asia', he urged. Not only would 'the food supplies of Japan and other Asiatic peoples in Siam [Thailand] and Burma be lost but Australia and New

Zealand would be threatened', the Japanese 'would turn towards Asiatic Communism', and nationalists in Morocco 'would rise against the French' in ways that would 'spread disquiet and disorder into Africa and the Middle East'. France could reject the EDC and opt for neutralism and NATO be 'destroyed'. This was 'the critical moment at which to make a stand against China', Radford insisted. The Soviet Union was 'frightened of war' and would not act to save the PRC. There was no time to lose, however, for 'every day that passed' meant a proportionate gain for the Communist powers at our expense'.[5]

For all the passion of the American's presentation, Churchill was unmoved. The fall of Dien Bien Phu might well be 'a critical moment in history', he conceded, but the

> British people would not be easily influenced by what happened in the distant jungles of S. E. Asia; but they did know that there was a powerful American base in East Anglia and that war with China, who would invoke the Sino-Russian Pact, might mean an assault by Hydrogen bombs on these islands. We could not commit ourselves at this moment, when all these matters were about to be discussed at Geneva, to a policy which might lead by slow stages to a catastrophe.

There was 'nothing more important' than Anglo-American amity, Churchill added, but 'we could not allow ourselves to be committed against our judgement to a policy which might lead us to destruction, the more so when we believed that the action which the Americans now proposed was almost certain to be ineffective'.[6]

When Colville's account reached Eden at Geneva, his jitters subsided; at the bottom of the record he jotted just one word, 'Good'.[7] Radford, meanwhile, returned to Washington 'greatly depressed' that Churchill's position had been 'in exact accord' with Eden's. Complaining about Britain's 'veto power' over US policy, he regretted that Churchill had been so worked up about 'that horrible thing' (as he referred to the H-bomb).[8] In the State Department, Merchant was more perceptive in identifying the source of UK 'timidity'. The British were 'scared of the H–bomb', he told Dulles. 'We frightened them badly'.[9]

In his memoirs, Eden described the restoration of peace in Indochina as 'the most dangerous … of the problems' facing him during his post-war Foreign Secretaryship.[10] But he did not confront the problem alone. At Geneva, he was able to call upon a talented team of advisors led by Denis Allen, Evelyn Shuckburgh and Harold Caccia, all of whom understood that only a successful outcome to the conference could defuse Indochina's potential as a catalyst for general war. They also understood that Vietminh's politico-military strength and corresponding French and Vietnamese weakness meant that the maintenance of Laos and Cambodia as independent states, and the partition of Vietnam into Vietminh and Franco-Vietnamese zones, was probably the best dénouement that could be managed. Initially, however, the British were reluctant to promote partition in case they were accused in certain quarters (not least the United States) of appeasement of communism. Instead, Eden and his team hoped that partition would emerge naturally during the course of the negotiations.[11]

The French were also reticent. In the lead-up to Geneva, the Laniel government, knowing that the State of Vietnam was adamantly opposed to partition (Bao Dai said the idea 'revolted' him), had declared publicly its respect for Vietnam's territorial integrity.[12] As the Quai d'Orsay acknowledged, this made it impossible for the French delegation to promote a division of Vietnam. The French were thus left to hope – like the British – that partition would emerge as a 'consequence … imposed by the circumstances', both at Geneva and in Vietnam. Or rather Jean Chauvel, the senior diplomat on the French delegation, and like-minded realists hoped that this would be the case.[13] Bidault, in contrast, was queasy about negotiating with Vietminh 'assassins', as he classified the DRV delegates. At Berlin, Bidault had fought hard to have Indochina placed on the Geneva agenda, but that did not mean that he was ready to propitiate France's enemies with territorial concessions.[14]

On the communist side, both the USSR and China arrived at Geneva accepting, privately, that a north-south partition of Vietnam was a viable compromise insofar as it would acknowledge Vietminh strength in Tonkin and serve China's security needs by establishing a friendly government on its south western border. The Chinese and Soviets identified the 16th parallel as the optimum dividing line, the likely key to achieving a settlement with France that would drive a wedge between the Americans and their Western allies and forestall US intervention, the Chinese government's greatest concern.[15] The United States, as we know, had already set its face against any settlement which ceded people or territory to the Vietminh. An agreement which risked letting the 'whole anti-communistic defense of that area crumble and disappear' was 'unacceptable', Eisenhower affirmed publicly.[16] In case Dulles failed to grasp his meaning, the President cabled him in Geneva to point out that 'any division or partition of Indo-China was not included in what I considered acceptable'.[17]

Eisenhower had no cause for concern. Dulles had recognized for some time that there was 'no possible negotiated solution' for Vietnam which did not 'boil down to (1) a face-saving formula to disguise the surrender of the French Union forces and the subsequent loss of the area to the Communists; or (2) a face-saving formula to cover the retreat of the Viet-Minh'. Given the military balance in Vietnam, alternative (1) was the leading contender, but this was as abhorrent to Dulles as it was to Eisenhower. This left alternative (2), unrealistic as it was. Or possibly a third (as yet unacknowledged) alternative – continued war with the United States joining France as a co-belligerent.[18] Even if Dulles had been inclined to compromise, his room for manoeuvre, the *Washington Post* pointed out, was 'cribbed, cabined and confined by Congress to the point where negotiation is impossible'.[19] But he was not so inclined. Under Dulles's stewardship, the US delegation was present at the Geneva conference more as observers than active questers after peace.[20]

If the French could not and the Americans and Vietnamese would not countenance partition, the British were left hoping that the Soviets and the Chinese would take the initiative. But what of the Vietminh? Ho and his comrades were on the brink of victory at Dien Bien Phu. Why should they compromise? One reason – and here contemporary Western suspicions are validated by communist sources made available since the end of the Cold War – was that the Soviets and Chinese, fearing the consequences of a wider war brought on by US intervention, compelled the DRV to explore diplomatic avenues. However, the Vietminh had also reasons of their own for doing so. After eight years of war, the PAVN was battle-weary, and morale amongst the Vietminh's political constituency was not as robust as its propaganda suggested. The French garrison at Dien Bien Phu might be facing annihilation, but DRV strategists knew that the overall balance of forces across all Indochinese fronts was such that the French had the capacity (if they could summon the will) to continue the war for some time to come.[21] Nor was nervousness about American intentions confined to the DRV's Sino-Soviet patrons. 'Our main enemy', observed Truong Chinh, a senior DRV figure, 'is the US empire'. Diplomacy, therefore, was worth considering if only to deter American intervention.[22]

Sino-Soviet-Vietminh perceptions of the United States and its interventionist outlook were not very far removed from those of the British. As previously discussed, Eden regarded America's conventional and nuclear military might as a double-edged sword; the threat of US intervention was helpful if it rendered the communist side amenable to compromise, but its realization was unthinkable. Nor did UK policymakers accept that the Americans were simply sabre-rattling, not with the memory of the nuclear discussions at Bermuda so fresh, the nuclear aspects of the New Look so flaunted and the Eisenhower administration so disapproving of the Geneva process.

Partition, then, was the UK government's preferred means to its policy ends, the restoration of peace in Indochina and the elimination of the danger of a wider war. But an important linked aim was to ensure that a settlement possessed longevity. Eden knew that any partition line in Vietnam would need to be guaranteed by a combination of the UK, United States, France, Australia, New Zealand and – if possible – the Colombo powers and other concerned Asian states. In time, this grouping might transcend its Indochinese genesis and become a fully fledged Southeast Asian security organization. But timing was everything. Eden remained concerned that overt moves to build an Asian NATO while Geneva was in session would antagonize the Chinese (who would see it as directed against them), estrange India and the other Asian neutrals (who would view it as incompatible with the pursuit of peace in Indochina) and condemn the conference to failure (permitting the war and its escalatory potential to endure). Given how avid the US administration was to build an alliance as soon as possible, the British were also concerned lest the Americans use a defence organization as multilateral cover for military intervention in Vietnam.

The achievement of British aims at Geneva in the face of American aloofness, Sino-Soviet manoeuvring and likely Vietminh obduracy posed a serious diplomatic challenge. But Eden and his team had also to contend with a French government riven by uncertainty as to what its best course of action should be. Personifying this doubt, Bidault oscillated between wanting to hold on in Vietnam in the hope that US intervention would rescue the French position and acceptance that the game was up and that France should get down to serious exit negotiations. 'They are like a dog in a trap,' Ambassador Jebb said of the French, 'and are counting on their allies to do something about extricating their paw'.[23] The problem was that France's two most important allies were divided on the method of extrication, with the Eisenhower administration's 'perpetual clamouring for military action' (as Shuckburgh put it) and its countervailing hostility to composing with the communists vying with the Churchill government's opposition to military action and its commitment to a serious exploration of negotiating angles.[24]

Interestingly, the most important inter-delegation relationship in terms of making a success of the Geneva conference turned out to be the one between the UK and USSR. Congruity of outlook on the part of these Cold War opponents was evident from the beginning. On the morning of 26 April, ahead of the opening of the conference-proper, Eden and Molotov met to discuss procedural matters. At Berlin, Molotov had lived up to his reputation for sternness and inflexibility, but at Geneva Eden encountered a more congenial interlocutor. 'Why don't you and I seize power?,' the Russian suggested. 'After all, it can't be America or China.' Behind this mischievous remark, Eden discerned a serious point: the UK and USSR both shared a desire to reach a diplomatic solution. On all procedural issues, Molotov was keen to be helpful. Regarding the Korean phase of the conference, which was to precede the Indochina phase, he was perfectly happy to rotate chairing duties with Eden and their Thai counterpart, Prince Wan Waithayakon. This and other technicalities, 'which the Americans had thought would take weeks' to sort out, were resolved 'in an hour', Eden informed London. As for Indochina, Molotov struck Eden as 'anxious to get into private talks with us'.[25]

Looking back, Eden ascribed the effectiveness of Anglo-Soviet relations to mutual nuclear nervousness:

> This was the first international meeting at which I was sharply conscious of the deterrent power of the hydrogen bomb. I was grateful for it. I do not believe that we should have got through the Geneva Conference and avoided a major war without it. Its effect was least on United States policy. This was natural, since America could not at that time be reached by bombs from Soviet Russia ... The same was not true of Soviet Russia or of ourselves, for we were sharply conscious of what the spread of an Indo-China conflict might mean.[26]

Eden also engaged in some early inter-Commonwealth diplomacy (he would be assiduous in keeping Australia, New Zealand, India and other Commonwealth states apprised of developments throughout the conference). At a luncheon meeting on 26 April with Richard Casey (Australia), Clifton Webb (New Zealand) and Lester Pearson (Canada), who were present for the Korean discussions, Eden was gratified to find all three foreign ministers 'emphatically in agreement' with the UK viewpoint on Indochina.[27] Fortified by this Commonwealth consensus, Eden went on to a meeting with Dulles during which he reaffirmed the UK's anti-intervention position and made clear that his government could not support a regional security grouping with a mandate for military action in Indochina. That said, if a settlement emerged from Geneva he was content for the Associated States to be included in the remit of a defence organization.[28]

Eden's advisors shared his basic outlook but also worried about his manner in dealing with Dulles. 'AE is so anti-American that it is hard to get him to look for positive ways of bringing Dulles to a more patient frame of mind,' Shuckburgh wrote. Together, Shuckburgh and his colleagues decided to confront Eden over 'the dangers of too great a split' with the Americans; the British public would no doubt be grateful to avoid a war in Indochina, they told him, but 'they would not be best pleased if they woke up to find the Communists rolling into Malaya, and all American sympathy and support withdrawn from us'.[29] Eden, though, was indifferent. 'It is probably inevitable that the Americans should feel a little sore just now', he cabled Churchill. 'They will get over it.'[30]

The Geneva conference formally opened at 3.30 pm on 26 April with a parade of delegations at the Palais des Nations, sixteen alone for the Korean side of the negotiations. However, it was the entrance of the Chinese that made the biggest stir, PRC diplomats having never before attended such a high-profile international gathering. 'Molotov appeared surrounded by hatchet-faced henchmen', the watching Clarissa Eden noted. 'Immediately behind come the 200 Chinese delegates … all looking about 14, delicate, dressed in loose, blue uniforms.'[31] One man above all others commanded attention: the PRC's Zhou Enlai. Shuckburgh, betraying casual racism, wrote of feeling 'upset' and 'frightened by the violent self-confidence of this man speaking for hundreds of millions of yellow men who … have become our enemies'. Almost as unnerving were 'the confident handshakes between Molotov and [Z]hou en-lai', all observed by Dulles in 'ashen anger'.[32]

'Molotov introduced me to Eden … who shook my hand and greeted me', Zhou cabled Mao that night, while Eden gained the impression that Zhou was a 'tough and uncompromising' operator.[33] Dulles, meanwhile, was determined to avoid any contact with the Chinese beyond the formal business of the conference. As the delegations melted away on the first afternoon, Zhou made to move towards Dulles with hand outstretched. Seeing what was coming, the US Secretary turned his ample back and gave Zhou the coldest of shoulders. U. Alexis Johnson, a Dulles aide, witnessed the snub. Zhou was 'deeply wounded', he recalled. It was 'a loss of face … I could see … reflected throughout the rest of the conference'.[34] Afterwards, Dulles's press chief, Carl McCardle, was asked by reporters if his boss planned any one-to-one meetings with Zhou. 'Not unless their limos crash into each other leaving the hall', he quipped. The reporters laughed. But McCardle was not joking.[35]

Now that the Korean fighting had ceased, Eden, in keeping with containment-and-compromise, was looking forward to engaging with Zhou at the conference table, but he drew the line at living with the Chinese. The UK delegation had been embarrassed to find itself sharing the Beau Rivage with its PRC counterpart (although Zhou himself stayed at the luxurious Grand Mont-Fleuri at Versoix). The British security detail was alarmed at the prospect of UK and Chinese diplomats operating cheek by jowl, but the initial advice offered to Eden to avoid being overheard in his suite – to 'accompany my talks with some "noises off", such as beating on the tables, which would confuse any would-be listeners' – would have graced the script of an Ealing comedy. Still, the issue was actually serious. When, at the end of April, it was discovered that the hotel had recently been re-wallpapered, and that communist agents might have taken advantage of the decorating to implant electronic listening devices, Eden and his advisors promptly decamped to a new base, the villa Le Reposoir, safe from 'Peeping Toms and flapping ears'.[36]

With the persiflage of the opening ceremony out of the way, Eden was impatient for real discussions to begin on Korea and even more so on Indochina. The Soviets and Chinese struck him as ready to 'talk business' on Vietnam. With the French cautious but essentially receptive to negotiations, this left the United States, opposed to any compromise with the communists, out on a limb. 'I find it difficult to assess what the Americans have in mind,' Eden cabled Churchill at the end of day one, 'but it is certainly not, in the first place, the Geneva conference'.[37] In the event, the formal Indochina talks would not get going until 8 May, almost a fortnight into the conference, but Eden came to appreciate the delay insofar as it bought time for the Western powers to try and reach an agreed position – no easy task with the UK favouring peace, the Americans preferring war and the French struggling to decide between the two extremes.

Eden, Dulles and Bidault managed an hour together on Indochina at the French delegation headquarters on 26 April. According to the US record, Bidault 'touched lightly on whole range of possibilities including collective defense, cease-fire and partition'. When Eden encouraged Bidault to develop his thoughts on a ceasefire, Dulles bridled. A general ceasefire or even a local ceasefire at Dien Bien Phu would amount to a disguised French surrender, he interjected. Fighting while negotiating was the only option. 'In my judgment', Dulles reported to the State Department afterwards, Eden's attitude proved that he had come to Geneva with 'instructions actively to encourage French into almost any settlement which will result in cessation hostilities in Indochina'. Eden embodied the 'British fear that if fighting continues, we will in one way or another become involved, thereby enhancing risk [of] Chinese intervention and possibility [of] further expansion of war'.[38]

On the morning of 27 April, Dulles and Eden met – and clashed – again. It was a 'great mistake' to usher the French towards a ceasefire, the American said. They should be kept 'in the mood to fight on'. Eden countered (with 'some heat', the American record tells us) that he was not advocating an immediate ceasefire but did feel that a ceasefire, and even better an armistice with safeguards and controls, ought not to be ruled out. Dulles was not placated. The Western position was hopelessly lacking in coordination, he complained. The British not only opposed US plans for ten-power discussions on regional security, including the defence of Indochina, but the French 'had in effect no government and were at a loss as to what to do'. As things stood, France was 'drifting toward disaster'. To Eden's mind, military intervention, even under the auspices of a defence organization, would itself tend towards disaster if it prompted Chinese counter-intervention. And even supposing the PRC stayed out, did Dulles not realize the scale of the effort needed to turn the war round? It would be 'a bigger affair than Korea'.[39]

In London that morning, the French Ambassador delivered a message to Churchill from Laniel asking that the Cabinet reverse its opposition to US intervention. Having seen Radford off the previous evening, Churchill, despite his sympathy for the French 'in their agony', now said no to Laniel.[40] He went on to House of Commons to deliver a statement clarifying the UK positon. A reported intensification of the Vietminh attack on Dien Bien Phu just as Geneva got going 'is not without significance but it must not be allowed to prejudice the sense of world proportion which should inspire the Conference', Churchill opined. He then affirmed (to applause from MPs) that his government was 'not prepared to give any undertakings about United Kingdom military action in Indo-China in advance of the results of Geneva'.[41]

In Cabinet the next day, Churchill said 'with a chuckle ... "I minded much more the British being chucked out of India, than I shall mind the French being chucked out of Indo-China".[42] The mordant humour reflected the tensions of recent days, but for Dulles the Prime Minister's Commons performance was no laughing matter. When Eden showed him a copy of the statement in Geneva, he 'lost his temper' and 'stalked out ... without a word' from a meeting intended to re-establish Anglo-American unity. Like Radford, Dulles may have hoped that Churchill, always so concerned for the well-being of the "special relationship", would eventually come to share the US outlook, sidelining Eden in the process. If so, he was as wrong as Radford had been. 'Our relations are very bad,' Shuckburgh wrote after Dulles left, 'and we shall have to be very careful'.[43] Eden, though, was unfazed. With Makins reporting that American policymakers were 'soft pedalling' the possibility of military action and that the public and political 'support which was certainly building up for a policy of intervention seems to be ebbing', his immediate objective to negate US-led intervention while Geneva was in session appeared to have been achieved.[44] Eden also believed that the brake he had put on early moves on regional defence had improved the chances of an Indochina settlement which the Colombo powers, and Asian opinion generally, could support.[45]

Had Makins read the Americans correctly, though? Meeting with Republican legislative leaders on the day Geneva opened, Eisenhower insisted that if or when the United States intervened in Vietnam, it would only be as a member of an international coalition. To go in alone on the side of France would be a 'tragic error' and a stain on America's reputation as a champion of freedom for colonial peoples. At present, however, he rated the chances of winning British support, the key to united action, as 'pretty grim'.[46] To that extent, Makins judged right. By 29 April, the Ambassador was rowing back. 'Reliable sources' indicated that Washington policymakers were 'giving the most serious consideration' to bypassing the UK and starting Southeast Asia pact discussions with such other allies as could be assembled, he told the Foreign Office. An approach to Congress for authority to commit American armed forces to Indochina was in the pipeline.[47]

The Ambassador's source was the US Under-Secretary of State.[48] At a meeting of the NSC that day (29 April), Smith, backed by Vice-President Nixon, advanced the idea of the United States building an alliance without the UK. If possessed of sufficient Asian content to counterbalance Britain's omission, the coalition, Smith averred, might be enough for the administration to win Congressional approval to deploy US air and naval power in Vietnam. If the military situation then stabilized and the United States took over the training of the Vietnamese armed forces, the Navarre Plan, which was 'fundamentally sound', could yet succeed. Eisenhower accepted that the formation of an alliance 'to the complete exclusion of the British' was a 'tough one' but 'I think that I would go along with the idea'. The President's frustration at the lack of allied support – Australia and New Zealand also remained non-committal – had grown in recent days and he now wondered aloud 'whether the right decision was not rather to launch a world war'. If America's allies 'were going to fall away in any case, it might be better for the United States to leap over the smaller obstacles and hit the biggest one with all the power we had'. However, this outburst aside, Eisenhower's default setting remained multilateralism and by the close of the NSC session Smith's recommendation that the administration explore the potential for building a regional security organization without the UK had been endorsed.[49]

At Geneva, it did not take long for the Korean negotiations – predicated on converting the armistice into a lasting peace – to become deadlocked. Still, as Molotov observed, this was tolerable because in Korea, unlike Vietnam, 'at least we are not shooting one another'.[50] Beyond the formal Korean plenary sessions, the Geneva principals worked on the attendance list for the Indochina phase. The wording of the Berlin conference communiqué specified that the United States, France, the UK, the USSR, China 'and other interested States' would participate in the negotiations. This combining of the Berlin four with China implied that the PRC had equal status as an inviting power, but the Americans refused to concede the Chinese a voice in determining who the 'other interested States' should be. The selection process thus devolved to the Berlin four. Later, the Eisenhower administration claimed a 'great victory' in denying China an elevation in status, but it was really the absence of serious protest from Molotov that prevented a protracted disagreement on a matter of procedure and further suggested that the USSR was taking the conference seriously.[51]

To begin with, the French were minded to negotiate on behalf of the Associated States, but Bao Dai, in a spoiling action, issued an impassioned public appeal for independent Vietnamese representation.[52] According to the Quai d'Orsay, 'Bao Dai's distrust of the conference was based on his conviction that only a compromise solution could be reached and that such a solution was bound to be against his own interests.' Of all possible outcomes, partition was the most repugnant.[53] The Americans were sympathetic to Bao Dai's outlook, in part because of their support for Vietnamese independence, and in part because the Vietnamese would be a natural ally in opposing partition. If the Associated States were invited, the Soviets would insist on DRV participation, but the French, British and even the Americans felt they could live with that.[54]

Alongside these Indochinese preliminaries, the Korean talks ground on inconclusively. Although an entirely separate set of negotiations, the unpleasant, ideologically charged polemics which characterized this phase of the conference generated tensions which threatened to impair the chances of constructive diplomacy when Indochina took centre stage. Nor were tensions exclusively East-West. At a plenary session on 29 April, when Molotov delivered a blistering denunciation of American policy in Asia, the failure of the British to rally to the US side did not go unnoticed by the communists – or by the Americans.[55] At noon the next day, Dulles called on Eden in a mood described by Shuckburgh as 'extremely grim'. The Western powers 'seemed to be in disarray before the world' and the communists 'having it all their own way'. Neither the British nor the French had spoken up in defence of the United States in the Korean plenary and it shocked Dulles that 'when the chips were down there was no cohesion between us' only a 'pathetic spectacle of drifting'. Eden offered no balm. If the Americans felt isolated on Korea, that was because of their backing for South Korea's wholly negative attitude to the peace process, he retorted. To support America was to endorse, by extension, Syngman Rhee's intractability. Dulles was not assuaged. If ever summoned by Congress to give an account of events at Geneva, the 'consequences', he warned, 'would be disastrous for … close United Kingdom-United States relations'.[56]

The testiness spilled over into Eden and Dulles's discussion of Southeast Asian defence, an issue already bedevilled by what Merchant described as 'British abandonment of ... the [London] communiqué of April 13'.[57] Denying any suggestion of bad faith, Eden reiterated that the UK government was happy to examine any proposals the Americans put forward with the dual proviso that regional defence planning did not jeopardize the Geneva process and that pact membership did not include a commitment to military action in Indochina. At this, Dulles offered a corrective of his own. Large-scale military intervention, never mind war with China, was not under consideration in Washington, although he appreciated that some of Radford's remarks might have conveyed a contrary impression. 'Radford, however, was not the spokesman of the United States,' Dulles said. 'Only the President and he could express their Government's opinion.' Nevertheless, the US administration did want regional security talks to be wide-ranging and address the question of whether bridgeheads could be held in Tonkin as platforms for regaining military control of all of northern Vietnam.[58]

Eden had gone into his meeting with Dulles buoyed by news of the progress of the Colombo conference, which opened on 28 April. He had worried that the leaders of India, Pakistan, Sri Lanka, Burma and Indonesia would put out a resolution condemning Western efforts to organize Southeast Asian security as an unwarranted neocolonial intrusion into Asian affairs. A blow in itself, such a resolution would also have damaged Indochina peace prospects. With the Cabinet's approval, he wrote to the prime ministers of the Commonwealth contingent, India, Pakistan and Sri Lanka, in advance of Colombo to assure them of his commitment to an Indochina agreement 'acceptable to Asian opinion as a whole'. He also said that the UK was ready to guarantee any emergent Indochina settlement and expressed the hope that their countries would do likewise.[59] This démarche made an impact. As the *Times* reported on 30 April, the Colombo conference 'feels that it has a friend in Geneva' in the British Foreign Secretary and 'may be open to any suggestion that Mr. Eden is likely to make'.[60]

The news from Colombo informed a memorandum Eden gave to Dulles at their meeting that day. Although not an official document, it encapsulated Eden's conviction that 'Communism in Asia cannot be checked by military means alone'. To the contrary, since the problem 'is as much political as military', to be effective any military combination 'must enjoy the widest possible measure of Asian support'. It might be expecting too much for an organization to win the 'active support' of the Colombo powers but their 'benevolent neutrality' was a minimum requirement. Beyond this, Eden believed that regional security needed to be carefully seeded and tended, not a 'hastily contrived expedient to meet the present crisis' of the kind Dulles appeared to have in mind. Realizing that his emphasis on the Colombo powers might be construed by US opinion as an excuse for inaction, Eden said that the UK was ready to join with the United States in an immediate and secret examination of 'the political and military problems involved in creating a collective defence for South-East Asia'.[61]

Eden was being disingenuous. Despite what he told Dulles, his preference for quiet UK-US politico-military talks was intended to delay the moment when the United States unveiled publicly its chosen pact line-up. In making his offer – in playing for time – Eden was reacting to three concerns. First, when it emerged that the only Asians involved in the US ten-power grouping were Thailand and the Philippines ('United States satellites,' Eden called them) and the Associated States, the good offices of the Colombo powers, never mind their association, would be lost. Second, if Beijing interpreted the nascent pact as anti-Chinese – statements from Beijing were already likening US plans to Japan's wartime conception of a Greater East Asian Co-Prosperity Sphere – a Zhou Enlai walkout from Geneva, the collapse of the peace process, the continuation of the war and, with it, the danger of US-led escalation were all possibilities. Lastly, with a defence grouping in place, the Americans would have their united action coalition.[62]

Eden was a fine diplomatist. But Dulles was good, too – good enough to see through the ruse. A secret Anglo-American examination 'might be useful', the American agreed, 'but … it would not be useful if that was all there was'. Furthermore, since the United States, UK, France, Australia, New Zealand, Thailand and the Philippines were already on board, and Vietnam, Laos and Cambodia effectively committed, why not move ahead straight away with this 'nucleus' and 'let it develop as seemed natural'? To this, the US record tells us, 'Mr. Eden made no reply.'[63]

After sparring inconclusively with Dulles, Eden lunched at Molotov's headquarters at the Hotel Metropole. Social interaction with the communists was repellent to Dulles on principle and to Bidault for reasons of propriety connected with Dien Bien Phu, but the British, who were in diplomatic relations with all principal Geneva participants (save the DRV), invested these encounters with high political value. Also present was Zhou Enlai. Acting the attentive host, Molotov reminded Shuckburgh of an 'anxious mother bringing a farouche daughter out into polite society'. The Russian also displayed further traces of humour which Eden, after the dourness of Dulles, seemed to appreciate. 'Mr. Molotov and I know each other well,' Eden told Zhou. 'I always know when he is cross with me and when he is pleased.' 'In that case', Molotov replied, 'I am a bad diplomat. I should conceal my feelings.'[64]

During the meal (caviar, ice cream and vodka were all on the menu), Eden twitted the Chinese Prime Minister over the PRC's refusal to enter into normal diplomatic relations with the UK. The previous Labour government had granted the Central People's Government de jure recognition in January 1950, but since then Beijing had refused to exchange ambassadors. Zhou agreed 'at once' to revisit the issue and, true to his word, there would be ongoing Anglo-Chinese discussions at Geneva in the weeks to come about regularizing relations. Eden also asked Zhou and Molotov if it would be possible to arrange a local truce at Dien Bien Phu so that the French wounded could be evacuated; the two communists felt that this was a matter for the French and Vietminh to arrange between themselves. The table talk became heated when the United States was the subject of discussion. Zhou was 'very bitter' towards the Americans, Shuckburgh wrote. Eden attempted to defend the 'peace-loving' United States, but Molotov, taking Zhou's part, suggested that the UK underestimated its 'power and influence' to moderate the extremes of US policy. 'You are flattering me,' Eden replied.[65]

The Chinese were the first to leave. It had been 'a useful lunch, do you not think[?],' Molotov said to Eden when they were alone (almost as if they 'had been dealing together with a strange fellow', Shuckburgh felt). Eden thought Zhou had been 'hard and cold and bitterly anti-American' but also gained the impression that 'Molotov himself felt that he had a rough client to deal with'.[66] Afterwards, Zhou sent a telegram to Mao in which he noted that Eden's support of America had been lukewarm. The 'United States is too impatient', he quoted Eden as saying; 'we [the UK] have nothing in common with the United States except the same language'.[67] For Eden, the abiding memory of the lunch was how 'terrified' the Chinese and Soviets were of US intervention in Vietnam.[68]

The mention by Molotov and Zhou of possible Franco-Vietminh truce consultations was a reminder to Eden that both the USSR and China wanted full DRV representation at the Indochina talks. By this point, the Berlin four had accepted that the Associated States should attend and did not contest countervailing Vietminh involvement. The French, however, struggled to sell this logic to the Vietnamese, and it was not until 3 May that Bao Dai's agreement was secured. In a statement issued from the Cote d'Azur, where he was sojourning, he accepted DRV participation but reiterated his opposition to partition and also made explicit his fears of an enlarged war in which his country would become 'an immense battlefield' and a possible proving ground for 'atomic or hydrogen bombs'.[69]

Bao Dai's statement begs the question as to what, exactly, the State of Vietnam wanted from Geneva, but for Dulles, the knowledge that the Vietnamese (to quote Foreign Minister Nguyen Quoc Dinh) were 'definitely resolved to resist any proposal of partition' was reassuring.[70] Soon after, it was confirmed that the Vietnamese delegation would be led by Dinh and Nguyen Trung Vinh, Vice-President of the Council of Ministers. Pham Van Dong, acting DRV Foreign Minister, and Ta Quang Buu, Vice-Minister of Defence, would head the Vietminh delegation. The Indochina starting line-up was settled: the UK, the United States, USSR, France, the PRC, the Associated States and the DRV.[71]

Eden could be forgiven for feeling he had put in a good shift on 30 April. His sparky encounter with Dulles had been followed by lunch with Molotov and Zhou and then afternoon talks on Korea. For a man who nearly died a year earlier and required a complex and powerful regimen of drugs to maintain his health, this was a demanding schedule. But his day was not finished. At an early evening tripartite discussion of Indochina, he found Bidault in the lowest of spirits. It was hard to envisage what France could offer in the Indochinese negotiations, the Frenchman confessed. Even if he was personally willing to countenance a territorial cleavage, the fact remained that France could not actively promote partition due to Vietnamese hostility. Meanwhile, there was no prospect of British backing for military action, and without this, united action could not be realized. In consequence, Bidault felt he had 'hardly a card in his hand, perhaps just a two of clubs or three of diamonds' and 'saw nothing to prevent a Communist victory throughout the whole area'.[72]

Dulles was taken aback by Bidault's pessimism. Alone with Eden later, the American cast about for a quick-fix method of restoring French morale and preventing a cave-in when the Indochina phase began. To that end, he proposed that multilateral talks begin immediately in Washington on a Southeast Asia pact. The memorandum Eden had given him earlier referred to confidential Anglo-American talks, but secrecy and bilateralism would neither lift French morale nor give the communists pause for thought as to the consequences of a continuation of the war if they failed to present the French with acceptable terms. Eden dug his heels in. 'If the talks were to be public, we should at once be asked whether we were going to help in Indo-China, which we could not do, or whether we were not, in which event the French would not be helped.'[73]

The tension in the Eden-Dulles relationship was palpable. On one side, Shuckburgh recorded, was 'the almost pathological rage and gloom of Foster Dulles'. On the other, Eden was 'fed up with Dulles, refuses to make concessions to his feelings, and almost resents seeing him'.[74] The one bright spot on this particular horizon was Dulles's imminent departure; the US Secretary had never hidden his intention of staying in Geneva for only a week or so and Eden looked forward to Smith taking over as head of the American delegation. Eden and Smith got on well, personally and professionally, having worked closely together during the Second World War. When Smith checked in at Geneva on 1 May, Shuckburgh was delighted at how 'effusively' he and Eden greeted one another.[75]

Dulles did not head home immediately which left time for an unpleasant Anglo-American dinner that evening at the US headquarters in the Hotel du Rhône. Dulles and Smith were joined on the American side of the table by Merchant and Walter Robertson, Assistant Secretary of State for Far Eastern Affairs, while Eden was accompanied by Lord Reading, one of his Foreign Office counsellors. In the interval between the main course and dessert, 'we were subjected to a prolonged, and at moments somewhat heated, onslaught upon our attitude', Eden informed London the next morning. Unlike previous conferences, Dulles said, America and Britain were 'in complete disarray'. Not on Korea, Eden retorted, only on Indochina. 'I simply did not know what it was that we were being asked to do', he told his hosts. If it was to intervene in Vietnam, that was 'impossible'. Dulles then asked bluntly whether the UK was prepared 'in any circumstances' to back the United States in military action, adding that the Eisenhower administration was no longer looking for 'material assistance' only 'moral support'. This was 'quite a new approach', Eden conceded, but because Dulles refused to spell out the kind of action London was being asked to condone, he was unable to sanction even this recalibrated US request. 'If the Americans went into the Indo-Chinese war', Eden reflected afterwards, 'the Chinese themselves would inevitably step up their participation. The next stage would be that the Americans and the Chinese would be fighting each other, and that was in all probability the beginning of the third world war'.[76]

Throughout the evening, Robertson kept up a 'theme song' to the effect that there were 300,000 troops in the VNA anxious to fight the Vietminh and looking to the United States and UK for encouragement. If they were so keen to fight, Eden eventually snapped, 'I could not understand why they did not do so'. The Americans then reverted to their desire to take over the training of the Vietnamese army, French efforts having proven deficient in this sphere. It might take two years to bring the VNA to a pitch of fighting ability. In the interim, the United States and its allies, working with France, would have to hold bridgeheads in Tonkin. When Reading commented that this meant 'things would remain on the boil for several years to come', Dulles thought that would be 'a very good thing'.[77]

The evening had been 'highly disturbing', Eden reported to the Foreign Office. It was 'apparent that the Americans were deeply aggrieved by our refusal to support them in such military measures as they might think advisable'. All those on the US side, save for Smith, seemed incapable of understanding the UK position. 'At the same time', Eden noted, 'they had no plans of their own, but were searching about for some expedient which would serve to restore, or at least hold the situation'. If no such expedient could be found, 'they may be ready to attribute the blame for their failure to us'.[78] 'Anthony certainly fought hard tonight to prevent the Americans launching a war,' Clarissa Eden wrote in her diary. 'Dulles ... said to Anthony ... that he felt isolated and that Britain had let the US down.'[79] Shuckburgh, though, was still worried about the fractiousness of UK-US relations and the way that his boss was 'all steamed up' with the Americans whom he accused of wanting to replace the French and run Indochina themselves. 'They want to replace us in Egypt too,' Eden added. 'They want to run the world.'[80] In a telegram to Washington, Dulles confirmed that he 'hit' Eden hard, but it had been necessary. The British now had a 'far clearer detailed picture of our intent and purposes' and had been 'definitely impressed' by the damage that failure 'to rally to our side' would do to Anglo-American relations.[81]

Awareness did not equal approval. 'My view is that we cannot give the Americans the moral support they seek,' Eden informed London on 2 May. This was also the view of his Canadian, Australian and New Zealand colleagues.

> I am conscious of the effect of our differences over this question upon Anglo-American relations. But I am sure our only wise course is to follow a consistent line. This means we must refuse, pending the outcome of negotiations here, not only to allow ourselves to be drawn into the Indo-China war but also to promise our moral support for measures of which we do not yet know the full scope.[82]

The next day, the Cabinet unanimously endorsed Eden's handling of matters.[83]

Dulles continued to try and pressurize the British via the Australians and New Zealanders. On 2 May, his last day in Geneva, he summoned Casey and Webb to an extraordinary ANZUS meeting at which he revealed that the French – to judge from Bidault's depressed demeanour – were on the brink of 'virtual unconditional surrender'. If he thought that Casey and Webb, prizing their ANZUS security ties to the Americans, would simply fall into line behind US proposals for remedial action, he was mistaken. To Casey, it was 'absolutely essential' to avoid war with China, which was a likelihood if there was Western intervention in Vietnam, while military action undertaken with Geneva still in session would destroy the peace process and outrage Asian opinion.[84] Try as he would, Dulles could never quite overcome Australian and New Zealand loyalty not just to Britain as head of the Commonwealth but to the merits of the UK approach on Indochina.[85]

One other feature of this ANZUS meeting is noteworthy. Dulles again stressed that the United States was not contemplating large-scale military intervention. US aims were limited to providing support to the French to keep the FEC fighting, should disaster befall Dien Bien Phu, and to taking over the training of the Vietnamese army. At the same time, the Americans saw no harm in letting the authorities in Beijing believe that in the event, say, of PRC intervention on the side of the Vietminh, the United States was prepared to retaliate by bombing and blockading China. The Eisenhower administration had 'no intention of getting into any provocative posture with Communist China', Dulles assured Casey and Webb. But if the PRC invaded, 'then another situation would be created'. The problem with this approach (and it was one Eden was alive to) was that it did not take account of the possibility, even probability, that any US or US-led intervention would prompt a Chinese countermove which the Americans might regard as just cause for launching full-scale war against the PRC. Dulles was doubtless sincere in saying that his government would do nothing to give the Chinese 'any justification to attack Indochina openly', yet he and the US administration generally continued to favour a policy which might provide that very rationale.[86]

After the meeting, Casey and Webb, along with Pearson, conveyed to a grateful Eden their concurrence with UK thinking on Indochina and Southeast Asian defence.[87] As for Dulles, having got nowhere with his ANZUS partners, he wrote to Eden to say that there was 'much' in the UK memorandum of 30 April 'with which we would go along'. But being more pessimistic than Eden about the chances of the French fighting on after the fall of Dien Bien Phu, the idea of secret, bilateral talks on regional security still struck him as 'inadequate'. Some 'new element' was required, perhaps staff talks between the United States, UK, Australia, New Zealand and France, and possibly Thailand. The knowledge that France's allies were making progress on defence coordination would give Bidault 'hope' that an alternative existed to 'a lonely, hopeless negotiation, which will amount to unconditional surrender'.[88]

Shuckburgh, Caccia and Allen all thought that Dulles's suggestion was a 'great advance' and a way to 'get back to Anglo-US cooperation'. The Five-Power Staff Agency, they felt, was perfect for this kind of study, but Eden spied 'a trap'. Five-power or ten-power talks, it made no difference if all the Americans wanted was a veneer of multilateral cover for intervention in Vietnam, while any publicized defence discussions remained a potential Geneva-wrecker. Nevertheless, Shuckburgh and his colleagues kept the pressure on Eden to respond generously and 'struck a slight spark' with the suggestion that the terms of reference of any staff talks be limited to considering action solely in the light of an agreement being reached at Geneva. Knowing that a settlement would require a guarantee, and admitting that he was 'perhaps ... seeing things out of proportion', Eden asked for London's view. Within twenty-four hours, the Foreign Office had approved a Five-Power Staff Agency study. And so, therefore, did Eden.[89] It was a rare moment of Anglo-American calm before the next storm.

The Fall of Dien Bien Phu, May 1954

On 3 May, Dulles left Geneva. Eden had been complaining privately for weeks about the way Dulles was trying to 'bulldoze' him 'to get the war he wanted in Indochina', but now, as the American prepared to board his plane at Cointrin, he told him to his face: 'The trouble with you, Foster, is that you want World War Three.'[1] Eden had only gone to the airport under pressure from his advisors to effect a conciliatory gesture, but 'I don't think it did much good,' he reflected.[2] He was right; no sooner was Dulles home than he was seething to Eisenhower about Eden's 'gall' in being photographed with him at the airport in a show of staged amity when 'he never said a word in defense of the US' during the conference.[3] Dulles's mood was not improved by the political flak he was attracting in America. On the Democratic side, former President Harry S. Truman and Senate Minority leader Lyndon B. Johnson claimed that the Secretary of State's failed Indochina policy left the United States 'naked and alone', while on the Republican right, Knowland accused Dulles of yielding to Anglo-French 'blackmail' and of preparing for a surrender to communism 'on the instalment plan'.[4]

Eden, meanwhile, having received approval from London for a Five-Power Staff Agency examination of Southeast Asian security, put off telling the Americans until he dined alone with Smith at Le Reposoir on 3 May – after Dulles had departed. By his own admission, Eden's instinct had been 'all against the slightest concession to Dulles', but he found Smith much more congenial.[5] Having said that, Smith, in a frisson of Radford's outlook, tried to persuade Eden that the Western powers 'could afford to take greater risks in our dealings with the Soviet Union today than would be possible in four of five years time' when the USSR's nuclear arms and delivery systems had advanced. As Smith viewed matters, the 'immediate problem in Indo-China was to encourage the French to hold on, not only in the battlefield but at the conference table, so as to gain time to organize a more effective defence, while bringing pressure to bear upon the Chinese and Russians to accept a tolerable settlement'. In response, Eden tabled his staff agency proposal. Those Asian states most intimately concerned, the Colombo powers and Thailand, should be kept apprised of progress and, if appropriate, invited to take part in a further study of the implications of guaranteeing an Indochina settlement. This initiative might in turn beget a larger collective defence organization. Smith, who professed to understand UK thinking, promised to convey Eden's offer to Washington.[6]

Those close to the British Foreign Secretary were relieved that the Anglo-American barometer had swung so quickly from stormy to fair, a development which they put down to the change in US leadership. Smith 'seems to agree entirely with the British attitude on Indo-China', Shuckburgh wrote. 'He thinks air/sea action futile to affect the present campaign and says American ground forces will go into Indo-China over his dead body.'[7] Eden, too, was upbeat. 'We have had a very difficult time with Dulles,' he admitted, 'but now that Bedell Smith has taken his place, I believe we may be able to get our policies closer together.'[8] From Washington, however, Makins cautioned that Smith might be easier to get along with but Dulles had greater influence with the President, while Cable, looking back, felt that Eden exaggerated how much Smith, a hawk on Indochina, really differed from Dulles in policy terms.[9]

On 4 May, Eden's staff agency proposal was put down in a formal memorandum which was then passed to Smith. The American, though, now wanted more. With the National Security Council poised to discuss Indochina, Smith said that its approval of Eden's plan was more likely if the terms of reference were expanded to cover not just success but failure at Geneva. From a US standpoint, two broad alternatives presented themselves: first, 'to make the best arrangement' possible at the conference; second, 'for the United States to go to war'. Smith 'did not exclude the second'. Public hostility in America to another land war in Asia 'could be changed overnight' by a President 'whose popularity was undimmed'. This appreciation unsettled Eden. Any outside intervention in Vietnam 'might well lead to the third world war', he countered. Hence, the UK aim remained a negotiated agreement with the communists which would 'save all we could' of Vietnam as well as Laos and Cambodia.[10]

If it had been Dulles who proposed widening the scope of the five-power talks, Eden would have gone into lockdown. But this was his friend, "Beetle" Smith, and he was torn between wanting to respond positively (and help repair the rift in UK-US relations) and the worry that an open-ended military survey would be interpreted by the Chinese and Soviets, not to mention the Colombo powers and UK opinion, as a vote of no confidence in Geneva. In the end, because the staff study was without commitment to governments, Eden opted to mend fences with Washington. The Cabinet was asked to approve a five-power military exploration of the situation 'both now and as it may be after the Geneva Conference'. That approval was forthcoming on 5 May.[11] Transmitting a reworked version of Eden's proposal to the State Department, Smith pronounced it a 'considerable compromise' on the UK's part.[12]

At this point, Eden developed 'cold feet'.[13] Having impressed upon Smith the importance of avoiding public statements exaggerating the scope of the proposed discussions, the Foreign Secretary was displeased to find the *Times* in London and *New York Herald Tribune* carrying well-informed stories concerning the five-power talks.[14] Convinced that the leak emanated from the US side, Eden fretted that his agreement to UK participation would be seen publicly 'as a victory for Dulles'. He also worried that he had 'thrown away ... the whole popular position he has established' in Asia.[15] The communiqué issued at the end of the Colombo conference on 2 May had delighted Eden in welcoming 'the earnest attempts being made at Geneva' to find a peaceful solution in Indochina.[16] Privately, Nehru also promised him that India would assist in promoting an Indochina agreement and would participate in a guarantee of a settlement provided it was supported by communists, non-communists and neutrals.[17] This was a great gain, as Eden knew. But was it now at risk? In his diary, he confirmed that in giving way to Smith his aim had been 'to bridge Anglo-US gap, in appearance especially'. But in so doing, he had 'gone as far as I can … & maybe too far'.[18]

Hoping to limit the damage from any further publicity, Eden wrote to the leaders of India, Pakistan and Sri Lanka to reassure them that the staff talks did not presage any weakening in his commitment to the Geneva process.[19] In his telegram to Nehru, Eden also expressed interest in the idea of an all-encompassing guarantee for a settlement and offered the 1925 Locarno treaty (an idealistic but failed effort to concretize European borders promoted by his early mentor, Austen Chamberlain) as a possible model.[20] Eden's attachment to a Southeast Asian Locarno would increase over the weeks ahead before emerging mid-year as yet another – and quite spectacular – source of Anglo-American friction.

In Washington on 6 May, the National Security Council discussed Indochina. Brushing aside Smith's support for Eden's proposal, Dulles argued that in showing willing to discuss regional security, and to include Indochina in that discussion while Geneva was in session, the British had merely brought the position back to where it had been before they 'backed out' of the London agreement. Eisenhower, for his part, was uneasy about moving ahead with an Agency comprised of 'five white nations' which 'left out the Asian states'. However, like Smith, he felt that the British proposal was 'such a significant advance' that the administration needed to 'follow it through'. Melding two key US objectives (immediate defence planning, which covered Indochina, and building a Southeast Asian security community), Eisenhower suggested that the 'real work' of planning could begin on a five-power basis before a wider defence grouping, including Asian states, consolidated what had been done. The NSC endorsed this dual-track approach: the Five-Power Staff Agency was designated 'a subsidiary body rather than the heart of a coalition', its study being recognized as a beginning, not an end.[21]

To Dulles, the regional perspective was important, but if Vietnam was lost, he feared that Southeast Asia might be beyond saving. For this reason, and disregarding whether Britain 'would act with us initially to try to save Indochina', he told the NSC that the United States needed to reach agreement with France on the terms under which American intervention in Vietnam could occur. He put forward four 'fundamentals': genuine independence for the Associated States, a leading role for the United States in training the Vietnamese National Army, joint Franco-American planning and command, and a French pledge to continue the fight rather than use US intervention as an excuse to liquidate the FEC. If the Laniel government accepted these conditions, the United States 'might go into Indochina on the gamble that the British would also ultimately join'. There was, though, 'a much greater chance of Chinese overt intervention' in response to US military action 'than would be the case if the British were in it with us'. Eisenhower, bristling, was quick to put Dulles straight. Unilateral intervention on the side of France 'would be completely inconsistent with our whole foreign policy'. Nor could there be 'US belligerency in Indochina without Congressional agreement' which, in turn, might well depend on the formation of a united action coalition.[22]

Back in Geneva, the satisfaction British officials derived from the Foreign Secretary's apparently diminishing anti-Americanism was offset by concern about his rising pro-Sovietism. It was one thing to be at loggerheads with Dulles, Shuckburgh felt, but another matter altogether to start 'thinking of Molotov as a sort of benevolent middle-man' just because 'he smiles so nicely and talks so gently to us'. If Eden persisted in playing the neutral East-West mediator, what would that do for UK-US relations given that Britain was supposed to be on America's side in the Cold War? The USSR was the enemy. Neutrality was not an option.[23] Eden disagreed. 'I am inside right, the Americans outside right,' he told his advisors. 'Molotov is inside left, [Z]hou outside left.' His meaning was clear enough even to those unfamiliar with football tactics: the UK and USSR occupied the centre circle; both wanted Geneva to succeed; but both had unpredictable allies on their respective wings who did not necessarily share their commitment to the peace process and who might yet come to blows.[24]

On the evening of 5 May, Eden hosted a dinner at Le Reposoir for Molotov and senior Soviet officials. 'Molotov was in an unusually relaxed mood' and 'seemed genuinely anxious that the conference should succeed' but was 'considerably worried over the situation in Indo-China', Eden cabled London the next morning. The two foreign ministers agreed to share the chairing of the Indochina phase between them on a rotating basis, an easy arrangement which cohered, Eden felt, to Molotov's 'theme that the success of the conference largely depended on him and me, and that it was our task to bring, in his case the Chinese, and in mine the Americans, into line'. Confronted by the double jeopardy of internationalization and escalation, Eden and Molotov were as one in viewing an armistice as the overriding priority. 'If the Indo-China situation was not effectively handled here', Eden remarked, 'there was real danger that the supporters of each side would go on increasing the degree of their participation until finally there was a clash between them, and if that happened it might well be the beginning of the third world war'. To all this, Molotov 'warmly agreed'.[25]

Eden was pleased by the success of the dinner. 'They had a hilarious evening, which went on quite late with screams of laughter and talk on all subjects,' Clarissa Eden wrote in her diary.

> Molotov speaking of the conference as someone completely detached and agreeing with Anthony on all points and making no difficulties about anything. He said he sees the world now as stable except for two restless powers – China and America. He sees Britain and Russia in analogous positions regarding the conference. Neither wants an extension of the war and both have belligerent allies.[26]

Eden's attentiveness to the Soviets was not appreciated by his officials, however. Allen had been 'shocked' at the eagerness with which he revealed to Molotov his ideas about 'the middle position of USSR and UK, with an implication that we deprecate the wildness of the Americans (and Chinese), the hopelessness of the French'. It was 'pretty terrible'.[27] The next day, Eden wrote to Churchill to say that the 'position at this conference is about as difficult and dangerous to Western unity as anything I have ever seen'.[28] Eden blamed the Americans, but Shuckburgh and Allen more than half blamed Eden for going straight 'to the Bosom of Auntie Mol'.[29]

The Foreign Secretary's advisors had a point about the negative impact that his modus operandi was having on Anglo-American relations. Before leaving Geneva, Dulles had warned Eden not to become 'a go-between for the Allies & Russia', but this had only redoubled his determination to act as peace-broker.[30] Back in Washington, Dulles told Eisenhower that the British were 'scared to death by the specter of nuclear bombs in the hands of the Russians' and consequently 'beguiled' by the prospect of détente with the post-Stalin leadership in the Kremlin.[31] Dulles was only partially correct. The British *were* scared – but it was the prospect of US military action in Asia at the risk of war with China, general war with the USSR and a Soviet nuclear assault on the UK, that unnerved them. Détente had become both a national security imperative and a means of containing America. On the US side, Eisenhower and Dulles acknowledged but still could not sympathize with UK nuclear insecurities. Instead, they expressed 'great disappointment ... in Eden's current behaviour'. By playing the noble-minded international statesman, Eisenhower surmised that he was looking to enhance his domestic standing and improve his chances of an early takeover from Churchill. If that was the case, commented Dulles, he 'hoped [Chancellor R. A.] Butler would be made the successor'.[32]

Dulles indulged in more Eden-bashing when he briefed Congressional leaders on 5 May. Blaming the UK Foreign Secretary for 'embarrassing' the administration by scuttling the London agreement, he offered the 'personal view' that he had caved in to pressure from Nehru. Dulles also scoffed at the Churchill government's 'almost pathological' fear of nuclear weapons which was preventing it from adopting any 'line of action which might bring on H-bomb devastation'. The UK rated 'much higher ... than we did ... the risk that open Western intervention in Indochina would lead to Chinese intervention and global war'.[33]

If the British and Soviets were keen for Geneva to succeed and the Americans fearful of what success might look like, the French, torn between getting on and getting out, struggled to formulate a coherent negotiating position as the Indochina negotiations drew nearer.[34] It did not help that the government Bidault represented was fighting for its political life. On 6 May, Laniel survived a vote of confidence in the National Assembly (311 to 262). Analysing the result, the UK Embassy in Paris concluded that a majority of French parliamentarians would continue to hold out for peace on acceptable terms even if that meant prolonging the war for a time. But this majority was fragile 'and would probably not stand up against any shocks'.[35]

To Bidault, the vote must have felt like a stay of execution. Unless there was something to show from Geneva, he told Eden, the Laniel government would fall and its successor pursue of a policy of cut and run.[36] But what did Bidault want from the conference? As the Frenchman acknowledged, the threat of US military intervention was helpful to the extent that the Soviets, Chinese and Vietminh, if sufficiently alarmed by American menaces, might offer acceptable terms.[37] But what constituted acceptable terms? Partition conceivably fitted the bill, but even if proposed by the communists, France could not accept this solution without outraging the State of Vietnam and antagonizing the United States.[38]

Bidault in Geneva and Laniel in Paris were in a triple-bind. To fight on meant internationalizing the war, but this would lead to an erosion of French authority in

Indochina and lend substance to the popular perception in France that the conflict was being waged less for French interests than for the anti-Chinese objectives of Eisenhower's America. Even supposing the Laniel administration managed to cling to office following the fall of Dien Bien Phu and the collapse of the peace process, internationalization risked unleashing not just war with China but general war with the USSR at a time when French opinion, no less than British opinion, was experiencing thermonuclear nervousness. Yet to strike a deal with the Vietminh on the basis of partition would not only betray Vietnam and alienate the United States but probably clear the way for the communization of all of Indochina as soon as the FEC pulled out. And that would equal peace with *dis*honour. No wonder Bidault sometimes appeared to be at his wits' end.

*

When French troops first occupied Dien Bien Phu, they called it *le camp retrenché* (the entrenched camp); after the battle commenced, it became *le merdier* (the shithole); with the onset of the rains at the end of April, it became simply *le bidet*.[39] The contrast between the horror of a battlefield in Tonkin and the tranquil beauty of Lac Léman could not have been greater. 'It is not easy always to remember, in these sunny Geneva surroundings, the ghastly horror of Dien Bien Phu,' wrote Shuckburgh.[40]

On 1 May, the PAVN, equipped with newly delivered Soviet bloc recoilless cannons and *Katyusha* multi-tube rocket launchers, began its final offensive.[41] The end for the French came six days later when Vietminh forces succeeded in overwhelming the remaining Centres of Resistance (CRs). After eight weeks of fierce combat, the guns fell silent. General de Castries had been captured in his command bunker at dusk on 6 May. The last CR, Isabelle, held out for a short time longer before the final capitulation. As infantrymen from the 308th and 312th PAVN Divisions took possession of the battlefield, dazed survivors emerged from their bunkers. French veterans later remarked upon the youth and nervousness of the Vietminh troops. 'It's all over?,' one boy soldier enquired of his French prisoner. 'Yes, it's all over.' 'No more shooting?' 'No more shooting.' During the battle, the French lost around 2,700 dead or missing in action, with 10,000 wounded/able-bodied troops taken prisoner. Deserters (the 'rats of Nam Yum') accounted for most of the remainder. Vietminh casualties were upwards of 25,000, including 10,000 killed.[42]

The news of de Castries's capture filtered into and around Paris – six hours behind Tonkin – from early morning on 7 May. That afternoon, an emotional Laniel spoke to the National Assembly. The 'central positon of Dien Bien Phu has fallen', he revealed, although the defenders of the Isabelle redoubt were believed to be still fighting. When it was confirmed soon after that the fortress had fallen, the Archbishop of Paris ordained a solemn Mass for the dead; television schedules were cancelled; theatres, restaurants and cinemas closed their doors; and radio networks replaced entertainment shows with programmes of sombre music, including, appropriately, Berlioz's *Requiem*.[43]

In Geneva, Eden sent Bidault a message of sympathy which elicited a response couched 'in exquisite moving words'.[44] Churchill wrote to Laniel. 'The loss of the fortress has been a bitter pang to me though I am sure there was nothing we could have done or ought to have tried to do in the last phase which would have averted its doom.' As for the future, he urged that one lost battle should not be regarded by the French as 'closing the hope of extracting an honourable settlement'.[45] There was no mention of a settlement in Eisenhower's message of condolence to French President René Coty, only praise for his nation's traditional resilience. France had suffered 'temporary defeats' in the past and had managed 'to continue as one of the world's leaders in all things that tend to bring greater richness to the lives of men'.[46] From his air-conditioned headquarters in Hanoi, Navarre explained the defeat by pointing to the scale of Chinese military aid which had enabled the PAVN 'to inaugurate a type of modern warfare that was entirely new to the Indochinese theatre of operations'. Critics would later interpret his words to mean that he and his senior advisors had committed the most basic sin of warfare: they had underestimated their enemy.[47]

Encountering Bidault at Geneva on 7 May, Smith found him 'in a very bad way' and expecting instructions from Paris to propose a ceasefire 'which would amount to a virtual surrender'.[48] Laniel, however, in a public statement that evening, struck a defiant note by announcing that the FEC's strength would be maintained and possibly boosted by reinforcements from Europe. The British Embassy in Paris applauded French resolve, but the US Embassy offered a more cynical assessment; Laniel's defiance was 'chiefly for the record' in the sense that if his government 'is to go down it should at least, like the heroes of Dien Bien Phu, be seen to go down fighting'.[49] The Americans were closer to the truth. According to orders issued to him by the Committee of National Defence in the aftermath of Dien Bien Phu, Navarre was to try to hold the Red River delta but not in ways that would 'risk the attrition of the expeditionary corps'. France would cling on, not fight on.[50]

At 4.00 pm the following day, 8 May, Eden chaired the first session of the Geneva conference on Indochina. It fell to Bidault to make the opening statement. With the DRV delegation looking on, he held his composure sufficiently to acknowledge the heroism of the Dien Bien Phu garrison before proposing that the conference adopt as its guiding principle 'a general cessation of hostilities in Indochina supported by essential guarantees of security'. In effect, just twenty-four hours after the French humiliation at Dien Bien Phu, Bidault called for an armistice without any regard for the strength of the Vietminh's military position. He could hardly do anything else without dishonouring the French fallen, but as a basis for a settlement there was nothing in it for the Vietminh.[51]

As the Geneva conference set about exploring the potentialities for peace, the US government remained preoccupied with the possibility of war. In a televised broadcast following the fall of Dien Bien Phu, Dulles stated that 'present conditions' did not provide 'a suitable basis for the United States to participate with its armed forces' in Vietnam.[52] From this, it would appear that Giap's boast that his troops had 'struck a rude blow against the intrigues of the French colonialist warmongers and the American interventionists' was merited.[53] But Dulles spoke only of the present. In secret, the Eisenhower administration continued to weigh its future options.

For Radford, the disaster at Dien Bien Phu confirmed the foolhardiness of attempting local defence in Southeast Asia and strengthened his conviction that targeting the Chinese People's Republic must be the US strategic object. 'There existed no local military method of preventing the surrender over a period of several years of the rest of the area by Communist infiltration and ... political accommodation,' he warned Dulles on 9 May. The 'only military solution was to go to the source of Communist power ... and destroy that power'. With Soviet quantitative and qualitative nuclear advances expected in the next few years, America's lead over the USSR in nuclear weapons was a diminishing asset. It followed, Radford argued, that with the United States presently immune from the danger of Soviet A-bomb or H-bomb retaliation, there would never again be 'as clear-cut a basis for taking measures directly against China as was the case now in Indochina'.[54]

Dulles found Radford's prescription too extreme. Believing that it was better to deter than to fight a war with the PRC, he still wanted to build a collective defence grouping and draw a line in Southeast Asia beyond which the United States and its allies would not permit the Chinese or their proxies to advance.[55] Dulles had not given up on Indochina, though. As the negotiations got underway at Geneva on 8 May, the National Security Council agreed that the French government should be apprised of the conditions – Dulles's fundamentals – which needed to be met if the United States was to consider entering the war.[56] That evening, Dulles called on Bonnet at his residence and told him that the US government was 'prepared to sit down and talk with the French about what the French called "internationalizing" the war'. The hurt of Dien Bien Phu was too raw for Laniel and his colleagues to think in these terms just yet, Dulles accepted, but they 'might change their mind after the full harshness of probable Communist terms was revealed'. Fight on with America and other allies and retrieve national pride, or negotiate a humiliating settlement with the communists; these, Dulles implied, were the only options for France.[57]

At Geneva, the Indochina negotiations had quickly descended into negativity. In the days following Bidault's opening statement, most of the other delegations delivered set-piece orations intended to reproach opponents, mollify allies or satisfy domestic constituencies more than advance the peace process. The plenary sessions became stages upon which diplomats struck attitudes reprised afterwards for the benefit of the news-hungry international press pack assembled at the Palais des Nations: the Americans condemned the Godless barbarism of the Chinese; the Chinese pilloried the West in general and the United States in particular for their militarism and imperialism; the DRV railed against a century of French colonial evil; the Vietminh and Chinese together played up to the non-aligned outlook of India and the other Colombo powers by demanding an Asia for Asians; and the Associated States called for the surrender of an enemy whose strength they ignored. As co-chairs, the British and Soviet foreign ministers did their best to steer the talks towards possible areas of compromise, although Molotov openly sided with China and the Vietminh whereas Eden strove to maintain a more neutral position.[58]

The French and DRV opening statements served one useful purpose in revealing the extent of the gulf separating the sides. Beyond seeking a cessation of fighting on all Indochinese fronts, Bidault wanted a regrouping of regular forces in Vietnam in a series of designated enclaves. This so-called leopard-skin approach, with zones/ spots to be defined by the conference, was not, he argued, a hard territorial division – in other words, partition. The French also wanted the disarmament of irregulars, the release of prisoners and the establishment of an international commission to oversee the settlement. The situation in Laos and Cambodia was different in that both countries were victims of communist aggression (the PAVN had invaded Laos in April and December 1953 and made incursions into Cambodia in spring 1954); hence all that was required was for the PAVN to withdraw. The French deliberately limited themselves to military proposals, the watchful presence of the Vietnamese militating against any consideration of political initiatives (a coalition government involving the DRV, nationwide elections and, above all, partition).[59]

The DRV, having coordinated its position with the USSR and PRC in bilateral and trilateral meetings ahead of the conference, began by advancing its maximalist position.[60] Pham Van Dong insisted that military and political questions be dealt with simultaneously; there should be a ceasefire in Vietnam, certainly, but this must be linked to the withdrawal of foreign forces (meaning in practice the FEC) and the granting by France of genuine independence. As bait to the war-weary French, Dong left open the possibility of French Union membership for a united Democratic Republic of Vietnam. On Laos and Cambodia, the DRV refused to confirm the presence of its forces in either country and instead made common cause with the Pathet Lao and Khmer Issarak, the local communist movements in Laos and Cambodia, respectively, whose rights and interests the conference needed to acknowledge. Elections would be required in Vietnam, Laos and Cambodia to produce governments of national unity. Confident that Vietminh popularity would deliver a victory at the polls in Vietnam, Dong evidently hoped to propel the DRV's protégés into power in Laos and Cambodia and thus establish an Indochinese federation under Ho Chi Minh's leadership. The DRV made no mention of international supervision, only of bilateral Franco-DRV commissions to effectuate the settlement.[61]

While diplomats continued to pose and posture in Geneva throughout the rest of May and into June, soldiers still fought and died in Vietnam. After winning at Dien Bien Phu, the Vietminh quickly turned their attention to the Red River delta and the ultimate prize, Hanoi, 'the Berlin of Southeast Asia', as de Lattre called it.[62] Defying exhaustion, the rainy season and Navarre's predictions, the PAVN moved steadily eastwards.[63] By mid-June, French intelligence assessed that Giap had at his disposal a *masse de manoeuvre* sufficient to launch an assault on Hanoi and threaten the port of Haiphong, the FEC's emergency escape hatch. The French and French Union enjoyed numerical superiority in the delta – nearly 200,000 troops compared with 80,000 Vietminh troops – but the bulk of this manpower was locked up in fixed positions while the PAVN possessed considerable mobility even in monsoon conditions. The delta had also been infiltrated by an estimated 100,000 Vietminh irregulars over the previous two years, perhaps fatally so given the already substantial "rice roots" support for Ho Chi Minh amongst the area's predominantly rural population of ten million.[64]

For Eden, military developments underscored the imperative of reaching a negotiated settlement before a PAVN attack on the Hanoi-Haiphong complex brought American retaliation. Harold Caccia, one of his close advisors, was by no means alone in predicting that the Vietminh and their Chinese backers were 'playing with World War III if they try to take too much advantage of their temporary military position in Indo-China'.[65] American military action would be 'fraught with danger', Lord Salisbury fretted in London. 'We should have no control over them at all. They might drop the H. Bomb.'⁶⁶ Churchill, too, was conscious of the 'danger that the Americans may become impatient' and that Indochina might become an excuse to target not just China but the USSR in a pre-emptive assault while the United States remained ahead in the nuclear arms race and largely invulnerable to Soviet counter-attack. 'They may get in a rage and say … Why should we not go it alone? Why wait until Russia overtakes us?'⁶⁷

After a run of Geneva plenary sessions notable only for polemical grandstanding, Eden tried to get the conference to focus on core issues. The obvious one was an armistice. After a halt to the fighting in Vietnam, the FEC and PAVN needed to disentangle and relocate to agreed regroupment zones. In Laos and Cambodia, Eden agreed with Bidault that the PAVN should withdraw unconditionally, although this left unresolved the status and rights of the Pathet Lao and Khmer Issarak. Lastly, if the principle of international supervision of a settlement was agreed, the next thing to consider was the membership and functions of a multinational commission. To get anywhere on these questions, Eden was persuaded (and in turn managed to persuade Molotov) that the plenary approach should be set aside in favour of restricted sessions limited to the heads of the nine delegations with just two or three advisors apiece. A news blackout was also essential. Between them, Eden and Molotov secured the consent of the other delegations, and the first restricted session took place on 17 May.⁶⁸

This procedure did not entirely end the ideological sniping or the feeding of the press pack, but from mid-May onwards, negotiations approximating the true sense of the word began to develop. Indeed, there were two immediate if small-scale breakthroughs attributable to the more serious-minded atmosphere. First, Molotov informed Eden that military issues should be prioritized ahead of political matters, a departure from the DRV's hitherto adamant insistence on simultaneous politico-military discussion.⁶⁹ Molotov was the conveyor of the news but it was Zhou Enlai who did most to persuade the DRV to comply in the interests of preserving the negotiations and lessening the risk of US intervention. 'We've lost too many men in Korea,' Zhou acknowledged going into the conference. 'We're in no condition to get involved in another war at this time.'⁷⁰ Secondly, the DRV followed through on a previously expressed readiness to permit the evacuation of the more grievously wounded French prisoners from the vicinity of Dien Bien Phu. On 19 May, French and DRV military representatives met to determine the practicalities of evacuation, and before long these bilateral military talks had expanded to cover possible POW exchanges.⁷¹

To Eden's disappointment, there was no comparable progress on the bigger overarching issues of the conference. Even in restricted session, the communists and non-communists rarely inhabited common ground. The composition of a commission to oversee an agreement proved to be a source of especial disputation. After the USSR proposed a four-power grouping of India, Pakistan, Poland and Czechoslovakia, the Western powers united in objection to the presence of two European communist states. The UK, keen to cultivate neutral Asian opinion, proposed the Colombo powers; being five in number, they would also be able to reach majority verdicts on contentious questions whereas the Soviet four-nation model could easily produce stalemate. To Molotov's mind, the Colombo powers were not as neutral as Eden made out. India, Pakistan and Sri Lanka were linked to Britain via the Commonwealth, while Pakistan was close to the United States. Smith, for the Americans, rejected any communist participation and pressed for the inclusion of what he called 'genuinely neutral' states. In Zhou's view, there were two sides to the war – France and the Vietminh – hence the Soviet proposal had a balanced logic: Poland and Czechoslovakia had diplomatic relations with the DRV, India and Pakistan with France. Bidault, however, siding with Smith, maintained that communist states could never be neutral, a judgement that produced the Molotovian barb that there was no logical reason why non-communist states could be neutral either.[72] And so, Eden recalled, 'session after session passed in mutual recrimination and endless argument'.[73]

The same description applied to the discussions on Laos and Cambodia wherein the communists insisted on a single settlement to cover all three Associated States, and the Western powers countered that Laos and Cambodia should be dealt with separately.[74] Although the communists dropped an early demand that the Pathet Lao and Khmer Issarak be permitted to attend the conference, they refused to budge on the principle of an all-encompassing settlement; whatever applied to the Vietminh in Vietnam should also apply to the 'resistance' governments and forces in the neighbouring Indochinese states.[75] On 20 May, Eden and Zhou met again. The conference was dealing with 'a single colonial war which the French had started', the PRC Premier argued, and there needed to be 'a single indivisible' settlement for all of Indochina. In addition, the Pathet Lao and Khmer Issarak should be universally recognized as governments-in-waiting. This irked Eden. To many in the West, he responded, those movements were regarded as DRV proxies possessing no great following even in their own countries and whose existence was merely a means by which Ho Chi Minh could 'grab the whole of Indo-China'. A 'one-sided view', Zhou admonished.[76]

Eden relayed the PRC perspective to Bidault and Smith later that day. An end to hostilities in Cambodia and Laos could be arranged easily, Bidault said. It was 'simply a problem of external forces'. The danger with Zhou's concept of comparability was that extending the regrouping principle from Vietnam to Laos and Cambodia would embed Vietnamese communist troops in those two countries. Smith agreed that this was intolerable. An armistice should certainly take in all of Indochina, but 'we must maintain our position regarding separate consideration [for] Laos and Cambodia'.[77]

After briefing his Franco-American colleagues, Eden went on to dine with Molotov. The Russian 'made the evening as easy as he could', Eden wrote in his diary, and still believed that 'he and I have a special task in this conference to try and facilitate agreement'. Molotov intimated that in addition to simultaneous ceasefires in Vietnam, Cambodia and Laos, there might be separate armistice arrangements reflecting the differing political situations in each country, a concession to the Western powers at the expense, it seemed, of the Vietminh and China. Molotov stressed that he was offering a personal viewpoint; he did not speak for the PRC which 'was very much her own master'.[78]

Nothing further was heard from the Soviets on the matter over the next few days (Eden presumed that much USSR-PRC-DRV argumentation was going on behind the scenes), but Molotov continued to demonstrate his interest in a successful conference in other ways. Meeting Eden on 25 May, he proposed adding 'impetus' to the negotiations by encouraging the French and DRV high commands to establish direct contact both in the field and via military representatives at Geneva. Eden, whose own thoughts had been running along similar lines, proposed – and all other delegations agreed – that these military discussions should commence as soon as possible and focus, in the first instance, on delineating regrouping zones in Vietnam.[79] The following week, the French and Vietminh commands came together at Geneva to pore over maps.[80] From then on, these military talks functioned almost as a sub-conference, a welcome development for which Eden gave the 'skilful and constructive' Molotov much credit.[81] Of separate treatment for Laos and Cambodia, no more was heard for the time being.

During this period, Eden's personal warmth towards Smith coexisted with resentment at the US government's lack of constructive engagement in the peace process ('Anthony very angry & anti-American', Clarissa noted in her diary on 14 May). To the extent that Smith was non-committal or remote, Eden supposed him to be acting on Dulles's orders.[82] The British also had to fight a rear-guard action against American efforts to reshape their proposal for five-power staff talks to meet US ends. On instructions from Washington, Smith pressed Eden to agree to ten-power political discussions on a regional defence pact to run concurrently with the five-power military talks, both sets of discussions to take place in Washington. To Eden's mind, this was yet another attempt to jump-start alliance-building on the basis of Dulles's favoured founder members. It would be 'fatal at this stage to begin discussions with a ten-power group', he told Smith. 'To do so before the results of the Conference are known would destroy any prospect of bringing along the Asian Powers who really matter.' Instead, he preferred to stick to the plan to use the Five-Power Staff Agency to evaluate the situation, although he was content for Thailand and the Philippines, along with the Colombo powers, to be kept informed of the progress of the discussions.[83]

The British found it hard to escape the conclusion that the lack of US commitment to the Geneva process reflected the Eisenhower administration's ongoing interest in a military solution. Indeed, confirmatory evidence was banking up. On 11 May, as Smith was entreating Eden to consider ten-power political talks, Dulles told a news conference in Washington that if the Associated States were members of a Southeast Asian defence pact, 'it would be appropriate to use force to put down attacks such as were now going on there.'[84] The next day, Salisbury, who had spoken to Winthrop Aldrich, the American Ambassador in London, relayed to Eden the disconcerting news that 'the President agrees with the lobby in the US who want the US to enter the Indo-China war alone'.[85] From Washington, Makins claimed to have 'grounds for thinking that in the Pentagon the army view as well as that of Radford now is that direct American military intervention in Indo-China is necessary'.[86]

This simmering issue boiled over on 15 May. Perusing the Swiss newspapers that morning, Eden was startled to read that French and American officials had been secretly discussing the conditions under which the United States might enter the war. Surprise quickly gave way to anger. Hunting out Smith, Eden demanded to know why he had been kept in the dark about so vital a development. Smith denied any knowledge of Franco-American collusion and implied that it was all a press fabrication. Far from satisfied, Eden then approached Roland de Margerie, a senior diplomat in the French delegation, who was much more forthcoming. Washington, de Margerie confirmed, had provided Paris with a list of intervention conditions. If these were satisfied,

President Eisenhower would seek Congressional approval for military intervention should the Geneva conference collapse or sooner if Laniel so desired. According to de Margerie, Eisenhower 'clearly hoped' for a request before Geneva had run its course.[87]

As conveyed to Eden, the US conditions were an amplification of the Dulles fundamentals: American military action could only be undertaken as part of 'an international effort' and with UN blessing; in that connection, a Southeast Asian defence organization should be established, with UK involvement 'if possible'; there needed to be advance Franco-American agreement on 'supreme command'; independence for the Associated States, including the right to secede from the French Union, remained essential; the French had to maintain their military effort at a fixed proportion of the eventual US effort; and all these arrangements needed to be endorsed by the National Assembly, not just the Laniel Cabinet. The French government was presently considering its response.[88]

Armed with this information, Eden confronted Smith again. In some distress and embarrassment, the American recanted. There *had* been US-French contacts but they were 'not anything like as serious as it appeared in the headlines' and had mostly concerned American involvement in training the VNA. Having spoken (without the American's knowledge) to de Margerie, Eden knew this to be an economical rendering of the truth. Smith attempted to atone for his previous lack of candour by showing Eden two confidential cables he had received from Washington which, ironically, confirmed a level of possible US action beyond simply working with the VNA. In a telegram to London that evening, Eden said it was clear that 'the intention was that we should not be informed' about the Franco-American discussions 'until they had been concluded'. It was equally evident that UK approval was no longer a condition of American-organized intervention. In view of these troubling developments, Eden had no choice but to 'reserve' his position on UK involvement in the five-power staff talks.[89]

'Bedell Smith had shown himself as slippery as Dulles,' James Cable later assessed. Put on the spot, Smith lied to Eden; then, when caught out, he tried to make amends by sharing his government's secrets with the British Foreign Secretary.[90] Yet, astonishingly, Eden's blind spot where Smith was concerned – 'it is such a comfort to have him to work with' – would remain for the rest of the conference.[91] This is not to say that affection for the messenger lessened Eden's dislike of the message. 'This new talk of intervention will have weakened what chances remain at this conference,' he wrote to Churchill. The communists 'have all along suspected that the Americans intend to intervene in Indo-China whatever arrangements we try to arrive at here', while the Chinese 'also believe the Americans plan hostilities against them'. Now, their suspicions seemingly concretized, the communists would be within their rights to denounce Geneva as a fraud. 'It looks as though the Radford policy has won through in Washington,' Eden lamented.[92]

What in fact had won through was an American refusal to allow the British a never-ending veto over united action. On 10 May, Laniel – prompted by Bonnet – had asked the US government to specify the circumstances and conditions under which American armed forces would enter the war.[93] The next day, following a discussion with Eisenhower and other senior figures in the administration, Dulles instructed Ambassador Dillon to pass on formally to the French government the NSC-agreed conditions for action. In addition to looking to America, Dulles wanted the French to seek assistance from Britain, Australia, New Zealand, the Philippines and Thailand. A UK refusal to help was likely but could not be permitted to derail united action. The 'implications' of going ahead without the Churchill government's support 'would be extremely serious and far-reaching', Dulles admitted, but must be accepted.[94] Laniel's preoccupation with parliamentary problems, including another (survived) confidence vote, meant that Dillon was unable to pass on the conditions until 14 May. Politely appreciative, Laniel undertook to consult his colleagues and formulate a response.[95] Details of these exchanges leaked almost immediately – Paris Radio carried a well-informed account that night – and by the following day the story was splashed everywhere, including in Eden's late edition Swiss newspapers.[96]

On 16 May, Eden wrote to Salisbury. 'The American attitude becomes increasingly disturbing,' he confided. 'It is no doubt true that they are irritated by their Allies – with the French because they won't fight without help, which in the end means troops, and with us because we want to give this conference a chance to reach agreement before we discuss in detail a Pacific pact.' He was doing 'everything I can' to bring along the Colombo powers, 'but the Americans are too impatient'. Nor was this all. 'I must say that I think they are jealous of our authority and following here. They like to give orders, and if they are not at once obeyed they become huffy. That is their conception of an alliance – of Dulles' anyway. Unhappily they have never put their weight behind this conference and made an effort to get an agreement.' What then *was* the US objective? 'You know that Radford's policy has for some time been intervention in Indo-China, and in China too,' wrote Eden in closing. 'Some aspects of American policy are only comprehensible to me if that view is held by others in addition to Radford.'[97]

The next day (17 May), an editorial in the *Times* declared that the Western powers were 'gripped in the most dangerous crisis since the end of the world war'.[98] In the House of Commons that afternoon, Churchill attempted to settle nerves. 'Until the outcome of the Conference is known, final decisions cannot be taken regarding the establishment of a collective defence in South-East Asia and the Western Pacific,' he affirmed to MPs. Nor had the government embarked on any negotiation involving commitments with regard to military action in Indochina.[99] When Dulles read Churchill's statement, he confessed to 'a certain righteous – I hope – indignation' at what he held to be yet another British misrepresentation of the London agreement.[100]

At Geneva, Shuckburgh was preparing to step down after more than two years as Eden's private secretary. In his diary, he offered some parting reflections on Indochina. 'If it were not for the very nasty faces which the Americans are making, I don't see why the Communists have any incentive to talk, or to stop the war,' he wrote. 'It is going so nicely for them. But Molotov is more afraid of a world war and atomic bombs than [Z] hou En-lai, partly because Russia is more open to attack, partly because she is more of a satisfied power and has a lot to lose, and partly because he is a wiser and calmer man.'[101] The fact that the revelations about Franco-US intervention exchanges did not trigger a Sino-Soviet walkout supports Shuckburgh's assessment, although evidence from Chinese sources confirms that the possibility of American escalation in Vietnam influenced the PRC approach to the conference at least as much as it focused Soviet thinking on the consequences of diplomatic failure. As historian Qiang Zhai notes, the Chinese took US 'bluster and threats seriously'.[102] As for Eden, he continued to appreciate the diplomatic purchase provided by US 'noises off', but he also worried that there was real intent behind the rhetoric. Even Shuckburgh sometimes wondered. 'We are very gloomy,' he confided to his diary, and concerned about the Americans 'losing patience and starting World War III'.[103]

The Americans were certainly losing patience – but mostly with the Churchill government. The 'big hurdle is should we be willing to act without the British' if the French accepted US terms for internationalization, Dulles and Radford agreed between themselves before deciding that yes, the UK could be bypassed.[104] Meeting with the President on 11 May, Dulles had adumbrated the 'disadvantages' of a situation 'where we were obviously subject to UK veto, which in turn was in Asian matters largely subject to Indian veto, which in turn was largely subject to Chinese Communist veto'. A chain was thereby forged 'which tended to make us impotent, and to encourage Chinese Communist aggression to a point where the whole position in the Pacific would be endangered and the risk of general war increased'.[105] Specious as this reasoning was – the UK link in the chain did not exist as Dulles depicted it – the Eisenhower administration would continue to equate appearances with reality.

'The Most Troubled International Scene
I Can Ever Recall'

Neither the press storm brought on by the leak of the US-French exchanges nor the British government's strong adverse reaction deflected the Eisenhower administration from its new course. On 17 May, Dulles drew up a draft Congressional resolution granting the President authority to dispatch US air and naval forces to Indochina if the French, having met the prescribed American conditions, requested such support. Action would still be on a multilateral basis (the French were to be encouraged to seek wide allied backing), but both President and Secretary of State agreed that UK participation was no longer a deal-breaker, not when Eden was promoting what Eisenhower called 'a second Munich'. Approving the text, the President said 'He would not necessarily exclude sending some Marines if we went in.'[1] At the same time, the US Joint Chiefs of Staff determined that 'atomic weapons will be used whenever it is to our military advantage', although, as Radford was keen to clarify, the object was to employ America's nuclear arsenal against the PRC rather than in Vietnam. The United States 'should adopt the concept of offensive action against the "military power of the aggressor", in this instance Communist China, rather than the concept of "reaction locally at the point of attack"', he told Wilson.[2]

By the time the National Security Council met on 20 May, Dillon was reporting that the chances of French acceptance of US conditions, particularly those relating to the French Union and the maintenance of the French war effort, were poor. A rueful Dulles told the NSC that US-French consultations were in danger of becoming 'an academic exercise'. Even if the Laniel government was minded to embrace the prerequisites, the National Assembly might still balk. But he was not yet ready to 'exclude ... all possibility that the French might ultimately agree to internationalize the conflict'.[3] By way of encouragement to the French, Dulles wanted Dillon to explain to Laniel that 'we would not exclude sending some marines, if this made military sense', as part of an intervention plan.[4]

The British, meanwhile, suspected that all was not as the French would have it appear. After meeting with Quai d'Orsay officials on 18 May, Jebb concluded that the French had deliberately leaked the details of their exchanges with the Americans on intervention. As far as the Laniel government was concerned, the projected talks were not intended as preparation for internationalization at all; rather, the mere fact of their existence, once made public, would serve as a diplomatic 'instrument'.[5] At Geneva,

Bidault virtually admitted that this was the case when telling Eden that the only 'good card' France possessed was the 'ability to play upon both Russian and Chinese fear of American intervention and an extension of hostilities'. Eden knew this, too. But he also knew that there was the finest of lines between threatening military action and having to follow through on the threat for reasons of maintaining credibility. Even if Laniel and Bidault were leading the Americans on, the French needed to be careful in case the tables were turned on them and the US government compelled rather than requested compliance with its intervention conditions.[6]

Concern about the Eisenhower administration's military intentions infused a message from Makins to Eden on 21 May. 'What disturbs me', the Ambassador wrote, 'is the effect on Anglo-American relations' if or when the Americans intervened and 'the British were standing aloof or were opposed to American policy. You do not need me to dilate on the consequences to us and the Commonwealth ... if we and the Americans came to a parting of the ways over South-East Asia, whether it came about that they intervened without us or that they failed to intervene because of us'.[7] Irritated by the extent to which Makins had "gone native" in backing the US line since March, Eden used his reply to spell out the differences separating UK and US policy:

> My purpose is to reach an agreed settlement at Geneva of the Indo-China problem, and then to institute measures for the collective defence of South East Asia in the light of that settlement ... At present the only deterrent is the risk of war, and its effectiveness depends solely on the apparent unity and determination of the Western Powers. Ultimately, however, India, Pakistan and to a very limited extent Ceylon [Sri Lanka], may be able to provide the local military backing that the Western Powers, because of commitments elsewhere, cannot furnish alone. Meanwhile, nothing must be done that would antagonise Asian opinion and jeopardise this prospect. When I suggested holding five-Power staff talks, I intended these to demonstrate Western unity and determination, as well as to enable the participants to make an agreed assessment of the situation and of possible future measures. By their repeated and publicised attempts to convert these staff talks into an alliance aimed primarily at restoring or holding the military situation in Indo-China, the United States Government have impaired the first of these objectives (thereby seriously weakening the Western negotiating position at Geneva) and have delayed the second.

Given the strength of the Vietminh's military and political position, especially in northern Vietnam, Eden reaffirmed his commitment to peace-via-partition as the only realistic way forward. The Americans, in contrast, were not only reluctant to acknowledge Vietminh primacy but seemed to want to build an alliance to 're-conquer Indo-China'.[8]

The success of Eden's Geneva strategy and the continuation of the conference itself now hinged on how the French responded to the US conditions for intervention. 'I think it is fair to say that this is the crucial moment in the conference', Eden wrote to Selwyn Lloyd on 21 May. The Americans might be planning for war, but 'the cessation of hostilities in Indo-China' remained 'my primary objective'. Eden went on to take issue with Eisenhower's falling domino thesis:

> I do not personally agree with the people who suggest that if Indo-China were to go, Siam [Thailand], Malaya, etc., must be indefensible. They would obviously be much more difficult to defend, but that is not in itself a reason for intervening in Indo-China, even if we could do so effectively at this stage. If something could be saved from the wreck of that country, well and good. But we do not want to bring a greater disaster upon our heads by trying to avert the immediate one.[9]

Privately, Dulles confirmed Eden's assessment: 'We are confronted by an unfortunate fact that most of the countries of the world do not share our view that Communist control of any government anywhere is in itself a danger and a threat.'[10]

At Geneva, Bidault eased Eden's immediate fears of US-orchestrated escalation by telling him that there was 'no question' of France asking the United States for military assistance before the conference reached a natural conclusion, although it was his 'duty' to plan for a future in which the war went on.[11] Reassured, Eden lifted the hold he had placed on UK participation in the five-power staff talks.[12] In a personal message to the prime ministers of India, Pakistan and Sri Lanka, he pronounced himself 'satisfied that there is no likelihood of immediate United States intervention in Indo-China' and that the Franco-American exchanges had been confined to contingencies connected to failure at Geneva. He also warned them that five-power military discussions would take place in the very near future.[13] The understanding responses this message elicited left the Foreign Secretary confident that the Colombo powers would still 'play their part after the Conference, whether it results in an agreement or not, or at least be benevolently neutral'. Partition might be the solution that dared not speak its name, but Eden was not without hope that the French and Vietminh would eventually accommodate themselves to a territorial division. Until then, it was essential to stop the United States making any military moves.[14]

'It is still even money we may reach an armistice,' Eden wrote to his wife on 22 May. 'I am more than ever convinced of dangers of 3rd world war if we don't.'[15] In London two days later to brief the Cabinet, he told his colleagues that he would persist at Geneva because he was 'gravely concerned about the dangers of the alternative courses of action which the United States Government were likely to favour if a settlement were not now secured by negotiation'.[16] 'Successful talk with Cabinet, who all appeared in full agreement,' Eden wrote in his diary afterwards.[17] The slight hesitancy ('appeared') derived from his position as East-West intermediary and the strain that this was placing on Anglo-American relations. As Churchill cautioned, although 'we dislike the way US are playing their hand, we mustn't forget whose side we are on'. The British needed to be 'very careful not to have a break with the Americans' who were 'the only people who can defend the free world even though they bring in Dulles to do it'.[18] Knowing that his role was especially open to misconstruction in the United States, Eden urged Makins to emphasize to 'more responsible Americans that we are no less aware of the dangers of Communist expansion in South-East Asia than they are [but] we have, and are entitled to have, our own ideas of how this can best be done'.[19]

On 25 May, the US government formally accepted the British proposal for five-power staff talks on Southeast Asia. The Pentagon would be the venue, with the rank of participants – the Chief of the Imperial General Staff, Field Marshal Harding, would lead for British – elevating the meeting considerably above the level of its staff agency origins.[20] On 28 May, the five governments issued identical public statements confirming that discussions would begin the following week, albeit 'without commitment'. Any Indochina settlement emerging from Geneva 'would require some sort of underwriting in order to make it real', the text noted. Equally, if nothing came of Geneva, 'other ways of halting aggression in the Far East will have to be agreed'.[21]

No sooner had the statement been issued than Eden learned from Makins that 'we are approaching another dangerous corner'. Contrary to what the British had been led to believe, the French now seemed 'likely' to accept the American conditions for internationalization. The reason was the deteriorating position in the Red River delta which, Makins feared, was 'quite likely to get out of hand if some agreement is not reached [at Geneva] within ten days or a fortnight'.[22] Jebb in Paris confirmed from his own sources that Franco-American agreement 'has now practically been reached'. If the Geneva negotiations collapsed, Jebb understood that Eisenhower would approach Congress for approval to commit US air and naval forces, including up to three divisions of marines. The next step was formal military discussions between the French and Americans to perfect a *plan d'ensemble*.[23]

Coming just twenty-four hours after the announcement of the Washington staff conference, this news left Eden feeling angry and manipulated. To go ahead now would lend the military talks 'an entirely different character from what we intended', he confided to his diary. 'They were not to be to prepare for a breakdown', as originally envisioned, 'but to prepare for intervention'.[24] US behaviour at Geneva increasingly made sense. If war was preferable to the Americans than compromise, why would they make any effort to make a success of the conference? 'The truth seems to be that the Americans are mortally afraid of any agreement, however innocuous, reached with the Communists', Eden cabled London on 29 May. 'Their delegation here have recently been expressing concern about the contacts … taking place between the French and the Vietminh delegations and seem to fear that they will do a deal on their own. I see no reason to worry about this. All such contacts can only serve to bring a settlement nearer and may save us much trouble.'[25]

The Americans had become noticeably more tense since it became clear that Franco-DRV military talks would take place. Within this bilateral forum, the PAVN's superiority on the ground in Vietnam was likely to be more determining than in the wider politico-diplomatic negotiations, a realization which heightened American apprehension about drastic French concessions, including the surrender of Tonkin. Partition, it seemed, was beginning to insinuate itself into the equation in form if not yet name. At any rate, Smith was 'quite certain' that when the two commands got together 'we will see a division of Vietnam, no matter what it is called, and that we will be lucky to save half of it, as we will be lucky if we do not lose a considerable northern slice of Laos'.[26]

This prospect, so unwelcome to the Americans, contributed to an extraordinary private outburst by Smith aimed in the direction of the British Foreign Secretary. As we know, Eden not only regarded Smith as a friend but believed him to be fundamentally supportive of the UK position. It is not hard to imagine Eden's distress, therefore, had he been privy to the contents of a telegram Smith sent to Dulles on 30 May. Accusing the British in general of seeking to 'distort and deceive' to achieve their ends, Smith then launched an ad hominem attack on Eden.

> I have done everything I possibly can here to retain an Anglo-American equilibrium, but I want you to know that I believe it will be a sad day for Britain and America when Eden becomes Prime Minister. I am convinced, after long association, that he is without moral or intellectual honesty, and his vanity and petulance are not counterbalanced, as in the case of Churchill, by genuine wisdom and great strength of character.[27]

The disconnect between Eden's sense of Smith's feelings towards him and the reality evidenced in this cable is staggering. Smith lied to Eden on 15 May. A fortnight later he traduced him privately in the most damning terms. Yet, for the remainder of the conference, Eden would continue to see only one of Smith's two faces.

On 31 May, Eden met Bidault who confirmed that progress had indeed been made in Franco-American discussions on post-Geneva military action. The Eisenhower administration, it transpired, was now prepared to accept Indochinese independence within rather than outside of the French Union. As for intervention, the Americans had in mind the commitment of three divisions of ground troops, as well as air and naval support. Bidault described the discussions, and the accompanying press speculation, as 'distant thunder which might help the Conference', a view which suggested that the French were still engaged in an elaborate bluff to use the Americans to frighten the communists into offering honourable terms. Eden, however, was much disturbed. The French might be playing games, but the Americans struck him as deadly serious and he reminded Bidault of what he had told him at Orly on 25 April, namely that there was 'no question of any commitment by us [the United Kingdom] for intervention in Indo-China' if the United States pressed ahead.[28]

Writing to his wife, Eden described the implications of the Franco-American collaboration as 'dynamite'. The American 'war party' was looking 'very powerful' and threatening to sweep the French along with it. The situation was 'all grim & disheartening'.[29] If it was not for the ongoing Geneva process, Eden told Iverach McDonald, 'I am convinced we would have been in World War Three by now'.[30] The situation in the Red River delta added to Eden's anxiety. Each day that passed brought more news of French setbacks. By the start of June, Graves was reporting that the military initiative was 'firmly held by the Viet Minh'. If Giap launched an onslaught in the second half of the month – the earliest he could do so according to French military intelligence – 'it is extremely doubtful whether Hanoi can be held'. The monsoon 'will not stop the enemy'.[31] In an attempt to ward off disaster, the Laniel government agreed to reinforce Vietnam to the tune of one infantry division and was believed to be considering the repeal of the law preventing national service personnel from deployment in zones of active conflict. UK observers, however, including the Joint Intelligence Committee, viewed such measures as too little, too late.[32]

Unknown to the British, the French Committee of National Defence had ordered the High Command in Indochina to prepare for the abandonment of the southern and western sectors of the delta, concentrating resources on the defence of Hanoi and Haiphong and prioritizing 'the safeguarding of the Expeditionary Corps'.[33] In one of his last pronouncements before being replaced as Commander-in-Chief by Ely, Navarre averred that if Geneva did not produce agreement by 15 June, France, the United States and their allies should take all necessary action to save the eastern delta.[34] The High Command was particularly exercised by the possibility of PRC air support for a PAVN offensive. Operating from bases in Hainan, Chinese fighter-bombers could remain over Haiphong for up to twenty minutes, long enough to do serious damage to the port and make a French sea evacuation, should the need arise, extremely hazardous. Chinese air attack, the Quai d'Orsay assessed, 'would drastically tip the scales in favour of the Viet Minh and make total defeat of French forces in the delta inevitable'.[35]

Whether the French were being deliberately alarmist in the hope of increasing the chances of US intervention without strings attached, Eden could not tell, but the general situation in the delta did nothing to lessen his worries about American military action. To the British, Radford remained the arch-interventionist. As for Dulles, Eden struggled to decide whether he was 'endorsing or restraining' the Admiral. From what the British learned from the French, however, he had lately been behaving like 'a man who had been bitten by a mosquito' and was 'determined on action of some kind'. The situation in Tonkin and Geneva was starting to resemble a 'race between war and peace', French diplomat Paul Boncour told Eden. If Geneva failed in its task, the war could be internationalized on or soon after Navarre's 15 June deadline.[36]

To Eden's dismay, a diplomatic settlement, the ultimate deterrent to a dangerously expanded war, had never seemed more remote. The Franco-DRV military discussions were a positive development, it was true, but on the main issues dividing the two sides, including the supervision commission and the position of Laos and Cambodia, there was no movement.[37] Adding to Eden's despondency was the prospect of an official visit with Churchill to Washington.[38] Back in April, Eisenhower suggested that a top-level meeting was needed to address some of 'the seemingly wide differences' afflicting US-UK relations, amongst them 'the war in Indo-China'.[39] Arrangements were duly made for a three-day conference to begin on 18 June, but Eden now pleaded with Churchill for a postponement. With the Indochina negotiations in need of a final push for peace, he felt that his place was in Geneva. There was 'only too much evidence ... that the main American concern is not now, if it has ever been, for the success of the conference, but with preparations for intervention', he warned the Prime Minister. As such, the British party could arrive in Washington 'just when the French were in grievous trouble and the American desire to intervene at its height'. Calls for the UK 'to take part in such an adventure would then be intensified and the strain on Anglo-American relations, when we had to decline, could be all the worse'. Indochina, Eden concluded sombrely, was at the heart of 'the most troubled international scene I can ever recall'.[40]

On 3 June, the five-power staff conference opened at the Pentagon with the object of determining 'possible courses of action to enable an effective line of resistance to further Communist aggression or infiltration in South East Asia to be established'. In going about their business, the delegations were to examine 'all possible courses of action' in light of the 'current situation and of the known capabilities of the anti-Communist countries concerned in Southeast Asia and the Western Pacific'.[41]

After a week of deliberation, the conference delivered a report to the five governments. Replicating numerous previous Allied assessments, the report emphasized how 'critical' the retention of the Red River delta was to the entire anti-communist position in Vietnam, hence in Indochina, hence in Southeast Asia. The difference with earlier studies was that the French hold on the delta was now tenuous. A French intelligence assessment undertaken ahead of the talks confirmed both the advance of PAVN forces in the direction of Hanoi and Haiphong and an ebbing of French and Vietnamese morale in the aftermath of Dien Bien Phu. The monsoon might yet delay a fully coordinated PAVN offensive until September, but if the French were to have any hope of maintaining a defence perimeter around Hanoi and Haiphong they would require reinforcements in the region of three well-trained and equipped divisions and three hundred aircraft. Even then, securing the delta would be an ongoing challenge unless the PAVN was 'destroyed' as a fighting force, a task requiring even more manpower and resources.[42]

In an echo of the reinforcement debate in London in 1952–1953, the conference accepted that the French government would struggle to find more troops unless it tapped into the professional French army in Europe. The revocation of the law limiting the use of French national service personnel was also desirable. However, given the febrile state of French public and parliamentary opinion, the Laniel government was bound to face strong opposition to increasing its military commitment. The Vietnamese armed forces – a 'rabble', Navarre called them – were not yet in a state to take on a major role. Accordingly, the conference was forced to consider the possibility of a French evacuation of Tonkin and the drawing of a new defence line running westwards from Thakhek in Laos to Dong Hoi on the central coast of Vietnam. But here, too, a large injection of resources would be needed to help the FEC and Vietnamese deal with the Vietminh threat within the retained portion of Vietnam while simultaneously resisting pressure from the PAVN in the north. Combatting this dual challenge would require as many as three-to-four extra divisions and supporting aircraft.[43]

There was another source of manpower: France's allies, the 'Free Nations' as the report termed them. The dangers attending internationalization remained obvious (a violent Chinese riposte, full-scale war with the PRC, general war with the USSR). Moreover, to judge from the tone of the discussions, the US government was not minded to draw a distinction between unprovoked Chinese intervention and Chinese intervention prompted by prior American-led action. In both instances, the US response – in keeping with NSC-5405 – would be a massive air offensive against targets in China. 'To achieve a maximum and lasting effect', the report observed, 'nuclear as well as conventional weapons should be used from the outset'. A naval blockade of PRC ports might also be imposed. In the end, the five delegations could not agree on whether the risk of global war arising from direct action against the PRC 'constituted a definite probability or whether its degree was merely problematical', but it was evident that the British took the former view, the Americans the latter.[44]

Admiral Robert Carney, US Chief of Naval Operations, led for the Americans in the discussions, but Radford continued to campaign hard for internationalization from the sidelines.[45] It was becoming clear from the briefings delivered by French military experts, however, that Radford's belief that American air and naval power alone would be enough to restore the positon in Tonkin was at odds with the situation on the ground. A substantial infantry commitment would also be needed. With the British, Australians and New Zealanders no more keen on united action than they had been at the start of the crisis, and in view of the acknowledged limitations of French resources, there could be no escaping the deployment of multiple American divisions.[46] According to one US Army assessment, ground forces to the tune of 275,000 might be needed.[47] As for the Chinese dimension, Radford admitted that there was a high probability that internationalization would bring on war with the PRC (an assessment since confirmed from Chinese sources).[48] But far from fearing this, as the British did, Radford almost welcomed it. 'China is very vulnerable,' he told Harding, 'and could be quickly and easily defeated, without serious risk of Russian intervention as long as Russian soil was not threatened'.[49]

Throughout the conference, the Eisenhower administration's New Look and its view that nuclear weapons had achieved conventional status hovered in the background. The week before, Eisenhower had been reminded of the judgement of the Joint Chiefs of Staff that 'there was little use discussing any "defense" of the Southeast Asia area'. Rather, 'United States power should be directed against the source of the peril which was ... China', and 'in this connection atomic weapons should be used'.[50] Concerned that this approach would alarm America's allies, Eisenhower told senior politico-military figures, including Radford, that 'we must take care not to frighten our friends ... by bellicose talk'. As it was, 'our friends thought we were belligerent, wanted to fight, and were immature; therefore, we must be careful not to alarm them'.[51]

No matter how US strategic thinking was packaged, there was no escaping its essentially nuclear thrust. On 2 June, the eve of the staff talks, the US Embassy in London reminded the State Department of the Churchill government's 'dread that the war in Indo-China might, if not soon arrested, spread into a world war in which the United Kingdom would suffer the consequences of atomic and hydrogen bombardment'.[52] That same day, Eisenhower and his senior staff agreed amongst themselves that 'unprovoked Chinese aggression' anywhere in Southeast Asia would mean that 'a state of war existed with Communist China'. With Congressional and hopefully allied backing, 'the US should then launch large-scale air and naval attacks on ports, airfields, and other military targets in mainland China, using as militarily appropriate "new weapons"'. Eisenhower himself opined that 'if the situation warranted it ... there should be a strike at Communist Russia in view of her treaty with China'.[53]

At the staff talks, Carney, heeding Eisenhower's injunction, was positively statesmanlike in his handling of nuclear questions. The conference report likewise dealt with nuclear arms in a practical rather than lurid manner. Nevertheless, if Eisenhower and his advisors supposed that adopting a circumspect posture during a week of discussions at the Pentagon would be sufficient to erase from the memory of America's allies the US government's menacing rhetoric in the six months since Bermuda, he was mistaken. In the case of the Churchill government, worries about

American nuclear recklessness not only outlasted the staff talks but contributed soon afterwards to one of the most momentous decisions in UK post-war national security.

In London on 16 June, Churchill, the Chiefs of Staff and a small group of ministers (collectively, the Defence Policy Committee, DPC) determined that Britain should possess its own thermonuclear weapons.[54] Historians usually explain the government's decision in terms of national prestige, with the H-bomb posited as a badge of great power status as well as a weapon in the nation's armoury.[55] Churchill and his colleagues were certainly aware of the H-bomb's value in this regard, but the Indochinese context within which their thermonuclear outlook was forged was crucial in ways seldom if ever acknowledged in the scholarship. The British H-bomb was conceived at the height of the Indochina crisis. That crisis, in turn, was a crisis in Anglo-American relations in which the British worked to thwart US plans for military action in Vietnam which risked war with China and potentially general nuclear (and thermonuclear) war with the USSR. The Prime Minister in particular was consumed by 'a terrible fear' of the impact of nuclear weapons, not just on the UK but on 'civilisation'.[56]

Churchill and his advisors – including the absent but supportive Eden – saw an independent thermonuclear capability as a means of elevating the UK's value as an ally in the eyes of the US government. Britain, they believed, would be better placed to offer (and have heeded) cautionary advice in time of crisis if it was a member of the H-bomb "club". Obviously, there was no UK hydrogen bomb to factor into Anglo-American relations in the present. But looking ahead, and using the situation in Indochina as his point of reference, Churchill maintained that it was imperative to deter the United States from using an incident in Asia to 'bring matters to a head' with the communist bloc. In global war, the UK stood to suffer terribly from nuclear attack. British strategists identified the years 1954 to 1958 as the most dangerous window of vulnerability, the period of time it was thought the USSR would need to develop long-range bombers or intercontinental rockets capable of hitting North America. Would the United States stay its hand during this time frame? Endorsing the DPC's decision, the full Cabinet agreed that the 'primary aim' of British foreign and defence policy 'must be to prevent a major war' and, to that end, it might be necessary to contain the United States as well as the Soviet Union. 'Influence' over Washington 'depended on possession of force', Churchill avowed, hence the need for a H-bomb.[57]

In 1957, the UK detonated its first hydrogen device. To the extent that it was conceived in part as a politico-diplomatic instrument to deflect the United States from taking action which portended general war, the weapon deserved to bear an 'Indochina 1954' hallmark.[58]

While the Geneva negotiations stagnated, in Washington the State Department continued to view Eden's 'activities as an "honest broker"' with 'dismay and disappointment'.[59] Eden himself blamed the Americans as much as the communists for the lack of progress. On another flying visit to London on 5 June, he told the Cabinet that the chances of a breakthrough had diminished in the fortnight since he last spoke to ministers in person. In addition to the 'uncertainties and hesitations' of the French, the US delegation was operating under close instructions from Washington where there was 'no desire to see a successful outcome from the negotiations'. It was obvious 'that influential sections of opinion in Washington were now interested only in the question of military intervention in South-East Asia'.[60]

After listening to this Geneva update, the Cabinet took a break. By the time ministers reassembled twenty minutes later, the Foreign Secretary's assessment of US policy had altered. Waiting for Eden outside the Cabinet room was a Foreign Office courier who handed him the latest telegrams from Makins. These showed that the Eisenhower administration had apparently arrived at the view that only direct PRC aggression warranted intervention in Vietnam. In that event, Dulles told Makins, the United States 'would not confine counter-action to Indo-China', but by the same token, he did not believe that the Chinese would go beyond their present level of indirect support for the Vietminh.[61] 'Heard from Makins that Foster … decided on new policy which was not to intervene in Indo-China unless Chinese Communists did so by arms and aeroplanes,' Eden wrote in his diary. If the reports were true, 'Radford … and other interventionists, probably including Dulles, have had a setback'.[62]

When the Cabinet reconvened, Eden shared with his colleagues the 'farcical' yet 'reassuring' news that the Americans 'seemed to be seeking to relate … military intervention in Indo-China to a situation which was most unlikely to arise in practice'. The PAVN threat to Hanoi remained. But if the PRC stayed out, the United States would too. Eden ascribed the shift in Washington's outlook to the concurrent five-power staff conference's interim conclusion that only a serious ground troop commitment – serviced almost entirely by the United States – could reverse the tide of war. For the Eisenhower administration, this conjured up once more the prospect of a new Korea. As for the impact of the American policy shift on Geneva, Eden suspected that when the French realized that their hopes for a US rescue mission had been extinguished 'they might be more willing to accept the best settlement they could get'. On the other hand, for the United States to declare its new position publicly would be to remove doubt from the minds of the communists as to US intentions and encourage them to negotiate in an even more hard-nosed manner.[63]

Dulles came close to confirming that US policy was now predicated on a new basis when he held a news conference on 8 June. The conditions for united action in Vietnam did not presently exist, he observed. Nor did the administration plan to intervene unilaterally unless 'the whole nature of the aggression should change'. Pressed by reporters for clarification, he defined such change as 'a resumption by Communist China of open aggression in that area or in any other area of the Far East'.[64] What Dulles did not vouchsafe was that his hopes of building a united action coalition without Britain had received a severe blow with confirmation that neither the Australian nor New Zealand governments would break rank with the UK.[65]

The French were understandably aggrieved by the US administration's altered position. A few days later, Bidault reminded Dulles (via Bonnet) that the Laniel government had already indicated a readiness to accept 'the major part of the US conditions' under which America would join the fight. Why, then, was the United States retreating from its previous undertaking? Things had changed, Dulles explained. As of mid-June, it 'would require four or five divisions and in effect commit our strategic reserve' to combat the Vietminh in Tonkin. Six weeks before, when the Americans and French first began discussing internationalization, 'it had appeared that sea and air forces with a token land force would have been sufficient'. However, as the report of the staff talks confirmed, that was no longer the case.[66]

On 17 June, Dulles told the National Security Council that the French 'are desperately anxious to get themselves out of Indochina'. In light of the military situation in Tonkin, and bearing in mind the potential, identified by the staff conference, to hold a defensive line further south, Dulles thought that 'it was probably best to let them quit' and 'try to rebuild from the foundations'.[67] This was a watershed statement, US historians agree, pregnant with long-range implications. Although never to be expressed publicly (Dulles even thought it was 'something we would have to gag about'), the State Department, if not yet the US government as a whole, was edging towards acceptance of partition.[68]

Eden, of course, did not know this. Instead, he focused on trying to reconcile in his mind the US position on no intervention unless China attacked Vietnam with the Eisenhower administration's persistent negativity towards the Geneva conference. The Americans 'will discuss nothing … with the Chinese', he complained to Churchill. 'This can only lead to war.'[69] It was a gloomy conclusion reflective of a downcast state of mind. The first half of June found Eden at his lowest ebb since the start of the crisis. 'I am struggling with the world's ills,' he wrote to Clarissa. 'This wretched conference continues as difficult as ever,' the negotiations 'hard & disappointing'.[70] His mood was not improved by continued uncertainty about Churchill's plans. On his visit to London on 5 June, Eden had prised from the old man a promise to retire at the end of July. A few days later, Churchill changed his mind – due, he said, to 'the unsettled international situation', including Indochina. 'Nobody is going to push me', he decided. 'Besides, there may be a war by August.'[71]

Eden also knew that the longer the Geneva stasis endured, the greater the chance that he would suffer personal and political embarrassment. Six weeks into the negotiations, the communists, even the cooperative Molotov, had still to make a single worthwhile concession on the big issues; the French cleaved to a duality of outlook – unsure whether to get on in Vietnam with US help or get out in the face of US objections – which was unconducive to effective diplomacy; and the Americans wanted to be anywhere but Geneva.[72] Early on, Eden had basked in the praise that came his way. 'It's Eden's conference,' Labour MP and journalist Desmond Donnelly wrote to him on 8 May. 'The British delegation are right on top.'[73] The UK and French press carried positive headlines, and even Chinese newspapers called him the 'King of the Conference'.[74] US news commentary was more critical, with digs at Eden the 'Municheer', but that was only to be expected.[75] On 8 June, however, when Dulles publicly charged the communists with deliberately 'dragging their feet on peace' while 'intensifying their efforts for war', Eden's Geneva sojourn became harder to justify.[76] In London, Salisbury decided it was 'high time' the Foreign Secretary came home. To stay 'talking to Molotov and [Z]hou En-lai while the French are being chased out of Indo-China' made Eden 'look ridiculous' and exposed the Western powers 'to general contempt'. Within the Conservative party, murmurings of disquiet, building since mid-May over the deterioration in Anglo-American relations resulting from Geneva, now grew louder. For a man who would be Prime Minister, keeping on the right side of the Tory faithful was obviously good politics.[77]

For a combination of reasons – the desire to protect his political future, a degree of wounded armour propre, and the growing Vietminh menace to Hanoi – Eden now questioned whether the negotiations could or should continue much longer. There were also Geneva-specific reasons for calling a halt. By 9 June, he had identified 'three definite issues on which the conference is divided': the form of supervision of an agreement, the composition of a supervisory authority to oversee a settlement, and the separation of the problems of Laos and Cambodia from those of Vietnam. 'If we have to break', he told the Foreign Office, 'these are clear issues which world opinion will be able to understand'. Whatever then happened in Vietnam, an appeal by Laos and Cambodia to the United Nations, on the ground that they have been invaded, seemed the obvious recourse.[78]

Eden reached this decision reluctantly and in the knowledge that shutting down the diplomatic track would clear the way for the United States to pursue high-risk military alternatives. According to the latest news from Makins, if the war went on and there was 'a debacle in the delta, involving the loss of Hanoi, danger to European women and children and so on, and the French made frantic appeals for help, then we might quickly be back in the emotional atmosphere of the Dien Bien Phu weekend'. The government needed to prepare 'for the possibility, perhaps the likelihood, that the Americans will act; and on this occasion, act alone'.[79] In actual fact, as we have seen, the Americans were getting close to giving up on building a coalition without the UK. As Dulles privately reflected, the 'sooner the British get into a mood where we can seriously talk with them about collective action the better off we shall be'. That, though, could not happen while Geneva remained a going concern.[80]

On 10 June, Eden administered shock treatment to the other delegates in the hope of reviving the failing peace process. The fact of the Franco-DRV military talks was encouraging, he told a plenary session, but the 'divergences' on the mainframe of peace were 'deep'. The UK was ready to continue to work for compromise, but 'if the positions remain as they are today, then it is our clear duty to say so to the world, and to admit that we have failed'.[81] The Americans were relieved. Channelling Dulles, Smith told Chauvel that 'things should be wound up here as quickly as possible so that we can get ahead on serious talks on collective action as only real means of improving situation'.[82] Eden, in contrast, hoped that his ultimatum had 'shaken the Communists' and that the negotiations had a future.[83]

To begin with, there were some slight signs that Eden's approach had worked. On 12 June, Bidault told him that French and DRV military representatives had been holding secret meetings in addition to the acknowledged inter-command talks. On ceasefire arrangements, the Vietminh had been veering between support for the leopard-spot model for regrouping and the withdrawal of contending forces to larger-scale zones in Vietnam. Now, Bidault revealed, the DRV, unknown to the Bao Dai delegation, had indicated that if the French were to surrender Tonkin, 'satisfactory arrangements could probably be made in relation to the rest of Viet Nam'. This two-zone idea was still inchoate but there was enough in it to suggest to Eden that partition had at last infiltrated the conference discourse, and he advised Bidault to waste no time in following up the opening.[84]

This, though, was as good as it got. That same day, the French government lost a confidence vote in the National Assembly. Laniel had been the first French premier to 'recognise the inevitable and admit willingness to make a negotiated peace', the British Embassy in Paris commented, but his actions since April, not least his attempt to secure US intervention in Vietnam, cast doubt on his commitment to peace.[85] On 13 June, Laniel tendered his resignation; Bidault would stay on at Geneva until a new foreign minister was named, but his freedom to negotiate was heavily circumscribed.[86] Eden's unease about the future of the conference was compounded by 'an almost wholly negative interview' with Molotov, an ominous sign given how helpful the Russian had been until this point.[87] Encountering Casey afterwards, Eden told him he was 'completely "stuck" by reason of lack of any Communist response'.[88]

The Americans added to Eden's worries. In a speech in Los Angeles on 11 June, Dulles indicated that US policy had again shifted on its axis. Reiterating that direct PRC intervention in Vietnam would justify a full-scale riposte, the US Secretary said that military action might also occur in response to a request for help from France. He then ventilated publicly for the first time the conditions the French needed to fulfil if US combat forces were to enter the war.[89] The speech reflected the Eisenhower administration's impatience with the Laniel government, which had yet to respond formally to its intervention conditions (the President sometimes thought that 'the French ... would rather abandon Indochina, or lose it as a result of military defeat, than save it through international intervention').[90] At the same time, in raising once more the issue of military action, Dulles provided Eden with a reminder of the price of diplomatic failure.

At Geneva, Smith was more direct. According to US intelligence, he told Eden on 12 June, 'The French were laying their plans to get out of Viet-Nam and ... only the presence of American ground forces could restore the position.' He then showed Eden a cable he had received from Eisenhower urging him 'to do everything in his power' to bring the conference to a conclusion before the situation in the delta went critical. The time was approaching, the President wrote, to draw a line in Southeast Asia and for the United States and its allies to declare to the communists, 'thus far and no further'.[91] The American view that Chinese aggression alone justified military action had come and gone in the space of a week. In consequence, as Eden cabled Churchill, it was likely that 'we will be asked, when in Washington, to discuss the possibility of intervention'. The start date for the Anglo-American conference had been put back a week, to 25 June, at the request of the Eisenhower administration, but Eden now pleaded with Churchill for a further delay.[92]

The Foreign Secretary had also been put out by a loaded historical analogy in Dulles's Los Angeles speech linking the UK pursuit of peace in Indochina to the failed appeasement policies of the 1930s. If that was the American government's view of British efforts, Eden saw little point in a high-level meeting.[93] Churchill, however, was insistent. Britain 'will in no circumstances intervene in Viet Nam', he reassured him, but with Indochina imposing such strain on Anglo-American relations, 'a meeting between us and the President could not occur at a more opportune and even vital moment'. As for Dulles, he advised Eden to ignore his 'chatter'.[94] 'I dread this American business,' Eden confided to Butler, 'but I fear that it has now to be endured'.[95]

14

Geneva: Phoenix Rising, June 1954

On 13 June, a dejected Eden wrote to Makins from Geneva to say that there was 'virtually no hope of agreement here'.[1] Two days later, the conference seemed to him to be 'nearer to breakdown than it had ever been'.[2] This tallied with Dulles's sense: 'Eden's efforts have been futile, as we expected.' Henceforward, the British could have 'no adequate reason for further delaying collective talks on SEA defense'.[3]

Yet, from this nadir, Eden's hopes suddenly and unexpectedly revived. As on several previous occasions, the purveyor of encouragement was Molotov. Meeting with Eden late on 15 June, the Soviet Foreign Minister said that the communist delegations had decided to abandon their previous insistence on the principle of unanimity in the projected supervisory commission and would accept the Western preference for simple majority decision-making. Eden gratefully accepted the offer and reflected afterwards that Molotov's climbdown indicated that the USSR at least 'still had an interest in reaching an agreement'. True, Eden conceded, the Soviet aim might be 'to keep me here, and to spin the negotiations out while the Viet Minh prepare to capture Hanoi', but his instinct told him that Molotov did not want Geneva to fail.[4]

The following day – 16 June – the communists offered a truly substantive concession which proved crucial in preserving the conference. After weeks of insisting that Vietnam, Laos and Cambodia be treated as a single problem requiring a single solution, Zhou Enlai told Eden that the position in the latter two countries was different after all and should be handled as such. Provided that the United States did not establish military bases in Laos and Cambodia, and that the Pathet Lao and Khmer Issarak were recognized as legitimate political entities, Zhou said that Vietnamese 'volunteers' would be withdrawn. This was the first time that a communist negotiator had acknowledged the presence of Vietminh forces in Laos and Cambodia in any form. The PRC, Zhou added, might even recognize the royal governments in Vientiane and Phnom Penh as members of the French Union. Eden, surprised but pleased, assured Zhou that 'the United States had no desire for any bases in these countries'.[5] Writing in his diary that night, Eden recorded his 'strong impression that [Z]hou En-lai wanted a settlement ... and was anxious that this part of the conference should not break down'. Suddenly, against all the odds, 'the door is open'.[6]

From whence did this communist concession spring? Molotov had hinted to Eden as far back as 20 May that segregating Laos and Cambodia from Vietnam made sense. Over the next month, nothing more was heard from the communists on the matter. To the contrary, Pham Van Dong stuck limpet-like to the principle of a universal settlement which he hoped would lead to an Indochinese federation under the Vietminh's sway. By early June, however, Zhou had grown nervous lest DRV obduracy precipitate the collapse of the negotiations, invite US intervention and threaten a Sino-American war. To avoid these incendiary possibilities, Zhou, backed by Molotov, leant on Dong to offer a significant concession 'so that the conference will continue'. Reluctantly, the Vietminh gave up on the idea of a 'shared destiny' for Vietnam, Laos and Cambodia.[7] This insight into Sino-Soviet-Vietminh diplomacy, based on communist sources made available to historians over the last quarter of a century, was denied to the Western powers at the time, but the value of the concession was fully recognized. As Casey remarked when Eden briefed him, it was 'the best thing for a long time – and alone justifies this Geneva Conference'.[8]

Prior to this, Eden had been planning to fly home to prepare for his trip to America.[9] Now, in light of his meeting with Zhou, a subsequent and constructive discussion between Zhou and Bidault (their first one-to-one meeting of the conference), and indications that Franco-DRV military representatives were making some progress on Vietnam ceasefire terms, he opted to stay a little longer.[10] In doing so, he defied Churchill who had become concerned that the communists were playing him for a fool. 'If disasters occur' in Tonkin, the Prime Minister warned, 'you or we may be charged with having been sucked in by very obvious manoeuvres'.[11] Eden knew that a protracted stay was out of the question (he was due to fly to Washington on 24 June), but in the three days following the Zhou opening he succeeded in arranging for the conference to continue on a semi-recessed basis in his absence. Heads of delegations would return home to consult their governments leaving officials to carry on the negotiations. Hoping for further progress, especially in the Franco-DRV military discussions, Eden anticipated the full conference reconvening around mid-July.[12]

Two further developments in the forty-eight hours before the delegation chiefs departed gave Eden confidence that the conference had a future: first, the Chinese, Soviets and Vietminh agreed in open plenary to respect Cambodian and Laotian independence (albeit on the understanding that both countries were neutralized); and second, the remit of the Franco-DRV military committee on Vietnam was widened to take in 'questions relating to the cessation of hostilities in Laos and Cambodia'.[13] From London, Churchill, his forebodings assuaged, telephoned Eden to congratulate him on having 'turned war into jaw', a view echoed by Nehru's roving emissary at Geneva, Krishna Menon, who declared that Eden's 'wisdom and patience' had 'averted what threatened to be the start of World War III'.[14]

These plaudits were well meant but premature. The recess at Geneva marked the end of the beginning, not the beginning of the end (to invoke the wartime Churchill). Molotov was more prosaic but realistic. Bidding farewell to Eden on 19 June, he said that the conference 'might have made a greater contribution to peace, but … the contribution which it had made had not been negligible'. Eden agreed, but he also knew that as long as the fighting continued, the danger of a wider war remained.[15] Taking leave of Zhou Enlai later that same day, Eden urged the Chinese government to use its influence with the Vietminh to deter the PAVN from intensifying military operations in the Red River delta during the recess. Zhou took note but pointed out that hostilities were 'mutual' and that the French, too, needed to show restraint.[16] The following day, however, Mao Zedong, prompted by Zhou, instructed the Chinese military advisory mission to the DRV to caution Giap against expanding military operations.[17]

Arguably the greatest boost to peace prospects at this time occurred in Paris. There, on 17 June, Pierre Mendès-France, a Radical parliamentarian and perennial opponent of the war, was elected Prime Minister by a large majority of the French National Assembly. Mendès-France promptly appointed himself Foreign Minister in order to take personal charge of the Geneva negotiations. A firm believer in 'peace through compromise', he told the Chamber of Deputies that the wisdom of this outlook was reinforced by 'a new and fearful danger' emanating from the crisis in Indochina, namely 'an international and perhaps atomic war'. He went on to make a bold headline-stealing declaration: if he failed to deliver peace by 20 July, he would resign the premiership.[18]

Eden was delighted. Here at last was a French leader who knew his mind (unlike Bidault who 'had really dithered long enough').[19] Better still, that mind was bent towards making a success of Geneva. 'M. Mendès-France had an intensive driving power and a ruthlessness which was necessary for the straits we were in,' Eden recalled. 'He was the man for the short lap.'[20] Eden also came to suspect – rightly – that communist concessions at Geneva were not unconnected with the advent of a new French leader. In Mendès-France, Molotov and Zhou divined an opportunity to obtain a settlement favourable not just to the Vietminh but to wider Sino-Soviet strategic interests. Were they to negotiate with Mendès-France in the tough manner of their dealings with Laniel and Bidault they could undermine his authority and prospects. Mendès-France might be disposed to compromise, but if he was confronted by humiliating terms, the negotiations could still founder, the war continue and the United States escalate the conflict into an East-West showdown.[21] Mendès-France 'is not a genuine leftist politician', Zhou told Mao Zedong, but 'he is different from Bidault … [W]e should lend a hand to France so as to achieve an armistice.' Moreover, if Mendès-France stayed in power, his anti-EDC outlook could reduce or even eliminate the danger of German rearmament, the top priority of Soviet security policy in Europe.[22]

June 1954 also saw a change of government in Saigon. Following Prince Buu Loc's resignation as Vietnamese premier, Bao Dai appointed Ngo Dinh Diem, an ultra-nationalist, Francophobic Roman Catholic in his stead. It was rumoured that Bao Dai chose Diem under pressure from the Americans, who were attracted by his anti-communist reputation, but Bao Dai himself insisted that there was simply 'no better choice'.[23] Be that as it may, Bedell Smith emerged as an early admirer. Diem was 'a real "find"', he sensed, a potential 'modern political Joan of Arc' who might yet 'rally the country behind him'.[24]

In Vietnam, Diem's elevation was met with approval not only from his core Catholic constituency but other sections of the non-communist nationalist community. As for the Vietminh, Diem's years living in the United States and his high-profile American supporters (amongst them New York's Cardinal Spellman and, in the US Congress, a certain John F. Kennedy) were more than enough to damn him as an 'American lackey'. Convinced that the Americans were the Saigon king-makers, the DRV saw in Diem confirmation of a US design to replace the French. In recent months, the Vietminh had been won round to the Sino-Soviet argument that diplomacy could be used to block US military intervention, but Ho Chi Minh and his comrades now saw a Geneva settlement as a way to counteract the spread of American political influence via Diem, the 'henchman of the US Empire'.[25]

Eden left Geneva on 20 June but broke his journey home with a stop in Paris to confer with Mendès-France. Over luncheon at the British Embassy the two men established an easy rapport. Mendès-France was keen to reassure Eden that he was no Cold War neutralist, an accusation often levelled at him in America. On Indochina, he said that he intended to make clear to the United States that France was no longer willing to continue the war and wished to secure the best possible negotiated settlement. Eden urged him to speak to Zhou Enlai, 'the dominating figure' on the communist side, as soon as possible, but advised against making a meeting 'conditional on American consent' since that meant 'it would never take place'. As for the shape of a settlement, Eden said that partition offered the best prospect for Vietnam, though here, too, he cautioned about US attitudes. The Americans 'would be opposed to any arrangement' worked out with the Vietminh and the 'best that could be hoped for was that they would do nothing to prevent it or to cause it to break down once it had been achieved'. Mendès-France had reasons of his own to be wary of the Americans. Diem, the new Vietnamese Prime Minister, was a 'fanatical Catholic and not at all well-disposed towards the French', and the Eisenhower administration 'might ... be tempted to do some deal with this gentleman over the heads of the French'.[26]

Buoyed by Eden's support, Mendès-France met Smith – who had also stopped over in Paris – later that same day. His goal was an honourable peace, not 'a surrender to the Viet Minh' or 'a disguised capitulation', he told the US Under-Secretary. Smith took this in his stride – it was not as though the Frenchman had kept his views a secret – but warned (as Eden predicted) that a meeting between Mendès-France and Zhou Enlai 'would have very bad repercussions in certain quarters of American opinion who would take it to mean *de facto* recognition of Communist China by France'. Mendès-France asked that the US government use such influence as it possessed with Diem, 'a fanatic much like Syngman Rhee', to make him accept whatever settlement was reached on Vietnam, a request which Smith, already a Diem supporter, parried.[27] The worry that the Americans would 'implicitly encourage' the Vietnamese to reject a settlement would stay with Mendès-France for the duration of the Geneva conference.[28] Then again, the Diem government hardly needed external US stimuli; as it was, the prospect of a meeting between Mendès-France and Zhou Enlai left the Vietnamese delegation at Geneva feeling 'very upset' and 'talking about packing up and leaving the conference'.[29]

Ignoring the potential for American and Vietnamese censure, Mendès-France flew to Bern on 23 June to confer face-to-face with the PRC Premier/Foreign Minister.[30] In a two-hour meeting at the French Embassy, Zhou was conciliatory. Having 'lived in France' in the past, he had 'good feelings towards the French people'. As to Indochina, he was hopeful that Franco-DRV military talks at Geneva would produce ceasefire agreements within three weeks. On the political front, he restated his (new) position on Laos and Cambodia: provided no attempt was made to establish US military bases on their territory, and as long as Pathet Lao and Khmer Issarak legitimacy was recognized, both countries could be dealt with as cases apart from Vietnam. Mendès-France responded warmly. There was 'no question of creating ... bases and the establishment of them does not come into our prospects', he insisted. On Vietnam, Zhou made no direct mention of partition beyond a reference to the need for large regrouping zones, but he did express support for 'a general election' to produce a 'national unification' government.[31]

Mendès-France emerged from this meeting persuaded, like Eden, that Zhou was sincere in wanting a settlement.[32] Although partition had been sidestepped, a temporary division of Vietnam had become intrinsic to any agreement. The following day (24 June), Mendès-France and his top Indochina advisors agreed on the need for a 'horizontal cut', the severing of Tonkin from the body of Vietnam on or around the 18th parallel. Chauvel was instructed to return to Geneva to negotiate with the Vietminh on this basis. Mendès-France hoped to retain Haiphong as a French port-city and to have the large Catholic bishoprics of Phat Diem and Bui Chu accepted as autonomous enclaves. But these caveats were not adamantly held and he recognized that all of the north might have to be surrendered in return for the evacuation of Vietminh forces from the south.[33] The contrast with Bidault's modus operandi was marked. According to *Le Monde*, it had been Bidault's 'visible revulsion' at having to negotiate with the communists that had posed the major obstacle to progress at Geneva.[34] Privately, Chauvel agreed. Bidault had blocked any serious consideration of partition and clung instead to his 'entirely impracticable and unenforceable' leopard-skin formulation. Now, finally, Chauvel was free to negotiate in realistic acknowledgement (not unrealistic denial) of Vietminh military and political strength.[35] Bidault, though, would never forgive Mendès-France for becoming 'the accomplice of our enemies'.[36]

Eden landed at Heathrow from Orly on the evening of 21 June and went straight to Downing Street to brief the Prime Minister on his meeting with Mendès-France. As coincidence would have it, he found Churchill mulling over a message from Eisenhower asking if he regarded 'the elevation of Mendes-France and the pledges he has made as evidence of a readiness on his part to surrender completely in Southeast Asia?'[37] Churchill's response, which Eden helped draft, was sent late that same night. 'I think Mendes-France ... has made his mind up to clear out on the best terms available,' Churchill told Eisenhower. 'I think he is right.' Looking ahead, there was obvious need for 'a SEATO corresponding to NATO', although the 'timing' of substantive moves in this direction should be considered 'in relation to Geneva'. Premature and public action, Churchill argued, could jeopardize the chances of an Indochina settlement by antagonizing China and estranging neutral Asian opinion, but secret Anglo-American preparations would not run the same risks. As to the military situation, Churchill reiterated that 'in no foreseeable circumstances, except possibly a local rescue, could British troops be used' in Vietnam. He ended on the H-bomb, his worries on this subject accentuated by the ongoing crisis in Indochina. If or when it came to decisions involving weapons of mass destruction, he was 'sure' that Eisenhower would 'not overlook the fact that by the Anglo-American base in East Anglia we have made ourselves for the next year or two the nearest and perhaps the only bull's eye of the target'.[38]

The Cabinet met on 22 June. After recounting the developments at Geneva which persuaded him that a negotiated settlement 'was not beyond reach', Eden explained that an Asian variant on NATO would be needed no matter how the conference ended. However, working on the optimistic assumption that Indochina might soon be at peace, he stressed that a settlement would require a guarantee. Here, he still favoured a Locarno-type arrangement with all parties – Western powers, communists, Asian neutrals – joining in a collective expression of faith in Indochina's future. The original Locarno treaty had failed because of an unwarranted supposition that all sides were satisfied with the status quo, but Eden sensed a real desire on the part of the communists at Geneva to make a peace that would last.[39] As for taking action in the event of a violation of an Indochina agreement, the Foreign Office felt it was 'essential to ensure that the participating states were able to act individually (as in the case of Article 4 of the Locarno Treaty) and that action was not made exclusively collective in such a way as to give the Communist powers a veto'.[40]

The following day – the eve of his departure for the United States – Eden delivered a statement to parliament on the position at Geneva. 'I have seldom known a situation in which the risks of a wider conflagration should be more apparent to all,' he told MPs. 'We have, therefore, very good reasons for wishing this Conference to succeed.' Recapitulating the events of the previous two months, he offered a strong rebuttal of US claims that he had reneged on the London agreement. He also asserted the UK's right to reach an independent judgement on matters of international moment and underscored his continued commitment to work with not against Asian opinion. There could never be 'real security in South-East Asia without the good will of the free Asian countries', hence if peace was restored in Indochina he hoped that the Colombo powers would be 'willing to take their part in supervising and guaranteeing the settlement'. Pondering the mechanics of a guarantee, Eden gave public voice to his desire for 'a reciprocal arrangement … such as Locarno'. This kind of guarantee, however, did not negate the need for 'a defensive alliance such as NATO is in Europe'. During the course of his statement, Eden thanked those who had helped him to keep alive both the Geneva conference and the chance of peace. Molotov, Zhou Enlai and Bedell Smith all got a name-check but there was no mention for Dulles.[41]

Having updated parliament, Eden turned his attention to the Anglo-American talks. The approach he intended to take on Indochina was codified in a memorandum approved by the Cabinet on 22 June:

1. We must persuade the Americans to give the French at least a chance of reaching a settlement in the next few weeks.
2. We must continue to make it clear that we cannot consider intervening in Indo-China and we must do our best to restrain the Americans from doing so.
3. We must again make it plain that we can accept no further commitments in regard to 'united action' in South-East Asia until the outcome of Geneva is known.
4. But we should express willingness to examine at once and in secret how best we can proceed to strengthen our common defences.
5. We should discuss how the principal Asian powers … can best be associated with this work.
6. But we should not agree, before Geneva is over, to any wider and more publicised meeting, at which Siam [Thailand] and the Philippines would be the only Asian countries present, to plan and proclaim an anti-Communist alliance.[42]

However, Eden's hopes for constructive dialogue with the Americans received a setback when US newspapers picked up on his House of Commons statement. As Makins reported, press commentary ranged from cool (at best) to critical and indignant. In the former category was the *New York Times* which suggested that Eden's emphasis on the 'independence of British policy' vis-à-vis the United States 'seemed to mark a turning point in the post-war relationship between the two nations'. At the harsher end of the scale, the Associated Press described the speech as 'bristling with criticism of the United States' and peppered with 'thinly disguised slaps at American policy'.[43] Aside from the alleged anti-Americanism of his statement, it was the referencing of Locarno that did most to generate a US press reaction described by Macmillan as 'more hostile than I can ever remember'.[44] In American popular-historical memory, Locarno was regarded as an early experiment in appeasement – wrongly so, Eden (rightly) maintained, since 'Locarno had nothing to do with Munich in either time or temper'.[45] Nevertheless, for many Americans, Locarno, like Munich and Yalta, was 'poison', and Eden found himself accused by the US press and sections of Congress of working to inveigle the United States into back-door approval of partition, hence of communist gains in Vietnam.[46]

On 24 June, Churchill, Eden and sundry aides and advisors took off from Heathrow aboard the strato-cruiser *Canopus* and flew west across the Atlantic. Also in the party was the Prime Minister's personal physician, Lord Moran. Alone together, Churchill confided to Moran his enduring admiration for the American people and his 'hope' that 'Anthony won't upset them'.[47] Ironically, thanks to what today might be called Locarno-gate, Eden managed to upset a great many people in America before even setting foot in the country. Yet, despite this most inauspicious prelude, the conference proved to be a success on a number of levels – so much so that Churchill confessed to having 'never had a more agreeable or fruitful visit'.[48]

The Prime Minister contributed a good deal to this satisfactory outcome. Ahead of the talks, the US Ambassador in London warned the State Department that Churchill, now nearly eighty, had declined physically and mentally in the six months since Bermuda. There were 'good and bad days but [the] former are becoming rarer', Aldrich felt.[49] As a general assessment, this was probably right, but in Washington, Churchill managed three good days in a row. Staying at the White House as the President's guest, he was greeted with warmth and affection wherever he went. Although Eisenhower sometimes felt the strain of keeping the old man happy, the result was worth the effort. At Bermuda, Churchill's sourness set the tone for a 'sod of a conference', as one member of the UK delegation wrote.[50] This time, his high spirits ensured a generally bonhomous atmosphere. 'First impressions', wrote Colville, 'surprisingly and immediately satisfactory while the world in general believes that there is at this moment greater Anglo-American friction than ever in history'.[51]

Adding further to Churchill's contentedness was Eisenhower's willingness to propitiate him on two policy issues close to his heart, détente and nuclear weapons. On the former, Eisenhower offered no particularly strong objection when Churchill proposed an Anglo-Soviet heads of government meeting, the precursor to what he hoped would be a full-scale East-West encounter between himself, Eisenhower and Malenkov. Later, it emerged that Churchill had misinterpreted the President's attitude, seeing positive approval and even enthusiasm where only ambivalence existed. Still, for the moment, his satisfaction was great. On nuclear matters, the Prime Minister made headway in his campaign to revive the UK-US intimacy of the war. Although Eisenhower refused to provide a cast-iron pledge to always consult with the British before nuclear weapons were used, he did agree to revisit the 1946 Atomic Energy Act (the McMahon Act) with a view to extending technical interchange. To Churchill, this welcome advance could yet be followed by others; having revealed to Eisenhower that the UK intended to proceed with development of a H-bomb, his hope was that Britain's emergence as a thermonuclear power would strengthen the case for a full Anglo-American nuclear alliance.[52]

Aside from Churchill's 'excited good humour', two other factors contributed to the smoothness of the conference.[53] First, what Macmillan described as the 'antipathy between Dulles and Eden', which had been such 'a feature of the American-British rift', fizzled without flaring.[54] On one occasion, noticing that Eden had been closeted with Dulles far longer than planned, Churchill grew nervous. 'Christ!', he exclaimed. 'I hope they haven't quarrelled and killed each other.'[55] He need not have worried: no blows were exchanged. Secondly, Indochina did not turn out to be the schismatic issue which many observers had predicted. To the contrary, the Americans seemed to have become fatalistic about the prospects for Geneva and were more than usually understanding of the UK position. The 'United States had believed in taking more positive action in Indochina than our allies believed desirable', Eisenhower told the National Security Council on the eve of the Anglo-American talks. 'We had lost the argument.' Dulles, agreeing, reflected on the nuclear aspect. A 'major problem' arising out of the launch of the New Look was 'the growing danger of atomic war', both generally and in relation to Indochina. 'In light of this, our "tough policy" was becoming increasingly unpopular throughout the free world; whereas the British "soft policy" was gaining prestige and acceptance both in Europe and Asia.'[56]

Indochina was always going to dominate the conference, but before the two sides got down to detailed discussion, the fallout from Eden's public promotion of a Southeast Asian Locarno needed to be cleared up. On the first afternoon (25 June), Anglo-American leaders gathered at the White House to map out an agenda. At the mention of Indochina, Eisenhower observed that some in Congress had reacted so negatively to Eden's Locarno proposal that there was talk of reconsidering US assistance to the UK under the Mutual Security Program. Eden, however, had no desire to be cast in the role of a latter-day Neville Chamberlain and declared himself 'bewildered by the ... reaction to his reference to Locarno'. All he had done was 'point out the unacceptability of a guarantee of a Geneva settlement which involved the retention of a veto on the part of any single guarantor'. He then snapped, testily, 'Change the name Locarno ... if it stinks in the United States.' It was an embarrassing moment, but rather than debate with Eden, Eisenhower steered the meeting on to other matters.[57]

Later, Eden wrote in his memoirs that the Americans 'not only understood' his Locarno proposal but 'seemed to like the idea', a strange conclusion at variance with the contemporary evidence.[58] On the first evening, he had a tête-à-tête with Aldrich, who had flown in from London. 'You know, Mr. Ambassador,' he told him, 'I am going to drop this Locarno matter.'[59] This was not an admission that a multilateral East-West guarantee was wrong, only that he ought to have avoided historical analogies. At the same time, Eden appreciated that the Anglo-American discussions on Indochina would not progress very far if he held fast to Locarno. Dulles seemed to appreciate the gesture. The 'grave objection' to the Locarno model from a US standpoint, he told him, was that it would amount to 'moral approval of a Communist success' should northern Vietnam pass into Vietminh hands. The most the United States would do was take note of a settlement and agree not to use force to overturn it. 'While we must accept the fact of Communist domination in large parts of the world', Dulles remarked, 'we do not believe in guaranteeing it anywhere'.[60]

With Locarno shunted into the sidings, Dulles and Eden were able to focus on Indochina. In the lead-up to the conference, the British were afforded a valuable insight into the state of US thinking courtesy of Australian Foreign Minister Casey who passed on an account of a frank conversation he had with Smith just before Geneva recessed. There had been 'no real clear-cut American policy on Indo-China until quite recently', Smith admitted. Instead, the administration 'had swung from one extreme to the other'. US officials issued 'widely varying public statements ... which had no doubt confused their friends as much as the enemy'. The administration's thinking 'had gradually crystallised on the need to salvage Laos and Cambodia from the wreck with as much as possible of Vietnam'. Intervention with American forces 'was "out"', Smith affirmed, 'although they did not want the Chinese to realise this too clearly'. As for partition, Casey was convinced that Smith was 'quite ready to accept the conception ... although he stresses that it must not be called partition but something else ... it is the *word* "partition" that is unacceptable in Washington'.[61]

The accuracy of Casey's report is confirmed by a memorandum Smith submitted to Dulles on his return to Washington. He wrote,

> I cannot escape the feeling that for us to disassociate ourselves from the harsh reality to which our friends are bowing would accelerate Communist momentum in Southeast Asia, decrease the prestige of the US as a realistic, responsible and reliable ally in the long period of struggle ahead, and thus possibly discredit or weaken our capacity to conduct US foreign policy.[62]

This counsel made an impression on Dulles. The day before the Anglo-American talks began, the US Secretary briefed Republican Congressional leaders. A settlement involving partition of Vietnam would be repugnant and regrettable, he observed, but borrowing Smith's phraseology, he suggested that it was still possible to 'salvage something' in Indochina; if southern Vietnam, Laos and Cambodia could be preserved – ideally 'free of the taint of French colonialism' – the United States would seek to 'hold this area' and 'fight subversion within with all the strength we have'. Dulles had in mind US military and economic aid to bolster internal security and stability, and a regional defence organization to offer NATO-like protection against external aggression.[63]

When Dulles and Eden met for their first Indochina session on 27 June, the American said that military intervention was extinct as an option. As for Geneva, if it came down to a choice between a Vietnam settlement based on partition and one which prioritized nationwide elections, the former was 'preferable' insofar as under 'almost any foreseeable circumstances the Communists would gain from elections', perhaps as much as 75 per cent of the vote. Even if the Vietminh failed to win an outright majority, 'their superior organisation in a coalition would allow them to take the country over as in Hungary'.[64] As Geoffrey Warner has noted, this was 'the first time an authoritative American spokesperson had been prepared to comment favourably on either alternative in conversation with the British'.[65] 'I *believe* it is not going too badly,' Eden wrote to Clarissa. 'Foster is all right outwardly at any rate.'[66]

Insofar as the Eisenhower administration's policy appeared to be moving away from a military solution and towards acceptance of a diplomatic compromise, it might be inferred that Mendès-France's coming to power played a determining role. To be sure, the new French government insisted that 'no French parliament would approve [the] conditions which the US had laid down for its intervention', and that the French delegation at Geneva consequently had 'no choice but [to] make the best deal they could [on Vietnam]'.[67] This outlook in turn left US policymakers with limited options. But the sobering conclusions of the five-power staff conference earlier in June – including the judgement that several divisions of US ground troops might be required to recover and then hold Tonkin – had begun to impact on the American outlook, certainly in the case of Smith, and increasingly so with Dulles, even before Mendès-France formed his ministry.[68] However, it was one thing for Dulles to concede privately (as he did to Eden) that partition was a lesser evil than all-Vietnam elections but quite another to express that view openly. For that would be to admit that the administration's Indochina policy was in shreds.

With the Americans seemingly prepared to face Indochinese realities, the importance the Eisenhower administration attached to a Southeast Asia defence organization increased commensurately. In addition to an alliance's region-wide role in deterring communist aggression, policymakers now saw it as the future guardian of Laos, Cambodia and whatever part of Vietnam remained beyond Vietminh control. Consequently, Eden found himself under pressure to approve immediate moves to conclude a security pact. Cognizant of the need to give the Americans some earnest of goodwill, he told Dulles that he was ready to explore on a purely Anglo-American basis – and, significantly, in advance of the outcome of Geneva – the broad outline of a Southeast Asia Treaty Organisation (SEATO).[69] To this end, agreement was reached on the establishment of an Anglo-American study group to explore how best to 'deter and if necessary combat Communist aggression' and assist regional states in dealing with 'Communist infiltration and subversion'. Bedell Smith and Walter Robertson from State and Rob Scott of the British Embassy would be the negotiators. The group would get down to business on 7 July. For public consumption, its deliberations would be presented as the natural outgrowth of the work of the five-power staff conference.[70]

In another sign that Anglo-American thinking on Indochina was beginning to converge, Dulles and Eden agreed to furnish Mendès-France with a document outlining the kind of settlement their two governments would feel able to endorse in public. In a memorandum composed on 28 June, the Americans and British undertook to 'respect' an Indochina agreement which:

1. Preserves the integrity and independence of Laos and Cambodia and assures the withdrawal of Vietminh forces therefrom;
2. Preserves at least the southern half of Vietnam, and if possible an enclave in the [Red River] delta; in this connection we would be unwilling to see the line of division of responsibility drawn further south on a line running generally west from Dong Hoi;
3. Does not impose on Laos, Cambodia, or retained Vietnam any restrictions materially impairing their capacity to maintain stable non-communist regimes; and especially restrictions impairing their right to maintain adequate forces for internal security, to import arms and to employ foreign advisers;
4. Does not contain political provisions which would risk loss of the retained area to communist control;
5. Does not exclude the possibility of ultimate reunification of Vietnam by peaceful means;
6. Provides for the peaceful and humane transfer, under international supervision, of those people desiring to be moved from one zone to another in Vietnam;
7. Provides effective machinery for international supervision of the agreement.[71]

The seven points were 'a turning point in American policy' towards Geneva, Makins reflected, and 'the first official recognition by the United States Government of the possibility that they might accept a solution by partition' in Vietnam.[72]

It was, in truth, a very limited recognition. No sooner were the seven points agreed than Anglo-American differences resurfaced with Eden instructing Jebb to offer Mendès-France a pledge of unstinting UK support in pursuing a settlement and Dulles refusing to counsel Dillon in like fashion.[73] The seven points spoke to what the Americans would tolerate, not to what they wanted. The United States 'could accept a settlement which passed the agreed tests', Dulles affirmed, but the administration 'would not wish to be associated as one of its promoters', both on moral grounds (since it involved a surrender to communism) and in domestic-political terms (given that the Republican Old Guard, the China lobby and others were certain to react negatively to any hint of appeasement).[74] In the end, Allen assessed, the seven points disguised rather than composed Anglo-American differences. If or when Geneva produced a settlement, even one resting on the seven pillars, 'the Americans will be looking for reasons to disapprove of the agreement, whereas our inclination will be to find good grounds for approving it'.[75]

The Washington conference ended on 28 June. A joint Eisenhower-Churchill statement (the Potomac Charter) reaffirmed the importance of the US-UK "special relationship", much to the Prime Minister's satisfaction. In the connected communiqué, the two leaders confirmed that Indochina had been discussed in relation both to the success and failure of the Geneva negotiations and that the two countries intended to 'press forward plans for collective defense' in Southeast Asia. The most striking feature of the communiqué was a veiled threat, inserted at the request of Mendès-

France: 'We are both convinced that if at Geneva the French Government is confronted with demands which prevent an acceptable agreement regarding Indochina, the international situation will be seriously aggravated.'[76]

Mendès-France might be a peace advocate but he was also shrewd enough to appreciate that a Geneva dénouement satisfactory to France and the Associated States still depended to some extent upon what he called 'the menace of American, and indeed wider, military intervention' should the war go on. By the same token, 'no immediate threat should appear to issue from Washington' since that would jeopardize the negotiations. All that was required was to make clear publicly that the collapse of the Geneva process 'would leave everyone free to take other decisions which might be extremely unpalatable to the Communists'.[77] Consequently, the French premier found the Washington communiqué 'very helpful' and later described the Anglo-American seven points as 'entirely on the right lines'.[78]

Taking an overview of his time in Washington, Eden thought it was 'astonishing how much was accomplished'.[79] In terms of the Indochina objectives he put to the Cabinet before leaving London, however, the outcome was rather mixed. On the positive side of the ledger, the Eisenhower administration seemed to have accepted the inevitability of a diplomatic settlement of the war, including partition of Vietnam, while the study group initiative spoke to a confluence of Anglo-American views on Southeast Asian security.[80] On the negative side, the US government made clear that it would do nothing to help bring about an Indochina settlement, even one based on the seven points, nor would it publicly approve or guarantee a settlement. As for the Dulles-Eden rapprochement, this was more apparent than real. Eden had barely vacated Washington before Dulles was complaining about the Foreign Secretary's 'efforts to conclude peace at any price', and throughout the remainder of the Geneva conference the American remained 'fearful' that 'Eden will try to push Mendès France into agreement far short of 7 points'.[81]

For his part, Eden was sceptical about Dulles's assurances that US military intervention was no longer an option. By this stage, the Foreign Secretary was preprogrammed to query almost anything the US Secretary of State said to him ('Dulles outwardly quite correct & almost friendly', he wrote to Clarissa on his final day in Washington, 'but I suspect otherwise within.')[82] Nevertheless, as he told ministerial colleagues when he got back to London, he found it hard 'to avoid conclusion that US don't want agreement' at Geneva, seven points or no seven points. And if diplomacy could not be ruled in, military action could not be ruled out. What if US aloofness at Geneva prompted the Soviets and Chinese to refuse to sign an Indochina agreement on the grounds that they would be committed while the Americans were free to pursue an independent course? In that situation, the negotiations would collapse, the war continue and the French, in desperation, might make another appeal for allied assistance.[83]

Eden's suspicions were not without foundation. A substantial body of opinion within the US government continued to favour a military solution over a diplomatic compromise. Strategists in the Pentagon, drawing on the report of the five-power staff conference, insisted that retention of the Red River delta was vital to the security of all of Southeast Asia. In the State Department, some members of the Policy Planning Staff even contemplated the creation of a military alliance between the United States and the Associated States, to the exclusion of France, to 'bust up' the Geneva conference and 'achieve a new climate' in which the fight against the Vietminh could continue.[84] The US Ambassador in Saigon, Donald Heath, summoned to Washington for consultations, concluded that 'all the people below the Secretary and Under Secretary are unanimous that we should intervene or rather make up our mind to intervene now with or without the French'.[85]

Heath's reference to the hierarchy at State is important. Both Smith and, in his own rueful way, Dulles, had become pragmatic partisans of partition, and that evolution in thinking mattered more than the complaints of mid-level Foreign Service officers and military planners. Eden, though, was too scarred by the mercurial nature of US policy to accept anything at face value. To his mind, success at Geneva remained the only certain barrier to US intervention. Nor were Dulles or Smith about to broadcast their conversion to partition at a moment when Knowland was busy whipping Congress into a frenzy over incipient appeasement at Geneva.[86] At a wider level, there were signs that the US government was beginning to accept that British nuclear apprehensions could not be dismissed; to the contrary, they were recognized as the engine driving not just UK Indochina policy but the UK approach to the Cold War. The British had 'no answer to the terrible threat of atomic attack', Dulles told the National Security Council on 1 July, and 'feel compelled to promote the idea of peaceful coexistence with the Soviet Union'. This outlook was 'widely shared both by the other free countries of Western Europe and by the free Asian states' and 'US policy must plainly recognize and take account of this fact'.[87]

In the days following the Washington conference, the French position in the Red River delta continued to deteriorate. As rumours of an impending Vietminh assault on Hanoi intensified, the French government announced plans to reinforce the FEC. As earnest of intent, French troops stationed in Germany were inoculated against tropical diseases.[88] Controversially, Mendès-France also made clear his intention of seeking parliamentary approval for the dispatch of conscripts to Vietnam if Geneva failed to end the fighting.[89] Then, on 1 July, French and Vietnamese soldiers and civilians began evacuating the south western delta and heading for the Hanoi-Haiphong complex, a contracted version of the old de Lattre defence perimeter.[90] In Saigon, where the move was widely interpreted as the prelude to total abandonment of Tonkin, the Diem administration had been given no advance warning and was reported to be 'at an almost insane pitch of hatred against [the] French'.[91]

The news from Vietnam alarmed the British. Recrossing the Atlantic at a stately pace aboard the RMS *Queen Elizabeth*, Churchill arrived back in London on 6 July. After reviewing the latest situation reports, he wrote to Eisenhower expressing his 'fear that grave military events impend in the Tonkin Delta and indeed throughout Indo-China'. Churchill was particularly concerned about the 'profound effect in the United States' that 'disaster and defeat' might produce.[92] 'I find no reason for taking a brighter view of the Tonkin Delta situation,' Eisenhower replied. The position was 'all the more exasperating to our people because ... this government has been suggesting and urging some internationalization of the Indo-China conflict'.[93]

The President's mood was not improved by speculation in the American press that PRC admission to the United Nations might be re-visited if Geneva was a success. In a cable to Churchill on 9 July, Eisenhower said there was zero prospect of rewarding the Chinese communists in this way. In a passive-aggressive barb prompted by the UK's pragmatic approach to the PRC, he told Churchill that he had 'no worries' about maintaining Anglo-American relations 'on a sound, friendly and cooperative basis as long as this one question, which looms so importantly in the American mind, does not rise up to plague us'.[94] Churchill harboured no tender feelings towards the Chinese communists and reassured Eisenhower that the UK would not support early PRC entry to the United Nations. But he disliked being lectured on the subject. Nor did he feel that anti-PRC fulminations in Washington would help the diplomatic prospect at Geneva. 'I cannot see why Anthony should not go on trying to persuade China to behave decently even if their conduct should make them more eligible for membership of the club', was his curt retort.[95]

In an effort to prevent an upsurge of violence in Vietnam, Eden had enlisted the good offices of Nehru. On learning that Zhou Enlai was planning to stop over in New Delhi, Eden sent the Indian Prime Minister an urgent cable describing Zhou's visit as 'good news' but also asking him to remind his guest that 'our whole effort will be imperilled if new large scale attacks are launched in Indo-China while the military committees [at Geneva] are trying to work out the terms of a cease fire'. Zhou's role as a pacifier was 'crucial', Eden argued. If he employed his 'influence on the side of moderation, I would not underrate the chances of a peaceful settlement'.[96] Nehru did as asked in talks with Zhou at the end of June. Agreeing that 'it was desirable to stop the killing', Zhou pointed out that 'the main reason for any increase in Viet Minh activity had been the increase in French bombing'. Still, Eden's point registered to the extent that Zhou 'hoped that both sides would avoid any major military operations while they were discussing the armistice'. In the event, Giap stayed his hand; there was skirmishing but no PAVN offensive.[97]

On 28 June, Nehru and Zhou issued a joint statement dedicating their countries to respect 'Five Principles of Peaceful Co-existence'. First set out in April as a basis for regulating Sino-Indian relations, Nehru and Zhou agreed that the code – the Panchsheel – offered a universally applicable framework for peace and security. Before long other Afro-Asian countries would also embrace the principles, to wit: mutual respect for the territorial integrity and sovereignty of all states, non-aggression, non-interference in the internal affairs of other countries, equality and mutual benefit, and peaceful coexistence.[98] In London, the Foreign Office took a cynical view of Chinese intentions. The Panchsheel offered Zhou 'a convenient peg' upon which to 'hang his Asian policy'. The underlying object was to create the impression that 'the Chinese were Asians first and Communists afterwards' and that US-led Western imperialism, not communism, was the greatest danger to Asian peoples.[99] Be that as it may, Eden could not ignore the Panchsheel in his quest for an Indochina settlement – a quest that was also now seriously time-limited, with precisely twenty-two days separating the issuance of the Panchsheel and the Mendès-France deadline.

The Geneva Settlement, July 1954

In London on 7 July, Eden delivered a brief statement in the House of Commons explaining the decision to establish an Anglo-American study group on Southeast Asia.[1] He also tabled a paper for discussion in Cabinet which assessed the prospects for Geneva when the negotiations resumed. If a settlement emerged in conformity with the Anglo-American seven points, all would be well, he felt, though the French would be 'lucky' to secure such an outcome. If a settlement was in view which departed from the seven points, it would be necessary for British diplomacy to display 'flexibility'. The overall objective was an agreement acceptable to France, the Associated States and Asian opinion and tolerable to the United States. However, if a settlement crystallized in a manner abhorrent to the Eisenhower administration but satisfactory to the Mendès-France government, Britain might have to jettison its respect for American sensibilities, especially if the Colombo powers approved of what impended.[2]

At Geneva itself there had been little progress during the absence of the heads of delegations. In the military talks, French and DRV representatives disagreed over where to draw the demarcation line in Vietnam; ostensibly, this line would delineate regrouping zones, but in reality it would establish the formal partition line between a communist north and non-communist south. The French insisted on a line running along the 18th parallel, close to the Tonkin-Annam boundary, while the Vietminh pressed for a line at least 300 miles further south along the 13th or at the outside the 14th parallel. Mendès-France's hope that an enclave in the north, ideally Haiphong, might be retained, and that Phat Diem and Bui Chu would be recognized as autonomous Catholic zones, had been quickly abandoned in the face of Vietminh insistence on control of all Tonkin.[3]

It was obvious to the British – and to the French and Americans – that failure to agree on a demarcation line, or to resolve the equally vexed question of the composition of a supervisory commission, would doom Geneva and ensure the continuation of the war. But what of the communist side? 'For all his brave words', Jebb said of Mendès-France in a dispatch to Eden on 29 June, 'the successful achievement of a cease-fire depends less on his own efforts than on the Chinese and Soviet policy in regard to Indo-China'.[4] This was a prescient observation. The following week (3–5 July), Zhou Enlai held a series of meetings with Ho Chi Minh and General Giap in Liuzhou in southern China. Looking back, the outcome of these talks made the difference between success and failure at Geneva.

The fact of the PRC-DRV consultations was known (the *New China News Agency* confirmed that 'the question of the restoration of peace in Indochina, and related questions' had been on the agenda), but no details were divulged publicly.[5] However, from communist sources we can now see that the Chinese placed considerable pressure on the Vietminh leaders to compromise at Geneva to save the conference and prevent a dangerously enlarged conflict. 'If we ask too much' in the negotiations 'and ... peace is not achieved, it is certain the US will intervene', Zhou told Ho and Giap. The outbreak of the Korean War was the PRC's reference point. In 1950, Zhou contended, 'If there had not been US intervention, the [communist] Korean People's Army would have been able to drive Syngman Rhee's [armies] into the ocean.' It followed that in Indochina the 'central issue' was 'to prevent America's intervention' and that required the DRV to compromise on demarcation and offer the French the 16th or even the 17th parallel. Failure to negotiate flexibly, Zhou warned, would see the Vietminh 'fall into the trap prepared by the US imperialists'.[6]

The DRV leaders accepted Zhou's analysis that if Mendès-France defaulted on his peace promise he would be forced to resign and a successor ministry might revive the dormant Franco-American intervention negotiations. Even without internationalization, Giap estimated that the FEC, with reinforcements pending and the VNA in support, could call on 470,000 troops, and it might take a damaged and weary PAVN five more years to achieve final victory. With US intervention, victory might never come.[7] The new communist negotiating position – demarcation in Vietnam at the 16th/17th parallel, along with a non-communist political solution for Cambodia and the securing of regrouping zones for the Pathet Lao in upper Laos – was codified in what became known as the 'July 5th Document'. This in turn was relayed to a reportedly disgruntled Pham Van Dong at Geneva.[8]

In later years, the Vietnamese communists came to regard the Liuzhou conference as a moment of betrayal, the point when the Chinese, placing their own national security interests ahead of the fortunes of the Vietnamese revolution, levered the DRV into accepting a division line further north than Vietminh military success and political ascendency merited. A quarter of a century later, Vietnamese resentment still broiled. In 1979, the government of the Socialist Republic of Vietnam issued the so-called White Book, a catalogue of criticisms of the PRC which, inter alia, condemned the way that Zhou Enlai had forced the Vietminh to compromise in 1954 when they were on the brink of total victory, both military and diplomatic. However, as R. B. Smith has demonstrated, the truth (rather than the propaganda) is that the 'military realities of 1954 had left no alternative' to Ho and Giap other than to fall in with Zhou, 'since without agreement the war would have escalated to a new level of violence'. Nor did the White Book acknowledge the extent to which the Vietminh had become dependent upon Chinese military assistance in the war with France, assistance which might have been withdrawn or at least reduced had DRV leaders failed to heed the PRC's plea for diplomatic flexibility. That was a second reality, Smith contended: 'Without Chinese aid the Viet-Minh would have faced disaster.'[9]

Whatever lay in store for Sino-Vietnamese relations in the future, in the summer of 1954, the outcome of the Liuzhou conference boosted Eden's hopes of a settlement at Geneva. On 8 July, Zhou sent him a message confirming that he had 'reached

[an] agreement with Ho Chi Minh on the way the Indo Chinese question could be settled' which would 'make it easier to get agreement at Geneva'.[10] Unfortunately, by the time the Cabinet discussed (and approved) Eden's Geneva position paper on 9 July, this encouraging news had been offset by a further hardening in Washington's attitude towards the conference. In a cable to Eden, Dulles revealed that neither Smith nor any American of ministerial rank would be in attendance when the conference resumed the following week; instead, leadership of the US delegation would devolve to a lower-level official.[11] Dulles subsequently made the same point at a news conference in Washington.[12] With Geneva's prospects 'on a knife-edge', Eden later wrote, the Eisenhower administration's decision to downgrade the importance it attached to the conference was as worrying as it was disappointing.[13]

It was just ten days since the end of the Anglo-American conference in Washington, but in that time US policymakers had experienced a recrudescence of revulsion towards a Geneva settlement, especially partition of Vietnam. As for the seven points, Dillon confided to Jebb that 'it now almost looked to him as if Mr. Dulles would be seeking any excuse to say that a settlement at Geneva did not carry out the intentions of a document whose very existence was probably a grave embarrassment to the Administration'.[14] The US government's misgivings were accentuated by the torrent of criticism emanating from Knowland and others in Congress towards a nascent Southeast Asian 'Munich'. 'Briefly, here is what we are all worried about,' Hagerty recorded on 6 July.

> First ... it looks as if the French are getting ready to almost completely capitulate to the Vietminh to partition Vietnam and withdraw from the entire north, leaving behind them many of the population of that territory who are Catholic and who have been strong anti-Red fighters ... [I]f that happens, these people will be brutally treated by the Communists and many will be liquidated.

The partition of Vietnam, meanwhile, 'will be badly received in this country and will be quite properly regarded as a tremendous triumph for Communism throughout the world'.[15]

These concerns informed the US administration's stance on representation at Geneva. As Makins reported to London, Dulles, fearing that the French might yet accept an agreement deviating from the seven points, refused to send Smith back to the conference to protect him from having to confront 'the choice of "doing something dramatic" e.g. walking out ... or, by remaining, giving the impression that the United States in some way accepts, or at least is associated with, a disastrous settlement'.[16] On 9 July, Eden informed the Cabinet of the American attitude. One way or another, he said, 'the next phase of the negotiations would be critical and difficult'.[17]

On 12 July, Eden flew back to Geneva for the resumption of the conference-proper leaving Churchill to deliver a statement on Indochina to the House of Commons. The situation in the Red River delta continued to cause 'deep anxiety ... lest the military events which are taking place become dominant, with a consequent serious increase of tension in every quarter', he told MPs. On a more upbeat note, the recent Anglo-American discussions in Washington had been 'realistic and constructive', and he looked forward to the reactivation of the Geneva process 'with some hope'. Any settlement, however, would need to be underwritten not just by the Geneva participants but by other countries 'with interests in the area', including the Colombo powers. A guarantee, together with 'arrangements for collective defence in South-East Asia', was amongst the issues currently being considered by the Anglo-American study group.[18]

Churchill made no reference to the US government's decision to reduce the status of its representation at Geneva. That morning's *Times* was not so coy, an editorial insisting that the 'position of Britain and France at the conference is ... weakened by the coldness, not to say suspicion, evinced by the American Administration'.[19] This was also Eden's sense. On arrival in Geneva, he found Mendès-France, Molotov, Zhou Enlai, Pham Van Dong and the heads of the Vietnamese, Laotian and Cambodian delegations already re-established. The State Department's U. Alexis Johnson, liked and trusted by the British, was in charge on the American side, but what Eden really wanted was Dulles or at least Smith as a symbol of US faith in the conference. With just eight days to go before the French deadline, he recalled, the 'atmosphere was taut'.[20]

The aloofness of the Eisenhower administration was also a blow to Mendès-France. Shortly after getting to Geneva, the French Prime Minister met with Zhou Enlai and proposed the 18th parallel as the demarcation line for Vietnam. Zhou neither accepted nor rejected the suggestion but remarked enigmatically that 'if France gives a little, the Democratic Republic of Vietnam will give a lot'.[21] When Mendès-France then met Pham Van Dong – the first top-level Franco-Vietminh political encounter of the conference – the influence of the July 5 Document was evident in the DRV's offer of the 16th parallel. This was quite a gesture by Dong but it was not good enough for Mendès-France who stood fast on the 18th parallel. Nevertheless, the two sides were getting closer, diplomatically and geographically (privately, Dong later praised the French premier's evident 'honesty and reliability'). In contrast, the American attitude to the work of the conference disturbed Mendès-France in that any evidence of Western disunity might encourage the Vietminh to stick on the 16th parallel or revert to demanding a more generous portion of Vietnam.[22]

Sharing the French leader's concern, Eden sent a personal message to Dulles imploring him to reconsider his government's decision on representation and promising to 'do his damndest to stick as closely as possible to the seven points'.[23] In response, Dulles agreed to fly to Paris on 13 July to explain his thinking in person. Mendès-France welcomed the offer despite the inconvenience; he had only just got to Geneva, but Dulles was adamant that Paris was the only possible venue. Eden was less enthusiastic but following conversations with Molotov and Zhou, which left him feeling that there was 'an even chance of agreement, provided we could persuade the Americans to join us', he relented.[24] 'I clearly had no option but to fall in with these arrangements,' he told Churchill. 'Indeed some good may come out of them' if he and Mendès-France could 'persuade Mr. Dulles to follow us back to Geneva'.[25] The next morning (13 July), Zhou Enlai told Mendès-France that the United States was 'trying to do everything possible to sabotage the conference'. A few hours later, the French leader was on a plane to Paris with the Edens fully intending to put Zhou's claim to the test when he met Dulles.[26]

'Anthony goes to dine at the Matignon [at 8.30 pm] with Mendès-France and Dulles,' Clarissa wrote in her diary once ensconced in the British Embassy. 'Comes back very late – 1.30 [am]. He says Mendès-France was terrific with Dulles – very different from Bidault. Wiped the floor with him. Stood by all his guns, aided by Anthony. Dulles got very cross and cornered.'[27] What the US Secretary ran into was a coordinated Anglo-French critique of his government's stance. Dulles 'cut a sorry figure', Eden wrote later. Concerned that the French would abandon the seven points, he 'kept quoting Yalta' in explaining how US opinion would not tolerate 'the subjugation of millions of Viet-Namese to Communist rule'. At the same time, he made clear that the French could not expect much in the way of US military assistance if Geneva failed to produce a settlement and the war went on. The position had 'changed fundamentally' since US-French intervention discussions commenced in May. Now, 'nothing but a large scale intervention of ground troops could hope to succeed'. Towards the end of the meeting, however, Dulles was forced into the striking admission that 'if the conference broke down a chain of events might follow which would result in United States "involvement" and a third world war'.[28]

Overnight, the US Secretary had a change of heart. In exchange for a letter from Mendès-France pledging that France would seek an agreement consonant with the seven points, he now agreed that Smith should return for the final phase of the negotiations. But he made it 'crystal clear that the US could never join in any guarantee to the Communists of the fruits of their aggression'.[29] What brought about this 'cave-in', as historian George Herring has termed it?[30] Pressure from Eden and Mendès-France played a part, as did Dulles's concern for the well-being of US-French relations, especially with the fate of the EDC still in the balance.[31] He was also undone by his own doom-laden logic: if no settlement at Geneva meant the Third World War, then a compromise with Ho Chi Minh was a vastly lesser evil. In addition, Eisenhower, increasingly anxious about the damaging spectacle of tripartite disunity, had already decided that Smith's presence would on balance do more good than harm, and Dulles had travelled to Paris knowing the presidential mind.[32] Above all, perhaps, Mendès-France's sincerity won Dulles's 'respect and admiration' and dissipated worries that his purportedly neutralist or fellow-travelling outlook would incline him to cut a deal with the USSR, trading the destruction of the EDC for an Indochina settlement. 'This guy is terrific!', emoted Dulles afterwards.[33]

Ultimately, Dulles and Eisenhower recognized that benefits could accrue from the United States taking – and being seen to take – the conference seriously. If a high-level diplomatic presence helped bring about a solution based upon, or closely related to, the seven points, including a partition line as far north in Vietnam as possible, that was about as good as the US administration could hope for at this late stage. Publicly, for domestic political reasons, it would be necessary to adopt a critical stance, but in private they and other US policymakers could take solace in the preservation of the southern half of Vietnam, Laos and Cambodia. 'Bedell, my boy, I've got some news for you,' Eisenhower told his old friend when he got him on the telephone. 'You're going back.'[34]

In Paris, Mendès-France and the Edens drove to Orly together for their return flight to Geneva. The details of the tripartite talks were secret but a communiqué rushed out on the afternoon of 14 July not only confirmed a US ministerial presence at the conference but emphasized Eden's contribution to this outcome. In consequence, the British Foreign Secretary was rather pleased to find himself the recipient of cries of 'merci Monsieur Eden' from members of the public as the Anglo-French motorcade snaked its way out of central Paris.[35]

✳

That same day, a cartoon by David Low in the *Manchester Guardian* fused one of the great sporting feats – Roger Bannister's breaking of the four-minute mile in Oxford in May – with Mendès-France's dash for the line at Geneva. Entitled 'Indo-China 4-Minute Mile', the cartoon showed the French Prime Minister, dressed in shorts and running vest, speeding towards the '20 July' finishing tape. Just behind him are Eden and Krishna Menon, Nehru's ambassador-at-large. Running in tandem, they symbolize the shared Anglo-Indian hope that Mendès-France would achieve his goal. Speeding alongside the edge of the track, parallel to the three runners, is a black diplomatic limousine; peering anxiously out of the windows are Zhou Enlai and Molotov, also keen, it seems, for the French leader to win the race. In the distance, a final figure can be seen sitting at the back of the viewing stand, not particularly interested in what is going on: Dulles. As a cartoonist, Low was renowned for his ability to capture complex political situations in a single image, and this cartoon is no exception.[36]

If Mendès-France was to win his race, three issues required urgent resolution. The first was the geographical positioning of the partition line in Vietnam. As we have seen, the Vietminh were offering the 16th parallel, albeit under some Sino-Soviet duress, and the French were holding firm on the 18th parallel. The second issue was the composition and jurisdiction of the supervisory commission to oversee an Indochina settlement. Eden remained keen to engage the services of the five Colombo powers, a solution Mendès-France found acceptable, but the Chinese, Soviets and Vietminh wanted a commission comprising two communist and two non-communist/neutral states. The final issue was the date of elections to reunify Vietnam. Having insisted on nationwide and democratic elections in Korea, the Western powers could hardly object to the same principle being applied to Vietnam even though Ho Chi Minh's popularity might well deliver the whole country to the Vietminh via the ballot box. Spurred by this unwelcome prospect, the French sought to delay the date of the poll as long as possible to allow the non-communists time to organize themselves to give the Vietminh an electoral run for their money. Pham Van Dong, however, demanded an early election to take advantage of the Vietminh's high post-Dien Bien Phu popular standing.[37]

For Eden, resolving these Indochina-specific issues was a daunting challenge, but as he discovered when he met with Zhou Enlai on 17 July, ongoing Anglo-American interest in regional collective security made his task even more difficult.[38] Basing himself on the communiqué issued after the recent Franco-UK-US meeting in Paris, Zhou said that it was evident that the Western powers were still determined to create a Southeast Asian Treaty Organisation (SEATO). Knowing that the Eisenhower administration was the main driving force, Zhou wanted to know whether the

Americans were planning to 'sabotage' the Geneva conference by including Vietnam, Laos and Cambodia in an anti-Chinese pact. 'If this were to be so, then peace would have no meaning other than preparation for new hostilities.' Eden assured him that SEATO was a purely defensive concept akin to NATO and analogous to the 1950 Sino-Soviet pact. So far as the British were aware, the Americans had no plans to recruit the Associated States as members, nor was the United States intending to establish military bases in Laos and Cambodia. Zhou then changed tack. What had happened, he asked, to Eden's Locarno proposal? A multilateral guarantee of a settlement appealed to Zhou as consistent with the coexistence principles he and Nehru had lately publicized. 'I have run into some trouble,' Eden replied, sheepishly. 'I used the word "Locarno" not knowing that the US did not like it'. At this, Zhou suggested that if all parties to a settlement issued statements supportive of its terms, that would produce a Locarno-type guarantee in effect if not in name, and that being so, there would be no need for SEATO. 'If the two were to exist at the same time', however, 'it would be unthinkable'. This comment drew from Eden a reiteration of SEATO's defensive purpose along with an assurance that it was also 'reconcilable and complementary' with any guarantee of peace in Indochina.[39]

Zhou's attitude unsettled Eden. Later that day, he called on Smith to check that his sense of American thinking was correct. The US Under-Secretary had arrived back at Geneva suffering from lumbago and ulcers, ailments he treated with a regimen of cigarettes, bourbon and Dexedrine, and his manner with Eden was consequently brusque to the point of rudeness. But the Foreign Secretary got what he wanted. 'The States of Indo-China', Smith said, 'would not become members of any South East Asia defence pact'.[40] Eden promptly sent Caccia to tell the Chinese that if a settlement materialized, Indochina 'absolutely would be ... neutralized'. In return, the Chinese agreed that the DRV would not be invited to join any Beijing-sponsored alliance.[41] But all was not quite as the British presented it. 'Although we have naturally said nothing to the Chinese,' Eden reported back to London, 'Bedell-Smith and I recognized that the territory of Laos, Cambodia and Southern Viet Nam might be covered by the South-East Asia Pact, even if the Associated States could not themselves be members.'[42]

This was not the only way in which SEATO impacted on Eden's efforts to seal an Indochina settlement in the last frenetic days at Geneva. On 17 July, the US-UK study group delivered its report. From Eden's standpoint, it did not make for entirely happy reading. Despite common terms of reference, the Anglo-Americans held markedly different views on what they were supposed to be doing. The British set out to consider the general principles underpinning a potential Southeast Asian pact – in other words, to do as charged and *study* the issues. The Americans were bent on drawing up a draft SEATO treaty, apprising the other American picks for membership (France, Australia, New Zealand, Thailand and the Philippines) of its terms, and issuing an early public declaration of collective intent to proceed to a full-blown alliance. 'Typically American, they want action – & they want it now,' Rob Scott, the UK negotiator, complained.[43]

Eden was aggrieved at what he saw as another attempt to kick-start regional security on the basis of US preferences. He was also worried that publicizing plans for what (by American lights) was an anti-Chinese alliance would cause the PRC to withdraw from the peace process. Furthermore, launching a pact with Thailand and the Philippines as the only regional states would convey the impression of a neocolonial construct, an essentially white organization with token or compromised Asian support. Few if any of the Colombo powers would ever join SEATO, Eden appreciated, but he was as keen as ever to obtain their blessing and benevolent support. In this regard, the American plan of action could easily trigger a denunciation by India and other Asian neutrals. Worse still, by going public as soon as Geneva ended, the Americans risked conflating SEATO and an Indochina settlement in a manner which could deter the Colombo powers from endorsing the fruits of the conference.[44]

In a pre-emptive damage limitation move, Eden handed Smith a memorandum specifying an itinerary of action to be followed if Geneva succeeded. The first priority was to appeal to the independent Asian bloc to back the settlement. Eden wanted to give India and other concerned states a period of post-Geneva grace to lodge their (hopefully positive) responses. The second initiative, to be launched no later than 7 August, was an Anglo-American invitation to the governments of France, Australia, New Zealand, India, Pakistan, Sri Lanka, Burma, Indonesia, the Philippines and Thailand to attend a conference to launch a Southeast Asian security system. That conference would convene on 1 September. In Eden's view, this staggered process would make clear to Asian opinion that the Indochina settlement and SEATO were not conjoined and that the former could be sanctioned without any pressure to participate in the latter.[45]

The Eisenhower administration accepted the UK's chronological sequencing on 20 July.[46] By then, Eden had taken out insurance against a failure at Geneva (his paper on sequencing being predicated on success). On 18 July, he sent telegrams to the governments of Australia, New Zealand and the Colombo Powers explaining that immediate action would be needed on SEATO if the Mendès-France deadline came and went without peace in Indochina. In that situation, he hoped that as many states as possible would join with Britain and the United States in a public declaration of readiness to create a collective defence system.[47] The response to Eden's message was much as expected: Australia and New Zealand were compliant; Indonesia, Burma and Sri Lanka were non-committal; Pakistan expressed measured interest in SEATO; and the Indian reaction crackled with displeasure. In keeping with the Panchsheel, India's 'foreign policy was based on not aligning herself with either side in the conflict between the Communist and non-Communist Powers', the Nehru government maintained.[48] As Eden knew, where India led, the Colombo powers, save Pakistan, usually followed.

As the clock ran down at Geneva, SEATO-connected issues were attenuated if not resolved: the Associated States would not become members of the organization, nor would anything be done publicly to advance SEATO until the key Asian powers had been given an opportunity to pronounce on an Indochina agreement. But would there be an agreement? In his memoirs, Eden wrote that the 'first indication that the Conference might be on the verge of success came on the afternoon of July 18th when [Z]hou En-lai proposed to me that the supervisory commission', one for each Associated State, 'should consist of India, Canada and Poland', with India as overall chair.[49] As a snapshot of the geopolitical state of international relations in 1954, Zhou's proposal could hardly be bettered: one neutral, one Western/NATO power and one Soviet bloc state. 'I am sorry to let go of the Colombo Powers,' Eden confided to his diary, 'but this could be a reasonable arrangement'.[50] When Molotov, Mendès-France and Smith gave their assent, this previously fractious issue was put to rest and the odds on a comprehensive settlement, which Eden had put at 'fifty-fifty' before his encounter with Zhou, started to shorten.[51]

Zhou had been the purveyor of the concession but it was Molotov whom Eden considered the architect. The Soviet Foreign Minister had been so helpful, not just on the commission line-up but on many smaller technical points, that Eden said to him 'that I thought he was going to give us all the presents from the Christmas tree'.[52] Throughout the conference, Molotov had been a largely consistent force for conciliation and compromise, and his effective working relationship with Eden was crucial in keeping the negotiations going. Ahead of Geneva, few Western observers would have predicted that Molotov, the legendary 'Nyet Negotiator', would transform himself into a diplomatic Santa Claus.[53] Eden put the change down to the passing of Stalin. Compared to when 'Joe' was alive, he told Churchill, Molotov was operating 'in a much more independent way ... as if the field of foreign affairs was his concern, without much, if any, interference from Malenkov ... or any other of his colleagues'.[54]

In contrast, most Americans at Geneva not only were suspicious of Molotov but continued privately to deride Eden for his gullibility in believing that the old Bolshevik had changed his outlook. Sitting next to a member of the US delegation at a conference function, Clarissa Eden was annoyed to see how he 'shook with over-simulated laughter when Molotov praised Anthony'.[55] Eden, though, was no dupe. 'Communist rulers' might be 'primitive and ruthless priests of a modern religion', as he put it, but that did not mean you could not do business with them in the international arena. Molotov stood for peace in Indochina, so Eden stood with him, whereas Dulles, and even Smith at times, seemed to stand for war. The Anglo-Soviet bonding agent, the ideology diluter, was nuclear and thermonuclear: 'It is the two countries likely to suffer most' in general war, 'ourselves and Russia', that were 'the most anxious to work out a settlement', Eden later reflected.[56]

On the evening of 19 July, Eden cabled Churchill to say that agreement on commission membership was a boost but 'we are not out of the wood'.[57] In fact, the last pieces of the Geneva settlement only slotted into place in the final twenty-four hours before the Mendès-France deadline. Late in the afternoon of 20 July, the French and DRV, pushed by Eden and Molotov, agreed that partition of Vietnam should be set at the 17th parallel. The French came down a parallel; the Vietminh went up one in a crude but effective split-the-difference compromise. As a senior Quai d'Orsay official at Geneva privately remarked, 'the division of the country at the 13th parallel would have more accurately reflected the true state of affairs', not least the primacy of the PAVN beyond the Hanoi-Haiphong corridor. Behind the scenes, however, Zhou and Molotov had ensured that the DRV would give the French a reasonably honourable way out.[58]

It was a similar story with the Vietnam election. Here, a belated Molotov intervention was decisive in resolving – substantially in France's favour – the deadlock between Pham Van Dong's desire for an early date for the poll and Mendès-France's preference for a vague commitment to a vote at some point in the more distant future. 'Shall we say two years?', the Soviet Foreign Minister proposed. Mendès-France readily agreed. Pham Van Dong also assented, but much less happily, and was later overheard muttering that the DRV's allies had 'double-crossed us'. Nevertheless, July 1956 was inscribed on the Vietnamese political calendar.[59]

Dong's disappointment is understandable. The DRV had not been levered by China and the USSR into negotiating at Geneva; as we have seen, evidence from the Vietminh side shows that Ho and his comrades had reasons of their own for wishing to go down the diplomatic track. However, the DRV was subsequently leant upon by its Sino-Soviet allies to accept terms unquestionably less favourable than the Vietminh's hard-won military success and political popularity deserved. As historian Fredrik Logevall had demonstrated, under Sino-Soviet pressure, the DRV did not so much make concessions at Geneva as 'surrender' in several vital respects.[60]

After the famous clock-stopping episode on the evening of 20 July, armistice agreements for Vietnam and Laos were signed in the early hours of 21 July, with the armistice for Cambodia following at midday (Sam Sary, the head of the Cambodian delegation, held out stubbornly and ultimately successfully for his country's right to accept outside military assistance despite its supposedly neutral status). In terms of the official Geneva documentation, all agreements were subsequently recorded as being reached by midnight on 20 July, a mark of respect for Mendès-France who was thus able to claim that he had succeeded in making his deadline.[61]

In Vietnam, the ceasefire was to be followed by the disentangling of the combatants and their regrouping either side of the 17th parallel within three hundred days, the Vietminh to the north, the French and Vietnamese armed forces to the south (the word 'partition' was eschewed in favour of 'military demarcation line'). The two sides were permitted to maintain their armed forces and arms stocks at existing levels; replacements, not reinforcements and augmentation, were allowed. The International Supervisory Commission would monitor the process. In Laos, the ceasefire would likewise be followed by disengagement and regrouping of forces and the withdrawal of PAVN troops. The FEC would also pull out apart from 3,500 troops and 1,500 military instructors who would remain in-country to assist the Laotian government in maintaining basic security. The Pathet Lao were to constellate in the north east pending a political settlement arising from elections projected for 1955. In Cambodia, the ceasefire would be followed by the separation of opposing forces, the withdrawal of both the FEC and the PAVN, and the assimilation of the Khmer Issarak into the wider community. Cambodia was permitted (thanks to Sam Sary's successful advocacy) to import arms and introduce military instructors for the purposes of self-defence. As with Vietnam, the tripartite supervisory commission would oversee the settlement in Laos and Cambodia.[62]

The armistice agreements were the only documents actually signed at Geneva as the delegations otherwise limited themselves to oral statements which were later entered into the conference record. Eden had wanted a collective – and signed – declaration of association with the settlement, but the United States refused to be formally tied to an outcome for which it had no liking; indeed, since Smith's return, the Americans, in obedience of Dulles's orders, had largely stood aside from the main business of the conference.[63] US objections were not unexpected (Dulles and Smith had both warned that this might happen), but Eden was still anxious about a possible diplomatic domino effect, with the Chinese, Soviets and Vietminh refusing to commit to undertakings which the United States did not share. If that happened, it would mean 'the continuation of the war with all that that will bring with it'.[64]

It was reassuring to Eden to know that he had full Cabinet support for his handling of this final difficulty, even to the extent of breaking with the Americans. 'The supreme Geneva objective is Cease Fire and stopping the war in Indo China,' Churchill told him, 'and no procedural differences with the United States should be allowed to prevent this'.[65] The Prime Minister, however, had an idea as to how another Anglo-American rupture could be avoided; rather than choose between a signed agreement or no agreement at all, he suggested that the Geneva delegates issue a simple statement taking note of what had been agreed.[66] For Eden, this was a far from perfect solution but it was better than no solution at all. Accordingly, having secured Soviet compliance, Eden and Molotov worked together to bring the rest of the conference into line.[67]

Repeatedly honed on 20–21 July, the Final Declaration of the Geneva conference contained an alphabetical listing of the participants in the Indochina phase of the negotiations followed by thirteen paragraphs, the majority of them beginning: 'The Conference takes note ....' The kernel of the Vietnam armistice agreement was recapitulated, but the Declaration's main focus was Vietnamese neutralization. The introduction of foreign troops, personnel, arms and munitions was forbidden, and the construction of military bases 'under the control of a foreign State' was strictly prohibited. Nor were the interim authorities of north and south Vietnam permitted to join 'any military alliance'. As for Laos and Cambodia, neither country was to request foreign aid, 'whether in war material, in personnel or in instructors except for the purpose of the effective defence of their territory', nor were they to participate in 'any ... military alliance not in conformity with the principles of the United Nations'. On Vietnam's political future, the Declaration described the military demarcation line as 'provisional' and made clear that it 'should not in any way be interpreted as constituting a political or territorial boundary'. The 1956 election, to be monitored by the International Supervisory Commission, would effectuate reunification. To prepare for the election, the authorities in the north and south would consult and plan together on or soon after 20 July 1955.[68]

The substitution of an orally adopted Final Declaration for a signed agreement saved both the conference and the peace in Indochina. But there was a cost. With no compulsion under international law to follow through on its provisions, the future of the settlement rested on goodwill. Of the nine delegations, seven (France, the UK, USSR, PRC, DRV, Laos and Cambodia) had reason to respect its terms. Two, the United States and Vietnam, had few. This was clear when Eden chaired the final plenary session of the conference at 3.00 pm on 21 July. Tran Van Do asked that it be 'officially noted' that the government of the State of Vietnam 'reserves for itself complete liberty of action' in the future 'in order to safeguard the sacred right of the Vietnamese people to territorial unity, national independence and liberty'. On behalf of the United States, Smith merely took note of the agreements and promised to 'refrain from the threat or the use of force to disturb them'.[69]

The settlement was not entirely satisfactory, Eden conceded in drawing the conference to a close, but it did end a war which had 'brought suffering and hardship to millions of people' and 'reduced international tension at a point of instant danger to world peace'. Looking to the future, he advised that 'all will now depend upon the *spirit* in which [the] agreements are observed and carried out'.[70]

As the nine delegations made speedy preparations to vacate Geneva – all hotel rooms and villas had been booked out from 22 July by a convention of dentists – Eden and Zhou Enlai managed a short farewell meeting. Although pleased by the outcome, Zhou remained 'concerned that the Americans might have some design on using Cambodia' for military purposes and would take advantage of the country's right to develop its national defence to establish a military presence. Eden said he was 'convinced' that the United States had no such plan. Reporting to London afterwards, however, he accepted that technically Cambodia would be within its rights to request US military advice and support and that the Americans would be within their rights to provide it. 'I am clear that this would be contrary to the spirit of these agreements,' he added, 'as well as being political folly'.[71]

There it was again: the 'spirit' of Geneva, the mystical glue that was supposed to hold the settlement together. Unfortunately, this adhesive was in short supply in Saigon and Washington. The day after the conference ended, Diem denounced a settlement 'concluded … without the concurrence of the Vietnamese delegation' and involving 'the enslavement of millions of compatriots faithful to the national ideal', and before long he had proclaimed 20 July, the date of the settlement, a 'national day of shame'.[72] On the American side, the public-political reaction was predictably critical, and not just of the settlement but of Eden. A *Time* magazine editorial took exception to his reputation, going back to the 1930s, as an anti-appeaser. Geneva, it argued, showed him to be the opposite:

> His friends picture him as the only real diplomat on the Western side. Is he not the only one who can lunch with the US's Bedell Smith or France's Bidault, yet take tea with Chou En-lai and dine with Molotov? The British newspapers are running over with enthusiasm for his exploits without stopping to consider whether anything is gained by drinking tea with the Chinese.[73]

Privately, US policymakers were mostly relieved at the preservation (for now at least) of half of Vietnam and all of Laos and Cambodia. Publicly, domestic political necessity required the Eisenhower administration to abandon *realpolitik* in favour of disappointment and fatalism. On 21 July, the President told a news conference that while he hoped the peace would hold, the United States was 'not party to or bound by the decisions taken by the Conference'. Pressed by reporters on whether the British and French had appeased the communists – as Knowland and the Old Guard claimed – Eisenhower replied that 'if I have no better plan, I am not going to criticize what they have done'.[74] Smith also rejected any Geneva/appeasement linkage. 'Munich is a damned poor term,' he told newsmen on his return to America. 'At Munich things were given away when there was no fighting. This is a war'.[75]

It fell to Dulles to point the way ahead for the United States. 'The important thing from now is not to mourn the past,' he declared on 23 July, 'but to seize the future opportunity to prevent the loss of Northern Viet-Nam from leading to the extension of Communism throughout South-East Asia and the South-West Pacific'.[76] In hindsight, it is hard not to interpret Dulles's words as the launch of an American campaign to ensure the non-communist future of southern Vietnam, Laos and Cambodia. If, in pursuit of this objective, the Geneva accords were stretched or even violated, so be it; as Eisenhower made clear, the United States was not bound by the settlement.

Whatever the future held, for now at least Indochina was at peace. From a Chinese perspective, that was a real gain. In a dispatch to Eden from Beijing, Humphrey Trevelyan, the British chargé d'affaires, reported that the official PRC line depicted Geneva as 'a major victory for the Indo-Chinese people, for peace and security, for the settlement of disputes through peaceful negotiations and for peaceful co-existence'. But there were other benefits more specific to China, Trevelyan suggested. The PRC had been treated by all delegations (bar the United States) 'as representatives of the only real Chinese government', and this might yet strengthen the case for its admission to the United Nations in place of Chiang's nationalist regime. In national security terms, the Chinese were guaranteed a 'Communist buffer-state ... on the border of their difficult Southern provinces' with every prospect that this would be extended through a Vietminh victory in the 1956 election. In totality, the settlement eliminated 'the danger of American intervention' in Indochina, 'with all its possible consequences'; China's 'security is improved'; the 'cause of Communism in South-East Asia has suffered no set-back'; and the 'respite from external preoccupations' should now permit the Chinese 'to concentrate their energies on ... industrialisation'.[77]

Trevelyan's assessment has since been corroborated by historians working from Chinese sources.[78] As to the other communist giant, the USSR's public commentary stressed the neutralization of the Indochinese states and highlighted the importance of the July 1956 election in Vietnam as a symbol of the 'defeat for those aggressive forces who sought to dismember Viet Nam with the object ... of converting South Viet Nam into one of the spring-boards of the projected new aggressive bloc in South-East Asia'. The Kremlin also accused the United States of trying – but failing – 'to prevent the work of the Conference being crowned by success'. As such, the settlement was 'an important victory for the forces of peace and a serious defeat for the forces of war'.[79]

In public, the DRV described the settlement as a victory even though privately its leaders harboured varying degrees of resentment towards the Chinese and Soviets for compelling them to abandon their hold on Laos and Cambodia, hence their dream of an Indochinese federation, and to accept a partition line in Vietnam requiring the retrocession of large swathes of territory and population under their jurisdiction for several years. On 22 July, Ho Chi Minh issued a statement to his followers lavish in its praise for the diplomatic support the USSR and China had given to the DRV. As to partition, this was a 'necessary measure' on the road to 'victory' for the socialist revolution, and Ho pledged to 'carry out faithfully' the terms of the Geneva settlement and work towards 'general free elections ... to realize national unification'.[80] A further gain was the precluding of US intervention, while recent research demonstrates that there was some confidence within the DRV leadership that the election would be held, and won, and that Geneva had therefore created 'favorable conditions' for the extension of socialism throughout Vietnam.[81]

Mendès-France delivered a radio address to the French people from Geneva on 21 July. 'Reason and peace have won the day,' he intoned. And though it was true that the accords contained 'cruel' clauses, he was 'certain that these conditions are the best we could hope for in the current state of affairs'.[82] The following day, drained and exhausted, Mendès-France spoke to the National Assembly in Paris. The settlement was 'a hard one', he reiterated, but that was because it 'reflected hard facts'. Looking forward, he said that France still had a role to play in the economic and cultural life of southern Vietnam, Laos and Cambodia and would continue to be responsible for military security for some time to come. He ended his statement with a few words on the subject of Anglo-French relations. 'I cannot refrain from saying how close and cordial our entente has been … Mr. Eden, who was one of the Presidents of the Conference, used the whole of his experience and authority to bring the two sides closer together and I wish to … address to him all the thanks of the French Government.' At that, French deputies (other than a small group of conservatives for whom Geneva was a badge of shame) burst into applause.[83]

Eden arrived back in London late on 21 July. The next day, after conferring with Churchill at Downing Street (the Cabinet, he learned, rejoiced in the 'success' of his 'patient persevering skill'), he delivered a statement to parliament. Outlining the nature of the settlement, he said that he was personally 'convinced' that the outcome of the conference was 'the best that could have been contrived'. No diplomatic compromise is ever ideal, but the 'only alternative' to the one just reached 'was continued fighting [and] further misery and suffering'. There had also been an 'ever-present risk that the conflict would spread, with measureless consequences'. In removing the conditions for general, even nuclear war, the Geneva settlement was 'a real gain for peace'.[84]

In Britain, the popular reaction to the settlement – and to Eden as the perceived architect of the settlement – was overwhelmingly positive.[85] The Foreign Secretary's 'prestige and authority will be much increased', Macmillan predicted, no bad thing for a man who would be Prime Minister.[86] Praise poured in to the Foreign Office from all corners of the Commonwealth including (and this gave Eden particular satisfaction) India, Pakistan and Sri Lanka.[87] The other two Colombo powers, Burma and Indonesia, were also fulsome in their congratulations.[88] 'There is cause for deep thankfulness in the agreement', the *Times* editorialized. True, northern Vietnam now appeared 'lost to the western world', but at the same time the settlement 'averted one of the most acute dangers of a great war that the world has faced since 1945'. For this, Mendès-France deserved great credit, but it was the 'unremitting imaginative skill' of Eden which kept the negotiations going 'often when the chances of success seemed nil'.[89] That sense of thankfulness imbued a special message to Eden from Her Majesty the Queen ('I am so delighted by your success'), and before the year was out he had been invested into the Order of the Garter.[90]

On 23 July, Eden spoke in Cabinet. In the Commons, he had been factual and circumspect. Now he offered a franker assessment of what the settlement portended. 'It must be assumed that, when elections came to be held, the majority of Vietnamese would place their hopes for the future in the leadership of Ho Chi Minh', and in consequence, the Vietminh 'will win'. The outlook for Laos and Cambodia was comparatively better as long as their neutralized status endured. In that connection, Eden stressed that it was 'essential' that 'the United States should not seek to establish any military influence' in those countries, 'which they will be tempted to do', because of the danger of provoking 'some counter-move by China' that would undermine the foundations of the whole Geneva edifice. As matters stood, Laos and Cambodia provided 'an independent and neutral buffer between China and Siam [Thailand]' and thus ensured Malaya's security to the north. And that was how Eden wanted it to stay.[91]

16

SEATO, 1954–1955

Eden took a much-needed vacation in August leaving his Foreign Office Asian experts to get on with finalizing a treaty to bring SEATO into being. In Washington, the State Department was similarly engaged. The deadline for the merging of the separate US and UK efforts into a single working text was tight: 1 September, the date when a working party of all projected SEATO members would meet in Manila to fine-tune the treaty in readiness for signature by ministers at a full conference the following week. Unfortunately, but predictably, the Anglo-American melding process did not go smoothly. Inevitable variations in detail and emphasis were honed away, but as the US-UK study group report had foreshadowed, differences on fundamentals remained.[1]

To begin with one of the less contentious issues, in the days immediately following the end of the Geneva conference, the Eisenhower administration indicated that it was no longer thinking of modelling SEATO on NATO; there would be no integrated command structure, no forces ear-marked for area defence and no commitment to automatic action in the face of aggression.[2] By mid-August, the British Embassy in Washington was reporting to London on a 'real somersault' in US thinking. According to Makins, American policymakers had developed objections to the NATO model on constitutional and political grounds. With the White House and Congress still locked in a dispute over the degree to which the President should possess a free hand in foreign policymaking, there were concerns that an attempt to extend to SEATO the commitment to automatic action embedded in the North Atlantic Treaty risked a humiliating rebuff by Congress. The State Department was also nervous about proceeding along NATO lines in case this generated 'unwelcome pressure' from Asian SEATO members for large-scale US military and financial assistance, an apprehension which accorded with 'signs of general reluctance' in Washington 'to accept fresh overseas commitments.'[3]

From a military perspective, the Pentagon and Joint Chiefs of Staff objected to the NATO model because of the potential curbs it would place on American military autonomy. Radford also considered it 'undesirable and unwise' to participate in an organization which risked US forces becoming engaged in local area defence. He was prepared to let SEATO go forward 'as a political exercise' provided that 'it does not lead to American military involvement in South East Asia', which was 'militarily indefensible by the West against a major attack'. Cleaving to his established outlook, Radford insisted that since 'serious trouble can come only from China – direct or indirect', the United

States should be free 'if need arises … to deal with the source of the trouble' rather than 'fritter away large resources in South East Asia.'[4] Dulles had developed similar doubts and was uneasy about an alliance which 'involved committing the prestige of the United States in an area where we had little control and where the situation was by no means promising'. At the same time, to simply shelve SEATO would 'mark a total abandonment of the area without a struggle'. On balance, he felt that a pact which offered protection to Laos, Cambodia and southern Vietnam, the main US concern in the post-Geneva period, was 'the lesser of two evils'. The President thought so too. On 17 August, he instructed Dulles to 'go ahead' with SEATO.[5]

As for the British, as recently as 23 June Eden had spoken in parliament of the prospects for 'a NATO system in South-East Asia'.[6] By the end of July, however, it was not just the Americans who were in retreat from the NATO model. The British Chiefs of Staff also pronounced in favour of 'some looser form of alliance or understanding'; the real danger in Southeast Asia, they argued, was not main-force Chinese aggression but subversion, a threat assessment which emphasized the need to help the countries of the region to develop internal police, self-defence and intelligence organizations and methods of countering communist infiltration. If an external threat developed, the COS saw merit in the suggestion of their US counterparts for a mobile strike force composed of troops and resources drawn from the militarily advanced 'white' members of SEATO and capable of intervention across the treaty zone.[7]

Confronted by this informal alliance of the US government and the UK service chiefs, the Foreign Office shelved the NATO model. In truth, despite Eden's parliamentary referencing of NATO, he and his officials had long recognized the value of non-military methods of combatting communism in the developing world and had themselves begun to question the relevance of a top-heavy NATO structure to the conditions obtaining in Southeast Asia. 'As you know we have for months been trying to persuade the Americans that the immediate problem of containing Communism in Asia is as much political as military,' the Foreign Office informed Makins. 'The new trend in their thinking … in the direction of a more modest military organisation less likely to alienate Asian opinion is therefore to be welcomed. In our view the security of South-East Asia depends first and foremost on the internal security of the countries on the periphery of China.'[8]

Compared with the ease with which the British and Americans agreed on the structure of SEATO, membership generated tensions redolent of the spring when Dulles first proposed united action. Eden remained adamant that if non-regional US allies like Nationalist China and South Korea were proposed for membership, SEATO's geopolitical and military remit would be greatly extended and the organization as a whole given a militantly anti-communist aura. Eden was still keen to secure the blessing of the Colombo powers. In view of their non-aligned outlook, India, Burma, Indonesia and Sri Lanka were unlikely to join SEATO as founder members, although Pakistan had shown some interest. However, their support from without might still be secured, Eden believed, if Chiang Kai-shek's China and Syngman Rhee's South Korea were excluded.[9]

Dulles was initially content to confine membership to anti-communist Southeast Asian states like Thailand and the Philippines alongside the United States, UK, France,

Australia and New Zealand in a seven-country starting line-up. What troubled him was the potential for the UK's promotion of the Colombo powers to generate pressure on the administration from Congress, the Old Guard and China lobby to bring in US allies – Japan as well as South Korea and Nationalist China – as counterweights. Apart from antagonizing Eden, this would complicate and delay alliance-building at a moment when Southeast Asia still required urgent attention. Even shorn of its potential to unleash a negative US domestic political reaction, 'the Eden position' on the Colombo powers 'might be seriously destructive of our efforts', the State Department judged. Apart from Pakistan, which was developing close ties to the United States, Washington policymakers were convinced that the Colombo states valued their neutralism too highly to endorse let alone sign up to SEATO. In which case, why waste time trying to win them round?[10] The British outlook also came in for criticism in the American press with a number of commentators arguing that the Churchill government was plainly in thrall to India and that Nehru had become 'the high priest of Britain's foreign policy in Asia'.[11] Dulles was inclined to agree. The 'great trouble', he told Eisenhower, 'is that the British are delaying, trying to get India in – & will waste 6 months trying to do so'.[12]

Eden, however, would not be deflected. In line with the chronological sequencing the Americans had accepted towards the end of the Geneva conference, he wrote to the leaders of the Colombo powers urging them to endorse the Indochina settlement. This they duly did. Encouraged, Eden wrote to them again on 30 July on the subject of SEATO. Conceived in accordance with the Charter of the United Nations, the planned pact was entirely defensive and concerned with regional economic and political stability as much as military security, he argued. The Geneva neutrality provisions meant that the Indochinese states would not become members of SEATO, but he saw no reason why the alliance should not aid them in preserving their freedom if they ever fell victim to external aggression. This, and other matters, would be addressed at Manila in September and he hoped that all five prime ministers would be willing to send delegations to the conference.[13]

The following week, in a joint public statement, the Colombo powers reiterated their 'deep satisfaction' at the restoration of peace in Indochina and voiced 'firm support' for the Geneva accords.[14] This was much to the good, Eden felt, and 'would give the settlement a better chance to survive'.[15] In comparison, the responses to his SEATO invitation were disappointing if predictable. Nehru was especially sharp in dismissing the pact as a fundamentally anti-Chinese alliance which would 'extend the area of the cold war … and the psychosis of hatred and suspicion in this part of the world'. Restating India's commitment to non-alignment, Nehru said he supported 'peace alliances' not 'military alliances'. As such, SEATO not only conflicted with the Panchsheel but posed a danger to the Geneva agreement by needlessly provoking China, a key prop of support for the settlement.[16] The leaders of Indonesia, Sri Lanka and Burma were less strident than Nehru but still withheld their backing for SEATO, although Pakistan's Mohammed Ali opted to attend Manila as an observer.[17]

In his memoirs, Eden put the best gloss he could on what was truly a diplomatic failure. It was 'clear that our policy of bringing the Asian powers into the picture at an early stage had been fruitful', he wrote. 'Even if we had not enlisted their positive support for SEATO, at least they understood what we were about, and had no ill feelings towards our action.'[18] It is hard to reconcile this recollection with the contemporary record. In a speech on 9 August, Nehru accused Anglo-American SEATO planners of using Orwellian 'double talk'. The United States in particular spoke oxymoronically of 'peace' in 'militant terms' and propounded policies 'in [the] name of preventing aggression [which] actually encouraged aggression'.[19] In the Foreign Office, Nehru's reaction was described as 'bitter' and in the weeks to come the Indian government would continue to criticize SEATO as 'unwise and even dangerous'.[20]

The Eisenhower administration had developed further doubts about SEATO based on what appeared to policymakers to be rapidly diminishing British interest in an alliance. Was it possible, Dulles wondered, that the United States could end up committed in SEATO without its most important ally at its side? Was this what Eden's focus on the Colombo powers was about? Would the British use Nehru's animus to justify their own non-involvement?[21] At several points during the Indochina intervention crisis and later during the Geneva conference, Dulles was content to do without the UK. Now, as SEATO neared realization, he seemed more concerned on that score. Alerted to Dulles's 'impression' that the UK was starting to look askance at SEATO, Ivone Kirkpatrick, the Foreign Office Permanent Under-Secretary, assured the US Ambassador in London that the opposite was the case. As a signal of the government's commitment, Eden would personally lead the British delegation at Manila.[22]

The value of this clarification quickly depreciated when a new Anglo-American difference of opinion blew up over threat-designation. Viewing SEATO through the lens of the Cold War, the Eisenhower administration insisted on specifying *communist* aggression as the primary danger the alliance was designed to combat. The Churchill government, committed to upholding the Geneva neutrality principles and still hopeful of winning at least moral support from the Colombo powers, preferred to avoid the prefix 'communist' and settle for aggression per se. In Eden's judgement, framing SEATO in overtly anti-communist terms was 'needlessly provocative' to China and 'calculated to make it very difficult for some of the Asian countries to adhere to the Treaty if at a later stage they wish to do so'.[23] The American counterargument – that an open-ended reference to aggression could suck SEATO into a conflict between, say, Pakistan and India – was a valid one, Eden acknowledged, but he still considered the risk to be acceptable.[24]

When Dulles learned of the British definitional preference, he was greatly put out. The United States might be 'better off by ourselves' after all, he assessed, especially if the price of working with allies was constant compromising on US principles. 'This running away from the word Communist' was an example. The British, and the French, too, were 'more concerned with trying not to annoy the Communists rather than stopping them'. Recalling Eisenhower's injunction to forge ahead regardless, Dulles could not just turn his back on SEATO. Instead, he would go and 'fight it out' at Manila. But with a week to go to the conference, he was still asking himself, 'Is it good to tie oneself up with people who are not willing to fight[?]'[25]

News from Europe, meanwhile, seemed likely to disrupt US and UK preparations for Manila. After vacillating for more than two years, the French government finally put the EDC treaty forward for ratification in the National Assembly on 30 August only to have it unceremoniously rejected. Since the launch of the EDC was dependent on the treaty's unanimous approval by the legislatures of all member states, the French vote killed the scheme and plunged NATO into crisis. Before long, rumours were flying that Mendès-France had concocted a 'secret deal' at Geneva whereby in return for an acceptable settlement on Indochina, he promised Molotov that he would bring about the demise of the EDC, a project he had never liked.[26] Speculation about a secret compact would never go away, but Mendès-France, while admitting to an occasional clumsy Soviet probe, declined to mix ('mélanger les genres') the issues.[27] For his part, Eden could find 'absolutely no evidence in support' of a trade-off, a judgement corroborated by Ilya Gaiduk in his study of the Soviet Union and Indochina.[28] What is more certain is the impact of the French vote on British planning for Manila. Eden had intended to lead the UK delegation to the SEATO conference. Now he decided that his place was in Europe. The immediate priority, he cabled Dulles on 1 September, was to prevent the wreck of the EDC taking NATO down with it.[29]

Dulles shared Eden's apprehension – the future of the US commitment to Western European security, or the commitment of Congress, at any rate, had come to depend on the launch of the EDC – and he was initially minded to focus on Europe himself at the expense of SEATO until Merchant persuaded him otherwise. Dulles and SEATO were 'so intimately associated' in the public mind, both in America and around the world, that his absence from Manila 'would cast a pall over the participants', Merchant counselled. His chief took the point.[30] 'American nerves are jangled and frayed by the disasters of this year', first Indochina and now EDC, Scott of the British Embassy in Washington reflected, with Dulles and his mournful mien almost personifying the failures of US foreign policy.[31] Eden, however, went from one diplomatic triumph to another. In September, he successfully shepherded the Atlantic Alliance towards acceptance of a British plan to replace the supra-national EDC with a less complex intergovernmental substitute, the Western European Union (WEU), which preserved a German military contribution to NATO and paved the way for the solemnization of the Federal Republic's sovereignty the following spring.[32]

At Manila on 1 September, a seven-power working group set out to shape a SEATO treaty from the Anglo-American draft in readiness for ministers to sign when the conference-proper opened a few days later. By now, the main points of dispute had narrowed. On threat-designation, the Americans denied that they were suffering from an 'addiction to the word Communist' but did have to respect 'the constitutional realities of the situation', namely that Congress would not ratify a treaty which failed to stress *communist* aggression. Therefore, despite being substantially isolated on this issue, American officials refused to compromise.[33] Allen, head of the UK team, feared that ministers might have no treaty to sign when they turned up at Manila and recommended to London that the US viewpoint be accommodated to some degree. 'No reason to give way now', Eden replied. 'We must stand up to the Americans on this resolutely.'[34]

By the time that Dulles got to Manila on 5 September for what he called 'one of the most important international conferences of our time', he was aware that the deadlock on threat-designation, if it rendered the meeting stillborn, would give the communist bloc a propaganda bonanza and leave US policy in Southeast Asia in ruins.[35] Weighing the matter, he shifted ground. The word 'communist' could be dropped from the treaty as long as he was permitted to publish a reservation stating that US obligations related exclusively to communist aggression. But that was as far as he would go. 'No reservation, no treaty,' he told Reading, Eden's locum.[36] As it happened, that was far enough for Britain and the other SEATO powers. Dulles got his reservation.

Another issue requiring resolution was the future security of Indochina, a delicate matter due to the neutralization features of the Geneva settlement. In a news conference in the immediate wake of Geneva, Dulles noted that the terms of the agreements as they affected Cambodia meant that the Phnom Penh government was at liberty to join any regional defence organization compatible with the UN Charter. Laos might well be free in this respect as well, although Vietnam's membership was 'unlikely'.[37] Eden was dismayed. 'Whatever may be technically the position … the whole understanding on which the agreements were reached was that none of the three Associated States … should be members of any South East Asia defence organisation.' At Geneva, his personal pledge to Zhou on this point had been 'an essential part of the settlement eventually reached'.[38] Eden reacted negatively again in August when the Americans proposed that observers from southern Vietnam, Laos and Cambodia be allowed to attend the Manila conference. If anything, he argued, 'protecting neutralisation was more important than to remove the word "Communist" from the [Manila] Treaty'.[39] Indochinese observers at Manila would 'not only arouse doubts in non-Communist countries in Asia and elsewhere as to whether this [neutralisation] understanding was being respected, but might provide the Communists with a pretext to upset or to fail to carry out the settlements', the British Embassy explained to a Diem government envoy in Washington.[40]

Dulles was not happy. He wrote to Eden:

If we are really determined to try and save [the Indochinese states] from Communism, it seems that we ought to try to build them up rather than to subject them to what I fear will be interpreted as humiliation in not being allowed to observe the making of a treaty which will presumably mention them by name and be designed for their benefit.[41]

Here, if needed, is confirmation that whatever else SEATO might go on to achieve, at this stage the Americans saw it as a means of engaging allies in an effort to ensure the non-communist future of what remained of the Associated States. Eden, however, continued to argue 'strongly' that 'the balance of advantage lies against having observers', and in due course this proved to be the consensus amongst the other SEATO states.[42]

When the Manila conference got underway, all delegations, including the American, agreed that the Associated States could not join SEATO in any formal sense without upsetting the Geneva neutralization provisions. At the same time, all delegations, including the British, wished to extend SEATO protection to the territory of Vietnam (or in practice southern Vietnam), Laos and Cambodia. But how could this desire be implanted in the body of the treaty without making the Indochinese states de facto members of SEATO? The contrivance arrived at was to add a special protocol to the treaty locating 'the States of Cambodia and Laos and the free territory under the jurisdiction of the State of Vietnam' within SEATO's geographical ambit, hence its security remit.[43] Whether this sleight of hand would persuade the USSR, PRC and Vietminh that neutralization was being respected remained to be seen, but Eden, even as he accepted the protocol, thought it doubtful. Having succeeded in stopping the Americans from turning SEATO into an overtly anti-communist construct, he genuinely believed that the pact posed no danger to China or to the integrity of the Indochina settlement. The protocol was a different matter. Extending SEATO coverage to southern Vietnam, Laos and Cambodia stretched neutralization to the limit. Clearly, there was a need to provide insurance for Indochina, even at some risk to the Geneva settlement, but while accepting its necessity, Eden privately admitted that 'I still don't like this protocol'.[44]

The Manila treaty was signed on 8 September 1954. Having arrived as an observer, Pakistan ended up as the eighth founder member of SEATO, a development which did nothing to lessen Indian dislike of the organization. In its final form, the treaty reflected US objections to any automatic commitment to respond collectively and in kind to external armed aggression. Instead, each member undertook to 'meet the common danger in accordance with its constitutional processes', a caveat which neither ruled in nor ruled out the use of military force.[45] In reality, the British Chiefs of Staff pointed out, the SEATO framework placed no restrictions on the unilateral exercise of US military power in a crisis. In the event of Chinese aggression, the COS expected Radford and the other Joint Chiefs to opt for widespread conventional and atomic bombing and a naval blockade of the PRC. Nor would the Americans be deterred from action by the absence of general SEATO support. Throughout the Manila discussions, the 'American attitude ... was very much conditioned by the fear of having their hands tied as regards action against China'. The Chiefs of Staff might have been referring to any of the five-power military conferences on regional security since 1951–1952. SEATO changed nothing other than to give the United States a carapace of international legitimacy for any action it might decide to take in the future.[46]

For now, the Manila conferees accepted that the immediate danger in Southeast Asia was not main-force PRC aggression but subversion. Here, though, the SEATO commitment to remedial action was extremely woolly; treaty signatories were merely obliged to 'consult' with each other 'on measures to be taken for common defense', a provision which spoke to the failure of the SEATO states to reach an agreed definition of what constituted indirect aggression, still less to determine what level of subversion would justify a collective reaction.[47] Structurally, a SEATO Council was to be established as a forum for 'consultation with regard to military and any other planning', though it would convene periodically rather than sit in permanent session. In terms of widening participation, the door was left open for future accession by other states.[48]

The SEATO treaty and protocol and the American reservation did not quite complete the Manila documentation.[49] Towards the end of proceedings, the Philippines government surprised the other delegations by tabling a Pacific Charter; intended to complement the treaty, the charter committed the SEATO powers to respect the principles of independence and self-government. The object, according to Filipino President Ramon Magsaysay, was to counteract communist attempts to depict SEATO as a colonial "front" organization – the membership of Britain and France offering an opening in this regard – and to make it easier for India and other anti-colonial states to join in the future.[50] On instructions from London, Reading initialled the charter ad referendum. The French, Australians and New Zealanders adopted a similarly provisional position.[51] On reflection, the Cabinet decided that it would be politic for the UK to sign up fully, as did the other previously hesitant states, and the charter was duly sanctioned at the end of September.[52]

The Manila treaty was approved by the House of Commons in November 1954.[53] By the time of the inaugural SEATO Council meeting in Bangkok in February 1955, all the other treaty powers had likewise ratified. Having missed Manila, Eden made a particular point of leading the British delegation at Bangkok and wrote later of his 'pleasant memories' of two days of 'easy as well as effective' discussions.[54] Dulles remembered things differently. Eden was 'listless and contributed little', he told Eisenhower, his thoughts 'largely elsewhere, perhaps at Downing Street' as Churchill moved closer to retirement.[55] On its first outing, the SEATO Council rarely strayed from discussion of structure and administrative procedures to deal with policy and strategy. Beyond the formal sessions, however, Dulles was in provocative form. At a news conference on 25 February, he remarked on the absence of Japan, Taiwan and South Korea, states which could have contributed to protecting Southeast Asia. The reason for their omission, he strongly implied, was excessive British sensibility towards the Colombo powers. But since none of the latter had joined SEATO (apart from Pakistan), 'I think that from now on it will be respectable in this circle to talk about international communism'.[56]

Some reflections are in order. At the close of the Manila conference, Dulles had been upbeat about what had been achieved. If SEATO 'had been in existence three or four months ago, I don't believe that the free world would have had to take the losses that it did take in Indo-China'.[57] Looking back at the end of 1954, he declared that SEATO was a 'defence weapon of great potential power'.[58] These claims, when juxtaposed with SEATO's subsequent and mostly ineffectual history, seem overblown. Even at the time, the limited liabilities incurred by the treaty signatories revealed a disconnect between Dullesian rhetoric and reality. The scope for opting out of action was extensive, and not just in respect of the hard-to-define matter of subversion but in the case of major external aggression. As a military alliance, SEATO was nothing without the United States, but notwithstanding Dulles's signature on the Manila treaty, the Eisenhower administration put nothing significant into nor accepted meaningful commitments on behalf of the alliance. The SEATO response to external aggression was conditional on the constitutional processes of member states, which in the American case left the final say to a Congress scarred by the experience of Korea and risk-averse to sending US troops into other potentially deadly quagmires on the Asian mainland. The SEATO commitment to combat subversion was a commitment to *talk* about combatting subversion.

It is little wonder that historians have been wont to dismiss SEATO as 'a zoo of paper tigers' and an alliance based on 'a fiction'.[59] To Dulles, the Manila treaty might have been conceived as a 'no trespassing sign', a warning to Beijing and Moscow to keep out of Southeast Asia, but from the outset SEATO was so conspicuously lacking in unity of intent and purpose that trespassers were never greatly deterred. At any rate, the absence of main-fore Chinese aggression in Southeast Asia in the years that followed was in spite of, not because of, SEATO. Eschewing signage metaphors, the diplomat-turned-historian James Cable likened SEATO to a 'fig leaf' covering 'the nakedness of American policy'. Even in the 1960s, at the height of the American war in Vietnam, SEATO 'never brought a man or a gun to Indochina', rather, the relationships that mattered continued to be bilateral, especially the US-South Vietnam relationship.[60]

But why did SEATO turn out to be such a hollow alliance? The answer is that in the wake of the Geneva conference, it became, for the British and Americans alike, something of an unwanted alliance. In August 1954, Cable (then of the Southeast Asia Department of the Foreign Office) reprised for colleagues the advantages of UK membership. SEATO would 'publicly define a limit' to communist expansion in an area of great importance to the UK; deter aggression and 'reduce the risk of blundering into World War III'; 'encourage' Thailand, the Associated States and their neighbours to better resist 'the threats and blandishments of Communism'; function as an 'umbrella beneath which we can hope to persuade the Americans to spend money on strengthening [regional] countries, economically even more than militarily'; offer an additional safeguard to Malaya; potentially 'supersede' ANZUS and so end the humiliation of Britain's exclusion from that pact; and in terms of power-by-proxy, 'ultimately prove the nucleus of a genuinely Asian defence organization that will relieve us of the burden of defending S. E. Asia'.[61]

Significantly, the way in which Cable pitched these benefits indicates a shift in the Foreign Office's outlook. 'If it be objected that most of these objectives could have been achieved without SEATO – perhaps better achieved in some cases – the answer is that account had to be taken of United States views. We could not achieve any of them without American help and the Americans insisted on SEATO.' The inference here is that if a US commitment could have been assured without SEATO, this would have been welcomed by the Foreign Office. Nor was this the extent of the post-Geneva rationalizing. Because the Americans appeared to be so sold on SEATO, Cable cautioned that it would risk another 'serious breach' in Anglo-American relations if Britain opted for non-involvement. But disassociation was impossible for another reason. SEATO, Cable stated, 'was the price of American acquiesce in the Geneva settlement, thus avoiding unilateral American intervention and the risk of war'. The UK wanted peace in Indochina; the Americans wanted SEATO; and so a co-relation – not a happy one – developed.[62]

According to the Cable analysis, the UK embraced SEATO largely to conciliate the Americans and protect the Indochina settlement. Another British Asia-hand of high reputation, Rob Scott, provides an alternate but compatible reading. SEATO, he recalled, was a 'sop' to the Eisenhower administration. It was 'part of the price of getting the Americans ... to Geneva', never mind bringing them round to acceptance of the final settlement.[63] There is evidence in American sources, too, of an implicit trade-off. Following the US government's decision in mid-July 1954 to send Smith back to Geneva, Dulles vouchsafed to Hagerty that he told Eden when he met him in Paris 'that we did not particularly like the idea of the partition of Vietnam but would go along with it if they [the British] would support the American effort to form promptly ... a Southeast Asia Treaty Organization'.[64]

The contrast between the Foreign Office's take-it-or-leave-it attitude to regional security in the high summer of 1954 and its approach for much of the period following Eden's return as Foreign Secretary in 1951 is striking. For several years, an Asian NATO had been the centrepiece of UK politico-military planning, a lure to draw the United States into contributing to Southeast Asian defence and consequently to easing the financial and military burden on Britain for area security. In addition, it was hoped that a defence organization would impose a check on US unilateralism vis-à-vis China. But then came the Indochina crisis. For Eden, the Eisenhower administration's drive to create a united action coalition as cover for intervention in Indochina demanded a rethink. In some respects, Dulles's proposal for united action was close to what the Foreign Office and Ministry of Defence had sought for several years: here, almost on a plate, was the coveted American commitment to Southeast Asia within a putative alliance framework. Yet, when united action revealed itself as a euphemism for military action in Vietnam, the Churchill government felt it had no option but to reject UK involvement or even support. By May 1954, US plans for a formal defence organization had superseded the original ad hoc coalition idea but Eden remained suspicious. 'The Americans ... appear to contemplate an organisation that would assist them to re-conquer Indo-China,' he remarked.[65] The following month, when Makins warned him that the Americans might lose interest in regional defence unless the UK government was more forthcoming, Eden shot back: 'I don't mind!'[66]

Makins was not far off the mark. Even before Geneva was over, the State Department and the Joint Chiefs of Staff had begun to doubt whether a full-blown alliance would necessarily serve US purposes. As we have seen, Eisenhower felt that his administration had become so identified with SEATO that there was no choice but to press on. Still, Eden's rejoinder to Makins is telling. The Indochina crisis demonstrated that there was something to be said for Britain retaining independence in Southeast Asian affairs – including the right to criticize American actions or distance the UK from US policy. The scope for free expression would be circumscribed in an alliance structure where the imperative of presenting a united front could lead to a victory by default for US preferences. Could an alliance-rooted Britain have resisted US plans for united action so successfully? Could Eden have worked with Molotov as effectively as he did at Geneva in pursuit of a negotiated settlement if he (Eden) had represented not just Britain but of a combination of powers, America included?

Furthermore, US adventurism in Indochina had been stymied despite the absence of an alliance based on collective responsibility and decision-making. What need was there, then, beyond financial and economic offset, for working with the United States in a formal defence system? Later, Henry Kissinger observed that the British 'almost certainly joined SEATO in order to gain a veto over what they considered the potential for rash American actions'. Kissinger was chronologically adrift. From 1951 to 1954, the British had seen a SEATO construct as a mechanism for containing America. By the summer of 1954, there was growing concern in London that SEATO might end up tying the UK to American extremism.[67]

Eden's own ambivalence deepened in the weeks after Geneva. US involvement in Southeast Asia still retained advantages for Britain – he had no argument with the Cable list – but significant disadvantages were banking up. An organization sponsored by or led by the United States was always going to resemble, in appearance if not actuality, an anti-communist league and consequently estrange those Asian Commonwealth and neutral states whose goodwill Eden prized so highly.[68] The involvement of Thailand and the Philippines, countries he regarded as American 'satellites', was no substitute for genuinely independent Asian support.[69] Dulles, despite his own growing uncertainty about SEATO in mid-1954, could not understand why the British seemed so blasé given that the 'primary purpose of the whole exercise was to save Malaya'.[70]

This was a common American refrain: the UK was bound to favour SEATO for Malaya-related reasons, US policymakers contended. But the Churchill government felt that *Ringlet* and *Irony* offered some prospect of protecting Malaya, albeit finding the manpower and resources in time of crisis would be a challenge. Even after the Songkhla strategy was revealed to them, the Americans continued to assume that protecting Malaya would guarantee British backing for SEATO. More generally, Dulles was convinced that 'American policy in the oil-rich Middle East as well as Asia has been badly handicapped by a tendency to support British and French "colonial" views'.[71] What he failed to see was that in Southeast Asia, his own noisy championing of the Philippines and Thailand did much to negate parallel British efforts to secure full Colombo power adherence. If SEATO was predominantly a 'white man's pact', and if, as Kissinger has attested, 'the [Asian] countries refusing to participate in SEATO were more significant than its members', this was due as much to US as to UK policy.[72]

The British, then, despite protestations to Washington to the contrary, *had* cooled on the idea of a defence organization. At the same time, the Americans themselves evinced serious doubts about the SEATO concept in the aftermath of Geneva. The Joint Chiefs of Staff had scant interest in mortgaging America's military freedom of action to any Asian organization, NATO based or otherwise, and Radford even thought that 'it might be necessary, in defense of the vital security interests of the United States, to act without our allies'.[73] On the eve of the inaugural SEATO Council, the Admiral averred privately 'that if overt aggression takes place, the US should strike at the source of such aggression', namely China, and that 'our strategy must be based on the use of appropriate atomic weapons'. As Radford knew, nothing in the Manila treaty prevented the United States going its own way in this regard.[74]

Later, the *Pentagon Papers* would suggest that Dulles's personal desire for a meaningful alliance was undermined by the refusal of the US Joint Chiefs to commit to SEATO.[75] In truth, Dulles was self-undermining. The inter-allied wrangling over membership and threat-designation (the British, with the French supporting them, 'are blocking everything we want to do') interacted with the US Secretary's pre-existing doubts about hard alliances to leave him hesitant about SEATO. 'The happiest day in his life', he confided to Henry Cabot Lodge, 'will be when we don't have to modify our policies … to keep up a façade of unity'.[76] Beyond this, in the lead-up to Manila, Dulles gave increasing attention to the old British thesis about containing communism by non-military means. A 'sense' of military security against Chinese aggression would be helpful to the states of Southeast Asia, he conceded, but it was also 'important to bolster them up … in the economic field'. Did that require SEATO? A Marshall Plan for Southeast Asia? More and more, Dulles thought not.[77]

In the end, the British went along with SEATO 'mainly to maintain Anglo-American solidarity', Eden admitted, not from any real belief in the necessity of the project.[78] Dulles occasionally divined this; the 'idea that they are signing the Treaty to please him does not please him at all', he commented a week before the Manila conference.[79] By the same token, the Americans stuck with SEATO because the Eisenhower administration's public championing of united action since March 1954 made it embarrassing to back away. The consequence of American half-heartedness was played out at Manila where the US delegation evinced no interest in making firm commitments to deal with aggression, or communist aggression, in a crisis. The British were happy to follow suit. Why would the United States or UK go further or do more for an alliance that neither particularly wanted?[80]

In hindsight, the most important document to come out of Manila was the SEATO protocol. As Fredrik Logevall has shown, if Dulles got what he wanted in terms of a treaty – 'an alliance that made few hard-and-fast commitments on its members' – he also got what he wanted in the protocol, namely 'a legal basis for intervention in Indochina'.[81] Following Geneva, Dulles maintained that American interest in Southeast Asia centred on trying 'to salvage what the Communists had ostensibly left out of their grasp in Indochina'.[82] In particular, he wanted to provide a 'mantle of protection' to ensure that the southern half of Vietnam, the trigger-domino, remained safe and secure within the Western Cold War camp.[83] The SEATO protocol was that mantle, a multilateral screen for any unilateral US intervention which might become necessary in the future – 'an aura of an interest bigger than just the big selfish United States … going in there', as Nixon put it – as well as a legal basis for intervention which the Eisenhower administration had lacked at the time of Dien Bien Phu.[84]

For the Churchill government, the overriding objective in post-Geneva Indochina was to preserve and implement a peace settlement Eden believed to be 'the best that our hands could devise'.[85] As previously noted, some of the Churchill government's concerns about the Manila treaty and protocol derived from their potential to destabilize the Geneva accords if the Sino-Soviet reaction proved to be excessively hostile. As it happened, the communist powers confined themselves to propagandistic condemnation rather than peace-menacing action: an editorial in *Pravda* accused the Americans of building an 'imitation … anti-Comintern pact', while the PRC denounced the Manila protocol for 'flagrantly violating the Geneva Conference Agreements' and lambasted SEATO itself as 'a hostile military alliance'.[86]

Eden, the 'man of Geneva', obviously had a considerable personal stake in the settlement but the Conservative government had additional and weighty reasons for wanting the accords to work. If the peace collapsed and hostilities resumed, the Eisenhower administration might press (or *re*-press) for a military solution on the ground that the UK preference for diplomacy had failed. The dilemma the British had confronted in spring 1954 would then resurface, only in more acute form. Could the UK defy the United States a second time on the question of intervention without causing grave harm to the "special relationship"? Yet, to go along with the Americans meant running a risk of war with China and even general – nuclear – war with the USSR. For the moment, the dilemma was theoretical. As long as the Indochinese states remained neutralized, and provided that preparations for the 1956 Vietnam election were on track, Eden and the Foreign Office reasoned that the DRV and its Sino-Soviet patrons would complain about but in the end accept SEATO.[87]

If the British, as well as the French, Soviets, Chinese and Vietminh had reason to abide by Geneva, the United States and the State of Vietnam were a different matter. In this connection, Eden and the Foreign Office found two particular aspects of the post-Geneva situation troubling. The first was American championing of Diem as the best (or least bad) leader of what, for convenience, if not yet constitutional accuracy, we will call South Vietnam. The second was the way in which the Eisenhower administration began undermining the residual French position in the south when, in the British view, it was only the French Expeditionary Corps which offered any assurance of security in the lead-up to the 1956 election. In combination, these two factors ended up suborning the Geneva settlement in ways that ensured that an American war in Vietnam succeeded the French war. 'US policy in Vietnam in 1954, and for a year or two afterwards, was not taken in accord with its allies,' Eden reflected in June 1965 as the US ground troop commitment to South Vietnam was gathering the momentum which, by 1968, would see over half-a-million American troops in-country. 'On the contrary, the French were then definitely against it and so, with less first-hand knowledge, were we.'[88] In a public lecture the following year, Eden accepted that the 'Geneva Conference fell short', but 'not by so wide a margin'.

As will be seen in the final chapter of this book, the falling short actually began while Eden was still Foreign Secretary.[89]

Geneva Suborned

With the termination of the Indochina War in July 1954, it might be supposed that the French colonial administration went into immediate liquidation and that Vietnam, or southern Vietnam, Laos and Cambodia embarked on independent futures. This, though, was not the case. For one thing, the three states remained members of the French Union and this afforded the French significant ongoing influence. For another, though committed to the Vietnam reunification election (to adopt any other approach seemed certain to provoke the Vietminh), the French were equally committed to finding ways to preserve the economic and commercial investment they had built up during a century of colonialism. This outlook extended to the whole country. In August, the Mendès-France government announced that Jean Sainteny, a diplomat trusted by Ho Chi Minh, was to be sent to the north as Delegate-General to seek a modus operandi with the DRV authorities.[1]

Back in July 1953, France had pledged to perfect the independence of the Associated States. Agreement was quickly reached with Laos confirming its freedom within the French Union, but it took France and Cambodia until mid-1954 to arrive at a similar arrangement. As for Vietnam, two agreements were drawn up in April 1954, one on the country's independence, the other defining the nature of future Franco-Vietnamese relations within the French Union framework. Both documents were initialled – not formally signed – in June.[2] The ensuing Geneva settlement bestowed de facto independence on Vietnam with the prospect, so the Mendès-France government claimed, of early de jure independence.[3] It soon transpired that the French expected the Diem government to sign a variant of the April agreements, thereby locking 'free' Vietnam into the French Union and preserving significant French prerogatives relating to finance, customs, judiciary, police and security forces. Diem held out for full and unfettered freedom, but the absence of any immediate legal or constitutional resolution left the French in a quasi-colonial position to the disappointment of the southern nationalist community.[4]

American policymakers found it hard to accept the French argument that Vietnam could be both independent and a member of the French Union.[5] Like their British counterparts, they appreciated that 'in the last analysis, Vietnamese security will be determined by the degree of French protection' in the lead-up to the 1956 election.[6] But they also expected the French to try and manipulate Vietnam's political and economic life to serve their own ends, a possibility which caused Dulles to dream from time to time of a future wherein the French 'get completely out' leaving the United States 'to work directly with the native leadership'.[7] For now, Washington wanted Diem to establish his credentials as an independent leader around whom the forces of non-communist nationalism could coalesce. Accordingly, the Eisenhower administration began treating his government as though it was already independent. In a letter to Mendès-France on 19 August, Dulles revealed that the United States wished to deal directly with Diem in the future in a number of key areas, including economic and military assistance. Anticipating the moment when South Vietnam was genuinely free, the Americans wished to encourage 'self-confidence and self-reliance'. There was also a domestic imperative at work insofar as Congressional backing for further appropriations for Vietnam could not be guaranteed if the French colonial administration remained the conduit of aid. For similar funding reasons, the United States proposed to take a more direct role in the training not just of the Vietnamese but the Cambodian armed forces.[8]

The French were shocked by what appeared to be a brazen attempt to lever them out of Indochina ahead of schedule. In particular, the diversion of security funding to the Vietnamese would make it financially prohibitive to maintain FEC force levels in the interregnum between Geneva and the 1956 election.[9] The British shared French dismay. If the FEC was forced to withdraw before the Vietnamese National Army was competent enough to assume sole responsibility for security, a military vacuum would be created which the Vietminh might be tempted to fill. 'This is bad', Eden commented. So was the US plan to take on a bigger role in training the Vietnamese military. It did not matter whether this was technically permissible under the self-defence aspects of the Geneva agreement; Eden worried that the communist side would regard the developing Washington-Saigon axis as incompatible with Vietnam's neutrality. 'The Americans', he concluded, 'are once again out to wreck the Geneva agreement.'[10]

Looking back, Eden credited US policy with a coherence it did not necessarily possess. American policymakers were certainly cynical about French intentions but they also knew that it would be 'militarily disastrous to demand the withdrawal of French forces from Vietnam before the creation of a new National Army'. The terms of the Geneva settlement barred any increase in force levels in Vietnam beyond those obtaining as of 20 July 1954, a prohibition which ruled out the US military simply taking over from the FEC had it wished to do so. Instead, the Eisenhower administration wanted to assume primary responsibility for the training of the Vietnamese with a view to the VNA taking on defence duties pari passu with the staggered rundown of French and French Union forces over the space of two years.[11] Appreciating that the prospects for South Vietnam's non-communist future were uncertain, Dulles came to see an ongoing French presence as useful for onus-shifting reasons. 'If we fail' in Vietnam, 'it will be a terrible blow to our prestige in that area', he commented privately. 'So far we have been able to say the losses in that area have been French failures.'[12]

As we will see, recognition of the value of the FEC presence did not prevent Dulles and the US administration generally from taking actions in 1954–1955 which cumulatively made it impossible for the French to maintain meaningful force levels. 'The US asked France to stay in Vietnam militarily, to get out of Vietnamese economic and political life, but at the same time Washington asked for French support and cooperation in implementing US programs,' the *Pentagon Papers* later said of the Eisenhower administration's policy. 'This was probably asking too much.'[13]

Turning to Diem, British policymakers had doubts about his leadership qualities and prospects from the very start. Aloof and austere, he lacked charisma and the common touch, presided over a cabinet of inexperienced ministers, possessed a political power base largely confined to the Catholic minority in a predominantly Buddhist country, relied on his immediate family for counsel (much of it dubious) and though an ardent patriot, seemed more likely to divide than unify the nation.[14] Yet, to the bewilderment of British observers, Diem (a 'dismal failure', according to Graves in Saigon) was seen by the Eisenhower administration and influential sections of the US Congress as South Vietnam's great hope.[15]

In fairness, the difficulties Diem faced from the summer of 1954 onwards would have challenged the leadership qualities of the most accomplished politician. To begin with, there was a severe refugee crisis to manage. Taking advantage of the Geneva provision allowing free movement of people for three hundred days from 20 July, large numbers of northerners headed south. In all, nearly 900,000 people joined what US-Diemist propaganda depicted as an exodus from tyranny. Without French and American support, the Saigon government would have been overwhelmed by the task of reception and resettlement.[16] There were also multiple challenges to Diem's political authority: from senior officers in the Vietnam National Army (the most serious of which was a coup plot involving General Nguyen Van Hinh, the Chief of Staff); from the politico-religious sects, the Cao Dai and Hoa Hao, with their private militias and a faithful of three million; from the Binh Xuyen, the Saigon "mafia" and its well-resourced private army; and Bao Dai, still Head of State and an inveterate intriguer. And lest we forget, there was also the French whom Diem – and the Americans – suspected of covertly aiding and abetting some or possibly all of these rebellious factions in the hope that Diem would be replaced by a leader more sympathetic to their interests.[17]

In London, the Foreign Office accepted that Diem was 'a poor horse to put one's money on' being merely 'the least bad candidate' for Prime Minister of Vietnam. At the same time, United States moves to denude the French Expeditionary Corps, an established force, in favour of channelling aid direct to Diem and the inexperienced VNA, struck the British as rash and risky.[18] The Americans were not without misgivings about Diem – a 'messiah without a message', unless it was 'blind hatred of the French', as the US chargé d'affaires in Saigon described him.[19] But for most US policymakers, Diem's impeccable anti-communist credentials compensated for his less positive attributes. The French, in contrast, saw no counterbalancing virtues.[20]

For a time, the Hinh challenge threatened to become serious, and the more the General looked to confront Diem, the more the CIA suspected the French of covertly urging him on.[21] In the event, the plot fizzled out. Advised by CIA agents that the moment he made an overtly threatening move, all US aid to Vietnam would cease, Hinh decided against a career in politics and left the country never to return.[22] But American mistrust of the French and their anti-Diemism lingered. The FEC might have an important security brief, yet as long as Diem was forced to operate in the shadow of the French tricolour, Washington policymakers doubted that he would ever win widespread nationalist support. This concern strongly informed the Eisenhower administration's decision to canalize military aid to the Vietnamese in a manner that 'cut out the French middle men'.[23]

A similar desire to bypass the residual colonial setup underlay American plans to extend the Military Assistance Advisory Group (MAAG) operating in Vietnam to Cambodia.[24] Mindful of negative communist reactions to any diminution of Cambodia's neutrality, the US Ambassador in Phnom Penh told the British that the MAAG initiative would be 'pianissimo'.[25] When Eden learned of what was afoot he was livid. 'If Americans cannot be stopped', he snapped, 'it is my view that Geneva agreements will be wrecked, with other loss as well'.[26] On the Foreign Secretary's instructions, Makins conveyed this view (in suitably diplomatic terms) to the State Department in late September. American policy, Under-Secretary Smith countered, was based on the right of the Associated States to defend themselves. Geneva acknowledged that right. Did the British not do so, too? As for the French, officially their policy was 'non-interference' in local politics, but US intelligence had discovered that 'a good deal of intrigue was in fact taking place'. In their desperation to protect their economic and commercial stake, Smith thought that the French were working to promote a Francophile government. Indeed, given that those interests existed north as well as south of the 17th parallel, the French might even be planning to work with the Vietminh.[27]

In trying to make sense of the British position, State and Defense Department officials wondered whether Eden, or Eden in cahoots with Mendès-France, had given 'side assurances to the Chinese Communists' at Geneva. Had the PRC been promised that neutralization would extend to blocking any efforts by outside powers to bolster the defence capacity of Vietnam, Laos and Cambodia?[28] In the end, though, Eden's displeasure did not alter the trajectory of American policy. On 29 September, a State Department press release confirmed that US military aid would soon go 'direct' to the Associated States.[29] The Joint Chiefs of Staff and the Pentagon had held out against assuming responsibility for training the Vietnamese Army in the absence of a 'reasonably strong, stable, civil government in control' in Saigon, but they had been won round to the State Department view, which was shared by the White House, that a US military commitment might strengthen Diem politically.[30]

Mendès-France 'deplored' the decision to redirect US aid straight to the Associated States; 'they did not need the dollars while France did', he told Dulles.[31] But recognizing a fait accompli when they saw one, the French moved swiftly to restore some amity to Franco-American relations. In London on 8 October, Mendès-France took time out from discussions on European security to talk to Dulles about Diem. Any successful nationalist leader in Vietnam 'would have to be somewhat anti-French', he appreciated. The real issue was Diem's 'apparent lack of administrative qualities and ability to get along with others'. Nevertheless, Mendès-France promised to 'give Diem a good try'.[32]

The next day – 9 October – PAVN units entered Hanoi, 'advancing like a tide as the French troops withdrew, sector by sector'. Cheering crowds thronged the pavements of a city festooned with Vietminh flags and banners ('Long Live Ho Chi Minh', 'Welcome to the Government coming back to its old home').[33] It was a little over nine years since Ho had stood in the city's Ba Dinh square to declare his country independent and announce the birth of the Democratic Republic of Vietnam. It was approaching eight years since Ho and his followers had been forced to flee Hanoi at the outbreak of the war with France. Now the Vietminh were back in what Giap called 'our beloved capital city', albeit with a formidable task of post-war reconstruction ahead of them.[34] Would similarly triumphal scenes be played out in Saigon in 1956 as a result of the all-Vietnam election? If Ho, Giap and their comrades dared to hope, they reckoned without the United States.

Two weeks after the Vietminh re-entered Hanoi, the Eisenhower administration deepened its commitment to Diem in a manner which, in hindsight, solidified the partition of Vietnam. On 22 October, the National Security Council approved 'a crash program to sustain the Diem government and establish security in Free Vietnam'.[35] On 24 October, the US Embassy in Saigon delivered to Diem a personal letter from Eisenhower – originally drafted in August – confirming that from January 1955 US aid would be given 'directly to your Government'. But US largesse was not extended unconditionally. To the contrary, the letter reflected in implicit form doubts about Diem's leadership and latent authoritarianism regularly ventilated in the White House, Pentagon, State Department and NSC. 'The Government of the United States expects that this aid ... combined with your own continuing efforts, will contribute effectively toward an independent Viet-Nam endowed with a strong government,' Eisenhower wrote. 'Such a government would, I hope, be so responsive to the nationalist aspirations of its people, so enlightened in purpose and effective in performance, that it will be respected both at home and abroad and discourage any who might wish to impose a foreign ideology on your free people.'[36]

Although the French knew what was coming, the subsequent publication of the Eisenhower letter still brought forth a 'very violent adverse reaction' from the Mendès-France government.[37] In London, the Chiefs of Staff were in process of approving a Joint Intelligence Study of the situation in Vietnam which described the Diem government as 'unstable and ineffective and ... losing such popular support as it had'. The COS signed off on the report (which reflected the Foreign Office outlook, too) on 23 October, the same day that Eisenhower's letter to Diem was dispatched.[38]

The divergence in the post-Geneva Anglo-American approach to Vietnam was most marked in regard to the 1956 election. No sooner was Geneva concluded than the Americans were seeking excuses for non-compliance with this central feature of the settlement. The first pretext advanced related to election monitoring. In Saigon, US Ambassador Heath told Graves that the prospect of the election was 'causing him and his colleagues a lot of concern', especially whether they could 'rely sufficiently on the neutrality or disinterestedness of the Indians', never mind the Poles, on the International Supervisory Commission.[39] The Diem government had a different objection. According to Foreign Minister Tran Van Do, 'it was mathematically certain the Vietminh would win' because the population of the north was bigger than that of the south (around 14 million and 11 million, respectively), and in any event, communist coercion would deliver 'a 100% vote' for Ho Chi Minh. For these reasons, 'elections were out of the question'.[40]

In London, officials in the Foreign Office held that Britain was morally obliged to work for the holding of the election. The fundamental issue, the Southeast Asia Department's William Paterson argued, was whether we should pay lip service to the ideas of democracy and at the same time subvert them in Communist fashion or whether we should take our chance (and probably lose) by permitting free elections. The Americans favour the former which will only result in another Chiang Kai Shek or S. Korean type of regime in the East. This will be a source of discord and will destroy any remaining Asian belief in our good intentions.[41]

To the Foreign Office, the UK commitment was 'an absolute one and could not be evaded simply because of fears that the elections might go the wrong way'.[42]

On 8 October, Dulles signalled a shift in the US approach away from objecting to the election because of concern about the robustness of monitoring and towards the Geneva settlement's insistence that the election be free. Meeting with senior advisors, he said that there was 'no possibility of fair elections in the North'. Where communism existed, there was no freedom; conversely, where freedom was, there was no communism. According to this (to Dulles) incontestable logic, 'when the time came, we would have ample grounds for postponing or declining to hold them [elections]'. Increasingly, the 'problem is not one of getting ready for a political election but combating subversion and infiltration'.[43] Dulles might have added (as a National Intelligence Estimate did) that even under the most fair conditions, 'the Viet Minh will almost certainly win', but this conclusion seems to have conflicted with his sense of how national self-determination functioned.[44] In Saigon, US Embassy officials were franker than their chief in explaining to their British counterparts the root cause of the American government's animus: 'Elections were certain to result in a Vietminh victory and therefore simply could not take place.'[45] The Mendès-France government, meanwhile, not wishing to give the Vietminh cause to renew hostilities while the FEC remained in Vietnam, urged Diem to at least show up for the scheduled north-south election planning conference on or after 20 July 1955.[46]

The US attitude continued to be criticized by London policymakers. In the Foreign Office, Kirkpatrick was put in mind of 'a crypto' he once met who 'only approved of free elections if they gave the desired result'. It was 'interesting to observe that Communist theory being taken over by the Americans'.[47] Speaking with the US Ambassador, Allen described the 'principle of genuinely free elections' as 'the whole basis of our policy'. The Churchill government was 'bound to stand by the results of such free elections even when, as in Indo-China, there was a risk that a majority might voluntarily, even if misguidedly, decide to vote Communist'.[48] The Foreign Office position was refined in a paper prepared by Cable of the Southeast Asia Department. 'Any attempt to frustrate the elections would be a major violation of the Geneva settlement and would give the Communists an admirable excuse for declaring the settlement null and void without outraging neutral Asian opinion.' If that happened, 'we should find ourselves back on the horns of that dilemma from which we temporarily escaped at Geneva: whether to intervene militarily in Indo-China at the risk of world war or to allow the whole country to succumb to Communist domination'. The paper went on:

If the worst came to the worst, it is better to let South Vietnam go than, by destroying the Geneva settlement, to face a renewed choice between the risk of

war and that of losing the whole of Indo-China … Our policy … should be to rub
Vietnamese noses in the inevitability of elections in the hope that we will thereby
galvanise their leaders into activity that will produce enough non-Communist
votes in the elections to enable us to postpone, if not indefinitely avoid, any
consequent transfer of power in South Vietnam to the Viet Minh.[49]

The Americans 'appear to realise that elections would result in Vietnam going
Communist but they deduce that the electoral process must ipso facto be corrupt and
they therefore mean to prevent its operation', Paterson commented in a postscript.[50]

In November, Eden proposed UK-US-French ministerial talks in an effort to
reach agreement on how to proceed on Indochina, still 'the central problem in South
East Asia'. At a minimum, he felt that the Diem government should be recast or
replaced to 'provide the non-Communist area of Viet-Nam with a reasonably firm
and competent administration'. This could not happen soon enough. 'We have already
lost 5 months of the time gained at Geneva,' he complained, 'and cannot afford to lose
more'.[51] When neither the Americans nor the French showed much interest, Eden
lost his temper:

> This is hopeless & very serious. If neither W'ton nor Paris will do anything,
> I consider that we should make clear … for the record … that it's not our fault
> that zero has happened in five months. There will be a grim reckoning over this
> miserable Indo-Chinese failure to attempt any rally of our friends. We must be
> alive to our own position. If our allies will do nothing – not even meet – then the
> responsibility must be placed squarely on them for the record.[52]

Makins in Washington and Jebb in Paris were ordered to try again to persuade
their host governments of the importance of tripartite unity in 'upholding Geneva
and in stopping the Communist-rot'.[53] In a cable to Sir Hugh Stephenson, Graves's
successor in Saigon, the Foreign Office summarized the wider state of play. While the
UK was committed to Geneva, the Americans 'do not consider themselves bound' by
the terms of the settlement and 'appear to believe that these will have to be violated if
Indo-China is to be preserved from Communist domination'. The French purported to
respect Geneva but it was hard to avoid the conclusion that 'they have written off South
Vietnam as lost and are pinning their hopes on a modus vivendi with the Viet Minh'.[54]
Worn down by British badgering, the Americans and the French eventually agreed to
set aside time for a tripartite discussion during the annual NATO Council meeting in
Paris in December.[55]

By now, the Eisenhower administration was in receipt of new and disturbing
assessments about Diem from the US Embassy and CIA station in Saigon. 'Diem is
rigid, unwilling to compromise, and inexperienced in the rough and tumble of politics,'
one estimate affirmed. On the basis of present trends, 'it is highly unlikely that South
Vietnam will develop the strength necessary to counter the growing Communist
subversion within its borders; it almost certainly would not be able to defeat the
Communists in country-wide elections'.[56] The administration had to take notice – and
did. Diem should 'adopt urgently and vigorously reforms', Dulles decided, 'including

broadening his government to bring in technical ability now lacking, counter propaganda, land redistribution and economic remedies tailored to fit new situation'.[57]

While the Americans sought to improve matters *through* Diem, the British, like the French, took the view than any improvement required the *removal* of Diem. In a brief prepared for Eden's use in the Paris talks, Foreign Office officials underlined the need for 'a reasonably firm and competent administration' in Saigon, an objective which necessitated 'the replacement of Mr. Diem'. The Americans, however, were seemingly bent on evading the 1956 poll and maintaining a separate South Vietnam and so rationalized that Diem the anti-communist opponent of Geneva cancelled out Diem the administrative incompetent. Nonetheless, Eden's advisors encouraged him to make clear in the talks that the UK 'cannot be a party to any plan for frustrating the elections' and that 'we cannot afford that the Geneva Settlement should break down'.[58]

On 16 December, the eve of the NATO Council, Eden and Dulles dined together at the British Embassy in Paris. When Eden remarked that the chances of effective government in South Vietnam were 'depressing' with Diem in power, Dulles did not demur. Diem lacked many qualities of leadership, he agreed, but the Americans had so far failed to identify a better alternative. Dulles also noted that the French were seeking to speed up the withdrawal of the FEC, reducing force levels to 80,000 by July 1955 and to just 25,000 by December 1955. The US decision to provide $500 million of military assistance direct to the Associated States and only $100 million to the French for the upkeep of the FEC, a quarter of what the French estimated they needed to maintain their forces, was clearly not unconnected with the revised timetable, though Dulles made no comment on cause and effect.[59]

Before leaving for Europe, Dulles confided to Hagerty that it was no longer 'desirable to have the French forces stay very long'.[60] Instead, as he proceeded to tell Eden in Paris, the Vietnamese Army was the future. It was 'no use trying to match the Vietminh' man for man, though. The 'wisest plan was to concentrate on producing a small but effective force which would take care of internal security'. For external defence, the United States looked to the deterrent power of SEATO and a concomitant Sino-Soviet 'reluctance to risk a major war'. Eden accepted Dulles's assurance that the United States was seeking to operate in Vietnam within parameters permissible under the Geneva agreements but he still felt that the "nobody else" thesis should be tested given that Diem had no great support beyond the Roman Catholics and sections of the rural land-owning class and urban educated elites. Again, Dulles did not disagree. Diem might not last but the longer he did the better. 'It might in the end still not prove possible to save Vietnam,' he conceded, 'but at least we could use the intervening period to strengthen Cambodia, Laos and Siam [Thailand] as much as possible. If we did this then we might be better able in a year's time to withstand the loss of Vietnam than we were now'.[61]

At tripartite talks at the Matignon on 18 December, the French confirmed that the Vietnamese Army was now under Diem's control and that the danger of a military coup had passed. Moreover, General Ely, High Commissioner in Indochina, and Eisenhower's special envoy in Saigon, General J. Lawton Collins, had agreed on a programme of reforms which, if implemented, would inject some stability and increase popular support for the Saigon government. However, because Diem had yet to agree to the programme, and might never do so, Mendès-France thought it prudent to look at alternatives. Dulles was less sure. 'Good indigenous leadership was not found ready-made in a young country and we must be content with something less than the best,' he observed. The 'only course was to continue to back Diem but to exert increasing pressure upon him to make the necessary changes in his Government'. If Diem refused to alter his approach, then the US government would be compelled to consider 'whether continued American investment' in Vietnam 'could be justified'.[62]

The British and French inferred an implied threat in Dulles's words – American abandonment of Vietnam unless their allies agreed to give Diem more time. In truth, Dulles's outlook reflected the current temper of the US Congress. A few weeks earlier, Senator Mike Mansfield of Montana, the foremost Asia expert on Capitol Hill, had produced a report based on a tour of inspection to Indochina. Endorsed by the Senate Foreign Relations Committee, the report concluded that if the Diem government fell, 'the United States should consider an immediate suspension of all aid to Vietnam and the French Union forces'.[63] Keen to cement bipartisan support for its post-Geneva effort, the Republican Eisenhower administration welcomed the Democrat Mansfield's report (but not as much as Diem who had 100,000 copies made and distributed all over South Vietnam).[64] Seen against this backdrop, Dulles's remarks were not agonizing reappraisal-like bluster. Sensing this, Mendès-France grew uneasy; if the Americans walked away from Vietnam, he reflected, the FEC might have to stay on. As for Eden, he felt that Western (in practice US) aid to Diem 'for another year would have a beneficial effect upon the neighbouring countries, particularly upon Cambodia and Laos and upon Siam [Thailand]'. And that 'would be an important gain'.[65]

Despite the thread of anxiety stitched into the Foreign Office's Indochina briefs for Paris, Eden returned home 'much reassured by all that Mr. Dulles had to say'.[66] Afterwards, he wrote to Nehru to say that the US Secretary had agreed with him on 'the paramount importance of upholding the Geneva Agreements'.[67] The Foreign Office was also gratified by the 'change of attitude' on the part of the Americans towards July 1956, particularly Dulles's readiness to 'accept the principle of elections'.[68] The British, however, had got ahead of themselves and of the Americans. A commitment to the principle of an election was not a commitment to hold one. Whether Eden was misled by Dulles or misconstrued US intentions is hard to determine, but it would not be long before the idea of an Anglo-American congruity of outlook, not just on the election but on Vietnam generally, was shown to be an illusion.

On 10 January 1955, Eden circulated a foreign policy stock-take to the Cabinet. On Indochina, he noted that while the Geneva settlement 'saved the French armies from imminent and complete destruction', the current outlook was 'dark'. In Vietnam, the communists had 'the advantage of being able to wave the nationalist flag'. Ho Chi Minh was 'much more than a Communist leader … [h]e is the nationalist leader' and for the Americans 'to bring in Diem, who is not only a bigoted Catholic but is known to have American backing and set him up in Saigon where his authority hardly stretches beyond his own front door, is no answer to this kind of appeal'. In the eighteen months remaining before the election, the challenge for British diplomacy was to find 'a national leader in the South' who was credible in the eyes of the Vietnamese and acceptable to both the Americans and the French. If that proved achievable, Eden felt there was a chance that the large post-partition Catholic influx from the north might help deliver a non-communist majority in the south at least.[69]

The following week, the Foreign Office surveyed Vietnamese prospects in more detail. According to Allen, the government's adherence to the principle of democratic elections was all very well, but it was a gamble to suppose – as some of his colleagues did – that Ho Chi Minh would prove to be an Asian 'Tito' and that Vietnam under the Vietminh would operate as an independent communist state, sympathetic to but not an agent of Beijing and Moscow. After much reflection, he had come to the conclusion that 'our interests would probably be best served by a continuance, with the tacit acquiescence of both sides, of the existing division'. This would offer 'a good chance' of containing the spread of communism beyond northern Vietnam and prevent Malaya from being menaced. For China, 'it has the important advantage of at least ensuring a friendly state on her southern frontier'. A UK proposal for an all-Vietnam constitution (offered in its capacity as continuing co-chair of the Geneva conference) might engender complex north-south negotiations. If these 'were to drift into deadlock and if the deadlock were in turn to lead gradually to acceptance by both sides of the idea of a semi-permanent division of Vietnam', the dual result might be the maintenance of peace and the protection of the UK against any charge of playing false by Geneva. Against this section of what he called Allen's 'able paper', Eden scribbled an approving 'Yes'.[70]

The idea of a semi-permanent division gained traction in London in February when the Washington Embassy reported that the Eisenhower administration, privately if not yet publicly, had come out strongly against the holding of the Vietnam election. UK policymakers were taken aback. What, they asked, had happened to Dulles's assurances to the contrary in Paris in December? As Eden prepared to head to Bangkok for the first meeting of the SEATO Council, his advisors were left to lament that 'we were wrong in thinking ... that the Americans now accept the principle of holding elections'.[71] Reluctant to abandon so critical a feature of the Geneva settlement, the Foreign Office adopted a pragmatic approach. There could be 'no further attempt ... to displace Mr. Diem', the Southeast Asia Department accepted, but this concession to the Americans ought to be traded for US support, if not for the election, then for the Diem government's participation in the north-south election coordination conference. Thereafter, if the conference threw up 'insuperable difficulties ... advantage could be taken of this to seek the postponement of the elections'.[72]

Over the next few weeks, the political situation in Vietnam began to stabilize, much to the surprise of British observers. As the Saigon government applied itself to implementing the Ely-Collins programme (widening its politico-demographic base, improving its administrative processes and pressing ahead with social and economic reforms), Eden had to admit that 'Diem is doing better'.[73] On a stopover in Saigon, Dulles was also 'favorably impressed by Diem who is much more of a personality than I had anticipated'.[74] The Vietminh, meanwhile, with their eyes focused on the electoral prize, bided their time.[75] As for the French, Mendès-France, whom the Americans had always suspected of playing a 'schizophrenic' double game (publicly backing Diem while secretly plotting his ouster and negotiating with the Vietminh via Sainteny), resigned in late February and was succeeded by Edgar Faure.[76]

During this time, Eden's concentration on Indochina, so intense for the past year, lessened. Apart from competition from other directions, notably difficulties in Egypt and a tour of Southeast Asia and the Middle East, Churchill had taken an apparently irreversible decision to resign at the start of April, and preparations for the prime-ministerial transition became a significant distraction. Even so, Eden did not fail to register a portentous development in Saigon in late March when the Cao Dai and the Hoa Hao sects joined forces with the Binh Xuyen in a United Front of Nationalist Forces. When Diem refused to accede to the Front's demand for a new genuinely representative cabinet, Saigon was plunged into turmoil. Armed skirmishes between the VNA and the Binh Xuyen's military wing increased and before long an ostensibly political crisis threatened to become a shooting war. The Eisenhower administration was disappointed when the French adopted a neutral position; refusing to lend Diem military support to put down 'this gangster outfit', as Dulles characterized the Binh Xuyen, Ely tried to broker a compromise between the semi-warring factions.[77] According to Makins, US officials viewed this 'French policy ... as a continuation of their earlier efforts to get rid of Diem'.[78]

With Diem clinging on in Saigon against a backdrop of mounting violence, in London a long anticipated (and peaceful) transfer of power was finally completed. On the morning of 5 April, Churchill presided at his last Cabinet before driving to Buckingham Palace to tender his resignation to the Queen. The next day, after more than a decade as Churchill's acknowledged successor, Eden got his hands on the keys to Number 10 Downing Street. 'You know that I will do everything I can to help the course of the relations between our two countries run smoothly', he wrote to Eisenhower.[79] The sentiment was sincere. But Vietnam soon provided a test of its practical application.

Amidst the swirl of crisis in Saigon, the Foreign Office, now headed by Harold Macmillan, accepted that an all-Vietnam election was unlikely to happen given the combined opposition of the Eisenhower administration and Diem government. However, UK policymakers still hoped to persuade their US counterparts to avoid a showdown with the Vietminh, China and the USSR a year earlier than necessary by forcing Diem to participate in the north-south election coordination conference, which was mandated to take place from 20 July onwards. If the conference was boycotted by the Saigon authorities and the DRV responded by renewing hostilities, 'public opinion in Great Britain would not wholeheartedly endorse counter action under the Manila Treaty', the State Department was told.[80] This was strong meat but it elicited no immediate response. That in itself was no surprise. Since the end of the Geneva conference, Cable complained, 'it has become quite clear that the US Government do not want us to have a voice in the shaping of their policy in Viet Nam'. From his new vantage point in Downing Street, Eden could only agree: 'We are treated like Australia.'[81]

As the stand-off between Diem and the United Front intensified during April, the Eisenhower administration began at last to reassess its policy. The catalyst of change was Presidential envoy General Collins. In a series of cogently argued cables from Saigon, and then in person on a visit to Washington, Collins convinced Eisenhower and Dulles that the crisis was largely of Diem's making, that similar crises would be a staple of Vietnamese politics while Diem remained head of government and that it was essential to find an alternative leader.[82] As recently as December, Dulles had told Eden that Diem might be a 'time-buying operation'; if he could hold South Vietnam together for a year or so, that would allow the United States to get on with creating a politico-military basis for containing communism which would endure irrespective of who was in power in Saigon.[83] Now, just four months on, Diem's time seemed to be up.

On 27 April, Dulles cabled the US embassies in Paris and Saigon confirming that the US government was ready to work for a 'new alignment' in South Vietnam. Bao Dai might be approached as Head of State to dismiss his prime minister.[84] Diem was on the brink. But he did not topple over it. The next day, events in Saigon took a dramatic turn when the Binh Xuyen launched a mortar attack on the Norodom Palace, the former seat of the French Commissariat-Général in which Diem had recently taken up residence. Other government positions in the city were also attacked. It is unclear whether the Binh Xuyen escalated the crisis of its own volition or was provoked by the government. Either way, Diem, who may have sensed that the Americans were preparing to abandon him, did something out of character: he showed leadership. With French forces more concerned with protecting French lives and property than in intervening to defuse the situation, Diem ordered 2,000 VNA regulars into battle. It was the boldest play of his premiership. To the surprise of many, especially Collins, the Binh Xuyen were routed in a week of street fighting.[85]

As historian George Herring has shown, Diem's proactivism, resilience and above all his victory in the Battle of Saigon 'produced an American policy reversal of momentous significance.'[86] As soon as news of the fighting reached Washington, Dulles ordered the US embassies in Paris and Saigon to destroy his regime-change cable.[87] By 1 May, with the Binh Xuyen in retreat, the Eisenhower administration's search for alternative leadership was called off and Diem was once again lauded as the 'symbol of Vietnamese nationalism struggling against French colonialism and corrupt backward elements.'[88] The South Vietnamese Premier outlasted his would-be nemesis, Collins; indeed, so fierce was the US administration's born-again faith in Diem that heretics like Collins were quietly removed from the centre of Vietnam decision-making.[89]

The American rededication to the Diemist cause was on show when the leading Western powers assembled in Paris shortly after the Battle of Saigon to witness the coming into force of the Western European Union. On 7 May – a year to the day since the fall of Dien Bien Phu – Dulles told Faure and Macmillan that Diem was 'the only means US sees to save South Vietnam'. No matter what the 'US view has been in [the] past, today [the] US must support Diem wholeheartedly'. The Eisenhower administration would 'not permit Diem to become another Kerensky'.[90] It was a powerful protestation but it did not impress Faure. 'Diem was notable only for his hatred of France,' he retorted. 'If maintained in power he would only bring about a Vietminh victory'. If the Americans would not cut their ties to Diem, 'France should withdraw from Indo-China and bring home the French expeditionary force as soon as possible'. Dulles was disconcerted; he certainly wanted the French out, but at a time and on terms of US choosing. 'Diem might have weaknesses, but he would not depart at the wave of our hands,' he countered. Nor was a US Congress in thrall to the Mansfield Report likely to approve economic and military assistance for any other Vietnamese government.[91]

By the time of the next round of tripartite discussions on Indochina on 10 May, Dulles was in receipt of a Joint Chiefs of Staff judgement that while the removal of the FEC might be the eventual aim of American policy, premature withdrawal would result in 'an increasingly unstable and precarious situation' which could only redound to the Vietminh's advantage. The JCS considered the Vietnamese Army incapable of maintaining internal security and even more so of countering outside aggression without assistance. At the same time, the Geneva freeze on force levels militated against any direct US commitment to defend Vietnam.[92] Dulles, taking on board this assessment, was emollient with Faure. 'Vietnam, though important, was not important enough to be allowed to become a source of serious discord between France and the US,' he said. 'It would be better to abandon Vietnam than to pursue antagonistic policies there.' After their last meeting, when Faure proposed a French withdrawal, Dulles had 'suggested US withdrawal' to his own government. But both options were counsels of despair. Far better, he believed, for America and France to work together. 'It was recognized that Diem was anti-French,' but if the Faure government could bring itself to lend Diem greater support, the Americans in turn would use their influence to ameliorate Diem's Francophobia.[93]

Faure, too, was conciliatory. If 'genuine Franco-American co-operation' could be assured, he was ready to back Diem, but the repatriation of the FEC would continue apace to demonstrate that France was not seeking to maintain colonial authority. Dulles was grateful. It was 'necessary to look upon [Diem] not as a calamity to be endured', he commented, 'but as representing the emergence of those nationalist anti-Communist forces which were needed if the country was to be saved from Communism'.[94] With that, a Franco-American entente was re-established, but it was fragile. Despite Dulles's soothing words about the importance of close US-French relations, now that Diem had proved his mettle in the Battle of Saigon, the Eisenhower administration was more than ever inclined to work independently of the French.[95]

There was a final tripartite meeting on 11 May focused on the Vietnam election. The French, fearing that cancellation would provoke the Vietminh into resuming hostilities, continued to take this central provision of the settlement extremely seriously. The British were also anxious to avoid giving Ho Chi Minh and his Sino-Soviet allies any grounds for suspecting that the election might not happen, which meant that the north-south planning conference needed to happen. As for the Americans, they had no desire to see the election take place but faced a dilemma over the degree to which they could publicly oppose a vote. Like the Western Alliance generally, the United States was a long-standing advocate of free elections in Germany and Korea. In those countries, however, the chances of the communists ever agreeing to a national ballot were minimal, and this allowed the Americans to inhabit the moral high ground without worrying about an actual communist victory. In Vietnam, an election monitored for fair play by an international commission was already in the diary – and likely to be won by Ho Chi Minh whose patriotic and nationalist credentials, Eisenhower conceded, were sure to attract many more Vietnamese than were repelled by his political ideology.[96] In the end, the US government attempted to evade this dilemma by continuing to oppose the election on the specific issue of freedom or rather the purported absence of freedom in northern Vietnam. Disregarding the monitoring functions of the International

Supervisory Commission, Dulles insisted that communists never permitted a free and open political process. This meant, ipso facto, that all-Vietnam elections, being only truly free in the south, should be postponed until such time as genuinely open governance prevailed north of the 17th parallel. In practice, this approach would permit indefinite delay, although tactically it was politic for the United States to follow not lead the Saigon government; Diem was never going to agree to the election, and US policy was to back him in this.[97]

On the eve of the Paris talks, the *Times* noted that Britain, despite the 'vital role' it had played at Geneva, was becoming marginalized in Indochinese decision-making.[98] It is true that Macmillan had contributed little to the inter-allied discussions, but at this final session he tried – albeit with limited success – to alter US thinking on the election. With two months to go before the planning conference could commence, it would be 'a disaster', he argued, if DRV representatives turned up while the Diem government stayed away. The psephological prospect admittedly 'offered no more than a sporting chance of success' for the non-communists, but 'it should not prove impossible to find a solution, especially if there were effective [Western] co-operation'. Dulles agreed that the election should take place, but only if it was held 'in conditions of freedom'. Not being a party to Geneva, the United States was chary about dictating to those that were, but this still struck him as 'sound policy'. Macmillan, deflated, offered no comeback.[99]

By June 1955, with no obvious sign that the Americans were trying to persuade Diem to participate in the north-south conference, and with the DRV warning publicly against 'any manoeuvres by American imperialists' to make partition permanent, officials in the British Foreign Office grew anxious. A South Vietnamese boycott of the conference would not only be exploited by communist propaganda, Asian experts contended, but could reignite the war.[100] This was also Eden's concern. As Prime Minister, he was unable to bring to Indochina the concentrated focus that characterized his approach as Foreign Secretary, but the reluctance of the Americans to push Diem on the election exercised him.[101] 'This could be very dangerous', he minuted to Macmillan on 17 June. 'The matter cannot be left as it is.' If the Americans remained inert, 'we will have to give Diem a solemn warning ourselves, whether it is effective or not'.[102] The Eisenhower administration's 'support of Diem has been obstinate and unhappily unsuccessful', he added. Did it 'have to continue whatever the price?'[103] To judge from what Dulles said at a news conference on 28 June, the answer was yes:

> The United States believes, broadly speaking, in the unification of countries which have a historic unity, where the people are akin. We also believe that, if there are conditions of really free elections, there is no serious risk that the Communists would win. The Communists have never yet won any free election. I don't think they ever will. Therefore, we are not afraid at all of elections, provided they are held under conditions of genuine freedom which the Geneva armistice agreement calls for. If those conditions can be provided we would be in favor of elections, because we believe that they would bring about the unification of the country under free government auspices.[104]

The Foreign Office was dismayed but directed its disappointment at the Vietnamese minister-resident in London rather than the Americans, Macmillan and Reading joining forces to lecture him on the perils of a 'breach' of Geneva. If, as result of Saigon obduracy, the fighting resumed, Diem should be aware that 'it would be impossible for HMG to give any support' to his government.[105] The Americans were the ones best placed to influence – or pressure – the Vietnamese, but as Makins reported from Washington, US policymakers insisted that there was a limit beyond which 'Diem's arm should not be twisted'. With Congress adopting an identical position, the likelihood of the election taking was dimming fast. 'If the US take this responsibility they will have to shoulder it before the world,' Eden wrote of the American attitude. As to the possibility of reviving Anglo-American tension if the UK hectored the US authorities on compliance with Geneva – a concern flagged by Makins – the Prime Minister was indifferent: 'We must not be frightened of this.'[106]

On 1 July, Macmillan offered a response to Eden's earlier implicit accusation that the Foreign Office had not been tough enough with the Americans. Lacking Eden's personal proprietorial interest in the Geneva settlement, and having witnessed first-hand in Paris in May the strength of American views, Macmillan felt that it might be time to accommodate British policy to post-Geneva realities and support rather than continue to contest the Eisenhower administration's approach.

> You asked whether the obstinate and unsuccessful American support of Diem has to continue whatever the price. One answer is that we have not found an effective reply to the American question 'who else?' In the past we and the French have of course repeatedly tried to persuade the Americans to agree to Diem's replacement. But in the recent struggle, Diem has displayed considerable ability as a revolutionary politician, and his firm handling of the Sects ... has strengthened his internal position. It is true that he has yet to demonstrate that he can run an effective administration; but for the present there is no serious rival for power ... In the circumstances I do not see any purpose in trying to persuade the Americans to change their minds. Diem is more firmly established, he has become the focus of nationalist and anti-communist sentiment in Vietnam and is free from the colonial taint. Our best tactics will be to go on urging the Americans to press for the strengthening and broadening of the Diem administration and for the opening of electoral consultations.[107]

Contrary to British supposition, the Americans *had* been trying to get Diem to engage with the election planning process – but only to give him a platform to contest the legitimacy of Geneva and question the impartiality of the International Supervisory Commission. In addition, as Dulles admitted privately, 'we were telling Diem to do everything possible to frustrate the holding of elections by insisting on conditions which the Communists could not possibly accept'.[108] Ultimately, no amount of US cajolery would bring Diem to commune with the Vietminh. The State Department was beginning to learn that if Diem was a US puppet – a charge levelled at him by opponents, and not just communist ones – he was 'a puppet who pulled his own strings'.[109]

On 16 July, four days before the notional start date for the north-south consultations, Diem issued a public statement. Accepting the principle of free elections, he argued that the 'regime of oppression as practised by the Viet Minh' meant that the poll could only be free in the south. The Saigon government wanted national reunification, but as a precondition the Vietminh needed to demonstrate that 'they put the superior interests of the national community above those of the communist'.[110] In a public response, the Churchill government made the best it could of the situation. On the plus side, Diem had committed himself to elections, albeit according to Saigon's subjective interpretation of freedom, and this, in the UK view, offered 'the best hope of achieving the unity of Viet Nam'. On the negative side, it was regrettable that Diem 'made no reference to consultations about the elections' in 1956 which needed to take place 'as soon as possible'.[111]

On 20 July, the first anniversary of the Geneva settlement, there were protests in Saigon against the accords and sporadic acts of violence directed at the offices of the International Supervisory Commission.[112] The Foreign Office complained to Diem about the 'deplorable impression' the unrest created, including the 'damage to the international standing of the Vietnamese Government which must inevitably result, and the effects on neutral opinion'. There was now a danger of 'a complete breakdown of the Geneva settlement'.[113] The DRV, meanwhile, delivered a strongly worded protest to the Eden government about Diem's violation of the settlement, conveying the message via the other co-chair, the USSR.[114]

By coincidence, British and Soviet leaders, along with the Americans and the French, were gathered together in Geneva at this time for a four-power East-West summit (Churchill's dream having been realized, ironically, just three months after he had retired). On 23 July, Eden spoke to Molotov about next moves. Both agreed to let the situation play itself out naturally in the short term rather than make any formal intervention as (ongoing) co-chairs. Eden felt that 'we should perhaps be thankful that the Geneva Agreements had so far worked as well as they had'. Despite obvious problems, the 'situation a year ago had been menacing and if we still had difficulties to face, they were not at present as threatening to world peace as they had been when the Geneva Conference met last year'.[115]

By now, a further difference of opinion had arisen between Eden and Macmillan. With no immediate prospect of an election, but equally no sign of a violent Vietminh reaction, Macmillan felt that partition was set to continue for some time. In that case, he recommended that the UK line-up behind the Americans in support of 'Diem and his friends who seem to be our best hope'. An unambiguous British commitment to South Vietnam, hence to a semi-permanent division of the country (the Allen thesis), would also go a long way towards reducing Anglo-American friction. Eden, though, still held out for full respect for Geneva, including the election provision, and blanched at every American violation, real or imagined.[116]

On 30 August, Dulles once again declared publicly that the US government supported Diem in rejecting an all-Vietnam election while the Vietminh controlled the north.[117] In the Foreign Office, if not yet in Number 10, there was growing acceptance of the status quo. 'So long as it remains probable that unification of Vietnam might lead to its domination by the Vietminh,' Allen commented, 'our interests will be best served by a perpetuation of the existing division of the country'. Bearing in mind the importance of appearing to stand by Geneva, Allen recommended that the best way forward was to continue to urge Diem to consult with the DRV on electoral planning 'in the hope that the argument about the necessary conditions for freedom will result in deadlock, which in turn will lead both sides to acquiesce in continued division of the country after July 1956'. This approach was endorsed by Macmillan, Kirkpatrick and the rest of the Foreign Office hierarchy.[118] Eden was distraught. 'Dulles moves further away from his position at Geneva every time he speaks,' he minuted. 'I hope we shall address the United States Government very seriously on this subject soon. If they are going to advise the wrecking of the Geneva agreement – for that is what this amounts to – we should make it clear it is their sole responsibility.'[119]

Complain as he might, Eden must have known that the die was cast. The elections would never take place. The Americans, however, do not bear 'sole responsibility' (as Eden maintained) for this betrayal of Geneva. Leaving aside the Diem government's anti-election viewpoint, there was what historian Kathryn Statler has described as an 'amazing lack of concern' on the part of the USSR and PRC.[120] Neither communist giant was prepared to support Vietminh protests or DRV calls for the reopening of the Geneva conference at the risk of confrontation with America. Under Nikita Khrushchev's leadership, the USSR was developing a policy of peaceful coexistence towards the West, and Macmillan, in his dealings with Molotov on Indochina, gained the impression that 'the Russians ... share our desire to leave well alone and keep the situation quiet'. The Chinese were focused on recovering from the combined ravages of the Second World War, a civil war and the Korean War, and rationalized that their security to the south was already assured by a communist North Vietnam. Supporting the Vietminh's reunification agenda would not improve that security if it served to inflame Sino-US relations.[121]

In October 1955, Diem succeeded Bao Dai as Chief of State in South Vietnam. In a referendum, essentially a vote-off between Diem and Bao Dai, the former secured 98.2 per cent of votes cast (including 605,000 votes from the 405,000 registered voters in Saigon). The result made a mockery of Diem's repeated assertion – which the Americans endorsed – that the communist north could not be trusted to conduct a free and fair election. Soon after, a new state, the southern Republic of Vietnam (RVN), was born. Nowhere in the RVN's founding constitution was there any mention of the French Union.[122] In December, Diem terminated all existing economic and financial agreements with France, called on Paris to denounce the Geneva agreement and break off diplomatic contacts with Hanoi and withdrew RVN representatives from the French Union Assembly. Accepting that its time in Vietnam was finally up, the French government brought home the remaining contingents of the Expeditionary Corps in March 1956. The following month, the French High Command was disestablished. Henceforward, the Diem government and the Americans, not the French, would be responsible for the fate of South Vietnam.[123]

Well before the planned election day of 20 July 1956, Vietnam succumbed to that Cold War default solution for vexed territorial problems, a temporary partition rendered permanent by local and geopolitical circumstances. The two Vietnams, Ho's Democratic Republic and Diem's Republic, took their place alongside the two

Germanys and the two Koreas.[124] For Dulles, the removal of the French promised a new beginning. 'We have a clean base there now, without a taint of colonialism,' he recorded with satisfaction. 'Dienbienphu was a blessing in disguise.'[125] History would show that the blessing fell upon the French, not the Americans and definitely not the Vietnamese. 'I fear there is no doubt that it was American policy then [1954–1956], Dulles' policy if you like, to reduce the French influence and even participation in Vietnam,' Eden wrote in September 1965 amidst the US air war against North Vietnam and the mounting US ground war in South Vietnam. 'There was also rejection of French advice about how to use Diem, which was a mistake because the advice was very good.'[126]

Conclusion: Eden, Indochina and Suez

Anthony Eden adored Shakespeare. He could quote word-perfectly huge swathes of the Bard's work, Shakespearean references litter his private correspondence, and as President of the Shakespeare Memorial Theatre in Stratford-upon-Avon from 1958 he presided over the venue's transformation into the Royal Shakespeare Theatre, the home of the Royal Shakespeare Company. Where Eden stood on *Henry VIII*, Shakespeare's late collaboration with fellow playwright John Fletcher, is unclear. But one line from the text would surely have resonated with him over two decades of retirement following his resignation as Prime Minister in 1957: 'Men's evil manners live in brass, their virtues we write in water'.[1] Today, Eden is still best remembered for Suez, his failure of statesmanship etched in permanence in popular historical consciousness. However, in this book, any 'evil manners' that may be ascribed to Eden over Suez have been set aside to concentrate on his 'virtues' or on one particularly virtuous foreign policy achievement. As has been shown, Eden's 1954 Indochinese diplomacy deserves the plaudits it has earned from historians. Geneva was 'a beautiful diplomatic operation'.[2] It was also the 'last example of an independent British policy exercising a significant influence in the resolution of a major international crisis'.[3] And it was unquestionably the 'glittering success' of Eden's annus mirabilis.[4]

However, where previous works have mostly ignored the nuclear dimension of Eden's diplomacy, this book has accorded it due and proper prominence. Fear of the nuclear war potential of the Indochina crisis was one of the main drivers – arguably the greatest driver – of Eden's determination not just to contest the American approach to the Franco-Vietminh war but to work to foil US plans to internationalize the conflict. The March 1954 convergence of Dien Bien Phu and Washington's call for united action with American H-bomb tests and international alarm over thermonuclear fallout is rarely noted let alone explored in the historical literature. In this book, it functions as an interpretative Rosetta Stone helping decipher the determinants of British policy. Coming just three months after Eisenhower and Dulles's disturbing nuclear performance at the Bermuda conference, these developments ensured that Eden did not have to try very hard to build a consensus in Whitehall in opposition to US plans for Vietnam and in support of giving Geneva a chance to bring about a peaceful settlement.

Anxieties over US adventurism in Indochina also provide the context to the June 1954 decision of the Cabinet's Defence Policy Committee to build a UK thermonuclear weapon. A hydrogen bomb made sense in terms of national security (a thermonuclear element adding obvious value to the UK's strategic deterrent) and was also an expression of national self-confidence (being a symbol of great power status as well as weapon).[5] But coming in the midst of the Indochina crisis and at a moment of great tension in Anglo-American relations, the H-bomb decision was also expressive of a need to arm Britain diplomatically against America. The Prime Minister, the Cabinet and the Ministry of Defence all believed that the United States would take a thermonuclear UK more seriously as an ally and increase its chances of successfully exercising restraint over US policy in any future crisis which threatened to turn the Cold War into a Hot War.[6] In retrospect, the limited sway the UK enjoyed over US decision-making in the years that followed suggests that the Churchill government suffered from excessive wishful thinking. Britain would also have gone on to develop a thermonuclear weapon at some point as a natural progression from its graduation as a nuclear power. Nevertheless, Indochina ensured that a UK hydrogen bomb programme commenced in 1954, rather than at a later date, and that the H-bomb possessed, at its point of conception, a diplomatic utility as an instrument for restraining, hence containing America.

Any discussion of British crisis management in 1954 – its nature and compulsion, nuclear or otherwise – must deal with a canard in the American historiography which claims that there was never any likelihood of US intervention in Vietnam. The origins of this notion can be traced to comments made by Dulles in a 1956 *Life* article by James Shepley ('How Dulles Averted War'). Reflecting on Indochina, Dulles agreed that the United States had talked as though it wanted to internationalize the war but this was deliberate rhetorical 'brinkmanship', a means of frightening the USSR, PRC and DRV into giving the French better terms at Geneva than their weak position merited. If, in the end, the Indochina settlement was better than the Americans had at one time feared, that was confirmation, in Dulles's view, of the efficacy of his approach. 'The ability to get to the verge without getting into the war is the necessary art,' he maintained. On Indochina, 'we walked to the brink and we looked it in the face'.[7]

Using the Shepley article as a platform, some historians have built a thesis to fit its brinkmanship conclusion.[8] In the aftermath of America's harrowing Korean experience, it is argued, neither Eisenhower nor Dulles had any desire to involve US forces in a new land war in Asia. However, having pledged in 1952 that a Republican administration would deal decisively with the communist danger, a do-nothing approach was impossible. On reflection, therefore, the White House and State Department decided to set conditions for military action (first-and-foremost allied support) that were reasonable in themselves but which Eisenhower and Dulles banked on being unfulfillable. In the case of the UK, the government's nervousness about war with China, and its interest in a general Asian settlement, made its backing for intervention unlikely. When the UK subsequently reacted as predicted, the US administration shelved its plans. Through this stratagem, Eisenhower and Dulles outmanoeuvred extremists in the administration like Radford and saved the United States from a second Korea. They were also able to accept the Geneva settlement without publicly endorsing its terms; bolster Laos, Cambodia, southern Vietnam and other dominos through SEATO; and redirect the anger and disappointment of the US

Congress and public over northern Vietnam's loss to communism on to the UK, their appeasement-minded ally.

Only a minority of historians subscribe to this "Ike and Dulles not serious" line of thought, and with good reason. Tortuous and tendentious, the thesis relies on a selective assembly of sources when, most scholars agree, the wider body of evidence points to real intent on the part of the US government.[9] In dealing with this issue from a British (and American) perspective, this book has amplified the seriousness of US purposes. The conditions set down by the Eisenhower administration, including UK participation in a coalition, were neither ruses nor subterfuges but honest prerequisites keyed to the post-Korea state of US political and popular opinion. It follows that if London had issued a green light, some level of US-led intervention would probably have occurred. Having repeatedly and publicly attested to the overriding importance of a non-communist Indochina, both to US and free world security, the Eisenhower administration could hardly have walked away from united action if British compliance fulfilled the key Congressionally endorsed criterion for carrying it out. The French, it is true, would still have had the final say on internationalization. But this caveat aside (and until the advent of Mendès-France, French acquiescence was as likely as French opposition), it is evident that in arresting the momentum towards united action, Eden helped counteract a real not a chimerical danger of US-initiated escalation.

For confirmation, one need to look no further than Eisenhower's letter to Churchill of 4 April 1954 in which he compared the urgent need for united action in Vietnam with the years of 'stark tragedy and desperate peril' that followed the failure of the democracies to unite in time to thwart Hitler, Hirohito and Mussolini. This was no routine request for support. This was a psychologically sophisticated appeal intended to hit all of Churchill's emotional and "special relationship" trigger points. If US political leaders were secretly hoping for a UK veto of united action, why try so hard to bring about the opposite result? The irony is that the President's appeal might well have succeeded had the Prime Minister not been so weighed down by thermonuclear worries caused by the Eisenhower administration's own New Look national security policy.

'What I really attempted to do was to get established in that region the conditions under which I felt the United States could properly intervene to protect its own interests,' Eisenhower wrote to his friend and confidant 'Swede' Hazlett in October 1954. 'A proper political foundation for any military action was essential.'[10] In blocking UK participation in united action, Eden denied Eisenhower that foundation ahead of Geneva. Then, at the conference itself, though prepared to use menacing US "noises off" as an aid to diplomacy, he determined to achieve a settlement for one overriding reason – to end a conflict which, if it continued, could foment full-scale war between the United States and China if not general nuclear war with the USSR.

At Geneva, Eden found a kindred spirit in the 'actively helpful' Molotov.[11] There were other proponents of peace, notably Mendès-France and Zhou Enlai, whose contributions were important, but in terms of holding the conference together in defiance of the United States it was Eden's relationship with Molotov that was critical. At times, Eden's closeness to his Soviet counterpart – and his remoteness from the Americans – worried his advisors. In the 1980s, when he was preparing his diaries for publication, Shuckburgh felt the need to tone down those entries recording Eden's diplomatic kinship with Molotov in case they made him look like a communist stooge.[12] Shuckburgh's care for his old master's reputation is touching, but even in 1954 he worried needlessly. In a world of multiplying weapons of mass destruction, Eden knew exactly what he was doing in eschewing ideological fixity in pursuit of peace. 'I do not believe ... that in any dispute one party is 100 per cent a black villain, and the other 100 per cent snow white,' he told the United Nations General Assembly shortly after returning as Foreign Secretary in 1951. 'All men are fallible and peace can only rest on mutual forbearing and restraint.'[13] At Geneva four years later, this attitude infused his diplomatic efforts. The contrast with Dulles's approach, predicated on a crusader's zeal to 'purge' the communists, could hardly have been greater.[14]

Eden's Indochina crisis management subjected Anglo-American relations to tremendous strain. Two years on, when the Suez crisis erupted, a significant residue of suspicion remained. Working separately but in consonance, a number of scholars have attempted to use this legacy of 1954 to establish an Indochina-Suez linkage. Although the present study has striven to remove Eden and his Indochinese diplomacy from the shadow of Suez, this linkage, if it can truly be shown to exist, may offer an answer to the great question about Eden posed by Anthony Nutting in his account of Suez, *No End of a Lesson*: 'How and why did the man, whose whole political career and reputation had been founded on his genius for negotiation, act so wildly out of character ... [and] come to play the decisive role in the sordid disaster of the Suez War?'[15]

The purported linkage takes two broad forms. Firstly, it is argued that Eden's success at Geneva, together with the other achievements of his annus mirabilis, led him to entertain 'delusions of grandeur'; more specifically, his Indochinese triumph gave him a 'distorted' view both of his ability to shape international events and of how far Britain could act independently or in defiance of the United States. Overconfidence, born of Indochina in 1954, came to maturity in 1956.[16] The second aspect concerns Suez more directly. Because Eden's success in thwarting united action in 1954 was achieved at the expense of the United States, it is suggested that he had only a shallow reservoir of American goodwill to draw on in 1956. Furthermore, because Indochina was such a personal victory for Eden over Dulles, the US Secretary of State is portrayed as nursing his resentment until Suez gave him the chance to exact his revenge.[17]

To test whether these claims rest on anything more than inference we need to dwell a little on Suez. The leading characters in 1956 were essentially the same as in 1954 (on the US side, Eisenhower and Dulles, and on the UK side, Churchill was gone but Eden remained). Significantly, though, the roles were reversed. In July 1956, the Eden government's reaction to Egyptian nationalization of the Anglo-French Suez Canal Company was a combination of outrage on imperialist grounds, concern for geostrategic reasons (Nasser's Egypt having recently gravitated towards the Soviet bloc), and alarm about the implications for UK economic security given that the canal fed essential supplies of Middle East oil into Britain. Together, these reactions produced a governmental consensus, replicated in Paris, in favour of forceful action to retake the canal. In contrast, then, to 1954, it was the UK, not the United States, that favoured a military solution to a serious international crisis.[18]

The Eisenhower administration was no less anxious about Nasser's links to the USSR and also acknowledged the 'transcendent worth of the Canal to the free world'.[19] Adding to American concerns was the prospect of a Nasser-coordinated Arab threat to Israel whose independence the United States had championed since 1948. All told, Washington had no reason to view Nasser, his government or his actions with equanimity, but this did not produce automatic support for a UK-led military solution to the Suez crisis. To the contrary, the Eisenhower administration had to weigh other considerations, including the danger that identification with British and French 'colonialism' could spark a regional backlash at a time when its relations with the Arab world were already troubled as a consequence of its support for Israel. Whatever Washington's private misgivings about Nasser, in public in 1956 it donned the mantle of peace-broker in contraposition to its role in 1954.[20]

The Suez crisis reached a climax in the autumn of 1956. Three months on from nationalization, the canal was functioning effectively under Egyptian control despite British predictions of chaos. This development seemed to have robbed the Eden government of a casus belli just as a British seaborne task force was closing in on Egypt. On 29 October, however, the vista was transformed when Israel invaded Egypt, its forces advancing into the Sinai in the direction of the Suez Canal. The British and French immediately issued an ultimatum; if the combatants refused to down arms, Anglo-French forces would enter the Canal Zone as peacekeepers to keep the armies apart and protect an international waterway.[21]

In Washington, the administration, suspecting the British and French of conniving with the Israelis to engineer a crisis to justify intervention, the recovery of the canal and (as an undeclared corollary) the toppling the Nasser government, reacted with a fury that Eden wholly failed to anticipate. As it happens, the US suspicion was well-founded; a deal between the UK, France and Israel had indeed been sealed in secret a few days before the Israeli attack.[22] However, the Eisenhower administration did not need corroboration to come out publicly against an Anglo-French policy which it regarded as depressingly redolent of nineteenth-century gunboat diplomacy not to mention dubious in terms of international law.[23] Eden had expected strong words but he was badly shaken when the United States went on to take the lead at the United Nations in marshalling opinion against Britain and France. Nevertheless, the Anglo-French ultimatum having been rejected, Eden held to his interventionist course. On 5 November, the eve of the US presidential election in which Eisenhower was seeking a second term in office, Anglo-French paratroopers landed at Port Said and Port Fuad, the prelude to full-scale amphibious operations the following day with the object – under the guise of peacekeeping – of retaking the canal.[24]

At this point, the US administration's verbal displeasure became transfigured into direct financial pressure and sanctions on Britain to abort the whole enterprise. Eden and the Cabinet were left reeling as a run on the pound developed and gold and sterling reserves began haemorrhaging. The contemporaneous crisis in Hungary – in which the USSR was violently suppressing a popular protest against communist rule – added to the severity of the American reaction in as much as US condemnation of the Soviet Union would lack moral authority if it did not take an equally strong position on Anglo-French action in Egypt.[25] On 5 November, when the Kremlin warned that it might have to intervene to punish the Anglo-French 'aggressors' (a possibility Eden dismissed as 'twaddle'), the Eisenhower administration had further cause to try and terminate the crisis as swiftly as possible.[26]

The Anglo-French operation in the Canal Zone had begun well enough but Israel's sudden acceptance of a UN call for a ceasefire stripped the British and French of any legitimacy as peacekeepers. Then, on 6 November, Eden was warned by the Treasury that unless American demands to halt military action were obeyed, national bankruptcy loomed. With his Cabinet split down the middle, a broken Eden accepted a ceasefire even though success – the recovery of the whole canal – seemed in sight. Even then, US financial pressure did not relent until he agreed to an unconditional military withdrawal.[27]

Humiliated and exhausted, Eden took off for the Caribbean on 23 November in search of rest and respite. The trip was justified on medical grounds; since his life-threatening illness in 1953, he was 'constantly having trouble with his insides' and his health had deteriorated markedly during the crisis.[28] On Eden's return to London in mid-December, his political position, already fragile, became untenable when he denied in the House of Commons that he had possessed any foreknowledge of the Israeli attack on Egypt. Few even in his own party truly believed him.[29] Eden stood down as Prime Minister on 9 January 1957. His resignation statement was truthful in citing medical advice as the reason for his decision; he was genuinely a sick man. But other things had collapsed along with his health. His reputation for honesty and integrity, for one. And his mastery of foreign affairs, seemingly so complete in 1954, for another.

This book has no remit to analyse the Suez crisis or seek to fathom why Eden decided 'to go berserk about Nasser'.[30] With regard to the historiographical Indochina-Suez linkage, however, it is permissible to offer some comment on whether Eden's actions in Egypt were influenced by his experience of Indochina. More particularly, can the legacy of 1954 help explain his grievous misjudgement of how Washington would react to Anglo-French intervention? As Robert Rhodes James has shown, Eden was 'absolutely convinced' that the Eisenhower administration would accept forcible Anglo-French repossession of the canal as a fait accompli even if publicly it was obliged to adopt a critical posture for reasons of domestic and foreign policy expediency.[31] 'Who could have accepted that they would have actively opposed us?', Eden asked in later years. He had expected 'grumbles & irritation' from the Americans, but also, in the final analysis, 'tepid neutrality'.[32]

According to the Indochina-Suez linkage, Eden emerged from Geneva and his wider annus mirabilis with a boosted but unrealistic sense of his ability to manage the United States. But did this lead him to downplay the likelihood of US actions (as opposed to words) in response to the Suez operation? There are circumstantial reasons for supposing so. Nutting described Eden as 'essentially more vain than most politicians', and Indochina and Geneva gave him a lot to be vain about.[33] Moreover, Eden believed in the linkage. 'Dulles never forgave me' for failing to support united action, he confessed in 1966, and that 'sentiment multiplied his unhelpfulness all through the Suez Crisis'.[34] Similarly, in 1976, the year before his death, he told an interviewer that Dulles 'resented' his refusal to back him over Indochina and this was 'one reason ... Dulles did not want to give us the time to finish the operation' to retake the canal.[35] However, those historians who wish to extend the linkage to argue for Indochina-Suez cause-and-effect have only inference, not evidence, to go on. Eden's post-retirement comments offer an unreliable (almost inadmissible) guide to what he really thought at the time of Suez.

Rather than back-project to 1954, it makes greater sense to root Eden's Suez decision-making – including his mistakes and misjudgements – wholly in 1956. For one thing, it is hard to argue that his health problems during Suez, and a powerful regimen of drugs since proven to cause insomnia, anxiety, irritability and overstimulation, did not have some negative impact on his handling of events. In 1954, he was well and thriving at Geneva. In 1956, he was ill and struggling. By the same token, 1956 offers a far better guide than 1954 to the American aspect of the issue. As Sean Greenwood has shown, throughout the Suez crisis Dulles pursued a 'schizophrenic policy', sometimes supportive, other times critical of Eden's preference for military action.[36] Eden had been very struck by Dulles's insistence early on that a way needed to be found to make Nasser 'disgorge' what he had taken. Eisenhower, too, in a letter to Eden at the time of nationalization, balanced hope for a peaceful compromise with acceptance that 'the use of force might become necessary to protect international rights'. Thereafter, although firm in his public opposition to military intervention, the President never commented on what his administration would do if the UK pressed ahead regardless with plans to retake the canal by force.[37]

Presented with a bifurcation in US thinking – itself an indication that the Americans were conflicted about the correct course to take – Eden chose to base his assessment of Washington's reaction to military moves on those signals that cohered most closely to his outlook (Dulles's 'disgorge' comment 'rang in my ears for months', he remembered).[38] Where does this leave the Indochina-Suez linkage? In truth, it is hard to evidence how the experience of Geneva in 1954 influenced Eden's assessment of US thinking. In any event, his expectation of public criticism/private compliance was clearly derived from contemporaneous or Suez-specific experience: the established US animus towards Nasser's Egypt; secret MI6-CIA intelligence exchanges on covert methods of regime-change; persistent American concern for the security of Israel; and the President's appreciation of the huge strategic value of the Suez Canal not just to the UK but to all NATO countries in Europe.[39]

The idea of Dulles the avenging diplomatic angel also falls down for want of evidence. Back in 1954, the criticism Dulles received in America for the failure of united action was amongst the most serious he encountered during all his time at the State Department, and as Victor Bator has observed, it would be 'only human for Dulles to have retained a feeling of resentment ... that might well have influenced his mind two years later in the Suez crisis'.[40] But if the antagonism was present, it was subconscious. There is no tangible evidence that Dulles permitted his Suez diplomacy to be influenced by ill will towards Eden stemming from the recent Indochinese past.[41] For Eden, though, the 'bitterly anti-British' Dulles would always occupy a special place in his personal demonology.[42] On 1 January 1957, with just eight days of his premiership remaining, he wrote in his pocket diary that Dulles 'was against anything in which UK and perhaps above all self could take a lead'. Then, with possibly a backwards glance to 1954, he added: 'A meanly jealous man.'[43]

*

'The wheel is come full circle,' remarks Edmund, Gloucester's bastard son, near the end of *King Lear*, another of Eden's favourite Shakespeare plays and the inspiration for the title of his memoirs (*Full Circle*) covering Indochina and Suez.[44] Whatever may be said about Suez – and plenty has, and plenty more will be – we, too, need to come full circle and recall another Eden, the Eden of Geneva in 1954. The Indochina crisis never attained the level of extreme nuclear danger characteristic of those frightening Cold War close calls over Cuba in 1962 and the Yom Kippur War in 1973. But in its local, regional and global war potentialities, Indochina, the first crisis of the thermonuclear age, did not lack for danger. Moreover, the fact that it never joined Cuba or Yom Kippur on the upper rung of the ladder of escalation was due in no small measure to the diplomatic creativity, negotiating skill and sheer perseverance of the British Foreign Secretary in 1954.

Those historians who have constructed complex analytical helixes to show that the United States was not serious about military action in Vietnam, and those who have created ingenious interfaces in an attempt to marry Indochina to Suez, are not only wrong in their basic conclusions but overlook a simpler reality. This was expressed by Eden himself on 21 July 1954 in closing the Geneva conference:

> The Agreements concluded today could not, in the nature of things, give complete satisfaction to everyone. But they have made it possible to stop a war which has lasted for eight years and brought suffering and hardship to millions of people. They have also, we hope, reduced international tension at a point of instant danger to world peace. These results are surely worth our many weeks of toil.[45]

'He was interested in settling problems, in bringing people together and working out agreements,' Shuckburgh later wrote of his old boss. 'And he was good at it.'[46] Somehow, Eden lost that gift in 1956, but it was present to dazzling effect in 1954.

Notes

Chapter 1

1 Anthony Eden, *Full Circle* (London: Cassell, 1960), p. 77.
2 From the large literature on the Franco-Vietminh war see in particular: Pierre Brocheux and Daniel Hémery, *Indochine: La colonisation ambiguë, 1858–1954* (Paris: Découverte, 2001 edition); Jacques Dalloz, *The War in Indo-China, 1945–54* (Dublin: Gill and Macmillan, 1990); Arthur J. Dommen, *The Indochinese Experience of the French and the Americans: Nationalism and Communism in Cambodia, Laos, and Vietnam* (Bloomington: Indiana University Press, 2001); Christopher E. Goscha, *Vietnam: un état né de la guerre, 1945–1954* (Paris: Armand Colin, 2011), and Christopher E. Goscha, *The Penguin History of Modern Vietnam* (London: Allen Lane, 2016); Mark Lawrence and Fredrik Logevall, *The First Vietnam War: Colonial Conflict and Cold War Crisis* (Cambridge, MA: Harvard University Press, 2007).
3 The literature on the United States and the Indochina War is extensive but the following are recommended: William J. Duiker, *US Containment Policy and the Conflict in Indochina* (Stanford: Stanford University Press, 1994); Lloyd C. Gardner, *Approaching Vietnam: From World War II through Dienbienphu* (New York: Norton, 1988); Lawrence S. Kaplan, Denise Artaud and Mark R. Rubin, eds, *Dienbienphu and the Crisis of Franco-American Relations, 1954–1955* (Wilmington: Scholarly Resources, 1990); Fredrik Logevall, *Embers of War: The Fall of an Empire and the Making of America's Vietnam* (New York: Random House, 2012).
4 Eisenhower news conference, 7 April 1954, *Public Papers of the Presidents 1954* (*The American Presidency Project*, University of California at Santa Barbara, hereafter *PPP 1954*), doc. 73.
5 Dulles speech, 29 March 1954, in Allan W. Cameron, ed., *Viet-Nam Crisis: A Documentary History, Volume I, 1940–1966* (Ithaca, NY: Cornell University Press, 1971, hereafter *VNC/I*), pp. 233–236.
6 Churchill-Eisenhower meeting, Bermuda, 5 December 1953, Dwight D. Eisenhower Library (DDEL) online archive.
7 On Korea, see William Stueck, *The Korean War: An International History* (Princeton: Princeton University Press, 1995).
8 Andrew Kelly, 'Discordant Allies: Trans-Tasman Relations in the Aftermath of the ANZUS Treaty, 1951–1955', *Journal of Australian Studies*, Vol. 4, No. 1 (2017), pp. 81–95.
9 C(54)155, 27 April 1954, record of Cabinet meetings, and Eden contributions, 11:00 am and 4:00 pm, 25 April 1954, CAB129/68; Eden to Clarissa Eden, 22 May 1954, Lord Avon Papers (AVO), University of Birmingham, AVO/AP20/45/49.
10 Eden, *Full Circle*, p. 139; Geneva telegrams 110 and 161 to FO, 2 and 6 May 1954, FO371/112058/379G and FO371/112060/446G.
11 Brian Crozier, Drew Middleton and Jeremy Murray-Brown, *This War Called Peace* (Chicago: Universe Books, 1985), p. 135; Brian Crozier, 'Post-Stockholm Euphoria', *National Review*, 7 November 1986.

12 Eighth (final) plenary session, Geneva, 21 July 1954, in Cameron, ed., *VNC/I*, pp. 308–318.

13 An exception is Geoffrey Warner, to whose pioneering archival work we are indebted. See Geoffrey Warner, 'The Settlement of the Indochina War', in John W. Young, ed., *The Foreign Policy of Churchill's Peacetime Administration 1951–1955* (Leicester: Leicester University Press, 1988); Geoffrey Warner, 'Britain and the Crisis over Dien Bien Phu, April 1954: The Failure of United Action', and 'From Geneva to Manila: British Policy towards Indochina and SEATO, May–September 1954', in Kaplan et al., *Dienbienphu*.

14 Anthony Adamthwaite, 'The Foreign Office and Policy-making', in Young, ed., *Churchill's Peacetime Administration*, p. 1.

15 For recent examples of the league table phenomenon, see *The Independent*, 16 October 2016, and *Tatler* magazine, 29 June 2016.

16 The literature on Suez is vast but see Simon C. Smith, ed., *Reassessing Suez: New Perspectives on the Crisis and Its Aftermath* (London: Routledge, 2008); Jonathan Pearson, *Sir Anthony Eden and the Suez Crisis: Reluctant Gamble* (Basingstoke: Palgrave, 2003).

17 Unless indicated, the following biographical sketch is a conflation of information drawn from Robert Rhodes James, *Anthony Eden* (London: Weidenfeld and Nicolson, 1986); David Dutton, *Anthony Eden: A Life and Reputation* (London: Arnold, 1997); and D. R. Thorpe, *Eden: The Life and Times of Anthony Eden, First Earl of Avon, 1897–1977* (London: Chatto and Windus, 2003).

18 Anthony Eden, *Another World, 1897–1917* (London: Allen Lane, 1976), p. 150.

19 Winston S. Churchill, *The Second World War, Volume I: The Gathering Storm* (London: Penguin, 1985 edition), p. 231.

20 Eden, *Full Circle*, pp. 247, 249.

21 Winston S. Churchill, *The Second World War, Volume VI: Triumph and Tragedy* (London: Penguin, 1985 edition), p. 521.

22 Elisabeth Barker, *Churchill and Eden at War* (London: Macmillan, 1978); also Avi Shlaim et al., eds, *British Foreign Secretaries since 1945* (Newton Abbot: David and Charles, 1977), pp. 84–86.

23 David Reynolds, 'Roosevelt, Churchill, and the Wartime Anglo-American Alliance, 1939–1945: Towards a New Synthesis', and Sir Michael Howard, 'Afterword: The "Special Relationship"', in William Roger Louis and Hedley Bull, eds, *The Special Relationship: Anglo-American Relations since 1945* (Oxford: Oxford University Press, 1989 edition), pp. 1, 387.

24 Churchill speech, Harvard, 6 September 1943, in Churchill Papers (Chartwell collection), Churchill Archives Centre, Churchill College, Cambridge, CHAR9/196A-B; Warren F. Kimball, 'Wheel within a Wheel: Churchill, Roosevelt and the Special Relationship', in William Roger Louis and Robert Blake, eds, *Churchill: A Major New Assessment of His Life in Peace and War* (Oxford: Oxford University Press, 1996), Chapter 17.

25 David Dutton, 'Anthony Eden', in T. G. Otte, ed., *The Makers of British Foreign Policy: From Pitt to Thatcher* (Basingstoke: Palgrave, 2002), p. 228.

26 Eden diary, 10 September 1943, AVO/AP20/1/23.

27 Eden diary, 3 July 1945, AVO/AP20/1/25.

28 Dutton, *Eden*, pp. 143. This judgement is echoed by other biographers, including James, *Eden*, pp. 352–353; Thorpe, *Eden*, p. 274; David Carlton, *Anthony Eden: A Biography* (London: Allen Lane, 1981), p. 299. p. 253; and Victor Rothwell, *Anthony*

Eden: A Political Biography (Manchester: Manchester University Press, 1992), pp. 116, 255.

29   Eden, *Full Circle*, p. 3.

30   Eden, 10 November 1938, Hansard, *House of Commons Debates* (hereafter *HCD*), Vol. 341, col. 377.

31   See for example, Adamthwaite, 'Foreign Office and Policy-making', p. 1; Corelli Barnett, *The Verdict of Peace: Britain between Her Yesterday and the Future* (London: Macmillan, 2001), p. 106; Richard Lamb, *The Failure of the Eden Government* (London: Sidgwick and Jackson, 1987), p. 117; Peter Lowe, *Contending with Nationalism and Communism: British Policy towards Southeast Asia, 1945–65* (Basingstoke: Palgrave, 2009), p. 72; Kenneth O. Morgan, *The People's Peace: British History 1945–1989* (Oxford: Oxford University Press, 1990), p. 132; Anthony Seldon, *Churchill's Indian Summer: The Conservative Government, 1951–55* (London: Hodder and Stoughton, 1981), p. 409.

32   James, *Eden*, p. 382, 389–390. Other biographers who concur include Thorpe, *Eden*, pp. 400, 410, 412, 415; Dutton, *Eden*, p. 345; Rothwell, *Eden*, pp. 139, 151; William Rees-Mogg, *Sir Anthony Eden* (London: Rockliff, 1956), pp. 101–102; Lewis Broad, *Sir Anthony Eden: Chronicles of a Career* (London: Hutchinson, 1955), p. 212. An exception is Carlton, *Eden*, pp. 355–356, for whom Eden was too eager to propitiate the communists at Geneva.

33   Randolph S. Churchill, *The Rise and Fall of Sir Anthony Eden* (London: Macgibbon and Kee, 1959), p. 191.

34   David Reynolds, 'Eden the Diplomatist, 1931–1956: Suezide of a Statesman?' *History*, Vol. 74, No. 1 (1989), p. 73; C. J. Bartlett, *British Foreign Policy in the Twentieth Century* (London: Macmillan, 1989), p. 95. Similarly, Robert Blake, *The Decline of Power, 1915–64* (London: Granada, 1985 edition), p. 351; Dutton, *Eden*, p. 352; Morgan, *People's Peace*, p. 132.

35   Anthony Nutting, 'Sir Anthony Eden', in Herbert Van Thal, ed., *The Prime Ministers*, Vol. II (London: Allen and Unwin, 1975), p. 337.

36   *King Henry IV, Part 2*, Act 2, Scene 2, in Richard Proudfoot, Ann Thompson and David Scott Kastan, eds, *The Arden Shakespeare Complete Works* (London: Thomson, 1998 edition), p. 403. Eden was President of the Royal Shakespeare Company from 1958 to 1966.

37   Reynolds, 'Suezide', p. 64.

38   James Cable, *The Geneva Conference of 1954 on Indochina* (London: Macmillan, 1986), p. 4.

39   Eisenhower to Congress, 17 February 1954, *PPP 1954*, doc. 38; John Lewis Gaddis, *Strategies of Containment: A Critical Appraisal of American National Security Policy during the Cold* War (Oxford: Oxford University Press, 2005 edition), pp. 165–167.

40   New York telegram 807 to FO, 15 November 1952, PREM11/323.

41   Kevin Ruane, *Churchill and the Bomb in War and Cold War* (London: Bloomsbury, 2016), pp. 234–240; Matthew Jones, 'Targeting China: US Nuclear Planning and "Massive Retaliation" in East Asia, 1953–1955', *Journal of Cold War Studies*, Vol. 10, No. 4 (2008), pp. 37–65.

42   Diary, 24 April 1954, in Clarissa Eden (with Cate Haste), *Clarissa Eden: A Memoir from Churchill to Eden* (London: Weidenfeld and Nicolson, 2007), p. 157; diary, 24 April 1954, in Evelyn Shuckburgh, *Descent to Suez: Diaries, 1951–56* (London: Weidenfeld and Nicolson, 1986, hereafter *Descent*), p. 172.

43   Matthew Jones, *After Hiroshima: The United States, Race and Nuclear Weapons in Asia, 1945–1965* (Cambridge: Cambridge University Press, 2012 edition), p. 213.

44   Dulles speech, 12 January 1954, in Denise Folliot, ed., *Documents on International Affairs 1954* (Oxford: Oxford University Press, 1957), pp. 265–267.On the New Look, see Saki Dockrill, *Eisenhower's New Look National Security Policy, 1953–61* (Basingstoke: Palgrave, 1996).

45   Wenner minute, 18 January 1954, Maitland letter, 2 February 1954, FO371/109135/1; Russell D. Buhite and Wm. Christopher Hamel, 'War for Peace: The Question of an American Preventive War against the Soviet Union, 1945–1955', *Diplomatic History*, Vol. 14, No. 3 (1990), p. 380.

46   Churchill, 15 February 1951, *HCD*, Vol. 484, cols 623–641.

47   Denise Artaud, 'Conclusion', in Kaplan et al., *Dienbienphu*, p. 274.

48   Diary, 26 June 1954, in Lord Moran, *Winston Churchill: The Struggle for Survival* (London: Constable, 1966), hereafter *Churchill*, p. 563.

49   Sir Nicholas Cheetham (31 January 1989) and Sir Frank Roberts (21 November 1989) both used this phrase in interviews with Kevin Ruane.

50   Several officials in the Foreign Office's Southeast Asia Department in the early 1950s confirmed this judgement in interviews or correspondence with Kevin Ruane: R. A. Burrows (24 October 1988), J. G. Tahourdin (3 January 1990), J. E. Cable (23 July 1990).

51   Eden, *Full Circle*, p. 12.

52   Ibid., pp. 81–82.

53   Ibid., p. 87.

54   COS Global Strategy papers, D(50)45, 7 June 1950, and D(52)26, 17 June 1952, CAB131/9 and /12.

55   FO memorandum, 18 March 1952, FO371/101261/43G.

56   On Malaya, see Karl Hack, *Defence and Decolonisation in Southeast Asia: Britain, Malaya and Singapore, 1945–1965* (London: Curzon, 2001);Karl Hack, 'The Origins of the Asian Cold War: Malaya 1948', *Journal of Southeast Asian Studies*, Vol. 40, No. 3 (2009), pp. 471–496.

57   Eden, *Full Circle*, p. 87; Cable, *Geneva*, p. 10; Olver, Strang and Eden minutes, 3–6 April 1952, FO371/101058/59G.

58   Harrison minute, 19 January 1952, Strang minute, 21 January 1952, FO371/101259/23G.

59   When the Tories returned to power, the colony's dollar earnings from rubber and tin amounted to almost two-thirds of the value of all UK exports to the United States and Canada. FO brief for Eden, 30 October 1951, FO371/92065/34; Lyttelton memorandum, 20 November 1951, CAB129/48, C(51)26.

60   FO position papers, 11 and 25 February 1952, FO371/101267/2G and 7G.

61   *HCD*, Vol. 510, col. 2066, 5 February 1953.

62   Eden to Lloyd, 21 May 1954, AVO/AP/17/15A.

63   Eden to Clarissa Eden, 22 May 1954, AVO/AP20/45/49; CC(54)35th meeting, 24 May 1954, CAB128/27.

64   On Eden's ideological fluidity, Herbert Feis, 'Anthony Eden and the Cacophony of Nations', *Foreign Affairs*, Vol. 44, No. 1 (1965), p. 78.

65   Carlton, *Eden*, pp. 295–298; Rothwell, *Eden*, p. 103; Shlaim et al., eds, *Foreign Secretaries*, pp. 90–91.

66   Dutton, 'Eden', pp. 221, 235, makes a similar but generalized case.

67   C(52)202, 18 June 1952, CAB129/53.

68 Alec Cairncross, *Years of Recovery: British Economic Policy 1945–1951* (London: Methuen, 1985), pp. 220–225.

69 Moran diary, 1 and 4 January 1952, *Churchill*, pp. 352–353.

70 C(52)202, 18 June 1952, CAB129/53.

71 David Reynolds, *Britannia Overruled: British Policy and World Power in the 20th Century* (Harlow: Longman, 1991), pp. 177–178.

72 John Williams, 'ANZUS: A Blow to Britain's Self-esteem', *Review of International Studies*, Vol. 13, No. 4 (1987), pp. 243–263.

73 On this issue, Kevin Ruane, 'SEATO, MEDO and the Baghdad Pact: Anthony Eden, British Foreign Policy and the Collective Defence of Southeast Asia and the Middle East, 1952–1955', *Diplomacy and Statecraft*, Vol. 16, No. 1 (2005), pp. 169–199.

74 Scott memorandum, 30 October 1951, and Eden annotations, FO371/92065/34; Strang minute, 21 January 1952, FO371/101259/22G.

75 S. R. Ashton, 'Keeping a Foot in the Door: Britain's China Policy, 1945–1950', *Diplomacy and Statecraft*, Vol. 15, No. 1 (2004), pp. 79–94; Tom Buchanan, *East Wind: China and the British Left, 1925–1976* (Oxford: Oxford University Press, 2012), especially Chapters 3 and 4.

76 Nancy Bernkopf Tucker, 'China and America: 1941–1991', *Foreign Affairs*, Vol. 70, No. 5 (1991–1992), pp. 79–80. On Anglo-American differences, Victor S. Kaufman, *Confronting Communism: US and British Policies toward China* (Columbia, MO: University of Missouri Press, 2001).

77 Victor S. Kaufman, '"Chirep": The Anglo-American Dispute over Chinese Representation in the United Nations, 1950–1971', *English Historical Review*, Vol. 115, No. 461 (2000), pp. 354–377, especially pp. 354–358.

78 Bradford Perkins, 'Unequal Partners: The Truman Administration and Great Britain', in Louis and Bull, eds, *Special Relationship*, p. 59; Jebb to Salisbury, 25 August 1953, FO371/103518/24G; FORD paper, 19 November 1953, FO371/103497/15.

79 FO telegram 4523 to Washington, 11 October 1950, and Bevin-Stikker meeting, 23 November 1950, FO371/83015/44G; Tripartite staff talks, 11 January 1952, JCS record, FO371/101260/26G.

80 Rosemary J. Foot, 'Anglo-American Relations in the Korean Crisis: The British Effort to Avert an Expanded War, December 1950–January 1951', *Diplomatic History*, Vol. 10, No. 1 (1986), pp. 43–57.

81 US-UK meeting, State Department, 12 September 1951, FO371/92067/21. In general, Thomas Hennessey, *Britain's Korean War: Cold War Diplomacy, Strategy and Security, 1950–53* (Manchester: Manchester University Press, 2015).

82 Eden to Churchill, 19 December 1951, FO371/92760/86G.

83 Reflections on containment-and-compromise in FO memorandum, 30 August 1951, FO371/92065/31G; Scott minute, 17 May 1952, FO371/99217/2; Scott to Eden, 5 December 1952, FO371/105179/1G; FO memorandum, 4 December 1953, FO371/105180/26.

84 Bevin to Roberts, 27 February 1951, FO800/470/2.

85 Attlee statement, 12 February 1951, *HCD*, Vol. 484, col. 63; Eden speech, New York, 12 March 1953, FO371/105180/6.

86 Geir Lundestad, *'Empire' by Integration: The United States and European Integration 1945–1997* (Oxford: Oxford University Press, 1998), pp. 13–28; Michael Lind, *The American Way of Strategy* (New York: Oxford University Press, 2006), pp. 113–115.

87 *HCD*, Vol. 429, cols 428–442, 23 June 1954.

88   Clarissa Eden diary, 3 May 1954, *Memoir*, p. 160.

89   See Kevin Ruane, 'The Origins of the Eden–Dulles Antagonism: The Yoshida Letter and the Cold War in East Asia 1951–1952', *Contemporary British History*, Vol. 25, No. 1 (2011), pp. 141–156.

90   Douglas Dillon, cited in Carlton, *Eden*, p. 342; U. Alexis Johnson, interview, 7 February 1982, for *Vietnam: A Television History*, WGBH Media Library & Archives.

91   Cable, *Geneva*, p. 143; Dutton, 'Eden', p. 232; Sean Greenwood, *Britain and the Cold War 1945–91* (Basingstoke: Macmillan, 2000), p. 135; Rothwell, *Eden*, p. 152.

92   Thorpe, *Eden*, p. 405.

Chapter 2

1   Eden note, n.d., early 1951, AVO/AP20/1/27.

2   Dalloz, *Indo-China*, pp. 125–129; Bernard Fall, *Street without Joy* (Mechanicsburg, PA: Stockdale, 1994 edition), p. 33.

3   Eden, *Full Circle*, p. 81.

4   Goscha, *Modern Vietnam*, p. 276.

5   Lucien Bodard, *The Quicksand War: Prelude to Vietnam* (London: Faber 1967), pp. 352–353.

6   Dalloz, *Indo-China*, p. 148.

7   COS(51)155th meeting, 4 October 1951, DEFE4/47; Morrison-de Lattre meeting, 5 October 1951, FO371/92427/59.

8   FO telegram 5320 to Washington, 25 October 1951, FO371/93084/133G.

9   FO 371/92065/37, FO brief for Eden, 1 November 1951; Paris telegram 669 to FO, 10 November 1951, FO371/93084/141G.

10   Rumbold minute, 21 November 1951, FO brief for Eden, 14 December 1951, Scott minute, 17 December 1951, FO371/93085/152G, 155G and 164G.

11   FO telegram 1932 to Paris, 22 December 1951, FO371/92412/15.

12   FO telegram 6258 to Washington, 24 December 1951, FO371/92412/23.

13   BJSM to MOD and Washington telegram 3980 to FO, 28 December 1951, FO371/92412/21 and 27.

14   JIC(51)130(Final), 27 December 1951, CAB158/13.

15   Duiker, *US Containment Policy*, pp. 118–121.

16   Makins to Eden, 29 November 1951, FO371/90938/41G; Saigon dispatch 7 to Eden, 18 January 1952, FO371/101047/6.

17   Ruane, *Churchill and the Bomb*, pp. 200–201.

18   Rome telegrams 653 and 654 to FO, 29 November 1951, FO371/92759/75G-76G.

19   Moran diary, 5 January 1952, *Churchill*, p. 355.

20   Sir Anthony Montague Browne, interview with Kevin Ruane, 13 September 1989.

21   Moran diary, 7 and 26 January 1952, *Churchill*, pp. 357 and 371.

22   US-UK talks, 5 January 1952, UK record, CAB21/3057.

23   US-UK talks, 6 January 1952, US record, Acheson Papers (ACH), Memoranda/Box#70, Harry S. Truman Presidential Library (HSTL), Independence, Missouri.

24   US-UK talks, 8 January 1952, UK record, CAB21/3057.

25   Webb-Truman meeting, 10 December 1951, US National Archives II (NARA), College Park, Maryland, RG59/Box#2769/611.41/12–1051.

26 US-UK talks, 8 January 1952, UK record, CAB21/3057; Martin Gilbert, *Never Despair: Winston S. Churchill, 1945–1965* (London: Heinemann, 1988), p. 680.

27 TCT D-5/12c, 2 January 1952, HSTL/PSF/General/Box#116.

28 Churchill address to Congress, 17 January 1952, CHUR5/46.

29 *Manchester Guardian* and *Daily Herald*, 18 January 1952.

30 *Times*, 27 February 1952; Moran diary, 29 February 1952, *Churchill*, p. 380.

31 Macmillan, 17 January 1952, in Peter Catterall, ed., *The Macmillan Diaries, Volume I: The Cabinet Years 1950–1957* (London: Macmillan, 2003, hereafter *Diaries*/I), p. 133.

32 Truman diary, 27 January 1952, HSTL/PSF/Longhand Notes/Box#333.

33 *Life*, 28 January 1952.

34 Alain Ruscio, 'L'opinion Française et la guerre d'Indochine (1945–1954): Sondages et témoignages', *Vingtième Siècle Revue d'histoire*, No. 29 (1991), pp. 35–45.

35 Tripartite talks, 11 January 1952, JCS record, FO371/101260/26G.

36 Ibid.

37 Scott minute, 15 January 1952, FO371/101259/12G; Murray minute, 8 February 1952, FO371/101260/30G.

38 COS(52)123, 15 February 1952, DEFE5/37; FO memorandum, 21 February 1952, FO371/101260/29G.

39 Strang minute, 21 January 1952, FO371/101259/22G.

40 JCS(LIS)24 to COS, 15 February 1952, and Annex B to COS(52)344, 16 February 1952, FO371/101260/31G.

41 Churchill-Elliot meeting, 16 February 1952, PREM11/369.

42 COS(52)38th meeting, 11 March 1952, FO371/101261/38G; McLean to Churchill, 18 March 1952, PREM 11/648.

43 Harrison minute, 19 January 1952, Strang minute, 21 January 1952, FO371/101259/23G.

44 Anthony Short, *The Origins of the Vietnam War* (London: Longman, 1989), p. 103.

45 William C. Gibbons, *The US Government and the Vietnam War: Part I, 1945–1960* (Princeton: Princeton University Press, 1986), p. 107.

46 Acheson memorandum, 5 March 1952, NARA/RG59/Box#4132/790.5/30552.

47 FO telegram 1181 to Washington, 12 March 1952, FO371/101057/49G; COS(52)38th meeting, 11 March 1952, FO371/101261/38G.

48 D(52)4, 14 March 1952, and discussion, D(52)2nd meeting, 19 March 1952, CAB131/12.

49 D(52)2nd meeting, ibid.

50 D(52)13, 29 April 1952, and D(52)4th meeting, 30 April 1952, CAB131/12; Alexander to Churchill, 2 May 1952, and Churchill acknowledgement, 8 May 1952, PREM11/648.

51 Eden-Acheson meeting, 26 May 1952, and FO telegrams 179 and 180 to Saigon, 30 May 1952, FO371/101058/72–73 and 78.

52 Ibid.

53 NSC 124/2, 25 June 1952, in *Foreign Relations of the United States, 1952–1954; Vol. XII, East Asia and the Pacific* (Washington: US Government Printing Office, 1984, hereafter *FR1952–54*/XII), pp. 127–134.

54 COS(52)84th meeting, 12 June 1952, FO371/101262/53G; C(52)202, Eden memorandum, 18 June 1952, CAB129/53.

55 FO memorandum, 21 February 1952, FO371/101260/29G; MB(52)18, 20 May 1952, PREM11/404.

56　Casey, 25 June 1952, in R. G. Casey, *Australian Foreign Minister: Diaries 1951–60* (London: Collins, 1972), p. 84; UK-US-French talks, London, 27 June 1952, FO371/99577/343.

57　Lloyd-DOS meeting, 25 June 1952, HSTL/ACH/Memoranda/Box#81.

58　Churchill to Lloyd, 26 August 1952, PREM11/301.

59　CC(52)62nd meeting, 24 June 1952, and 63rd meeting, 26 June 1952, CAB128/25 and CAB195/10;.

60　CC(52)63rd meeting, 26 June 1952, CAB128/25.

61　UK-US talks, 26 June 1952, FO371/99577/344; Secto-14 to DOS, 26 June 1952, HSTL/HST/Korean War/Box#13; Dean G. Acheson, *Present at the Creation: My Years in the State Department* (New York: Norton, 1969), pp. 656–657.

62　Churchill statement, *HCD*, Vol. 503, cols 269–274, 1 July 1952.

63　UK-US-French talks, 27 June 1952, FO371/99577/343; Lloyd-DOS meeting, 25 June 1952, HSTL/ACH/Memoranda/Box#81.

64　Paris telegram 367 to FO, 26 June 1952, FO371/101738/1.

65　Eden-Acheson meeting, 26 June 1952, HSTL/ACH/Memoranda/Box#71.

66　Acheson-Franks meeting, 17 June 1952, HSTL/ACH/Memoranda/Box#70; Washington telegram 1168 to FO, 18 June 1952, FO371/101262/60G.

67　Eden minute, 15 June 1952, FO telegram 2379 to Washington, 13 June 1952, FO brief, 20 June 1952, FO371/101262/52G–53G, and 60G.

68　Minutes by Tahourdin, Eden and Shuckburgh, 24–26 July 1952, FO371/101263/74G.

69　Churchill statement, *HCD*, Vol. 503, cols 269–286, 1 July 1952; Eden to Churchill, 1 August 1952, FO371/101263/74G.

70　Washington telegram 1485 to FO, 5 August 1952, FO 371/101263/78G.

71　FO telegram 3515 to Washington, 1 September 1952, FO371/101263/83G; London telegram 1210 to DOS, 2 September 1952, NARA/RG59/Box#4132A/790.5/9–252.

72　BJSM telegram ELL479 to MOD, 15 October 1952, FO371/101264/117G; COS(52)147th meeting, 21 October 1952, DEFE 4/57; Lovett to Acheson, 5 December 1952, NARA/RG59/Box#4132A/790.5/12–552; COS(52)690, 18 December 1952, Appendix, DEFE5/43.

73　COS(52)663, 5 December 1952, DEFE5/43.

74　FO brief, 17 November 1952, FO371/101264/127G.

75　Tahourdin minute, 19 September 1952, FO371/101263/101G.

76　FO telegram 4424 to Paris, 24 December 1952, FO371/101265/152G.

77　FO telegram 94 to Washington, 10 January 1953, FO371/106990/5G.

78　Scott memorandum, 30 August 1952, FO371/101263/99G, emphasis added; Eden, *Full Circle*, p. 143.

79　Scott memorandum, 10 January 1953, FO telegram 94 to Washington, 10 January 1953, and COS(53)4th meeting, 13 January 1953, FO371/106990/5G, 13G and 22G.

80　Scott, Reading and Eden minutes, 13–17 January 1953, FO371/106990/16G and 17.

81　FO telegram 94 to Beijing, 16 December 1952, FO371/101265/135G.

82　Tahourdin minute, 15 January 1953, FO371/106765/1G.

Chapter 3

1　Harvey dispatch 4 to Eden, 2 January 1952, FO371/101056/3.

2　Harvey dispatch 30 to Eden, 19 January 1952, FO959/126.

3   Graves despatch 14 to Eden, 24 January 1952, FO371/101047/8.
4   *Times*, 7 January 1952.
5   Dalloz, *Indo-China*, p. 147; Philippe Devilliers and Jean Lacouture, *End of a War: Indochina 1954* (London: Pall Mall Press, 1969), pp. 30–32; Ruscio, 'L'opinion Française', pp. 35–45.
6   Kevin Ruane, *The Rise and Fall of the European Defence Community: Anglo-American Relations and the Crisis of European Defence, 1950–1955* (Basingstoke: Macmillan, 2000), pp. 38, 83–84.
7   Scott minute, 3 March 1952, FO371/101056/26G; Reading to Eden, 17 March 1952, FO371/101057/30G.
8   D(52)5, 14 March 1952, CAB131/12; Hack, *Defence and Decolonisation*, p. 89.
9   D(52)2nd meeting, 19 March 1952, CAB131/12.
10 Olver, Strang and Eden minutes, 3–6 April 1952, FO371/101058/59G; FO brief, 25 February 1952, FO371/101267/7G.
11 To meet communist infiltration of Malaya following the loss of Indochina, an additional infantry brigade would be needed, but to deal with a potential PRC/ Vietminh invasion, there would need to be a major degree of mobilization to provide three infantry divisions, 500 aircraft and a substantial naval deployment. D(53)1, 22 January 1953, CAB131/13.
12 D(52)2nd meeting, 19 March 1952, and D(52)5, 14 March 1952, CAB131/12; FO memorandum, 24 May 1952, FO371/101058/67G.
13 *HCD*, Vol. 504, col. 1509, 30 July 1952.
14 Harvey dispatch 179 to Eden, 16 April 1952, FO371/101057/48G; Peter Calvocoressi, *Survey of International Affairs 1952* (London: Oxford University Press, 1955), p. 411.
15 Logevall, *Embers of War*, p. 316.
16 Paris dispatch 149 to Eden, 25 March 1952, FO371/101057/33G.
17 François Guillemot, '"Be men!": Fighting and Dying for the State of Vietnam (1951–54)', *War and Society*, Vol. 31, No. 2 (2012), pp. 184–212.
18 Graves dispatch 50 to Eden, 18 April 1952, FO371/101078/4; Graves dispatches 56, 25 April 1952, and 63, 8 May 1952, FO371/101058/58 and 65; Calvocoressi, *Survey 1952*, pp. 414–415.
19 *Times*, 22 April 1952.
20 Olver minute, 2 April 1952, FO371/101048/2G.
21 Letourneau speech, 17 June 1952, FO3710101059/103; FO telegram 181 to Saigon, 30 May 1952, FO371/101058/74; Nicholas Tarling, *Britain, Southeast Asia and the Impact of the Korean War* (Singapore: National University of Singapore Press, 2005), pp. 192–193.
22 Eden-Acheson meeting, 26 May 1952, FO371/101058/78.
23 US-French communiqué, 18 June 1952, FO371/101059/85.
24 Eden, *Full Circle*, p. 84; Calvocoressi, *Survey 1952*, p. 423.
25 Saigon dispatch 53 to Eden, 18 April 1952, FO371/101058/52; Graves to Scott, 10 June 1952, FO371/101055/36; Saigon telegram 195 to FO, 22 June 1952, FO371/101059/87.
26 Murray minute, 25 June 1952, FO371/101262/58G; Scott to Graves, 6 August 1952, FO371/101059/108G.
27 *Scotsman*, 15 July 1952; Graves to Scott, 18 July 1952, FO371/101059/108G; Graves to Scott, 22 August 1952, FO371/101060/117G.
28 Graves to Tahourdin, 22 September 1952, FO371/101060/120G; COS(52)133rd meeting and Tahourdin memorandum, 19 September 1952, FO371/101263/100G-101G.

29 SEAD paper, 27 September 1952, and Eden annotations, FO371/101264/106G.
30 Eden to Alexander, 30 September 1952, Alexander reply, 6 October 1952, and COS(52)545, 3 October 1952, FO371/101264/106G and 110G; COS(52)158th meeting, 18 November 1952, FO371/101264/129G.
31 Head to Eden, 15 December 1952, FO371/101061/151; Roberts minute, 11 December 1952, FO371/101267/19; Hayter to Scott, 2 January 1953, FO371/106765/1G; Singapore telegram 680 to FO, 8 December 1952, FO371/101061/136; FE(O)(52)1st meeting, 13 January 1953, CAB134/898.
32 Calvocoressi, *Survey 1952*, p. 428; Paris telegram 431 to FO, 24 October 1952, FO371/101070/42; Chancery Saigon to FO, 28 October 1952, FO371/101071/49.
33 Eden, *Full Circle*, p. 84; Harvey dispatch 606 to Eden, 19 November 1952, FO371/101060/130.
34 COS Secretariat to Scott, 28 November 1952, FO371/101265/136G.
35 Eden minute, 4 December 1952, ibid.
36 Dixon minute, 25 October 1952, FO371/101264/123G.
37 *Economist*, 1 November 1952.
38 French troops constituted just 56,000 out of a total military strength of 490,000, the balance being made up of North African, Foreign Legion and Vietnamese troops. Lowe, *Contending with Nationalism and Communism*, p. 62.
39 Cheetham minute, 16 December 1952, FO371/101061/136; *HCD*, Vol. 504, col. 1506, 30 July 1952.
40 Harvey dispatch 606 to Eden, 19 November 1952, FO371/101061/130.
41 Hayter to Reilly, 25 September 1952, Scott to Hayter, 10 November 1952, COS(52)158th meeting, 18 November 1952, FO371/101264/104G, 122G, and 129G.
42 Eden dispatch 1181 to Paris, 22 December 1952, FO371/101743/2. In general on British policy, see Ruane, *European Defence Community*.
43 CC(52)102nd meeting, 4 December 1952, CAB128/25; C(52)434, 10 December 1952, CAB129/57; Ruane, *European Defence Community*, pp. 31–36.
44 Olver minute, 11 December 1952, and various responses, FO371/101061/126; SEAD submission, 18 February 1953, FO371/106765/18.
45 Scott minute, 24 January 1953, FO371/105182/1G; FO brief, 10 February 1953, FO371/106765/14G; Tahourdin minutes, 15 January and 19 February 1953, Cheetham minute, 16 January 1953, FO371/106765/1G, and 9–10.
46 PUSD memorandum, 6 November 1952, FO371/125009/4.
47 FO telegram 4713 to Washington, 5 November 1952, PREM11/572.
48 Colville diary, 9 November 1952, in John Colville, *The Fringes of Power: Downing Street Diaries 1939–1955* (London: Hodder and Stoughton, 1985, hereafter *Fringes*), p. 654.
49 Gilbert, *Never Despair*, pp. 773–774.
50 *Daily Express*, 6 February 1953.
51 Paul Gore-Booth, *With Great Truth and Respect* (London: Constable, 1974), p. 183; Roderick Barclay, *Ernest Bevin and the Foreign Office, 1932–1969* (London: Barclay, 1975), p. 117; Moran diary, 7 December 1953, *Churchill*, p. 540.
52 Richard Immerman, *John Foster Dulles: Piety, Pragmatism and Power in US Foreign Policy* (Wilmington: Scholarly Resources, 1999), pp. 38–43; John Young, *Churchill's Last Campaign: Britain and the Cold War, 1951–1955* (Oxford: Clarendon Press, 1996), pp. 106–107.

53   Dwight D. Eisenhower, *Mandate for Change: The White House Years, 1953–1956* (London: Heinemann, 1963), pp. 72–73.

54   New York telegram 807 to FO, 15 November 1952, PREM11/323.

55   Stephen Hess, 'Foreign Policy and Presidential Campaigns', *Foreign Policy*, No. 8 (1972), p. 10.

56   FORD memorandum, 24 November 1952, FO462/6.

57   CC(52)102nd meeting, 4 December 1952, CAB128/25.

58   Lloyd to Eden, 20 and 26 December 1952, AP20/15/22A and 24A.

59   Eden dispatch 1198 to Paris, 30 December 1952, PREM11/438.

60   Eisenhower diary, 6 January 1953, in Robert H. Ferrell, ed., *The Eisenhower Diaries* (New York: Norton, 1981), pp. 222–224.

61   Churchill telegram 7 to Eden, 6 January 1953, PREM11/404; Washington telegram 34 to FO, 8 January 1953, FO800/838/1; Makins to Eden, 9 January 1953, AP20/16/21.

62   Truman to Minton, 6 September 1958, in Robert H. Ferrell, ed., *Off the Record: The Private Papers of Harry S. Truman* (Columbia: University of Missouri Press, 1980), p. 368.

63   Eisenhower, State of the Union address, 2 February 1953, *PPP 1953 online* (doc. 6).

64   FO telegram 428 to Washington, 31 January 1953, FO371/105196/9.

65   Washington telegram 206 to FO, 31 January 1953, PREM 11/867; CC(53)6th meeting, 3 February 1953, CAB128/26; Washington telegram 100 to FO, 7 February 1953, FO371/103495/6.

66   Churchill to Eisenhower, 7 February 1953, in Peter Boyle, ed., *The Churchill-Eisenhower Correspondence 1953–1955* (Chapel Hill: University of North Carolina Press, 1990, hereafter *CEC*), p. 21; CC(53)6th meeting, 3 February 1953, CAB195/11.

67   FO telegram 428 to Washington, 31 January 1953, FO371/105196/9; Eden statement, 3 February 1953, *HCD*, Vol. 510, cols 1672–1673.

68   Scott to Eden, 4 February 1953, and Shuckburgh to Makins, 6 February 1953, FO371/105196/27 and 40.

69   *HCD*, Vol. 510, cols 2057–2067, 5 February 1953.

70   FO telegram 565 to Washington, 7 February 1953, FO371/105180/2.

71   Tomlinson to Scott, 19 February 1953, FO371/105180/5G; Wilkinson to Maitland and enclosure, 11 March 1953, FO371/103513/31.

72   Eden-Dulles meeting, 4 February 1953, and Eden dispatch 101 to Singapore, 26 February 1953, FO371/106765/13G; Eden dispatch 237 to Washington, 21 February 1953, FO371/103512/16.

73   Harvey dispatch 36 to Eden, 28 January 1953, FO371/106765/7.

74   Burrows minute, 30 January 1953, ibid.

75   Graves dispatch 34 to Eden, 19 February 1953, Burrows minute, 3 March 1953, FO371/106751/12.

76   CRO to FO, 26 March 1953, FO371/106765/33.

77   The term 'Vietnamization', though usually associated with the American war in Vietnam in and after 1969, was in currency in the Foreign Office in the early 1950s. See Olver minute, 27 November 1952, FO371/101060/13G.

78   Ruane, *Churchill and the Bomb*, pp. 223–226.

79   Scott brief for Eden, 25 February 1953, FO371/105182/6G.

80   Conflation of US record of Dulles-Eden talks, 5 March 1953, NARA/RG59/Box#2770/611.41/3–553, Dulles to Eisenhower, 6 March 1953, Dwight D. Eisenhower Presidential Library (DDEL), Abilene, Kansas, AWF/International/Box#17, and Washington telegram 193 to FO, 7 March 1953, FO371/105182/5G.

81 Ibid.

82 Ibid.

83 Eisenhower-Eden meeting, 6 March 1953, PREM11/431.

84 State telegram 5001 to Paris, 27 March 1953, NARA/RG59/Box#2815/611.51/3–2753; US-French communiqué, 28 March 1953, in Cameron, ed., *VNC/I*, pp. 198–199.

85 US-French talks, FPT-Min-2, 26 March 1953, NARA/RG59/Box#2815/611.51/4–653; Paris telegram 115 to FO, 1 April 1953, FO371/107443/11.

86 *Life*, 26 January 1953, p. 34.

87 US-French talks, FPT-Min-2, 26 March 1953, NARA/RG59/Box#2815/611.51/4–253; Ronald H. Spector, *Advice and Support: The Early Years of the US Army in Vietnam, 1941–1960* (New York: Free Press, 1985), p. 170.

88 Tahourdin minute, 17 April 1953, and Tahourdin to Joy, 21 April 1953, FO371/106765/42 and 55G; Summary of COS views, 1 April 1953, FO371/106751/18.

Chapter 4

1   Paris telegram 111 to FO, 9 April 1953, FO371/107434/5; Peter Calvocoressi, *Survey of International Affairs, 1953* (Oxford: Oxford University Press, 1956), pp. 16–18.

2   Eisenhower to Churchill, 6 April 1953, CHUR/6/3.

3   Ruane, *Churchill and the Bomb*, pp. 223–226.

4   *The Pentagon Papers*, US National Archives online, *PP/II/p.* A–50.

5   Martin Windrow, *The Last Valley: Dien Bien Phu and the French Defeat in Vietnam* (London: Weidenfeld and Nicolson, 2004), pp. 126–127.

6   NSC 141st meeting, 28 April 1953, *Foreign Relations of the United States 1952–54*, Vol. XIII (Washington: Government Printing Office, 1982, hereafter *FR1952–54/ XIII*), pp. 516–519.

7   FE(O)(53)5th meeting, 13 May 1953, CAB134/898; FO position paper, 2 May 1953, FO371/107015/20; Malcolm MacDonald Papers, University of Durham, MacDonald dispatch 31, 13 June 1953, MaC/18/11/21.

8   Templer-Salisbury meeting, 19 May 1953, GEN.425/4, CAB130/83.

9   Churchill dispatch 256 to Singapore, 20 June 1953, FO371/106997/22G.

10 MacDonald dispatch 28 to Churchill, 29 May 1953, FO371/106745/48.

11 FE(O)(53)4, 6 June 1953, and CO memorandum, 13 June 1953, CAB134/898.

12 GEN.425/1st meeting, 1 April 1953, CAB130/83; MOD (draft) to Washington, 22 April 1953, FO371/106999/10G; D(53)26, 26 April 1953, and D(53)7th meeting, 29 April 1953, CAB131/13.

13 FO brief, 29 April 1953, FO371/106999/11G.

14 Templer-Salisbury meeting, 19 May 1953, GEN.425/4, CAB130/83; FO memorandum, November 1953, FO371/106956/42.

15 D(53)7th meeting, 29 April 1953, CAB131/13.

16 Churchill to Salisbury, 2 May 1953, FO371/106999/12G, original emphasis.

17 JP(53)(79)(Final), 5 May 1953, DEFE4/62; COS(53)79th meeting, 25 June 1953, DEFE4/63.

18 Joy to Tahourdin, 29 April 1953, FO371/106776/69.

19 Tahourdin minute, 25 April 1953, Alison minute, 30 May 1953, FO371/106751/52.

20 Joy dispatch 69 to Churchill, 16 May 1953, FO371/106777/83.

21   NSC 143rd meeting, 6 May 1953, and Eisenhower to Dillon, 7 May 1953, *FR1952–54/* XIII, pp. 548, 550–551.
22   Jules Roy, *The Battle of Dienbienphu* (London: Faber, 1965), p. 7.
23   MacDonald note, 29 May 1953, MACD/20/14/9–33.
24   Henri Navarre, *Agonie De L'Indochine, 1953–4* (Paris: Plon, 1956), pp. 1–5.
25   Logevall, *Embers of War*, p. 349.
26   D(53)7th meeting, 29 April 1953, CAB131/13.
27   D(53)26, 26 April 1953, and D(53)7th meeting, 29 April 1953. CAB131/13; Duff minute (containing Lloyd's view), 4 May 1953, FO371/106767/116.
28   Head to Churchill, 30 April 1953, PREM 11/645.
29   Joy to Tahourdin, 13 May 1953, FO371/106751/48.
30   Dixon diary, 2 May 1953, DIX/Piers Dixon collection.
31   Churchill to Head, 2 May 1953, PREM11/645.
32   Ibid.
33   *HCD*, Vol. 515, col. 891, 11 May 1953; Harrison minute, 15 May 1953, FO371/106767/120G.
34   R. A. Burrows, interview with Kevin Ruane, 24 October 1988.
35   Lloyd to Churchill, 19 May 1953, PREM11/613; Tahourdin minute, 20 May 1953, FO371/106751/45.
36   Scott memorandum, 7 May 1953, FO371/106767/120G.
37   Dixon, Reading and Strang minutes, 7–8 May 1953, ibid.
38   FO meeting, 21 May 1953, FO371/106767/122G.
39   *Le Monde*, 27 June 1953; *Times*, 27 June 1953.
40   Indochina brief, 24 June 1953, FO371/106768/134G.
41   Ibid.
42   *CEC*, pp. 81–82, medical report.
43   WSC to Eisenhower, 1 July 1953, CHUR6/3.
44   Harrison minute, 30 June 1953, Allen minute, 1 July 1953, FO371/107437/83; Lyttelton to Salisbury, 7 July 1953, FO371./106768/134G.
45   Salisbury to Emrys-Evans, 3 July 1953, EMR/BL/58241.
46   Harvey dispatch 251 to Salisbury, 26 June 1953, FO371/107437/83.
47   Devilliers and Lacouture, *End of a War*, pp. 31–32.
48   Acheson-de Lattre meeting, 14 September 1951, HSTL/ACH/Memoranda/Box#69.
49   Duiker, *US Containment Policy*, p. 141.
50   New York telegram 807 to FO, 15 November 1952, PREM11/323; Pre-inaugural Cabinet meeting, 10 December 1952, in Stephen E. Ambrose, *Eisenhower the President, 1952–1969* (London: Allen and Unwin, 1984), p. 173.
51   Alexander Werth, *France, 1940–1955* (London: Hale, 1956), p. 608; Allison minute, 24 June 1953, FO371/107437/76.
52   Laniel statement, 3 July 1953, Cameron, ed., *VNC/*I, pp. 199–200.
53   Navarre, *Agonie De L'Indochine*, p. 76.
54   Ibid., p. 87; Bernard Fall, *Hell in a Very Small Place: The Siege of Dien Bien Phu* (Cambridge, MA: Da Capo Press, 2002 edition), p. 32; Windrow, *Last Valley*, pp. 209–212.
55   Paris telegram 273 to FO, 30 July 1953, Tahourdin minute, 4 August 1953, FO371/106754/184G.
56   NSC 161st meeting, 9 September 1953, *FR1952–1954/*XIII, pp. 780–789; Washington telegram 754 to FO, 11 September 1953, FO371/106770/180.
57   Franco-American communiqué, 30 September, Cameron, ed., *VNC/*I, pp. 206–207.

58 Paris telegrams 234 and 256 to FO, 4 and 9 July 1953, FO371/106753/124 and 137; Tahourdin minute, 8 July 1953, FO371/106756/261; Dommen, *Indochinese Experience*, p. 214.

59 Indochina brief, 24 June 1953, FO371/106768/134G; Burrows minute, 6 July 1953, FO371/106753/122.

60 Joy to Tahourdin, 5 September 1953, FO371/106756/243; Robert Shaplen, *The Lost Revolution: Vietnam, 1945–1965* (London: Deutsch, 1966), p. 93.

61 Devilliers and Lacouture, *End of a War*, pp. 35–36.

62 Burrows minute, 31 July 1953, Tahourdin minute, 4 August 1953, FO371/106754/184G.

63 General Paul Ely, *Mémoires: L'Indochine dans la Tourmente* (Paris: Plon, 1964), p. 25; Pierre Rocolle, *Pourquoi Dien Bien Phu?* (Paris: Flammarian, 1968), p. 21; Roy, *Dienbienphu*, pp. 17–19.

64 Reading minute, 6 August 1953, FO371/106755/198G.

65 MA Paris to WO, 11 July 1953, Burrows minute, 4 August 1953, FO371/106778/102 and 105; Paris telegram 340 to FO, 2 October 1953, FO371/106770/193.

66 Burrows and Tahourdin minutes, 4 and 6 August 1953, FO371/106778/105; Chancery Paris to FO, 6 August 1953, FO371/106769/163; Graves dispatch 131, 14 September 1953, FO371/106756/246.

67 Navarre, *Agonie De L'Indochine*, pp. 1–5.

68 Salisbury-Bidault meeting, 13 July 1953, PREM11/425; Washington telegrams 1477 and 1485 to FO, 13 July 1953, and Burrows minute, 14 July 1953, FO371/106768/136 and 139.

69 Ibid.

70 Scott minute, 17 May 1952, FO371/99217/2; Scott memorandum for Eden, 5 December 1952, FO371/105179/1G.

71 *HCD*, Vol. 518, cols 893–895, 27 July 1953.

72 Calvocoressi, *Survey 1953*, p. 210.

73 Makins dispatch 387 to Salisbury, 11 August 1953, FO371/103497/17.

74 Salisbury dispatch 653 to Paris, 1 August 1953, FO371/106768/157; Joy to Tahourdin, 7 August 1953, FO371/106755/215.

75 Dalloz, *Indo-China*, pp. 163–164.

76 Reilly dispatch 342 to Salisbury, 10 August 1953, FO371/106769/165.

77 Tripartite meeting, 13 July 1953, UK record, FO371/105179/13G; Cmd. 8938, *Special Report of the Unified Command on the Korean Armistice Agreement signed at Panmunjom on July 27, 1953* (London: HMSO, 1953), pp. 4–5.

78 Calvocoressi, *Survey 1953*, pp. 214–221.

79 NIACT-168 to State, 12 December 1953, *Foreign Relations of the United States 1952–54*. Vol. XV, hereafter *FR1952–54/XV*, pp. 1655–1657; Robert F. Randle, *Geneva 1954: The Settlement of the Indochinese War* (Princeton: Princeton University Press, 1969), p. 21.

80 NSC 170/1, 20 November 1953, and Bowie to Dulles, 3 December 1953, *FR1952–54/XV*, pp. 1620–1624, 1634–1636; *Times*, 15 December 1953.

Chapter 5

1 Dulles speech, 2 September 1953, Cameron, ed., *VNC/I*, pp. 204–205.

2 *Manchester Guardian*, 3 September 1953; Statler, *Replacing France*, p. 74.

3 *Pravda*, 2 September 1953; Paris telegram 302, 3 September 1953, FO371/106769/172.

4 *Manchester Guardian*, 3 September 1953.

5 *New China News Agency*, 3 September 1953.

6 Burrows memorandum, 8 September 1953, FO371/106769/175.

7 Tahourdin minute, 3 September 1953, Selby to Graves, 16 September 1953, FO371/106769/172, and 175.

8 CC(53)48th–50th meetings, 18–25 August 1953, CAB128/26; Paris telegram 312 to FO, 11 September 1953, FO371/106769/179; Dixon minute, 23 September 1953, FO371/106770/184.

9 Selby to Graves, 16 September 1953, FO371/106769/175; Cable, *Geneva*, p. 28.

10 Ambassador Harvey called the French 'past masters' in this regard. Paris dispatch 4 to Eden, 2 January 1952, FO371/101056/3.

11 Tahourdin to Joy, 21 April 1953, FO371/106765/42.

12 Paris telegram 819 to DOS, 29 August 1953, *FR1952–54*/XIII, pp. 740–741, emphasis added.

13 Logevall, *Embers of War*, p. 357.

14 Calvocoressi, *Survey 1953*, p. 295; Paris telegram 340 to FO, 2 October 1953, FO371/106770/193.

15 Paris telegram 341 to FO, 2 October 1953, FO371/106770/194.

16 Paris telegram 344 to FO, 5 October 1953, Burrows minute, 6 October 1953, FO371/106770/195.

17 Spector, *Advice and Support*, pp. 176–177.

18 DOS report to NSC, 5 August 1953, *FR1952–54*/XIII, p. 717.

19 Ogburn memorandum, 8 September 1953, and Bonsal to Johnson, 9 September 1953, emphasis added, *FR1952–54*/XIII, pp. 762–766, 794.

20 Makins to Strang, 11 August 1953, SHER/525, views of Eisenhower as disclosed on 7 August 1953.

21 *Pentagon Papers*, US National Archives online, PP/II/pp. A38–40, original emphasis.

22 Burrows minute, 8 September 1953, FO371/106769/175.

23 Cable, *Geneva*, p. 30; Ted Morgan, *Valley of Death: The Tragedy at Dien Bien Phu that led America into the Vietnam War* (New York: Random House, 2010), p. 192.

24 Fall, *Hell in a Very Small Place*, pp. 15–21.

25 Windrow, *Last Valley*, p. 291; Roy, *Dienbienphu*, p. 66.

26 Roy, *Dienbienphu*, p. 64.

27 Morgan, *Valley of Death*, p. 228.

28 JIC(54)2nd meeting, 7 January 1954, CAB159/15.

29 Pierre Asselin, 'New Perspectives on Dien Bien Phu', *Explorations in Southeast Asian Studies*, Vol. 1, No. 2 (1997), pp. 12–21.

30 Thorpe, *Eden*, pp. 392–396.

31 HCD, Vol. 520, cols 309–311, 5 November 1953.

32 D(53)14th meeting, 14 October 1953, and D(53)45, COS report, 1 October 1953, CAB131/13.

33 COS(53)132nd meeting, 24 November 1953, and COS(53)135th meeting, 27 November 1953, DEFE4/67.

34 Dixon memorandum, 15 October 1953, DIXON/Piers Dixon collection; FO memorandum, November 1953, FO371/106956/42.

35 C(53)330, 24 November 1953, CAB129/64; CC(53)72nd meeting, 26 November 1953, CAB128/26.

36   Young, *Churchill's Last Campaign*, pp. 215–217.

37   Calvocoressi, *Survey 1953*, p. 35.

38   Ellen J. Hammer, *The Struggle for Indochina* (Stanford: Stanford University Press, 1954), pp. 311–312.

39   Cameron, ed., *VNC/I*, pp. 223–224.

40   Burrows minute, 2 December 1953, SEAD to Chancery Saigon, 3 December 1953, and associated minutes, Chancery Moscow to FO, 1 December 1953, FO371/106749/43–50; State Department press release 678, 29 December 1953, FO371/112047/3.

41   Zhou memorandum, 2 March 1954, and Zhou presentation to PRC delegation, 20 April 1954, *Cold War International History Project*, Digital Archive, hereafter *CWIHP*/DA; Tao Wang, 'Neutralizing Indochina: The 1954 Geneva Conference and China's Efforts to Isolate the United States', *Journal of Cold War Studies*, Vol. 19, No. 2 (2017), pp. 4–5; Chen Jian, *Mao's China and the Cold War* (Chapel Hill: University of North Carolina Press, 2001), pp. 139–140.

42   Pierre Asselin, 'The Democratic Republic of Vietnam and the 1954 Geneva Conference: A Revisionist Critique', *Cold War History*, Vol. 11, No. 2 (2011), pp. 161–163.

43   Logevall, *Embers of War*, p. 372.

44   Devilliers and Lacouture, *End of a War*, p. 41.

45   Asselin, 'Revisionist Critique', p. 162.

46   *Le Populaire*, 4 December 1953; FO to Chancery Saigon, 3 December 1953, Paris telegram 434 to FO, 3 December 1953, FO371/106749/43 and 53.

47   Calvocoressi, *Survey 1953*, pp. 292–294.

48   *Times*, 9 December 1953.

49   Campbell to Gore-Booth, 18 January 1954, GOR/Ms.Eng.c.4553.

50   Colville diary, 4 December 1953, *Fringes*, p. 683.

51   Calvocoressi, *Survey 1953*, p. 36.

52   BC(P)(53)6th meeting, UK record, 7 December 1953, PREM11/645.

53   Ibid.

54   Eisenhower diary, 4–8 December 1953, DDEL/AWF/International/Box#3.

55   *HCD*, Vol. 520, cols 311, 309–311, 5 November 1953.

56   Bermuda telegram 151 to FO, 8 December 1953, 105211/11; US record of meeting, 7 December 1953, DDEL/DUL/Subjects/Box#1.

57   Colville diary, 5 December 1953, *Fringes*, p. 684.

58   NSC 173rd meeting, 3 December 1953, *FR1952–54/XV*, pp. 1636–1645; Jones, 'Targeting China', pp. 37–65.

59   Eisenhower notes, 4 December 1953, DDEL/AWF/International/Box#3; Gilbert, *Never Despair*, p. 918.

60   Shuckburgh diary, 5 December 1953, *Descent*, p. 114; Eden to Clarissa Eden, 6 December 1953, AVO/AP20/45/34.

61   Eden to Churchill, 4 December 1953, AVO/AP20/16/90.

62   Ruane, *Churchill and the Bomb*, p. 237.

63   Jones, 'US Nuclear Planning', p. 47.

64   Ruane, *Churchill and the Bomb*, pp. 193–205.

65   *HCD*, Vol. 484, cols 623–641, 15 February 1951, and Vol. 494, cols 2591–2609, 6 December 1951.

66   Truman-Churchill communiqué, 9 January 1952, *Foreign Relations of the United States 1952–54*, Vol. VI (Washington: Government Printing Office, 1986, hereafter *FR1952–54/VI*), p. 837.

67 A(52)1st meeting, 26 March 1952, CAB134/734.
68 AEC press release 56, 16 November 1952, FO371/99748/92.
69 *New York Times*, 17 November 1952; *Times*, 17 November 1952.
70 Lorna Arnold, *Britain and the H-Bomb* (Basingstoke: Palgrave, 2001), p. 17.
71 Macmillan, 22 February 1953, *Diaries/I*, p. 215.
72 Harold Caccia, n.d., Lord Caccia Papers, Eton College, CAC/9.
73 HDC(53)5(Revise), CAB134/942, May 1953, in Peter Hennessy, *Having It So Good: Britain in the Fifties* (London: Allen Lane, 2006), p. 165.
74 Steven J. Zaloga, *The Kremlin's Nuclear Shield: The Rise and Fall of Russia's Strategic Nuclear Forces, 1945–2000* (Washington: Smithsonian, 2014), pp. 18, 21.
75 Moran diary, 16 August 1953, *Churchill*, p. 451.
76 *Times*, 21 August 1953.
77 Colville diary, August 1953, *Fringes*, pp. 675–676; Moran diary, 27 July, 16 August 1953 and 2 September 1953, *Churchill*, pp. 446, 452, 465.
78 Ruane, *Churchill and the Bomb*, pp. 234–239.
79 Eisenhower diary, 5 December 1953, DDEL/AWF/International/Box#3.
80 PM to the Queen, 11 December 1953, CAB21/3074.
81 Eden to Churchill, 4 and 7 December 1953, AVO/AP20/16/90–91; D(54)8, 1 February 1954, CAB131/14.
82 Hagerty diary, 5 January 1954, in Robert H. Ferrell, ed., *The Diary of James C. Hagerty: Eisenhower in Mid-course, 1954–1955* (Bloomington: Indiana University Press, 1983), p. 3.

Chapter 6

1   *Times*, 30 December 1953. In general on the New Look, Gaddis, *Strategies of Containment*, pp. 125–234.
2   Dulles speech, 12 January 1954,Folliot, *Documents on International Affairs 1954*, pp. 265–267.
3   Wenner minute, 18 January 1954, Maitland letter, 2 February 1954, FO371/109135/1.
4   D(54)8, 1 February 1954, CAB131/14.
5   Eden, *Full Circle*, pp. 81–82.
6   Ibid., p. 87.
7   C(54)13, 11 January 1954, CAB129/65.
8   Harvey to Allen, 12 January 1954, FO371/112038/5.
9   FO memorandum, 15 January 1954, FO371/112047/8; Kevin Ruane, 'Anthony Eden, British Diplomacy and the Origins of the Geneva Conference of 1954', *Historical Journal*, Vol. 37, No. 1 (1994), pp. 153–160.
10 Berlin communiqué, 18 February 1954, Cameron, ed., *VNC/I*, pp. 229–230.
11 Shuckburgh diary, 27 January 1954, unpublished/original version kindly supplied to the authors by Professor John Charmley.
12 Berlin telegram 13 to FO, 25 January 1954, CAB21/3077.
13 Cmnd 9080, *Documents Relating to the Meeting of Foreign Ministers in Berlin* (London: HMSO, 1954), pp. 17–18, 21–22; Shuckburgh diary (unpublished), 26 January 1954; Plenary, 27 January 1954, UK record, FO371/109277/282.
14 CC(54)5th meeting, 26 January 1954, CAB128/27; Churchill to Eden, 26 January 1954, PREM11/665; FO telegram 40 to Berlin, 27 January 1954, PREM11/664.

15 Shuckburgh diary (unpublished), 26 January 1954; Tripartite meeting, UK record, 23 January 1954, FO371/109276/262; Berlin telegram 12 to FO, 25 January 1954, CAB21/3077.

16 CC(54)5th meeting, 26 January 1954, CAB128/27; FO telegram 40 to Berlin, 27 January 1954, PREM11/664.

17 Berlin telegram 12 to FO, 25 January 1954, PREM11/648; Shuckburgh diary (unpublished), 27 January 1954, and 15 March 1954, *Descent*, p. 148.

18 Berlin telegram 31 to FO, 27 January 1954, CAB21/3077; MacArthur memorandum, 27 January 1954, *FR1952–54*/XIII, pp. 999–1000.

19 Shuckburgh diary (unpublished), 27 January 1954; Berlin telegram 36 to FO, 28 January 1954, PREM11/664; Eden to Clarissa Eden, 27 January 1954, AVO/AP20/45/39.

20 Dulte 6 to DOS, 26 January 1954, DDEL/AWF/Dulles-Herter/Box#2.

21 Shuckburgh diary (unpublished), 22 January 1954.

22 Berlin telegram 37 to FO, 28 January 1954, CAB21/3077.

23 Berlin plenary, UK record, 28 January 1954, FO371/109278/311.

24 Eden to Clarissa Eden, 1 February 1954, AVO/AP20/45/43.

25 Dulte 42 to DOS, 6 February 1954, DDEL/AWF/Dulles-Herter/Box#2.

26 Berlin telegram 120 to FO, 8 February 1954, FO800/785/7; CC(54)8th meeting, 10 February 1954, CAB128/27.

27 Berlin 1st and 2nd restricted sessions, 8 and 11 February 1954, UK record, FO371/109286/489 and 543; Shuckburgh diary, 11 February 1954, *Descent*, pp. 132–133.

28 NSC 186th meeting, 26 February 1954, DDEL/AWF/NSC/Box#5.

29 CC(54)8th meeting, 10 February 1954, CAB195/11.

30 FO telegrams 17 and 31 to Berlin, 25–26 January 1954, CAB21/3077.

31 FO telegrams 23, 134 and 199 to Berlin, 26 January 1954, 8 and 13 February 1954, CAB21/3077; C(54)8th meeting, 10 February 1954, CAB195/11.

32 Berlin telegram 166 to FO, 14 February 1954, PREM11/665.

33 FO telegrams 199 and 222 to Berlin, 13 and 15 February 1954, Berlin telegram 192 to FO, 16 February 1954, PREM11/664.

34 CC(54)10th meeting, 22 February 1954, CAB195/11.

35 Berlin communiqué, 18 February 1954, Cameron, ed., *VNC*/I, pp. 229–230.

36 Berlin telegram 4 to FO, 24 January 1954, FO371/109276/238; Dulte 42 and Dulte 54 to DOS, 6 and 9 February 1954, DDEL/AWF/Dulles-Herter/Box#2; Georges Bidault, *Resistance: the Political Biography of Georges Bidault* (London: Weidenfeld and Nicolson, 1967), p. 194.

37 Berlin telegram 34 to FO, 28 January 1954, FO 371/109277/274G; CC(54)8th meeting, 10 February 1954, CAB195/11; Shuckburgh diary (unpublished), 16 February 1954.

38 Gruenther to Eisenhower, 7 February 1954, DDEL/AWF/Admin/Box#16.

39 *The Spectator*, 13 November 1953; Ruane, 'Geneva Conference', 168–170.

40 FO telegram 160 to Berlin, 10 February 1954, FO800/785/9; CC(54)8th meeting, 10 February 1954, CAB128/27; Logevall, *Embers of War*, p. 434.

41 Washington telegrams 314 and 325 to FO, 23 February 1954, PREM11/618; NSC 186th meeting, 26 February 1954, DDEL/AWF/NSC/Box#5; Jackson to Eisenhower, 12 March 1954, DDEL/AWF/Admin/Box#22; Werth, *France*, p. 664.

42 Dulte 42 to DOS, 6 February 1954, DDEL/AWF/Dulles-Herter/Box#2.

43 Shuckburgh diary, 17 February 1954, *Descent*, p. 133.

44 CC(54)10th meeting, 22 February 1954, CAB128/27.

45 *New York Times*, 23 February 1954; MacArthur to Morton, 24 February 1954, *FR1952–54*/XIII, pp. 1074–1075; Washington telegram 465 to FO, 27 February

1954, PREM11/649; Victor Bator, *Vietnam – A Diplomatic Tragedy: Origins of US Involvement* (London: Faber and Faber, 1965), p. 32.

46   Randle, *Geneva*, p. 48.
47   Allen minute, 22 February 1954, FO371/112047/35.
48   Ruane, 'Geneva Conference', p. 158; BBC monitoring report, 19 February 1954, FO371/112047/28.
49   Washington telegram 771 to Taipei, 13 March 1954, *Foreign Relations of the United States 1952–1954, Vol. XVI, The Geneva Conference* (Washington: Government Printing Office, 1981, hereafter *FR1952–54/XVI*), pp. 457–458.
50   NSC 186th meeting, 26 February 1954, DDEL/AWF/NSC/Box#5; Kitchen to Smith, 1 March 1954, *FR1952–54/XVI*, p. 428.
51   Dulte 87 to DOS, 18 February 1954, *Foreign Relations of the United States 1952–1954, Vol. VII, Germany and Austria* (Washington: Government Printing Office, 1986, hereafter *FR1952–54/VII*), p. 1162.
52   *Times*, 23 February 1954.
53   Saigon despatch 34 to Eden, 8 March 1954, FO371/112039/39; MacDonald report, 12 March 1954, MACD/12/14/1–8; *New Statesman*, 'The Markos Hypothesis', 13 March 1954; Werth, *France*, pp. 664–666.
54   Paris telegram 3315 to DOS, 11 March 1954, *FR1952–54/XIII*, pp. 1106–1107.
55   Allen and Kirkpatrick minutes, 23–24 March 1954, Eden minute, 26 March 1954, FO371/112048/63.
56   Paris telegram 124 to FO, 30 March 1954, FO371/112049/109.
57   US memorandum, 6 April 1954, *FR1952–54/XVI*, pp. 496–497.
58   Rumbold to Tahourdin, 16 March 1954, FO371/112048/63.
59   Saigon telegram 64 to FO, 23 February 1954, FO371/112033/13G; Graves telegram 106 to FO, 25 March 1954, FO371/112049/87G; Eden minute, 20 March 1954, FO371/112103/18.
60   Eden, *Full Circle*, p. 87; Tahourdin to Kevin Ruane, 3 January 1990.
61   FORD memorandum, 26 February 1954, FO371/112033/22.
62   Ibid.
63   Burrows minute, 18 March 1954, FO371/112033/22; Graves to Allen, 15 March 1954, Singapore telegram 129 to FO, 18 and 22 March 1954, FO371/112048/61 and 69; Singapore telegram 143 to FO, 26 March 1954, FO371/112049/89; COS(54)36th meeting, 31 March 1954, FO371/112050/135G.
64   Shuckburgh diary (unpublished), 9 and 15 March 1954.
65   Shuckburgh diary, 11 March 1954, *Descent*, p. 145; Butler note, 11 March 1954, BUT/G27/18–19; Macmillan diary, 14 March 1954, MACM/dep.c.16.
66   FO brief, 9 March 1954, FO371/112034/30.
67   Allen minute, 23 March 1954, Eden minute, 25 March 1954, FO371/112049/104.
68   Graves to Selby, 13 October 1953, FO371/106771/206; Saigon telegram MA2 to MOD, 22 March 1954, FO371/112103/33; John Prados, 'Reassessing Dien Bien Phu', in Lawrence, and Logevall, eds, *First Vietnam War*, p. 219.
69   Fall, *Hell in a Very Small Place*, p. 48; *Times*, 20 February 1954.
70   Morgan, *Valley of Death*, p. 246.
71   Goscha, *Modern Vietnam*, pp. 284–285.
72   Windrow, *Last Valley*, pp. 170, 193, 222; Dalloz, *Indo-China*, p. 170.
73   James Waite, *The End of the First Indochina War: A Global History* (London: Routledge, 2012), p. 42.
74   Roy, *Dienbienphu*, p. 157.
75   Ibid., p. 161; Jian, *Mao's China*, pp. 134–135.

76 The classic account of the battle is Fall, *Hell in a Very Small Place* (1966), but more recently Windrow, *Last Valley* (2004) has produced a magisterial amplification. Both works are drawn on in the account of the battle in the pages that follow.
77 Saigon telegram 97 to FO, 18 March 1954, PREM11/645.
78 Harding to Alexander, 19 March 1954, PREM11/645.
79 Paris telegram 135 to FO, 16 March 1954, FO371/112103/22.
80 Bidault, *Resistance*, p. 195.
81 FO memorandum, 31 March 1954, Eden minute, 1 April 1954, FO371/112049/103G.

Chapter 7

1   Eisenhower message to Congress, 21 January 1954, *PPP 1954 online* (doc. 14).
2   On this, Waite, *First Indochina War*, p. 34.
3   *Times*, 8 February 1954; Eisenhower, 8 February 1954, in Ferrell, ed., *Diaries*, p. 275. There were already 125 technicians in-country.
4   Randle, *Geneva*, p. 29.
5   Hagerty, 8 February 1954, in Ferrell, ed., *Diary*, p. 15.
6   Emmet Hughes, *The Ordeal of Power: A Political Memoir of the Eisenhower Years* (New York: Atheneum, 1963), p. 142. The Republicans held slim majorities in both houses (48-47-1 in the Senate, and 221-213-1 in the House).
7   Philip A. Grant, 'The Bricker Amendment Controversy', *Presidential Studies Quarterly*, Vol. 15, No. 3 (1985), pp. 572–582.
8   Eisenhower diary, 1 April 1953, in Ferrell, ed., *Diaries*, p. 234.
9   Eisenhower, *Mandate for Change*, p. 316.
10 Washington telegram 241 to FO, 8 February 1954, FO371/112047/19.
11 Eisenhower news conference, 10 February 1954, *PPP 1954 online* (doc. 33).
12 Gardner, *Approaching Vietnam*, p. 170.
13 Joy to Tahourdin 13 February 1954, FO371/112047/26.
14 Washington telegram 288 to FO, 17 February 1954, FO371/112047/28.
15 NSC 179th meeting, 8 January 1954, *FR1952–54*/XIII, pp. 947–954.
16 Ibid.
17 NSC-5405, 16 January 1954, *FR1952–54*/XIII, pp. 971–976.
18 Smith to Eisenhower, 18 January 1954, DDEL/SmithMS/Box#25.
19 Smith committee, 29 January 1954, and Kyes to Talbott, 29 January 1954, *FR1952–54*/XIII, pp. 1002–1007.
20 Washington telegram 299 to FO, 19 February 1954, FO371/112047/32.
21 Allen to Scott, 24 February 1954, FO371/112047/28; Warner, 'Settlement of the Indochina War', p. 240.
22 Smith committee report, 2 March 1954, *FR1952–54*/XIII, pp. 1109–1116.
23 Gardner, *Approaching Vietnam*, p. 177.
24 NSC 186th meeting, 26 February 1954, DDEL/AWF/NSC Series/Box#5.
25 See Kevin Ruane, 'Agonizing Reappraisals: Anthony Eden, John Foster Dulles and the Crisis of European Defence, 1953–54', *Diplomacy and Statecraft*, Vol. 13, No. 4 (2010), pp. 151–185.
26 Scott to Allen, 10 March 1954, circulated as C(54)108, 18 March 1954, CAB129/67, original emphasis.

27 NSC 189th meeting, 18 March 1954, *FR1952-54*/XIII, pp. 1132–1133.

28 Anderson to Radford, 21 March 1954, *FR1952-54*/XIII, pp. 1137–1140.

29 Hagerty, 20 March 1954, in Ferrell, ed., *Diary*, p. 32.

30 Ely, *Mémoires*, p. 32; Morgan, *Valley of Death*, pp. 312–313; Jones to Merchant, 23 March 1954, *FR1952-54*/XIII, p. 1145.

31 Ely, *Mémoires*, pp. 67–88; Spector, *Advice and Support*, pp. 193–194.

32 Stephen Jurika, ed., *From Pearl Harbor to Vietnam: The Memoirs of Admiral Arthur W. Radford* (Stanford: Hoover Institution Press, 1980), pp. 391–401; Morgan, *Valley of Death*, p. 321.

33 George G. Herring and Richard H. Immerman. 'Eisenhower, Dulles, and Dien Bien Phu: "The Day We Didn't Go to War" Revisited', in Kaplan et al., eds, *Dienbienphu*, p. 85.

34 Radford to Eisenhower, 24 March 1954, *FR1952-54*/ XIII, p. 1159.

35 NSC 190th meeting, 25 March 1954, *FR1952-54*/XIII, pp. 1163–1168.

36 Lacouture and Devilliers, *End of a War*, pp. 73–75; Ely, *Mémoires*, pp. 82–87.

37 Dulles news conference, 23 March 1954, Cameron, ed., *VNC*/I, pp. 231–233.

38 Eisenhower news conference, 24 March 1954, *PPP 1954 online* (doc. 63).

39 Dulles-Eisenhower meeting, 24 March 1954, DDEL/DullesMS/WHMeetings/Box#1.

40 Ridgway to JCS, 2 April 1954 and 6 April 1954, *FR1952-54*/XIII, pp. 1220–1221 and 1269.

41 Spector, *Advice and Support*, pp. 200–202; Logevall, *Embers of War*, p. 464.

42 Dulles to Radford, 24 March 1954, *FR1952-54*/XIII, p. 1151.

43 Hagerty, 26 March 1954, in Ferrell, ed., *Diary*, p. 35.

44 NSC 190th meeting, 25 March 1954, *FR1952-54*/XIII, pp. 1163–1168.

45 Richard Nixon, *RN: The Memoirs of Richard Nixon* (London: Sidgwick and Jackson, 1978), p. 151.

46 Dulles to Knowland, DDEL/DULLES/Telcons/Box#2, 30 March 1954.

47 Dulles speech, 29 March 1954, Cameron, ed., *VNC*/I, pp. 233–236; Dulles to Eisenhower, 26 March 1954, Mudd/DULLES/Box#80.

48 Anderson to Radford, 21 March 1954, *FR1952-54*/XIII, pp. 1137–1140.

49 *PP*/I, pp. 99–100; John Prados, *The Sky Would Fall: Operation Vulture – the Secret US Bombing Mission to Vietnam, 1954* (New York: Dial Press, 1983), p. 142.

50 Washington telegram 524, 27 March 1954, FO371/112049/100.

51 Gardner, *Approaching Vietnam*, p. 191, is one of the few to note the juxtaposition.

52 *Times*, 3 February 1954.

53 Eisenhower to Congress, 17 February 1954, *PPP 1954 online*, doc. 38.

54 Eisenhower to Churchill, 9 February 1954, *FR1952-54*/VI, pp.1012–1014.

55 Macmillan diary, 27 February 1954, MAC/dep.c.16.

56 Shuckburgh diary, 1 March 1954, *Descent*, p. 137.

57 Eden to Churchill, 2 March 1954, PREM11/1074.

58 *Manchester Guardian*, 18 February 1954.

59 Churchill to Eisenhower, 9 March 1954, *CEC*, pp. 122–124.

60 Ruane, *Churchill and the Bomb*, pp. 245–248.

61 'The H-Bomb and World Opinion', *Bulletin of Atomic Scientists*, Vol. 10, No. 5 (May 1954), p. 165; *Daily Mirror*, 2 April 1954.

62 Eisenhower to Churchill, 19 March 1954, CHUR6/3B.

63 CC(54)21st conclusions, 22 March 1954, CAB195/12, original emphases.

64 Shuckburgh diary, 26 March 1954, *Descent*, pp. 153–154.

65 *Daily Mirror*, 1 April 1954.

66 Ibid.

67 Ibid.

68 Ibid.

69 Allen minute, 31 March 1954, Eden minute, 1 April 1954, FO371/112049/103G; COS(54)36th meeting, FO371/112050/135G.

70 Randle, *Geneva*, pp. 74, 81.

71 Bidault note, 7 April 1954, in Waite, *First Indochina War*, p. 110.

72 Washington telegram 548, 30 March 1954, FO371/112049/107.

73 FO telegram 1324 to Washington, 1 April 1954, FO371/112049/103G; Cable, *Geneva*, p. 49.

74 Washington telegram 579, 3 April 1954, FO371/112049/121G; Dulles-Makins meeting, 2 April 1954, FO371/112050/134G.

75 Ibid.

76 Washington telegrams 580 and 588, 3–4 April 1954, and Eden minute, 6 April 1954, FO371/112049/121G-122G.

77 Rocolle, *Pourquoi Dien Bien Phu?* p. 466; Morgan, *Valley of Death*, p. 379.

78 NSC 191st meeting, 1 April 1954, *FR1952-54/*XIII, pp. 1200–1202.

79 Hagerty, 1 April 1954, in Ferrell, ed., *Diary*, p. 39.

80 *FR1952-54/*XIII, p. 1202, note 3; Dulles-Eisenhower telcon, 1 April 1954, DDEL/AWF/Diary/Box#5.

81 White House meeting, 2 April 1954, and draft resolution, *FR1952-54/*XIII, pp. 1210–1212.

82 Ibid; Gibbons, *US Government and the Vietnam War*, p. 195.

83 Dulles-Radford-Congressional leaders' meeting, 3 April 1954, *FR1952-54/*XIII, pp. 1224–1225.

84 Dulles-Eisenhower telcon, 3 April 1954, *FR1952-54/*XIII, p. 1230.

85 Mark Lawrence and Fredrik Logevall, 'Introduction', in Lawrence and Logevall, eds, *First Vietnam War*, p. 12.

Chapter 8

1 Washington telegram 599, 6 April 1954, FO371/112050/131G.

2 Australian record of Dulles-Spender-Munro meeting, 4 April 1954, FO371/112051/164G.

3 Ibid.

4 US record of Dulles-Spender-Munro meeting, 4 April, *FR1952–54/*XIII, pp. 1231–1235.

5 DOS telegram 5090 to London, 1 April 1954, *FR1952–54/*XIII, pp. 1202–1204.

6 Cable, *Geneva*, pp. 54–56.

7 Munro telegrams 540 and 552 to Auckland, 6 April 1954, FO371112052/207G.

8 Dulles-Eisenhower telcon, 3 April 1954, *FR1952–54/*XIII, p. 1230.

9 Sherman Adams, *First-hand Report: The Inside Story of the Eisenhower Administration* (London: Hutchison, 1962), p. 103.

10 Eisenhower to Churchill, 4 April 1954, Boyle, ed., *CEC*, pp. 136–138.

11 Ibid.

12 Ibid.

13 Moran diary, 26 March 1954, *Churchill*, p. 530.

14 Dulles-Strauss telcon, 29 March 1954, *FR1952–54/*II, pp. 1379–1380.

15 Eisenhower-Strauss news conference, 31 March 1954, *PPP 1954 online* (doc. 68).
16 *New York Times*, 1 April 1954.
17 *HCD* Vol. 526, cols 36–153, 5 April 1954; Woolton diary, 6 April 1954, WOOL/3.
18 London telegram 4384, 6 April 1954, DDEL/AWF/International/Box#19.
19 Munro telegram 552 to Auckland, 6 April 1954, FO371/112052/207G.
20 Churchill to Eisenhower, 6 April 1954, Boyle, ed., *CEC*, p. 138.
21 Washington telegram 616, 7 April 1954, FO371/112050/144G; Washington telegram 642, 8 April 1954, FO371/112052/208G.
22 *Times*, 6 April 1954.
23 Laurent Césari and Jacques de Folin, 'Military Necessity, Political Impossibility: The French Viewpoint on Operation *Vautour*', in Kaplan et al., eds, *Dienbienphu*, p. 109.
24 Paris telegram 3710, 5 April 1954, *FR1952–54*/XIII, pp. 1236–1238.
25 Dulles-Eisenhower telcon, 5 April 1954, *FR1952–54*/XIII, pp. 1241–1242.
26 State telegram 3482 to Paris, 5 April 1954, and Paris telegram 3729 to State, 5 April 1954, *FR1952–54*/XIII (docs 695–696), pp. 1242–1243; Washington telegram 616 to FO, 7 April 1954, FO371/112050/144G.
27 NSC 1074-a, *The Pentagon Papers: The Defense Department History of United States Decisonmaking on Vietnam: Senator Gravel Edition*, Vol. I (Boston: Beacon Press, 1971), pp. 462–476; Morgan, *Valley of Death*, pp. 414–415.
28 NSC 192nd meeting, 6 April 1954, *FR1952–54*/XIII, pp. 1250–1265.
29 Ibid.
30 NSC 192nd meeting, 6 April 1954, *FR1952–54*/XIII, pp. 1250–1265.
31 NSC 1074-a, *Pentagon Papers – Gravel Edition*, Vol. I, pp. 462–476.
32 Dulles-Dean telcon, 22 March 1954, DDEL/DullesMS/Telcons/Box#2.
33 Eden dispatch 337 to Washington, 6 April 1954, Kirkpatrick minute, 7 April 1954, and US memorandum, 6 April 1954, FO371/112050/143G, 159G; London telegram 4382, 6 April 1954, *FR1952–54*/ XIII, pp. 1248–1249.
34 CC(54)26th meeting, 7 April 1954. CAB195/12.
35 *Times*, 9 April 1954.
36 HC Delhi telegram 350 to CRO, 10 April 1954, and Eden minute, n.d., FO371/112051/181.
37 Morgan, *Valley of Death*, p. 294.
38 C(54)134, 7 April 1954, CAB129/67.
39 Ibid.
40 CC(54)26th meeting, 7 April 1954, CAB128/27.
41 Ibid., CAB195/12.
42 Churchill to Eisenhower, 7 April 1954, Boyle, ed., *CEC*, p. 139.
43 Eisenhower, *Mandate for Change*, p. 347.
44 Allen paper, 9 April 1954, and brief for Dulles visit, n.d., COS(54)42nd meeting, 10 April 1954, FO371/112052/202G.
45 FO telegram 1458 to Washington, 7 April 1954, FO371/112050/140G.
46 Washington telegrams 617–619, 7 April 1954, FO371/112050/146–147 and 151G; Washington telegrams 679–680, 10 April 1954, FO371/112051/173–174.
47 Ibid.
48 Cable minute, 12 April 1954, FO371/112051/174.
49 *New York Times*, 7 and 9 April 1954; Cable minute, 10 April 1954, FO371/112051/169.
50 Washington telegram 164, 10 April 1954, FO371/109100/17; Cable minute, 12 April 1954, FO371/112051/175.

51 Eisenhower news conference, 7 April 1954, *PPP 1954 online* (doc. 73).
52 Eisenhower, *Mandate for Change*, p. 96.
53 MacArthur to Dulles, 7 April 1954, *FR1952–54*/XIII, pp. 1270–1272.
54 Paris telegram 3756 to DOS, 7 April 1954, *FR1952–54*/XIII, pp. 1272–1273.
55 DOS telegram 3520 to Paris, 7 April 1954, *FR1952–54*/XIII, pp. 1274–1275.
56 Dulles-Heeney meeting, 7 April 1954, *FR1952–54*/XIII, p. 1276; DDEL/Dulles/Telcons/box#2, Dulles-Wiley, 7 April 1954.
57 Dulles-Bonnet meeting, 8 April 1954, *FR1952–54*/XIII, pp. 1290–1292.
58 Paris telegram 149, 10 April 1954, FO371/112051/180.
59 Eden dispatch 269 to Paris, 9 April 1954, FO371/112051/182G.
60 Dulles statement, 10 April 1954, *FR1952–54*/XIII, pp. 1302–1303.
61 Washington telegram 688, 10 April 1954, FO371/112051/176.
62 Casey diary, 12 April 1954, *Diaries 1951–60*, p. 125.
63 Hagerty diary, 7 April 1954, DDEL/Hagerty/Box#1.

Chapter 9

1 Eden-Dulles meeting, 11 April 1954, FO371/112054/267G.
2 Ibid.
3 Ibid.
4 Ibid.
5 Ibid.
6 London telegram 4490, 12 April 1954, *FR1952–54*/VI, p. 1023.
7 Allen minute, 8 April 1954, Eden annotation, n.d., FO371/112051/197; Eden, *Full Circle*, p. 94.
8 Sulzberger diary, 23 November 1954, in C. L. Sulzberger, *A Long Row of Candles: Memoirs and Diaries, 1934–1954* (Toronto: Macmillan, 1969), p. 770.
9 Salisbury-Knowland meeting, 30 September 1953, FO800/784/90.
10 CRO memorandum, 10 April 1954, FO371/112052/202G.
11 US record of Eden-Dulles talks, 11 April 1954, *FR1952–54*/XIII, pp.1307–1309.
12 US-UK officials' talks, and US draft of declaration of common purpose, 12 April 1954, and Tahourdin minute, 14 April 1954, FO371/112054/268G and 296; US record in *FR1952–54*/XIII, pp. 1311–1313.
13 Ibid.
14 Eden-Dulles meeting, 12 April 1954, FO371/112054/268G.
15 Ibid.
16 Ibid.
17 Ibid.
18 Secto 1 to DOS, 13 April 1954, *FR1952–54*/XIII, p. 1320.
19 GEN.463/1st meeting, 12 April 1954, PREM11/645. Eden made the same points to the full Cabinet the next day. CC(54)28th meeting, 13 April 1954, CAB128/27.
20 Eden-Dulles meeting, 13 April 1954, FO371/112054/252G; Secto 2 to DOS, 13 April 1954, *FR1952–54*/XIII, p. 1321.
21 Ibid.
22 Ibid.
23 *HCD*, Vol. 526, cols 969–975, 13 April 1954.
24 *Times*, 13 and 14 April 1954.

25 Shuckburgh diary, 12 April 1954, *Descent*, p. 164, original emphasis; also Allen minute, 14 April 1954, FO371/112053/224.

26 Bidault-Dulles talks, 14 April 1954, *FR1952–54*/XIII, pp. 1328–1334.

27 Ibid. Also Dulles-Laniel-Bidault meeting, 14 April 1954 and Franco-American communiqué, 14 April 1954, *FR1952–54*/XIII, pp. 1335–1338.

28 FO telegram 1627 to Washington, 14 April 1954, FO371/112053/223G.

29 Allen to US-UK officials' meeting, 12 April 1954, *FR1952–54*/XIII, pp. 1311–1313.

30 FO telegram 1627 to Washington, 14 April 1954, FO371/112053/223G.

31 Washington telegram 742 to FO, 16 April 1954, ibid.

32 FO telegram 1674 to Washington, 17 April 1954, ibid.

33 FO telegrams 1675 to Washington and FO telegram 179 to Rangoon, 17 April 1954, FO371/112053/232G; FO telegram 1676 to Washington, 17 April 1954, FO800/785/18; Eden dispatch 535 to Washington and annex, 12 June 1954, FO371/112085/1018.

34 Washington telegram 750, 18 April 1954, FO371/112053/232G; Smith-Makins meeting, 18 April 1954, *FR1952–54*/XIII. pp. 1349–1350.

35 Washington telegrams 753 and 754, 18 April 1954, FO371/112053/238G.

36 FO telegram 1691 to Washington, 19 April 1954, ibid.

37 Ibid.

38 FO telegram 1692 to Washington, 19 April 1954, ibid.

39 FO telegram 1696, ibid.

40 Mosley, *Dulles*, p. 358.

41 Interview with U. Alexis Johnson, 7 February 1982, for *Vietnam: a Television History*, WGBH Media Library & Archives.

42 Cited in Carlton, *Eden*, p. 342.

43 Klaus Larres, *Churchill's Cold War: The Politics of Personal Diplomacy* (New Haven: Yale University Press, 2002), p. 331; Warner, 'Settlement of the Indochina War', p. 250; John Charmley, *Churchill's Grand Alliance: The Anglo-American Special Relationship 1940–57* (London: Hodder and Stoughton, 1995), pp. 279–280; John Dickie, *'Special' No More – Anglo-American Relations: Rhetoric and Reality* (London: Weidenfeld and Nicolson, 1994), p. 88.

44 Washington telegram 1094 to FO, 4 June 1954, FO800/842/59.

45 Cable, *Geneva*, p. 57.

46 Secto 10 to DOS, 13 April 1954, *FR1952–54*/XIII, pp. 1322–1323.

47 Bidault-Dulles talks, 14 April 1954, *FR1952–54*/XIII, p. 1331.

48 Shuckburgh diary, 13 April 1954, *Descent*, p. 164.

49 Eisenhower diary, 14 May 1953, in Ferrell, ed., *Diaries*, p. 237.

50 *New York Times*, 15 April 1954.

51 Hagerty diary, 19 April 1954, DDEL/Hagerty/Box#1.

52 Makins to Kirkpatrick, 21 April 1954, FO 371/112059/409G.

53 Shuckburgh diary, 3 May 1954, *Descent*, p. 189.

54 Peck to Stewart, 27 November 1964, FO371/175503/215.

55 Morgan, *Valley of Death*, p. 439.

56 Bator, *Vietnam*, pp. 68–69. Similarly, Prados, *Sky Would Fall*, p. 126.

57 Historians who find against Eden include Carlton, *Eden*, p. 343; Rothwell, *Eden*, p. 145; and Young, *Churchill's Last Campaign*, p. 261. James, *Eden*, p. 377, finds in his favour. Warner, 'Settlement of the Indochina War', pp. 244–247, and Charmley, *Churchill's Grand Alliance*, pp. 279–280 find some fault on both sides.

58 Cable, *Geneva*, pp. 57, 59.

59 Paterson and Speaight minutes, 26–27 April 1954, FO371/112059/409G.

60 Kirkpatrick to Makins, 30 April 1954, ibid.
61 London telegram 4523 to DOS, 13 April 1954, *FR1952–54*/XIII, p. 1322, note 1.
62 State telegram 183 to Canberra, 15 April 1954, NARA/RG59/790.5/4–1554.
63 Colville to Massigli and enclosure, 18 April 1954, PREM11/645.
64 Washington telegram 770 to FO, 20 April 1954, FO371/112054/255.
65 Hagerty, 24 April 1954, in Ferrell, ed., *Diary*, p. 48.
66 FO memorandum, 21 April 1954, FO371/112101/2.
67 Shuckburgh diary, 22 April 1954, *Descent*, p. 168.
68 Dulte 3 to DOS, 22 April 1954, *FR1952–54*/XIII, pp. 1362–1363.
69 Paris telegram 244 to FO, 22 April 1954, FO371/112054/279G.
70 Cable, *Geneva*, p. 64.
71 Dulte 3 to DOS, 22 April 1954, *FR1952–54*/XIII, pp.1362–1363.
72 Cited in Chalmers Roberts, *First Rough Draft* (New York: Praeger, 1973), p. 121.
73 Dulte 3 to DOS, 22 April 1954, *FR1952–54*/XIII, pp. 1362–1363.
74 Cable, *Geneva*, pp. 13, 60; Shuckburgh diary, 15 April 1954, *Descent*, p. 166.
75 Allen minute, 8 April 1954, Eden minute, n.d., FO371/112051/197; Allen to Paterson, 23 April 1954, FO371/112055/301.
76 Cable, *Geneva*, p. 60; *Pentagon Papers*, US National Archives online, II/B/p. B-27.

Chapter 10

1   Morgan, *Valley of Death*, pp. 429, 460–461.
2   Casey, 15 April 1954, *Diaries 1951–60*, p. 128.
3   Navarre note, 21 April 1954, in Waite, *First Indochina War*, p. 100; Logevall, *Embers of War*, p. 496; Césari and de Folin, 'Military Necessity', p. 113.
4   Dulles-Nixon telcon, 19 April 1954, DDEL/Dulles/Telcons/box#2.
5   Dulte 2 to DOS, 22 April 1954, *FR1952–54*/XIII, pp. 1361–1362.
6   Tedul 5 to Paris, 23 April 1954, *FR1952–54*/XIII, pp. 1366–1367.
7   Paris telegram 245, 22 April 1954, FO371/112055/280G, and US record in Dulte 3, 22 April 1954, *FR1952–54*/XIII, pp. 1362–1363.
8   Shuckburgh diary, 22 April 1954, *Descent*, p. 169.
9   Paris telegram 246 to FO, 22 April 1954, FO371/112055/281G.
10 Shuckburgh diary, 22 April 1954, *Descent*, p. 169; Paris telegrams 246–247 to FO, 22 April 1954, FO371/112055/281G–282G.
11 Shuckburgh diary 23 April 1954, *Descent*, pp. 169–170.
12 Laniel-MacArthur meeting, 23 April 1954, *FR1952–54*/XIII, pp. 1371–1373.
13 Dulte 7 to DOS, 23 April 1954, *FR1952–54*/XIII, p. 1374.
14 Paris telegram 257 to FO, 23 April 1954, FO371/112055/305G.
15 Dulte 8 and Dulte 10 to DOS, 23 April 1954, *FR1952–54*/XIII, pp. 1374–1375.
16 Shuckburgh diary, 23 April 1954, *Descent*, pp. 170–171.
17 Eden, *Full Circle*, p. 102.
18 Dulles statement, 23 April 1954, *FR1952–54*/V, pp. 509–514.
19 Shuckburgh diary, 24 April 1954, *Descent*, p. 171.
20 Paris telegram 262 to FO, 24 April 1954, FO371/112056/314G; Dulles-Eden meeting, 24 April 1954, and note 1, Dulte 18 to DOS, 24 April 1954, *FR1952–54*/XIII, pp. 1386–1391.
21 Ibid.
22 Shuckburgh diary, 24 April 1954, *Descent*, p. 172.

23 Clarissa Eden diary, 24 April 1954, *Memoir*, p. 157.
24 Merchant-Pearson meeting, 30 April 1954, *FR1952–54*/XVI, pp. 626–629.
25 Paris telegram 267 to FO, 24 April 1954, FO371/112056/315G; Dulte 15 to DOS, 24 April 1954, and Dulte 19 to DOS, 24 April 1954, *FR1952–54*/XIII, pp. 1391–1393.
26 Devilliers and Lacouture, *End of a War*, p. 96, note 8; Randle, *Geneva*, pp. 99–100.
27 Paris telegram 267 to FO, 24 April 1954, FO371/112056/315G.
28 Shuckburgh diary, 24 April 1954, *Descent*, pp. 172–173.
29 Dulte 15, 24 April 1954, *FR1952–54*/XIII, pp. 1391–1393.
30 Bidault, *Resistance*, pp. 196–197.
31 David L. Anderson, *Trapped by Success: The Eisenhower Administration and Vietnam, 1953–61* (New York: Columbia University Press, 1991), p. 27.
32 Morgan, *Valley of Death*, pp. 479–481.
33 Spector, *Advice and Support*, p. 200; Logevall, *Embers of War*, p. 499.
34 Prados, *Sky Would Fall*, p. 92.
35 DOS telegram 501 to Paris, 9 August 1954, *FR1952–54*/XIII, pp. 1928.
36 Fredrik Logevall, '"We might give them a few": Did the US offer to drop Atom bombs at Dien Bien Phu?' *Bulletin of Atomic Scientists*, 26 February 2016.
37 Text of Dulles to Bidault, 25 April 1954, *FR1952–54*/XIII, pp. 1398–1399.
38 Iverach McDonald, *A Man of the Times* (London: Hamish Hamilton, 1976).
39 Dulte 18 to DOS, 24 April 1954, *FR1952–54*/XIII, p. 1386, note 1.
40 Shuckburgh diary, 24 April 1954, *Descent*, p. 173.
41 Shuckburgh minute and enclosure, 25 April 1954, FO371/112056/323G.
42 Shuckburgh diary, 24 April 1954, *Descent*, p. 173.
43 Bidault to Dulles, 25 April 1954, *FR1952–54*/XIII, p. 1401.
44 CC(54)155, 27 April 1954, record of Cabinet discussion, 11.00 am, 25 April 1954, CAB129/68.
45 Ibid.
46 Ibid.
47 FO telegram 924 to Paris, 25 April 1954, FO371/112056/321G.
48 Ibid.
49 Shuckburgh diary, 25 April 1954, *Descent*, p. 175.
50 C(54)155, 27 April 1954, record of Cabinet meeting, 4.00 pm, 25 April 1954, CAB129/68.
51 Macmillan diary, 25 April 1954, Catterall, ed., *Diaries*/I, pp. 309–310, original emphasis.
52 CC(54)30th meeting, 25 April 1954, CAB195/12.
53 Shuckburgh diary, 25 April 1954, *Descent*, p. 175, 25 April 1954.
54 Chalmers Roberts, 'The Day We Didn't Go to War', *The Reporter*, 14 September 1954, pp. 31–35.
55 Roberts, *First Rough Draft*, p. 114.
56 Dulte 17 to DOS, 24 April 1954, *FR1952–54*/XIII, pp. 1394–1396.
57 Paris telegram 4060 to DOS, 25 April 1954, *FR1952–54*/XIII, pp. 1402–1403.
58 Tedul 4 to Geneva, 25 April 1954, *FR1952–54*/XIII, pp. 1403–1404.
59 Eisenhower to Gruenther, 26 April 1954, DDEL/AWF/Admin/Box#16; Adams, *First-hand Report*, p. 104.
60 Dulte 3 to DOS, 25 April 1954, *FR1952–54*/XIII, pp. 1404–1405.
61 Shuckburgh diary, 25 April 1954, *Descent*, pp. 175–176; Geneva telegram 6 to FO, 25 April 1954, FO371/112055/308G.
62 Eden, *Full Circle*, p. 107.

63 Shuckburgh diary, 25 April 1954, *Descent*, p. 176.
64 Geneva telegram 7 to FO, 26 April 1954, FO371/112055/309G; US record in *FR1952–54*/XVI, pp. 553–557.
65 Ibid.
66 Secto 1 to DOS, 24 April 1954, *FR1952–54*/XVI, pp. 552–553.
67 Washington telegram 801 to FO, 26 April 1954, FO371/112056/324G.
68 Geneva telegram 9 to FO, 26 April 1954, FO371/112056/315G.
69 Clarissa Eden, *Memoirs*, p. 160.
70 Shuckburgh diary, 22 and 25 April 1954, *Descent*, pp. 169, 176.
71 Geneva telegram 7 to FO, 26 April 1954, FO371/112056/309G.
72 Dulte 21 to DOS, 29 April 1954, *FR1952–54*/XVI, p. 607.
73 Eisenhower to Hazlett, 27 April 1954, DDEL/AWF/DDE Diary Series/Box#6.
74 Tarling, *Impact of the Korean War*, p. 343.

Chapter 11

1   Eisenhower-Smith telcon, 24 April 1954, *FR1952–54*/XIII, pp. 1381–1383.
2   FO telegram 28 to Geneva, 27 April 1954, FO371/112057/344G.
3   COS(54)54th meeting, 29 April 1954, ibid.
4   Colville to Makins, 28 April 1954, PREM11/666; Eden cited in Jones, *After Hiroshima*, p. 213.
5   Record of Churchill-Radford dinner, 26 April 1954, FO371/112057/360G.
6   Ibid.
7   Eden annotation, ibid.
8   JCS-960578 to Dulles, 27 April 1954, *FR1952–54*/VI, pp. 1030–1032; Tedul 15 to Geneva, 28 April 1954, *FR1952–54*/XVI, p. 594; Jurika/Radford, *Pearl Harbor to Vietnam*, pp. 408–409; Townsend Hoopes, *The Devil and John Foster Dulles* (Boston: Little, Brown, 1973), p. 358.
9   Merchant to Dulles, 29 April 1954, *FR1952–54*/XVI, pp. 619–620.
10 Eden, *Full Circle*, p. 77.
11 CC(54)155, 27 April 1954, Cabinet discussion, 11.00 am, 25 April 1954, CAB129/68.
12 Bao Dai statement, 25 April 1954, Cameron, ed., *VNC*/I, p. 242; Dalloz, *Indo-China War*, p. 176.
13 Quai d'Orsay directive, 31 March 1954, in Kathryn Statler, *Replacing France: The Origins of American Intervention in Vietnam* (Lexington: University of Kentucky Press, 2007), p. 96.
14 Lacouture, Mendès-France, p. 205.
15 Ilya Gaiduk, *Confronting Vietnam: Soviet Policy toward the Indochina Conflict, 1954–1963* (Stanford: Stanford University Press, 2003), p. 18; Wang, 'Neutralizing Indochina', pp. 3, 7; Zhou cable to Ho, 11 March 1954, *CWIHP Digital Archive*.
16 Eisenhower news conference, 29 April 1954, *PPP 1954 online* (doc. 92).
17 Tedul 26 to Geneva, 1 May 1954, *FR1952–54*/XVI, pp. 640–641.
18 Dulles-Bonnet meeting, 3 April 1954, *FR1952–54*/XIII, p. 1226.
19 *Washington Post*, 1 May 1954.
20 Gary R. Hess, 'Redefining the American Position in Southeast Asia: The United States and the Geneva and Manila Conferences', in Kaplan et al., eds, *Dienbienphu*, p. 130.
21 In general, Asselin, 'Revisionist Critique', pp. 155–195.

22   Logevall, *Embers of War*, p. 520.

23   Paris telegram 302, 3 May 1954, FO371/112058/398G.

24   Shuckburgh diary, 26 April 1954, *Descent*, pp. 178–179.

25   Geneva telegram 19 to FO, 26 April 1954, FO371/112056/326G; Clarissa Eden, diary, 27 April 1954, *Memoir*, pp. 158–159.

26   Eden, *Full Circle*, p. 123.

27   Geneva telegram 18 to FO, 26 April 1954, FO371/112056/325G; Shuckburgh diary, 26 April 1954, *Descent*, p. 177.

28   Dulte 7 to DOS, 26 April 1954, *FR1952–54*/XVI, pp. 570–571.

29   Shuckburgh diary, 26 April 1954, *Descent*, pp. 177–179.

30   Geneva telegram 45 to FO, 28 April 1954, PREM11/666.

31   Clarissa Eden diary, 27 April 1954, *Memoir*, p. 158.

32   Shuckburgh diary, 27 April 1954, *Descent*, p. 181.

33   Zhou telegram to Mao, 26 April 1954, *CWIHP Digital Archive*; Eden diary, 28 April 1954, AVO/AP20/1/3.

34   Kinzer, *Brothers*, p. 191.

35   Hoopes, *Dulles*, p. 361.

36   Clarissa Eden, *Memoir*, pp. 157–158; Eden, *Full Circle*, p. 108.

37   Geneva telegram 19 to FO, 26 April 1954, FO371/112056/326G.

38   Dulte 9 to DOS, 26 April 1954, *FR1952–54*/XVI, pp. 575–576.

39   Dulte 13 to DOS, 27 April 1954, *FR1952–54*/XVI, pp. 576–577.

40   FO telegram 37 to Geneva, 27 April 1954, FO800/790/2.

41   *HCD*, Vol. 526, cols 1455–1456, 27 April 1954.

42   Macmillan diary, 28 April 1954, MAC/dep.c.16.

43   Shuckburgh diary, 28 April 1954, *Descent*, p. 180.

44   Washington telegram 807 to FO, 26 April 1954, FO371/112056/334; Washington telegram 825 to FO, 28 April 1954, FO371/112057/350.

45   Eden, *Full Circle*, pp. 108–110.

46   Tedul 16 to Geneva, 28 April 1954 (meeting took place on 26 April), *FR1952–54*/XVI, pp. 599–600.

47   Washington telegram 832 to FO, 29 April 1954, FO371/112057/366.

48   Tedul 20 to Geneva, 29 April 1954, *FR1952–54*/XVI, pp. 615–617.

49   NSC 194th meeting, 29 April 1954, *FR1952–54*/XIII, pp. 1441–1444 and Eisenhower memorandum, 27 April 1954, *FR1952–54*/XIII, pp. 1422–1423.

50   Shuckburgh diary, 13 May 1954, *Descent*, p. 202.

51   Hagerty diary, 26 April 1954, DDEL/Hagerty/Box#1; Cameron, ed., *VNC*/I, pp. 229–230.

52   *Times*, 26 April 1954.

53   Paris telegram 304 to FO, 3 May 1954, FO371/112059/411.

54   Geneva telegram 28 to FO, 27 April 1954, FO371/112057/339G; Shuckburgh diary, 27 April 1954, *Descent*, pp. 179–180.

55   Zhou telegram to Mao, 1 May 1954, in Wang, 'Geneva Conference', p. 18.

56   Geneva telegram 86 to FO, 30 April 1954, FO371/112058/374G; Dulte 33 to DOS, 30 April 1954, *FR1952–54*/XVI, pp. 165–168.

57   Merchant-Caccia-Shuckburgh meeting, 27 April 1954, *FR1952–54*/XVI, p. 578.

58   Geneva telegram 86 to FO, 30 April 1954, FO371/112058/374G; Dulte 33 to DOS, 30 April 1954, *FR1952–54*/XVI, pp. 165–168.

59   CC(54)30th meeting, 28 April 1954, CAB128/27; CRO circular telegram to New Delhi, Karachi and Colombo, 28 April 1954, FO371/112057/338G.

60 *Times*, 30 April 1954.

61 Geneva telegrams 86 and 87 to FO, 30 April 1954, FO371/112058/374G.

62 Eden to Makins, 26 May 1954, AVO/AP/20/17/18B; Qiang Zhai, *China and the Vietnam Wars, 1950–1975* (Chapel Hill: University of North Carolina Press, 2000), p. 54.

63 Dulte 13 to DOS, 27 April 1954, *FR1952–54/XVI*, pp. 165–168.

64 Geneva telegram 82 to FO, 30 April 1954, FO371/112085/1018; Shuckburgh diary, 30 April 1954, *Descent*, pp. 183–185.

65 Ibid.

66 Ibid.

67 Zhou telegram to Mao, 1 May 1954, *CWIHP Digital Archive*; Zhou to Beijing, 3–4 May 1954, in Wang, 'Neutralizing Indochina', p. 18.

68 Clarissa Eden diary, 1 May 1954, *Memoir*, p. 160.

69 *Times*, 5 May 1954; Saigon telegram 10 to FO, 8 May 1954, FO371/112025/60.

70 Dulte 50 to DOS, 4 May 1954, *FR1952–54/XVI*, pp. 666–667.

71 Paris telegram 314 to FO, 5 May 1954, FO371/112060/430; Devilliers and Lacouture, *End of a War*, p. 125. Dinh would be replaced by Tran Van Do in June.

72 Geneva telegram 88 to FO, 30 April 1954, FO371/112058/378G; Dulte 34 to DOS, 30 April 1954, *FR1952–54/XVI*, pp. 638–639.

73 Ibid.

74 Shuckburgh diary, 30 April 1954, *Descent*, p. 185.

75 Ibid., p. 186, 1 May 1954.

76 Geneva telegram 110 to FO, 2 May 1954, FO371/112058/379G.

77 Ibid.

78 Ibid.

79 Clarissa Eden diary, 1 May 1954, *Memoir*, p. 160.

80 Shuckburgh diary, 2 May 1954, *Descent*, p. 187.

81 Dulte 42 to DOS, 2 May 1954, *FR1952–54/XVI*, pp. 648–649.

82 Geneva telegram 113 to FO, 2 May 1954, FO371/112058/379G.

83 CC(54)31st meeting, 3 May 1954, CAB128/27; Eden, *Full Circle*, p. 113.

84 ANZUS meeting, 2 May 1954, *FR1952–54/XVI*, pp. 654–665.

85 Waite, *First Indochina War*, pp. 106–108.

86 Ibid.

87 Eden, *Full Circle*, p. 114.

88 Dulles to Eden, 2 May 1954, *FR1952–54/XVI*, p. 665.

89 Shuckburgh diary, 2–3 May 1954, *Descent*, pp. 188–189; Geneva telegram 119 to FO, 3 May 1954, FO371/112058/397G; FO telegram 173 to Geneva, 3 May 1954, FO800/785/27.

Chapter 12

1 Hoopes, *Dulles*, pp. 357–358; Clarissa Eden diary, 3 May 1954, *Memoirs*, p. 160.

2 Eden diary, 3 May 1954, AVO/AP20/1/30.

3 Dulles-Eisenhower meeting, 5 May 1954, *FR1952–54/XIII*, pp. 1466–1470.

4 Waite, *First Indochina War*, pp. 121–122.

5 Shuckburgh diary, 3 May 1954, *Descent*, p. 189.

6 Geneva telegram 137 to FO, 4 May 1954, FO371/112059/416G.

7   Shuckburgh diary, 3 May 1954, *Descent*, p. 190; Reading to Lloyd, 5 May 1954, SELO/5/21.
8   Eden to Swinton, 4 May 1954, AVO/AP20/17/16A.
9   Makins to Kirkpatrick, 6 May 1954, FO371/112064/520; Cable, *Geneva*, p. 70.
10   Geneva telegram 154 to FO, 5 May 1954, FO371/112060/431G.
11   Geneva telegram 155 to FO, 5 May 1954, FO371/112060/432G; Geneva telegram 157 to FO, 5 May 1954, FO800/785/31; CC(54)32nd meeting, 5 May 1954, CAB128/27.
12   Dulte 51 to DOS, 5 May 1954, *FR1952-54*/XVI, p. 698–699.
13   Shuckburgh diary, 5 May 1954, *Descent*, p. 192.
14   *Times*, 5 May 1954; *New York Herald Tribune*, 6 May 1954.
15   Shuckburgh diary, 5 May 1954, *Descent*, p. 192; Geneva telegram 162 to FO, 6 May 1954, FO371/112060/432G.
16   Colombo conference communiqué, 2 May 1954, FO371/112085/1018.
17   New Delhi telegram 441 to CRO, 5 May 1954, FO371/112060/439.
18   Eden diary, 5 May 1954, AVO/AP20/1/30.
19   Geneva telegram 176 to FO for circulation, 7 May 1954, FO371/112061/470G.
20   Anita Inder Singh, *The Limits of British Influence: South Asia and the Anglo-American Relationship, 1947–1956* (London: Pinter, 1993), pp. 171–172.
21   NSC 195th meeting, 6 May 1954, *FR1952-54*/XIII, pp. 1481–1493.
22   Ibid.
23   Shuckburgh diary, 28 April 1954, *Descent*, pp. 181–182.
24   Shuckburgh diary, 4 May 1954, *Descent*, p. 190.
25   Geneva telegram 161 to FO, FO371/112060/446G, 6 May 1954.
26   Clarissa Eden diary, 5 May 1954, *Memoir*, p. 161.
27   Shuckburgh diary, 5 May 1954, *Descent*, pp. 192–193. Shuckburgh was not at the dinner.
28   Geneva telegram 144 to FO, 5 May 1954, AVO/AP20/17/35A.
29   Shuckburgh, unpublished diary, 5 May 1954.
30   Clarissa Eden diary, 28 April 1954, *Memoir*, p. 159.
31   Eisenhower-Dulles meeting, 5 May 1954, *FR1952-1954*/XIII, p. 1466–1470.
32   Ibid.
33   Dulles briefing of Congressional leaders, 5 May 1954, *FR1952-54*/XIII, pp. 1471–1477.
34   Geneva telegram 185 to FO, 7 May 1954, FO371/112061/467G.
35   Paris telegrams 323 and 324 to FO, 7 May 1954, FO371/112061/465.
36   Geneva telegram 145 to FO, 5 May 1954, FO371/112059/419G.
37   Geneva telegram 329 to FO, 17 May 1954, FO371/112067/561G.
38   Logevall, *Embers of War*, pp. 562, 569.
39   Morgan, *Valley of Death*, p. 517.
40   Shuckburgh diary, 27 April 1954, *Descent*, p. 179.
41   Zhai, *China and the Vietnam Wars*, p. 49.
42   Windrow, *Last Valley*, pp. 616, 624; Asselin, 'Revisionist Critique', p. 166.
43   Fall, *Hell in a Very Small Place*, pp. 415–416.
44   Eden to Bidault, 7 May 1954, FO371/112105/71; Shuckburgh diary, 7 May 1954, *Descent*, pp. 194–195.
45   FO telegram 287 to Geneva, 8 May 1954, FO800/785/36.
46   Eisenhower to Coty, 7 May 1954, *FR1952-54*/XIII, p. 1501.
47   Fall, *Hell in a Very Small Place*, p. 422; John Colvin, *Volcano under Snow: Vo Nguyen Giap* (London: Quartet, 1996), p. 124.

48   Shuckburgh diary, 7 May 1954, *Descent*, p. 195; Geneva telegram 186 to FO, 7 May 1954, FO371/112085/1018.
49   Paris telegrams 327 and 328, 8 May 1954, FO371/112039/56.
50   Randle, *Geneva*, pp. 248–249.
51   Bidault statement, 8 May 1954, Cameron, ed., *VNC*/I, pp. 257–260.
52   Dulles statement, 7 May 1954, ibid., p. 256.
53   Giap declaration in Fall, *Hell in a Very Small Place*, pp. 422–423.
54   Dulles-Radford-staff meeting, 9 May 1954, *FR1952–54*/XII, 9 May 1954, pp. 463–465.
55   Ibid.
56   NSC 196th meeting, 8 May 1954, *FR1952–54*/XIII, pp. 1505–1511.
57   Dulles-Bonnet meeting, 8 May 1954, *FR1952–54*/XIII, p. 1516.
58   Eden, *Full Circle*, p. 118.
59   Bidault statement, 8 May 1954, Cameron, ed., *VNC*/I, pp. 257–260.
60   Zhai, *China and the Vietnam Wars*, pp. 51–52.
61   Pham Van Dong statement, 10 May 1954, ibid., 261–264.
62   Cited in R. E. M. Irving, *The First Indochina War* (London: Croom Helm, 1975), p. 103.
63   Navarre, *Agonie De L'Indochine*, pp. 262–263.
64   Dalloz, *Indo-China War*, p. 160; Logevall, *Embers of War*, p. 537.
65   Shuckburgh diary, 12 May 1954, *Descent*, p. 201.
66   Salisbury to Eden, 9 May 1954, AVO/AP20/17/118.
67   Moran diary, 4 May 1954, *Churchill*, pp. 544–545.
68   Geneva telegram 259 to FO, 12 May 1954, FO371/112085/1018; Geneva telegram 279, 14 May 1954, FO371/112065/535; Eden, *Full Circle*, p. 118.
69   Eden to Clarissa Eden, 17 May 1954, AVO/AP20/45/48.
70   Asselin, 'Revisionist Critique', p. 175; Zhai, *China and the Vietnam Wars*, p. 53.
71   Geneva telegram 279 to FO, 14 May 1954, FO371/112065/535; Cable, *Geneva*, pp. 86–87.
72   Geneva telegrams 476, 551, 552 and 626 to FO, 27 May, 1 and 8 June 1954, FO371/112068/599 and FO371/112069/623 and 626, FO371/112070/656; Singh, *Limits of British Influence*, p. 172.
73   Eden, *Full Circle*, pp. 127–128.
74   Geneva telegram 227 to FO, 11 May 1954, FO112063/500; Cable, *Geneva*, p. 83.
75   Eden, *Full Circle*, pp. 118–119.
76   Geneva telegram 386 to FO, 20 May 1954, PREM11/646.
77   Secto 267 to DOS, 20 May 1954, *FR1952–54*/XVI, pp. 863–864.
78   Geneva telegram 395 to FO, 21 May 1954, FO371/112085/1018; Eden diary, 20 May 1954, AVO/AP/17/231.
79   Geneva telegram 447 to FO, 25 May 1954, FO371/112067/589.
80   Eden, *Full Circle*, p. 126; Geneva telegrams 498 and 499 to FO, 29 May 1954, FO371/112068/609.
81   Eden to CC(54)35th meeting, 24 May 1954, CAB128/27.
82   Clarissa Eden diary, 14 May 1954, *Memoir*, p. 162.
83   Smith to Eden, 10 May 1954, *FR1952–54*/XVI, pp. 761–762; FO telegrams 230 and 231, 11 May 1954, FO371/112063/505G.
84   *Times*, 12 May 1954.
85   Clarissa Eden diary, 12 May 1954, *Memoir*, p. 161.
86   Washington telegram 930 to FO, 15 May 1954, PREM11/666.
87   Geneva telegrams 293 and 294 to FO, 15 May 1954, FO371/112065/540G.

88   Ibid.
89   Geneva telegram 301 to FO, 15 May 1954, FO800/785/47.
90   Cable, *Geneva*, p. 78; Eden comments on Smith to CC(54)35th meeting, 24 May 1954, CAB128/27.
91   Eden to Makins, 13 June 1954, SHER/d.527; Eden, *Full Circle*, p. 143.
92   Geneva telegram 308, 16 May 1954, FO800/785/50.
93   Paris telegram 4287 to DOS, 10 May 1954, *FR1952–54*/XIII, pp. 1522–1525.
94   DOS telegram 4023 to Paris, 11 May 1954, *FR1952–54*/XIII, pp. 1534–1536.
95   Paris telegram 4383 to DOS, 14 May 1954, *FR1952–54*/XIII, pp. 1566–1568; Joseph Laniel, *Le drame Indochinois: de Dien-Bien-Phu au pari de Genève* (Paris: Plon, 1957).p. 110.
96   BBC monitoring report, 14 May 1954, FO371/112089/3.
97   Eden to Salisbury, 16 May 1954, AVO/AP20/17/118A.
98   *Times*, 17 May 1954.
99   Hansard, *HCD*, Vol. 527, col. 1692, 17 May 1954.
100 Tedul 99 to Geneva, 20 May 1954, *FR1952–54*/XVI, pp. 869–870.
101 Shuckburgh diary, 9 May 1954, *Descent*, p. 198.
102 Zhai, *China and the Vietnam Wars*, p. 54.
103 Shuckburgh diary, 10 May 1954, *Descent*, p. 198.
104 Dulles-Radford telcon, 10 May 1954, *FR1952*–54/XIII, p. 1526, note 3.
105 Eisenhower-Dulles meeting, 11 May 1954, *FR1952–54*/XIII, pp. 1532–1533.

Chapter 13

1   Eisenhower-Dulles meeting, 19 May 1954, and annex (draft resolution, 17 May 1954), *FR1952–54*/XIII, pp. 1583–1585.
2   JCS memorandum, 20 May 1954, *FR1952–54*/XIII, pp. 1590–1592; Radford to Wilson, 21 May 1954, enclosure to NARA/RG49/Box#4132C/790.5/5–2554; Gardner, *Approaching Vietnam*, p. 279.
3   NSC 198th meeting, 20 May 1954, *FR1952–54*/XIII, pp. 1588–1589.
4   DOS telegram 4194 to DOS, 21 May 1954, *FR1952–54*/XIII, pp. 1594–1595.
5   Paris telegram 353 to FO, 18 May 1954, PREM11/646.
6   FO telegram 319 to FO, 17 May 1954, FO371/112067/561G.
7   Makins to Eden, 21 May 1954, AVO/AP/17/18A.
8   Geneva telegram 125 to Washington, 22 May 1954, FO371/112085/1018; Rothwell, *Eden*, p. 140.
9   Eden to Lloyd, 21 May 1954, AVO/AP/17/15A.
10   Adams, *First-hand Report*, p. 105.
11   Geneva telegram 329 to FO, 17 May 1954, FO371/112067/561G.
12   Geneva telegram 339 to FO, 18 May 1954, PREM11/649.
13   Geneva telegram 333 to FO for Colombo powers distribution, 17 May 1954, FO371/112066/553G.
14   FO telegram 2353 to Washington, 23 May 1954, FO800/785/56.
15   Eden to Clarissa Eden, 22 May 1954, AVO/AP20/45/49. Clarissa had returned to England from Geneva on 15 May.
16   CC(54)35th meeting, 24 May 1954, CAB128/27.
17   Eden diary, 24 May 1954, AVO/AP/17/231.

18 CC(54)35th meeting, 24 May 1954, CAB195/12; Churchill to Clementine Churchill, 25 May 1954, in Mary Soames, ed., *Speaking for Themselves: The Personal Letters of Winston and Clementine Churchill* (London: Black Swan, 1999), p. 579.

19 Eden to Makins, 26 May 1954, AVO/AP/17/18B.

20 Geneva telegrams 431 and 432 to FO, 25 May 1954, PREM11/649.

21 *Times*, 29 May 1954.

22 Makins to Eden, 29 May 1954, SHE/d.527.

23 Paris telegrams 387 and 389, 29 May 1954, PREM11/646.

24 Eden diary, 30 May 1954, AVO/AP/17/231.

25 Geneva telegram 507 to FO, 29 May 1954, FO371/112068/611.

26 Dulte 136 to DOS, 31 May 1954 *FR1952–54*/XVI, pp. 992–993.

27 Smith to Dulles, 30 May 1954, DDEL/JFD/Subjects/Box#9. The more damning passages were omitted from the published version of the cable in *FR1952–54*/XVI, pp. 977–978.

28 Geneva telegram 527 to FO, 31 May 1954, FO371/112085/1018.

29 Eden to Clarissa Eden, 31 May 1954, AVO/AP20/45/50.

30 McDonald, *Man of the Times*, p. 136.

31 Saigon telegrams 205 and 208 to FO, 4 June 1954, FO371/112106/100 and 101.

32 Paris telegram 386 to FO, 29 May 1954, PREM11/649; JIC(54)51st meeting, 3 June 1954, CAB159/16.

33 Laniel, *Le Drame Indochinois*, pp. 106–107.

34 Geneva telegram 480 to FO, 28 May 1954, FO371/112068/607G.

35 Paris telegram 4607 to DOS, 30 May 1954, *FR1952–54*/XIII, pp. 1639–1641.

36 Geneva telegram 313 to FO, 16 May 1954, PREM11/666; Geneva telegram 547 to FO, 1 June 1954, FO371/112069/620.

37 Eden, *Full Circle*, pp. 127–128.

38 Geneva telegram 313 to FO, 16 May 1954, FO800/841/43.

39 Eisenhower to Churchill, 26 April 1954, *CEC*, p. 140.

40 Geneva telegram 540 to FO, 1 June 1954, PREM11/666.

41 Report of the Five-power Military Conference (hereafter RFPMC), 11 June 1954, *FR1952–54*/XII, p. 554.

42 RFPMC, *FR1952–54*/XII, pp. 555–557.

43 Ibid., pp. 557–558; Duiker, *US Containment Policy*, p. 174.

44 RFPMC, *FR1952–54*/XII, p. 562; BJSM telegram JH2 to MOD, 4 June 1954, FO371/112069/646G.

45 BJSM telegram JH2 to MOD, 4 June 1954, FO371/112069/646G.

46 RFPMC, *FR1952–54*/XII, p. 557.

47 Prados, *Sky Would Fall*, pp. 188–190.

48 Jian, *Mao's China*, pp. 139–140.

49 BJSM telegram JH2 to MOD, 4 June 1954, FO371/112069/646G.

50 Eisenhower-Dulles meeting, 25 May 1954, DDEL/JFD/WHMemos/Box#1.

51 Eisenhower-senior staff/advisors meeting, 28 May 1954, *FR1952–54*/XII, pp. 521–524.

52 London dispatch 3933 to DOS, 2 June 1954, NARA/RG59/Box#2771/611.41/6–254.

53 Eisenhower-staff meeting, and Cutler to Dulles, 2 June 1954, DDEL/AWF/Admin/Box#10/Cutler#4.

54 DP(54)3rd meeting, 16 June 1954, CAB134/808; CC(54)53, 26 July 1954, CAB128/27.

55 Graham Farmelo, *Churchill's Bomb: A Hidden History of Science, War and Politics* (London: Faber and Faber, 2013), p. 426, for a recent example.

56 Butler memorandum, 18 April 1957, BUT/G31/88.

57 C(54)249, 23 July 1954, CAB129/69; CC(54)53, 26 July 1954, CAB128/27; DP(54)1st and 2nd meetings, 4 and 19 May 1954, CAB134/808.

58 Ruane, *Churchill and the Bomb*, p. 281.

59 Merchant-Heeney meeting, 3 June 1954, USNA/RG59/Box#2771/611.41/6-354.

60 CC(54)39th meeting, 5 Jun 1954, CAB128/27 and CAB195/12.

61 Washington telegrams 1109, 1110 and 1112 to FO, 4 June 1954, PREM11/646.

62 Eden diary, 6 June 1954, AVO/AP/17/231.

63 CC(54)39th meeting, 5 Jun 1954, CAB128/27; Macmillan diary, 6 June 1954, *Diaries*/I, p. 316.

64 Dulles news conference, 8 June 1954, Cameron, ed., *VNC*/I, p. 272.

65 Waite, *First Indochina War*, pp. 107-108.

66 Dulles-Bonnet meeting, 16 June 1954, *FR1952-54*/XIII, pp. 1710-1713.

67 NSC 202nd meeting, 17 June 1954, *FR1952-54*/XIII, pp. 1713-1718.

68 Logevall, *Embers of War*, p. 575; Duiker, *US Containment Policy*, p. 177; George C. Herring, *America's Longest War: The United States and Vietnam, 1950-1975* (New York: McGraw Hill, 2002 edition).

69 Geneva telegram 731 to FO, 15 June 1954, FO800/785/65.

70 Eden to Clarissa, 1 and 2 June 1954, AVO/AP/20/51 and 55.

71 Clarissa Eden diary, 5 and 21 June 1954, *Memoir*, pp. 162-163; Eden to Hailes, 13 June 1954, HAIS/4/11.

72 Geneva telegrams 628 and 676 to FO, 9 and 12 June 1954, PREM11/666 and 646.

73 Donnelly to Eden, 8 May 1954, FO800/761/42.

74 Morgan, *Valley of Death*, p. 370; Clarissa Eden diary, 1 May 1954, *Memoir*, p. 160; Shuckburgh diary, 14 May 1954, *Descent*, p. 203.

75 Bator, *Vietnam*, p. 94.

76 Dulles news conference, 8 June 1954, *FR1952-54*/XVI, pp. 1067-1069.

77 Shuckburgh diary, 14 May and 11 June 1954, *Descent*, pp. 203 and 220; Salisbury to Churchill 12 June 1954, PREM11/646.

78 Geneva telegram 635 to FO, 9 June 1954, FO800/785/58.

79 Makins to Kirkpatrick, 8 June 1954, FO371/112090/33.

80 Dulles (San Francisco) to DOS, 10 June 1954, *FR1952-54*/XVI, p. 1117.

81 Eden statement, 10 June 1954, FO371/112071/688.

82 Dulte 179 to DOS, 14 June 1954, *FR1952-54*/XVI, pp. 1132-1134.

83 Eden to Clarissa Eden, 11 June 1954, AVO/AP20/45/56.

84 Pham Van Dong statement, 25 May 1954, Cameron, ed., *VNC*/I, p. 267; Geneva telegram 671 to FO, 12 June 1954, FO371/112071/683G.

85 Reilly dispatch 241 to Eden, 21 June 1954, FO371/112780/60.

86 Randle, *Geneva*, p. 276.

87 Geneva telegram 679 to FO, 12 June 1954, FO800/761/65.

88 Casey telegram to Canberra, 13 June 1954, FO371/125137/4G.

89 Dulles speech, 11 June 1954, Cameron, ed., *VNC*/I, pp. 273-274.

90 Eisenhower, *Mandate for Change*, p. 345.

91 Geneva telegram 677 to FO, 12 June 1954, FO800/785/61.

92 Geneva telegram 678 to FO, 12 June 1954, FO371/112071/684G.

93 Geneva telegram 679 to FO, 12 June 1954, FO800/761/65.

94   FO telegrams 1082 and 1083 to Geneva, 13 June 1954, FO800/785/62 and PREM11/666.
95   Eden to Butler, 13 June 1954, BUT/G27/49.

Chapter 14

1   Eden to Makins, 13 June 1954, SHE/d.527.
2   Eden, *Full Circle*, p. 128; Geneva telegram 728 to FO, FO371/112073/710.
3   Dulles-Knowland telcon, 12 June 1954, DDEL/JFDP/Telcons/Box#2; Tedul 196 to Geneva, 14 June 1954, *FR1952–54*/XVI, pp. 1146–1147.
4   Geneva telegrams 726 and 727 to FO, 15 June 1954, FO371/112073/709 and 715.
5   Geneva telegrams 747 and 751 to FO, 16 June 1954, FO371/112073/719G.
6   Eden diary, 16 June 1954, AVO/AP20/17/231.
7   Zhou telegram to Mao, 30 May 1954, and PRC record of PRC-USSR-DRV meeting, Geneva, 15 June 1954, *CWIHP Digital Archive*; Wang, 'Neutralizing Indochina', pp. 13, 22, 25.
8   Casey diary, 16 June 1954, FO371/125137/4G.
9   Eden to Makins, 13 June 1954, SHE/d.527.
10   Eden diary, 17 June 1954, AVO/AP20/17/231; Geneva telegrams 769 and 770 to FO, 17 June 1954, FO371/112073/727G and 728G.
11   FO telegram 1148 to Geneva, 16 June 1954, FO800/785/67.
12   Eden, *Full Circle*, pp. 129–130.
13   Geneva telegrams 769, 770 and 774 to FO, 17 June 1954, FO371/112073/728 and 729; Wang, 'Neutralizing Indochina', p. 25.
14   Casey diary, 17 June 1954, FO371/125137/4G; Menon to Eden, 21 June 1954, FO371/112081/934.
15   Geneva telegram 807, 19 June 1954, FO371/112074/740.
16   Zhou telegram to Mao, 22 June 1954, *CWIHIP Digital Archive*; Cable, *Geneva*, p. 100.
17   Jian, *Mao's China*, p. 141.
18   Mendès-France statement, 17 June 1954, Cameron, ed., *VNC*/I, pp. 275–277.
19   Eden diary, 18 June 1954, AVO/AP20/17/231.
20   Eden, *Full Circle*, p. 130.
21   Logevall, *Embers of War*, pp. 580–581.
22   Zhou telegram to Mao, 19 June 1954, *CWIHP Digital Archive*; Wang, 'Neutralizing Indochina', p. 26.
23   Graves dispatch 89 to Eden, 12 July 1954, FO371/112026/91; Bao Dai, *Dragon d'Annam* (Paris: Plon, 1980), p. 329. In general on the US-Diem relationship see Edward Miller, *Misalliance: Ngo Dinh Diem, the United States and the Fate of South Vietnam* (Cambridge, MA: Harvard University Press, 2013), and Jessica M. Chapman, *Cauldron of Resistance: Ngo Dinh Diem, the United States and 1950s Southern Vietnam* (Ithaca, NY: Cornell University Press, 2013).
24   Australian delegation Geneva to DEA Canberra, 18 June 1954, FO371/112075/766G; Anderson, *Trapped by Success*, p. 56.
25   Asselin, 'Revisionist Critique', pp. 168–171.
26   Eden-Mendès-France meeting, 20 June 1954, FO800/785/70; Paris telegram 434 to FO, FO371/112074/744G.
27   Paris telegram 4944 to DOS, 20 June 1954, *FR1952–1954*/XIII, pp. 1725–1727.

28 FO telegram 375 to Saigon, 29 June 1954, FO371/112075/785; Roberts minute, 28 June 1954, FO371/112076/800.

29 Geneva telegram 837 to FO, 22 June 1954, FO371/112074/754G.

30 Werth, *France*, p. 679.

31 Mendès-France-Zhou Enlai meeting, 23 June 1954, PRC record, *CWIHP Digital Archive*; Chen Jian, 'China and the Indochina Settlement at the Geneva Conference of 1954', in Lawrence and Logevall, eds, *First Vietnam War*, p. 253.

32 Jean Lacouture, *Pierre Mendes France* (New York: Holmes and Meir, 1984, trans. George Holloch), p. 222.

33 FO telegram 375 to Saigon, 29 June 1954 (text of French aide-memoire), FO371/112075/785; Devilliers and Lacouture, *End of a War*, pp. 255–258.

34 *Le Monde*, 29 June 1954.

35 Dulte 195 to DOS, 18 June 1954, *FR1952-54*/XVI, pp. 1176–1178; Waite, *First Indochina War*, pp. 147, 154–155.

36 Bidault, *Resistance*, p. 204.

37 Eisenhower to Churchill, 18 June 1954, *CEC*, p. 146.

38 Churchill to Eisenhower, 21 June 1954, ibid., p. 147.

39 CC(54)43rd meeting, 22 June 1954, CAB128/27; Eden, *Full Circle*, p. 132.

40 Allen minute, 24 June 1954, approved by Eden, n.d., FO371/111867/155.

41 *HCD*, Vol. 429, cols 428–442, 23 June 1954.

42 C(54)207, 22 June 1954, CAB129/69.

43 Washington telegram 1269 to FO, 24 June 1954, FO371/112075/771; *New York Times*, 24 June 1954.

44 Macmillan, 25 June 1954, *Diaries*/I, p. 319.

45 Eden, *Full Circle*, p. 133.

46 Washington telegram 1269 to FO, 24 June 1954, FO371/112075/771; Eden, *Full Circle*, p. 133.

47 Moran diary, 24 June 1954, *Churchill*, pp. 559–560.

48 Moran diary, 26 June 1954, *Churchill*, p. 562.

49 London telegram 5841 to DOS, 18 June 1954, DDEL/AWF/Dulles-Herter/Box#2.

50 Ismay cited in Sulzberger diary, 8 December 1953, in Sulzberger, *Candles*, p. 779.

51 Colville diary, 25 June 1954, *Fringes*, p. 692.

52 Ruane, *Churchill and the Bomb*, pp. 266–270.

53 Colville diary, 26 June 1954, *Fringes*, p. 692.

54 Macmillan diary, 25 June 1954, MAC/dep.c.16.

55 Moran diary, 27 June 1954, *Churchill*, p. 566.

56 NSC 204th meeting, 24 June 1954, *FR1952-54*/II, pp. 694–695.

57 US-UK meetings (CEV/MC-2 and MC-3), 25 June 1954, *FR1952-54*/VI, pp. 1077–1084.

58 Eden, *Full Circle*, p. 133.

59 Hagerty, 25 June 1954, in Ferrell, ed., *Diary*, p. 77.

60 US-UK meeting (CEV/MC-4), 27 June 1954, *FR1952-54*/VI, p. 1090.

61 Casey telegrams to Canberra, 13 and 18 June 1954, FO371/115137/4G, original emphasis.

62 Smith to Dulles, 23 June 1954, *FR1952-54*/XIII, pp. 1733–1734.

63 Herring, *Longest War*, pp. 47–48.

64 US-UK meeting (CEV/MC-4), 27 June 1954, *FR1952-54*/VI, p. 1086–1094; Washington telegram 298 to FO, 27 June 1954, FO371/112075/792.

65 Warner, 'Settlement of the Indochina War', p. 255.

66 Eden to Clarissa Eden, 26 June 1954, original emphasis, AVO/AP20/45/59.

67 Chauvel-Johnson meeting, 18 June 1954, *FR1952-54*/XVI, p. 1178.

68 DOS telegram 4570 to Paris, 14 June 1954, *FR1952-54*/XIII, pp. 1689–1690.

69 *FR1952-54*/XII, pp. 574–576; Washington telegram 1300 to FO, 27 June 1954, PREM11/646.

70 C(54)225, 7 July 1954, CAB129/69; US-UK talks, Washington, 27 June 1954, FO371/111869/212G.

71 Washington telegrams 1303 and 1326 to FO, 27 and 29 June 1954, FO371/112075/786.

72 Makins dispatch 388 to Eden, 3 August 1954, FO371/112084/1012.

73 DOS telegram 4853 to Paris, 28 June 1954, *FR1952-54*/XVI, pp. 1256–1257.

74 Dulles-Eden meeting, 29 June 1954, FO371/112075/786; DOS telegram 52 to Paris, 3 July 1954, *FR1952-54*/XIII, pp. 1780–1782.

75 Allen to Jebb, 1 July 1954, PRO, FO 371/112076/807.

76 US-UK communiqué, 28 June 1954, *PPP 1954 online* (doc. 154); FO telegram 375 to Saigon, 29 June 1954, text of French aide-memoire.

77 Mendès-France cited in Roberts minute, 28 June 1954, FO371/112076/800.

78 Dillon to Dulles, 30 June 143, JFD/MUDD/Box#80; Paris telegrams 247 Saving and 461 to FO, 29 and 30 June 1954, FO371/112075/794 and 798.

79 Eden to Dulles, 2 July 1954, JFD/MUDD/Box#80.

80 Allen to Jebb, 1 July 1954, FO371/112076/807.

81 Heath to Bonsal, citing Dulles, 4 July 1954, *FR1952-54*/XVI, p. 1282 and Tosec 565 to Geneva, 18 July 1954, *FR1952-54*/XVI, pp. 1429–1430.

82 Eden to Clarissa Eden, 28 June 1954, AVO/AP20/45/60.

83 CC(54)49th meeting, 9 July 1954, CAB195/12.

84 Stelle to Bowie, 24 June 1954, *FR1952-54*/XIII, pp. 1741–1742; Duiker, *US Containment* Policy, pp. 184–185; Gardner, *Approaching Vietnam*, p. 285.

85 Heath to Bonsal, 4 July 1954, *FR1952-54*/XVI, pp. 1280–1282.

86 Dulles draft memorandum to Eisenhower, 1 July 1954, *FR1952-54*/XIII, pp. 1774–1776; Hagerty, 6 July 1954, in Ferrell, ed., *Diary*, p. 84.

87 NSC 205th meeting, 1 July 1954, *FR1952-54*/VI, pp. 1133–1137.

88 Donald Lancaster, *The Emancipation of French Indochina* (London: Oxford University Press, 1961), p. 327.

89 Randle, *Geneva*, p. 314.

90 Cable, *Geneva*, p. 107.

91 Saigon telegram 48 to DOS, 4 July 1953, *FR1952-54*/XIII, pp. 1782–1784.

92 Churchill to Eisenhower, 8 July 1954, *CEC*, pp. 154–155.

93 Eisenhower to Churchill, ibid., pp. 156–157.

94 Churchill to Eisenhower, and Eisenhower reply, 8 July 1954, ibid., pp. 154–157.

95 Churchill to Eisenhower, 9 July 1954, ibid., pp. 157–160.

96 CRO telegram 1073 to New Delhi, 23 June 1954, FO371/112081/934.

97 CRO Rangoon telegram 318 to FO, 29 June 1954, PRO, FO 371/112075/788; CRO circular telegram Y268, 30 June 1954, PREM11/646.

98 *Panchsheel* (Five Principles), 28 June 1954, Indian Ministry of External Affairs online archive; Gilles Boquérat, 'India's Commitment to Peaceful Coexistence and the Settlement of the Indochina War', *Cold War History*, Vol. 5, No. 2 (2005), p. 219.

99 Humphrey Trevelyan, *Worlds Apart: China, 1953-55, USSR 1962-65* (London: Macmillan, 1971), pp. 73–74.

Chapter 15

1   *HCD*, Vol. 529, col. 2153, 7 July 1954.
2   C(54)227, 8 July 1954, CAB129/69.
3   Paterson minute, 8 July 1954, FO371/112077/845; Geneva telegrams 886 and 900 to FO, 9 and 12 July 1954, FO381/112085/1018.
4   Jebb dispatch 263 to Eden, 29 June 1954, PREM11/900.
5   PRC-DRV communiqué, 5 July 1954, Cameron, ed., *VNC*/I, p. 283.
6   Zhou presentations, Liuzhou conference, 3–5 July 1954, *CWIHP Digital Archive*.
7   Jian, 'China and the Indochina Settlement', pp. 254–258.
8   Logevall, *Embers of War*, pp. 597–598.
9   R. B. Smith, *An International History of the Vietnam War: Volume I – Revolutions versus Containment 1955–61* (Basingstoke: Macmillan, 1987 edition), pp. 24, 59–60.
10 Beijing telegram 453 to FO, 8 July 1954, FO371/112076/825.
11 DOS telegram 101 to London (Dulles to Eden), 7 July 1954, *FR1952–54*/XIII, p. 1788.
12 *Times*, 9 July 1954.
13 Eden, *Full Circle*, pp. 138–139.
14 Jebb to Eden, 5 July 1954, FO371/112081/943.
15 Hagerty, 6 July 1954, in Ferrell, ed., *Diary*, pp. 83–84.
16 Washington telegram 1412 to FO, 7 July 1954, FO371/112077/836.
17 CC(54)49th meeting, 9 July 1954, CAB128/27 and CAB195/12.
18 *HCD*, Vol. 530, cols 34–49, 12 July 1954.
19 *Times*, 12 July 1954.
20 Eden, *Full Circle*, p. 138.
21 Waite, *Indochina War*, pp. 175–176.
22 Paris telegram 118 to DOS, 9 July 1954, *FR1952–54*/XIII, pp. 1801–1803; Zhou-Dong meeting, 12 July 1954, *CWIHP Digital Archive*.
23 London telegram 201 to DOS, 12 July 1954, NARA/RG59/Box#2816/611.51/7-1254.
24 Geneva telegram 893 to FO, 12 July 1954, FO800/762/75; Eden, *Full Circle*, p. 138.
25 Geneva telegram 901 to FO, 12 July 1954, FO800/790/14.
26 Zhou-Mendès-France meeting, 13 July 1954, PRC record, *CWIHP Digital Archive*.
27 Clarissa Eden diary. 13 July 1954, *Memoir*, p. 166.
28 Paris telegrams 488, 490 and 491 to FO, 13–14 July 1954, FO371/112085/1018; US record, 13 July 1954, *FR1952–54*/XVI, pp. 1348–1355.
29 US record of tripartite meeting, US Embassy, Paris, 14 July 1954, DDEL/AWF/JFD-HERTER/Box#3; Geneva telegrams 496 to 499 to FO, 14 July 1954, FO371/112077/857G–859G.
30 George C. Herring "'A Good Stout Effort": John Foster Dulles and the Indochina Crisis, 1954–1955', in Richard Immerman, ed., *John Foster Dulles and the Diplomacy of the Cold War*, p. 225.
31 Dulles to NSC 206th meeting, 15 July 1954, *FR1952–54*/XIII, pp. 1834–1840.
32 Hagerty, 11 July 1954, in Ferrell, ed., *Diary*, p. 88; Herring, 'Good Stout Effort', p. 224.
33 Tosec 544 to Geneva (Dulles to Mendès-France), 15 July 1954, *FR1952–54*/XIII, pp. 1381–1382; Statler, *Replacing France*, pp. 103–105; Lacouture, *Mendes France*, p. 227.
34 Hagerty diary, 14 July 1954, DDEL/Hagerty/Box#1.
35 Tripartite communiqué, 14 July 1954, Cameron, ed., *VNC*/I. pp. 283–284; Paris telegram 495 to FO, 14 July 1954, FO371/112077/857G; Sir Patrick Reilly, interview with Kevin Ruane, 14 January 1990.

36   *Manchester Guardian,* 14 July 1954.
37   SEAD memorandum, 16 July 1954, FO371/112079/883; Geneva telegram 952 to FO, 17 July 1954, FO371/11208195/1018.
38   Allen to Paterson, 18 July 1954, FO371/112080/907.
39   Zhou-Eden meeting, 17 July 1954, conflation of PRC record in *CWIHP Digital Archive* and UK record at FO371/112080/907.
40   Geneva telegram 959 to FO, 17 July 1954, FO 371/112079/885; Antony Beevor, 'Eisenhower's Pit Bull', *Wall Street Journal,* 23 October 2010.
41   Caccia-Zhang meeting, 19 July 1954, PRC record, *CWIHP Digital Archive*; Geneva telegram 960 to FO, 18 July 1954, FO371/112079/886.
42   Geneva telegram 982 to FO, 19 July 1954, FO371/112080/902.
43   Scott to MacDonald, 12 July 1954, MACD/23/2/58.
44   Geneva telegram 899 to FO, 12 July 1954, PREM11/650; Warner, 'Settlement of the Indochina War', p. 255.
45   Geneva telegrams 962, 963 and 967 to FO, 18 July 1954, FO 371/112079/887, 888 and 890; Paterson minute, 19 July 1954, FO371/111872/254.
46   Geneva telegrams 987 and 988 to FO, 20 July 1954, PREM11/650; Geneva telegram 995 to FO, 20 July 1954, FO371/112085/1018.
47   Geneva telegrams 962 and 963 to FO, 18 July 1954, FO371/112079/887 and 888.
48   See responses in FO371/112079/887 and FO371/112081/940 and most notably HC New Delhi telegram 686 to CRO, 20 July 1954.
49   Eden, *Full Circle*, p. 141.
50   Eden diary, 18 July 1954, AVO/AP20/17/231.
51   Geneva telegrams 966 and 967 to FO, 18 July 1954, FO371/112079/889 and 890.
52   Eden diary, 18 July 1954, AVO/AP20/17/231.
53   Victor Israelyan, *On the Battlefields of the Cold War: A Soviet Ambassador's Confession* (University Park: University of Pennsylvania Press, 2003), p. 9.
54   Geneva telegram 957 to FO, 17 July 1954, FO800/762/79. This seems to be a correct reading. See Ilya V. Gaiduk, 'Developing an Alliance: The Soviet Union and Vietnam, 1954–75', in Peter Lowe, ed., *The Vietnam War* (London: Palgrave, 1998), pp. 134–135.
55   Clarissa Eden, *Memoir,* p. 167.
56   Eden, *Full Circle*, p. 431; McDonald, *Man of the Times*, p. 136.
57   Geneva telegram 980 to FO, 19 July 1954, FO800/786/77.
58   Devilliers and Lacouture, *End of a War*, p. 309; Lacouture, *Mendes France*, p. 235.
59   Stanley Karnow, *Vietnam: A History* (London: Guild Publishing, 1985 edition), p. 204.
60   Logevall, *Embers of War,* pp. 609–610.
61   Geneva telegrams 996, 1000, 1007 and 1010, 20–21 July 1954, FO371/112080/912, 915, 919 and 920.
62   Tahourdin memorandum, summary of Geneva settlement, 26 July 1954, FO371/112084/990; Cameron, ed., *VNC/I*, pp. 286–318.
63   Dulles to Smith, 16 July 1954, *FR1952–54/*XVI, pp. 1389–1390; Chester Cooper, *The Lost Crusade: America in Vietnam* (New York: Dodd, Mead and Col, 1970), p. 97.
64   Geneva telegram 984 to FO, 19 July 1954, FO371/112080/904.
65   CC(54)52nd meeting, 20 July 1954, CAB195/12; FO telegram 1517 to Geneva, 20 July 1954, FO800/786/78.
66   Anthony Montague-Browne, interview with Kevin Ruane, 23 February 1990.
67   Geneva telegram 1007 to FO, 21 July 1954, FO371/112080/919; Eden, *Full Circle*, p. 142.

68 Final Declaration, 21 July 1954, Cameron, ed., *VNC*/I, pp. 305–307.
69 Eighth (final) plenary session, Geneva, 21 July 1954, Cameron, ed., *VNC*/I,
pp. 308–318.
70 Ibid., p. 316, emphasis added.
71 Geneva telegram 1009 to FO, 21 July 1954, FO371/112080/921.
72 Diem statement, 22 July 1954, Cameron, ed., *VNC*/I, p. 325; Ramesh Thakur,
Peacekeeping in Vietnam: Canada, India, Poland, and the International Commission
(Edmonton: University of Alberta Press, 1984), p. 167.
73 Cited in Broad, *Eden*, p. 214.
74 Eisenhower news conference, 21 July 1954, *PPP 1954 online* (doc. 168); Hagerty, 22
July 1954, in Ferrell, ed., *Diary,* p. 95.
75 *New York Times*, 24 July 1954.
76 Dulles news conference, 23 July 1954, Cameron, ed., *VNC*/I, pp. 325–327.
77 Trevelyan dispatch 284 to Eden, 31 August 1954, FO371/110216/9.
78 Zhai, *China and the Vietnam Wars*, p. 50; Jian, *Mao's China*, pp. 143–144.
79 USSR government statement, 23 July 1954, Cameron, ed., *VNC*/I, pp. 327–329.
80 Ho Chi Minh statement, 22 July 1954, Cameron, ed., *VNC*/I, pp. 322–325.
81 Pierre Asselin, 'Choosing Peace: Hanoi and the Geneva Agreement on Vietnam,
1954–1955', *Journal of Cold War Studies*, Vol. 9, No. 2 (2007), pp. 102–103.
82 *Times,* 22 July 1954; Lacouture, *Mendes France*, p. 238.
83 Paris telegram 281 to FO, 23 July 1954, FO371/112082/952.
84 *HCD,* Vol. 530, cols 1570–1574, 22 July 1954.
85 During the conference, *Punch* had published a cartoon of Eden wearing Neville
Chamberlain's swallow-tail coat and carrying the legendary umbrella of appeasement,
but this snipe was out of keeping with the wider and positive reaction in Britain.
Broad, *Eden,* p. 214.
86 Macmillan, 20 July 1954, *Diaries*/I, p. 335.
87 HC New Delhi telegram 691 to CRO, 21 July 1954, and HC Karachi telegram 997
to CRO, PREM11/646; HC Wellington telegram 243 to CRO, 22 July 1954, HC
Colombo telegram 271 to CRO, 23 July 1954, FO371/112081/923, 941.
88 Djakarta telegram 2004 to FO, 23 July 1954, FO371/112081/948.
89 *Times,* editorial, 21 July 1954.
90 FO telegram 1550 to Geneva (HM to Eden), 21 July 1954, FO800/762/83.
91 CC(54)52nd meeting, 23 July 1954, CAB128/27 and CAB195/12.

Chapter 16

1 US-UK report, 17 July 1954, FO371/111871/250.
2 State telegram 589 to London, 28 July 1954, *FR1952–54*/XII, pp. 680–681;
Washington telegram 1645, 29 July 1954, FO371/111874/283G.
3 NSC 210th meeting, 12th August 1954, *FR1952–54*/XII, pp. 724–732; Washington
telegram 1815, 21 August 1954, FO371/111880/445; Washington telegram 1883 to
FO, 26 August 1954, FO371/111874/283G.
4 DOS-JCS meeting, 23 July 1954, and VP-CIA-DOS-DOD meeting, 24 July 1954,
FR1952–54/XII, pp. 653–657, 665–671; Washington telegram 1645, 29 July 1954,
FO371/111874/283G; Roger Dingman, 'John Foster Dulles and the Creation of the
Southeast Asia Treaty Organisation in 1954', *International History Review*, Vol. XI,
No. 3 (1989), pp. 461–463.

5   Dulles-Eisenhower meeting, 17 August 1954, DDEL/JFD/WHMS/box#1.

6   *HCD*, Vol. 529, col. 433, 23 June 1954.

7   COS(54)83rd meeting, 16 July 1954, DEFE4/71; Paterson minute, 20 July 1954,
     FO371/111872/254; Powell to Brittain, 26 August 1954, enclosing MOD assessment,
     FO 371/111883/501G.

8   FO telegram 3825 to Washington, 31 July 1954, FO371/111874/283G.

9   Eden, *Full Circle*, pp. 143–144; Washington telegrams 1658 and 1674, 2 and 4 August
     1954, FO371/111874/294 and 315.

10   Dulles/Staff meeting, 30 July 1954 and Galloway memorandum, 3 August 1954,
     FR1952–54/XII, pp. 684–686; Ruane, 'SEATO, MEDO', pp. 176–180.

11   Dulles-Merchant telcon, 3 August 1954, DDEL/DullesMS/Telcons/Box#2; Dulles to
     Eisenhower, 1 September 1954, DDEL/JFD/WHMS/Box#1.

12   Eisenhower-Dulles telcon, 21 July 1954, DDEL/AWF/DDE Diary Series/Box#7.

13   FO telegram 274 to Djakarta, 30 July 1954, and copied to other posts,
     FO371/111874/293.

14   *Times*, 5 August 1954.

15   Eden, *Full Circle*, p. 144.

16   HC New Delhi telegram 739 to CRO, 31 July 1954, FO371/111075/303.

17   Djakarta telegram 211 to FO, 2 August 1954, FO371/111075/295; HC Colombo
     telegram 289 to CRO, 3 August 1954, HC Karachi telegram 1084 to CRO, and
     Burmese Embassy Note to FO, 4 August 1954, FO371/111876/317, 323 and 331.

18   Eden, *Full Circle*, p. 144.

19   HC New Delhi telegram 898 to CRO, 10 September 1954, FO371/111886/625.

20   Paterson minute, 24 September 1954, and HC New Delhi telegram 988 to CRO, 30
     September 1954, FO371/111889/676 and 689.

21   Dulles/Staff meeting, 30 July 1954, *FR1952–54*/XII, pp. 685–686.

22   FO dispatch 738 to Washington, 10 August 1954, FO 371/111877/351; Kirkpatrick
     minute, 7 August 1954, FO371/111878/355.

23   FO telegram 4266 to Washington, 25 August 1954, FO371/111881/456; C(54)275. 26
     August 1954, CAB129/70.

24   Washington telegram 1809 and 1819, 20 and 21 August 1954, FO371/111881/446 and
     447; Eden minute, 8 September 1954, FO371/111886/612.

25   Dulles-Merchant telcon, 30 August 1954, DDEL/DullesMS/Telcons/box#2.

26   Jebb dispatch 372 to Eden, 4 September 1954, FO371/109440/5.

27   Pierre Mendès-France *OEuvres complètes, Vol. III: Gouverner c'est choisir* (Paris:
     Éditions Gallimard, 1986), pp. 113–114, 137–142.

28   Eden to Churchill, 29 September 1954, PREM11/900; Gaiduk, *Confronting Vietnam*,
     pp. 23, 50.

29   FO telegram 4395 to Washington, 1 September 1954, FO371/111884/538.

30   Dulles-Merchant telcon, 30 August 1954, DDEL/DullesMS/Telcons/Box#2.

31   Washington telegram 1815 to FO, 21 August 1954, FO371/111880/445; Scott to
     Makins, 2 September 1954, SHE/d.525.

32   See Ruane, *European Defence Community*, pp. 130–172 passim.

33   Manila telegram 28 to FO, 2 September 1954, FO371/111884/547.

34   Paterson minute, 3 September 1954, and Eden annotation, n.d., FO371/111884/547.

35   *Times*, 8 September 1954; MacArthur to Smith, 28 August, *FR1952–54*/XII, pp.
     706–708.

36   Manila telegram 65 to FO, 6 September 1954, FO371/111885/585; Reading to Eden,
     15 September 1954, FO371/111865/102G.

37 *Times*, 24 July 1954.
38 FO telegram 3649 to Washington, 24 July 1954, FO371/112081/928; FO telegram 3752 to Washington, 28 July 1954, FO371/111873/270.
39 FO telegram 4216 to Washington, 21 August 1954, FO371/112122/1; Rumbold minute, 2 September 1954, FO371/111882/492.
40 Washington telegram 1896 to FO, 28 August 1954, FO371/111882/49.
41 Dulles to Eden, 30 August 1954, *FR1952–54*/XII, pp. 822–823.
42 Eden to Dulles, 1 September 1954, *FR1952–54*/XII, p. 823, note 3.
43 Manila conference, third plenary session, 7 September 1954, *FR1952–54*/XII, pp. 862–884.
44 Eden minute, 8 September 1954, FO371/111885/598.
45 Manila Treaty, 8 September 1954, Yale Law School/Avalon Project online.
46 COS(54)98th meeting, 15 September 1954, FO371/111886/614.
47 Manila Treaty, 8 September 1954, Yale Law School/Avalon Project online.
48 Ibid.
49 Ibid.
50 Manila telegram 36 to FO, 2 September 1954, and FO telegram 44 to Manila, 2 September 1954, FO371/111884/551.
51 Manila telegram 91 to FO, 8 September 1954, FO371/111885/600.
52 CC(54)61st meeting, 21 September 1954, CAB128/27.
53 HCD, Vol. 532, cols 926–927, 8 November 1954.
54 Eden, *Full Circle*, p. 145.
55 Dulte 6 to DOS, 24 February 1955, *Foreign Relations of the United States 1955–57*, Vol XI (Washington: Government Printing Office, 1990, hereafter *FR1955–57*/XI), pp. 45–46.
56 Gardner, *Approaching Vietnam*, p. 347.
57 Ibid., p. 325.
58 *New York Times*, 1 January 1955.
59 Bator, *Vietnam*, p. 154; Cable, *Geneva*, p. 139.
60 Cable, *Geneva*, p. 139.
61 Cable minute, 20 August 1954, FO 371/111883/504.
62 Ibid.
63 Verbatim transcript of Scott interview with Anthony Seldon, 1980, SCO/ACC8181/18/Box#2.
64 Hagerty, 15 July 1954, in Ferrell, ed., *Diary*, p. 91.
65 Lowe, *Contending with Nationalism and Communism*, p. 84.
66 Makins to Eden, 21 June 1954, FO800/842/82, and Eden marginal comment.
67 Henry Kissinger, *Diplomacy* (London: Simon and Schuster, 1994). p. 637.
68 FO (Eden) telegram 274 to Djakarta, 30 July 1954, FO 371/111874/293.
69 Warner, 'From Geneva to Manila', p. 160.
70 Dulles/Staff meeting, 30 July 1954, *FR1952–54*/XII, pp. 685–686.
71 Cited in Lamb, *Eden Government*, p. 157.
72 Kissinger, *Diplomacy*, p. 637.
73 Radford to NSC 211th meeting, 18 August 1954, *FR1952–54*/XII, p. 750.
74 MacArthur memorandum, 14 February 1955, *FR1955–57*/XI, pp. 34–36.
75 *PP*/IV/A-3/p. 3, NARA online.
76 Dulles-Merchant telcon, 30 August 1954, DDEL/DullesMS/Telcons/Box#2; Dulles-Lodge telcon, 25 June 1954, DDEL/JFDP/Telcons/Box#2.

77   Washington telegram 1598, 26 July 1954, FO371/111873/270, Dulles-Makins meeting; NSC 210th meeting, 12 August 1954, *FR1952–54*/XII, pp. 724–732.
78   Eden to Churchill, 25 August 1954, AVO/AP20/17/86.
79   Dulles-Merchant telcon, 30 August 1954, DDEL/DullesMS/Telcons/Box#2.
80   Randle, *Geneva*, pp. 364–365.
81   Marilyn B. Young, *The Vietnam Wars, 1945–1990* (New York: Harper Perennial, 1991 edition), p. 47.
82   Dulles to NSC 207th meeting, 22 July 1954, *FR1952–54*/XII, p. 651.
83   Bator, *Vietnam*, p. 151.
84   Anderson, *Trapped by Success*, pp. 72–73.
85   Devilliers and Lacouture, *End of a War*, p. 313.
86   Moscow telegram 881 to FO, 6 September 1954, FO371/111885/585; Beijing telegrams 209 and 211 to FO, 25 February 1955, PREM11/1310.
87   Ex-Foreign Office figures Sir Nicholas Cheetham (31 January 1989) and Sir Frank Roberts (21 November 1989) both used the term 'man of Geneva' in interviews with Kevin Ruane.
88   Eden to Armstrong, 30 June 1965, Hamilton Fish Armstrong (HFA) papers, Princeton University, Box 26.
89   Anthony Eden, *Towards Peace in Indo-China* (Oxford: RIIA, 1966), p. xii.

Chapter 17

1   Graves dispatch 122 to Eden, 30 August 1954, FO371/112040/86.
2   Cameron, ed., *VNC*/I, pp. 268–271.
3   Geneva telegram 925 to FO, 15 July 1954, FO371/112040/76.
4   Kathryn C. Statler, 'After Geneva: The French Presence in Vietnam, 1954–1963', in Lawrence and Logevall, eds, *First Vietnam War*, pp. 263–276.
5   Dulles to ANZUS meeting, Geneva, 2 May 1954, *FR1952–54*/XVI, p. 655.
6   NIE 63–5–54, 3 August 1954, *FR1952–54*/XIII, pp. 1905–1914.
7   Dulles to NSC 207th meeting, 22 July 1954, *FR1952–54*/XIII, pp. 1869–1870.
8   Eisenhower-Dulles meeting, 17 August 1954, and Dulles to Mendès-France, 19 August 1954, *FR1952–54*/XIII, pp. 1953, 1957–1959.
9   Kirkpatrick to Eden, 27 August 1954, and FO telegram 4858 to Washington, 25 September 1954, FO371/112041/3 and 5.
10   Eden minute, 28 August 1954, FO371/112041/3.
11   Dulles to Wilson, 18 August 1954, *FR1952–54*/XIII, pp. 1954–1956.
12   Dulles-Anderson telcon, 19 November 1954, *FR1952–54*/XIII, pp. 2270–2271.
13   *PP*/IV/A-3/p. 6, NARA online.
14   Arthur Combs, 'The Path Not Taken: The British Alternative to U.S. Policy in Vietnam, 1954–1956', *Diplomatic History*, Vol. 19, No. 1 (1995), p. 40.
15   Graves to Allen, 2 October 1954, FO371/112027/162.
16   Dommen, *Indochinese Experience*, p. 269.
17   Ibid., pp. 262–283; *PP*/IV/A-3/p. 1, NARA online.
18   Dean to Scott, and FO telegram 2049 to Paris, 28 August 1954, FO371/112041/2 and 3; Allen to Graves, 12 October 1954, FO371/112027/162.
19   Saigon telegram 48 to DOS, 4 July 1954, *FR1952–54*/XIII, p. 1782–1784.
20   CIA report, 23 August 1954, *FR1952–54*/XIII, pp. 1977–1980.

21   DCI to NSC 215th meeting, 24 September 1954, *FR1952–54*/XIII, p. 2058.
22   James M. Carter, *Inventing Vietnam: The United States and State Building, 1954–1968* (New York: Cambridge University Press, 2008), p. 60.
23   *PP*/IV/A-3/p. ii, NARA online.
24   William J. Rust, *Eisenhower and Cambodia: Diplomacy, Covert Action and the Origins of the Second Indochina War* (Lexington: University Press of Kentucky, 2016), p. 63.
25   Allen minute, 23 September 1954, FO371/112041/5.
26   Eden minute, 26 September 1954, ibid.
27   Washington telegram 2075 to FO, 27 September 1954, FO371/112040/93.
28   US record of Dulles-Eden meeting, London, 26 September 1954, USNA/RG59/Box#2771/611.41/9–2754; DOS-DOD-FOA meeting, 27 September 1954, *FR1952–54*/XIII, p. 2079.
29   DOS press release 521, 29 September 1954, *FR1952–54*/XIII, pp. 2097–2098.
30   Wilson to Dulles, 12 August 1954 and 28 September 1954, *FR1952–54*/XIII, pp. 1938–1939, 2088–2091.
31   Dulte 11 to DOS, 30 September 1954, *FR1952–54*/XIII, p. 2103.
32   Dulles-Mendès-France meeting, 8 October 1954, *FR1952–54*/XIII, p. 2115.
33   *Times*, 11 October 1954.
34   Logevall, *Embers of War*, pp. 617–619.
35   NSC 218th meeting, 22 October 1954, *FR1952–54*/XIII, pp. 2153–2158.
36   Eisenhower to Diem, 24 October 1954, *FR1952–54*/XIII, pp. 2166–2167.
37   NSC 219th meeting, 26 October 1954, *FR1952–54*/XIII, pp. 2183–2186.
38   JIC(54)75(Final), October 1954, CAB 158/18.
39   Graves to Tahourdin, 16 August 1954, FO371/112026/114.
40   Graves to Tahourdin, 30 October 1954, FO 371/112030/216.
41   Paterson minute and related SEAD comments, 11–12 November 1954, ibid.
42   Allen minute, 19 November 1954, FO371/112030/234.
43   Dulles/Staff meeting, 8 October 1954, *FR1952–54*/XIII, pp. 2122–2125.
44   NIE 63-4-54, 3 August 1954, *FR1952–54*/XIII, pp. 1905–1914.
45   Etherington-Smith to Tahourdin, 1 November 1954, FO371/112030/217.
46   *PP*/IV/A-3/p. 38, NARA online.
47   Kirkpatrick annotation, n.d., to Scott letter to Allen, 29 November 1954, FO371/112031/250.
48   Allen to Scott, 26 November 1954, FO371/112031/250.
49   Cable paper, 3 December 1954, FO371/112044/44.
50   Paterson minute, 4 December 1954, ibid.
51   FO telegram 5668 to Washington, 17 November 1954, and CRO telegram 1279 to Ottawa, 15 November 1954, FO371/111893/748 and 751; Makins to Dulles, 19 November 1954, FO371/111894/768, FO telegram 5730 to Washington, 23 November 1954, DO35/5997.
52   Eden minute, 29 November 1954, FO371/112100/8.
53   FO telegram 5899 to Washington, 1 December 1954, DO35/5997.
54   Allen to Stephenson, 9 December 1954, FO 371/112044/4.
55   Washington telegram 2993 to FO, 2 December 1954, and FO telegram 2853 to Paris, 7 December 1954, FO371/112100/2 and 9.
56   NIE 63-7-54, 23 November 1954, *FR1952–54*/XIII, pp. 2286–2301.
57   Dulles telegram 1964 to Paris, 28 November 1954, *FR1952–54*/XIII, pp. 2314–2315.
58   FO briefs, 15 December 1954, FO371/112100/18 and 24, and FO371/117115/13.

59 UK-US talks, Paris, 16 December 1954, FO371/112100/24; SECTO-11 to DOS, 17 December 1954, *FR1952–54*/XIII, pp. 2385–2387; Editorial note, *Foreign Relations of the United States 1955–57*, Vol. I (Washington: Government Printing Office, 1985, hereafter *FR1955–57*/I), pp. 323–324.

60 Hagerty, 14 December 1954, in Ferrell, ed., *Diary*, p. 139.

61 UK-US talks, Paris, 16 December 1954, FO371/112100/24; SECTO-11 to DOS, 17 December 1954, *FR1952–54*/XIII, pp. 2385–2387.

62 Tripartite talks, Paris, 18 December 1954, FO371/112100/24; Paris telegram 837 to FO, 18 December 1954, PREM11/1310.

63 *Report of Senator Mike Mansfield on a Study Mission to Vietnam, Cambodia, Laos, October 15, 1954* (Washington: Government Printing Office, 1954).

64 Seth Jacobs, *Cold War Mandarin: Ngo Dinh Diem and the Origins of America's War in Vietnam, 1950–1963* (Lanham: Rowman and Littlefield, 2006), pp. 63–64.

65 Tripartite talks, Paris, 18 December 1954, FO371/112100/24; Paris telegram 2601 to DOS, 19 December 1954, *FR1952–54*/XIII, pp. 2400–2405.

66 Allen to Scott, 20 December 1954, FO 371/112100/23.

67 Eden to Nehru, 23 December 1954, PREM11/1310.

68 Tomlinson minute, 20 December 1954, Cable minute, 31 December 1954, FO371/117115/13.

69 C(55)4, Eden memorandum, 10 January 1955, CAB129/73.

70 Allen memorandum, 17 January 1955, and Eden annotation, 18 January 1955, FO371/117176/10.

71 Allen memorandum, 10 February 1955, and FO brief for Eden, 14 February 1955, FO371/117115/13 and 38.

72 Cable minute, 18 February 1955; Combs, 'Path Not Taken', p. 49.

73 Eden annotation, n.d., on Paris telegram 20, 12 January 1955, FO371/117115/14.

74 Dulte 18 to DOS, 1 March 1955, *FR1955–57*/I, pp. 96–97.

75 Asselin, 'Choosing Peace', p. 96.

76 Paris telegram 4116 to DOS, 25 March 1955, *FR1955–57*/I, pp. 147–148; *PP*/IV/A-3/p. 7, NARA online.

77 DOS telegram 3507 to Paris, 3 April 1955 and NSC 244th meeting, 7 April 1955, *FR1955–57*/I, pp. 193–194 and 212–214.

78 Washington telegram 811 to FO, 8 April 1954, FO371/117117/98.

79 Eden to Eisenhower, 11 April 1955, AVO/AP20/18/19B.

80 Combs, 'Path Not Taken', p. 50.

81 Cable minute, 26 April 1955, Eden annotation, FO371/117176/47.

82 See David Anderson, 'J. Lawton Collins, John Foster Dulles and the Eisenhower Administrations "Point of No Return" in Vietnam', *Diplomatic History*, Vol. 12, No. 1 (1988), pp. 134–148.

83 Heath to Robertson, 17 December 1954, *FR1952–54*/XIII, pp. 2391–2 392.

84 DOS telegram 3829 to Paris, 27 April 1955, *FR1955–57*/I, pp. 297–298.

85 Anderson, 'Point of No Return', pp. 138–142. Also, Jessica Chapman, 'The Sect Crisis of 1955 and the American Commitment to Ngo Dinh Diem', *Journal of Vietnamese Studies*, Vol. 5, No. 1 (2010), pp. 37–85.

86 Herring, *Longest War*, p. 65.

87 DOS telegram 3837 to Paris, 27 April 1955, *FR1955–57*/I, p. 301; *PP*/IV/A-3/p. 32, NARA online.

88 DOS telegram 4831 to Saigon, 1 May 1955, *FR1955–57*/I, pp. 346; *New York Times*, 7 May 1955.

89   Chapman, 'Sect Crisis', p. 72.
90   SECTO-8 to DOS, 8 May 1955, *FR1955–57*/I, pp. 372–376.
91   UK record of tripartite meeting, Paris, 7 May 1955, DO35/5997.
92   *PP*/IV/A-3/p. v, NARA online.
93   Tripartite meeting, Paris, 10 May 1955, DO35/5997; SECTO-36 to DOS, 11 May 1955, *FR1955–57*/I, pp. 393–399.
94   Ibid.
95   Statler, *Replacing France*, pp. 142–144; Spector, *Advice and Support*, p. 251.
96   George McT. Kahin, *Intervention: How America Became Involved in Vietnam* (New York: Knopf, 1986 edition), p. 90; Eisenhower, *Mandate for Change*, p. 372.
97   Herring, *Longest War*, p. 67.
98   *Times*, 30 April 1955.
99   Tripartite meeting, Paris, 11 May 1955, DO35/5997.
100 Hanoi telegram 140 to FO, 7 June 1955, FO371/117142/21; FO telegram 1080 to Paris, 10 June 1955, PREM11/1310.
101 Washington telegram 1389 to FO, 13 June 1955, FO371/117142/28.
102 Eden minute, 17 June 1955, and FO telegram 2878 to Washington, 18 June 1955, PREM11/1310.
103 De Zuluetta to Graham, 27 June 1955, PREM11/1310.
104 Dulles news conference, 28 June 1955, Yale Law School/Avalon Project online.
105 Macmillan dispatch 77 to Saigon, 1 July 1955, PREM11/1310.
106 Washington telegram 1569 to FO, 7 July 1955, and Eden annotations, PREM11/1310.
107 Macmillan to Eden, 1 July 1955, PREM11/1310.
108 NSC-5519, 17 May 1955, *FR1955–57*/I, pp. 410–412; Dulles-Staff meeting, 8 June 1955, *FR1955–57*/I, pp. 439–441.
109 Saigon telegram 165 to DOS, 15 July 1955, *FR1955–57*/I, pp. 487–488; Henry Kamm, *Dragon Ascending: Vietnam and the Vietnamese* (New York: Arcade, 1996), p. 108.
110 Statement in Saigon telegram 394 to FO, 16 July 1954, PREM11/1310.
111 FO telegram 18 to Geneva, 18 July 1955, PREM11/1310.
112 FO telegram 67 to Geneva, 20 July 1955, PREM11/1310.
113 Saigon telegram 398 to FO, 20 July 1955, PREM11/1310.
114 Molotov note and enclosure, 21 July 1955, PREM11/1310.
115 CRO telegrams 1549 and 1599 to New Delhi, 20 and 24 July 1955, PREM11/1310; DOS telegram 293 to Saigon, 26 July 1955, *FR1955–57*/I, pp, 497–498.
116 Lowe, *Contending with Nationalism and Communism*, p. 131.
117 *Times*, 31 August 1955.
118 Allen memorandum, 5 September 1955, and related minutes, FO371/117145/143.
119 Washington telegram 2061, 30 August 1955, and Eden annotations, FO371/117145/132.
120 Statler, *Replacing France*, p. 170.
121 Macmillan to Scott, 12 December 1955, FO371/117177/26; Mari Olsen, *Soviet-Vietnam Relations and the Role of China, 1949–64: Changing Alliances* (London: Routledge, 2006), p. 58.
122 Herring, *Longest War*, p. 66.
123 *PP*/IV/A-3/p. v, NARA online.
124 Bator, *Vietnam*, p. 130.
125 Hughes, *Ordeal of Power*, p. 208.
126 Eden to Armstrong, 8 September 1965, HFA/Box#26.

Chapter 18

1   *King Henry VIII*, Act 4, Scene 2, in Proudfoot et al., eds, *Arden Complete Shakespeare*, p. 593; Thorpe, *Eden*, p. 606.
2   A. J. P. Taylor, *Time*, 24 January 1977.
3   Cable, *Geneva*, p. 3.
4   Hugh Thomas, *The Suez Affair* (London: Tinling, 1967 edition), p. 54.
5   See discussion in Matthew Jones, *The Official History of the UK Strategic Nuclear Deterrent: Volume I – from the V-Bomber Era to the Arrival of Polaris, 1945–1964* (London: Routledge, 2017), pp. 30–32; and Ruane, *Churchill and the Bomb*, pp. 259–263.
6   DP(54)1st, 2nd and 3rd meetings, 4 May, 19 May and 16 June 1954, CAB134/808; C(54)249, 23 July 1954, CAB129/69; CC(54)53, 26 July 1954, CAB128/27.
7   James Shepley, 'How Dulles Averted War: Three Times, New Disclosures Show, Brought US Back from the Brink', *Life*, Vol. 40, No. 3 (16 January 1956), pp. 70–80.
8   The most sustained version of the thesis is Melanie Billings-Yun, *Decision against War: Eisenhower and Dien Bien Phu* (New York: Columbia University Press, 1988). See also Ambrose, *Eisenhower the President*, pp. 177–178, 209; Mark Moyar, *Triumph Forsaken: The Vietnam War, 1954–1965* (Cambridge: Cambridge University Press, 2006), p. 28.
9   For example, Anderson, *Trapped by Success*, pp. 28, 35, 38; James R. Arnold, *The First Domino: Eisenhower, the Military and America's Intervention in Vietnam* (New York: Morrow, 1991), pp. 167–169; Duiker, *US Containment Policy*, p. 172; Logevall, *Embers of War*, p. 472; John Prados, *Vietnam: The History of an Unwinnable War, 1945–1975* (Lawrence: University of Kansas Press, 2009), p. 30; Statler, *Replacing France*, pp. 93–94.
10 Eisenhower to Hazlett, DDEL/AWF/Names/Box#18.
11 Anthony Eden, 'The Burden of Leadership', *Foreign Affairs*, Vol. 44, No. 2 (1966), p. 234.
12 Charmley, *Churchill's Grand Alliance*, p. 284.
13 Eden speech at UN General Assembly, Paris, 12 November 1951, FO800/758.
14 Secto 1 to DOS, 24 April 1954, *FR1952–54/XVI*, pp. 552–553.
15 Anthony Nutting, *No End of a Lesson: The Story of Suez* (London, 1967), p. 18.
16 Greenwood, *Britain and the Cold War*, p. 135; Rothwell, *Eden*, p. 152; Thorpe, *Eden*, p. 412; Douglas Hurd, *Choose Your Weapons – the British Foreign Secretary: 200 Years of Arguments, Successes and Failures* (London: Weidenfeld and Nicolson, 2010), p. 359.
17 Dutton, 'Eden', p. 232; Thorpe, *Eden*, p. 405.
18 On these issues see David Carlton, *Britain and the Suez Crisis* (Oxford: Blackwell, 1988); Keith Kyle, *Suez* (London: Weidenfeld and Nicolson, 1991); W. Scott Lucas, *Divided We Stand: Britain, the US and the Suez Crisis* (London: Hodder and Stoughton, 1996).
19 Eisenhower to Eden, 31 July 1956, in Peter G. Boyle, ed., *The Eden-Eisenhower Corrspondence,1953–1957* (Chapel Hill: University of North Carolina Press, 2005), p. 156.
20 Geoffrey Warner, 'The United States and the Suez Crisis', *International Affairs*, Vol. 67, No. 2 (1991), pp. 303–317; Simon C. Smith, 'The Anglo-American "Special

Relationship" and the Middle East, 1945–1973', *Asian Affairs*, Vol. XLV, No. 111 (2014), especially pp. 425–434.

21 Eden statement, 30 October 1956, *HCD*, Vol.558, col.1275.

22 CM(56)73 and 74, 24–25 October 1956, CAB128/30.

23 W. Scott Lucas, ed., *Britain and Suez: The Lion's Last Roar* (Manchester: Manchester University Press, 1996), pp. 89–101; Diane B. Kunz, *The Economic Diplomacy of the Suez Crisis* (Chapel Hill: University of North Carolina Press, 1991), pp. 2–4.

24 Carlton, *Suez Crisis*, pp. 69–80.

25 Ambrose, *Eisenhower the President*, pp. 371–373; Smith, '"Special Relationship" and the Middle East', pp. 431–432.

26 Eden press secretary William Clark, cited in *New York Times*, 25 November 1979; Lucas, *Britain and Suez*, pp. 103–104; Eden, *Full Circle*, pp. 555–556.

27 Kyle, *Suez*, p. 501.

28 Shuckburgh, *Descent*, p. 14.

29 *HCD*, Vol. 562, col. 1518, 20 December 1956.

30 Shuckburgh to Jebb, 13 November 1986, Lord Gladwyn Papers, Churchill College, Cambridge, GLAD/1/1/18.

31 James, *Eden*, p. 544.

32 Eden-Dixon meeting, 17 April 1958, Thorpe, *Eden*, p. 557.

33 Nutting, 'Eden', p. 334.

34 Eden to Caccia, 9 September 1966, AVO/AP/14/34A.

35 Henry Brandon, *Special Relationships: A Foreign Correspondent's Memoirs from Roosevelt to Reagan* (New York: Atheneum, 1988), p. 134.

36 Greenwood, *Britain and the Cold War*, p. 137.

37 Eisenhower to Eden, 31 July 1956, in Boyle, ed., *Eden-Eisenhower Correspondence*, p. 156.

38 Eden, *Full Circle*, p. 487.

39 On intelligence, Douglas Little, 'Mission Impossible: The CIA and the Cult of Covert Action in the Middle East', *Diplomatic History*, Vol. 28, No. 5 (2004), pp. 663–701, especially pp. 680–681; Lucas, ed., *Britain and Suez*, pp. 38–39.

40 Bator, *Vietnam*, pp. 70–71.

41 Cable, *Geneva*, p. 137.

42 Eden to Salisbury, 8 April 1964, AVO/AP23/60/115A.

43 Eden pocket diary, 1 January 1957, AVO/AP20/2/5.

44 *King Lear*, Act 5, Scene 3, in Proudfoot et al., eds, *Arden Complete Shakespeare*, p. 665.

45 Cameron, ed., *VNC*, p. 316.

46 Shuckburgh, *Descent*, p. 15.

Bibliography

Archival/manuscript sources

Bodleian Library, Oxford

- Papers of Lord (Paul) Gore-Booth (GOR)
- Papers of Harold Macmillan, Earl of Stockton (MAC)
- Papers of Lord Nomanbrook (NOR)
- Papers of Lord Sherfield (SHE)
- Papers of Lord Woolton (WOO)

British Library, London

- Papers of Paul Emrys-Evans (EMR)

Cadbury Research Library, University of Birmingham

- Papers of Lord Avon/Anthony Eden (AVO)

Churchill Archives Centre, Churchill College, University of Cambridge

- Papers of Sir Winston Churchill (CHUR). Online version courtesy of the online Churchill Archive, Bloomsbury publishers, London
- Papers of Lord Gladwyn (GLA)

Dixon, Piers (private collection), London

- Papers of Pierson Dixon (DIX)

Durham University

- Papers of Malcolm MacDonald (MaC)

Dwight D. Eisenhower Presidential Library (DDEL), Abilene, Kansas

- Papers of John Foster Dulles (DUL)
- Papers of James. C. Hagerty (HAG)
- Papers of C. D. Jackson (CDJ)
- Whitman (Anne) file (AWF): Eisenhower diary, International and NSC series
- DDEL online documents archive

Eton College, Library and Archive

- Papers of Lord (Harold) Caccia

8

National Library of Scotland, Edinburgh
- Papers of R. H. Scott (SCO)

Princeton University, New Jersey: Mudd Library
- Papers of Hamilton Fish Armstrong (HFA)
- Papers of John Foster Dulles (DUL)

Sir Evelyn Shuckburgh
- Unpublished diary, copy in possession of Professor John Charmley

Harry S. Truman Library (HSTL), *Independence, Missouri*
- Papers of Dean G. Acheson (ACH)
- Papers of Harry S. Truman (HST)
- President's Secretary's files (PSF)
- Online documents archive
- White House Central files (WHCF)

Trinity College, Cambridge
- Papers of R. A. Butler (BUTLER)

UK National Archives, Kew, London
- CAB, Cabinet Office files
- DEFE, Ministry of Defence files
- DO, Dominions Office files
- FO, Foreign Office files
- PREM, Prime Minister's Private Office files
- T, Treasury files

US National Archives and Records Administration (NARA), *College Park, Maryland: Archives II*
- State Department, RG59, decimal and lot files

Primary sources (published)

Cameron, Allan W., ed., *Viet-Nam Crisis: A Documentary History, Volume I, 1940–1966* (Ithaca, NY: Cornell University Press, 1971).

Cold War International History Project, Digital Archive (*CWIHP*/DA): 'The 1954 Geneva Conference'.

Folliot, Denise, ed., *Documents on International Affairs 1954* (Oxford: Oxford University Press, 1957).

Foreign Relations of the United States (Washington, DC: State Department, Government Printing Office), online editions:

- *1952–1954, Vol. VI, Western Europe and Canada* (1986)
- *1952–1954, Vol. VII, Germany and Austria* (1986)
- *1952–1954, Vol. XII, East Asia and the Pacific* (1984)
- *1952–1954, Vol. XIII, Indochina* (1982)
- *1952–1954, Vol. XV, Korea* (1984)
- *1952–1954, Vol. XVI, The Geneva Conference* (1981)
- *1955–1957, Vol. I, Vietnam* (1985)
- *1955–1957, Vol. XI, East Asian Security* (1990)

Hansard, *House of Commons Debates* (HCD) and *House of Lords Debates* (HLD), online at millbanksystems.com.
The Pentagon Papers: The Defense Department History of United States Decisionmaking on Vietnam, US National Archives online resources.
The Pentagon Papers: The Defense Department History of United States Decisionmaking on Vietnam: Senator Gravel Edition, Vol. I (Boston: Beacon Press, 1971).
Public Papers of the Presidents of the United States (*PPP*), various volumes online at The American Presidency Project, University of California at Santa Barbara.

Published diaries and correspondence

Boyle, Peter, ed., *The Churchill-Eisenhower Correspondence 1953–1955* (Chapel Hill: University of North Carolina Press, 1990).
Boyle, Peter, ed., *The Eden-Eisenhower Correspondence, 1955–1957* (Chapel Hill: University of North Carolina Press, 2005).
Catterall, Peter, ed., *The Macmillan Diaries, Volume I: The Cabinet Years 1950–1957* (London: Macmillan, 2003).
Colville, John, *The Fringes of Power: Downing Street Diaries 1939–1955* (London: Hodder and Stoughton, 1985).
Ferrell, Robert H., ed., *Off the Record: The Private Papers of Harry S. Truman* (Columbia: University of Missouri Press, 1980).
Ferrell, Robert H., ed., *The Eisenhower Diaries* (New York: Norton, 1981)
Ferrell, Robert H., ed., *The Diary of James C. Hagerty: Eisenhower in Mid-Course, 1954–1955* (Bloomington: Indiana University Press, 1983).
Mendès-France, Pierre, *OEuvres complètes, Vol. III : Gouverner c'est choisir* (Paris: Éditions Gallimard. 1986).
Moran, Lord, *Winston Churchill: The Struggle for Survival* (London: Constable, 1966).
Nicolson, Nigel, ed., *Harold Nicolson: Diaries and Letters, Volume III, 1945–1962* (London: Collins, 1968).
Norwich, John Julius, ed., *The Duff Cooper Diaries* (London: Phoenix, 2006 edition).
Shuckburgh, Evelyn, *Descent to Suez: Diaries, 1951–56* (London: Weidenfeld and Nicolson, 1986).
Soames, Mary, ed., *Speaking for Themselves: The Personal Letters of Winston and Clementine Churchill* (London: Black Swan, 1999).
Sulzberger, C. L., *A Long Row of Candles: Memoirs and Diaries, 1934–1954* (Toronto: Macmillan, 1969).

Memoirs

Acheson, Dean G., *Present at the Creation: My Years in the State Department* (New York: Norton, 1969).

Adams, Sherman, *First-hand Report: The Inside Story of the Eisenhower Administration* (London: Hutchison, 1962).

Bao Dai, *Dragon d'Annam* (Paris: Plon, 1980).

Bidault, Georges, *Resistance: The Political Biography of Georges Bidault* (London: Weidenfeld and Nicolson, 1967).

Brandon, Henry, *Special Relationships: A Foreign Correspondent's Memoirs from Roosevelt to Reagan* (New York: Atheneum, 1988).

Butler, R. A., *The Art of the Possible* (London: Hamish Hamilton, 1971).

Casey, R. G., *Australian Foreign Minister: Diaries 1951-60* (London: Collins, 1972).

Eden, Anthony, *Memoirs: Full Circle* (London: Cassell, 1960).

Eden, Anthony, *Memoirs: The Reckoning* (London: Cassell, 1965)

Eden, Anthony, *Another World, 1897-1917* (London: Allen Lane, 1976).

Eden, Clarissa (with Cate Haste), *Clarissa Eden: A Memoir from Churchill to Eden* (London: Weidenfeld and Nicolson, 2007).

Eisenhower, Dwight D., *Mandate for Change: The White House Years, 1953-1956* (London: Heinemann, 1963).

Ely, General Paul, *Mémoires: L'Indochine dans la Tourmente* (Paris: Plon, 1964).

Gore-Booth, Paul, *With Great Truth and Respect* (London: Constable, 1974).

Gromyko, Andrei, *Memoirs* (New York: Doubleday, 1989).

Hayter, William, *A Double Life: The Memoirs of Sir William Hayter* (London: Hamish Hamilton, 1974).

Hughes, Emmet, *The Ordeal of Power: A Political Memoir of the Eisenhower Years* (New York: Atheneum, 1963).

Ismay, Lord, *The Memoirs of General the Lord Ismay* (London: Heinemann, 1960).

Jurika, Stephen, ed., *From Pearl Harbor to Vietnam: The Memoirs of Admiral Arthur W. Radford* (Stanford, CA: Hoover Institution Press, 1980).

Khrushchev, Sergei, ed., *The Memoirs of Nikita Khrushchev*, Vol. I (University Park: Pennsylvania State University Press, 2004).

Laniel, Joseph, *Le drame Indochinois: de Dien-Bien-Phu au pari de Genève* (Paris: Plon, 1957)

Macmillan, Harold, *Tides of Fortune, 1945-1955* (London: Macmillan, 1969).

McDonald, Iverach, *A Man of the Times* (London: Hamish Hamilton, 1976).

Montague Browne, Anthony, *Long Sunset: Memoirs of Winston Churchill's Last Private Secretary* (London: Cassell, 1995).

Navarre, Henri, *Agonie De L'Indochine, 1953-4* (Paris: Plon, 1956).

Nixon, Richard, *RN: The Memoirs of Richard Nixon* (London: Sidgwick and Jackson, 1978).

Resis, A., ed., *Molotov Remembers: Conversations with Felix Chuev* (Chicago: Ivan R. Dee, 1993).

Roberts, Chalmers, *First Rough Draft* (New York: Praeger, 1973).

Trevelyan, Humphrey, *Worlds Apart: China, 1953-55, USSR 1962-65* (London: Macmillan, 1971).

Truman, Harry S., *Memoirs: Year of Decisions* (New York: Doubleday, 1955).

Truman, Harry S., *Memoirs: Years of Trial and Hope* (New York: Doubleday, 1956).

General works

Ambrose, Stephen E., *Eisenhower the President, 1952–1969* (London: Allen and Unwin, 1984).

Anderson, David L., *Trapped by Success: The Eisenhower Administration and Vietnam, 1953–1961* (New York: Columbia University Press, 1991).

Arnold, James R., *The First Domino: Eisenhower, the Military and America's Intervention in Vietnam* (New York: Morrow, 1991).

Arnold, Lorna, *Britain and the H-Bomb* (Basingstoke: Palgrave, 2001).

Barclay, Roderick, *Ernest Bevin and the Foreign Office, 1932–1969* (London: Barclay, 1975).

Barker, Elisabeth, *Churchill and Eden at War* (London: Macmillan, 1978).

Barnett, Corelli, *The Verdict of Peace: Britain between Her Yesterday and the Future* (London: Macmillan, 2001).

Bator, Victor, *Vietnam – A Diplomatic Tragedy: Origins of US Involvement* (London: Faber and Faber, 1965).

Billings-Yun, Melanie, *Decision against War: Eisenhower and Dien Bien Phu* (New York: Columbia University Press, 1988).

Blake, Robert, *The Decline of Power, 1915–64* (London: Granada, 1985 edition).

Bodard, Lucien, *The Quicksand War: Prelude to Vietnam* (London: Faber 1967).

Broad, Lewis, *Sir Anthony Eden: Chronicles of a Career* (London: Hutchinson, 1955).

Brocheux, Pierre and Daniel Hémery, *Indochine: La colonisation ambiguë, 1858–1954* (Paris: Découverte, 2001 edition).

Buchanan, Tom, *East Wind: China and the British Left, 1925–1976* (Oxford: Oxford University Press, 2012).

Cable, James, *The Geneva Conference of 1954 on Indochina* (London: Macmillan, 1986).

Cairncross, Alec, *Years of Recovery: British Economic Policy 1945–1951* (London: Methuen, 1985).

Calvocoressi, Peter, *Survey of International Affairs, 1952* (Oxford: Oxford University Press, 1955).

Calvocoressi, Peter, *Survey of International Affairs, 1953* (Oxford: Oxford University Press, 1956).

Calvocoressi, Peter, *Survey of International Affairs, 1954* (Oxford: Oxford University Press, 1957).

Carlton, David, *Anthony Eden: A Biography* (London: Allen Lane, 1981).

Carlton, David, *Britain and the Suez Crisis* (Oxford: Blackwell, 1988).

Carter, James M., *Inventing Vietnam: The United States and State Building, 1954–1968* (New York: Cambridge University Press, 2008).

Chapman, Jessica M., *Cauldron of Resistance: Ngo Dinh Diem, the United States and 1950s Southern Vietnam* (Ithaca, NY: Cornell University Press, 2013).

Charmley, John, *Churchill's Grand Alliance: The Anglo-American Special Relationship 1940–57* (London: Hodder and Stoughton, 1995).

Churchill, Randolph S., *The Rise and Fall of Sir Anthony Eden* (London: Macgibbon and Kee, 1959).

Churchill, Winston S., *The Second World War, Volume I: The Gathering Storm* (London: Penguin, 1985 edition).

Churchill, Winston S., *The Second World War, Volume VI: Triumph and Tragedy* (London: Penguin, 1985 edition).

Colvin, John, *Volcano under Snow: Vo Nguyen Giap* (London: Quartet, 1996).

Cooper, Chester, *The Lost Crusade: America in Vietnam* (New York: Dodd, Mead and Col, 1970).

Crozier, Brian et al., *This War Called Peace* (Chicago: Universe Books, 1985).

Dallek, Robert, *Franklin D. Roosevelt and American Foreign Policy 1932–1945* (New York: Oxford University Press, 1995 edition).

Dalloz, Jacques, *The War in Indo-China, 1945–54* (Dublin: Gill and Macmillan, 1990).

Devilliers, Philippe, and Jean Lacouture, *End of a War: Indochina 1954* (London: Pall Mall Press, 1969).

Dickie, John, *'Special' No More – Anglo-American Relations: Rhetoric and Reality* (London: Weidenfeld and Nicolson, 1994).

Divine, Robert A., *Blowing on the Wind: The Nuclear Test Ban Debate, 1954–1968* (New York: Oxford University Press, 1978).

Dockrill, Saki, *Eisenhower's New Look National Security Policy, 1953–61* (Basingstoke: Palgrave, 1996).

Dommen, Arthur J., *The Indochinese Experience of the French and the Americans: Nationalism and Communism in Cambodia, Laos, and Vietnam* (Bloomington: Indiana University Press, 2001).

Duiker, William J., *US Containment Policy and the Conflict in Indochina* (Stanford, CA: Stanford University Press, 1994).

Dutton, David, *Anthony Eden: A Life and Reputation* (London: Arnold, 1997).

Eden, Anthony, *Towards Peace in Indo-China* (Oxford: RIIA, 1966).

Fall, Bernard, *Street without Joy* (Mechanicsburg, PA: Stockdale, 1994 edition).

Fall, Bernard, *Hell in a Very Small Place: The Siege of Dien Bien Phu* (Cambridge, MA: Da Capo Press, 2002 edition).

Farmelo, Graham, *Churchill's Bomb: A Hidden History of Science, War and Politics* (London: Faber and Faber, 2013)

Foot, Rosemary J., 'Anglo-American Relations in the Korean Crisis: The British Effort to Avert an Expanded War, December 1950–January 1951', *Diplomatic History*, Vol. 10, No. 1 (1986), pp. 43–57.

Gaddis, John Lewis, *The Cold War* (London: Allen Lane, 2005).

Gaddis, John Lewis, *Strategies of Containment: A Critical Appraisal of American National Security Policy during the Cold War* (Oxford: Oxford University Press, 2005 edition).

Gaiduk, Ilya, *Confronting Vietnam: Soviet Policy toward the Indochina Conflict, 1954–1963* (Stanford, CA: Stanford University Press, 2003).

Gardner, Lloyd C., *Approaching Vietnam: From World War II through Dienbienphu* (New York: Norton, 1988).

Gibbons, William C., *The US Government and the Vietnam War: Part I, 1945–1960* (Princeton, NJ: Princeton University Press, 1986).

Gilbert, Martin, *Never Despair: Winston S. Churchill, 1945–1965* (London: Heinemann, 1988).

Goscha, Christopher, *Vietnam: un état né de la guerre, 1945–1954* (Paris: Armand Colin, 2011).

Goscha, Christopher, *The Penguin History of Modern Vietnam* (London: Allen Lane, 2016).

Greenwood, Sean, *Britain and the Cold War, 1945–91* (Basingstoke: Macmillan, 2000).

Hack, Karl, *Defence and Decolonisation in Southeast Asia: Britain, Malaya and Singapore, 1945–1965* (London: Curzon, 2001).

Hammer, Ellen J., *The Struggle for Indochina* (Stanford, CA: Stanford University Press, 1954).

Hennessy, Peter, *Having It So Good: Britain in the Fifties* (London: Allen Lane, 2006).

Hennessey, Thomas, *Britain's Korean War: Cold War Diplomacy, Strategy and Security, 1950–53* (Manchester: Manchester University Press, 2015).

Herring, George C., *America's Longest War: The United States and Vietnam, 1950–1975* (New York: McGraw Hill, 2002 edition).

Hoopes, Townsend, *The Devil and John Foster Dulles* (Boston: Little, Brown, 1973).

Hurd, Douglas, *Choose Your Weapons – the British Foreign Secretary: 200 Years of Arguments, Successes and Failures* (London: Weidenfeld and Nicolson, 2010).

Immerman, Richard H., ed., *John Foster Dulles and the Diplomacy of the Cold War* (Princeton, NJ: Princeton University Press, 1990).

Immerman, Richard H., *John Foster Dulles: Piety, Pragmatism and Power in US Foreign Policy* (Wilmington: Scholarly Resources, 1999).

Irving, R. E. M., *The First Indochina War* (London: Croom Helm, 1975).

Israelyan, Victor, *On the Battlefields of the Cold War: A Soviet Ambassador's Confession* (University Park: University of Pennsylvania Press, 2003).

Jacobs, Seth, *Cold War Mandarin: Ngo Dinh Diem and the Origins of America's War in Vietnam, 1950–1963* (Lanham, MD: Rowman and Littlefield, 2006).

James, Robert Rhodes, *Anthony Eden* (London: Weidenfeld and Nicolson, 1986).

Jian, Chen, *Mao's China and the Cold War* (Chapel Hill: University of North Carolina Press, 2001).

Jones, Matthew, *After Hiroshima: The United States, Race and Nuclear Weapons in Asia, 1945–1965* (Cambridge: Cambridge University Press, 2012 edition).

Jones, Matthew, *The Official History of the UK Strategic Nuclear Deterrent: Volume I – from the V-Bomber era to the arrival of Polaris, 1945–1964* (London: Routledge, 2017).

Kamm, Henry, *Dragon Ascending: Vietnam and the Vietnamese* (New York: Arcade, 1996).

Kaplan, Lawrence S., Denise Artaud and Mark R. Rubin, eds, *Dien Bien Phu and the Crisis of Franco-American Relations, 1954–1955* (Wilmington: Scholarly Resources, 1990).

Karnow, Stanley, *Vietnam: A History* (London: Guild Publishing, 1985 edition).

Kaufman, Victor S., *Confronting Communism: US and British Policies toward China* (Columbia, MO: University of Missouri Press, 2001).

Kissinger, Henry, *Diplomacy* (London: Simon and Schuster, 1994).

Kunz, Diane B., *The Economic Diplomacy of the Suez Crisis* (Chapel Hill: University of North Carolina Press, 1991).

Kyle, Keith, *Suez* (London: Weidenfeld and Nicolson, 1991).

Kynaston, David, *Family Britain, 1951–1957* (London: Bloomsbury, 2009).

Lacouture, Jean, *Pierre Mendes France* (New York: Holmes and Meir, 1984, trans. George Holloch)

Lamb, Richard, *The Failure of the Eden Government* (London: Sidgwick and Jackson, 1987).

Lancaster, Donald, *The Emancipation of French Indochina* (London: Oxford University Press, 1961).

Larres, Klaus, *Churchill's Cold War: The Politics of Personal Diplomacy* (New Haven, CT: Yale University Press, 2002).

Lawrence, Mark, *Assuming the Burden: Europe and the American Commitment to War in Vietnam* (Berkeley: University of California Press, 2005).

Lawrence, Mark Atwood, and Fredrik Logevall, *The First Vietnam War: Colonial Conflict and Cold War Crisis* (Cambridge, MA: Harvard University Press, 2007).

Lind, Michael, *The American Way of Strategy* (New York: Oxford University Press, 2006).

Logevall, Fredrik, *Embers of War: The Fall of an Empire and the Making of America's Vietnam* (New York: Random House, 2012).

Louis, William Roger, and Hedley Bull, eds, *The Special Relationship: Anglo-American Relations since 1945* (Oxford: Oxford University Press, 1989 edition).

Louis, William Roger, and Robert Blake, eds, *Churchill: A Major New Assessment of his Life in Peace and War* (Oxford: Oxford University Press, 1996).

Lowe, Peter, *Contending with Nationalism and Communism: British Policy towards Southeast Asia, 1945–65* (Basingstoke: Palgrave, 2009).

Lowe, Peter, ed., *The Vietnam War* (London: Palgrave, 1998).

Lucas, W. Scott, ed., *Britain and Suez: The Lion's Last Roar* (Manchester: Manchester University Press, 1996).

Lucas, W. Scott, *Divided We Stand: Britain, the US and the Suez Crisis* (London: Hodder and Stoughton, 1996).

Lundestad, Geir, *'Empire' by Integration: The United States and European Integration 1945–1997* (Oxford: Oxford University Press, 1998).

Miller, Edward, *Misalliance: Ngo Dinh Diem, the United States and the Fate of South Vietnam* (Cambridge, MA: Harvard University Press, 2013).

Morgan, Kenneth O., *The People's Peace: British History 1945–1989* (Oxford: Oxford University Press, 1990), p. 132.

Morgan, Ted, *Valley of Death: The Tragedy at Dien Bien Phu That Led America into the Vietnam War* (New York: Random House, 2010).

Moyar, Mark, *Triumph Forsaken: The Vietnam War, 1954–1965* (Cambridge: Cambridge University Press, 2006).

Nutting, Anthony, *No End of a Lesson: The Story of Suez* (London, 1967).

Olsen, Mari, *Soviet-Vietnam Relations and the Role of China, 1949–64: Changing Alliances* (London: Routledge, 2006).

Otte, T. G., ed., *The Makers of British Foreign Policy: From Pitt to Thatcher* (Basingstoke: Palgrave, 2002).

Pearson, Jonathan, *Sir Anthony Eden and the Suez Crisis: Reluctant Gamble* (Basingstoke: Palgrave, 2003).

Prados, John, *The Sky Would Fall: Operation Vulture – the Secret US Bombing Mission to Vietnam, 1954* (New York: Dial Press, 1983).

Prados, John, *Vietnam: The History of an Unwinnable War, 1945–1975* (Lawrence: University of Kansas Press, 2009).

Qiang Zhai, *The Dragon, the Lion and the Eagle: Chinese-British-American Relations, 1949–1958* (Kent, OH: Kent State University Press, 1994).

Qiang Zhai, *China and the Vietnam Wars, 1950–1975* (Chapel Hill: University of North Carolina Press, 2000).

Randle, Robert F., *Geneva, 1954: The Settlement of the Indochinese War* (Princeton, NJ: Princeton University Press, 1969).

Rees-Mogg, William, *Sir Anthony Eden* (London: Rockliff, 1956).

Reynolds, David, *Britannia Overruled: British Policy and Power in the 20th Century* (Harlow: Longman, 1991).

Rioux, Jean-Pierre, *The Fourth Republic, 1944–1958* (Cambridge: Cambridge University Press, 1989 edition, trans.).

Rocolle, Pierre, *Pourquoi Dien Bien Phu?* (Paris: Flammarian, 1968).

Rothwell, Victor, *Anthony Eden: A Political Biography* (Manchester: Manchester University Press, 1992).

Roy, Jules, *The Battle of Dienbienphu* (London: Faber, 1965).

Ruane, Kevin, *The Rise and Fall of the European Defence Community: Anglo-American Relations and the Crisis of European Defence, 1950–1955* (Basingstoke: Macmillan, 2000).

Ruane, Kevin, *Churchill and the Bomb in War and Cold War* (London: Bloomsbury, 2016).

Rust, William J., *Eisenhower and Cambodia: Diplomacy, Covert Action and the Origins of the Second Indochina War* (Lexington: University Press of Kentucky, 2016).

Seldon, Anthony, *Churchill's Indian Summer: The Conservative Government, 1951–55* (London: Hodder and Stoughton, 1981).

Shaplen, Robert, *The Lost Revolution: Vietnam, 1945–1965* (London: Deutsch, 1966).

Shlaim, Avi et al., eds, *British Foreign Secretaries since 1945* (Newton Abbot: David and Charles, 1977).

Short, Anthony, *The Origins of the Vietnam War* (London: Longman, 1989).

Singh, Anita Inder, *The Limits of British Influence: South Asia and the Anglo-American Relationship, 1947–1956* (London: Pinter, 1993).

Smith, R. B., *An International History of the Vietnam War: Volume I – Revolutions versus Containment 1955–61* (Basingstoke: Macmillan, 1987 edition).

Smith, Simon C. ed., *Reassessing Suez: New Perspectives on the Crisis and Its Aftermath* (London: Routledge, 2008).

Spector, Ronald H., *Advice and Support: The Early Years of the US Army in Vietnam, 1941–1960* (New York: Free Press, 1985).

Statler, Kathryn C., *Replacing France: The Origins of American Intervention in Vietnam* (Lexington: University Press of Kentucky, 2007).

Stueck, William, *The Korean War: An International History* (Princeton, NJ: Princeton University Press, 1995).

Tarling, Nicholas, *Britain, Southeast Asia and the Impact of the Korean War* (Singapore: National University of Singapore Press, 2005).

Thakur, Ramesh, *Peacekeeping in Vietnam: Canada, India, Poland, and the International Commission* (Edmonton: University of Alberta Press, 1984).

Thal, Herbert Van, ed., *The Prime Ministers*, Vol. II (London: Allen and Unwin, 1975).

Thomas, Hugh, *The Suez Affair* (London: Tinling, 1967 edition).

Thorpe, D. R., *Eden: The Life and Times of Anthony Eden, First Earl of Avon, 1897–1977* (London: Chatto and Windus, 2003).

Waite, James, *The End of the First Indochina War: A Global History* (London: Routledge, 2012).

Werth, Alexander, *France, 1940–1955* (London: Hale, 1956).

Windrow, Martin, *The Last Valley: Dien Bien Phu and the French Defeat in Vietnam* (London: Weidenfeld and Nicolson, 2004).

Yergin, Daniel, *Shattered Peace: The Origins of the Cold War and the National Security State* (London: Deutsch, 1978).

Young, John, *Churchill's Last Campaign: Britain and the Cold War, 1951–1955* (Oxford: Clarendon Press, 1996).

Young, John, ed., *The Foreign Policy of Churchill's Peacetime Administration, 1951–1955* (Leicester: Leicester University Press, 1988).

Young, John, Effie Pedaliu and Michael Kandiah, eds, *Britain in Global Politics: Vol. 2, From Churchill to Blair* (Basingstoke: Palgrave Macmillan, 2013).

Young, Marilyn B., *The Vietnam Wars, 1945–1990* (New York: Harper Perennial, 1991 edition).

Zaloga, Steven J., *The Kremlin's Nuclear Shield: The Rise and Fall of Russia's Strategic Nuclear Forces, 1945–2000* (Washington: Smithsonian, 2014).

Articles, professional papers and chapters in edited collections

Adamthwaite, Anthony, 'The Foreign Office and Policy-making', in Young, ed., *Peacetime Administration*, 'Introduction'.

Anderson, David L., 'J. Lawton Collins, John Foster Dulles and the Eisenhower Administrations "Point of No Return" in Vietnam', *Diplomatic History*, Vol. 12, No. 1 (1988), pp. 127–147.

Artaud, Denise, 'Conclusion', in Kaplan et al., eds, *Dienbienphu*.

Ashton, S. R., 'Keeping a Foot in the Door: Britain's China Policy, 1945–1950', *Diplomacy and Statecraft*, Vol. 15, No. 1 (2004), pp. 79–94.

Asselin, Pierre, 'New Perspectives on Dien Bien Phu', *Explorations in Southeast Asian Studies*, Vol. 1, No. 2 (1997), pp. 12–21.

Asselin, Pierre, 'Choosing Peace: Hanoi and the Geneva Agreement on Vietnam, 1954–1955', *Journal of Cold War Studies*, Vol. 9, No. 2 (2007), pp. 95–127.

Asselin, Pierre, 'The Democratic Republic of Vietnam and the 1954 Geneva Conference: A Revisionist Critique', *Cold War History*, Vol. 11, No. 2 (2011), pp. 155–195.

Boquérat, Gilles, 'India's Commitment to Peaceful Coexistence and the Settlement of the Indochina War', *Cold War History*, Vol. 5, No. 2 (2005), pp. 211–234.

Boyle, Peter, 'The "Special Relationship" with Washington', in Young, ed., *Churchill's Peacetime Administration*, chapter 1.

Boyle, Peter, 'The Personalities', in Boyle, ed., *Eden-Eisenhower Correspondence*.

Buhite, Russell D., and Wm. Christopher Hamel, 'War for Peace: The Question of an American Preventive War against the Soviet Union, 1945–1955', *Diplomatic History*, Vol. 14, No. 3 (1990), pp. 367–384.

Césari, Laurent, and Jacques de Folin, 'Military Necessity, Political Impossibility: The French Viewpoint on Operation *Vautour*', in Kaplan et al., eds, *Dienbienphu*.

Chapman, Jessica, 'The Sect Crisis of 1955 and the American Commitment to Ngo Dinh Diem', *Journal of Vietnamese Studies*, Vol. 5, No. 1 (2010), pp. 37–85.

Combs, Arthur, 'The Path Not Taken: The British Alternative to U.S. Policy in Vietnam, 1954–1956', *Diplomatic History*, Vol. 19, No. 1 (1995), pp. 33–57.

Crozier, Brian, 'Post-Stockholm Euphoria', *National Review*, 7 November 1986.

Dingman, Roger, 'Atomic Diplomacy during the Korean War', *International Security*, Vol. 13, No. 3 (1988–1989), pp. 50–91.

Dingman, Roger, 'John Foster Dulles and the Creation of the Southeast Asia Treaty Organisation in 1954', *International History Review*, Vol. XI, No. 3 (1989), pp. 457–477.

Dutton, David, 'Anthony Eden', in Otte, ed., *Makers of British Foreign Policy*.

Eden, Anthony, 'The Burden of Leadership', *Foreign Affairs*, Vol. 44, No. 2, pp. 229–238.

Feis, Herbert, 'Anthony Eden and the Cacophony of Nations', *Foreign Affairs*, Vol. 44, No. 1 (1965), pp. 78–89.

Gaiduk, Ilya V., 'Developing an Alliance: The Soviet Union and Vietnam, 1954–75', in Lowe, ed., *Vietnam War*.

Grant, Philip A., 'The Bricker Amendment Controversy', *Presidential Studies Quarterly*, Vol. 15, No. 3 (1985), pp. 572–582.

Guillemot, François, '"Be men!": Fighting and Dying for the State of Vietnam (1951–54)', *War and Society*, Vol. 31, No. 2 (2012), pp. 184–212.

Hack, Karl, 'The Origins of the Asian Cold War: Malaya 1948', *Journal of Southeast Asian Studies*, Vol. 40, No. 3 (2009), pp. 471–496.

Herring, George C., 'Franco-American Conflict in Indochina, 1950–1954', in Kaplan et al., eds, *Dienbienphu*.

Herring, George C., '"A Good Stout Effort": John Foster Dulles and the Indochina Crisis, 1954–1955', in Immerman, ed., *Dulles*.

Herring, George C., and Richard H. Immerman, 'Eisenhower, Dulles, and Dien Bien Phu: "The Day We Didn't Go to War" Revisited', in Kaplan et al., eds, *Dienbienphu*.

Hess, Gary R., 'Redefining the American Position in Southeast Asia: The United States and the Geneva and Manila Conferences', in Kaplan et al., eds, *Dienbienphu*.

Hess, Stephen, 'Foreign Policy and Presidential Campaigns', *Foreign Policy*, No. 8 (1972), pp. 3–22.

Howard, Sir Michael, 'Afterword: The "Special Relationship"', in Louis and Bull, eds, *Special Relationship*.

Jian, Chen, 'China and the Indochina Settlement at the Geneva Conference of 1954', in Lawrence and Logevall, eds, *First Vietnam War*.

Jenkins, Roy, 'Churchill: The Government of 1951–1955', in Blake and Louis, *Churchill*, chapter 28.

Jones, Matthew, 'Targeting China: US Nuclear Planning and "Massive Retaliation" in East Asia, 1953–1955', *Journal of Cold War Studies*, Vol. 10, No. 4 (2008), pp. 37–65.

Jones, Matthew, 'Great Britain, the United States, and Consultation over Use of the Atomic Bomb, 1950–1954', *Historical Journal*, Vol. 54, No. 3 (2011), pp. 797–828.

Kahin, George McT., *Intervention: How America Became Involved in Vietnam* (New York: Knopf, 1986 edition).

Kaufman, Victor S., '"Chirep": The Anglo-American Dispute over Chinese Representation in the United Nations, 1950–1971', *English Historical Review*, Vol. 115, No. 461 (2000), pp. 354–377.

Kelly, Andrew, 'Discordant Allies: Trans-Tasman Relations in the Aftermath of the ANZUS Treaty, 1951–1955', *Journal of Australian Studies*, Vol. 4, No. 1 (2017), pp. 81–95.

Kimball, Warren F., 'Wheel within a Wheel: Churchill, Roosevelt and the Special Relationship', in Louis and Blake, eds, *Churchill*.

Lawrence, Mark, and Fredrik Logevall, 'Introduction', in Lawrence and Logevall, eds, *First Vietnam War*.

Little, Douglas, 'Mission Impossible: The CIA and the Cult of Covert Action in the Middle East', *Diplomatic History*, Vol. 28, No. 5 (2004), pp. 663–701.

Logevall, Fredrik, '"We Might Give Them a Few": Did the US Offer to Drop Atom Bombs at Dien Bien Phu?' Bulletin of Atomic Scientists, 26 February 2016.

Louis, William Roger, 'Dulles, Suez and the British', in. Immerman, ed., *Diplomacy of the Cold War*.

Nutting, Anthony, 'Sir Anthony Eden', in Herbert Van Thal, ed., *The Prime Ministers*, Vol. II.

Perkins, Bradford, 'Unequal Partners: The Truman Administration and Great Britain', in Louis and Bull, *Special Relationship*.

Prados, John, 'Reassessing Dien Bien Phu', in Lawrence and Logevall, eds, *First Vietnam War*.

Proudfoot, Richard, Ann Thompson and David Scott Kastan, eds, *The Arden Shakespeare Complete Works* (London: Thomson, 1998 edition).

Reynolds, David, 'Rethinking Anglo-American Relations', *International Affairs*, Vol. 65, No. 1 (1988–1989), pp. 89–111.

Reynolds, David, 'Eden the Diplomatist, 1931–1956: Suezide of a Statesman?' *History*, Vol. 74, No. 1 (1989), pp. 64–84.

Reynolds, David, 'Roosevelt, Churchill, and the Wartime Anglo-American Alliance, 1939–1945: Towards a New Synthesis', in Louis and Bull, eds, *Special Relationship*.

Roberts, Chalmers, 'The Day We Didn't Go to War', *The Reporter*, 14 September 1954, pp. 31–35.

Ruane, Kevin, 'Britain, the United States and the Issue of "Limited War" with China, 1950–54', in Young et al., eds, *Churchill to Blair*, chapter 4.

Ruane, Kevin, 'Anthony Eden, British Diplomacy and the Origins of the Geneva Conference of 1954', *Historical Journal*, Vol. 37, No. 1 (1994), pp. 153–172.

Ruane, Kevin, 'Containing America: Aspects of British Foreign Policy and the Cold War in South-East Asia, 1951–54', *Diplomacy and Statecraft*, Vol. 7, No. 1 (1996), pp. 141–174.

Ruane, Kevin, 'SEATO, MEDO and the Baghdad Pact: Anthony Eden, British Foreign Policy and the Collective Defence of Southeast Asia and the Middle East, 1952–1955', *Diplomacy and Statecraft*, Vol. 16, No. 1 (2005), pp. 169–199.

Ruane, Kevin, 'Agonizing Reappraisals: Anthony Eden, John Foster Dulles and the Crisis of European Defence, 1953–54', *Diplomacy and Statecraft*, Vol. 13, No. 4 (2010), pp. 151–185.

Ruane, Kevin, 'The Origins of the Eden–Dulles Antagonism: The Yoshida Letter and the Cold War in East Asia 1951–1952', *Contemporary British History*, Vol. 25, No. 1 (2011), pp. 141–156.

Ruscio, Alain, 'L'opinion Française et la guerre d'Indochine (1945–1954): Sondages et témoignages', *Vingtième Siècle Revue d'histoire*, No. 29 (1991), pp. 35–45.

Shepley, James, 'How Dulles Averted War: Three Times, New Disclosures Show, Brought US Back from the Brink', *Life* (16 January 1956), pp. 70–80.

Smith, Simon C., 'The Anglo-American "Special Relationship" and the Middle East, 1945–1973', *Asian Affairs*, Vol. XLV, No. 111 (2014), pp. 425–448.

Statler, Kathryn C., 'After Geneva: The French Presence in Vietnam, 1954–1963', in Lawrence and Logevall, eds, *First Vietnam War*.

Trachtenberg, Marc, 'A "Wasting Asset": American Strategy and the Shifting Nuclear Balance, 1949–1954', *International Security*, Vol. 13, No. 3 (1988–89), pp. 5–49.

Tucker, Nancy Bernkopf, 'China and America: 1941–1991', *Foreign Affairs*, Vol. 70, No. 5 (1991–1992), pp. 75–92.

Wang, Tao, 'Neutralizing Indochina: The 1954 Geneva Conference and China's Efforts to Isolate the United States', *Journal of Cold War Studies*, Vol. 19, No. 2 (2017), pp. 3–32.

Warner, Geoffrey, 'The Settlement of the Indochina War', in Young, ed., *Churchill's Peacetime Administration*.

Warner, Geoffrey, 'The United States and the Suez Crisis', *International Affairs*, Vol. 67, No. 2 (1991), pp. 303–317.

Warner, Geoffrey, 'Britain and the Crisis over Dien Bien Phu, April 1954: The Failure of United Action', in Kaplan et al., eds, *Dienbienphu*.

Warner, Geoffrey, 'From Geneva to Manila: British Policy towards Indochina and SEATO, May–September 1954', in Kaplan et al., eds, *Dienbienphu*.

Williams, John, 'ANZUS: A Blow to Britain's Self-esteem', *Review of International Studies*, Vol. 13, No. 4 (1987), pp. 243–263.

Young, John, 'Cold War and Détente with Moscow', in Young, ed., *Churchill's Peacetime Administration*, chapter 2.

Interviews and correspondence

- *British Diplomatic Oral History Programme* (Churchill Archives Centre, Churchill College, Cambridge), online archive.
- Kevin Ruane interviews/correspondence with: Reginald Burrows; Sir James Cable; Sir Nicholas Cheetham; Sir Anthony Montague-Browne; Sir Patrick Reilly; Sir Frank Roberts; Sir Evelyn Shuckburgh; J. G. Tahourdin.
- U. Alexis Johnson, interview, 7 February 1982, for *Vietnam: A Television History*, WGBH Media Library & Archives.

Selected press, magazine and web publications
Newspapers and magazines

Chartwell Bulletin; Chicago Tribune; Christian Science Monitor; Daily Express; Daily Herald; Daily Mail; Daily Mirror; Economist; Finest Hour; Guardian; Life; Illustrated London News; Independent; Le Monde; Le Populaire; Life: Listener; London Review of Books; Manchester Guardian; Nash's Pall Mall; New China News Agency; New Statesman; New York Herald Tribune; New York Times; Observer; Pravda; Punch; Reynold's News; Scotsman; Spectator; Strand; Sunday Pictorial; Tatler, Tribune; Washington Post; Yorkshire Post.

Miscellaneous

British Pathé, 'H-Bomb', 8 April 1954.

Command Paper, Cmd. 8938, *Special Report of the Unified Command on the Korean Armistice Agreement Signed at Panmunjom on July 27, 1953* (London: HMSO, 1953).

Command Paper, Cmnd 9080, *Documents Relating to the Meeting of Foreign Ministers in Berlin* (London: HMSO, 1954).

Command paper, Cmd. 9391, *Statement on Defence* (London: HMSO, 1955).

Oxford Dictionary of National Biography, online.

'The H-Bomb and World Opinion', *Bulletin of Atomic Scientists*, Vol. 10, No. 5 (May 1954), pp. 163–168.

Report of Senator Mike Mansfield on a Study Mission to Vietnam, Cambodia, Laos, October 15, 1954 (Washington: Government Printing Office, 1954).

Index

Acheson, Dean 21–3, 27–30, 37
Adams, Sherman 106
Adamthwaite, Anthony 4
Ad Hoc Committee (1952) 25
Aldrich, Winthrop 105, 108, 111–12, 174,
    199–200
Alexander, Lord 37
Ali, Mohammed 225
Allen, Denis 86, 92–3, 114, 120, 122,
    125–6, 128–9, 139
  Geneva conference 148, 161, 166, 252–3
  SEATO 227
  Vietnamese elections 242, 246
Anderson, George 115
Annam 25, 55, 57, 67, 207
ANZUS. See Australia/New Zealand/US
    'Pacific Pact'
Associated States 35–6, 49, 66, 69, 102,
    130, 141, 244. See also Cambodia;
    Laos; Vietnam
  Geneva conference 126, 151, 155–6,
    158, 170, 173–4, 204–5, 207
  independence of 34, 46, 57–9, 71, 92,
    100, 105, 119, 123–4, 143, 155, 175,
    237
  MAAG 240
  SEATO 120–1, 151, 174, 213–14,
    228–9, 231
Attlee, Clement 14–15, 23, 108, 123
Auriol, Vincent 70
Australia 96, 142, 151, 247. See also
    Australia/New Zealand/US 'Pacific
    Pact' (ANZUS)
  Pacific Charter (1954) 230
  SEATO 213, 225, 231
  Vietnam 2–3, 25, 30–1, 102, 104, 106,
    109–10, 115, 118, 119–20, 147, 150,
    154, 157, 160–1, 176, 186
Australia/New Zealand/US 'Pacific Pact'
    (ANZUS) 102, 105, 110, 112, 119,
    122, 160–1

  British exclusion from 13, 102
  SEATO 231

Baie d'Along 19
Bangkok 230, 246
Bao Dai 55, 59, 61, 65, 70, 136, 155, 158,
    190, 195, 239, 253
  Diem, dismissal of 248
  partition of Vietnam 85, 148
Barclay, Roderick 126–7
Bator, Victor 129, 261
Beria, Lavrenti 49
Berlin conference (1954) 71, 78–82, 87,
    155, 158
Bermuda conference (December 1953)
    55–7, 59, 64, 69–75, 77, 97–8, 136,
    146, 150, 186, 199, 255
  Little Bermuda (July 1953) 56, 60, 64
Bevan, Aneurin 123–4
Bevin, Ernest 15
Bidault, Georges 60–1, 65, 124, 127, 188
  armistice in Indochina 169–73, 183,
    190, 194
  Berlin conference 79–83
  Bermuda conference 70–1
  Dien Bien Phu, battle at 88, 101, 109,
    116–17, 131, 133–41, 143–4, 153,
    157, 160, 168–9
  Geneva conference 82, 84, 101, 146,
    149–50, 153, 157–8, 160, 167–9,
    180–1, 183, 190–1,194–5, 197, 218
  memoirs 138
Binh Xuyen 239, 247–8
blockades
  against People's Republic of China 22,
    24–8, 31, 62, 68, 101, 142, 146, 160,
    185
  against Soviet ports in Far East 26–7
Bodard, Lucien 20
Boncour, Paul 184
Bonnet, Henri 117, 141, 143, 170, 175, 188

Bonsal, Philip 66
Bradley, Omar 20, 22, 24–5
Bricker Amendment 89–90
Brook, Norman 113, 142
Bui Chu 197, 207
Burma 120, 126, 156, 220. *See also*
    Colombo conference/powers
    communist threat to 11, 34–5, 106,
    147
    SEATO 214, 224–6
Butler, Rab 56, 167, 191
Buu, Loc 195
Buu, Ta Quang 158

Cable, James 8, 92, 101, 115, 127, 129, 131,
    164, 175
    SEATO 231–2, 247
    Vietnamese elections 242–3
Caccia, Harold 148, 161, 171, 213
Cambodia 3, 88, 114, 125, 157. *See also*
    Associated States; Khmer Issarak
    American military bases 213, 218
    armistice 216–17
    communist threat to 1, 10, 38, 100,
    106, 130, 164, 171–2
    elections 171
    Final Declaration of Geneva
    conference 217–21, 225
    independence 33–4, 57, 59, 148, 190,
    193–4, 196, 201, 203, 221, 237
    MAAG 240
    peace negotiations for Indochina
    171–4, 184, 193, 196, 203, 210–11
    SEATO 224, 228–9, 256
Canada 142, 160, 214
Cao Dai 239, 247
Carney, Admiral Robert 185–6
Casey, Richard 117, 151, 160–1, 191, 194,
    201
Chamberlain, Austen 5, 165
Chamberlain, Neville 5, 200
Chauvel, Jean 138, 149, 190, 197
Chiang Kai-shek 14, 22, 43–4, 60, 128,
    219, 242
    SEATO 224
China. *See* Nationalist China; People's
    Republic of China
Chinh, Truong 150
Churchill, Randolph 7

Churchill, Sir Winston 5–6, 12, 54, 183,
    209–10
    as acting Foreign Secretary (1953) 50
    Berlin conference 80, 82–3
    Bermuda conference 55–6, 59, 64,
    69–72, 75, 97
    Congress, address to (1952) 23, 72
    Defence Committee, as chair of 35
    Dien Bien Phu, battle of 129, 134, 144,
    147–8, 153–4, 168
    economic issues 13
    and Eisenhower 40–3, 51, 56, 97–8,
    106–8, 112–13, 146, 167, 184, 186,
    191, 197, 199–200, 203, 205–6, 257
    Fulton (Iron Curtain) speech (1946) 6
    Geneva conference 83, 148, 151, 153,
    175–6, 210, 215, 217, 220
    health issues 56, 68
    history books by 6
    India 22, 140, 225
    Laos 52–3
    and Malenkov 49
    nuclear weapons 9, 72–4, 97–8,
    107–10, 187, 197, 199–200, 257
    as "peacemaker" in Cold War 41, 54
    Potomac Charter (1954) 203–4
    PRC, possible bombing of 23, 27,
    29–30, 42
    and Radford 147–8
    retirement/resignation as Prime
    Minister 15, 86, 167, 230, 247, 252,
    258
    and Roosevelt 6, 42, 108
    SEATO 225–6, 233–4
    "special relationship" with US 6, 21, 42,
    154, 257
    Thailand 50–1
    US intervention in Indochina 2–3, 15,
    21–4, 26, 28–9, 35, 72–4, 82, 101,
    104–8, 111–13, 138–44, 146, 147–8,
    150, 153–4, 175–6, 186–7, 189, 191,
    232, 256–7
    Vietnamese elections 242
Cochinchina 25, 57
Cold War 5, 36, 97, 145, 205, 234, 256. *See
    also* nuclear weapons
    Asian 1–2, 8, 11–12, 22, 33, 41–2, 49,
    52–3, 60, 68, 73, 82, 225–6
    and Churchill as "peacemaker" 41

Cuba 262
and Eden 1, 7–8, 11–12, 151, 166
neutralism 120–1, 150, 196
SEATO 225–6
Cole, Sterling 98
Collins, General J. Lawton 244, 246–8
Colombo conference (1954)/powers 126–7,
131–2, 150, 156–7, 163–4, 170, 172,
174, 181, 198, 207, 210, 212. *See also*
Burma; India; Indonesia; Pakistan;
Sri Lanka
SEATO 214, 224–5, 230
Colville, Jock 72, 147–8, 199
Coty, René 169
Cutler, Robert 111
Czechoslovakia 172–3

Davis, Vice-Admiral Arthur C. 25
Dean, Arthur 62
de Castries, General Christian Marie
Ferdinand de la Croix 67, 87, 129,
133, 168
Dejean, Maurice 61
de Lattre de Tassigny, General Jean 19–20,
22, 36, 51–2, 57, 67
de Lattre line 19–20, 205
death of 24–5, 33
de Margerie, Roland 174
détente 49, 81–2, 167, 199
Devilliers, Philippe 70
Dickson, Sir William 32
Diem, Ngo Diem 195–6, 205, 218, 235,
237, 243
Battle of Saigon (1955) 248–9
as Chief of State of Vietnam 253
elections in Vietnam 241–2, 247, 250–3
possible removal from power 243–6,
248
SEATO 228
United Front of Nationalist Forces
247
US support for 238–41, 244–52
Dien Bien Phu, battle (1954) 2, 11, 66–7,
86–8, 91–6, 101–2, 106, 114, 129,
131, 143, 149–50, 157, 254
casualties 102, 133, 168, 172
ceasefire, possible 133, 135, 153, 157
fall of 3, 116, 135, 137, 145, 147–8, 161,
168–9, 171, 185, 190

nuclear weapons 115, 119, 136, 138,
172, 179, 185–6, 255
US intervention, possible 92, 94–6,
99–100, 103, 109, 111–12, 115–17,
120, 124, 133–7, 141, 143–5, 147–8,
160–1, 234
Dillon, Douglas 64, 109, 116, 127, 133,
136, 143–4, 175, 179, 203, 209
Dinh, Nguyen Quoc 158
Do, Tran Van 217, 241
Dong Hoi 185, 203
Dong, Pham Van 158, 171, 194, 208, 210
elections 212, 215–16
Dong Trieu 19, 87
Donnelly, Desmond 189
Dulles, Allen 91, 94
Dulles, John Foster 8, 13, 94
Berlin conference 79–83
Bermuda conference 71, 75
brinkmanship 256
and Diem 238, 240, 246–8, 251–2
Dien Bien Phu, battle 95–7, 133–9,
141, 143–4, 154, 234, 254
and Eden 16–17, 41, 43–5, 111–17,
120–3, 125–32, 134–9, 144–5, 151,
153–61, 163–7, 184, 191, 193, 198,
200–2, 204, 210–11, 215–16, 227,
230–1, 234, 244–5, 258, 260
Five-Power Staff Agency 164–5, 174
Geneva conference 82, 84, 96, 117, 123,
131, 143, 149, 151–9, 163, 167, 189,
209–12, 226, 246, 256
Indochina, armistice and Final
Declaration 216, 218–19
Indochina, US intervention 2, 45,
63, 95–7, 100–18, 119–32, 133–9,
141–6, 148–9, 153, 155, 160–1,
165, 169–70, 174–7, 179, 181, 183,
188–91, 211, 215, 218–19, 231, 234,
237–8, 240, 244–5, 248–9, 252, 254,
256–8
Korean War 41–2, 45–6, 57, 60, 63,
77, 256
London, visit to (April 1954) 107–8,
113, 116–18, 119–25, 128
NATO 93, 131, 133–8
New Look 77–8, 80
North Atlantic Councils 131, 133–8
partition of Vietnam 205, 252

PRC, possible US attack on 101,
117–18, 119–20, 155, 160–1, 170
SEATO 224–8, 230–4, 244
Suez crisis 16–17, 258, 260–1
Dutton, David 6

EDC. *See* European Defence Community
Eden, Anthony 33, 37–9, 71. *See also*
Eden, Clarissa
and Acheson 21–3, 27–9, 37
and Allen 92–3, 125, 129, 139, 161, 166
all-Vietnam constitution 246
'British Overseas Obligations' paper
12–14, 20, 28
Churchill, closeness to 5–6
Cold War 1, 7–8, 11–12, 151, 166
death 260
and Diem 243–6, 254
Dien Bien Phu, battle 11, 133–41, 145
"dual containment" 15–16, 28
and Dulles 16–17, 41, 43–5, 111–17,
120–3, 125–32, 134–9, 144–5, 151,
153–61, 163–7, 184, 191, 193, 198,
200–2, 204, 210–11, 215–16, 227,
230–1, 234, 244–5, 258, 260
education 4–5
and Eisenhower 1, 43, 45, 98–9,
111–12, 167, 200, 257
European Defence Community 39–40
Five-Power Staff Agency 31–2, 68, 161,
163–5, 174, 181
Geneva conference 3, 10–12, 147–8,
150–61, 163–77, 235, 243–6, 251–3,
255, 258, 260–2
Armistice in Indochina 216–17
arrangement armistice of 82–3,
99–100
as co-chair 1, 4, 169–70, 217, 220
Final Declaration 4, 217, 220, 251
International Supervisory
Commission 212, 214–16
partition of Vietnam 10–12, 113,
117, 120–6, 148, 150, 199, 217,
231
peace negotiations for Indochina
169–77, 179–84, 187–91, 193–8,
204, 206, 207–18
praise for work at 4, 7–8, 16, 220,
260–2

pre-conference discussions 99,
111–13, 129, 131, 134, 144–6,
257
German rearmament 68
and Harvey 33
health issues 50, 56, 67, 158, 260–1
Indochina, US intervention 21–32,
43–4, 68–9, 101, 111–14, 120–32,
134–42, 144–5, 151, 153–61, 163–4,
174–6, 179–81, 189, 191, 198–9,
212, 220–1, 235, 240
Korea 68, 113, 159
Locarno treaty 165, 198–201, 213
MAAG 240
and Makins 44, 97, 114, 117, 125–9,
145, 154, 164, 180, 182, 188, 190,
193, 199, 203, 209, 232, 240
memoirs 10, 78, 85, 148, 200, 225–6,
262
and Mendès-France 16, 195–7, 206–7,
210–12, 220, 240
and Molotov 1, 16, 151–2, 157–8, 166,
172–4, 189, 191, 193–4, 198, 210,
215, 217–18, 232, 252, 257–8
Most Noble Order of the Garter,
induction to 7
and Nehru 206, 214, 245
North Atlantic Council 130, 133–8
nuclear weapons, fear of 1, 8–9, 72–3,
75, 78, 97–9, 142, 150, 172, 186,
255, 258
Panchsheel 206
parliamentary career 5
'Politician of the Year' 7
as Prime Minister 4, 16, 183, 189, 220,
247, 250
resignation as Prime Minister (1957) 4,
255, 260–1
SEATO 13–14, 16, 212–14, 234–5
Bangkok Council meeting (1955)
230, 246
creation of 223–9, 231–2
Manila conference (1954) 227–8,
230
Shakespeare, love of 8, 255, 262
and Smith 159, 163–5, 174–5, 183, 191,
198, 213–16, 218, 240
and Stalin, death of 45
Suez canal 4, 7–8, 16–17, 255, 258–62

Trieste 7
and Truman 21–4
United Nations 13, 258
Vietnamese National Army 37
Washington conference (1954)
    199–204
Wateler Peace Prize, award of (1954) 7
World War I 4–5, 7
World War II 4, 159
and Zhou Enlai 15–16, 152, 157–8,
    173, 189, 193–4, 196, 198, 206,
    208–10, 212–15, 218, 228, 257
Eden, Clarissa 81, 86, 137,174, 183, 189,
    204
    Geneva conference 144, 152, 160, 166,
    215
Eisenhower, President Dwight D.
    Berlin conference 79–81
    Bermuda conference 55, 69, 71–2,
        74–5, 77, 255
    Bricker Amendment 89–90
    and Churchill 40–3, 51, 56, 97–8,
        106–8, 112–13, 146, 167, 184, 186,
        191, 197, 199–200, 203, 205–6, 257
    and Diem 238–41, 243–5, 247–9
    Dien Bien Phu, battle 11, 94–6, 144,
        169
    election of (1952) 40
    'falling domino' principle 2, 115, 181
    Five-Power Staff Agency 165
    Geneva conference 84, 149, 154, 163,
        191, 207, 209–11, 218–19
    India 121
    Indochina, US intervention 1–3, 8, 11,
        13, 46, 49, 51–2, 58, 64–6, 89–97,
        99–100, 103–9, 111–12, 115–16,
        127–9, 134–8, 140–2, 144–5, 149,
        154–5, 159–60, 165, 168, 174–7,
        179–80, 182–3, 186, 191, 196, 200,
        202, 212, 232, 238–41, 246, 256–7
    Korea 8, 41–3, 45–6, 57, 72, 74–5, 89,
        256
    and Malenkov 49
    Navarre Plan 65–6
    New Look 8–9, 77, 80, 99, 146, 150,
        186, 257
    NSC-5405 91
    nuclear weapons 8–9, 72, 75, 77, 80,
        97–9, 146, 150, 167, 186, 255, 257

PRC 8, 42, 103–8, 140, 155, 160–1, 186
Potomac Charter (1954) 203–4
SEATO 13, 212, 214, 223–6, 230–2, 234
Stalin, death of 45
Suez crisis 16, 258–61
Thailand 50–1
Vietnam
    Elections proposed in 246–7, 249, 251
    partitioning of 149
    Washington conference (1954)
        199–200, 203–4
Elizabeth II, Queen 220
Elliot, Air Chief Marshal Sir William
    25–6, 31
Ely, Paul, General 59, 94–6, 109, 133, 138,
    143, 244, 246–7
    Ad Hoc Committee 25
European Defence Community (EDC) 45,
    57, 68, 93, 135
    collapse of (1954) 7
    France and 34, 38–40, 42, 53, 63, 83–4,
        93, 148, 195, 211, 226–7
    Germany, Federal Republic and 34,
        38, 53
    Soviet Union and 79, 83

Falkland Islands 13
Faure, Edgar 33, 246, 248
FEC. *See* French Expeditionary Corps
Five-Power Staff Agency (FPSA)/
    conference 31–2, 68, 161, 163–5,
    174, 181–2, 184–6
Fletcher, John 255
Foch, Marshal Ferdinand 24
Formosa. *See* Taiwan
Fox, Jean 67
FPSA. *See* Five-Power Staff Agency
Franks, Sir Oliver 21, 30
French Expeditionary Corps (FEC) 19, 38,
    46, 51, 60, 185, 242. *See also* Dien
    Bien Phu, battle
    disengagement of 34, 36–8, 44, 47,
        58–9, 84–5, 100, 116, 119, 165, 168,
        171, 172, 184, 216, 238–40, 244–5,
        249, 253
    Operation Castor (1953) 66–7
    troop numbers 66, 71, 87, 169, 205, 208
    US financing of 65, 238, 244
    Vietnam elections 235, 238–40

Gaiduk, Ilya 227
Geneva conference (1954) 1–4, 79, 81–2,
    93, 96, 99, 105–7, 113–14, 200–2,
    121–2, 241–5, 150–1, 255, 258. *See
    also under* Bidault; Dulles; Eden;
    Eisenhower; India; Laniel; Mendès-
    France; Molotov; Smith; Zhou
  all-Vietnam constitution 246
  armistice agreements 216–17
  arrangement of 82–5, 87, 92, 100–1,
    106
  clocks, stopping of 4, 216
  Commonwealth 151, 160
  Dien Bien Phu, battle 13, 88, 133–4,
    153, 157, 169
  International Supervisory Commission
    212, 214–17
  and Korea 82, 126, 151–2, 155, 158
  opening of 147, 152, 154
  partitioning of Vietnam 3, 113–14,
    148–50, 153, 158, 181, 190, 196–7,
    199, 207–11, 215, 217, 219
  peace negotiations for Indochina
    169–77, 179–84, 187–91, 193–8,
    202–5, 206, 207–18
  PRC, participation at 82, 117, 123,
    149–50, 152, 155, 157–8, 163–5,
    167, 170 (*see also under* Zhou
    Enlai)
  pre-conference discussions 99, 111–13,
    129, 131, 134, 144–6, 257
  SEATO 14, 223, 225–6, 231–5
  settlement for Indochina (Final
    Declaration) 4, 217–20, 228,
    238–40, 242, 251–2, 256
  US ambivalence towards 111–12, 117,
    120, 123–4, 149, 152–3, 182, 189,
    191, 193, 200, 204–5, 209–11, 213,
    216–17, 250
  USSR at 1, 16, 149, 151–2, 155, 166–7,
    170, 176 (*see also under* Molotov,
    Vyacheslav)
  Vietminh and 1, 3, 7, 12, 149–50, 158,
    160, 167–70, 174, 182, 193–6, 205,
    207–8, 210, 235
Germany, Federal Republic of 34–5,
    39–40, 68, 81
Giap, General Vo Nguyen 19, 37, 49, 206,
    241

Dien Bien Phu, battle 66–7, 87–8, 102,
    116, 169
  peace negotiations 207–8
  Red River delta 171, 183, 195
Gilbert, Martin 41
Granville, Lord 5
Graves, Hubert 33, 36–7, 44, 85–6, 183,
    239, 241
Greene, Graham 87
Greenwood, Sean 261
Grey, Sir Edward 4
Gruenther, Alfred 83

Hagerty, James 94, 103, 209, 231, 244
Hainan 184
Haiphong 19, 171, 184–5, 197, 205, 207,
    215
Hanoi 19–20, 25, 36, 66, 87, 95, 169
  communist threat to 171, 183–5,
    188–9, 193, 205, 215
  diplomatic contacts 253
  Vietminh and PAVN threat to 19, 171,
    184–5, 188, 240–1
Harding, Field Marshal Sir John 38, 50, 68,
    147, 182, 186
Harvey, Sir Oliver 33, 36, 38–9, 44, 56,
    79, 88
Hazlett, "Swede" 257
Head, Antony 52–4
Heath, Donald 205, 241
Herring, George C. 211, 248
Hinh, General Nguyen Van 239
Hirohito, Emperor 107, 257
Hitler, Adolf 107, 257
Hoa Binh 33
Hoa Hao 239, 247
Ho Chi Minh 1, 12, 20, 59, 84, 112, 237,
    240–1, 253
  Elections in Vietnam 212, 220, 241,
    245–6, 249
  Final Declaration of Geneva
    conference 219
  Indochinese federation 171
  peace negotiations 61, 63, 69–71,
    85, 88, 116, 149, 173, 196, 207–8,
    211
Hong Kong 14, 27, 43, 107, 110–12, 114,
    122, 136, 146
Huang Hua 62

India 97, 138, 177, 180–1. *See also*
    Colombo conference/powers;
    Nehru
  Geneva conference 112, 120–3, 125,
    151, 164–5
  independence 22, 140, 153
  neutralism 62, 121–2, 125, 132, 150,
    170, 214
  SEATO 122, 150, 156, 172–3, 214,
    224–6, 230
Indochina. *See* Associated States;
    Cambodia; Dejean; Dien Bien
    Phu; French Expeditionary Corps;
    Geneva conference; Laos; Salan;
    Tonkin; Vietminh; Vietnam;
    Vietnamese National Army; *See
    also under* Bidault; Churchill,
    Winston; Dulles; Eden; Laniel;
    Molotov
Indonesia 106, 120, 126, 156, 220. *See also*
    Colombo conference/powers
  SEATO 214, 224–5
International Supervisory Commission
    212, 214–17
Irony Malaya defence plan 35, 110–11,
    114, 122, 141, 145, 233

Jackson, C. D. 92
James, Robert Rhodes 7, 260
Japan 5, 15, 50, 121, 157
  communist threat to 106, 148
  nuclear bombing of (1945) 9
  SEATO 225, 230
  strategic importance of 22, 27, 115
  thermonuclear testing 99, 108
Jebb, Sir Gladwyn 141, 144, 150, 182, 203,
    207, 209, 243
Johnson, Lyndon B. 128–9, 163
Johnson, U. Alexis 127, 152, 210
Joy, Michael 53, 90
Juin, General Alphonse-Pierre 24–5

Kennedy, John F. 195
Khmer Issarak 171–3, 193, 196, 216
Khrushchev, Nikita 253
Kirkpatrick, Ivone 85, 126, 128–9, 226,
    242, 253
Ki Sok Pok, North Korean negotiator 62
Kissinger, Henry 232–3

Knowland, William F. 90, 115, 121, 163,
    205, 209, 218
Korea. *See* Korea, South; Korean Political
    Conference; Korean War
Korea, South 61–2, 102, 121–2, 128,
    155, 242. *See also* Korean Political
    Conference; Korean War; Saigon
  armed forces 37, 41, 82, 100
  partition 61, 254
  SEATO 224–5, 230
  and Taiwan 131
Korean Political Conference 24, 60–4, 68,
    79–80, 82
Korean War 9, 20, 65–6, 89, 137, 140,
    153, 253, 256–7. *See also* Korean
    Political Conference
  armistice (1953) 2, 15, 21, 23, 56–7,
    60–3, 72, 80, 82, 84, 155
  Berlin conference and 80–1, 83–4
  Bermuda conference and 72–3
  casualties 2
  and Eisenhower 8, 41–3, 45–6, 57, 72,
    74–5, 89, 256
  elections 212
  Geneva conference 82, 126, 151–2,
    155, 158
  Joint Policy Declaration (1953) 61–2,
    72
  mutual defence treaty with US (1953)
    61
  outbreak of (1950) 2, 12, 14, 43, 53,
    208
  partition 61, 254
  PRC 15, 19, 21–2, 24–7, 29–32, 45,
    61–2, 68, 70, 72, 78, 113, 155
  prisoner-of-war exchanges 62
  resumption of fighting threatened 72,
    74, 80, 94, 100
  United Nations 22, 24, 26, 45, 60–2,
    126
Kyes, Roger M. 91

Lacouture, Jean 70
Laniel, Joseph 90–1, 183, 185
  Bermuda conference 69–70
  Dien Bien Phu, battle 94, 100, 103, 109,
    116–17, 135–6, 143, 153, 168–70
  Elevation to premiership (1953) 55,
    57, 78

Geneva conference 94, 117, 123–4,
    135–6, 148–9, 167–8, 175, 179–80
partition of Vietnam 148–9
peace negotiations in Indochina 55–9,
    63–5, 69, 78, 94, 100, 117, 124, 135,
    143, 167–8, 195
resignation as prime minister (1954)
    191
US intervention in Indochina 58, 64–5,
    85, 94, 109, 116, 123–4, 135–6, 143,
    153, 165, 175, 179–80, 188, 191
votes of confidence in French assembly
    83, 167, 176, 190–1
Laos 1, 52, 88, 114, 125, 157, 244–5.
    See also Associated States; Luang
    Prabang; Pathet Lao; Thakhek
armistice 216–17
communist threat to 10, 38, 49–51, 53,
    66–7, 100, 106, 130, 164, 171–2,
    182, 190
Final Declaration of Geneva
    conference 217–21
independence of 3, 34, 57, 59, 148,
    193–4, 196, 201, 203, 221, 237
MAAG 240
PAVN threat to 49, 51, 66–7, 171–2,
    216
SEATO 224, 228–9, 256
US military bases 213
Vietminh attack on (1953) 49–51, 53,
    66–7
Letourneau, Jean 35, 44–5, 61, 64
Lind, Michael 15
Liuzhou conference (1954) 207–8
Lloyd, Selwyn 42, 52, 54, 60, 180
Locarno treaty (1925) 165, 198–201, 213
Lodge, Henry Cabot 233
Logevall, Fredrik 138, 216, 234
Lovett, Robert 22
Low, David 212
Luang Prabang 49
Lundestad, Geir 15

MAAG. *See* Military Assistance Advisory
    Group
MacArthur, Doug 115–16, 120, 122, 135,
    143
McCardle, Carl 152
McCarthy, Joseph. *See* McCarthyism

McCarthyism 14, 41, 82, 90
McCormack, John W. 142
McDonald, Iverach 112, 139, 183
MacDonald, Malcolm 52, 86
Macmillan, Harold 98, 142, 199–200, 220
    as Foreign Minister 247–8, 250–3
    and Molotov 253
Magsaysay, Ramon 229
Makins, Roger 44
    as British ambassador in Washington
        54, 61, 90, 92, 101–2, 105, 108, 110,
        115, 118, 174, 243, 247, 251
    and Eden 44, 97, 114, 117, 125–9, 145,
        154, 164, 180, 182, 188, 190, 193,
        199, 203, 209, 232, 240
    SEATO 223–4
Malaya 27, 39, 45, 110–12, 137, 221
    ANZUS 122
    as "buffer" state 50
    communist threat to 11–12, 20, 23,
        34–5, 46, 50, 106, 130, 140–1, 145,
        151, 181, 246
    Dien Bien Phu, battle at 88
    economic value of 12, 55
    independence 111
    Malayan Communist Party 50
    Malayan Emergency 11, 50
    SEATO 233
    UK aircraft 136
Malenkov, Georgi 49, 71, 74, 199, 215
Manila. *See under* South East Asia Treaty
    Organisation (SEATO)
Mansfield, Senator Mike 245
Mansfield Report (1954) 248
Mao Khe, battle (1951) 19, 87
Mao Zedong 60, 84, 152, 157, 195
Marshall Plan 39, 233
Massigli, René 61, 117, 141
Mayer, René 46, 51–2, 54–5
Mendès-France, Pierre 57, 237–8, 240–1
    armistice for Indochina and Final
        Declaration of Geneva conference
        216, 219–20
    and Diem 242, 244–6
    EDC 227
    and Eden 16, 195–7, 206–7, 210–12,
        220, 240
    Geneva conference 1, 3–4, 16, 195–7,
        204–6, 207, 210–12, 214–16, 227, 257

Potomac Charter 203–4
  resignation of 246
  Vietnamese elections 242
Menon, Krishna 194, 212
Merchant, Livingston 121, 125, 144, 148, 155, 159, 227
Military Assistance Advisory Group (MAAG) 240
Molotov, Vyacheslav 49
  Berlin conference 79–83
  East-West summit 252
  EDC 227
  and Eden 1, 16, 151–2, 157–8, 166, 172–4, 189, 191, 193–4, 198, 210, 215, 217–18, 232, 252, 257–8
  Geneva conference 1, 16, 151–2, 155, 157–8, 166, 170, 172–4, 176, 189, 191, 193–5, 198, 210, 212, 227, 232, 257–8
    Armistice in Indochina 217
    International Supervisory Commission 215
Moran, Lord 22, 199
Morgan, Ted 129
Morocco 39, 148
Morrison, Herbert 20
Morton, Thruston 103
Munro, Leslie 105–6
Mussolini, Benito 107, 257

Nasser, Colonel Gamel Abdel 258–61
Nationalist China 84, 96, 102, 111, 121, 128. *See also* Chiang Kai-shek
  SEATO 224–5
NATO. *See* North Atlantic Treaty Organisation
Navarre, General Henri 52, 54, 66–7
  Dien Bien Phu, battle 86–8, 95, 103, 109, 133, 135, 169
  Navarre Plan 57–60, 64–6, 84, 92, 154
  Red River delta 169, 171, 185
  replacement of 184
Nehru, Jawaharlal 132, 164–5, 167, 194, 206, 245
  Neutralism and 121–2
  SEATO 213–14, 225–6
New Look. *See under* Dulles; Eisenhower; nuclear weapons

New Zealand 2–3, 96, 151. *See also* Australia/New Zealand/US 'Pacific Pact' (ANZUS)
  Pacific Charter 230
  SEATO 213, 225
  Vietnam 25, 30–1, 102, 104, 106, 109–10, 115, 118, 119–20, 147–8, 150, 154, 157, 160–1, 176, 186
Nixon, Richard 90, 95, 154
North Atlantic Council 31, 93, 129, 133–6
North Atlantic Treaty Organisation (NATO) 1, 39, 53–4, 82, 93, 106, 115, 133, 198, 214, 243–4. *See also* European Defence Community; North Atlantic Council
  British commitment to 13, 40, 53
  destabilization of 7, 53–4, 63, 148
  and Eden 7, 13, 130, 133–8
  Germany, Federal Republic 34
  Korea, North 22, 30
  SEATO, model for 28, 112–13, 124, 150, 197, 201, 213, 223–4, 231, 233
  Soviet threat to 2, 117
  and Stalin, death of 45
nuclear weapons 45, 62, 176, 199, 205, 255. *See also* World War III, possibility of
  British 73–5, 99, 106–7, 113, 148, 186, 197, 200, 255–6
  Castle-Bravo test (1954) 98–9
  Dien Bien Phu, possible use at 115, 119, 136, 138, 172, 179, 185–6, 255
  Eisenhower 8–9, 72, 75, 77, 80, 97–9, 146, 150, 167, 186, 255, 257
  Ivy-Mike test (1952) 73, 97–8
  and Japan 9, 73–4
  New Look 8–9, 77, 99, 108, 146, 150, 186, 200, 257
  PRC, possible use against 1, 9, 23, 25, 68, 72, 101, 107–9, 142, 229, 233–4, 257
  Quebec agreement (1943) 108
  Soviet 72–4, 98–9, 108, 167, 170, 186, 257
  thermonuclear (hydrogen) 9, 11, 73–4, 97–9, 107–10, 113, 116, 136, 148, 158, 167–8, 170, 172, 186, 255–6
  US Atomic Energy Act 73, 200
Nutting, Anthony 8, 258, 260

Ogburn, Charlton 66

Pacific Charter (1954) 229–30
Pakistan 120, 126, 156, 165, 172–3, 180–1,
    220. *See also* Colombo conference/
    powers
    SEATO 214, 224–6, 229–30
Panchsheel 206, 214, 225
Panmunjom 21. *See also* Korean Political
    Conference
Paterson, William 241–3
Pathet Lao 171–3, 193, 196, 208, 216
PAVN. *See* People's Army of Vietnam
Pearson, Lester 137, 151, 161
Peck, Edward 128
People's Army of Vietnam (PAVN) 59,
        70, 90, 182, 215. *See also* Dien Bien
        Phu; Giap; Red River delta; Tonkin;
        Vietminh
    Cambodia 171–2
    Hanoi 19, 171, 184–5, 188, 240
    Laos 49, 51, 66–7, 171–2, 216
    morale issues 70, 149, 185, 208
    PRC support of 87, 184
    Soviet support of 168–9
People's Republic of China (PRC). *See also*
        Dien Bien Phu; Hainan; Liuzhou
        conference; Mao Zedong; Yalu
        River; Zhou Enlai; *See also under*
        blockades; Churchill; Dulles;
        Eisenhower; Geneva conference;
        Korean War; People's Army
        of Vietnam; Radford; Tonkin;
        Truman; United Nations; Vietminh
    Berlin conference 79–80
    birth of (1949) 60
    Central People's Government (CPG)
        14
    Chinese Civil War 1
    Chinese People's Liberation Army 50
    Final Declaration of Geneva
        conference 219
    nuclear weapons, possible use against
        1, 9, 23, 25, 68, 72, 101, 107–9, 142,
        229, 233–4, 257
    recognition of 84, 111
    SEATO 213, 224–6, 228–9, 234
    United Nations, admission to 206,
        219

Phat Diem 19, 197, 207
Philippines 96, 102, 109, 115, 118, 120,
    125–7, 141, 156–7, 176
    Indochina peace negotiations 174, 198
    Pacific Charter 229–30
    SEATO 213–14, 223–4, 229, 232
Pinay, Antoine 33, 36, 39, 46
Pleven, René 84–5, 143
Poland 172–3, 214
Port Fuad 259
Port Said 259
Potomac Charter (1954) 203–4
PRC. *See* People's Republic of China

Quebec agreement (1943) 108

Radford, Admiral Arthur W. 92, 111, 130,
    142, 163, 174–7, 184, 256
    Dien Bien Phu, battle 91, 94–5, 109,
        115, 119, 136–7, 141, 147–8, 153–4,
        169, 185–6
    PRC, action against 8–9, 15, 72, 95,
        103, 105, 109, 118, 137–8, 140–1,
        146, 147–8, 156, 169–70, 186, 188
    SEATO 223, 229, 233
Reading, Lord 159, 228, 230, 251
Red River delta 19, 25, 32–3, 51, 57, 66–7,
    137, 169, 171, 182–5, 194, 203–5,
    209. *See also* Tonkin
Reilly, Patrick 61
Republic of Vietnam (RVN). *See under*
    Vietnam
Reynolds, David 8
Rhee, Syngman 128, 155, 196, 208, 224
Ridgway, General Matthew B. 29, 95, 103
Ringlet Malaya defence plan 10–11, 35,
    114, 122, 141, 145, 233
Roberts, Chalmers 142
Robertson, Walter 159, 202
Roosevelt, President Franklin D. 6, 42,
    108
Russell, Senator Richard 103

Saigon 20, 36–7, 44, 51, 59, 66, 70, 85, 195,
    205, 239–41, 243–4
    Battle of (1955) 248–9
    Ely-Collins programme 246
    Final Declaration of Geneva
        conference 218

United Front of Nationalist Forces
247–8
Sainteny, Jean 237, 246
Salan, General Raoul 33, 51–2, 60, 66
Salisbury, Lord 50–1, 56, 60–1, 98–9,
171–2, 174, 176, 189
Sary, Sam 216
Schuman, Robert 30, 33
Schumann, Maurice 65, 138, 143
Scott, Robert 31–2, 54, 92–3, 101, 213,
231
SEATO. *See* Southeast Asia Treaty
Organisation
Senegal 39
Shakespeare, William
Henry IV (Part 2) 8
Henry VIII 255
King Lear 262
Shepley, James 256
Short, Anthony 27
Shuckburgh, Evelyn 79, 83, 99, 124, 126,
128–9, 134, 136–40, 144, 146, 176,
262
Geneva conference 148, 150–2, 154–5,
157, 159, 161, 164, 166, 168, 176–7,
258
Siam. *See* Thailand
Singapore 11
Sino-Soviet treaty (1950) 14, 113, 115,
121, 148, 150, 213
Slessor, Air Chief Marshal Sir John 26, 32
Slim, Field Marshal Sir William 24–5
Smith, R. B. 208
Smith, Walter Bedell 89–93, 101, 111, 120,
126, 130–1, 141, 143–5, 154, 202,
240
armistice in Indochina and Final
Declaration of Geneva conference
216–18
and Diem 195
and Eden 159, 163–5, 173–5, 183, 191,
198, 213–16, 218, 240
Geneva conference 159, 163–5, 169,
173–5, 190, 196, 198, 201, 209–11,
213, 215–17, 231
Korea 84
partition of Vietnam 182, 205
Songkhla (and Songkhla "strategy") 34,
50–1, 137, 145

Southeast Asia Treaty Organisation
(SEATO) 13, 197, 202, 212–14,
244
Bangkok Council meeting (1955) 230,
233, 246
effectiveness of 14, 230–5, 256
Manila conference (1954) 223, 225–30,
233–4, 247
membership of 224–5, 228–33
NATO as model for 28, 112–13, 124,
150, 197, 201, 213, 223–4, 231, 233
structure of 224–6, 229
treaty (1954), signing of 229–30, 234,
247
Spellman, Cardinal Francis Joseph 195
Spender, Sir Percy 105–6, 113, 129
Sri Lanka 120, 126, 156, 165, 172, 180–1, 220.
See also Colombo conference/powers
SEATO 214, 224–5
Stalin, Joseph 167
death of 45, 49, 71, 82, 215
Statler, Kathryn 253
Stephenson, Sir Hugh 243
Strang, Sir William 26, 54, 85
Strauss, Lewis L. 107, 116
Suez canal 20, 40, 255
British disengagement 258–60
crisis (1956) 4, 8, 16–17, 255, 258–62
Soviet approach to 258–60
Suez Canal Company 16, 258

Tahourdin, John 31, 85
Taiwan (Formosa) 14, 22, 29, 42, 63, 70,
102, 115, 122
communist threat to 43, 84, 102
Korean War 43, 61
SEATO 230
Templer, General Sir Gerald 50
Thailand (Siam) 35, 96, 102, 109, 118, 120,
125–7, 156–7, 161, 163, 176, 221,
244–5. *See also* Bangkok; Songkhla
communist threat to 11, 34, 50–1, 106,
140, 147, 181
Indochina peace negotiations 174, 198
SEATO 213–14, 224, 231–2
Thakhek 185
thermonuclear weapons. *See under*
nuclear weapons
Tonkin (Tongking) 11, 57, 145, 168, 184

and PRC, aggression towards 19–21,
    25–6, 30, 35, 38, 75, 92, 94, 149
surrender of 12, 182, 185–6, 190, 194,
    197, 205
US intervention 20, 92, 136, 156, 159,
    186, 188–9, 202
Trevelyan, Sir Humphrey 219
Trieste 7, 68
Truman, President Harry S. 36–7, 40, 163
    Eden and Churchill, meeting with
        (1952) 21–4
    Korean War 43, 89
    nuclear weapons 73
    and PRC 14–15, 24, 26, 28, 30–1, 35
Twining, Air Force General Nathan F. 95,
    138–9

UN. *See* United Nations
United Front of Nationalist Forces 247–8
United Nations (UN) 50, 80
    British commitment to 13
    Charter of 123, 125, 225, 228
    Final Declaration of Geneva
        conference 217
    Korea 22, 24, 26, 45, 60–2, 126
    PRC 14, 60–1, 69, 84, 206, 219
    Suez crisis 259
US Military Assistance Advisory Group
    92, 240

Vafiadis, Markos 84
Vautour air-strike plan 95, 101, 133, 135,
    141, 143–4
Verdaguer, Sauveur 112
Vietminh 11, 19, 23, 33, 36, 46–7, 49, 55,
    65, 173, 205, 241, 244, 249. *See also*
    Dong; French Expeditionary Corps;
    Ho Chi Minh; People's Army of
    Vietnam; *See also under* Hanoi;
    Laos
    Armistice for Indochina 190, 216, 235
    Elections in Vietnam 171, 202, 212,
        219–20, 237–8, 241–3, 246–7,
        251–2
    military success 2, 19–20, 32, 34, 38,
        50, 52, 59, 66, 86, 90–2, 148–9, 180,
        183–5, 190, 197, 201, 206, 209, 216
        (*see also* Dien Bien Phu; Mao Khe;
        Red River delta; Tonkin)

morale issues 149, 185
negotiations and 10, 34, 38, 57, 59–61,
    63, 66, 69–70, 78, 85, 93, 100, 158,
    167, 171–7, 179–82, 190, 193–4,
    195–7, 207–8, 216, 251 (*see also
    under* Geneva conference)
partitioning of Vietnam 10, 12, 130,
    149, 168, 181, 196–7, 201, 207–10,
    212, 215, 240
PRC support of 1, 9, 20, 24–5, 28, 34,
    37, 61, 70–1, 84–5, 90, 96, 101–2,
    105–9, 113–14, 118, 129, 160, 165,
    184, 188–9, 194, 208, 240
reunification of Vietnam 252–3
SEATO 229
Soviet support of 70
Vietnam. *See also* Associated States; Baie
    d'Along; Bao Dai; Binh Xuyen;
    Buu, Loc; Buu, Ta Quang; Cao
    Dai; Chinh; Diem; Dien Bien Phu;
    Do; Dong; Dong Hoi; Dong Trieu;
    French Expeditionary Corps;
    Haiphong; Hanoi; Hoa Binh; Ho
    Chi Minh; Hoa Hao; Hinh; Mao
    Khe; People's Army of Vietnam;
    Phat Diem; Red River delta;
    Tonkin; Vinh; Viet Tri; Vietminh;
    Vietnamese National Army; Vinh
    Yen
    all-Vietnam constitution 246
    armistice for Indochina 171–3, 216–17
    Final Declaration of Geneva
        conference 217–20
    independence of 34, 55, 57–9, 70, 143,
        155, 171, 183, 193–4, 237, 241
    "loss" of possible 34–5, 38, 90, 106, 111
    MAAG 240
    partitioning of 3, 10–12, 78, 85–6, 88,
        92, 113–14, 125, 129, 140, 148–50,
        158, 164, 168, 181, 190, 196–7, 201,
        203, 207–12, 215–20, 231, 241,
        252–3
    Republic of Vietnam (RVN), founding
        of 253
    reunification 253
    SEATO 213, 224, 228–9, 256
    US intervention 92, 240 (*see also
        under* Dien Bien Phu; Tonkin; *and
        see* US intervention in Indochina

under Churchill; Dulles; Eden;
    Eisenhower; Laniel)
'Vietnamization' 55, 58, 65
Vietnamese National Army 44–5, 47,
    58–9, 65, 71, 87, 100, 154, 208,
    238–9, 247–9
  size 36–7, 159, 244, 247–8
  US training of 175
Viet Tri 19
Vinh, Nguyen Trung 158
Vinh Yen, battle (1951) 19, 87

Wan Waithayakon, Prince 151
Warner, Geoffrey 8, 202, 262 (note 13)
Wateler Peace Prize 7
Webb, Clifton 151, 160–1
Western European Union (WEU) 227, 248
West Germany. *See* Germany, Federal
    Republic of
WEU. *See* Western European Union
White Book 208

Wilson, Charles E. 95, 103, 109, 111, 179
Woolton, Lord 108
World War III, possibility of 1, 3, 12, 16,
    23, 28, 72, 113, 121, 136–8, 140,
    142, 146, 163, 171, 176–7, 183, 194,
    211, 231. *See also* nuclear weapons

Yalu River 29–30, 68, 72
Yom Kippur War (1973) 262

Zhai, Qiang 176
Zhou Enlai 15–16
  and Eden 15–16, 152, 157–8, 173,
    189, 193–4, 196, 198, 206, 208–10,
    212–15, 218, 228, 257
  Geneva conference 157–8, 172–3, 189,
    193–7, 207–8, 210, 212–13, 218,
    228, 257
  Liuzhou conference (1954) 207–9
  and Nehru 206
  SEATO 213–14, 228